ROLF STURM'S
MAJOR METHOD

For Guitar Theory And Improvisation

Volume 2
Chords & Arpeggios

WATER STREET MUSIC PUBLICATIONS

PO Box 224,

Fairview, NJ 07022

ISBN: 978-0-578-10638-0
© Copyright 2010 by Rolf Sturm

All rights reserved. This book, or parts thereof, may not be reproduced in any manner without written permission from the publisher.

ACKNOWLEDGEMENTS

Thanks to John Abercrombie for his kind words and his contributions to jazz guitar.

Thanks to Jody Espina for his kind words and encouragement towards this book.

Thanks to John Stroud for the fantastic cover design.

Thanks to Alan Brady for help with proofreading this book.

Thanks to Rob Henke, Jody Espina, Leese Walker, Frank Fagnano, Tomas Ulrich, Tony Trischka, Walter Thompson, Joe Gallant, Pablo Aslan, Raul Jalrena, Brian Babcock, Grisha Alexiev, Kermit Driscoll ... and others, just too numerous to mention here (you know who you are!) for sharing your time and talents in helping to make such wonderful music.

Thanks to Joe Pass, Jim Hall, John Abercrombie, Bill Frisell, Steve Brown, and Harry Leahey for sharing your musical knowledge with me.

Thanks to Margie & Douglas Sturm, Leese Walker, Hans, Jackie & Wolfgang Sturm, for their unending support, love and caring.

NOTES

Chord voicings are almost always explained through the piano or keyboard because the theory is all laid out in front of you from left to right. The information contained in this book deals with the question: "What does all of this stuff look like on the neck of the guitar?"

The "MAJOR METHOD" is an approach to understanding music theory for guitarists. Almost all of the scales needed for improvisation are learned through the major scale, usually by changing only one note or by omitting a couple of notes. This dramatically reduces the amount of time and effort that it takes to learn these other scales. All of this information is covered in Volume 1 of the MAJOR METHOD. It is the theory behind the note numbering used in the diagrams in Volume 2. One doesn't have to have a complete understanding of the MAJOR METHOD in order to learn all of the information contained in this book. I have depicted each of the chord/inversion sets using two different diagrams: one that shows the basic shapes of these chords within a parent scale without numbers AND one that shows how these chords fit into a parent scale with the MAJOR METHOD numbering system.

Throughout this book I have used diagrams that are drawn in a similar way to how tabliture is constructed. This means that the headstock of the guitar is on the left and the body of the guitar is on the right, as if you are looking down at your guitar while you are playing. I've done this because, while you'll never encounter tabliture in a professional playing situation, it *is* widely used in the guitar education community and it might be confusing to many of our guitar brethren if I drew the diagrams any other way.

Also, I have NOT included "suggested fingerings" for any of the chord diagrams in Volume 2. At this point in your study of the guitar, you should be able to figure out workable fingerings for these voicings. HOWEVER, there are some chord voicings in this book that are impractical, if not impossible, using standard guitar-playing technique. Some of the larger, stretched out voicings can only be played using the tapping technique (unless you have incredibly long fingers!) I've included these voicings for a couple of reasons:

1. Guitar players should know their chord inversions! ALL of the chords presented in Volume 2 are presented along with ALL of their inversions (no matter how impractical these other inversions are). Sometimes, one inversion of a chord is very playable, but its other inversions aren't. It's useful to see what the other inversions look like on the neck. It gives you a context of the family of chords that the playable chord comes from. And remember, you *can* just play part of an impractical chord inversion.

2. In order to expand your knowledge of what music theory looks like and sounds like on the neck of the guitar, it's important to see and understand as much of the neck as you can. Besides, with tapping, you can play these awkward to impractical chords.

It should also be noted that some of the chords in this book are easier to play when using right hand "finger-style" technique (as opposed to using a plectrum or a pick). When using a pick on the chord voicings that skip strings, you'll have to muffle the strings that are not part of the chord or jump over these strings when strumming. This can get tricky, so I'd recommend using your right hand fingers instead of a pick when you encounter these kinds of chords.

If you're in a hurry to expand your chord vocabulary, and you want to get right to the most playable chord voicings, here is a general playability guide to the diatonic seventh chord section of this book (the triads are all playable):

Diatonic Seventh Chords
3 sets of Closed.............................Impractical (root positions are mostly good)
3 sets of Drop 2............................Good
2 sets of Drop 3............................Good
2 sets of Drop 2 & 3......................Mostly Good
1 set of Drop 4..............................Awkward (root positions are good)
2 sets of Drop 2 & 4......................Good
1 set of Drop 3 & 4.......................Awkward to Impractical (root positions are good)
1 set of Drop 2, 3 & 4...................Impractical (first inversions are good)
1 set of Double Drop 2 & Drop 4..........Good

The MAJOR METHOD Volume 2 primarily presents chords that include all of their chord tones, without any doubling. The only time a chord is presented that doesn't include all of its chord tones is when there is an extension or an alteration added to the chord. In these cases, one of the chord tones is sacrificed in order to play the desired chordal extension or alteration. There are many other ways to play chords on the guitar where you double or omit chord tones. I haven't included these chords in order to focus on a consistent and clear method where each full chord is presented with all of its inversions. This volume is intended to vastly expand your chord vocabulary and understanding of the neck. It provides a visual repesentation of the chord theory and chord construction that is taught in music theory classes and in private instruction. It is not intended to replace these experiences. There is no substitute for having face-to-face lessons with a well qualified teacher. Having said this, I *have* included some introductory explanations about chord tonalities, voicings, and inversions for those of you who haven't yet been introduced to these concepts. After reading these sections, if you still have questions, sign up for a class, or get a good private teacher. I realize that in this "do-it-yourself" day and age, everyone wants to get to the information as quickly as possible. So, here is A LOT of information …

TABLE OF CONTENTS

Major Method	i
Introducing Chords	1
Diatonic Triads	7
Closed	9
Drop 2	23
Drop 3	51
Drop 2 & 3	62
Altered Triads	66
Major #11	68
Major #5 (Augmented)	76
Diatonic Seventh Chords	84
Closed	86
Drop 2	97
Drop 3	107
Drop 2 & 3	114
Drop 4	121
Drop 2 & 4	125
Drop 3 & 4	132
Drop 2, 3 & 4	135
Double Drop 2 & Drop 4	139
Chordal Extensions	143
Minor 11 & Dominant 7(sus 4) Chords	147
13th Chords	155

<u>Altered Seventh Chords</u>	191
Major 7#11	193
Major 7#5	199
Minor Major 7	205
Dominant 7#11	211
Dominant 7#5	217
Dominant 7#9	223
Dominant 7b9	230
<u>Diatonic Seventh Chord Arpeggios</u>	236
"1" Chord Arpeggio	238
"2" Chord Arpeggio	242
"3" Chord Arpeggio	246
"4" Chord Arpeggio	250
"5" Chord Arpeggio	254
"6" Chord Arpeggio	258
"7" Chord Arpeggio	262
<u>Altered Seventh Chord Arpeggios</u>	266
Major 7#11 Arpeggio	268
Major 7#5 Arpeggio	271
Minor Major 7 Arpeggio	274
Dominant 7#11 Arpeggio	277
Dominant 7#5 Arpeggio	280
Dominant 7#9 Arpeggio	283
Dominant 7b9 Arpeggio	286
<u>What To Do & Chord Charts</u>	289

MAJOR METHOD

The MAJOR METHOD is an approach to learning music theory on the neck of the guitar. The neck of the guitar has a lot of different patterns and shapes to learn in order to know one simple major scale. In order to improvise using the whole neck, you have to tie all of these patterns together so that they appear as one huge pattern.

To approach "major", "pure/natural minor", "major pentatonic", "minor pentatonic", "blues", "harmonic minor", and "melodic minor" all as completely different and distinct intervalic structures (each requiring a whole new set of patterns), makes for an enormous pile of work!

It doesn't have to be so difficult... PARTICULARLY WHEN ALL OF THESE SCALES SHARE SO MANY OF THE SAME BASIC SHAPES!!

The MAJOR METHOD relates ALL of these scales back to the shapes and patterns of the major scale ... hence the name "MAJOR METHOD"... catchy, eh?

While the theory of this system will work for any instrument, it is particularly designed for the guitar. Music theory on the guitar is extremely visual (at least in the beginning). "Seeing" all of the notes of one major scale on the entire neck of the guitar is a fairly large task. Most of the other scales that one needs to know in order to become an accomplished improviser use EXACTLY the same shapes as the major scale, with the exception (usually) of just one or two notes per octave.

PURE/NATURAL MINOR
(MAJOR METHOD VS TRADITIONAL)

Every major scale has 7 different scale degrees (notes). Every major scale's letter name comes from its "starting" pitch (from the 1). **Every major scale also has a relative minor name.** The minor scale's letter name comes from the scale's 6th pitch. In the G major scale, "G" is the 1st pitch and "E" is the 6th pitch. "E" is the relative minor of G major. Technically this is the E "pure minor" or the E "natural minor" scale. Many times the words "pure" or "natural" are dropped when referring to this scale and it is just called the minor scale. These words are used to distinguish it from the two other minor scales that are commonly used when improvising: the harmonic minor and the melodic minor. These scales are always referred to as "harmonic" minor and "melodic" minor.

Most music theorists like to think of the "pure/natural" minor scale as a separate entity from the major scale and will assign a whole new set of numbers to the scale degrees. These new numbers are all based on how the minor scale's intervals relate to a major scale's intervals. Their reasoning is that since the 6th note of the major scale is the new "starting" pitch of the "pure/natural" minor scale, it should now be called the 1, the 7 becomes the new 2, the 1 becomes the new b3, etc ... They call this third pitch a "b"3 because the distance between the 1 and the 3 of a minor scale is a half step less than the distance between the 1 and the 3 of a major scale. This kind of thinking becomes obsolete when one realizes the visualization that is required to learn these scales on the neck of the guitar:

1) All of the shapes on the neck of the guitar **are exactly the same** for the major scale as they are for the natural minor scale. And you already have the pitches numbered as a point of reference, so why not just use the numbers that are already there?

2) When improvising, you don't have to "start" on the first pitch of any scale, so its not important to call the theoretical first pitch of the scale a "1". What is important is that you know where all of the available notes are and that you can begin to use them to make music.

Also, by always using one set of pitch numbers, you create less confusion when learning the shapes of other scales (particularly when the other scales share so many of the same or similar shapes).

TRADITIONALLY, the natural minor scale is taught as being a major scale with a b3, a b6, & a b7.

```
                  1   2   3   4  5   6   7   1
        E major:  E  F#  G#  A  B  C#  D#  E

                  1   2  b3   4  5  b6  b7   1
E natural minor:  E  F#   G   A  B   C   D   E
```

The MAJOR METHOD teaches that the natural minor scale is the same as its relative major scale, starting on the 6th scale degree. So E natural minor is the same as the G major scale, starting on the 6th scale degree:

```
                  1  2  3  4  5  6   7  1
        G major:  G  A  B  C  D  E  F#  G
                                 6  7  1  2  3  4  5  6
               E natural minor:  E  F#  G  A  B  C  D  E
```

The numbers stay the same.

HARMONIC MINOR
(MAJOR METHOD VS TRADITIONAL)

TRADITIONALLY, the harmonic minor scale is taught as being the same as a major scale with a b3 and a b6... or the same as a natural minor scale (major scale with a b3, a b6, & a b7) where the 7 is NOT flatted.

```
                 1   2   3   4  5   6   7  1
      E major:   E   F#  G#  A  B   C#  D# E

                 1   2   b3  4  5   b6  b7 1
E natural minor: E   F#  G   A  B   C   D  E

                 1   2   b3  4  5   b6  7  1
E harmonic minor: E  F#  G   A  B   C   D# E
```

The MAJOR METHOD teaches that the harmonic minor scale is the same as its relative major scale with a #5. This "5" that is being raised a half step, is the same number 5 that was introduced in the major scale patterns.

```
                 1  2  3  4  5  6  7   1
     G major:    G  A  B  C  D  E  F#  G

                 6   7   1  2  3  4  5   6
E natural minor: E   F#  G  A  B  C  D   E

                 6   7   1  2  3  4  #5  6
E harmonic minor: E  F#  G  A  B  C  D#  E
```

Remember that this G major scale with a sharped 5 is ALWAYS referred to by its minor name: "E harmonic minor".

Learning the harmonic minor scale this way could be somewhat difficult and confusing for other instruments. But for guitarists, with the large visual labyrinth of shapes that we need to know just to play a simple major scale, this is an incredibly fast and efficient way to learn the harmonic minor scale.

MELODIC MINOR
(MAJOR METHOD VS TRADITIONAL)

TRADITIONALLY, the melodic minor scale ascends with one set of notes and descends with another set of notes. The descending scale (mode) is THE SAME as the natural minor scale, so it doesn't introduce any new patterns on the neck of the guitar. The ascending scale (mode) is the same as a natural minor scale with the 6th & 7th scale degrees raised by a half step. This is the part of the scale that provides for new and different patterns on the neck of the guitar. In contemporary improvisational theory, the term "melodic minor" refers only to this ascending mode of the traditional melodic minor scale.

```
                          1   2   3   4  5   6   7  1
               E major:   E   F#  G#  A  B   C#  D# E

                          1   2   b3  4  5   b6  b7 1
       E natural minor:   E   F#  G   A  B   C   D  E

                          1   2   b3  4  5   6   7  1
(ascending) E melodic minor: E  F#  G   A  B   C#  D# E
```

When looking at this scale, one realizes that the ascending mode of the melodic minor scale is THE SAME as the major scale with a b3, so …

The MAJOR METHOD teaches the melodic minor scale as a major scale with a b3. All of the patterns and numbers remain the same except that everytime you get to a 3, you flat it (you lower it one fret).

```
                          1   2   3   4  5   6   7  1
               E major:   E   F#  G#  A  B   C#  D# E

                          1   2   b3  4  5   6   7  1
       E melodic minor:   E   F#  G   A  B   C#  D# E
```

With the MAJOR METHOD, you only have to change one note per octave, and you're good to go. Just keep in mind that with the MAJOR METHOD, the melodic minor scale and the major scale share the same letter name. G melodic minor scale is **the same** as the G major scale with a b3. For other instruments, this might seem like a distraction from the way that they think of these other scales, but for the guitar, it provides you with all of the possible notes for soloing and chord construction on the entire neck with the LEAST amount of effort … beyond learning the major scale patterns.

There are many ways to organize the information that you'll need in order to become an improvising guitarist. The MAJOR METHOD Volume 2 presents a fairly extensive compilation of the triads and seventh chords on the neck of the guitar. I have also included some of the basic arpeggios that you'll need to know.

"Are there any chords or arpeggios that aren't included in Volume 2?" ABSOLUTELY! But this is more than enough information to really get to know the neck of the guitar. In fact, this much information can be a little overwhelming. If you JUST learn the 3 sets of "drop 2" and the 2 sets of "drop 3" seventh chord inversions, extensions, and alterations, you will have a HUGE chord vocabulary that will get you through most of the playing situations that you're likely to encounter. Pace yourself, and enjoy.

The material covered in Volume 2 includes:

I <u>TRIADS</u>:
    1) Diatonic Triads
    2) Altered Triads

II <u>SEVENTH CHORDS</u>:
    1) Diatonic Seventh Chords
    2) Chordal Extensions for Diatonic Seventh Chords
    3) Altered Seventh Chords

III <u>ARPEGGIOS</u>:
    1) Diatonic Seventh Chord Arpeggios
    2) Altered Seventh Chord Arpeggios

This is a HUGE chunk of raw information that will move you far along on your guitar improv quest. There is, of course, more information that you will need to know.

You will also need to learn:

- What are the different ways that one can use all of this information?

- What are the relationships between all of the scales from Volume 1 and all of these chords and arpeggios from Volume 2?

This information will be provided in ... Volume 3.

INTRODUCING CHORDS

Chords are built from the notes of scales. You can build a chord starting on any one of the notes in a scale. That starting note that you choose to build a chord on is called the "root" of the chord.

Since the major scale has 7 different notes in it, you can build 7 different chords from it. Because these 7 chords all come from the same scale, they are referred to as "diatonic" to that major scale. If you're writing a tune in the key of G major (from the scale of G major), all of the 7 chords that come from this scale are available for you to use in your composition ... provided that you want to stay in one key. Most tunes that stay in one key do not use **all** of the chords that come from that scale.

There are two basic ways of playing these seven diatonic chords:
    1. Triads (chords that are built with 3 different notes)
    2. Seventh Chords (chords that are built with 4 different notes)

Whether you are using triads or seventh chords, all chords are built in thirds. This means that a chord is made up of every other note in the scale, starting from the root of the chord, and ascending until you have your 3 or 4 notes (chord tones). We've been working with the key of G major, so lets figure out what chords are in the key of G major. The 7 notes in the key of G major are:

                G A B C D E F#
                1 2 3 4 5 6 7

If you start with the G (the 1 chord) ... G is now the root.
The triad would be spelled: G, B, D.
The seventh chord would be spelled: G, B, D, F#.

If you start with the A (the 2 chord) ... A is now the root.
The triad would be spelled: A, C, E.
The seventh chord would be spelled: A, C, E, G.

The three notes of a triad are referred to as:
1. the "root"
2. the "third"
3. the "fifth"

The four notes of a seventh chord are referred to as:
1. the "root"
2. the "third"
3. the "fifth"
4. the "seventh"

In the G major triad (G, B, D):
The G is the root.
The B is the third.
The D is the fifth.

In the G major seventh chord (G, B, D, F#):
The G is the root.
The B is the third.
The D is the fifth.
The F# is the seventh.

NAMES?!

Music theorists love to name things. It is hoped that these names will help identify and organize the information that you'll need for a greater understanding of how things work. Every guitar chord that you play can be referred to by its letter name, its tonality, its function, its inversion, its voicing (the order of the notes from the top to the bottom), or its string grouping.

1. The Letter Name
2. The Tonality
3. The Function
4. The Inversion
5. The Voicing
6. The String Grouping

The function, inversion, voicing, and string grouping categories all use numbers in order to explain things. The numbers used in these different categories are different sets of numbers and they don't always come from the same place. A "2" chord, a chord in 2nd inversion, a drop 2 chord, and the string grouping "6, 4, 3, 2", ALL use the number "2". But each "2" refers to a different concept. I'll explain these differences in the sections that follow.

1. The Letter Name

The letter name assigned to any chord is the letter that is the root of that chord.

2. The Tonality

Remember that each of the 7 notes of the major scale can have a chord built on it. Each of these 7 chords that come from the major scale has its own sound or its own "tonality". The words that are used to describe these tonalities are as follows:

TRIAD TONALITY
1 Chord = Major
2 Chord = Minor
3 Chord = Minor
4 Chord = Major
5 Chord = Major
6 Chord = Minor
7 Chord = Minor b5 or Diminished

SEVENTH CHORD TONALITY
1 Chord = Major 7
2 Chord = Minor 7
3 Chord = Minor 7
4 Chord = Major 7
5 Chord = Dominant 7
6 Chord = Minor 7
7 Chord = Minor 7 b5 or Half Diminished

3. The Function

Notice, that if you build a chord on the first scale degree, it is called a "1" chord. If you build a chord on the second scale degree, it is called the "2" chord. This is what is meant by the "function" of the chord, i.e., how this chord functions within a scale (as a "1" chord or as a "2" chord, etc …). Each of these chords has its own harmonic tendencies (different chords tug at one's ear in different ways). Also remember that the "1" note is always the letter name of the major scale and the "6" note is always the letter name of the natural minor scale.

4. The Inversion

The inversion name has to do with which note of the chord is placed in the lowest position of the chord that you play.

TRIADS:

Because chords are built in 3rds (every other note of a scale), a "G major" chord would be spelled: G, B, D. This chord starts with the root of the chord on the bottom, so it is said to be in **"root position"**. When played from bottom to top, it would look like this:

   (top) -> D <- (fifth of the chord)
           B <- (third of the chord)
(bottom) -> G <- (root of the chord)

If you were to start with the "B" (the third of the chord) as the lowest note and spell the chord up from there, it would be spelled: B, D, G. This chord starts with the third of the chord on the bottom, so it is said to be in **"first inversion"**. When played from bottom to top, it would look like this:

    (top) -> G <- (root of the chord)
            D <- (fifth of the chord)
(bottom) -> B <- (third of the chord)

If you were to start with the "D" (the fifth of the chord) as the lowest note and spell the chord up from there, it would be spelled: D, G, B. This chord starts with the fifth of the chord on the bottom, so it is said to be in **"second inversion"**. When played from bottom to top, it would look like this:

    (top) -> B <- (third of the chord)
            G <- (root of the chord)
(bottom) -> D <- (fifth of the chord)

SEVENTH CHORDS:

A "G major 7" chord is spelled: G, B, D, F#. This chord starts with the root of the chord on the bottom, so it is said to be in **"root position"**. When played from bottom to top, it would look like this:

    (top) -> F# <- (seventh of the chord)
            D <- (fifth of the chord)
            B <- (third of the chord)
(bottom) -> G <- (root of the chord)

If you were to start with the "B" (the third of the chord) as the lowest note and spell the chord up from there, it would be spelled: B, D, F#, G. This chord starts with the third of the chord on the bottom, so it is said to be in **"first inversion"**. When played from bottom to top, it would look like this:

    (top) -> G <- (root of the chord)
            F# <- (seventh of the chord)
            D <- (fifth of the chord)
(bottom) -> B <- (third of the chord)

If you were to start with the "D" (the fifth of the chord) as the lowest note and spell the chord up from there, it would be spelled: D, F#, G, B. This chord starts with the fifth of the chord on the bottom, so it is said to be in **"second inversion"**. When played from bottom to top, it would look like this:

    (top) -> B <- (third of the chord)
            G <- (root of the chord)
            F# <- (seventh of the chord)
(bottom) -> D <- (fifth of the chord)

If you were to start with the "F#" (the seventh of the chord) as the lowest note and spell the chord up from there, it would be spelled: F#, G, B, D. This chord starts with the seventh of the chord on the bottom, so it is said to be in **"third inversion"**. When played from bottom to top, it would look like this:

    (top) -> D <- (fifth of the chord)
            B <- (third of the chord)
            G <- (root of the chord)
(bottom) -> F# <- (seventh of the chord)

5. The Voicing

How one "voices" a chord has to do with the order of the notes within a chord, from the top to the bottom. All of the chord examples presented in the previous section on "inversions", are examples of "closed" chord voicings, which is to say that all of the notes of the chords are stacked in order of the musical alphabet. These "closed" voicings and their inversions are easy to play on the piano, but they can be difficult, if not impossible, to play on the guitar. More open type voicings are available, and more comfortable for guitar players. To open a voicing, one can "drop" one of the notes down an octave. Even though the same notes (letter names) are being used and the name of the chord doesn't change, the ORDER of the notes being played from top to bottom *has* changed and, more than likely, the inversion of the chord (which note is on the bottom) has also been changed.

Here is the "root position", "closed" voicing for a G major 7 chord (G, B, D, F#):

(seventh of the chord) -> F# <- (top note)
   (fifth of the chord) -> D <- (2nd note from the top note)
   (third of the chord) -> B <- (3rd note from the top note)
    (root of the chord) -> G <- (4th note from the top note)

If one were to take the 2nd highest note (the "D") and "drop" it an octave, one would have a voicing that looks like this:

(seventh of the chord) -> F#
  (third of the chord) -> B
   (root of the chord) -> G
 (fifth of the chord) -> D

This voicing is called a "drop 2" voicing because you've dropped the 2nd highest note down an octave. Since you've dropped the 2nd highest note of the chord down an octave, that note now sounds on the bottom of the chord. Yes, this is still a G major 7 chord. But instead of it being called a "closed" voicing G major 7 chord in "root position", it is now called a "drop 2" G major 7 chord in "second inversion".

And yes, you could have a "drop 3" chord voicing. This would be spelled: B, G, D, F#. The "B" is the 3rd highest note of the chord, so in a "drop 3" voicing this is the note that gets "dropped" an octave. This "B" is, coincidentally, also the 3rd of the chord. And since this 3rd of the chord would be the lowest note of the chord, now the chord would be in "first inversion".

NOTE:
If one were to take a closed voicing, third inversion G major 7 chord: F#, G, B, D and play it as a "drop 3" voicing (the 3rd highest note of this chord is the "G"), the "G" would now be the lowest note of the chord. This "drop 3" approach would turn this closed G major 7 in third inversion into a "drop 3" G major 7 chord in "root position" because the "G" would now be the lowest note in this chord voicing.

You could also have combinations of dropped notes, like a "drop 2 & 3" G major 7 chord voicing: B, D, G, F#. Are your eyes starting to glaze over?

You get the picture. Music theorists love to name everything. And all of this information *can* be quite fascinating ... and helpful. It is intended to provide a clear way of thinking and talking about music. And while it can seem like pretty heady stuff and a bit of a distraction from playing the instrument, it is meant to speed one's understanding of music and all of the musical possibilities available on one's instrument. Even though the MAJOR METHOD Volume 2 has organized the chords by voicing types, string groupings, and inversions, I believe that getting your hands on these chords, starting to memorize the shapes and beginning to use them in your day to day playing is far more important than memorizing terms like "drop 2" or "third inversion". The MAJOR METHOD is intended to provide guitar players with a visual answer to the question: "What does all of this stuff look like on the neck of the guitar?".

6. The String Grouping

This is pretty self-explanatory. The guitar strings are numbered from the high E string (1) down to the low E string (6):

1 - High E String
2 - B String
3 - G String
4 - D String
5 - A String
6 - Low E String

So if you were playing a chord that used the following strings: low E, D, G, B, this would be the 6, 4, 3, 2 string grouping.

DIATONIC TRIADS

In Volume 1, we discussed the type of triads called "barre chords". These chords generally double some of their 3 notes in different octaves in order to create a more full and powerful sound. In Volume 2 we are going to explore many of the other ways that you can play 3 note chords (triads) on the neck of the guitar that don't double any notes.

Again, the "root" of a chord is the letter name that the chord is built on. So the root of a G major chord is the G. The root of an A minor chord is the A.

Also remember that there are seven diatonic triads that come from the major scale. These seven triads have the following tonalities:

1, 4, & 5 chords = Major
2, 3, & 6 chords = Minor
7 chord = Diminished (Minor b5)

Now what you need to know is:
 1) What do these chords look like on a chord chart?
 2) What do these chords look like on the neck of the guitar?

While there is no one standard notation for writing out chord symbols on chord charts, there are some symbols that are used more frequently then others.

I'll use the letter "C" as a constant to show you some of these symbols:

C Major = C, C Maj, C M, C Major, C△

C Minor = C-, C min, C mi, C m

C Diminished (Minorb5) = C°, Cminb5, C mi(b5), C-(b5)

These symbols are pretty self-explanatory. Your job will be to remember what they look like. Of course, you'll also have to learn the shapes of these chord types on the neck of the guitar. There are many places on the guitar that one can play each of these chord types.

NOTE:
Because of the way the neck of the guitar is structured, any one triad will have many different places where it can be played. These different places may contain the exact same notes in the exact same order, but they may use a different string grouping, a different fingering, and may have a slightly different timbre (a brighter or a darker sound) from each other. Rather than organizing all of the triads by how they look on the music staff (thereby having to present multiple string groupings at the same time), I have organized all of them by their string groupings along with their corresponding inversions. I have also included a parent scale in the diagrams so you can see how all of the chords live within the scale patterns. This allows for a more practical, working knowledge of the neck of the guitar and how the inversions and scales relate to each other.

REMEMBER:
When the root of the chord is the lowest note of the chord voicing, the chord is in:
"root position".
When the third of the chord is the lowest note of the chord voicing, the chord is in:
"first inversion".
When the fifth of the chord is the lowest note of the chord voicing, the chord is in:
"second inversion".

All of the triad diagrams in The MAJOR METHOD use the following shapes:
O = Root Position Chord
☐ = First Inversion Chord
⬭ = Second Inversion Chord

Here we go ...

DIATONIC TRIADS

○ = Root Position Triad
□ = First Inversion Triad
⬭ = Second Inversion Triad

CLOSED:
654 STRING GROUPING
The "1" Chord: Major Triad Inversions In "G" Major
G Major Triads

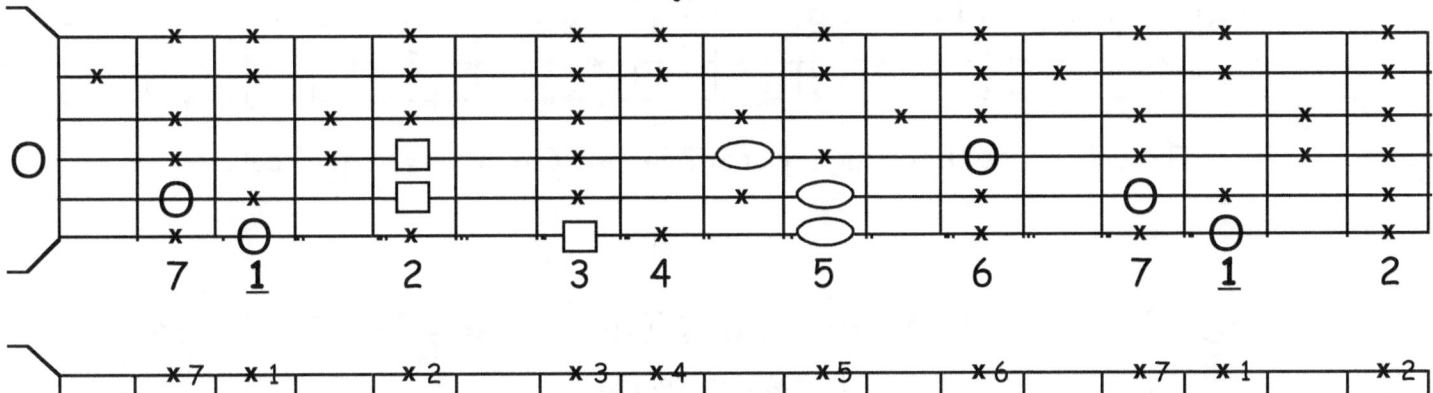

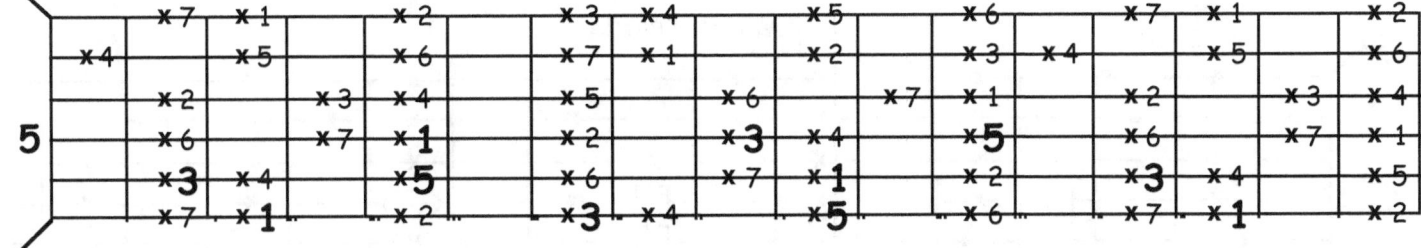

Notice that the only notes that you play are: 1, 3, and 5 of the G major scale. See how the major scale pattern lives underneath these chord inversions. For all of these diatonic triad chord diagrams, the only notes that you play are the notes of the chord within the major scale:

    For the "1" chords, you are playing the 1, 3, and 5 (major triad).
    For the "2" chords, you are playing the 2, 4, and 6 (minor triad).
    For the "3" chords, you are playing the 3, 5, and 7 (minor triad).
    For the "4" chords, you are playing the 4, 6, and 1 (major triad).
    For the "5" chords, you are playing the 5, 7, and 2 (major triad).
    For the "6" chords, you are playing the 6, 1, and 3 (minor triad).
    For the "7" chords, you are playing the 7, 2, and 4 (diminished triad).

654 STRING GROUPING

The "2" Chord: Minor Triad Inversions In "G" Major
A Minor Triads

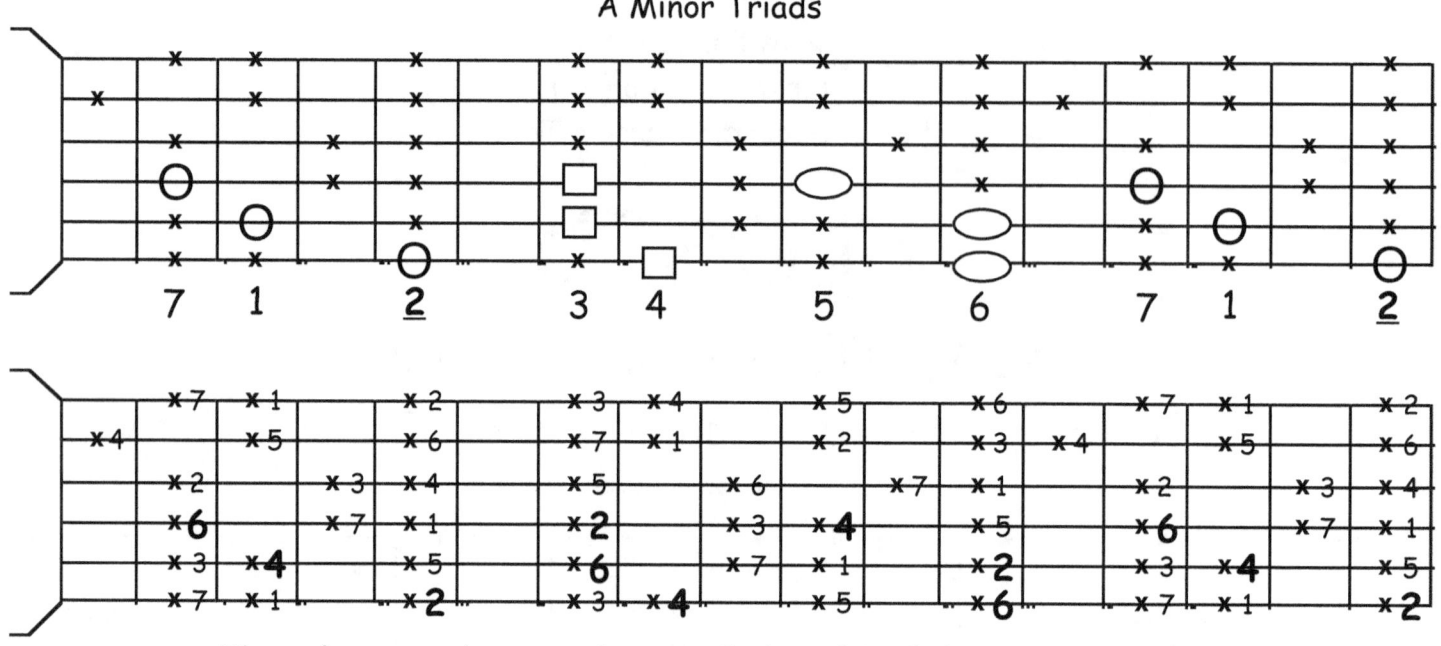

The only notes that you play are: 2, 4, and 6 of the G major scale.

The "3" Chord: Minor Triad Inversions In "G" Major
B Minor Triads

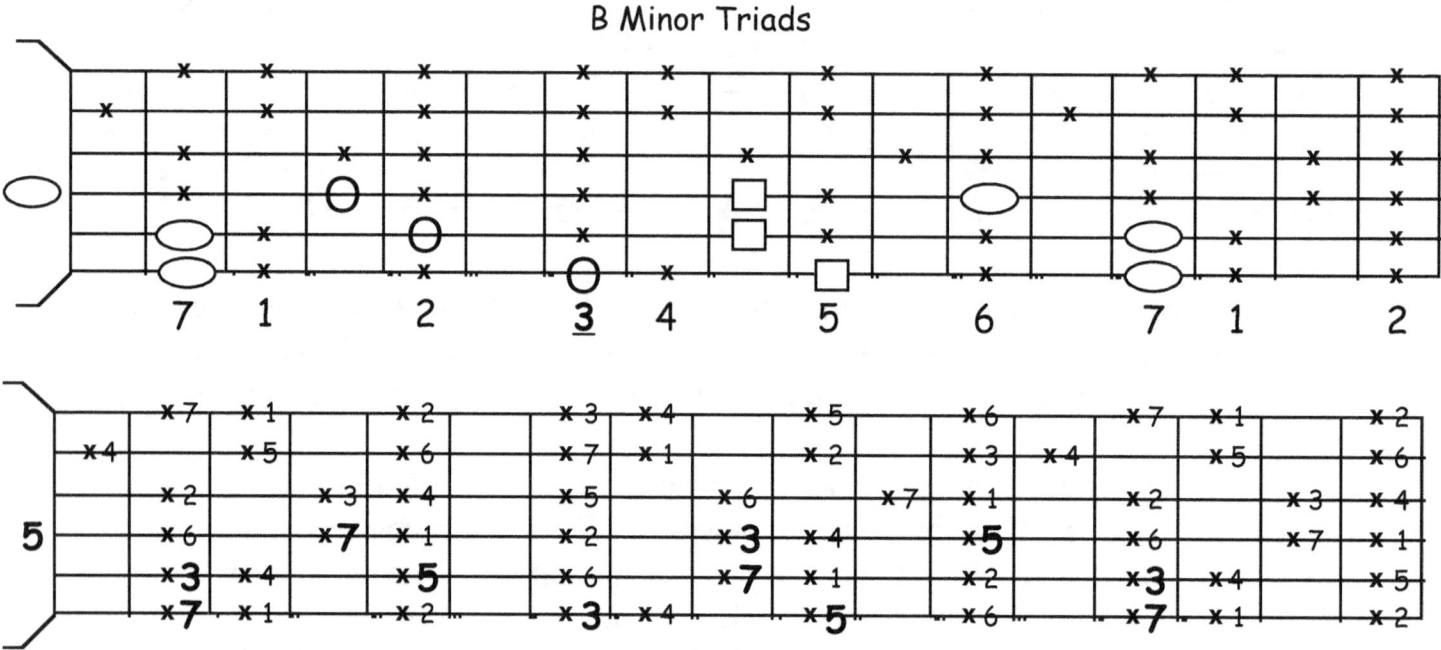

The only notes that you play are: 3, 5, and 7 of the G major scale.

654 STRING GROUPING

The "4" Chord: Major Triad Inversions In "G" Major
C Major Triads

The only notes that you play are: 4, 6, and 1 of the G major scale.

The "5" Chord: Major Triad Inversions In "G" Major
D Major Triads

The only notes that you play are: 5, 7, and 2 of the G major scale.

654 STRING GROUPING

The "6" Chord: Minor Triad Inversions In "G" Major
E Minor Triads

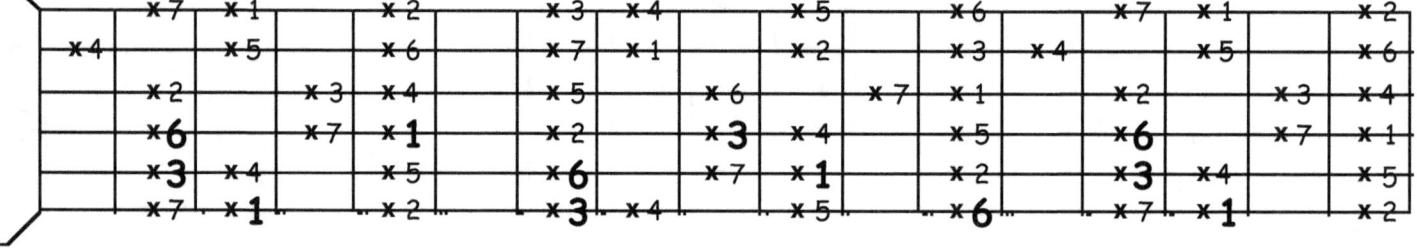

The only notes that you play are: 6, 1, and 3 of the G major scale.

The "7" Chord: Diminished Triad Inversions In "G" Major
F# Diminished Triads

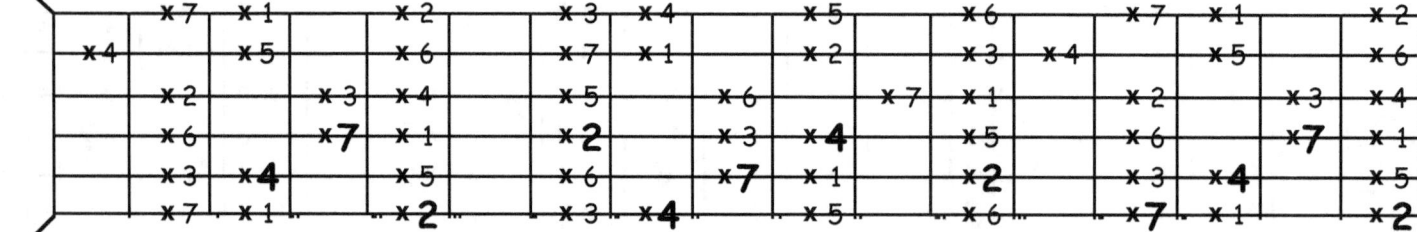

The only notes that you play are: 7, 2, and 4 of the G major scale.

CLOSED:
543 STRING GROUPING
The "1" Chord: Major Triad Inversions In "G" Major
G Major Triads

The only notes that you play are: 1, 3, and 5 of the G major scale.

The "2" Chord: Minor Triad Inversions In "G" Major
A Minor Triads

The only notes that you play are: 2, 4, and 6 of the G major scale.

543 STRING GROUPING

The "3" Chord: Minor Triad Inversions In "G" Major

B Minor Triads

The only notes that you play are: 3, 5, and 7 of the G major scale.

The "4" Chord: Major Triad Inversions In "G" Major

C Major Triads

The only notes that you play are: 4, 6, and 1 of the G major scale.

543 STRING GROUPING

The "5" Chord: Major Triad Inversions In "G" Major

D Major Triads

The only notes that you play are: 5, 7, and 2 of the G major scale.

The "6" Chord: Minor Triad Inversions In "G" Major

E Minor Triads

The only notes that you play are: 6, 1, and 3 of the G major scale.

543 STRING GROUPING
The "7" Chord: Diminished Triad Inversions In "G" Major
F# Diminished Triads

The only notes that you play are: 7, 2, and 4 of the G major scale.

CLOSED:
432 STRING GROUPING
The "1" Chord: Major Triad Inversions In "G" Major
G Major Triads

The only notes that you play are: 1, 3, and 5 of the G major scale.

432 STRING GROUPING

The "2" Chord: Minor Triad Inversions In "G" Major
A Minor Triads

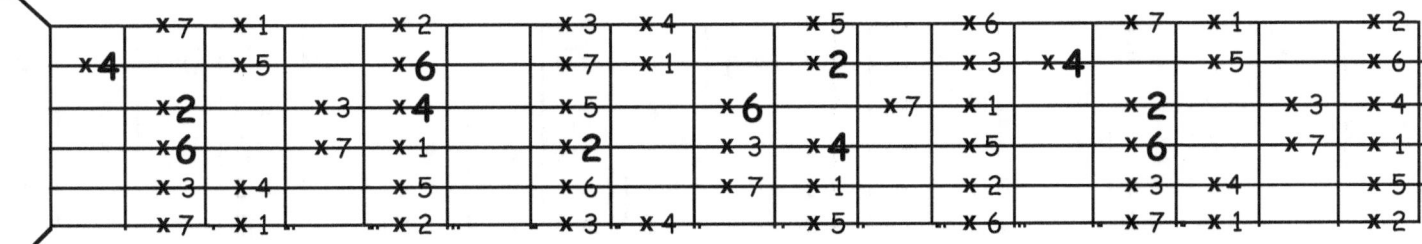

The only notes that you play are: 2, 4, and 6 of the G major scale.

The "3" Chord: Minor Triad Inversions In "G" Major
B Minor Triads

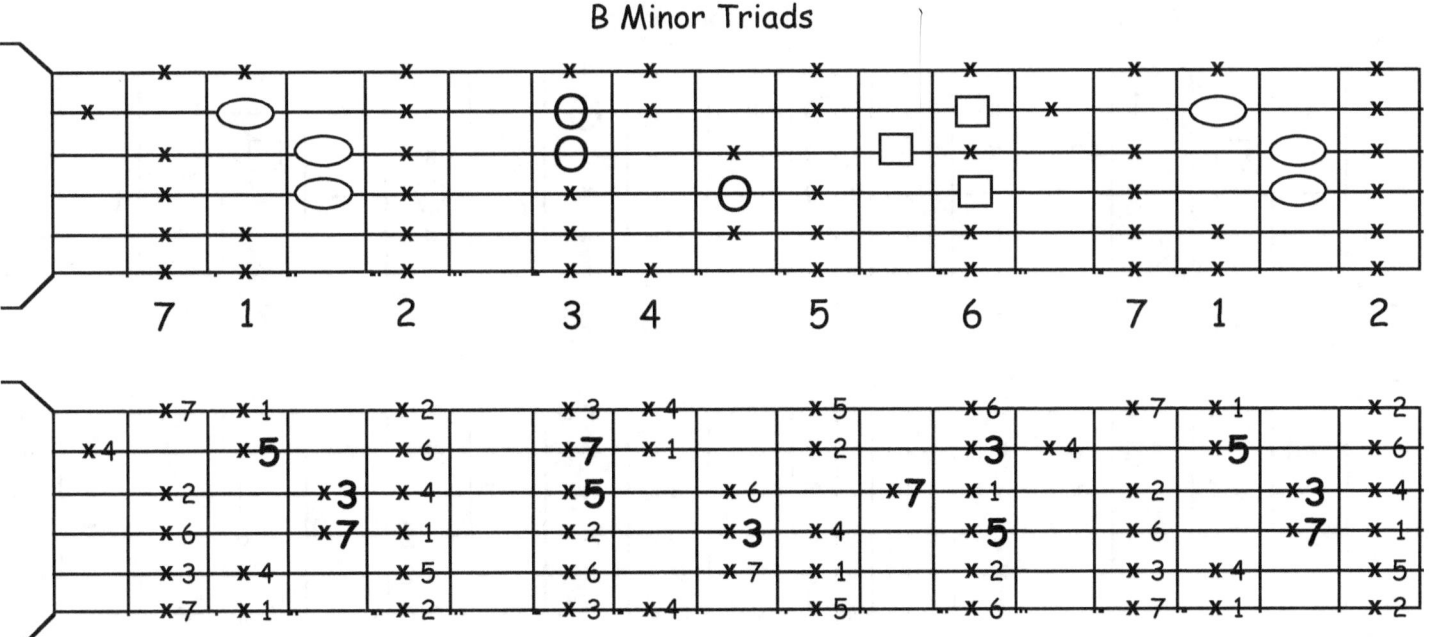

The only notes that you play are: 3, 5, and 7 of the G major scale.

432 STRING GROUPING

The "4" Chord: Major Triad Inversions In "G" Major
C Major Triads

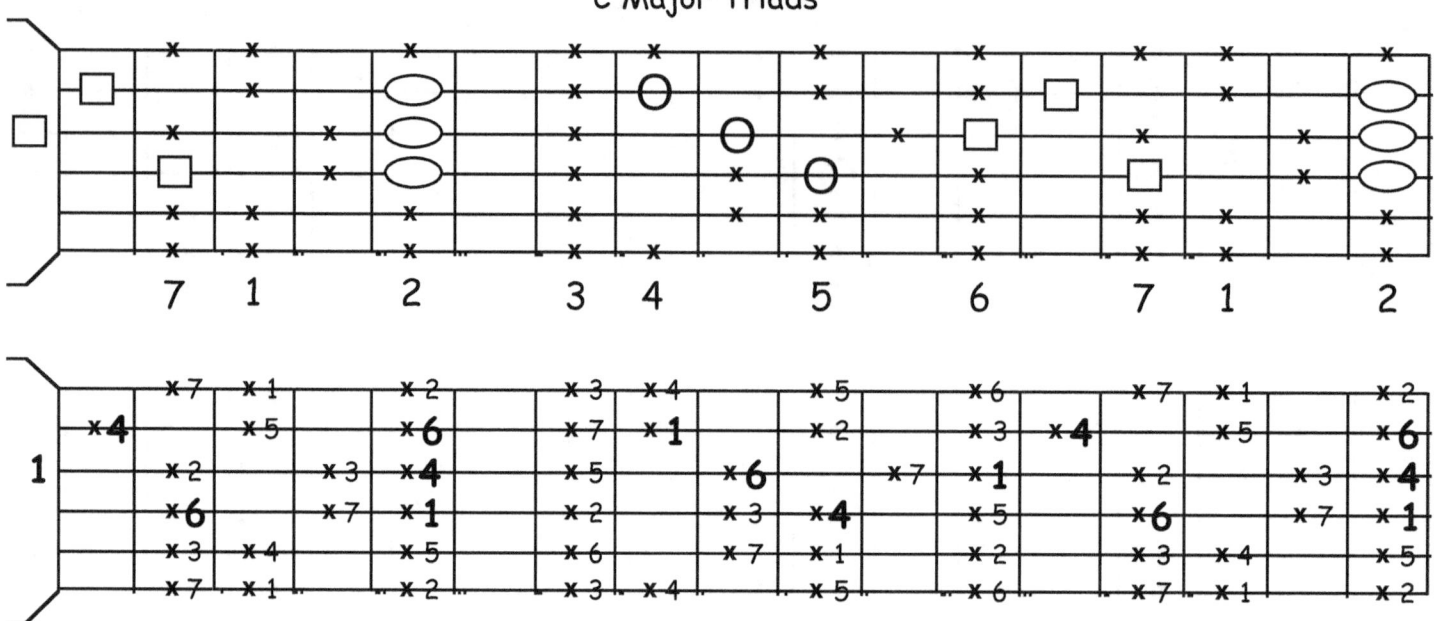

The only notes that you play are: 4, 6, and 1 of the G major scale.

The "5" Chord: Major Triad Inversions In "G" Major
D Major Triads

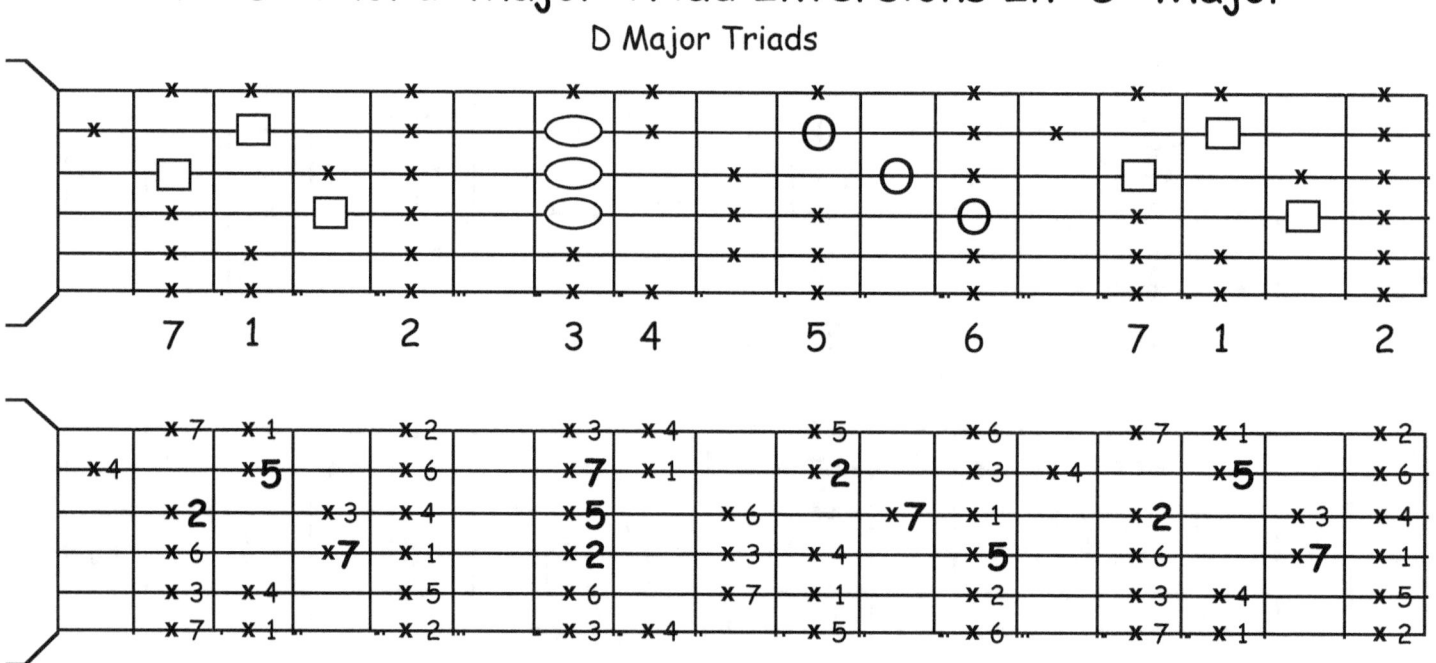

The only notes that you play are: 5, 7, and 2 of the G major scale.

432 STRING GROUPING

The "6" Chord: Minor Triad Inversions In "G" Major
E Minor Triads

The only notes that you play are: 6, 1, and 3 of the G major scale.

The "7" Chord: Diminished Triad Inversions In "G" Major
F# Diminished Triads

The only notes that you play are: 7, 2, and 4 of the G major scale.

CLOSED:
321 STRING GROUPING
The "1" Chord: Major Triad Inversions In "G" Major
G Major Triads

The only notes that you play are: 1, 3, and 5 of the G major scale.

The "2" Chord: Minor Triad Inversions In "G" Major
A Minor Triads

The only notes that you play are: 2, 4, and 6 of the G major scale.

321 STRING GROUPING

The "3" Chord: Minor Triad Inversions In "G" Major

B Minor Triads

The only notes that you play are: 3, 5, and 7 of the G major scale.

The "4" Chord: Major Triad Inversions In "G" Major

C Major Triads

The only notes that you play are: 4, 6, and 1 of the G major scale.

321 STRING GROUPING

The "5" Chord: Major Triad Inversions In "G" Major

D Major Triads

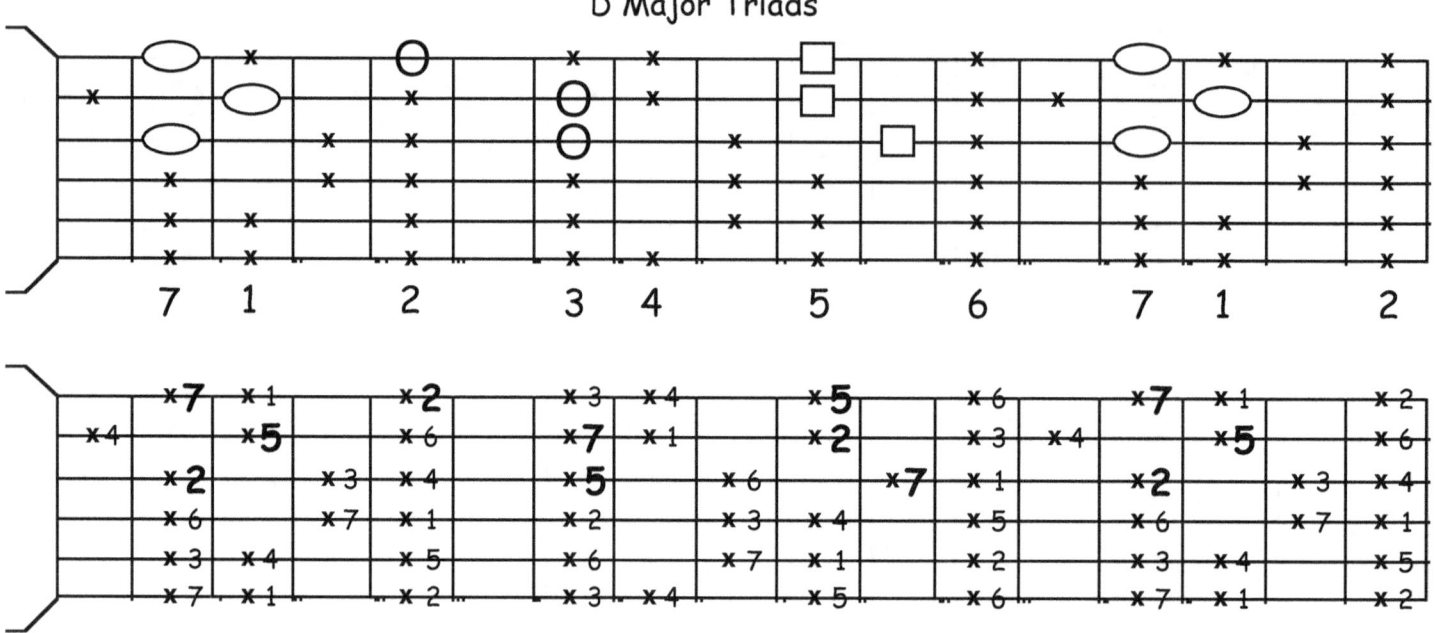

The only notes that you play are: 5, 7, and 2 of the G major scale.

The "6" Chord: Minor Triad Inversions In "G" Major

E Minor Triads

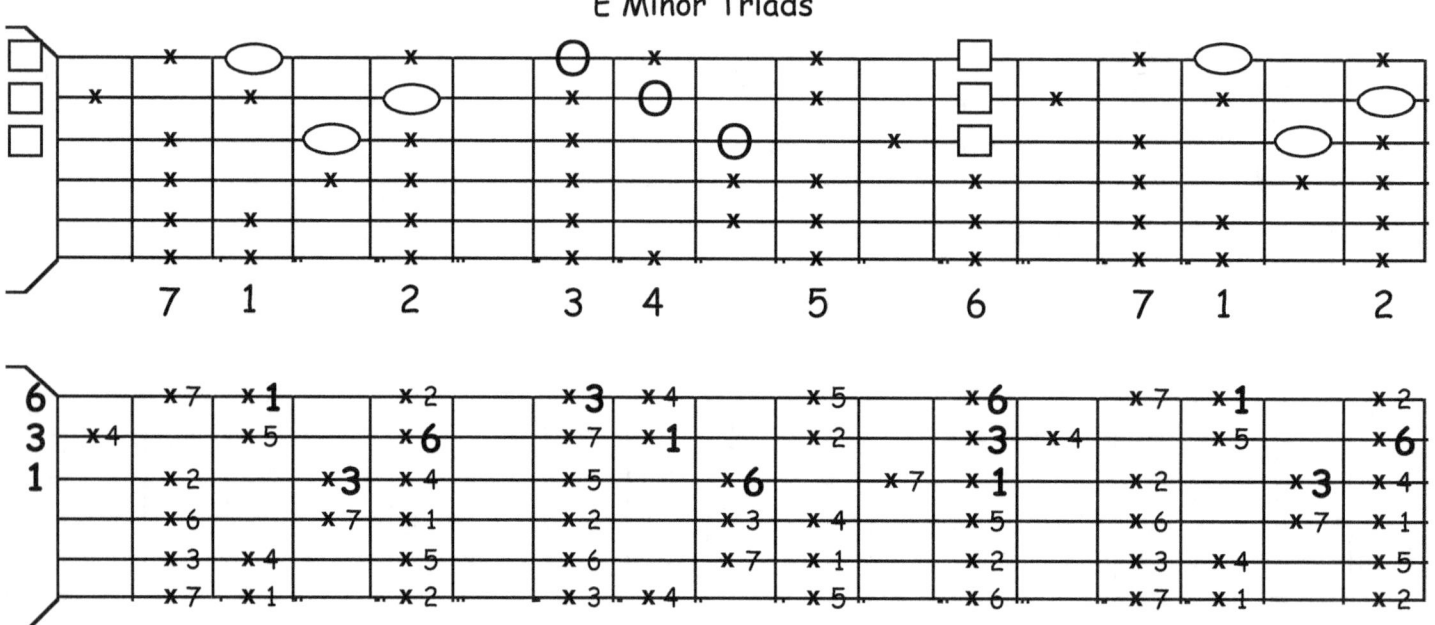

The only notes that you play are: 6, 1, and 3 of the G major scale.

321 STRING GROUPING
The "7" Chord: Diminished Triad Inversions In "G" Major
F# Diminished Triads

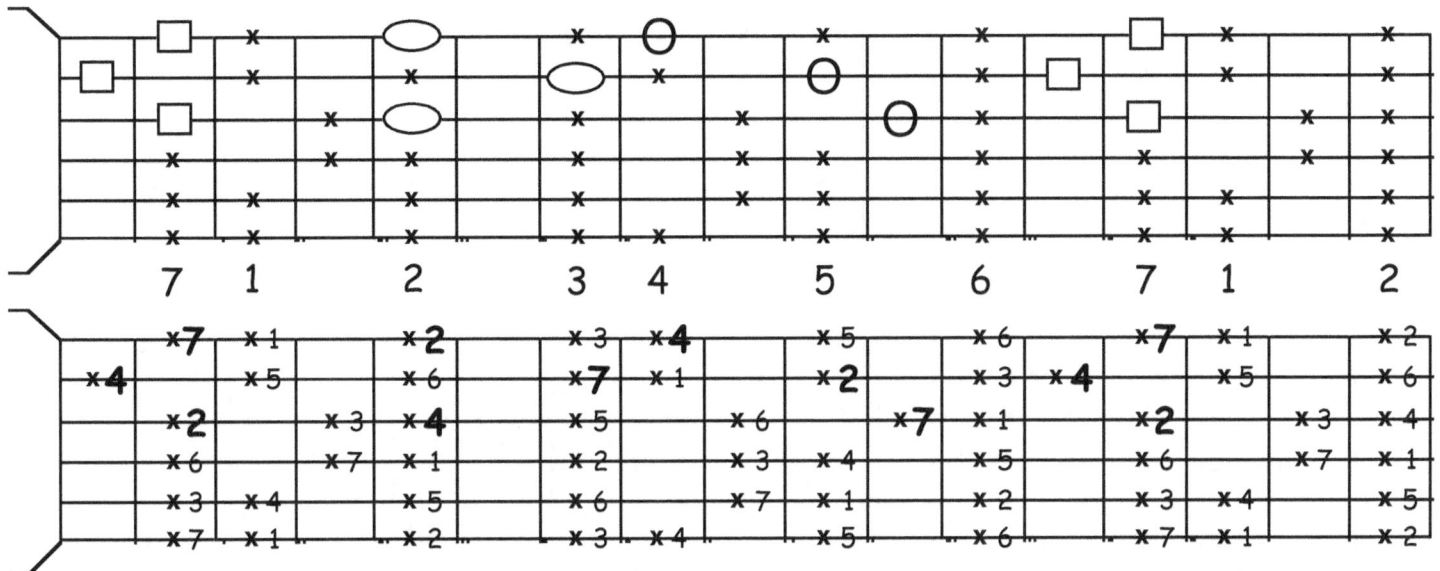

The only notes that you play are: 7, 2, and 4 of the G major scale.

DROP 2:
653 STRING GROUPING
The "1" Chord: Major Triad Inversions In "G" Major
G Major Triads

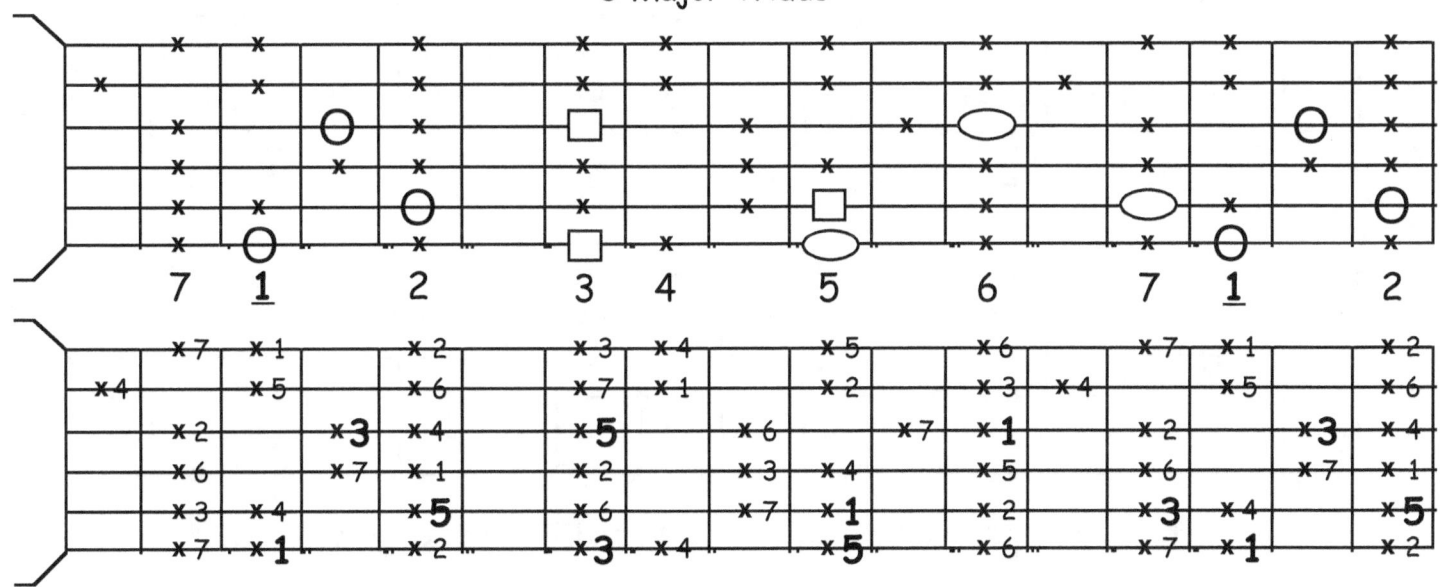

The only notes that you play are: 1, 3, and 5 of the G major scale.

653 STRING GROUPING

The "2" Chord: Minor Triad Inversions In "G" Major
A Minor Triads

The only notes that you play are: 2, 4, and 6 of the G major scale.

The "3" Chord: Minor Triad Inversions In "G" Major
B Minor Triads

The only notes that you play are: 3, 5, and 7 of the G major scale.

653 STRING GROUPING

The "4" Chord: Major Triad Inversions In "G" Major
C Major Triads

The only notes that you play are: 4, 6, and 1 of the G major scale.

The "5" Chord: Major Triad Inversions In "G" Major
D Major Triads

The only notes that you play are: 5, 7, and 2 of the G major scale.

653 STRING GROUPING

The "6" Chord: Minor Triad Inversions In "G" Major
E Minor Triads

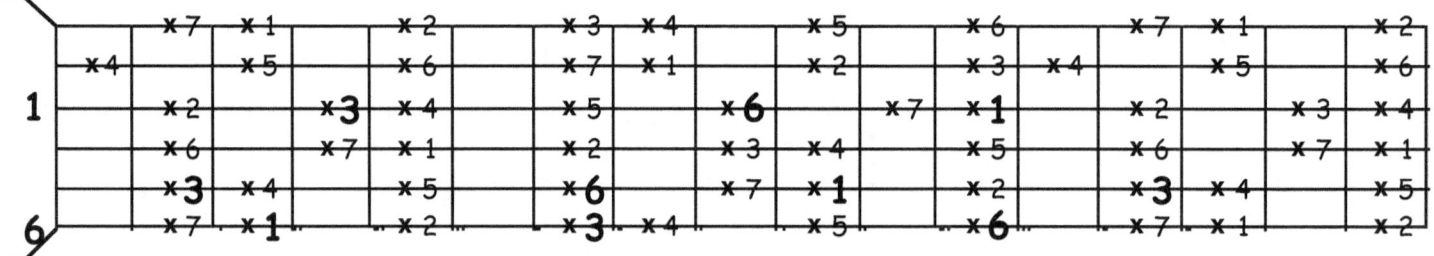

The only notes that you play are: 6, 1, and 3 of the G major scale.

The "7" Chord: Diminished Triad Inversions In "G" Major
F# Diminished Triads

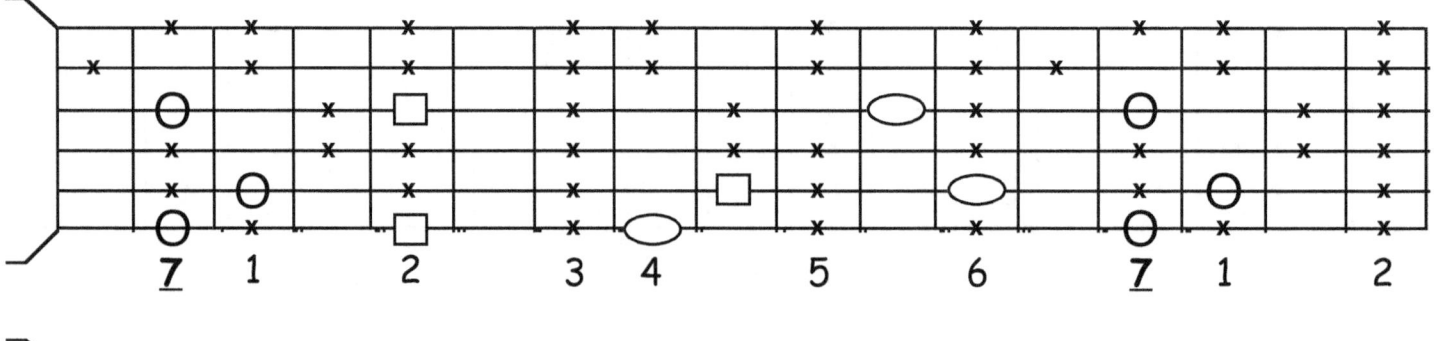

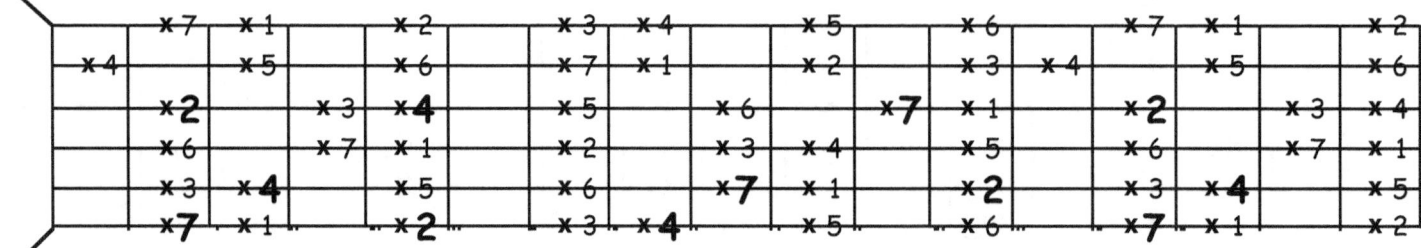

The only notes that you play are: 7, 2, and 4 of the G major scale.

DROP 2:
542 STRING GROUPING

The "1" Chord: Major Triad Inversions In "G" Major
G Major Triads

The only notes that you play are: 1, 3, and 5 of the G major scale.

The "2" Chord: Minor Triad Inversions In "G" Major
A Minor Triads

The only notes that you play are: 2, 4, and 6 of the G major scale.

542 STRING GROUPING

The "3" Chord: Minor Triad Inversions In "G" Major
B Minor Triads

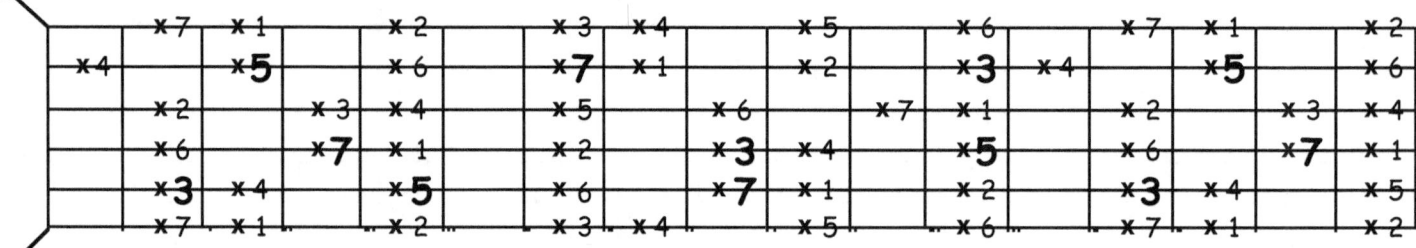

The only notes that you play are: 3, 5, and 7 of the G major scale.

The "4" Chord: Major Triad Inversions In "G" Major
C Major Triads

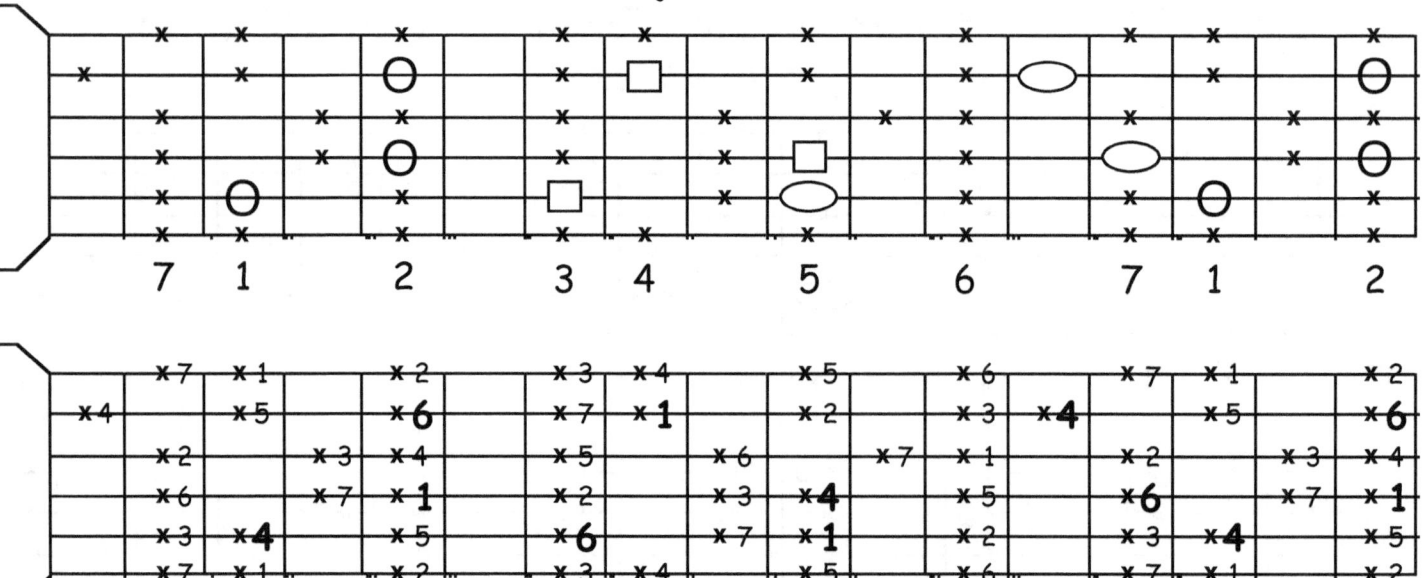

The only notes that you play are: 4, 6, and 1 of the G major scale.

542 STRING GROUPING
The "5" Chord: Major Triad Inversions In "G" Major
D Major Triads

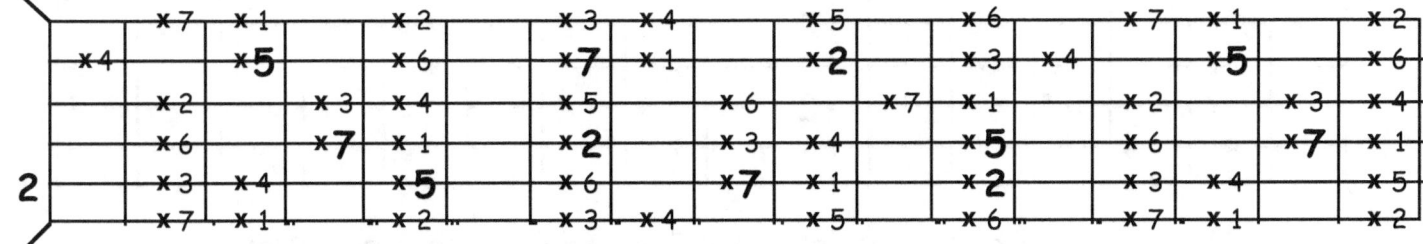

The only notes that you play are: 5, 7, and 2 of the G major scale.

The "6" Chord: Minor Triad Inversions In "G" Major
E Minor Triads

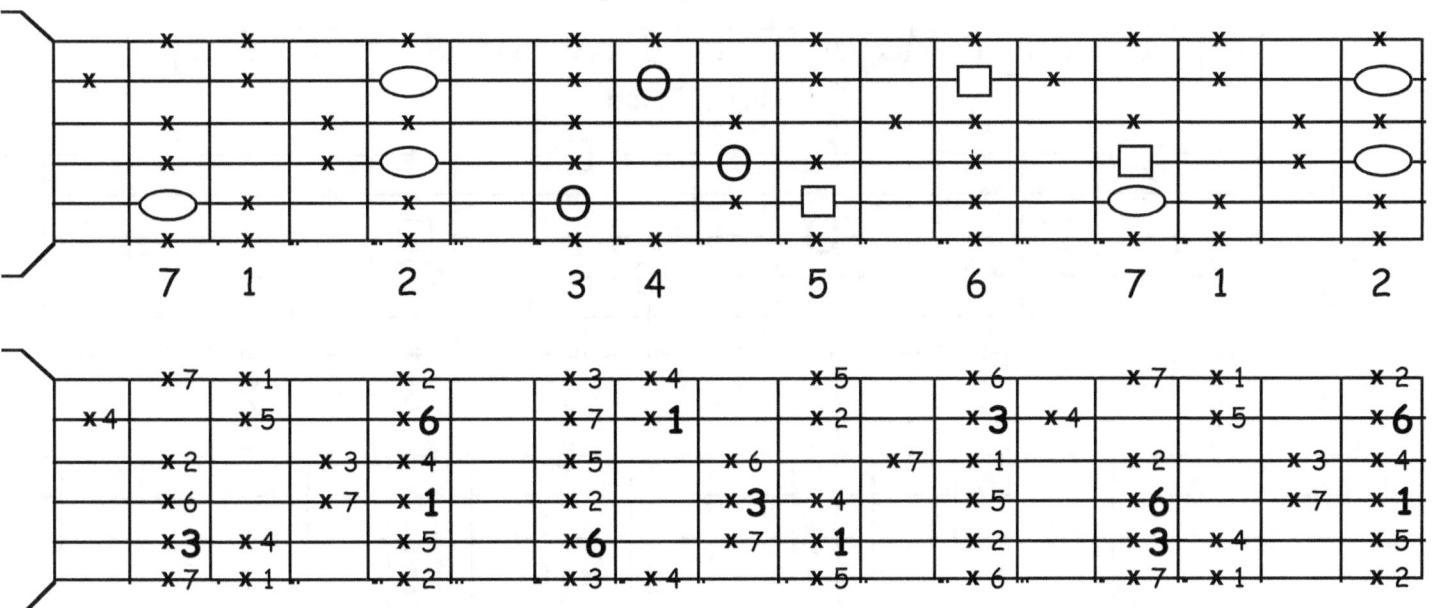

The only notes that you play are: 6, 1, and 3 of the G major scale.

542 STRING GROUPING
The "7" Chord: Diminished Triad Inversions In "G" Major
F# Diminished Triads

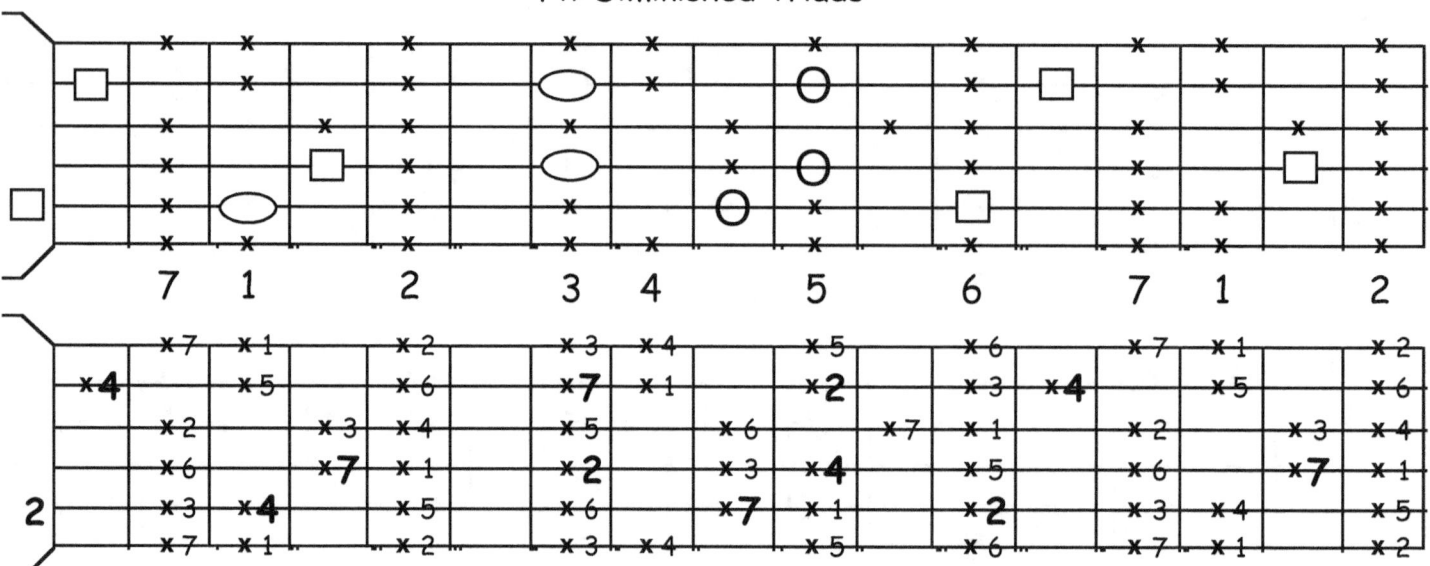

The only notes that you play are: 7, 2, and 4 of the G major scale.

DROP 2:

431 STRING GROUPING
The "1" Chord: Major Triad Inversions In "G" Major
G Major Triads

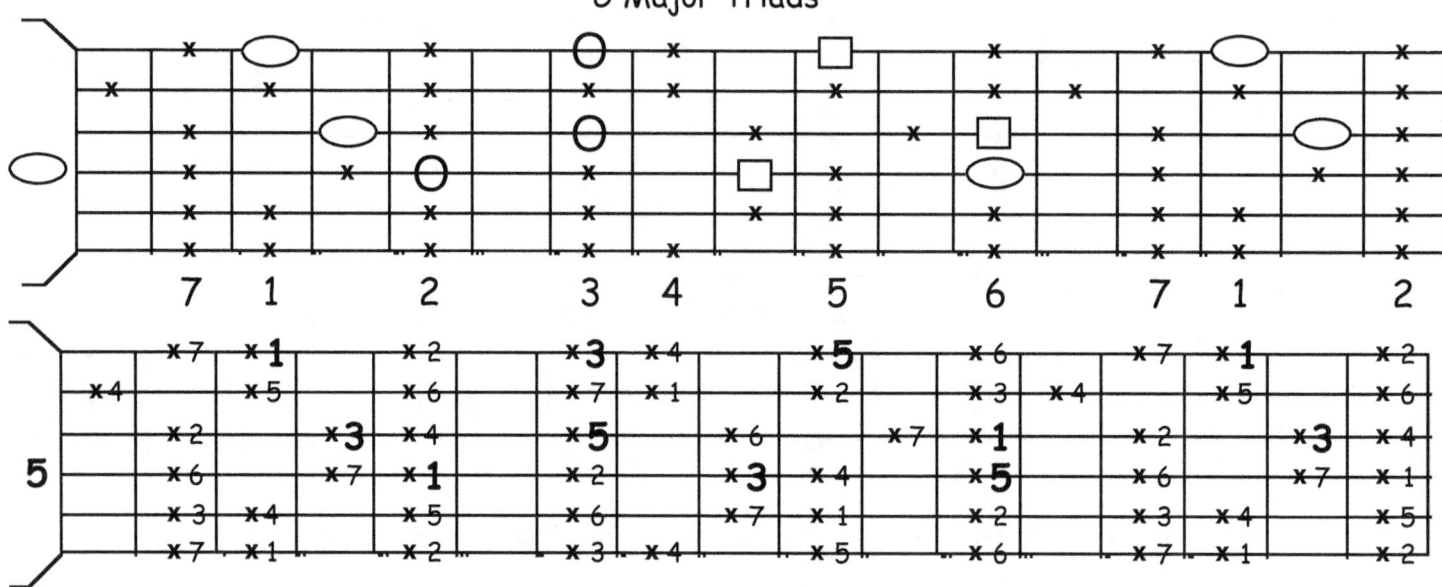

The only notes that you play are: 1, 3, and 5 of the G major scale.

431 STRING GROUPING

The "2" Chord: Minor Triad Inversions In "G" Major
A Minor Triads

The only notes that you play are: 2, 4, and 6 of the G major scale.

The "3" Chord: Minor Triad Inversions In "G" Major
B Minor Triads

The only notes that you play are: 3, 5, and 7 of the G major scale.

431 STRING GROUPING

The "4" Chord: Major Triad Inversions In "G" Major
C Major Triads

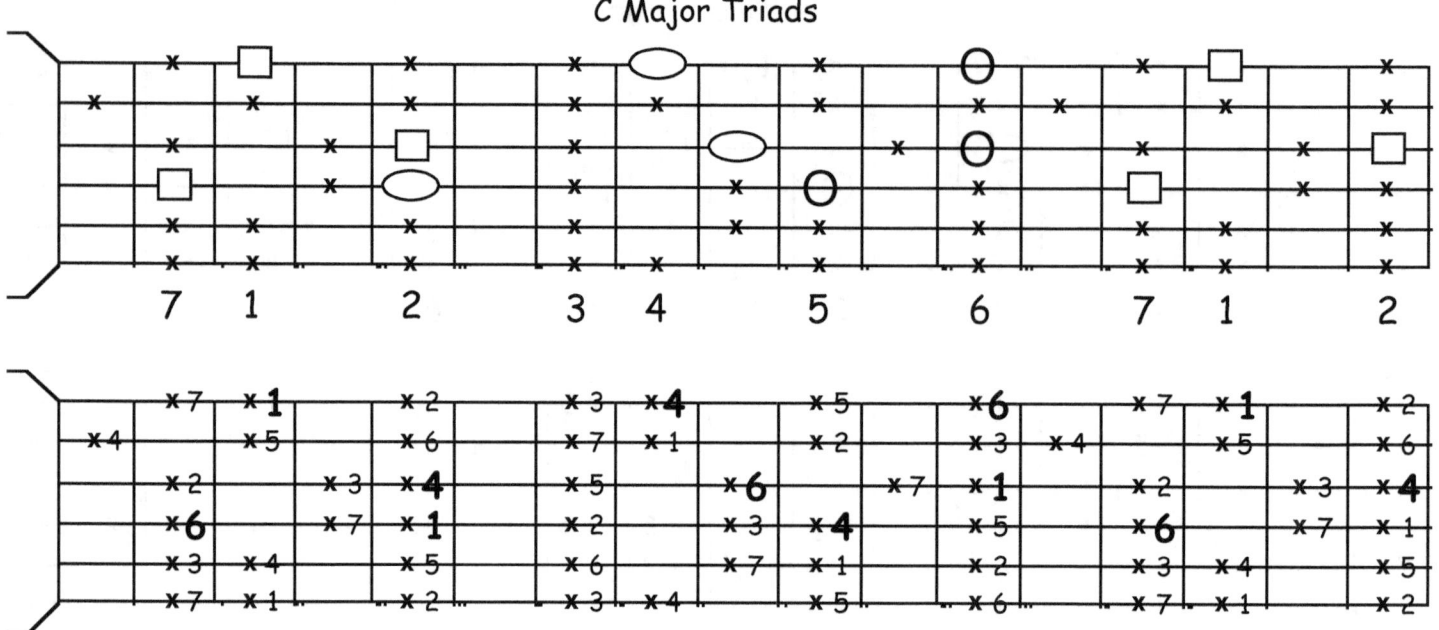

The only notes that you play are: 4, 6, and 1 of the G major scale.

The "5" Chord: Major Triad Inversions In "G" Major
D Major Triads

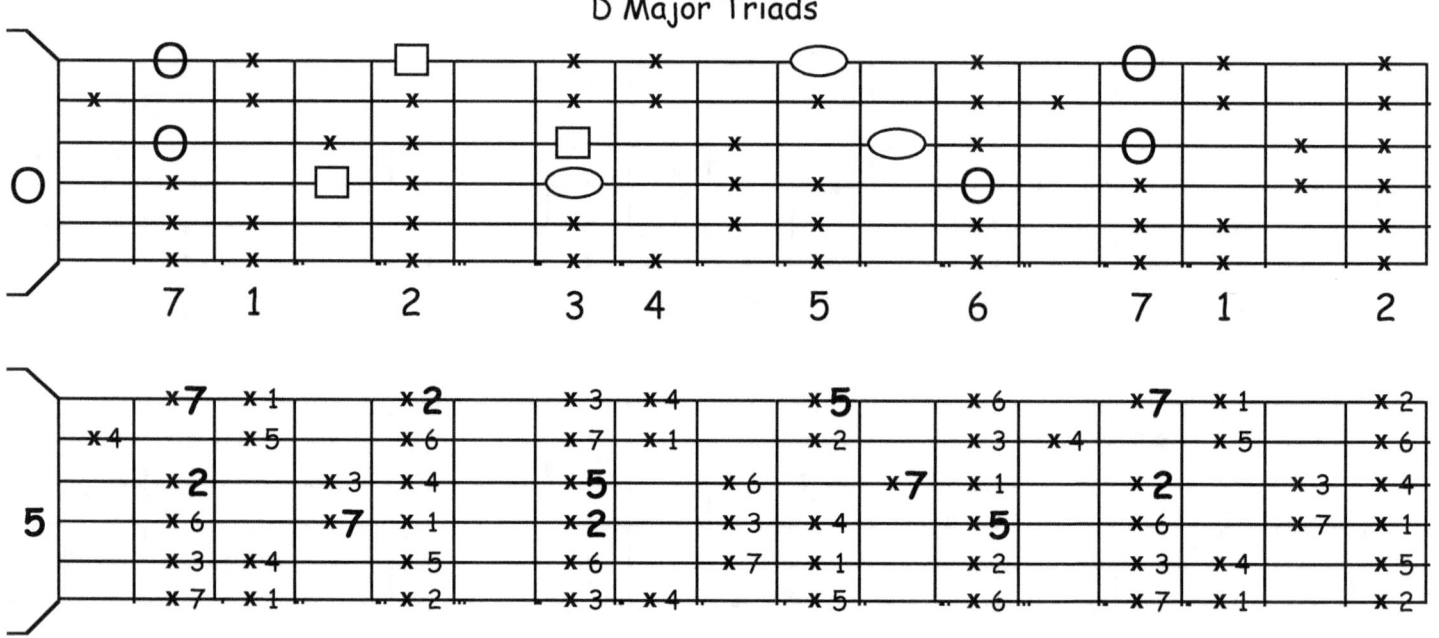

The only notes that you play are: 5, 7, and 2 of the G major scale.

431 STRING GROUPING

The "6" Chord: Minor Triad Inversions In "G" Major
E Minor Triads

The only notes that you play are: 6, 1, and 3 of the G major scale.

The "7" Chord: Diminished Triad Inversions In "G" Major
F# Diminished Triads

The only notes that you play are: 7, 2, and 4 of the G major scale.

DROP 2:
643 STRING GROUPING
(Same notes as 653 String Grouping, but a little brighter)
The "1" Chord: Major Triad Inversions In "G" Major
G Major Triads

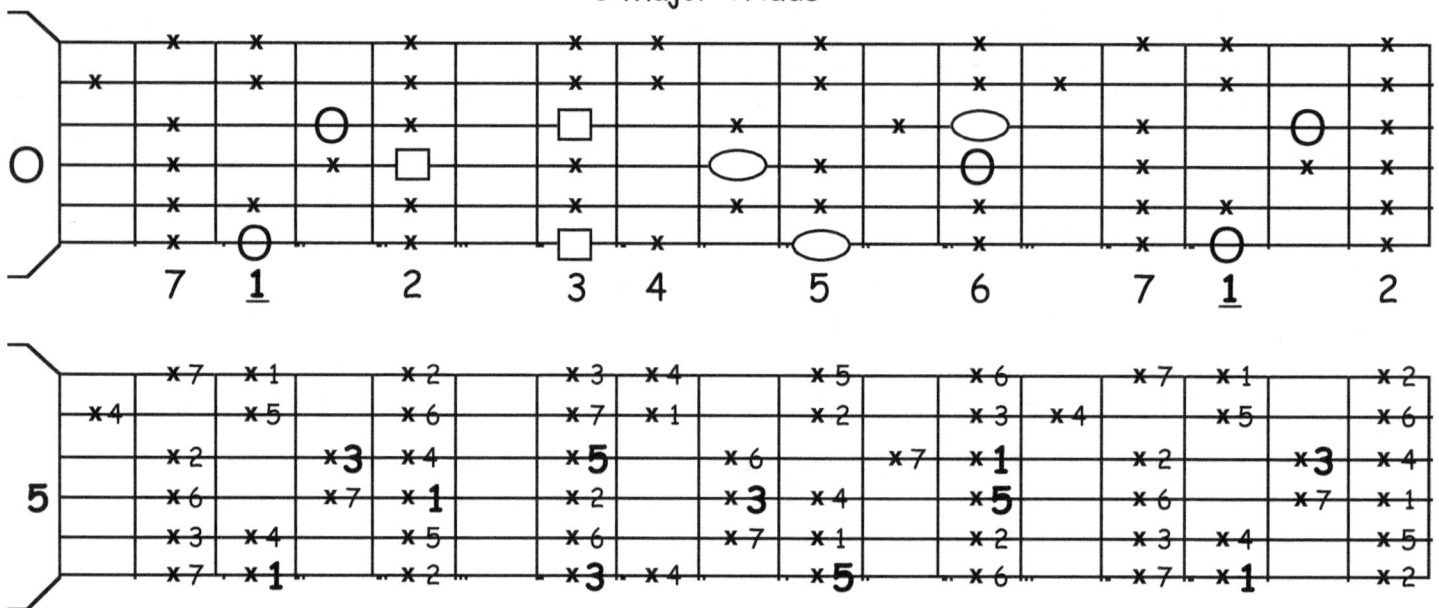

The only notes that you play are: 1, 3, and 5 of the G major scale.

The "2" Chord: Minor Triad Inversions In "G" Major
A Minor Triads

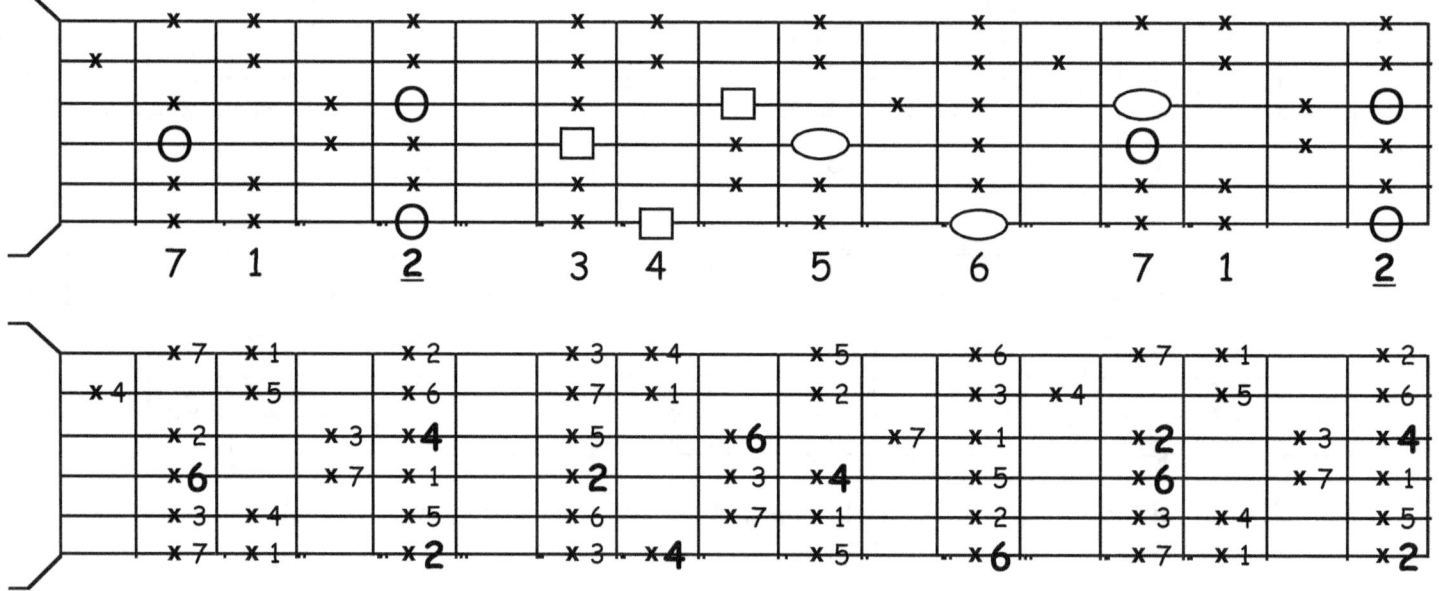

The only notes that you play are: 2, 4, and 6 of the G major scale.

643 STRING GROUPING

The "3" Chord: Minor Triad Inversions In "G" Major
B Minor Triads

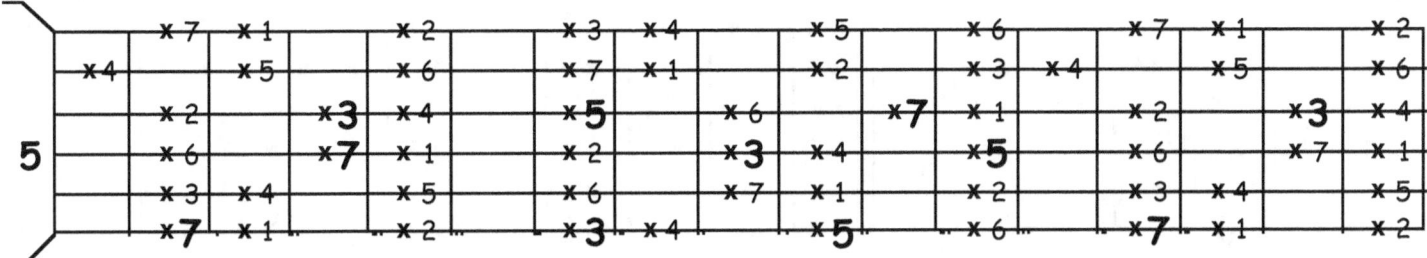

The only notes that you play are: 3, 5, and 7 of the G major scale.

The "4" Chord: Major Triad Inversions In "G" Major
C Major Triads

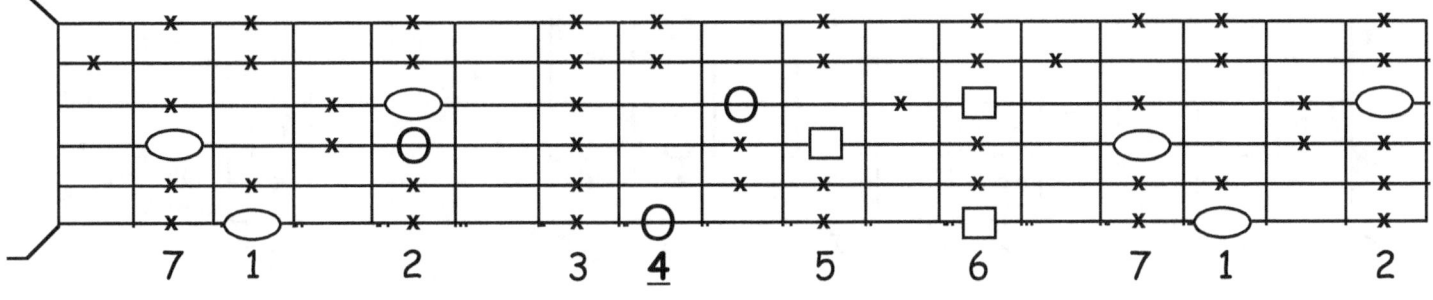

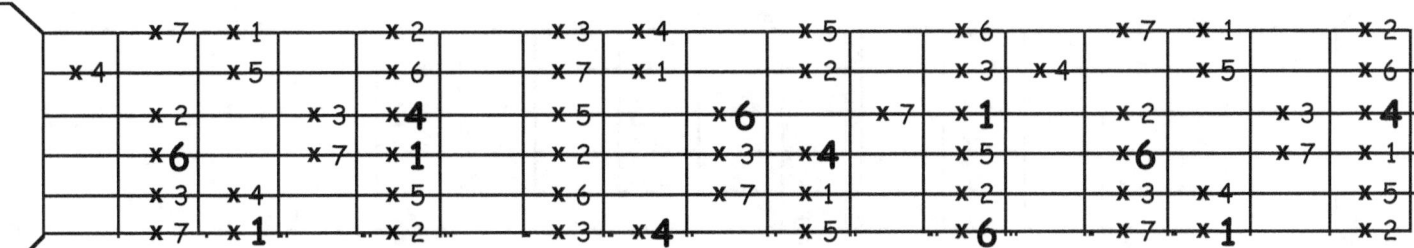

The only notes that you play are: 4, 6, and 1 of the G major scale.

643 STRING GROUPING

The "5" Chord: Major Triad Inversions In "G" Major
D Major Triads

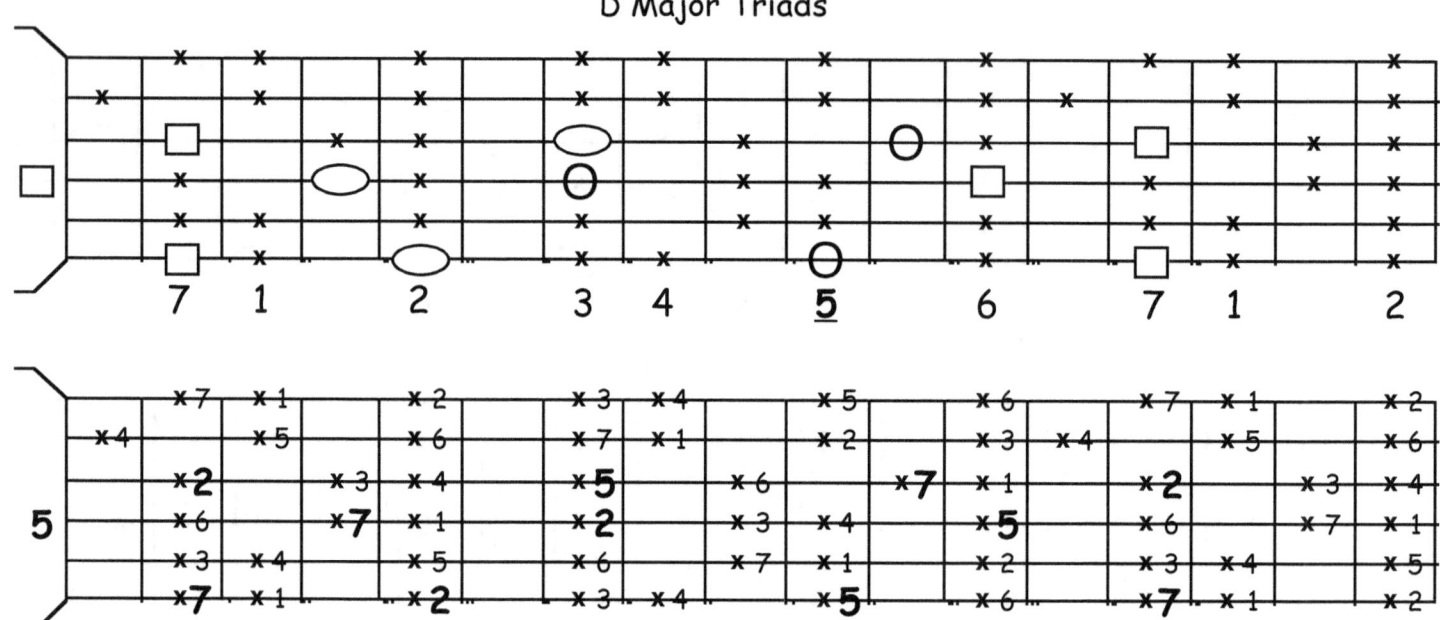

The only notes that you play are: 5, 7, and 2 of the G major scale.

The "6" Chord: Minor Triad Inversions In "G" Major
E Minor Triads

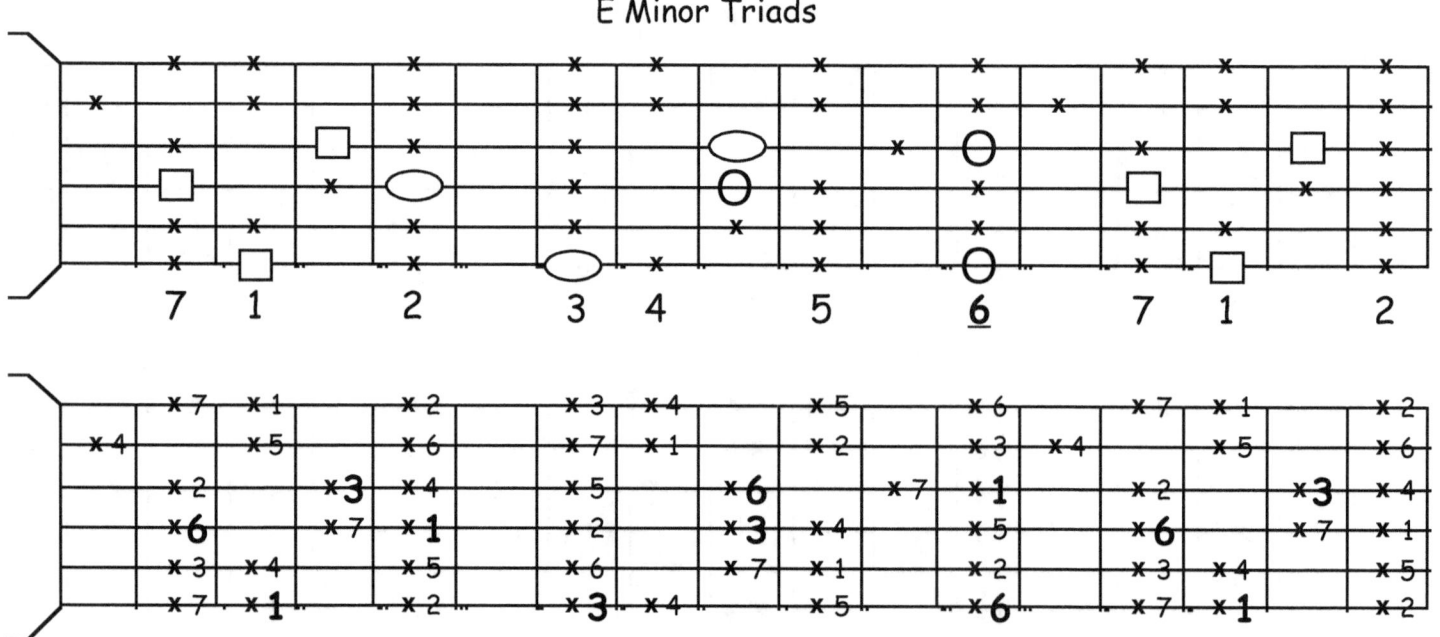

The only notes that you play are: 6, 1, and 3 of the G major scale.

643 STRING GROUPING
The "7" Chord: Diminished Triad Inversions In "G" Major
F# Diminished Triads

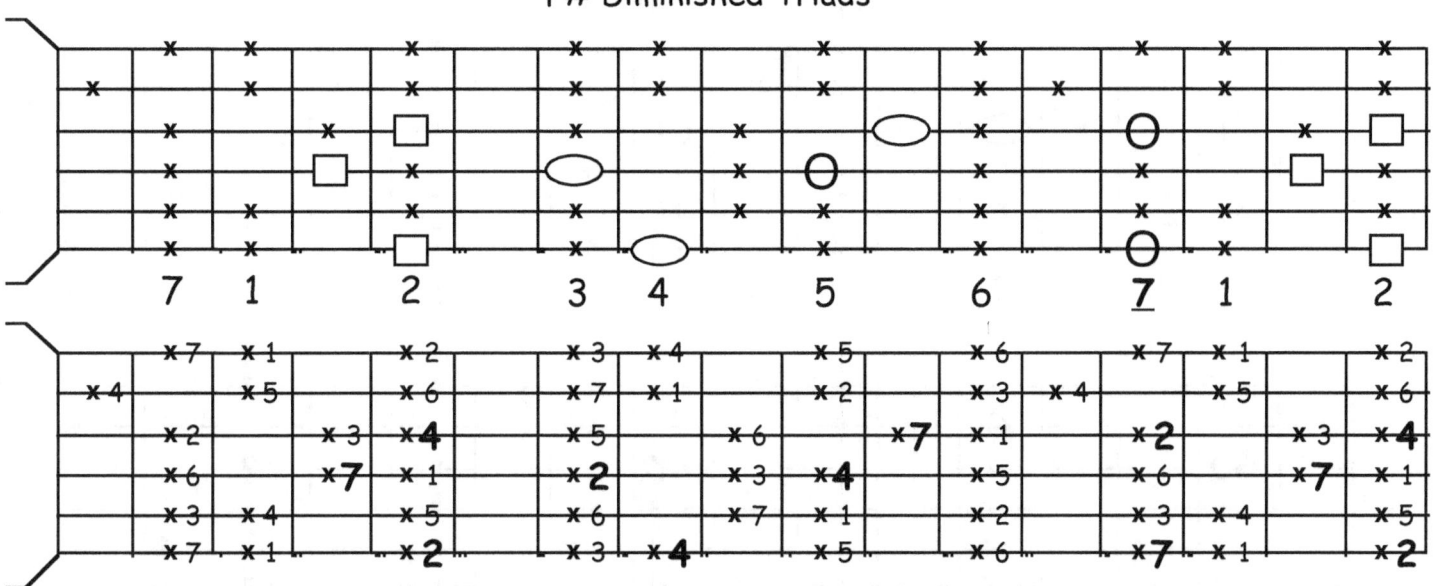

The only notes that you play are: 7, 2, and 4 of the G major scale.

DROP 2:

532 STRING GROUPING
(Same notes as 542 String Grouping, but a little brighter)
The "1" Chord: Major Triad Inversions In "G" Major
G Major Triads

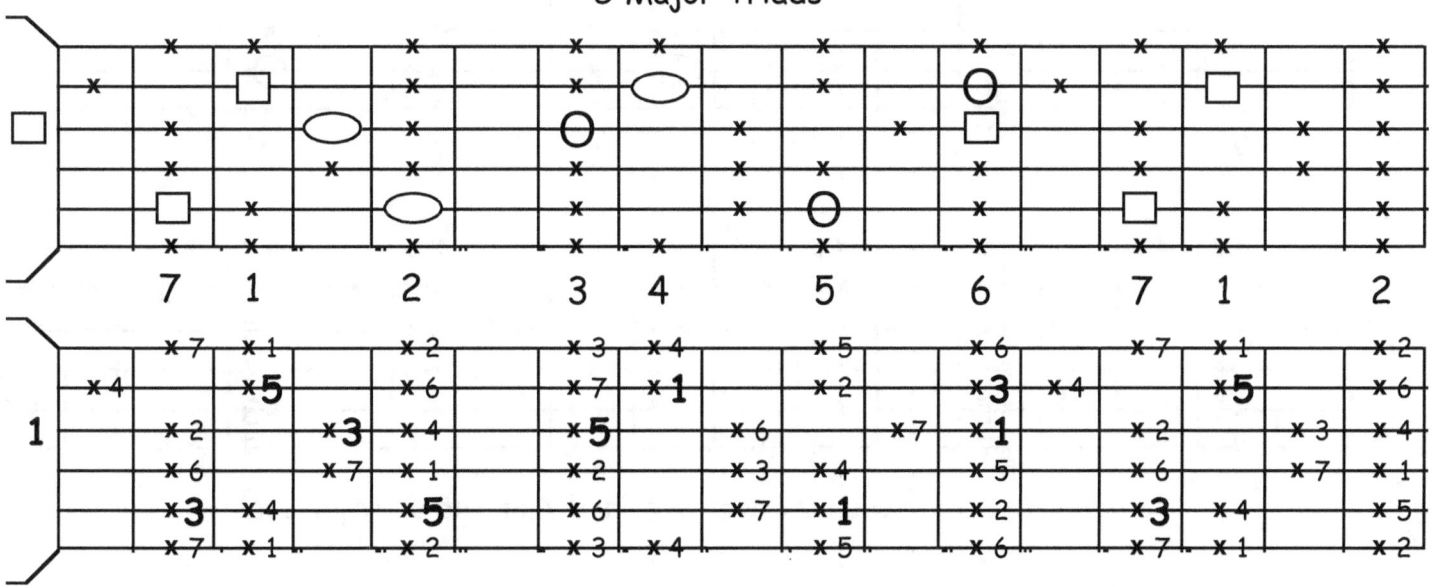

The only notes that you play are: 1, 3, and 5 of the G major scale.

532 STRING GROUPING

The "2" Chord: Minor Triad Inversions In "G" Major
A Minor Triads

The only notes that you play are: 2, 4, and 6 of the G major scale.

The "3" Chord: Minor Triad Inversions In "G" Major
B Minor Triads

The only notes that you play are: 3, 5, and 7 of the G major scale.

532 STRING GROUPING

The "4" Chord: Major Triad Inversions In "G" Major
C Major Triads

The only notes that you play are: 4, 6, and 1 of the G major scale.

The "5" Chord: Major Triad Inversions In "G" Major
D Major Triads

The only notes that you play are: 5, 7, and 2 of the G major scale.

532 STRING GROUPING

The "6" Chord: Minor Triad Inversions In "G" Major
E Minor Triads

The only notes that you play are: 6, 1, and 3 of the G major scale.

The "7" Chord: Diminished Triad Inversions In "G" Major
F# Diminished Triads

The only notes that you play are: 7, 2, and 4 of the G major scale.

DROP 2:
421 STRING GROUPING
(Same notes as 431 String Grouping, but a little brighter)

The "1" Chord: Major Triad Inversions In "G" Major
G Major Triads

The only notes that you play are: 1, 3, and 5 of the G major scale.

The "2" Chord: Minor Triad Inversions In "G" Major
A Minor Triads

The only notes that you play are: 2, 4, and 6 of the G major scale.

421 STRING GROUPING

The "3" Chord: Minor Triad Inversions In "G" Major

B Minor Triads

The only notes that you play are: 3, 5, and 7 of the G major scale.

The "4" Chord: Major Triad Inversions In "G" Major

C Major Triads

The only notes that you play are: 4, 6, and 1 of the G major scale.

421 STRING GROUPING

The "5" Chord: Major Triad Inversions In "G" Major
D Major Triads

The only notes that you play are: 5, 7, and 2 of the G major scale.

The "6" Chord: Minor Triad Inversions In "G" Major
E Minor Triads

The only notes that you play are: 6, 1, and 3 of the G major scale.

421 STRING GROUPING
The "7" Chord: Diminished Triad Inversions In "G" Major
F# Diminished Triads

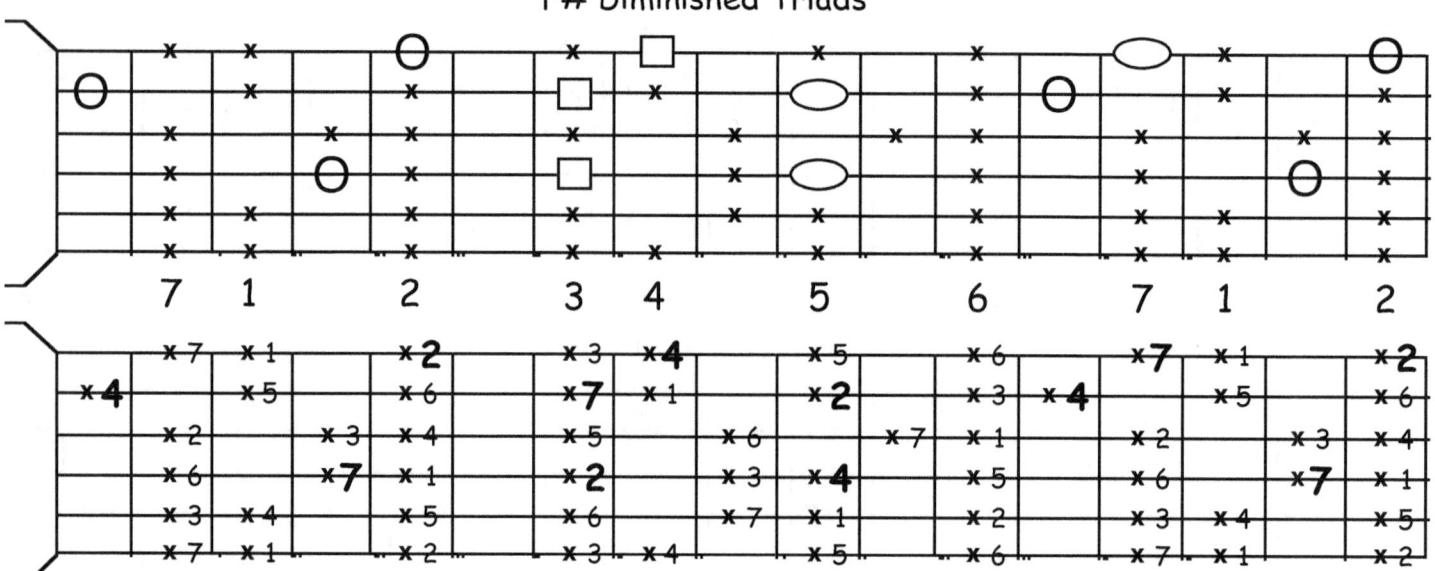

The only notes that you play are: 7, 2, and 4 of the G major scale.

DROP 2:

642 STRING GROUPING
(Same notes as 653 & 643 String Groupings, but even brighter)
The "1" Chord: Major Triad Inversions In "G" Major
G Major Triads

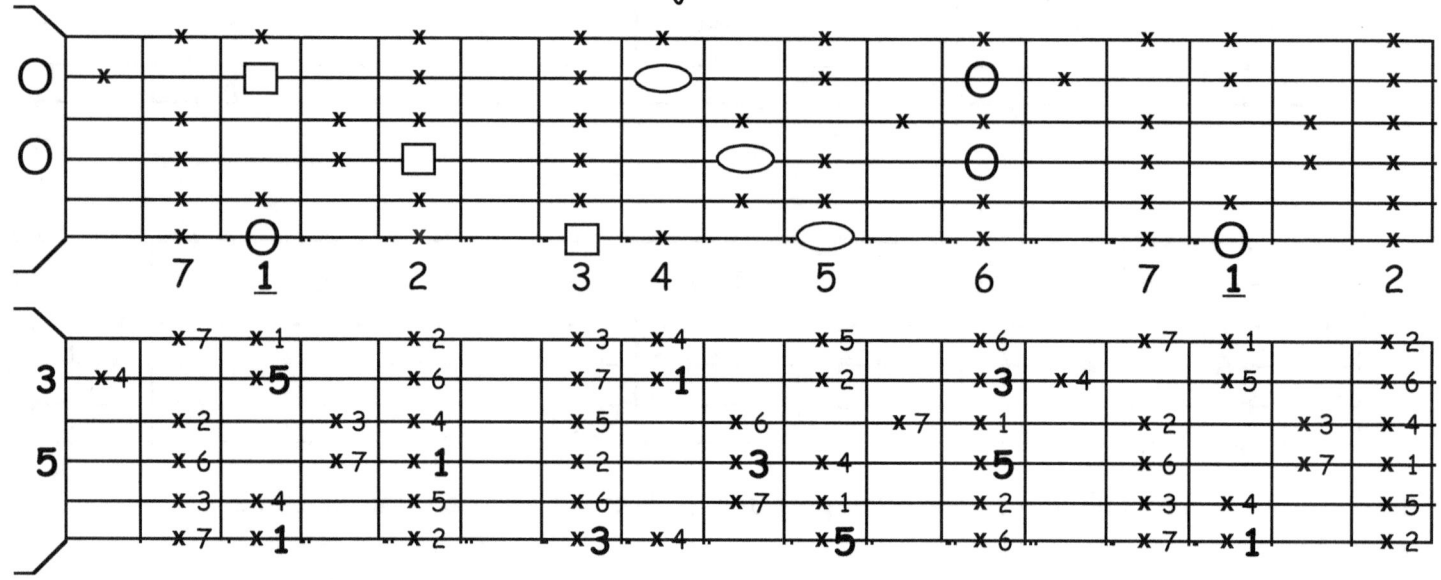

The only notes that you play are: 1, 3, and 5 of the G major scale.

642 STRING GROUPING

The "2" Chord: Minor Triad Inversions In "G" Major
A Minor Triads

The only notes that you play are: 2, 4, and 6 of the G major scale.

The "3" Chord: Minor Triad Inversions In "G" Major
B Minor Triads

The only notes that you play are: 3, 5, and 7 of the G major scale.

642 STRING GROUPING

The "4" Chord: Major Triad Inversions In "G" Major
C Major Triads

The only notes that you play are: 4, 6, and 1 of the G major scale.

The "5" Chord: Major Triad Inversions In "G" Major
D Major Triads

The only notes that you play are: 5, 7, and 2 of the G major scale.

642 STRING GROUPING

The "6" Chord: Minor Triad Inversions In "G" Major
E Minor Triads

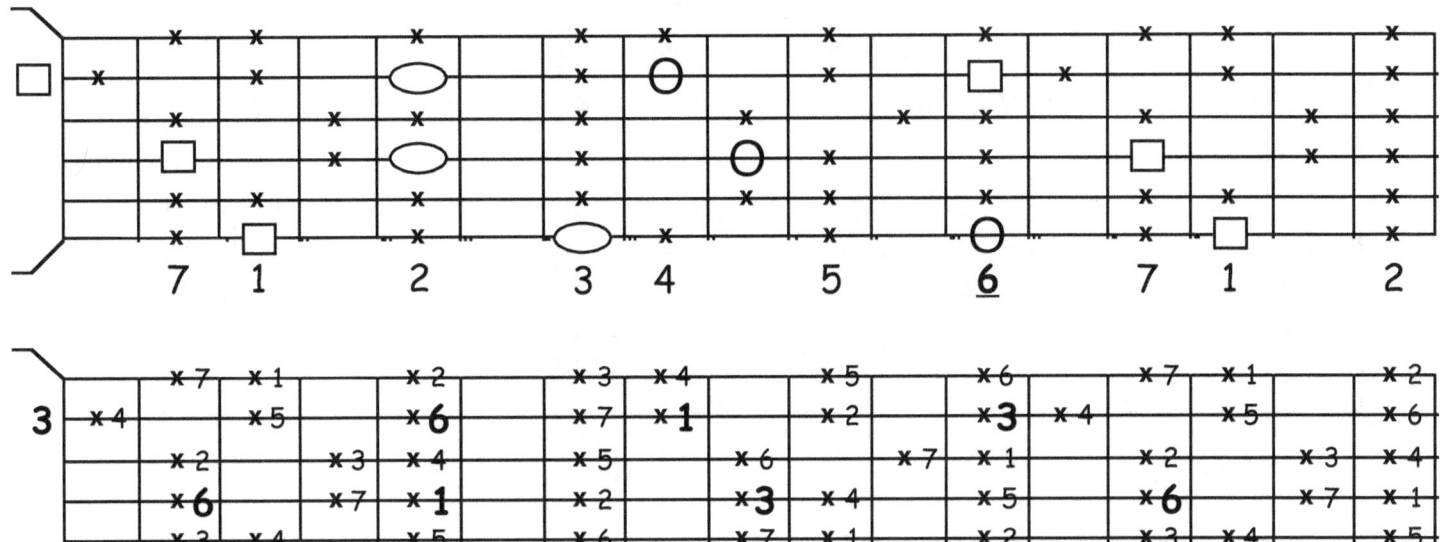

The only notes that you play are: 6, 1, and 3 of the G major scale.

The "7" Chord: Diminished Triad Inversions In "G" Major
F# Diminished Triads

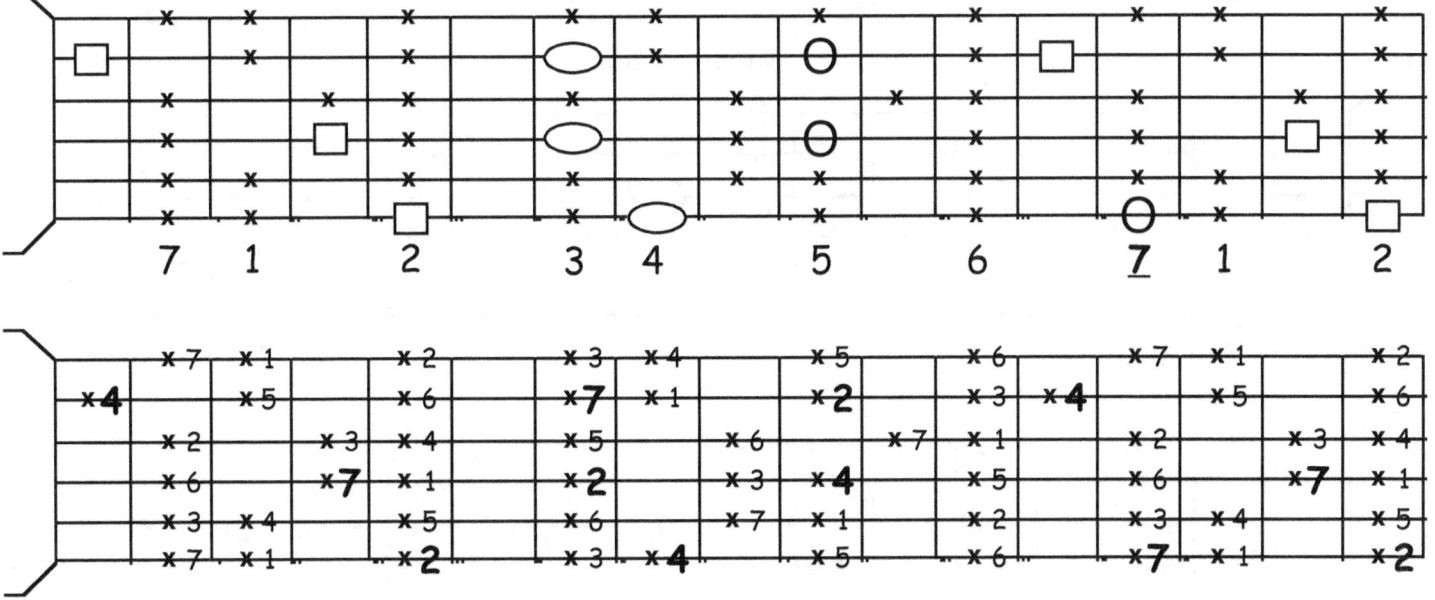

The only notes that you play are: 7, 2, and 4 of the G major scale.

DROP 2:
531 STRING GROUPING
(Same notes as 542 & 532 String Groupings, but even brighter)
The "1" Chord: Major Triad Inversions In "G" Major
G Major Triads

The only notes that you play are: 1, 3, and 5 of the G major scale.

The "2" Chord: Minor Triad Inversions In "G" Major
A Minor Triads

The only notes that you play are: 2, 4, and 6 of the G major scale.

531 STRING GROUPING

The "3" Chord: Minor Triad Inversions In "G" Major
B Minor Triads

The only notes that you play are: 3, 5, and 7 of the G major scale.

The "4" Chord: Major Triad Inversions In "G" Major
C Major Triads

The only notes that you play are: 4, 6, and 1 of the G major scale.

531 STRING GROUPING

The "5" Chord: Major Triad Inversions In "G" Major
D Major Triads

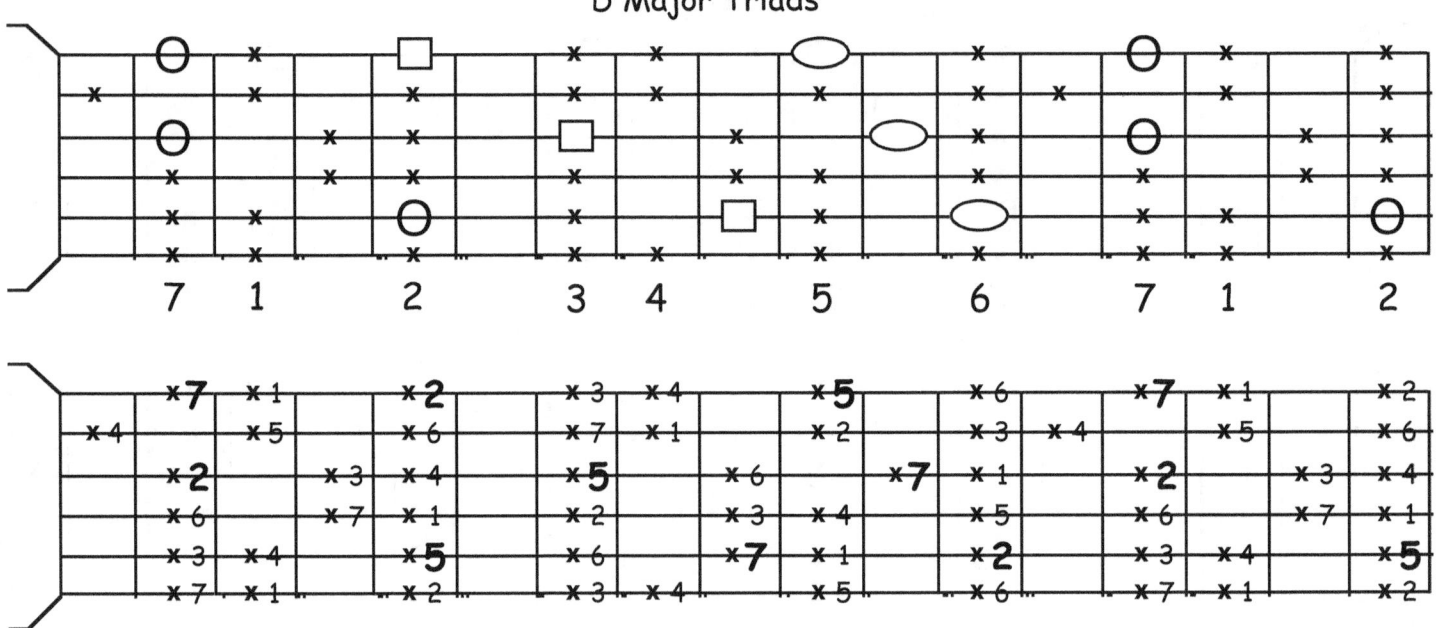

The only notes that you play are: 5, 7, and 2 of the G major scale.

The "6" Chord: Minor Triad Inversions In "G" Major
E Minor Triads

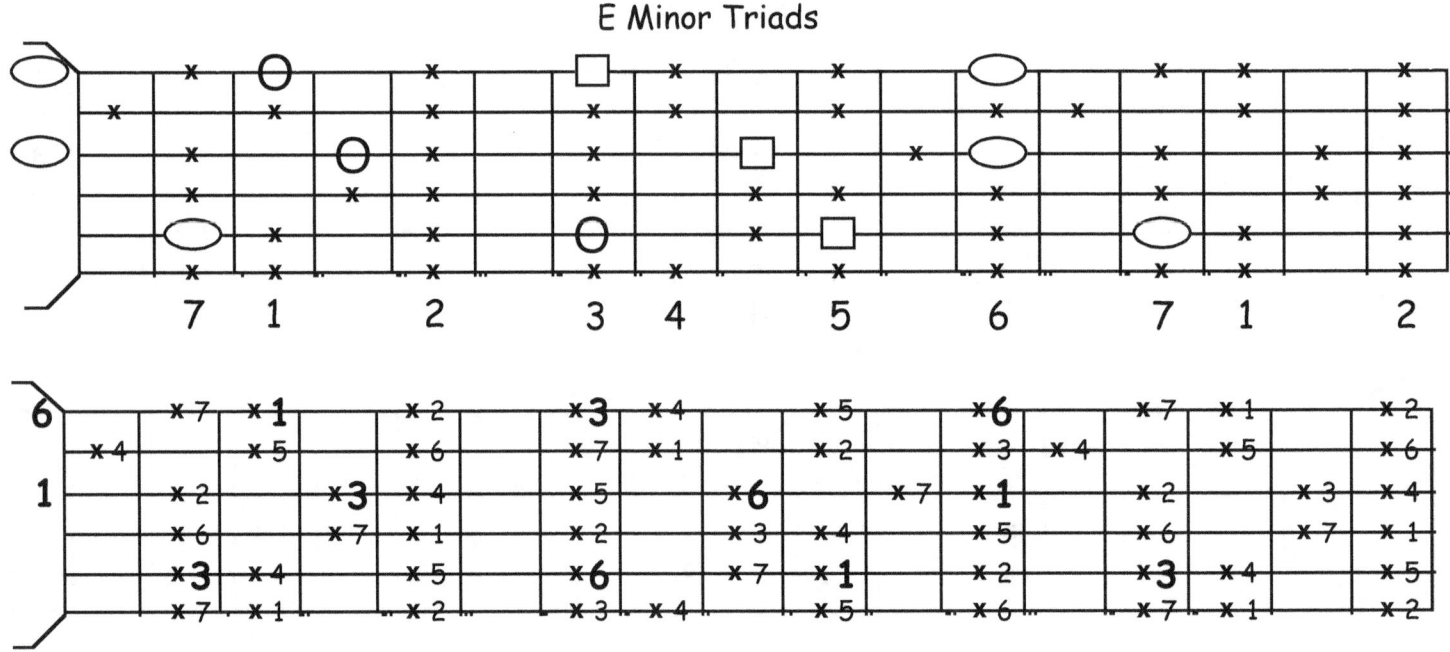

The only notes that you play are: 6, 1, and 3 of the G major scale.

531 STRING GROUPING
The "7" Chord: Diminished Triad Inversions In "G" Major
F# Diminished Triads

The only notes that you play are: 7, 2, and 4 of the G major scale.

DROP 3:

632 STRING GROUPING
The "1" Chord: Major Triad Inversions In "G" Major
G Major Triads

The only notes that you play are: 1, 3, and 5 of the G major scale.

632 STRING GROUPING

The "2" Chord: Minor Triad Inversions In "G" Major
A Minor Triads

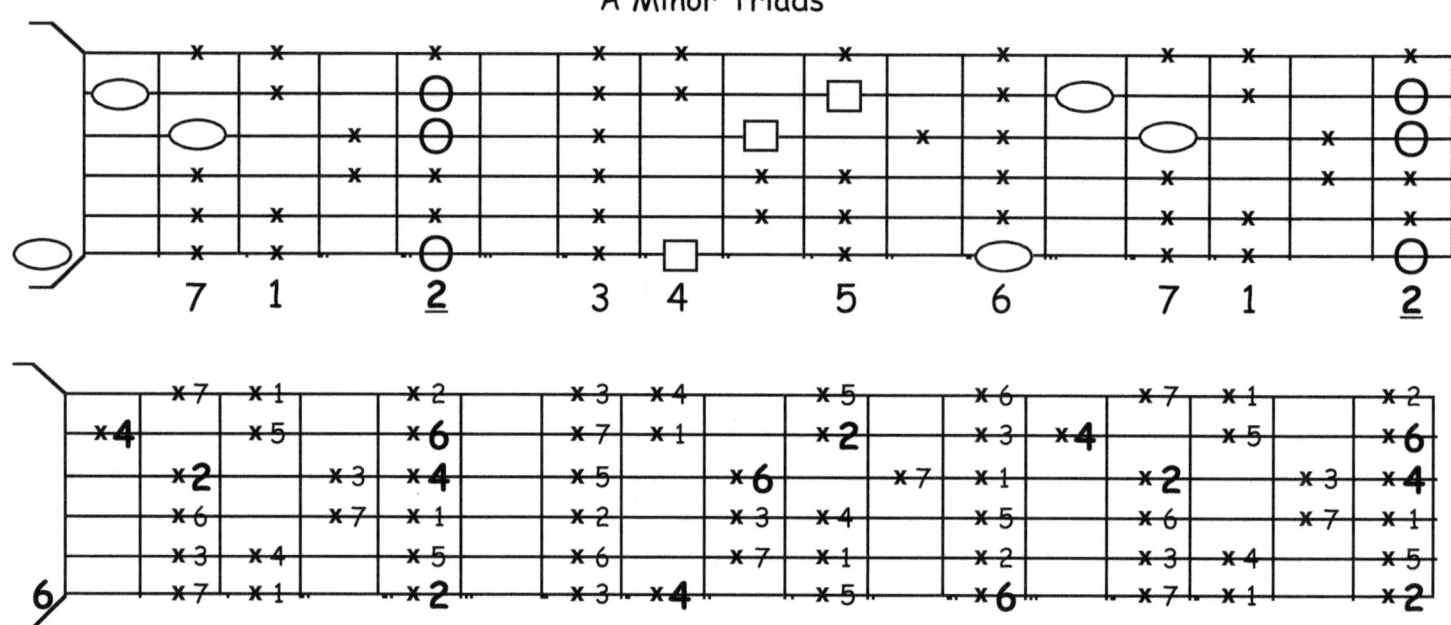

The only notes that you play are: 2, 4, and 6 of the G major scale.

The "3" Chord: Minor Triad Inversions In "G" Major
B Minor Triads

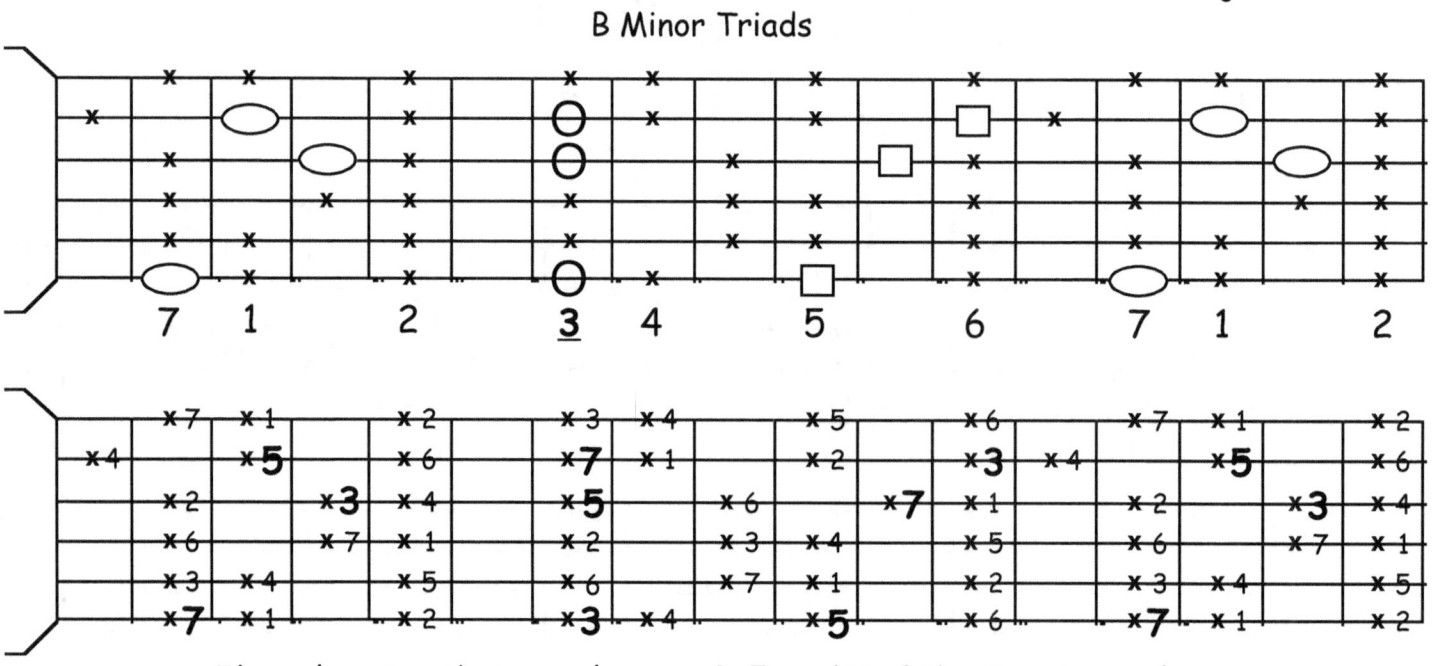

The only notes that you play are: 3, 5, and 7 of the G major scale.

632 STRING GROUPING

The "4" Chord: Major Triad Inversions In "G" Major
C Major Triads

The only notes that you play are: 4, 6, and 1 of the G major scale.

The "5" Chord: Major Triad Inversions In "G" Major
D Major Triads

The only notes that you play are: 5, 7, and 2 of the G major scale.

632 STRING GROUPING

The "6" Chord: Minor Triad Inversions In "G" Major
E Minor Triads

The only notes that you play are: 6, 1, and 3 of the G major scale.

The "7" Chord: Diminished Triad Inversions In "G" Major
F# Diminished Triads

The only notes that you play are: 7, 2, and 4 of the G major scale.

DROP 3:
521 STRING GROUPING
The "1" Chord: Major Triad Inversions In "G" Major
G Major Triads

The only notes that you play are: 1, 3, and 5 of the G major scale.

The "2" Chord: Minor Triad Inversions In "G" Major
A Minor Triads

The only notes that you play are: 2, 4, and 6 of the G major scale.

521 STRING GROUPING

The "3" Chord: Minor Triad Inversions In "G" Major

B Minor Triads

The only notes that you play are: 3, 5, and 7 of the G major scale.

The "4" Chord: Major Triad Inversions In "G" Major

C Major Triads

The only notes that you play are: 4, 6, and 1 of the G major scale.

521 STRING GROUPING

The "5" Chord: Major Triad Inversions In "G" Major
D Major Triads

The only notes that you play are: 5, 7, and 2 of the G major scale.

The "6" Chord: Minor Triad Inversions In "G" Major
E Minor Triads

The only notes that you play are: 6, 1, and 3 of the G major scale.

521 STRING GROUPING
The "7" Chord: Diminished Triad Inversions In "G" Major
F# Diminished Triads

The only notes that you play are: 7, 2, and 4 of the G major scale.

DROP 2 & 3:
652 STRING GROUPING
The "1" Chord: Major Triad Inversions In "G" Major
G Major Triads

The only notes that you play are: 1, 3, and 5 of the G major scale.

652 STRING GROUPING

The "2" Chord: Minor Triad Inversions In "G" Major
A Minor Triads

The only notes that you play are: 2, 4, and 6 of the G major scale.

The "3" Chord: Minor Triad Inversions In "G" Major
B Minor Triads

The only notes that you play are: 3, 5, and 7 of the G major scale.

652 STRING GROUPING
The "4" Chord: Major Triad Inversions In "G" Major
C Major Triads

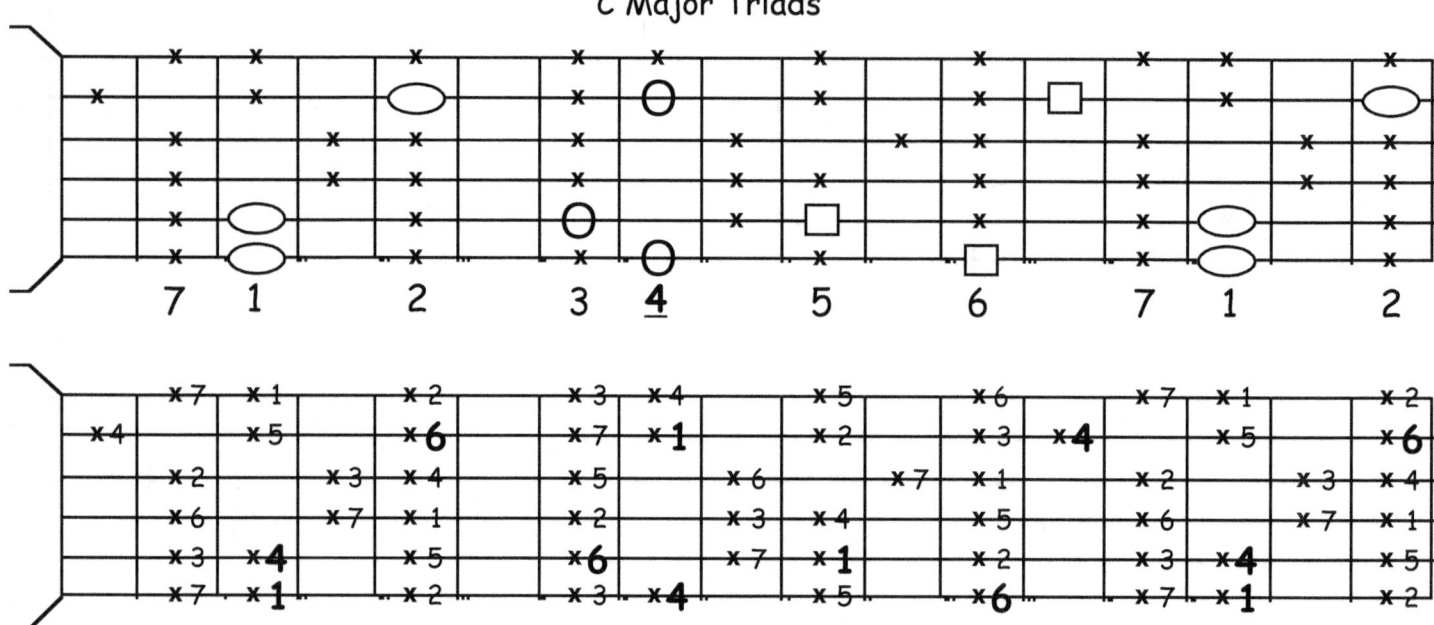

The only notes that you play are: 4, 6, and 1 of the G major scale.

The "5" Chord: Major Triad Inversions In "G" Major
D Major Triads

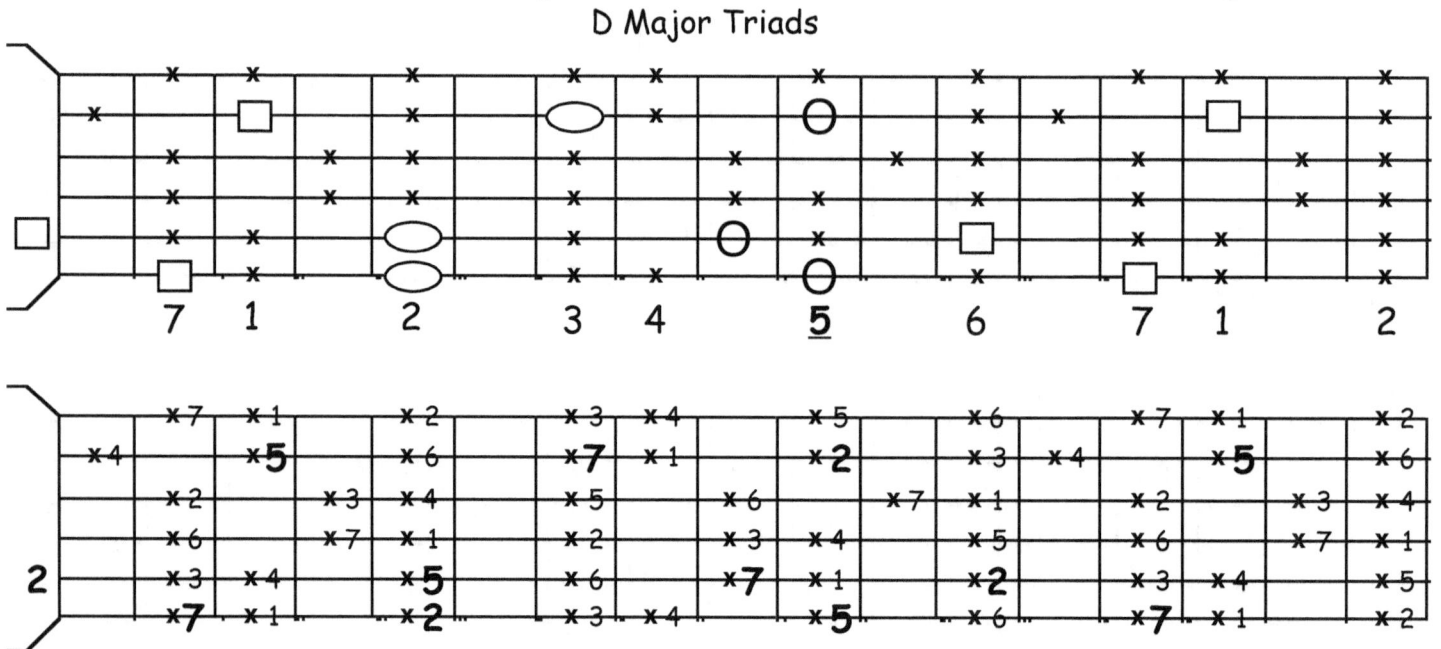

The only notes that you play are: 5, 7, and 2 of the G major scale.

652 STRING GROUPING

The "6" Chord: Minor Triad Inversions In "G" Major
E Minor Triads

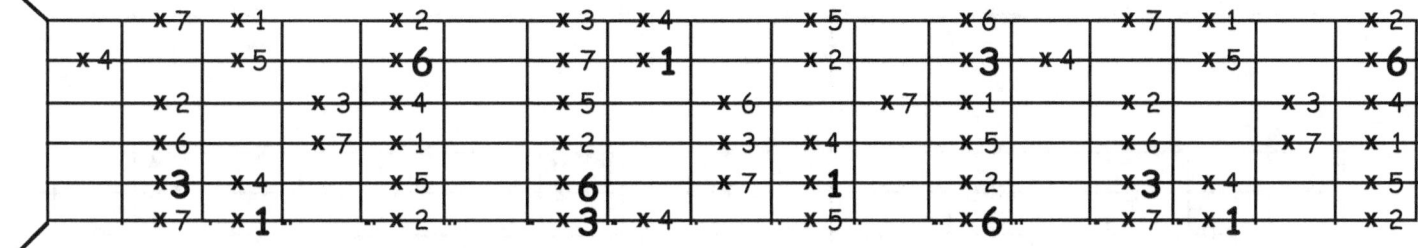

The only notes that you play are: 6, 1, and 3 of the G major scale.

The "7" Chord: Diminished Triad Inversions In "G" Major
F# Diminished Triads

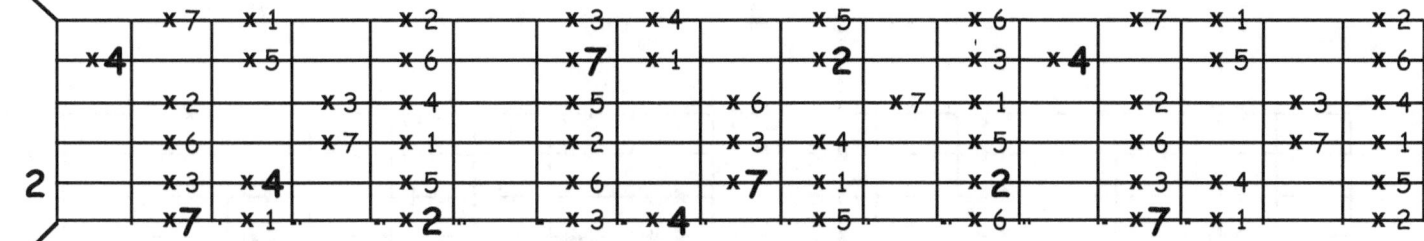

The only notes that you play are: 7, 2, and 4 of the G major scale.

DROP 2 & 3:
541 STRING GROUPING
The "1" Chord: Major Triad Inversions In "G" Major

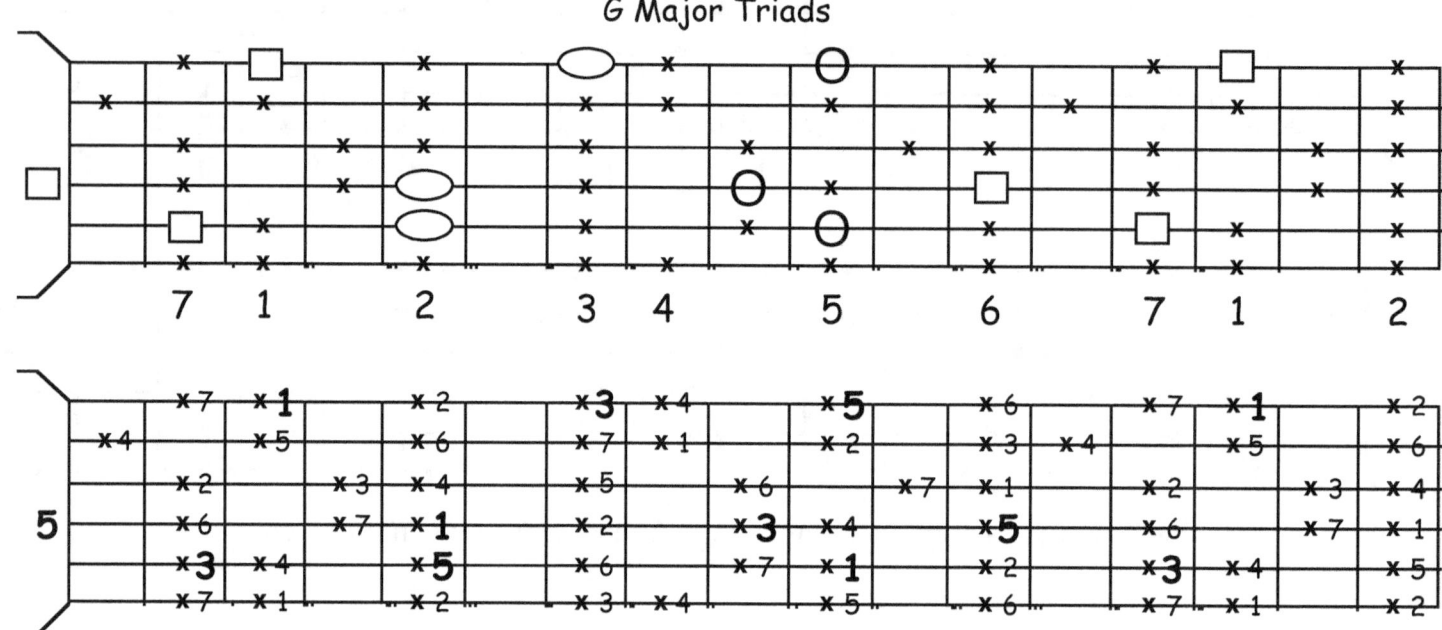

The only notes that you play are: 1, 3, and 5 of the G major scale.

The "2" Chord: Minor Triad Inversions In "G" Major

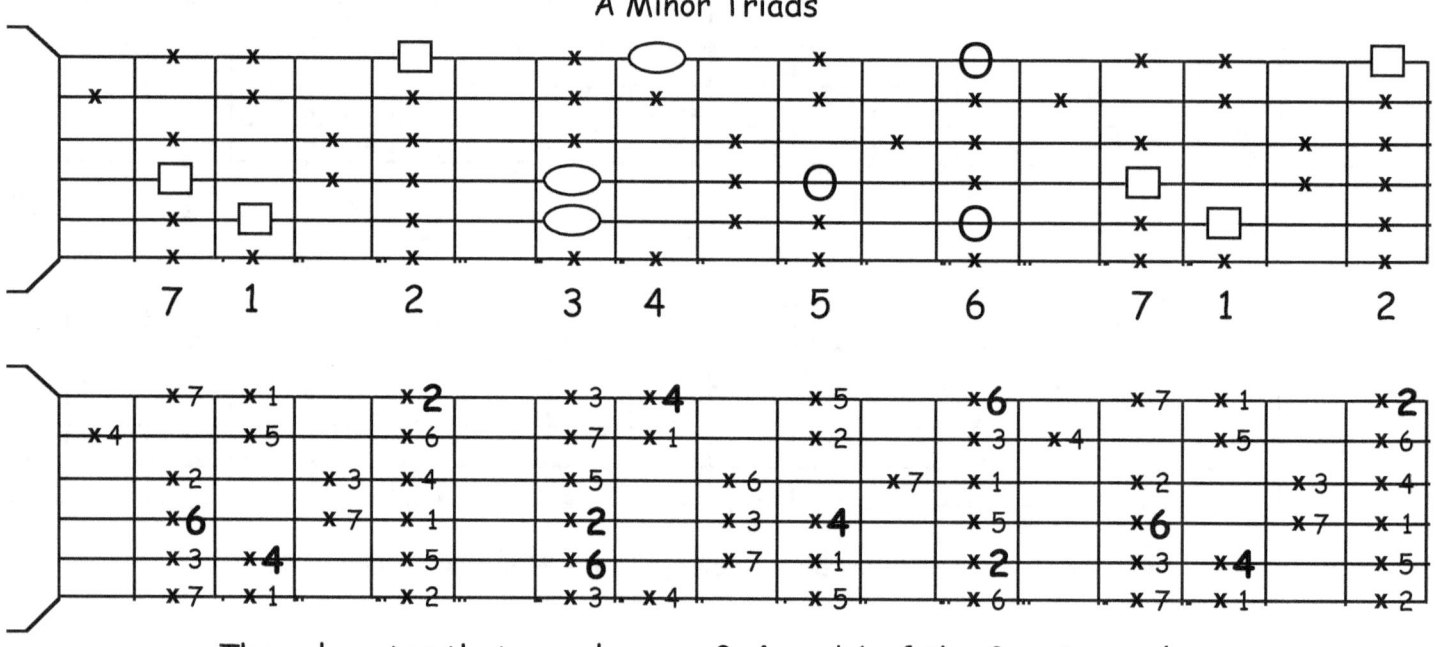

The only notes that you play are: 2, 4, and 6 of the G major scale.

541 STRING GROUPING

The "3" Chord: Minor Triad Inversions In "G" Major
B Minor Triads

The only notes that you play are: 3, 5, and 7 of the G major scale.

The "4" Chord: Major Triad Inversions In "G" Major
C Major Triads

The only notes that you play are: 4, 6, and 1 of the G major scale.

541 STRING GROUPING

The "5" Chord: Major Triad Inversions In "G" Major
D Major Triads

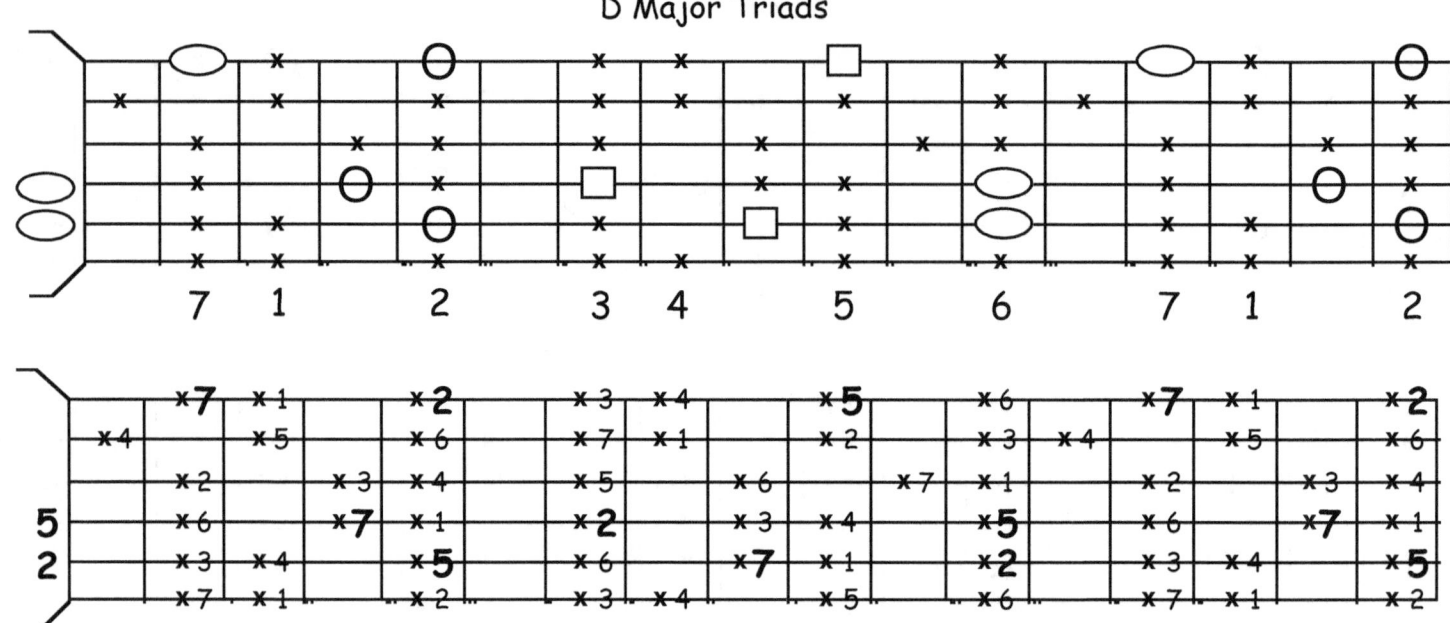

The only notes that you play are: 5, 7, and 2 of the G major scale.

The "6" Chord: Minor Triad Inversions In "G" Major
E Minor Triads

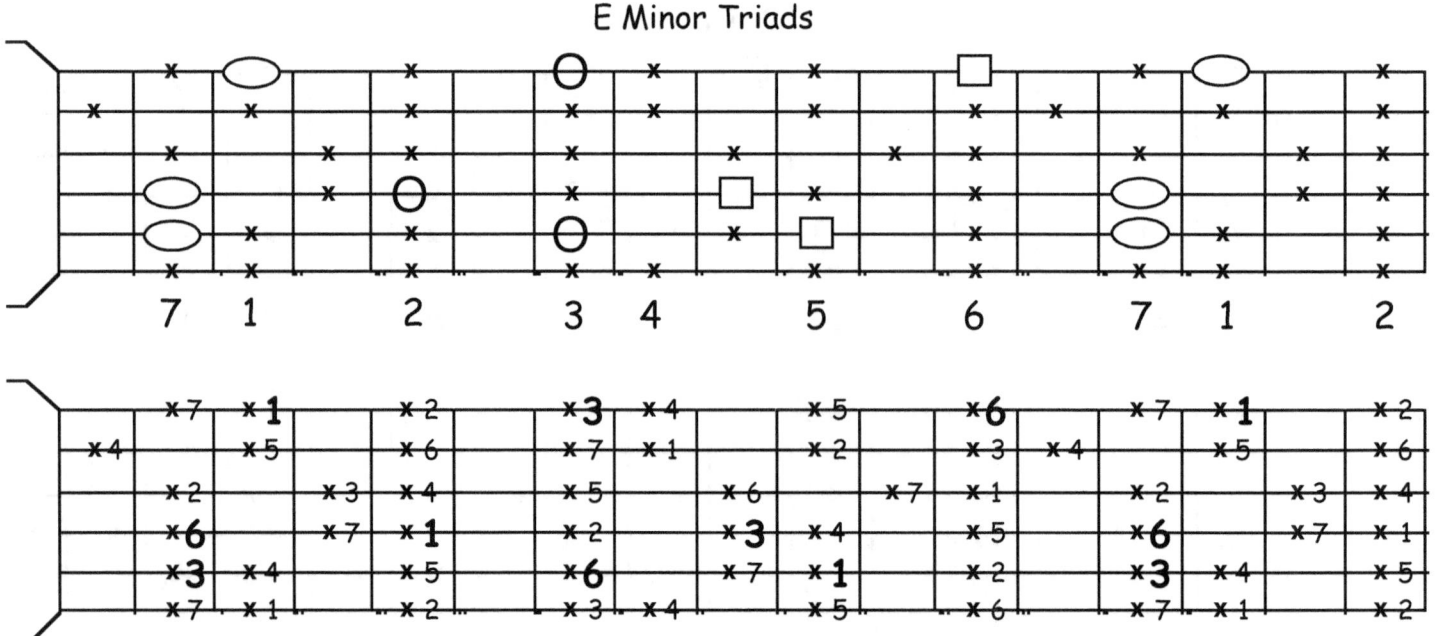

The only notes that you play are: 6, 1, and 3 of the G major scale.

541 STRING GROUPING
The "7" Chord: Diminished Triad Inversions In "G" Major
F# Diminished Triads

The only notes that you play are: 7, 2, and 4 of the G major scale.

ALTERED TRIADS

You now know that there are seven diatonic triads that come from the major scale and that these seven triads have the following tonalities:

1, 4, & 5 chords = Major
2, 3, & 6 chords = Minor
7 chord = Diminished (Minor b5)

The most common ways of altering these triads is by raising (#) or lowering (b) the 5th of these chords. A lowered 5th can also be referred to as a #11. When lowering the 5th of a minor triad, the note is usualluy called "b5". When lowering the 5th of a major triad, the note is usaually called "#11".

MINOR b5 TRIAD:
The "7" chord of a major scale is an example of a minor triad with a lowered 5th (b5).

MINOR #5 TRIAD:
The minor triad with a #5 is not that common. However, if you want to play one, a minor triad with a #5 is the same thing as a different diatonic major triad. Let me explain. If you play the "2" chord triad from the G major scale, you'd be playing an A minor triad: A, C, E. If you raise the 5th (the E) a half step, the "E" becomes an "E#" (enharmonically, this is the same thing as an "F"). What you're left with is: A, C, F. Looking at these three notes, you can see that this is an F major triad (F, A, C) in first inversion. So, if you want to play a minor triad with a #5, just play a major triad where the third of the chord is the root of your desired minor #5 triad.

MAJOR #11 TRIAD:
The best example of the major #11 (or b5) triad is available when looking at the "4" chord of a major scale. The "4" chord is spelled: 4, 6, 1. The 5th of this chord is the 1. In a major scale, the 1 can be lowered by a half step to the 7 without changing the scale. This gives you a chord that is spelled: 4, 6, 7 (4 = root, 6 = 3rd, 7 = #11th or b5th). I have included 16 sets of major #11 triads and their inversions in the MAJOR #11 TRIAD section of this book.

MAJOR #5 TRIAD:
The major #5 triad (also called an augmented triad) is a chord that fits very easily and simply into the whole tone scale. However, it also fits into other scales. One of these other scales is the harmonic minor scale. It would be more instructive to see how the major #5 triads fit within the harmonic minor scale, so this is how they are presented here. I have included 16 sets of major #5 triads and their inversions in the MAJOR #5 TRIAD section of this book.

Remember that the MAJOR METHOD introduces the harmonic minor scale with the same numbers that are used in its relative major scale. The E harmonic minor scale has THE SAME numbers (notes) as a G major scale with a #5. The "1" chord of this scale IS a major #5 triad.

If you are a guitarist who has been introduced to music theory through "Common Practice Period" theory and the MAJOR METHOD system of learning the neck of the guitar seems strange, have no fear. Remember that I have depicted each of the chord/inversion sets using two different diagrams: one that shows the basic shapes of these chords within a parent scale without numbers AND one that shows how these chords fit into a parent scale with the MAJOR METHOD numbering system.

NOTE:
Because of the way the neck of the guitar is structured, any one triad may have many different places where it can be played. These different places may contain the exact same notes in the exact same order, but they may use a different string grouping, a different fingering, and may have a slightly different timbre (a brighter or a darker sound) from each other. Rather than organizing all of the triads by how they look on the music staff (thereby having to present multiple string groupings at the same time), I have organized them all by individual string groupings along with their corresponding inversions. I have also included a parent scale in the diagrams so you can see how all of the chords live within the scale patterns. This allows for a more practical, working knowledge of the neck of the guitar and how the inversions and scales relate to each other.

REMEMBER:
When the root of the chord is the lowest note of the chord voicing, the chord is in:
"root position".
When the third of the chord is the lowest note of the chord voicing, the chord is in:
"first inversion".
When the fifth of the chord is the lowest note of the chord voicing, the chord is in:
"second inversion".

All of the triad diagrams in the MAJOR METHOD use the following shapes:

O = Root Position Chord
□ = First Inversion Chord
⌒ = Second Inversion Chord

Keep in mind that with the altered chords, one of the chord tones will be raised or lowered in order to create the desired "altered" note. When playing an inversion that calls for this affected chord tone in the bass, the "altered" note will be the note in the bass. Here we go ...

MAJOR #11 TRIADS

The only notes you play for these chords are: 4, 6, and 7 of the G major scale.

CLOSED:

The "4" Chord: Major #11 Triad Inversions In "G" Major

654 STRING GROUPING
C Major #11 Triad

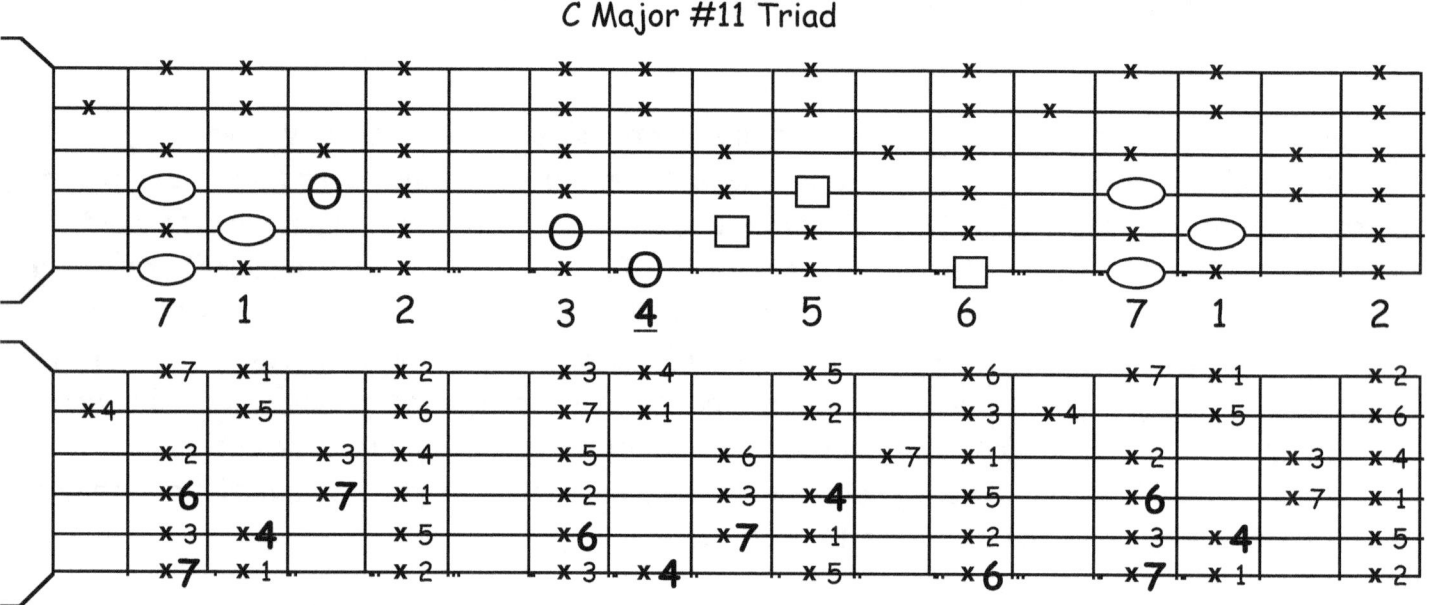

543 STRING GROUPING
C Major #11 Triad

The "4" Chord: Major #11 Triad Inversions In "G" Major

The only notes you play for these chords are: 4, 6, and 7 of the G major scale.

432 STRING GROUPING
C Major #11 Triad

321 STRING GROUPING
C Major #11 Triad

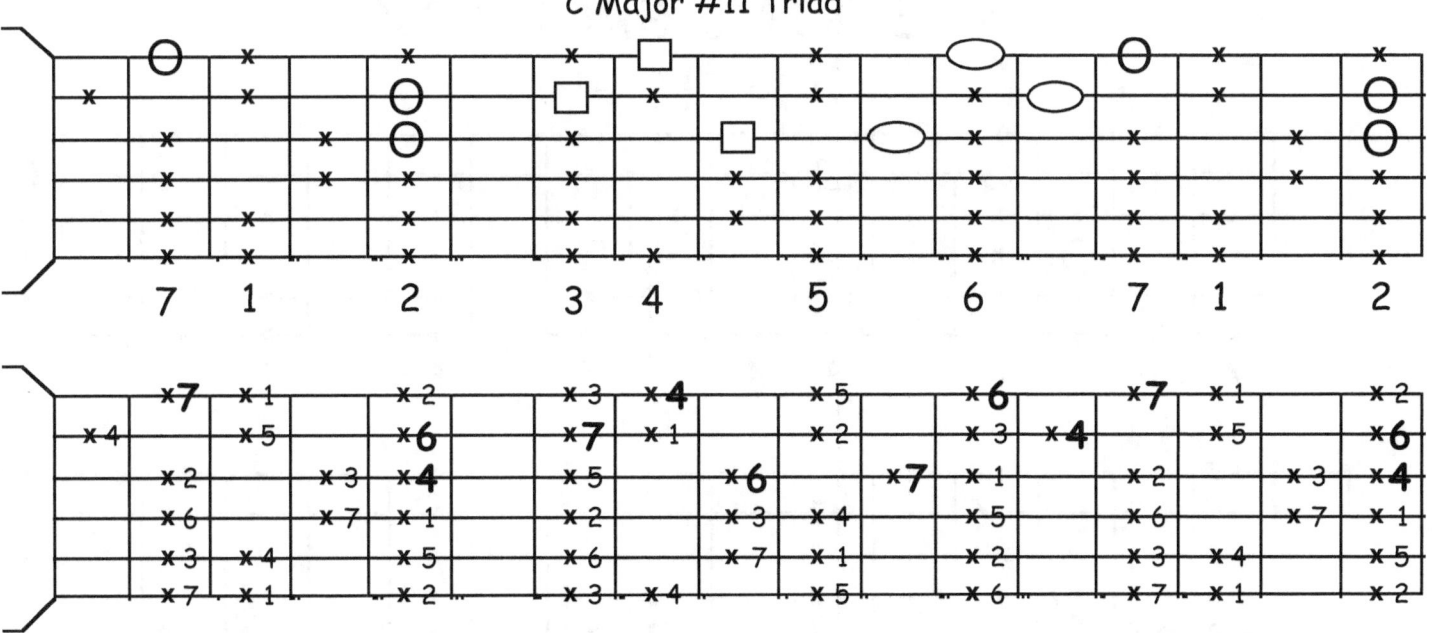

DROP 2:

The "4" Chord: Major #11 Triad Inversions In "G" Major
The only notes you play for these chords are: 4, 6, and 7 of the G major scale.

653 STRING GROUPING
C Major #11 Triads

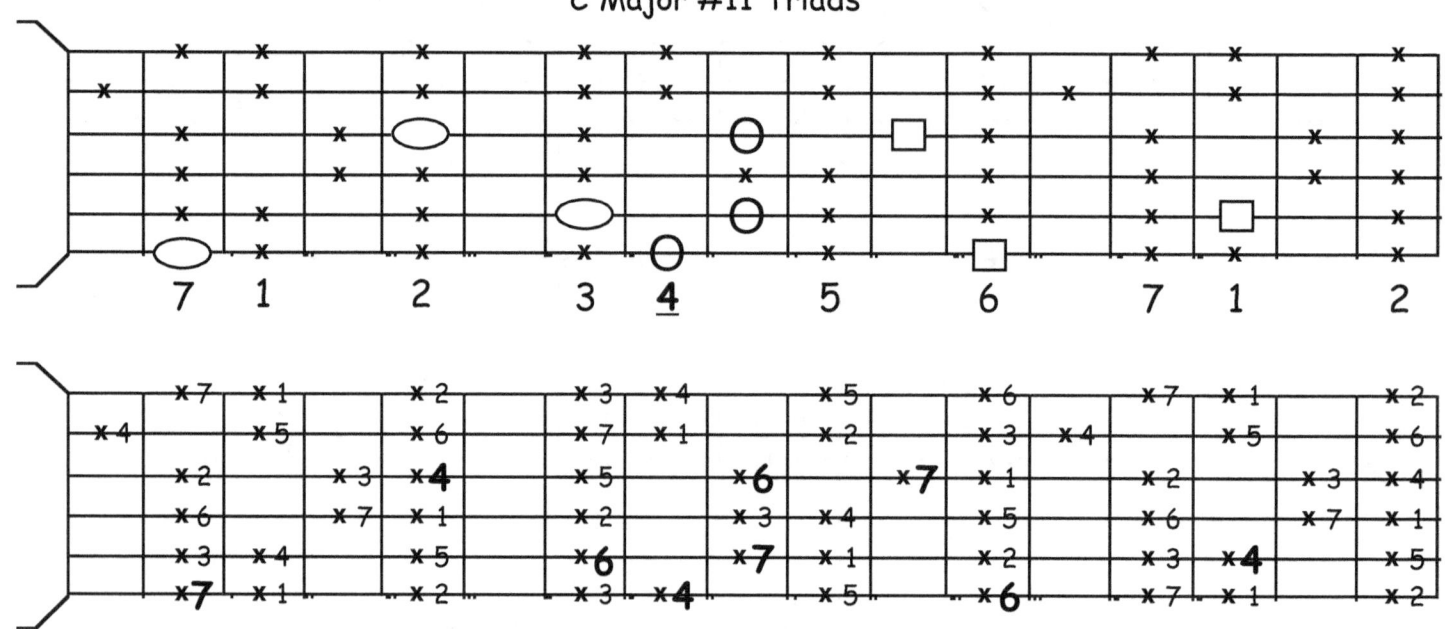

542 STRING GROUPING
C major #11 Triads

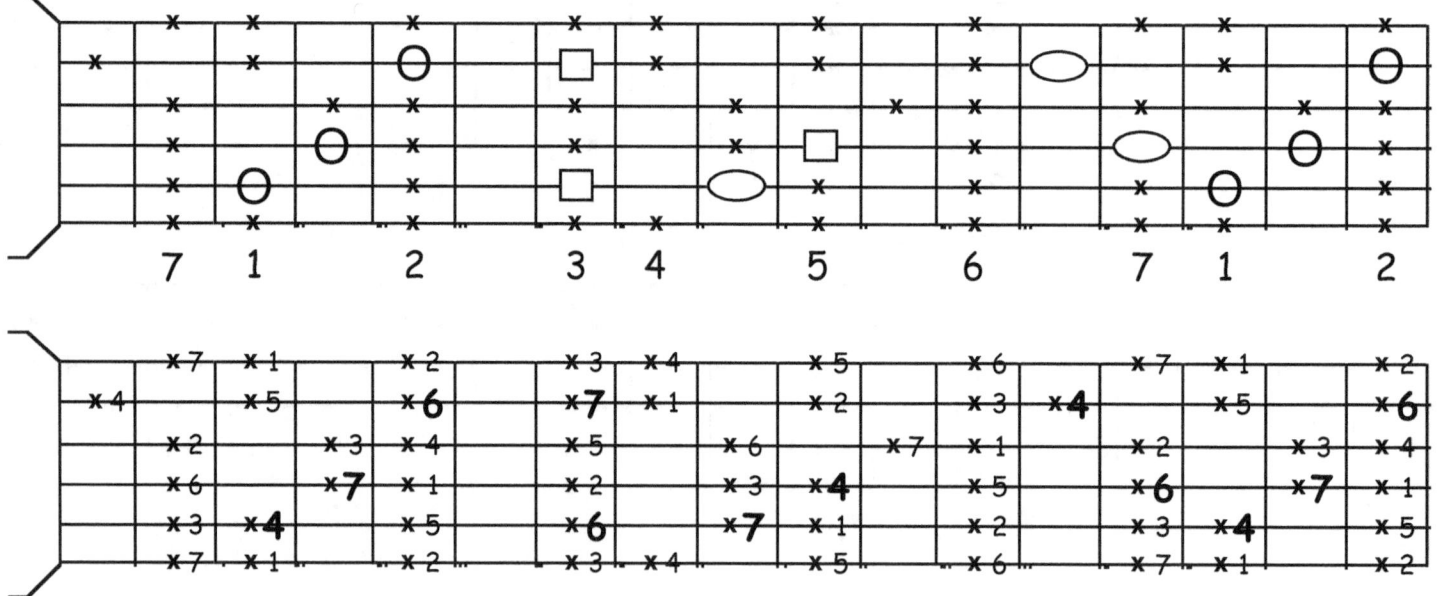

The "4" Chord: Major #11 Triad Inversions In "G" Major

The only notes you play for these chords are: 4, 6, and 7 of the G major scale.

431 STRING GROUPING
C Major #11 Triads

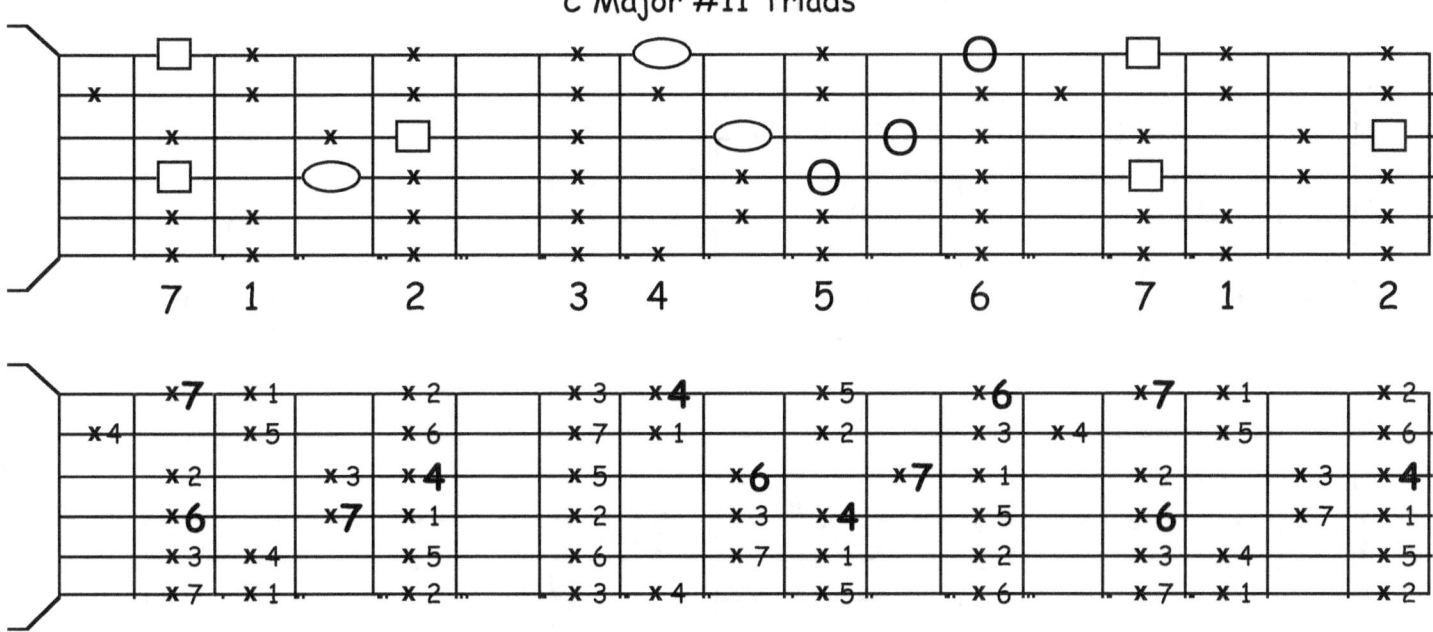

643 STRING GROUPING
(Same notes as 653 String Grouping, but a little brighter)
C Major #11 Triads

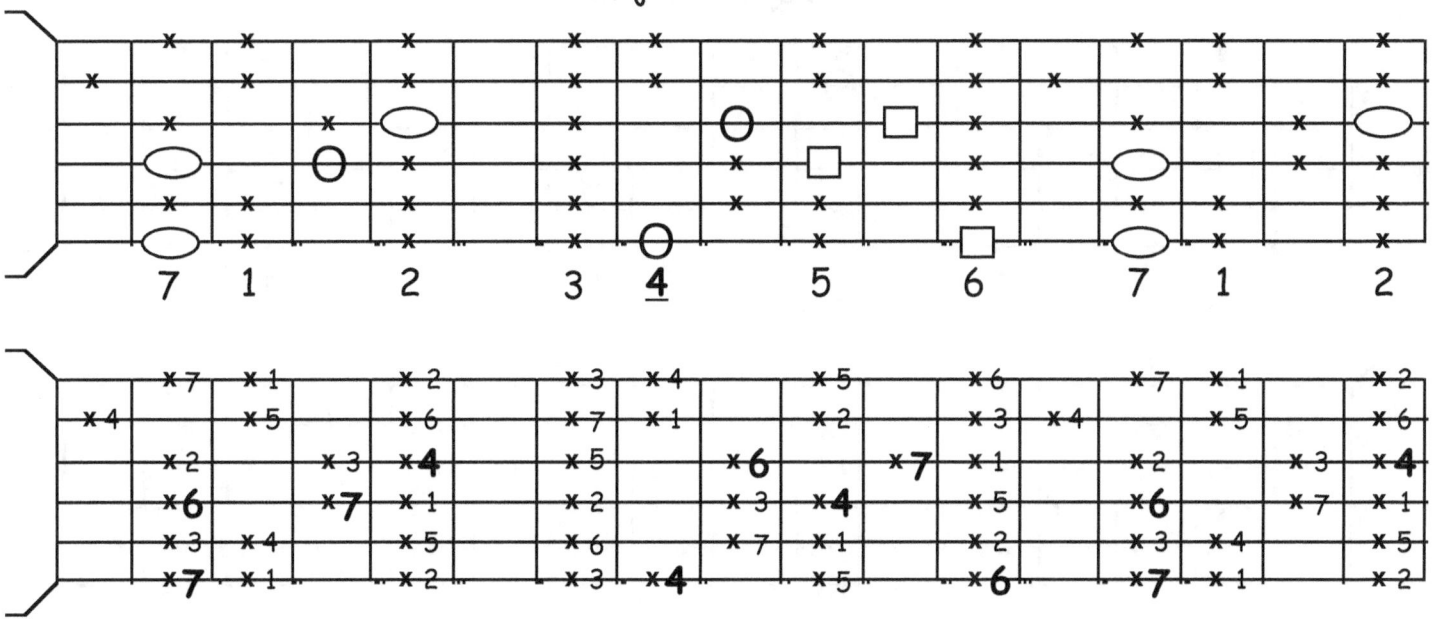

The "4" Chord: Major #11 Triad Inversions In "G" Major

The only notes you play for these chords are: 4, 6, and 7 of the G major scale.

532 STRING GROUPING

(Same notes as 542 String Grouping, but a little brighter)

C Major #11 Triads

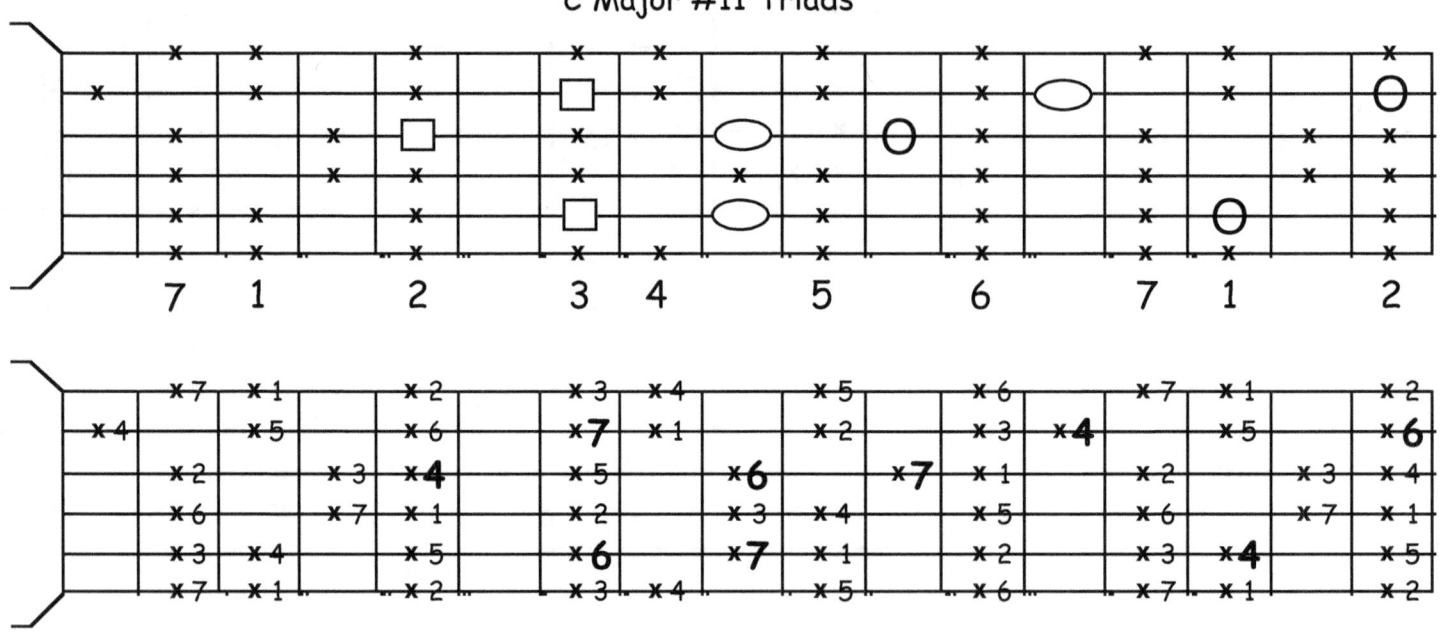

421 STRING GROUPING

(Same notes as 431 String Grouping, but a little brighter)

C Major #11 Triads

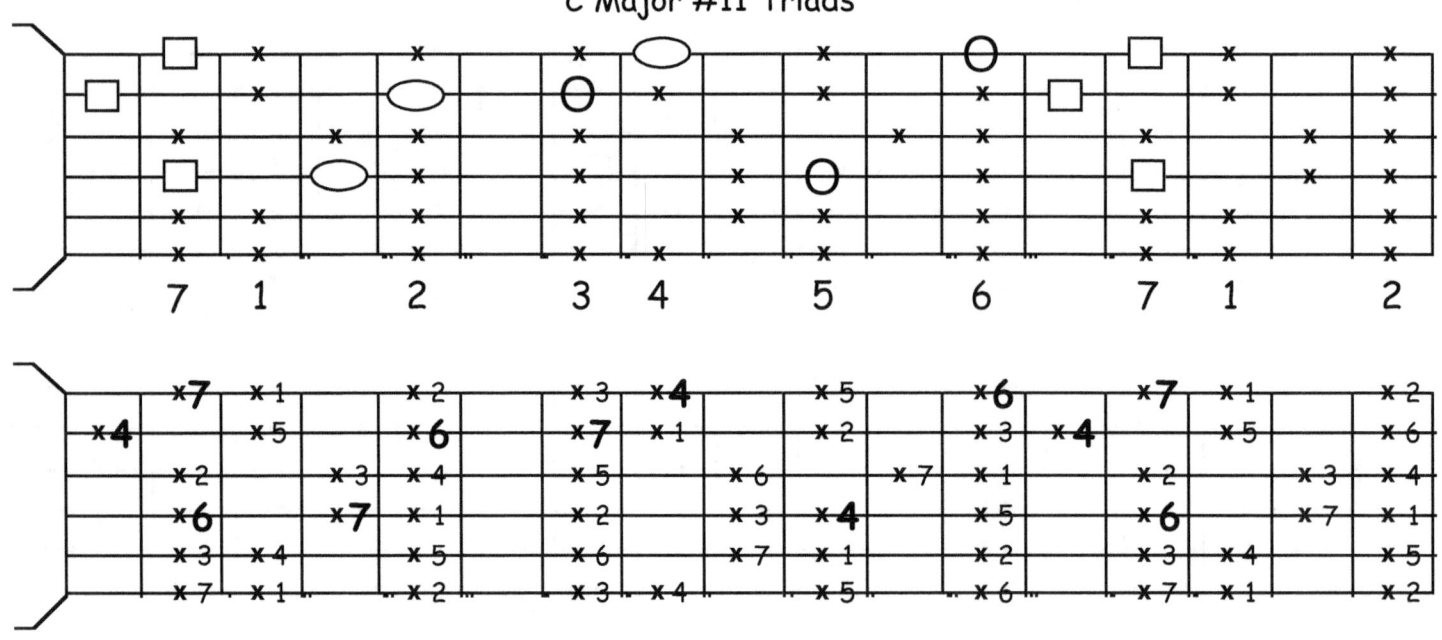

The "4" Chord: Major #11 Triad Inversions In "G" Major

The only notes you play for these chords are: 4, 6, and 7 of the G major scale.

642 STRING GROUPING

(Same notes as 653 & 643 String Groupings, but even brighter)

C Major #11 Triads

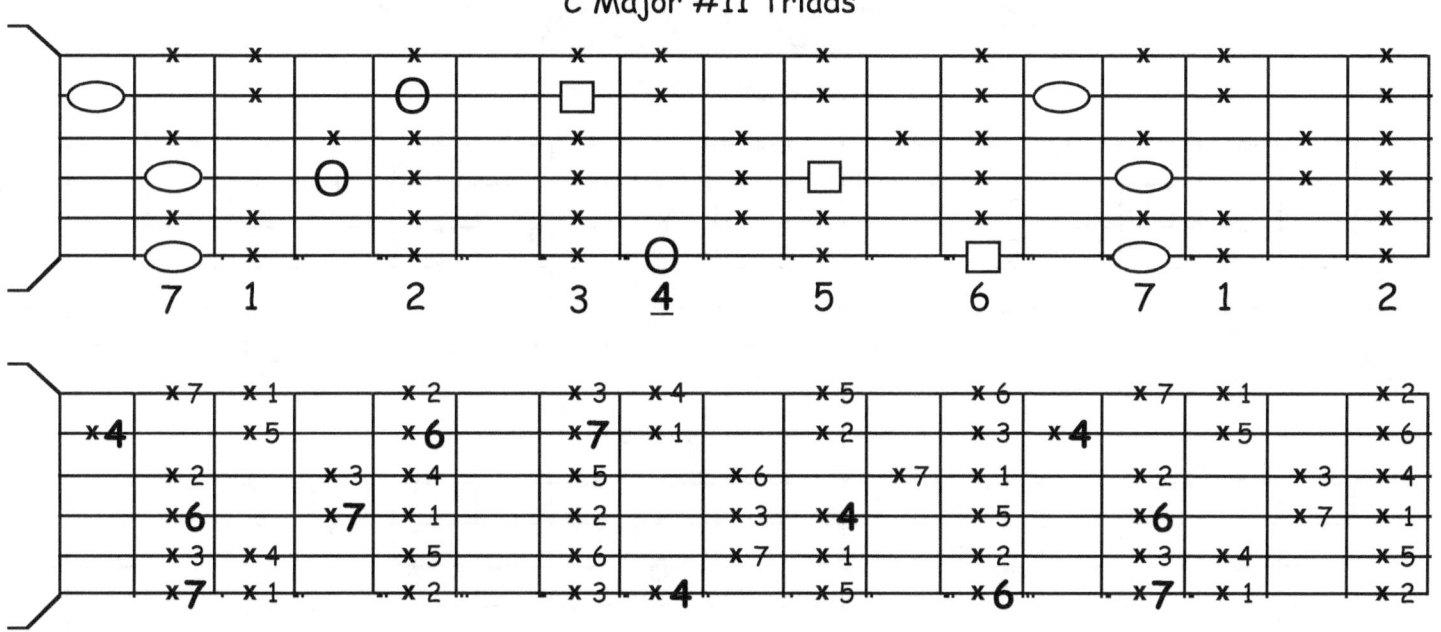

531 STRING GROUPING

(Same notes as 542 & 532 String Groupings, but even brighter)

C Major #11 Triads

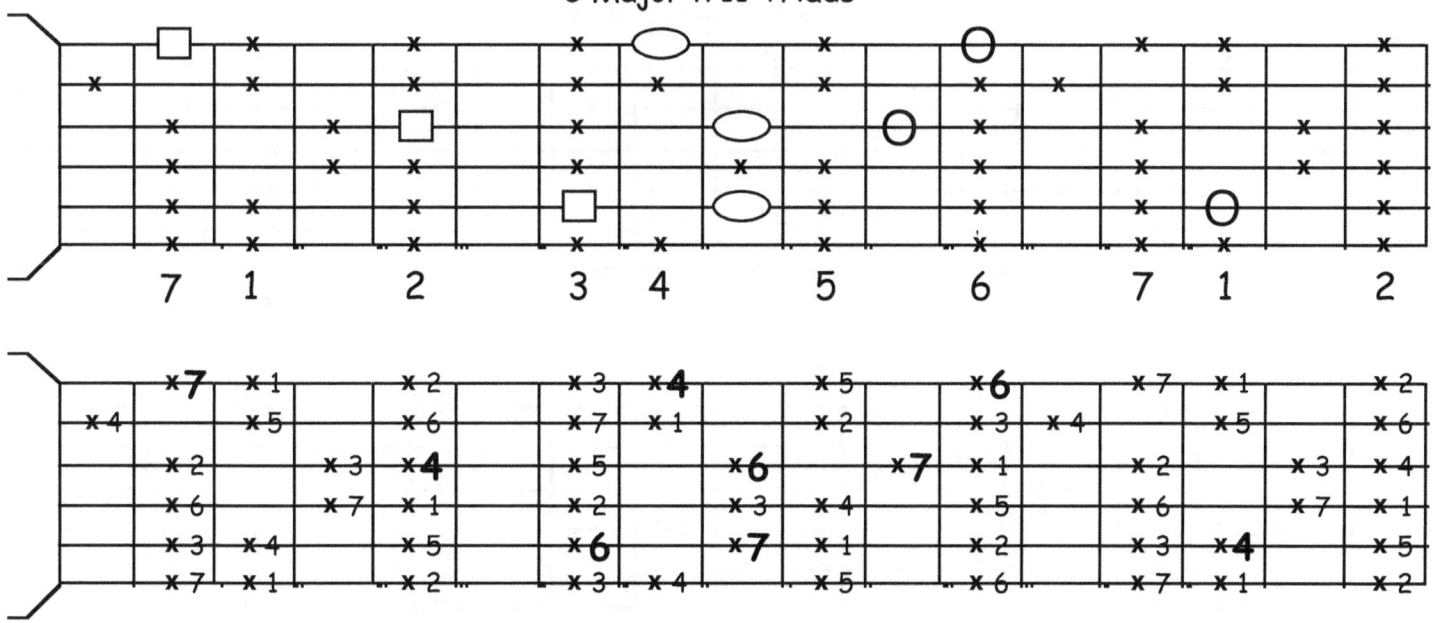

DROP 3:
The "4" Chord: Major #11 Triad Inversions In "G" Major
The only notes you play for these chords are: 4, 6, and 7 of the G major scale.

632 STRING GROUPING
C Major #11 Triads

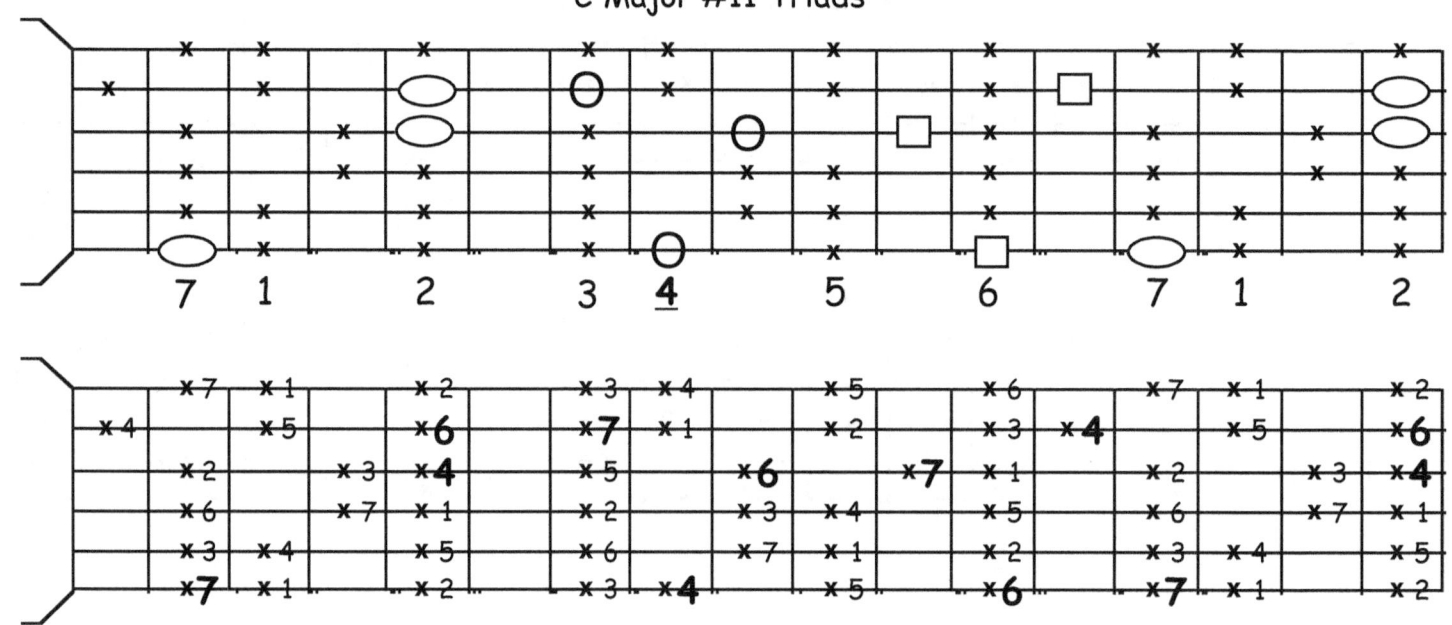

521 STRING GROUPING
C Major #11 Triad

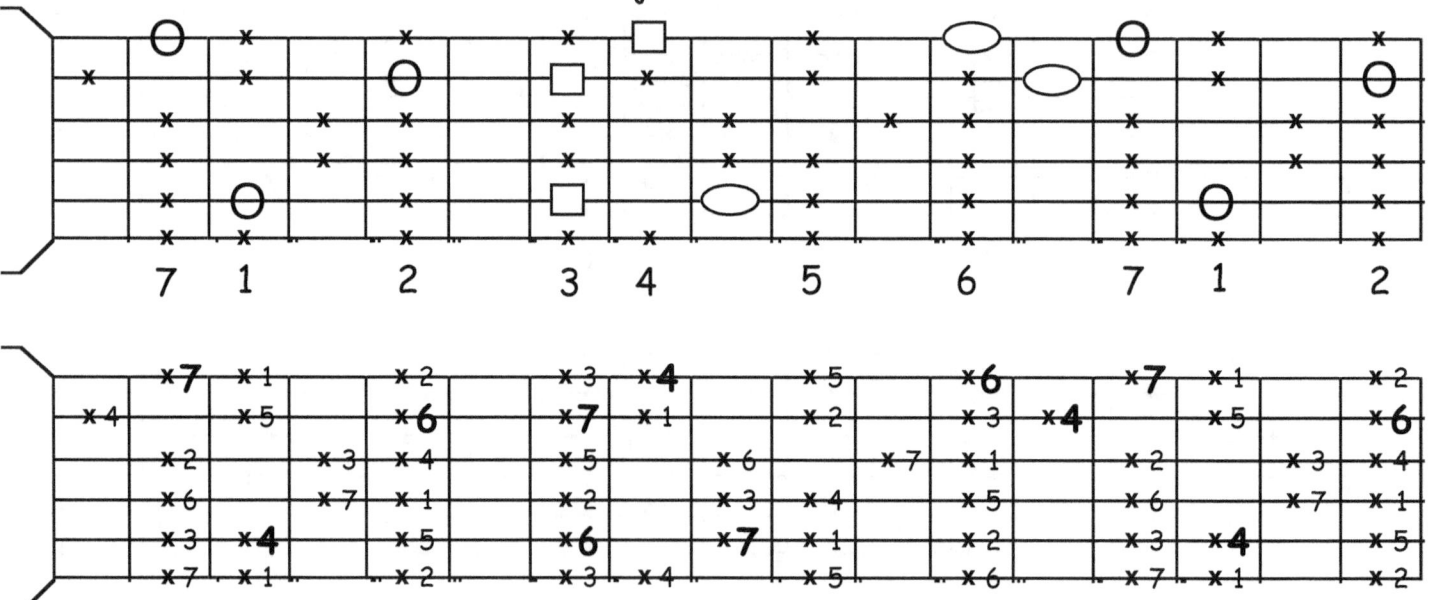

DROP 2 & 3:
The "4" Chord: Major #11 Triad Inversions In "G" Major
The only notes you play for these chords are: 4, 6, and 7 of the G major scale.

652 STRING GROUPING
C Major #11 Triads

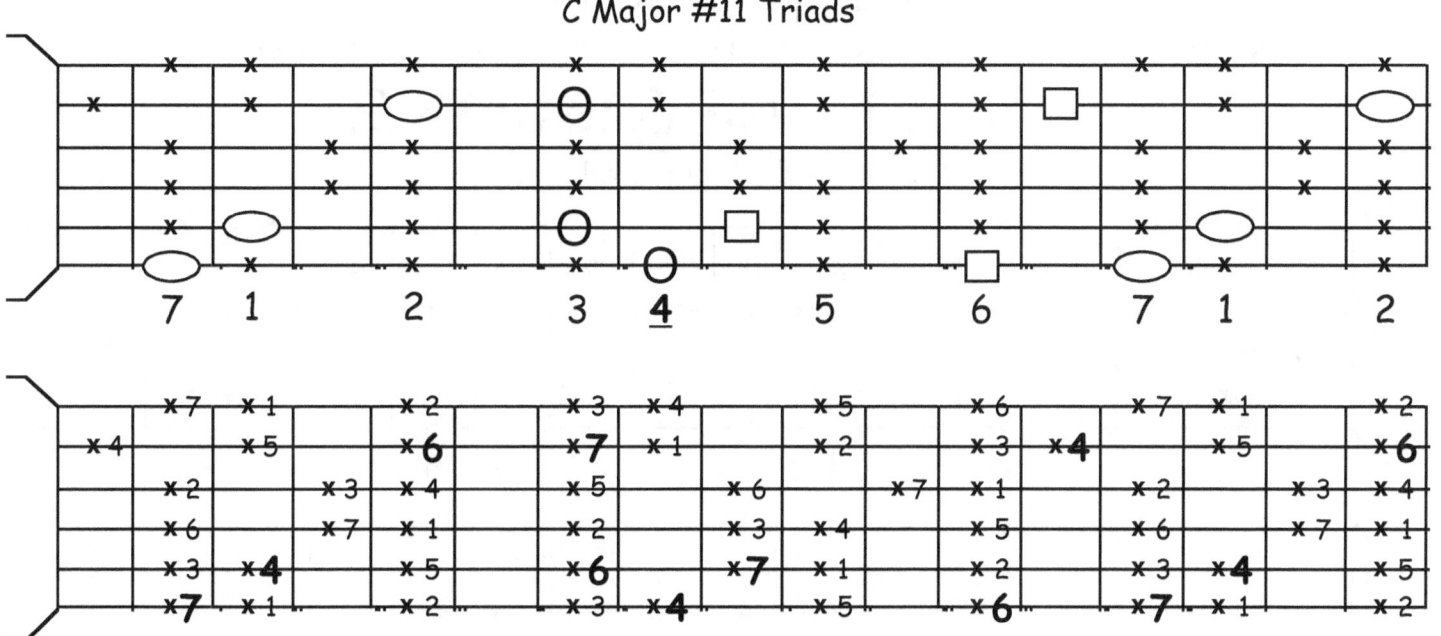

541 STRING GROUPING
C Major #11 Triads

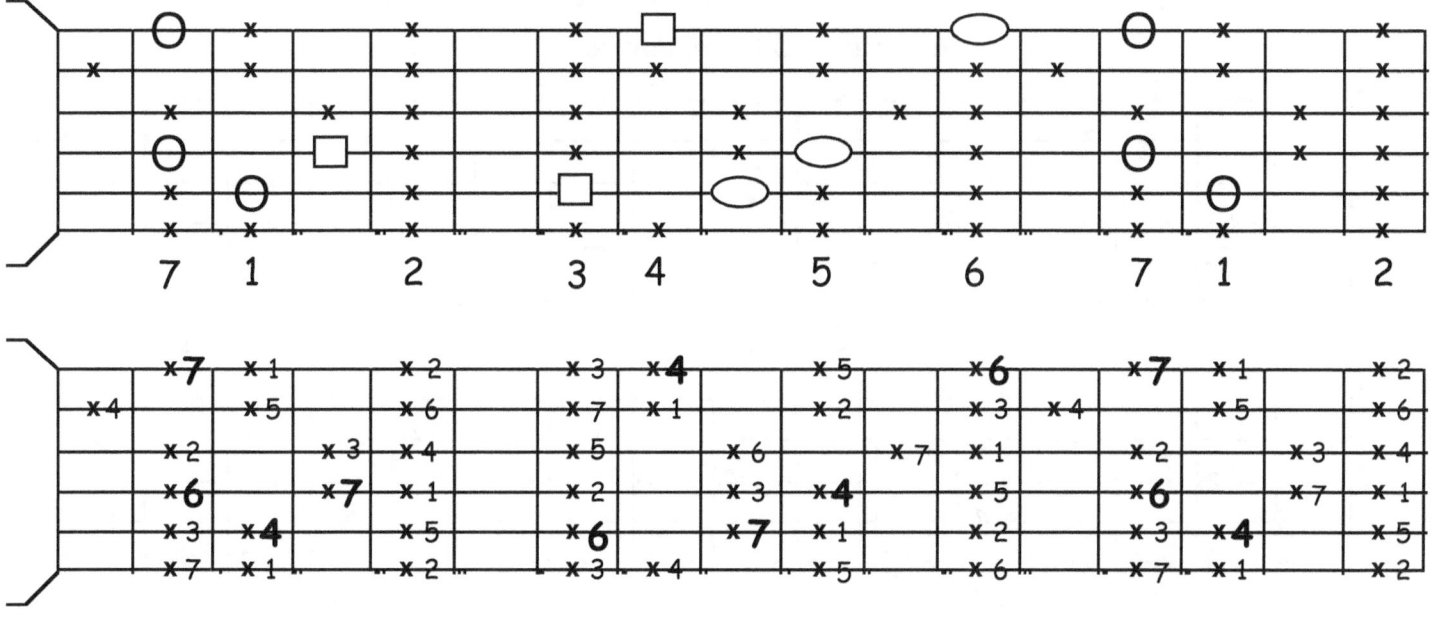

MAJOR #5 TRIADS
CLOSED:

The "1" Chord: Major #5 Triad Inversions
In E Harmonic Minor

The only notes you play for these chords are: 1, 3, and #5 of the E harmonic minor scale.

654 STRING GROUPING
G Major #5 (Augmented) Triads

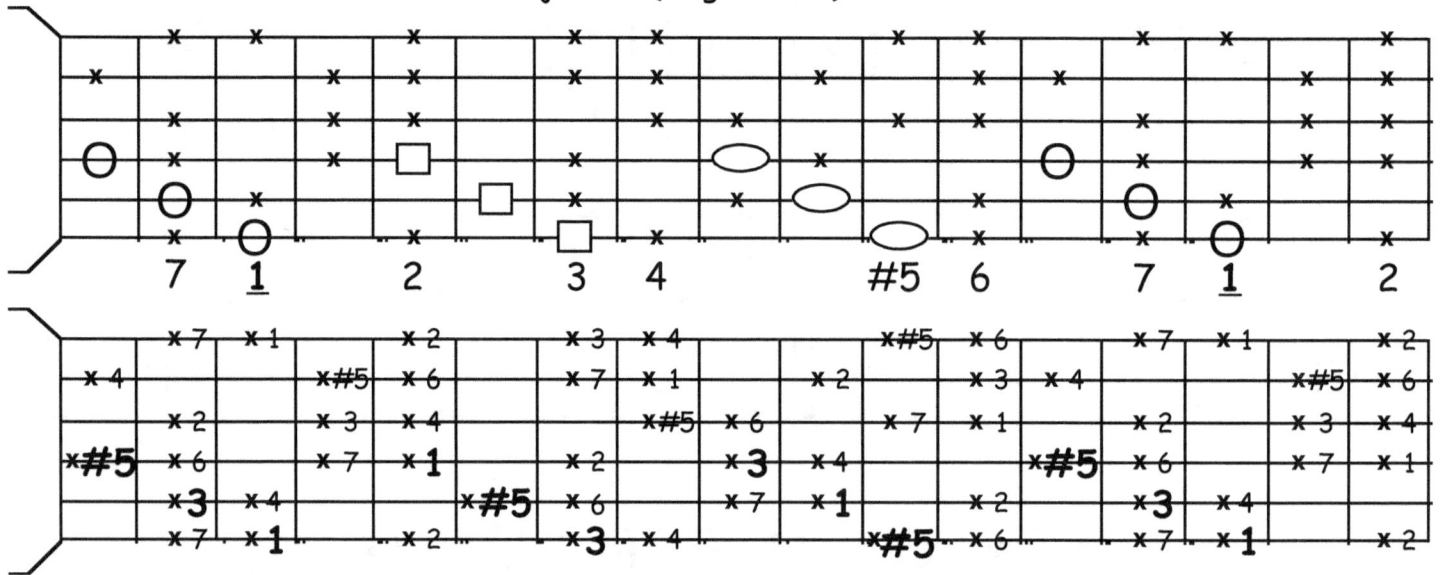

543 STRING GROUPING
G Major #5 (Augmented) Triads

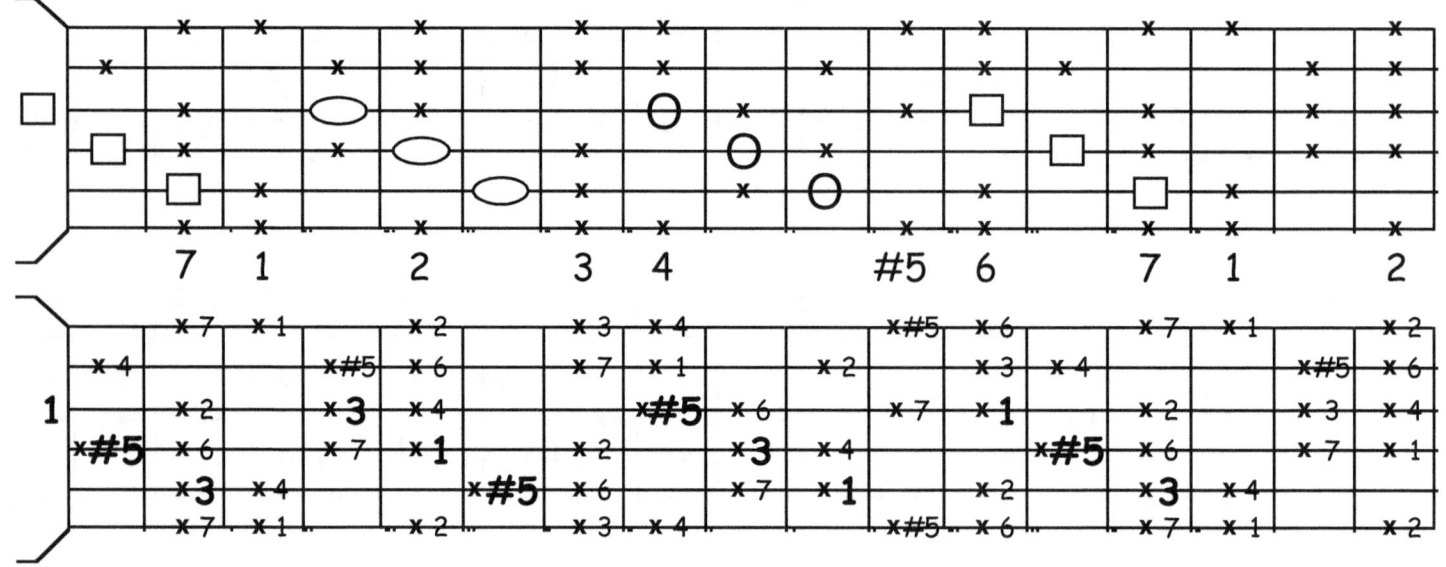

The "1" Chord: Major #5 Triad Inversions
In E Harmonic Minor

The only notes you play for these chords are: 1, 3, and #5 of the E harmonic minor scale.

432 STRING GROUPING
G Major #5 (Augmented) Triads

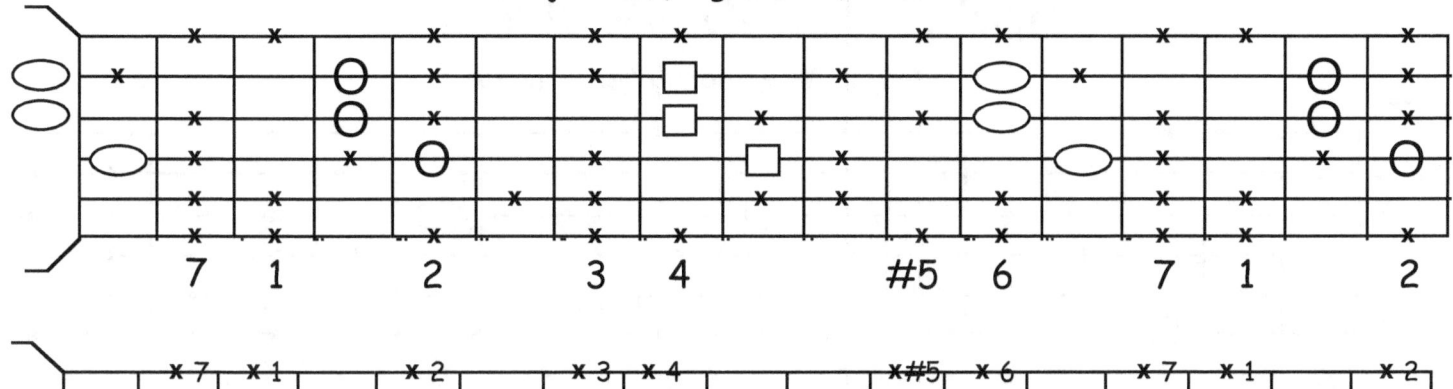

321 STRING GROUPING
G Major #5 (Augmented) Triads

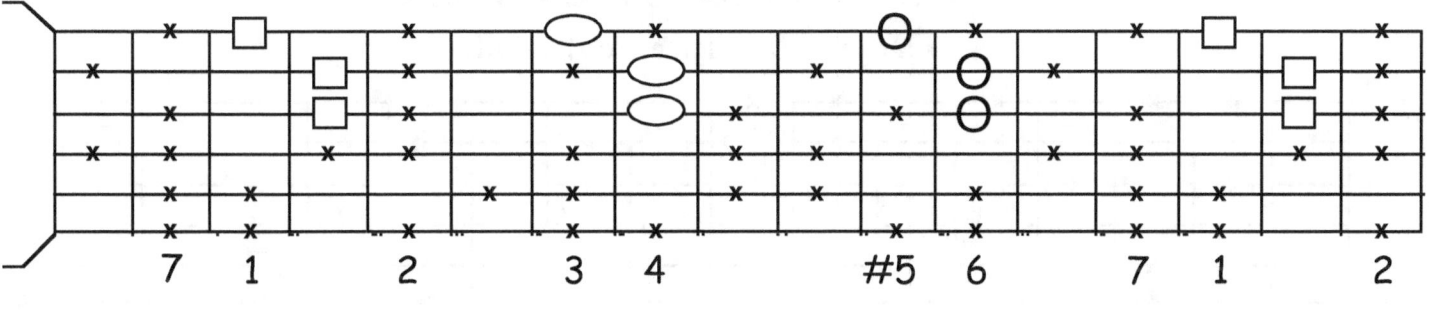

DROP 2:
The "1" Chord: Major #5 Triad Inversions
In E Harmonic Minor

The only notes you play for these chords are: 1, 3, and #5 of the E harmonic minor scale.

653 STRING GROUPING
G Major #5 (Augmented) Triads

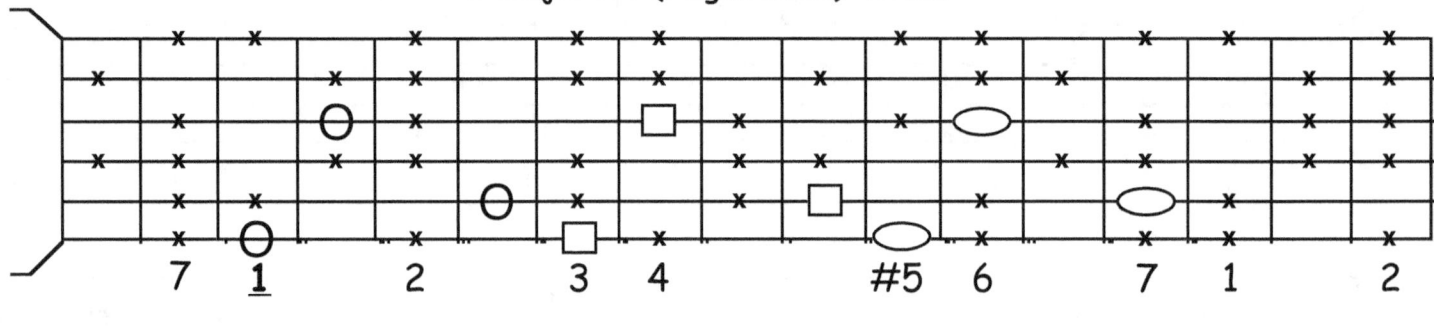

542 STRING GROUPING
G Major #5 (Augmented) Triads

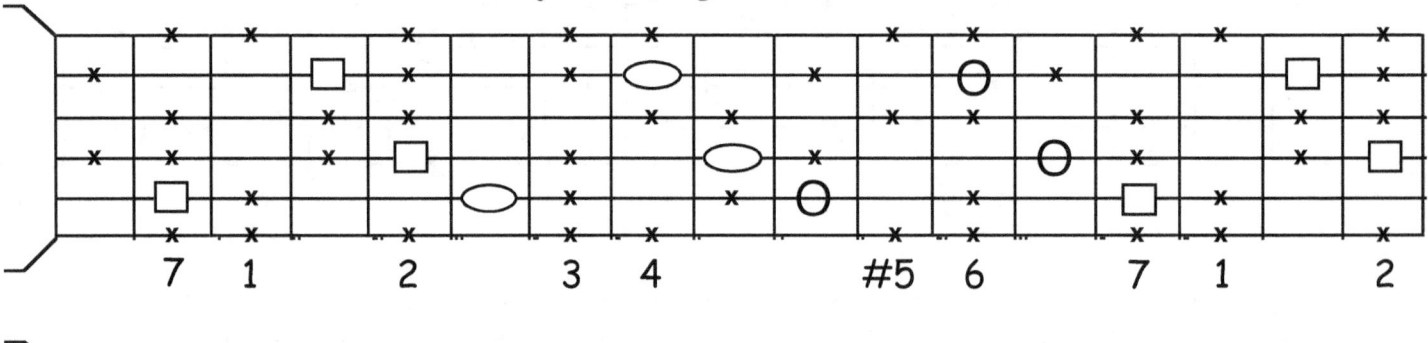

The "1" Chord: Major #5 Triad Inversions
In E Harmonic Minor

The only notes you play for these chords are: 1, 3, and #5 of the E harmonic minor scale.

431 STRING GROUPING
G Major #5 (Augmented) Triads

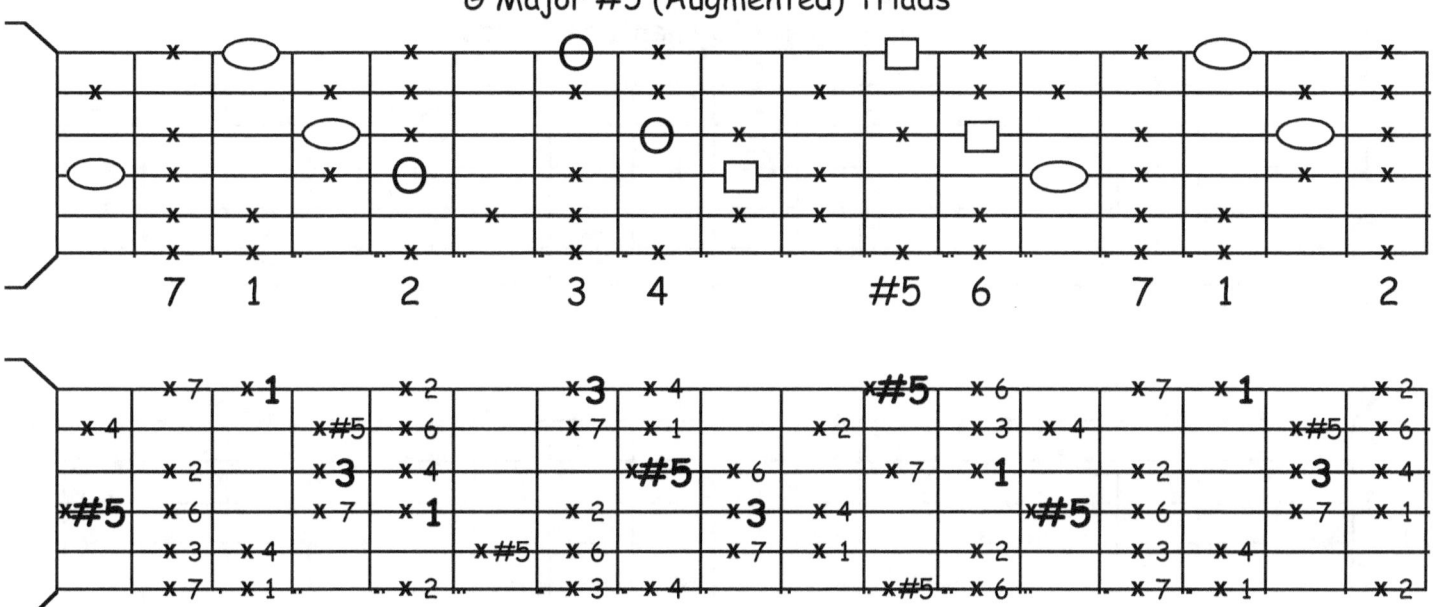

643 STRING GROUPING
(Same notes as 653 String Grouping, but a little brighter)
G Major #5 (Augmented) Triads

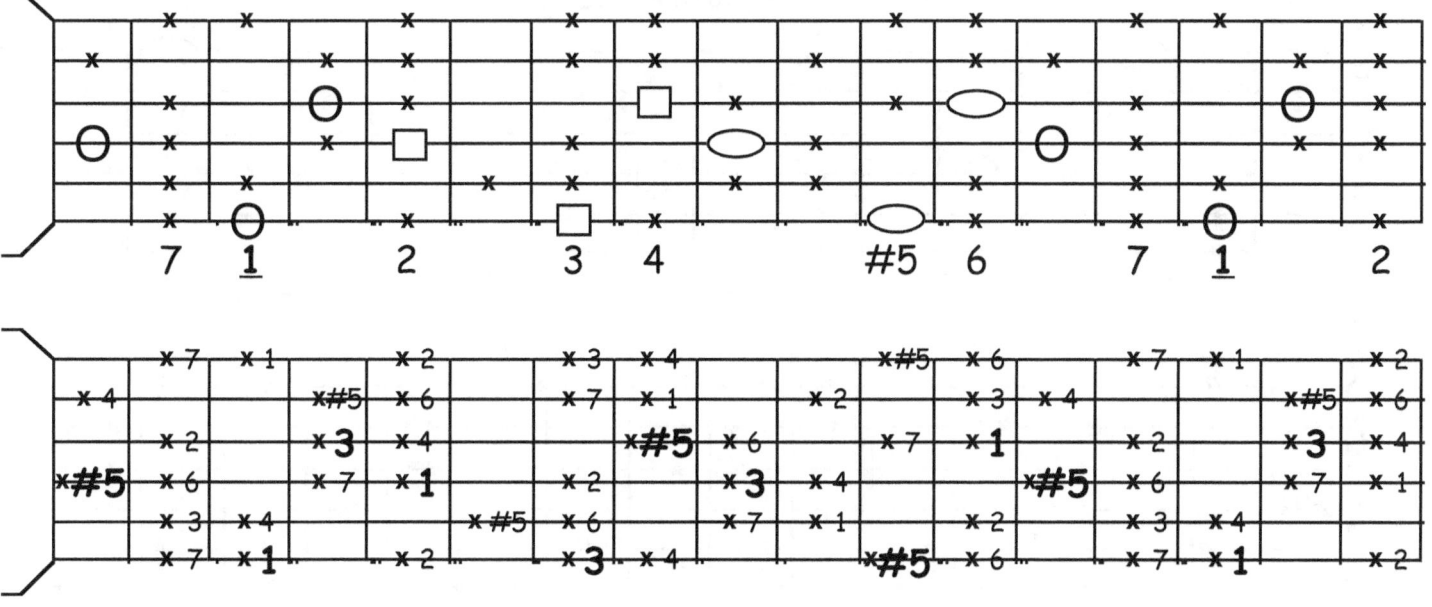

The "1" Chord: Major #5 Triad Inversions
In E Harmonic Minor

The only notes you play for these chords are: 1, 3, and #5 of the E harmonic minor scale.

532 STRING GROUPING

(Same notes as 542 String Grouping, but a little brighter)
G Major #5 (Augmented) Triads

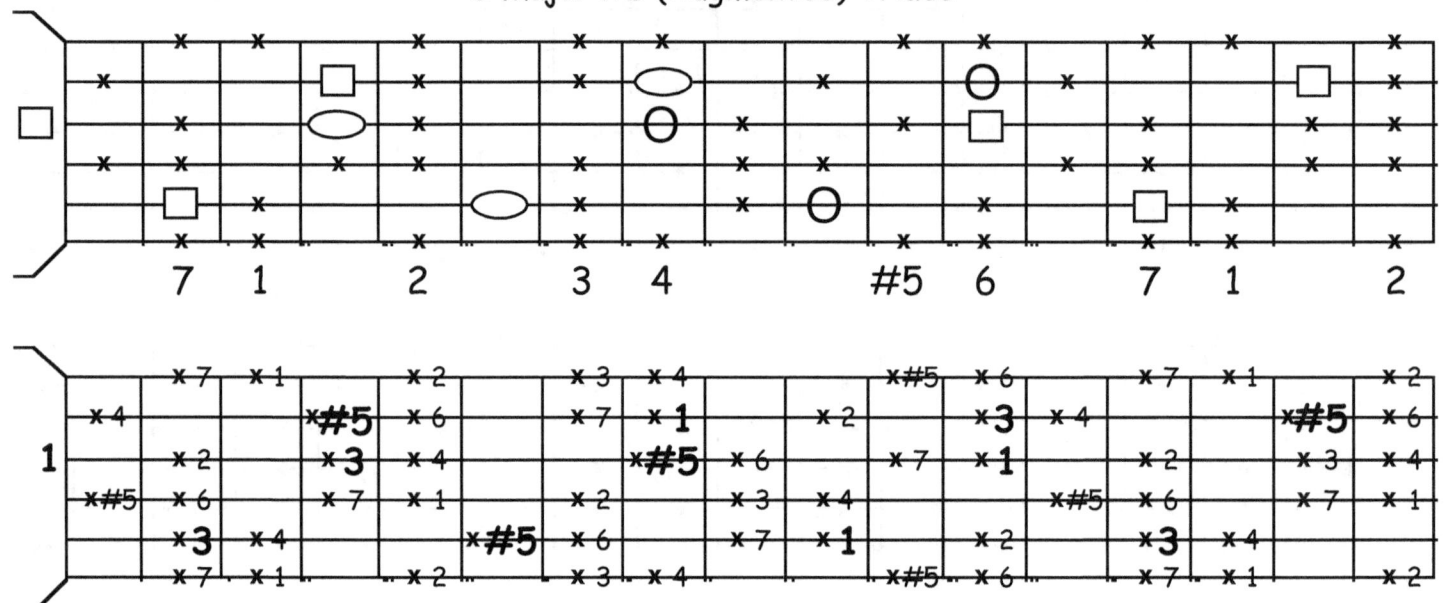

421 STRING GROUPING

(Same notes as 431 String Grouping, but a little brighter)
G Major #5 (Augmented) Triads

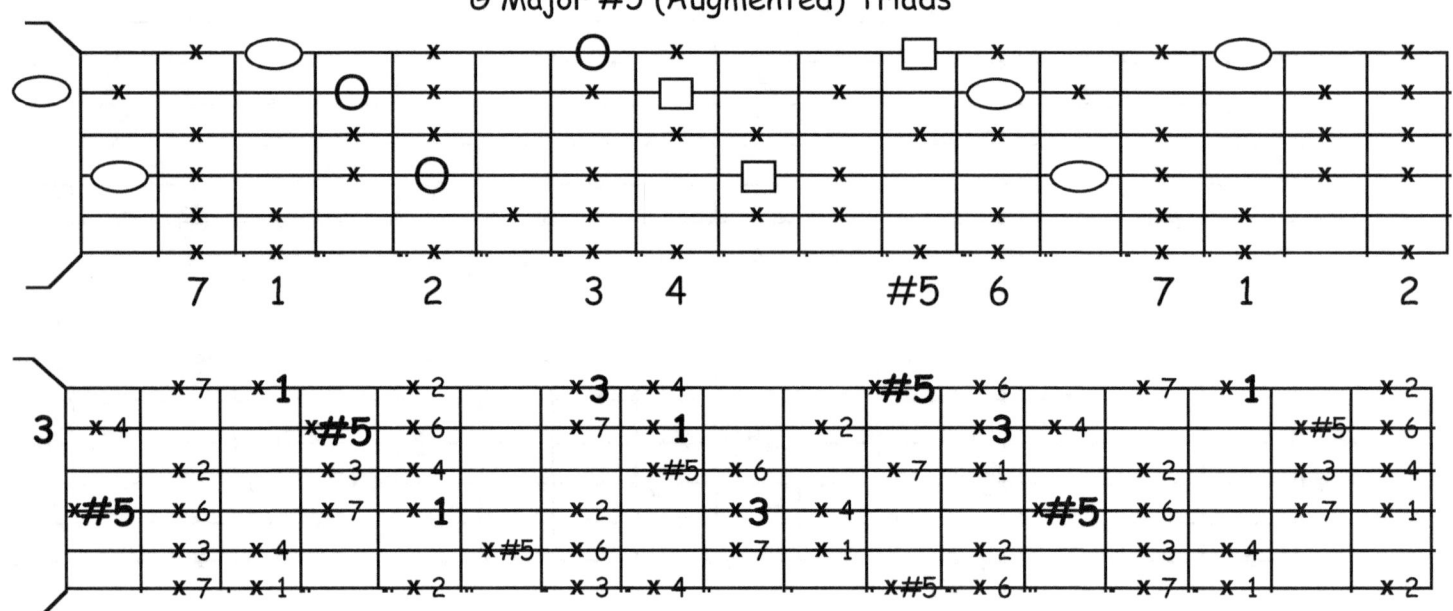

The "1" Chord: Major #5 Triad Inversions
In E Harmonic Minor

The only notes you play for these chords are: 1, 3, and #5 of the E harmonic minor scale.

642 STRING GROUPING

(Same notes as 653 & 643 String Groupings, but even brighter)
G Major #5 (Augmented) Triads

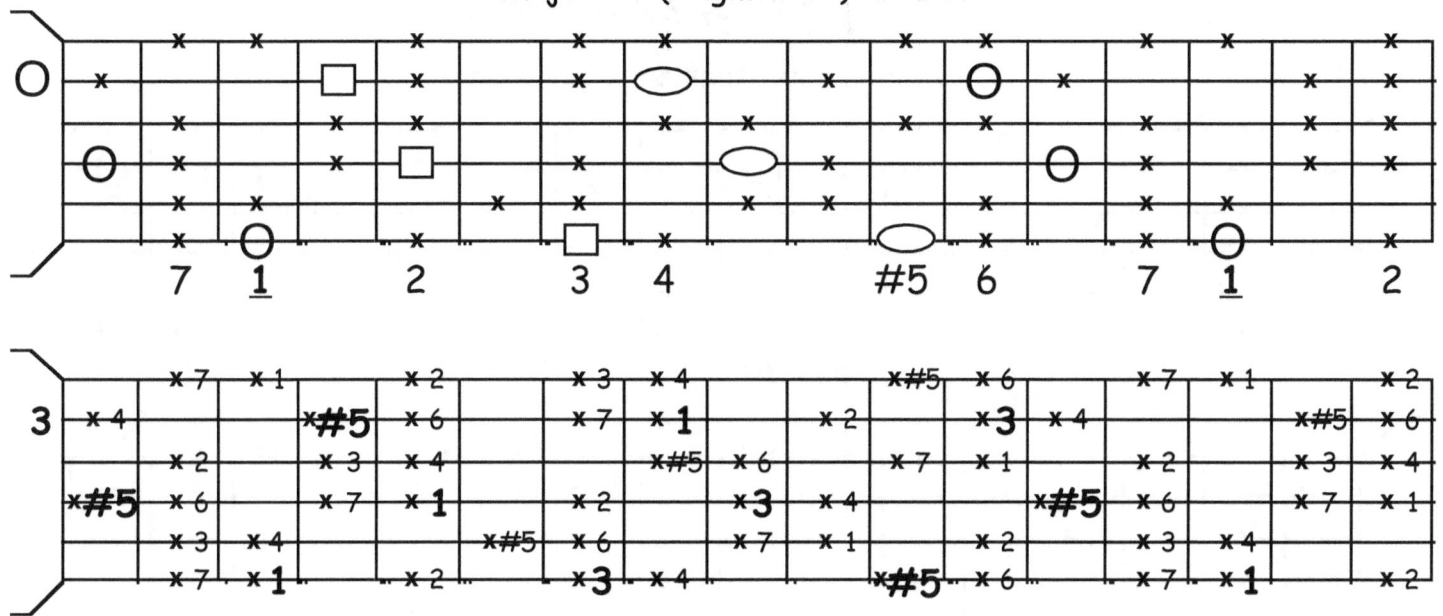

531 STRING GROUPING

(Same notes as 542 & 532 String Groupings, but even brighter)
G Major #5 (Augmented) Triads

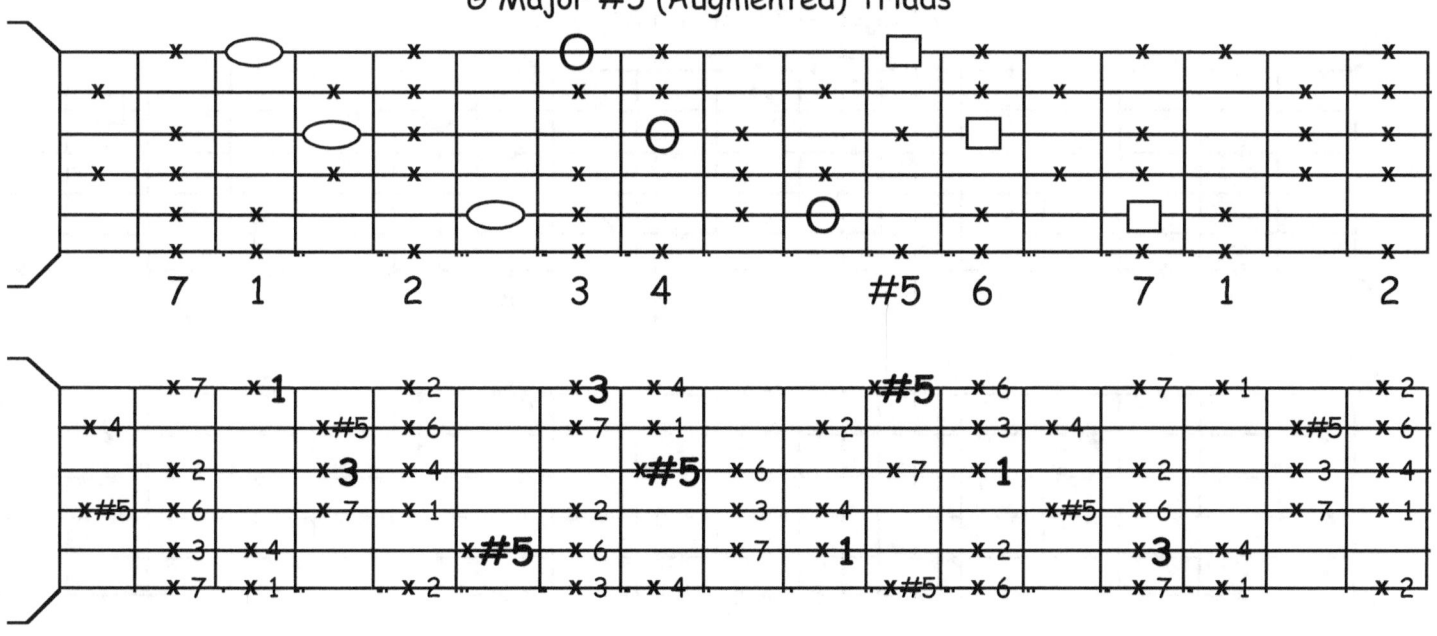

DROP 3:
The "1" Chord: Major #5 Triad Inversions
In E Harmonic Minor

The only notes you play for these chords are: 1, 3, and #5 of the E harmonic minor scale.

632 STRING GROUPING
G Major #5 (Augmented) Triads

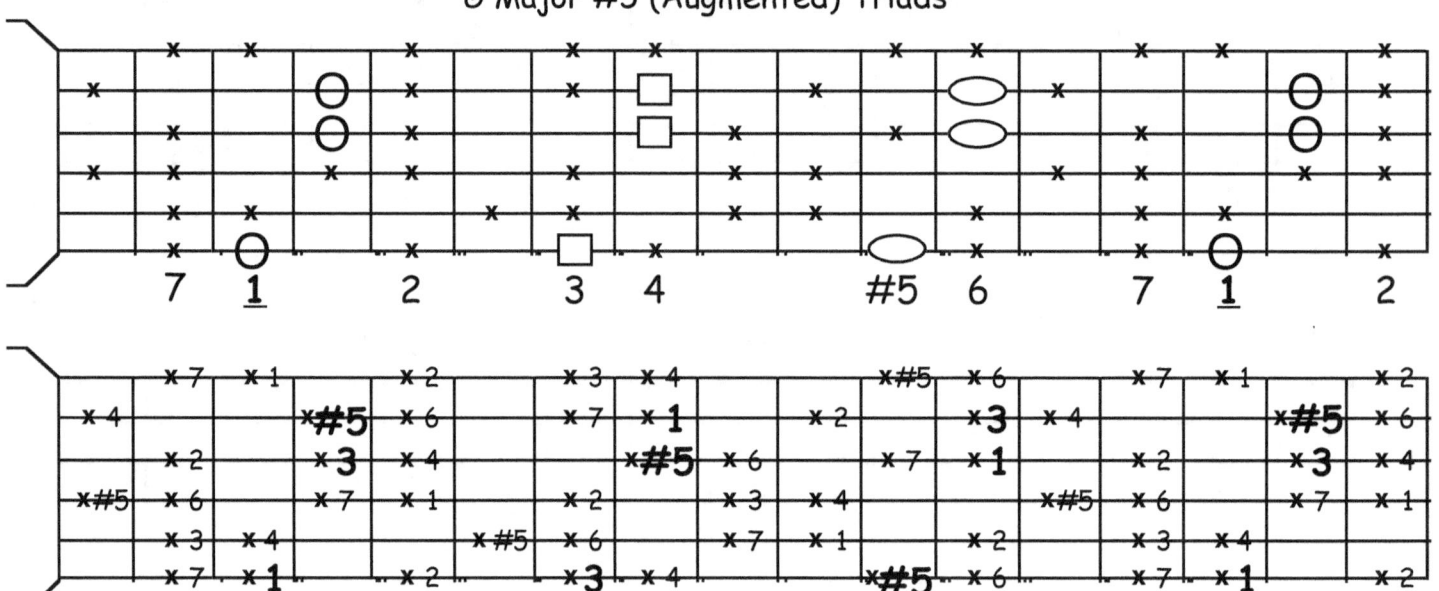

521 STRING GROUPING
G Major #5 (Augmented) Triads

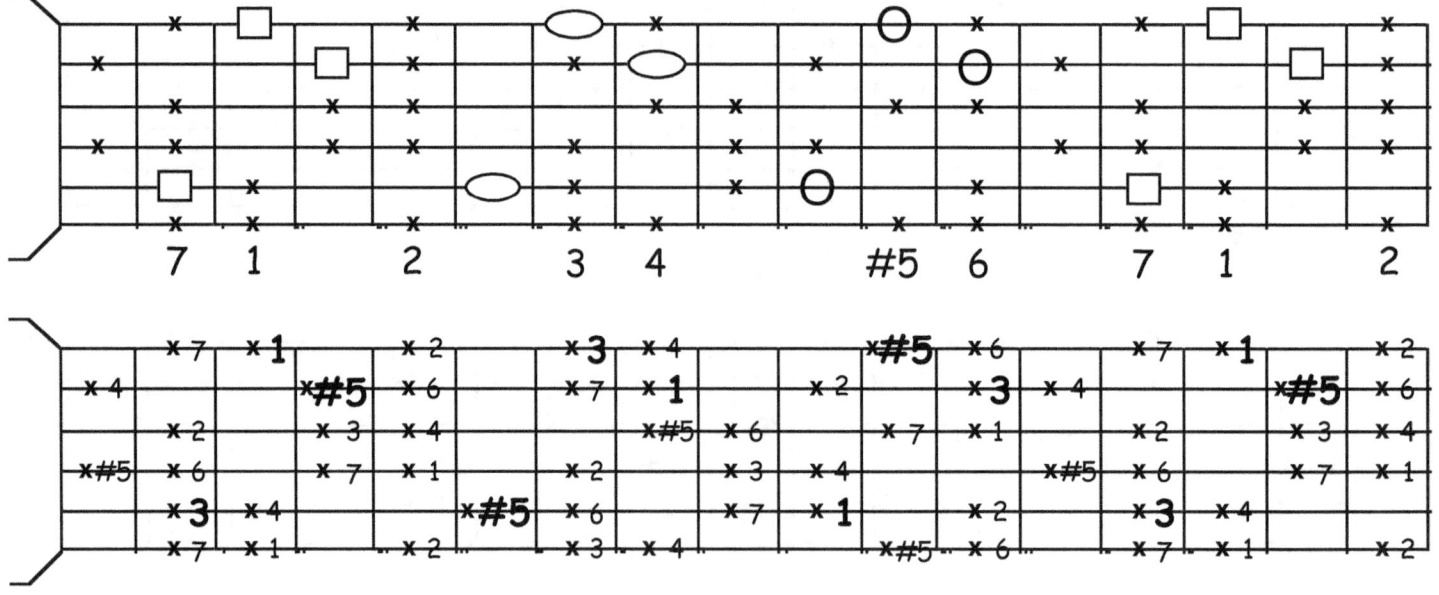

DROP 2 & 3:
The "1" Chord: Major #5 Triad Inversions
In E Harmonic Minor
The only notes you play for these chords are: 1, 3, and #5 of the E harmonic minor scale.

652 STRING GROUPING
G Major #5 (Augmented) Triads

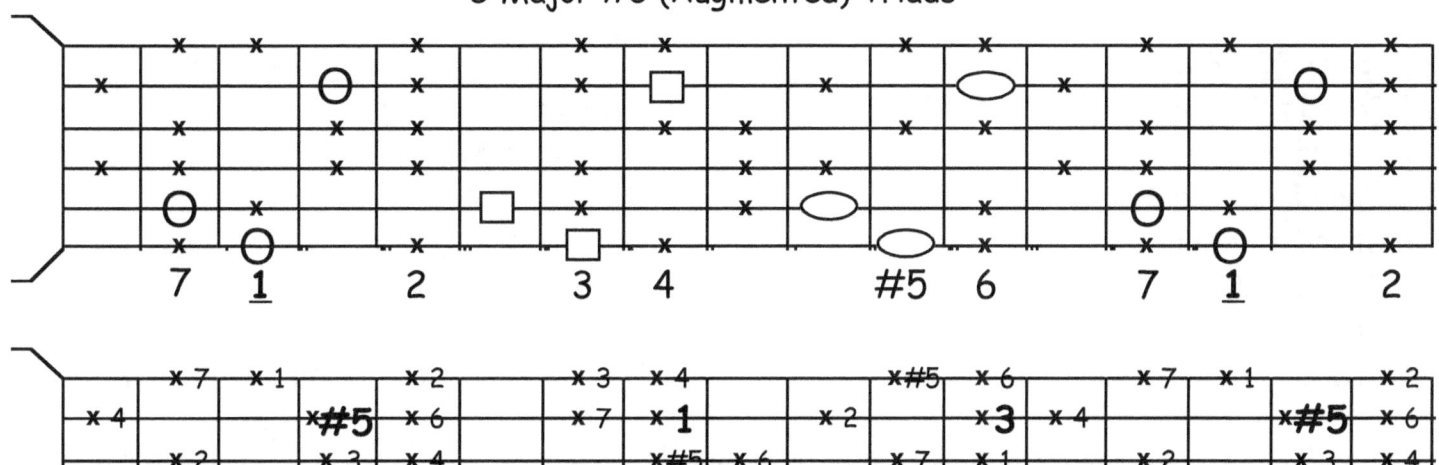

541 STRING GROUPING
G Major #5 (Augmented) Triads

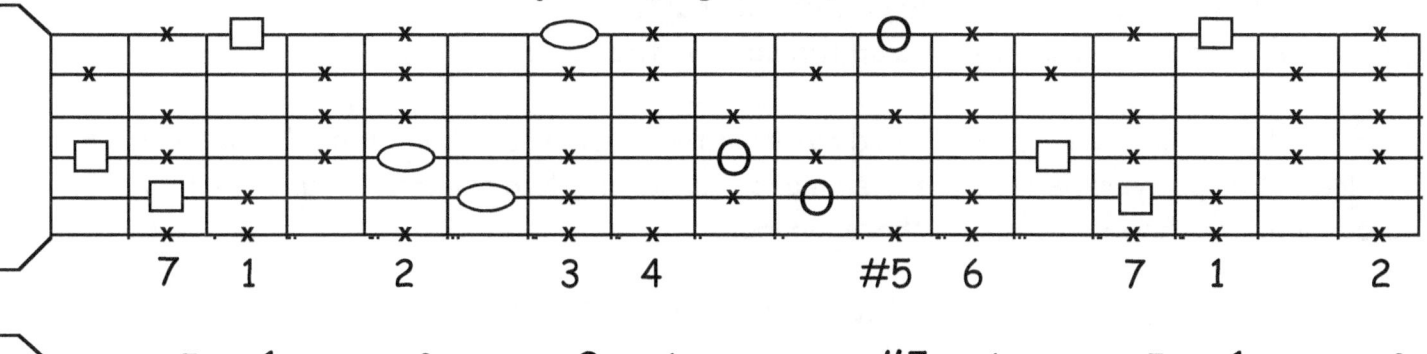

83

DIATONIC SEVENTH CHORDS

Remember that each of the 7 notes of the major scale can have a chord built on it. And each of these 7 chords that come from the major scale has its own sound or its own "tonality". The words that are used to describe these tonalities are as follows:

TRIAD TONALITY
1 Chord = Major
2 Chord = Minor
3 Chord = Minor
4 Chord = Major
5 Chord = Major
6 Chord = Minor
7 Chord = Minor b5 or Diminished

SEVENTH CHORD TONALITY
1 Chord = Major 7
2 Chord = Minor 7
3 Chord = Minor 7
4 Chord = Major 7
5 Chord = Dominant 7
6 Chord = Minor 7
7 Chord = Minor 7 b5 or Half Diminished

When dealing with seventh chords (4 note chords), you will have to know the "tonality" of each of the 7 chords that come from the major scale (THIS IS IMPORTANT):

        1 & 4 chords = Major 7
        2, 3, & 6 chords = Minor 7
        5 chord = Dominant 7
        7 chord = Minor 7b5 (or half diminished)

Now what you need to know is:
1) What do these chords look like on a chord chart?
2) What do these chords look like on the neck of the guitar?

Again, while there is no one standard notation for writing out chord symbols on chord charts, there are some symbols that are used more frequently then others. I'll use the letter "C" as a constant to show you some of these symbols:

      C Major 7 = C Maj7, C M7, C Major7, C∆7, C Ma7

      C Minor 7 = C-7, C min7, C m7, C mi7

      C Dominant 7 = C7 (This symbol is pretty universal)

      C Minor 7b5 = C-7b5, Cø7, Cmin7b5, C mi7b5

Of course, you'll also have to learn the shapes for each of these chord types on the neck of the guitar. Because of the way the neck of the guitar is structured, any seventh chord may have different places where it can be played. These different places may contain the exact same notes in the exact same order, but they may use a different string grouping, a different fingering, and may have a slightly different timbre (a brighter or a darker sound) from each other. Rather than organizing all of the seventh chords by how they look on the music staff (thereby having to present multiple string groupings at the same time), I have organized all of them by their string groupings along with their corresponding inversions. I have also included a parent scale in the diagrams so you can see how all of the chords live within the scale patterns. This allows for a more practical, working knowledge of the neck of the guitar and how the inversions and scales relate to each other ... sound familiar?

IMPORTANT NOTE: Even though there are plenty of other seventh chord voicings on the guitar, this is a fairly thorough representation of the seventh chords. Some are more practical than others. I have included the 3 sets of "closed" voicings because they are the basic piano voicings that many people learn when they study traditional theory. HOWEVER, they are not very guitaristic. Some of their inversions are impractical if not impossible. The same could be said for some of the "drop 4", "drop 3 & 4", and "drop 2, 3, & 4" inversions. Don't get overwhelmed by the amount of information here. You would have a VERY good chord vocabulary if you just learned the 3 sets of "drop 2" and the 2 sets of "drop 3" chord inversion, extensions, and alterations.

AND REMEMBER:
When the root of the chord is the lowest note of the chord voicing, the chord is in:
"root position".
When the third of the chord is the lowest note of the chord voicing, the chord is in:
"first inversion".
When the fifth of the chord is the lowest note of the chord voicing, the chord is in:
"second inversion".
When the seventh of the chord is the lowest note of the chord voicing, the chord is in:
"third inversion".
AND:
All of the seventh chord diagrams in The MAJOR METHOD use the following shapes:

O = Root Position Chord

☐ = First Inversion Chord

⬭ = Second Inversion Chord

X = Third Inversion Chord

Here are the diatonic seventh chords ...

DIATONIC 7th CHORDS

◯ = Root Position 7th Chord

☐ = First Inversion 7th Chord

⬭ = Second Inversion 7th Chord

X = Third Inversion 7th Chord

CLOSED:
6543 STRING GROUPING
The "1" Chord: Major 7 Inversions In "G" Major
G Major 7

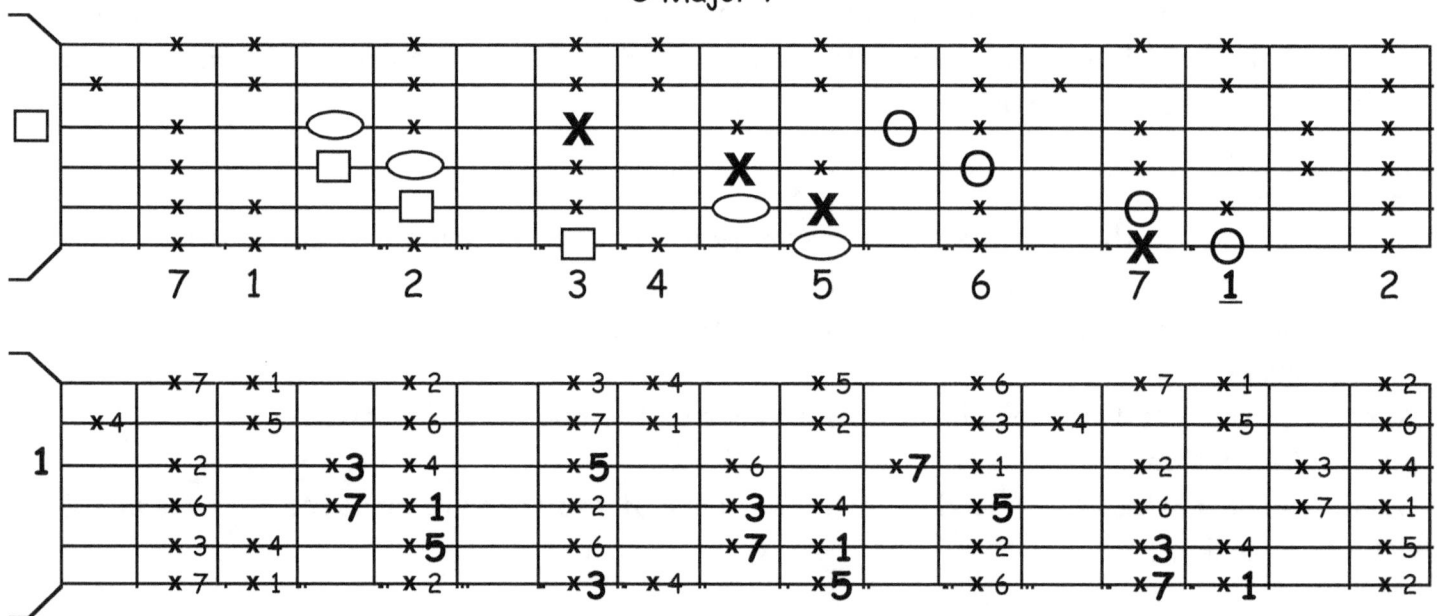

The only notes that you play are: 1, 3, 5, and 7 of the G major scale.

As you can see, these are NOT very practical chord voicings! But, I have included them so that you can see what these basic piano voicings look like on the neck of the guitar. Also, if you are a practitioner of "tapping" on the neck of the guitar, you may find these helpful. If you want to move along to more practical (left hand friendly) seventh chord voicings, you can jump forward to the "drop 2" chord voicings on page 97.

6543 STRING GROUPING
The "2" Chord: Minor 7 Inversions In "G" Major
A Minor 7

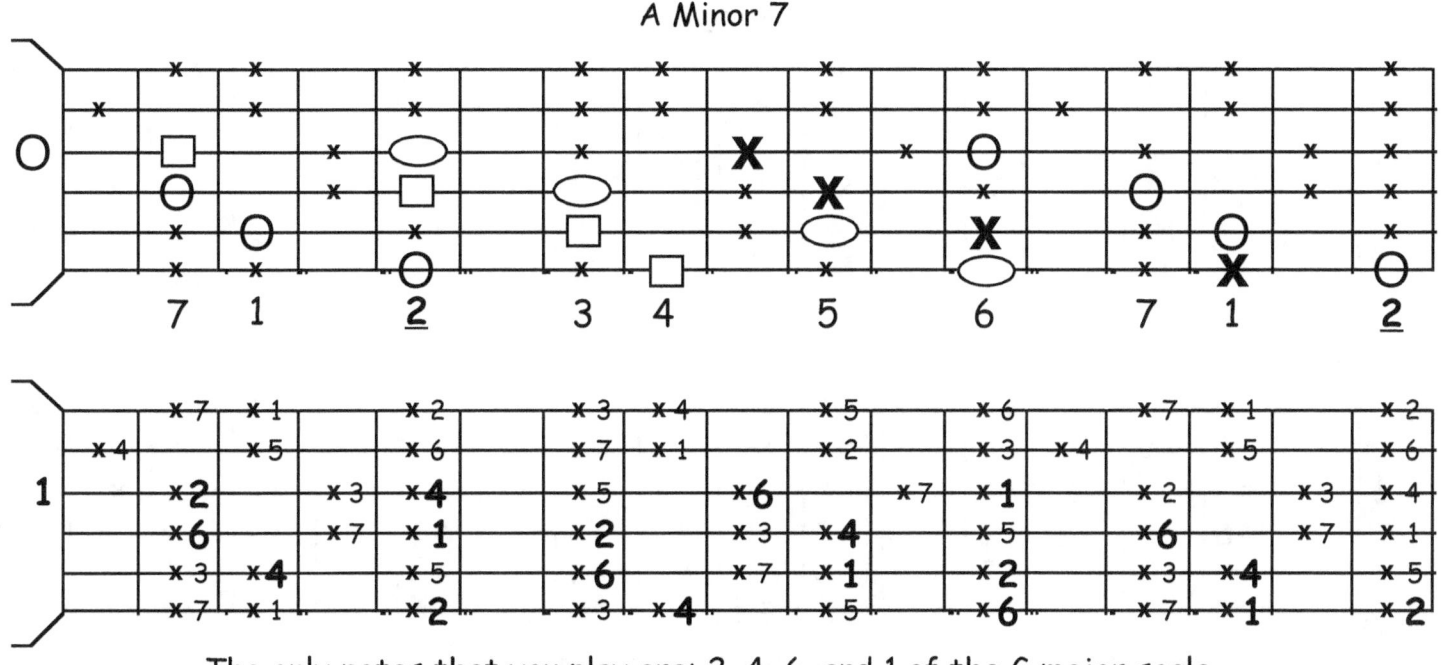

The only notes that you play are: 2, 4, 6, and 1 of the G major scale.

The "3" Chord: Minor 7 Inversions In "G" Major
B Minor 7

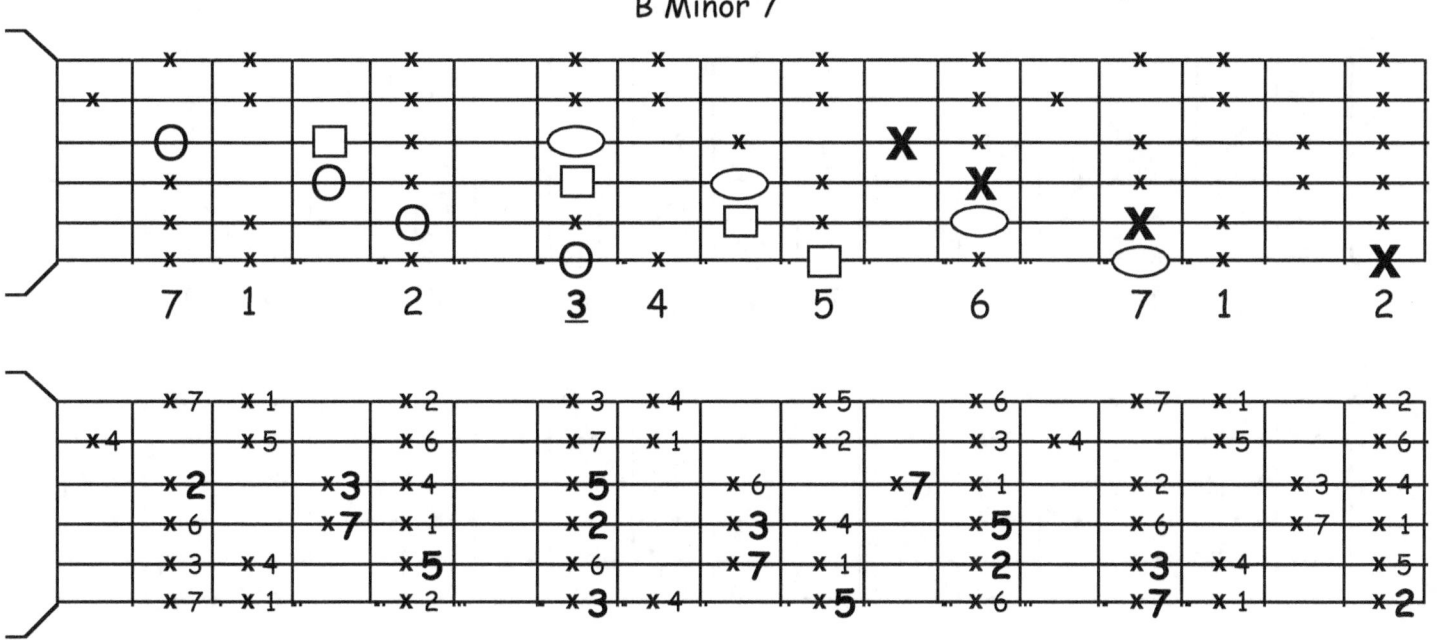

The only notes that you play are: 3, 5, 7, and 2 of the G major scale.

6543 STRING GROUPING

The "4" Chord: Major 7 Inversions In "G" Major

C Major 7

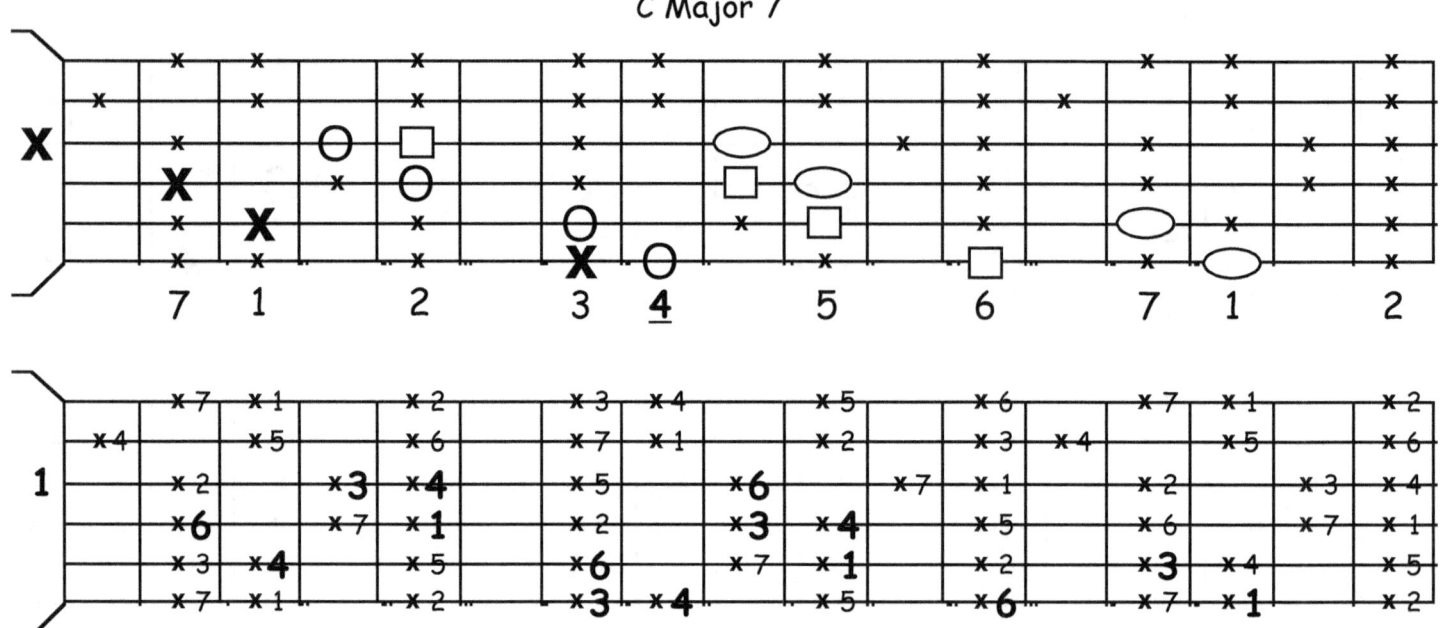

The only notes that you play are: 4, 6, 1, and 3 of the G major scale.

The "5" Chord: Dominant 7 Inversions In "G" Major

D Dominant 7

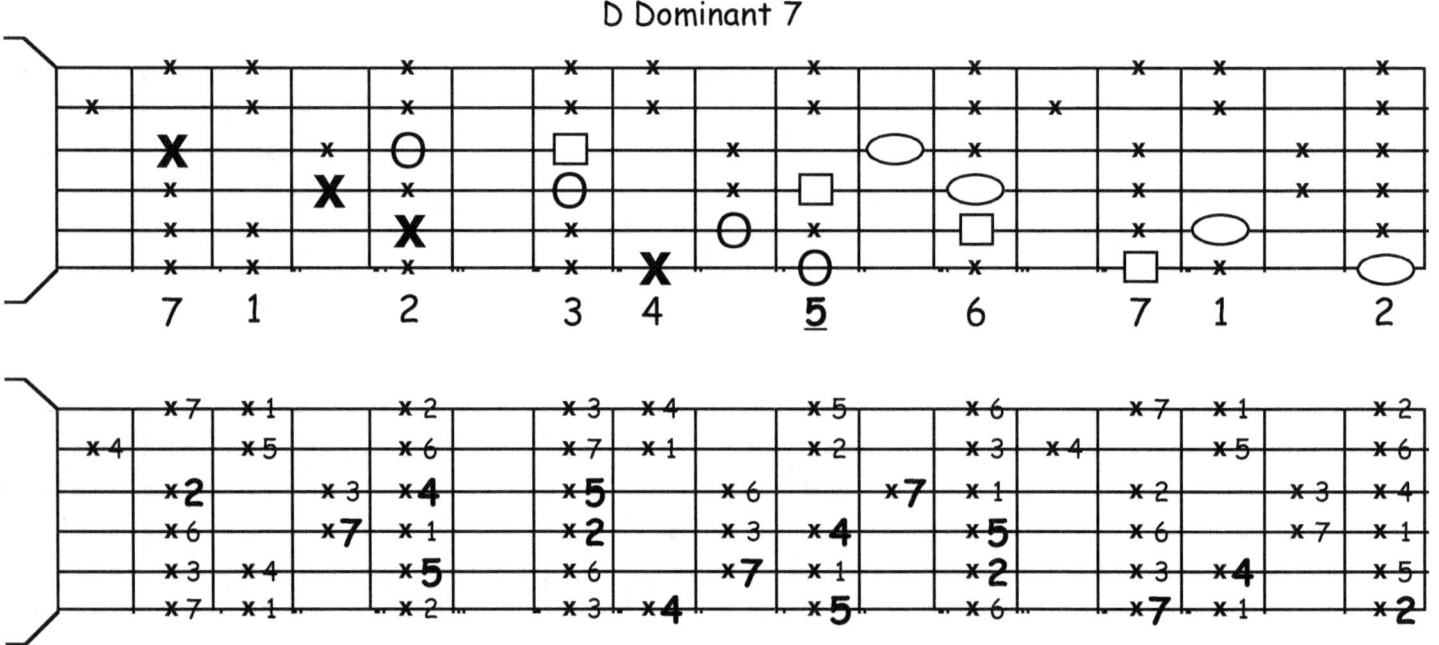

The only notes that you play are: 5, 7, 2, and 4 of the G major scale.

6543 STRING GROUPING

The "6" Chord: Minor 7 Inversions In "G" Major
E Minor 7

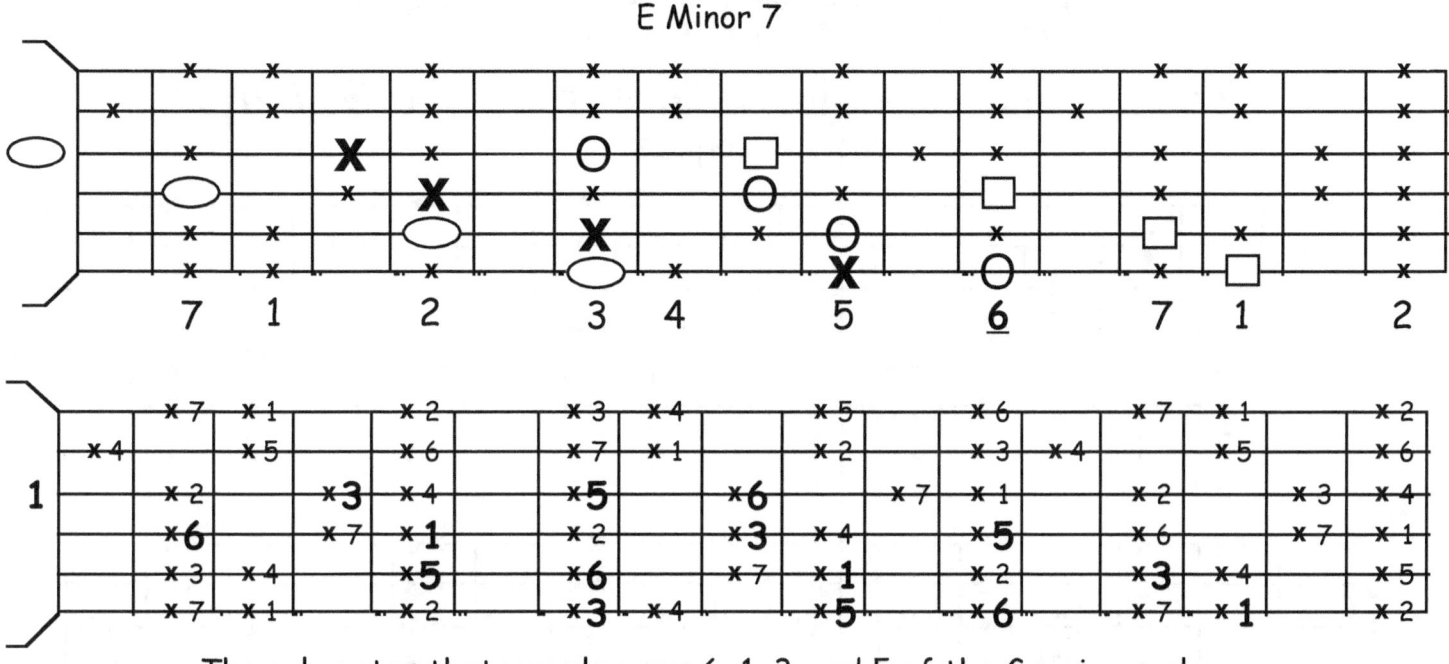

The only notes that you play are: 6, 1, 3, and 5 of the G major scale.

The "7" Chord: Minor 7b5 Inversions In "G" Major
F# Minor 7b5

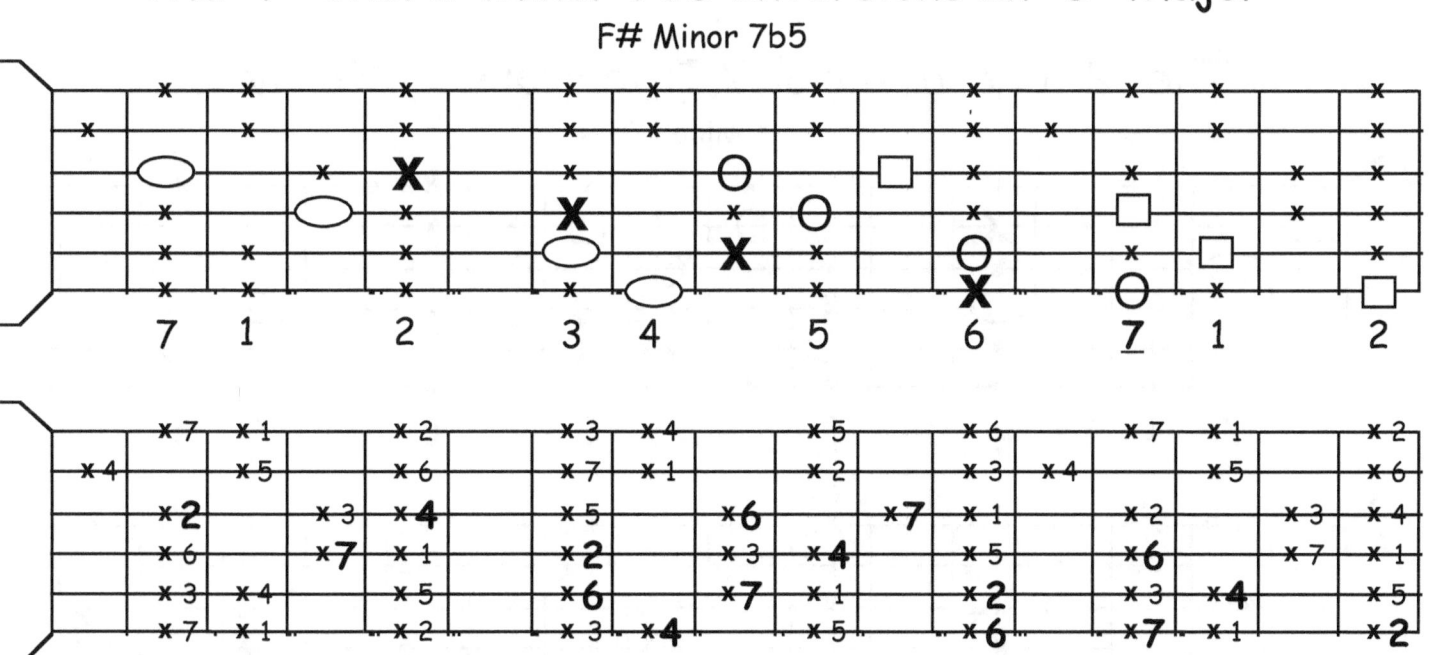

The only notes that you play are: 7, 2, 4, and 6 of the G major scale.

CLOSED:
5432 STRING GROUPING
The "1" Chord: Major 7 Inversions In "G" Major
G Major 7

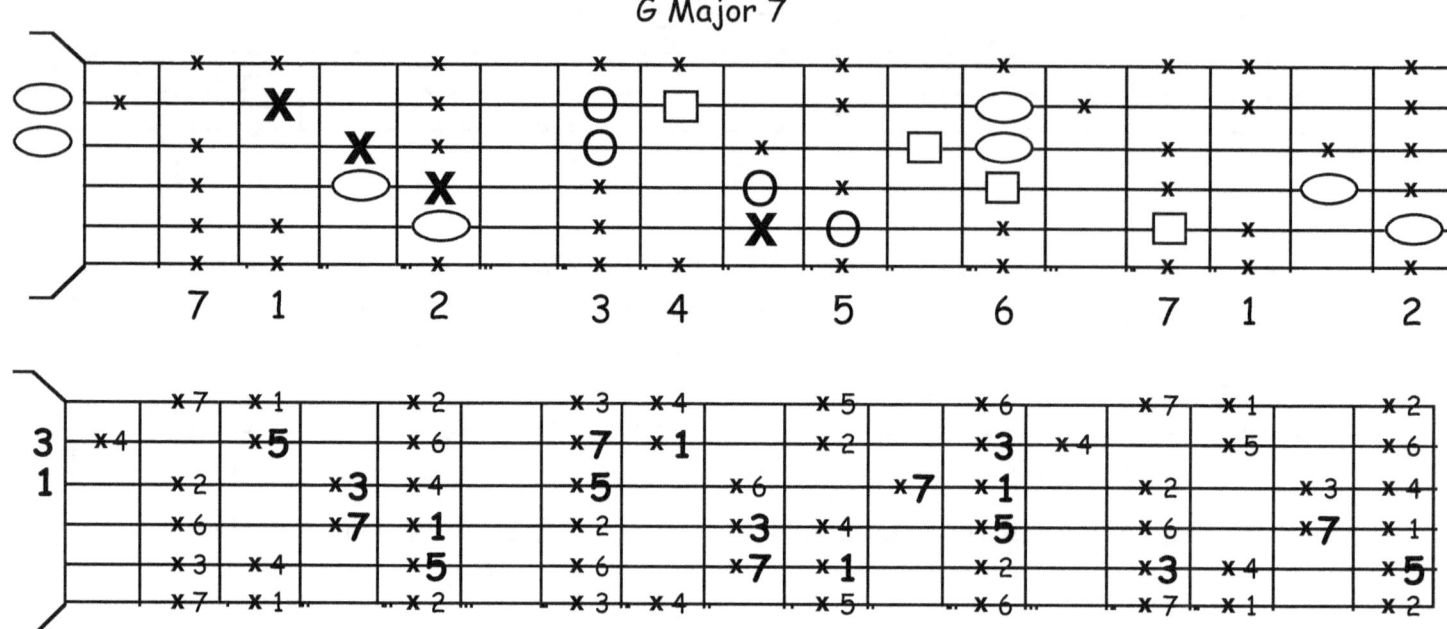

The only notes that you play are: 1, 3, 5, and 7 of the G major scale.

The "2" Chord: Minor 7 Inversions In "G" Major
A Minor 7

The only notes that you play are: 2, 4, 6, and 1 of the G major scale.

5432 STRING GROUPING
The "3" Chord: Minor 7 Inversions In "G" Major
B Minor 7

The only notes that you play are: 3, 5, 7, and 2 of the G major scale.

The "4" Chord: Major 7 Inversions In "G" Major
C Major 7

The only notes that you play are: 4, 6, 1, and 3 of the G major scale.

5432 STRING GROUPING

The "5" Chord: Dominant 7 Inversions In "G" Major

D Dominant 7

The only notes that you play are: 5, 7, 2, and 4 of the G major scale.

The "6" Chord: Minor 7 Inversions In "G" Major

E Minor 7

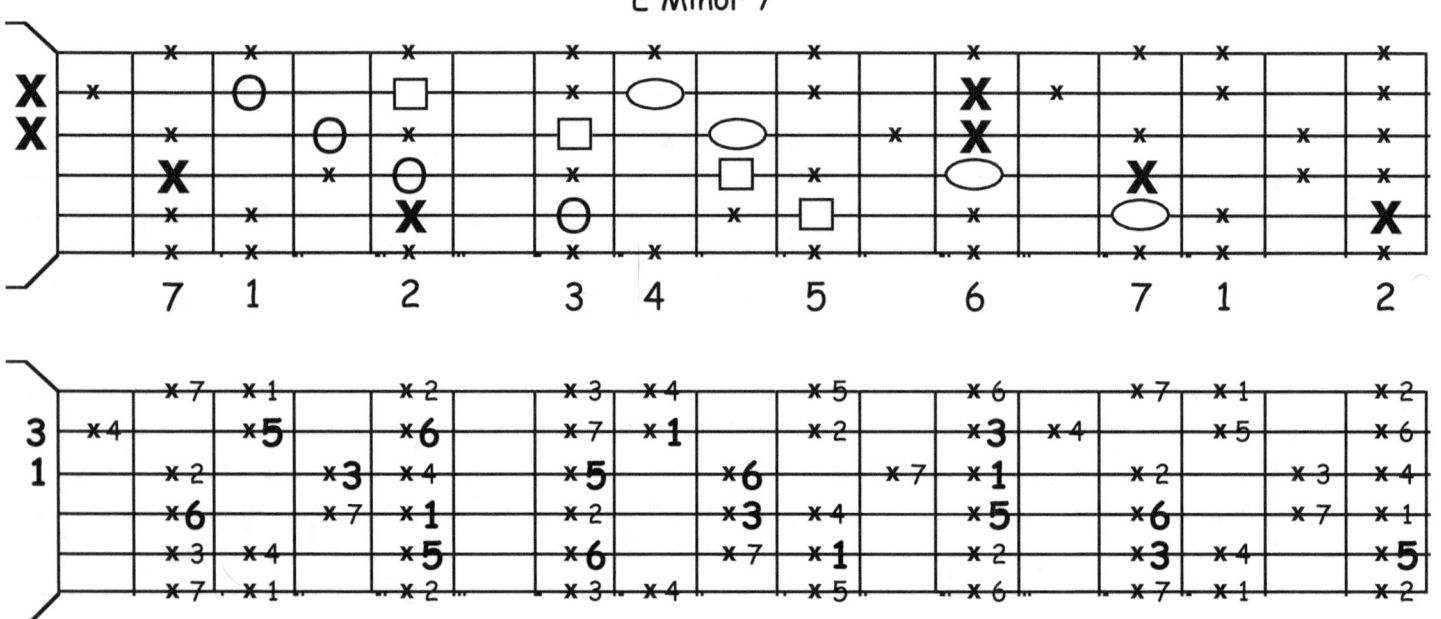

The only notes that you play are: 6, 1, 3, and 5 of the G major scale.

5432 STRING GROUPING
The "7" Chord: Minor 7b5 Inversions In "G" Major
F# Minor 7b5

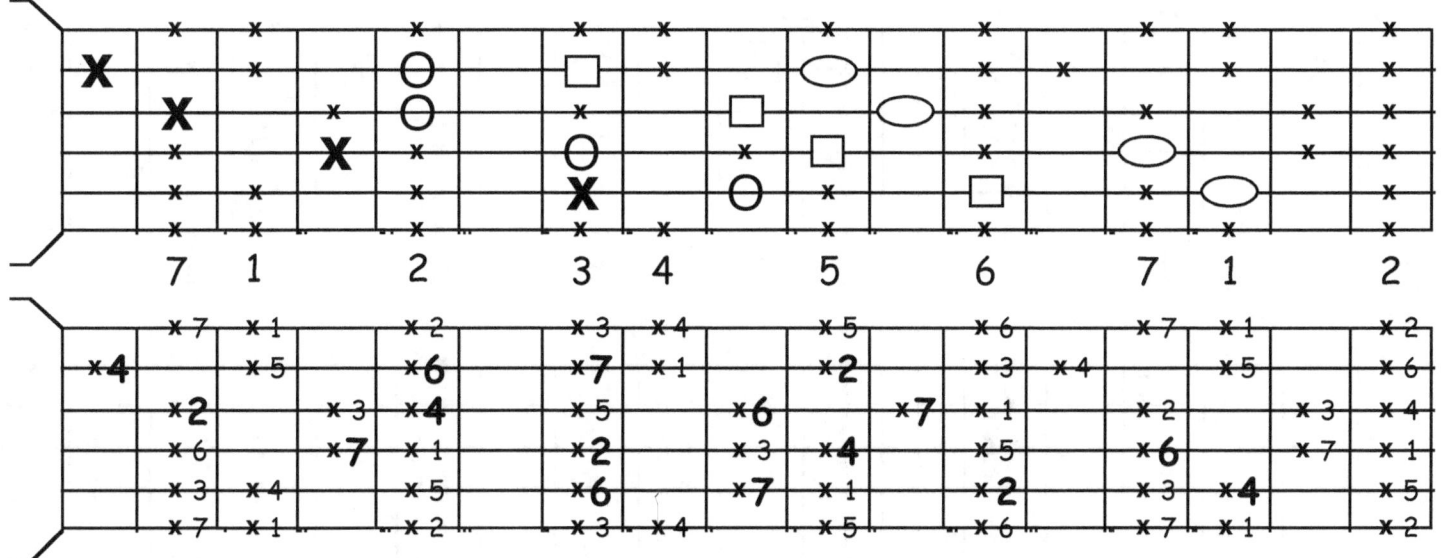

The only notes that you play are: 7, 2, 4, and 6 of the G major scale.

CLOSED:
4321 STRING GROUPING
The "1" Chord: Major 7 Inversions In "G" Major
G Major 7

The only notes that you play are: 1, 3, 5, and 7 of the G major scale.

4321 STRING GROUPING

The "2" Chord: Minor 7 Inversions In "G" Major

A Minor 7

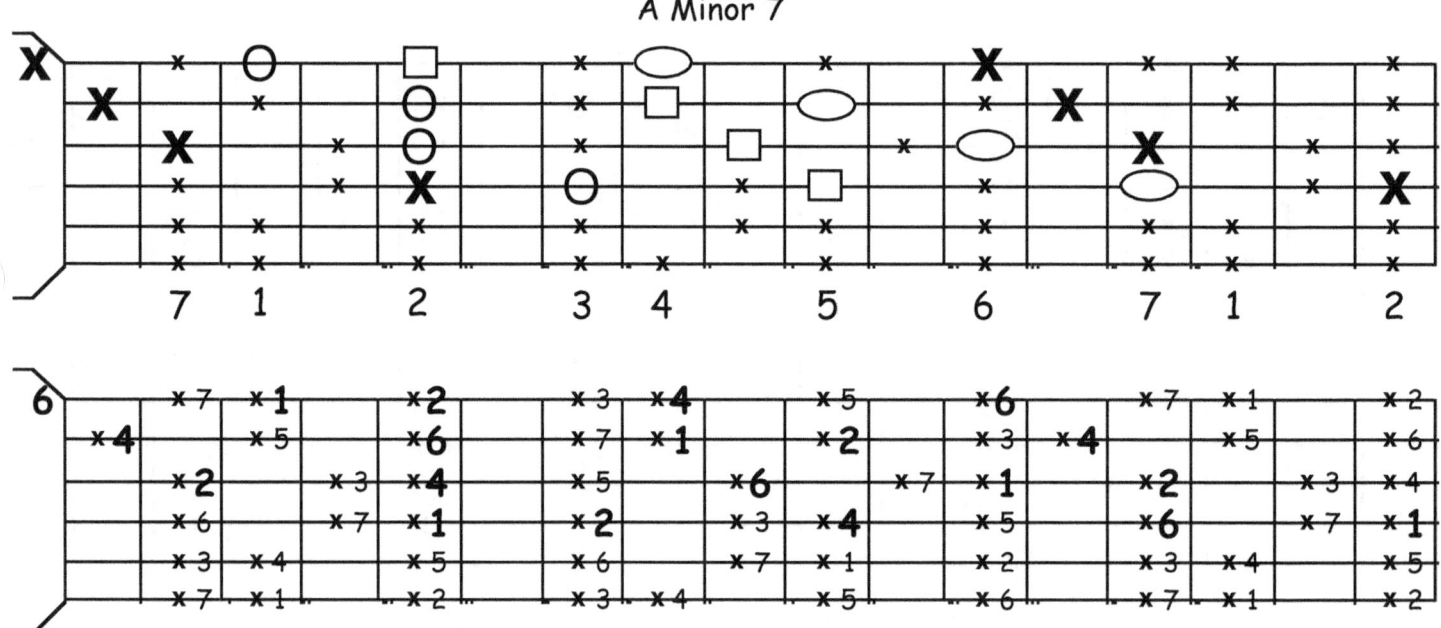

The only notes that you play are: 2, 4, 6, and 1 of the G major scale.

The "3" Chord: Minor 7 Inversions In "G" Major

B Minor 7

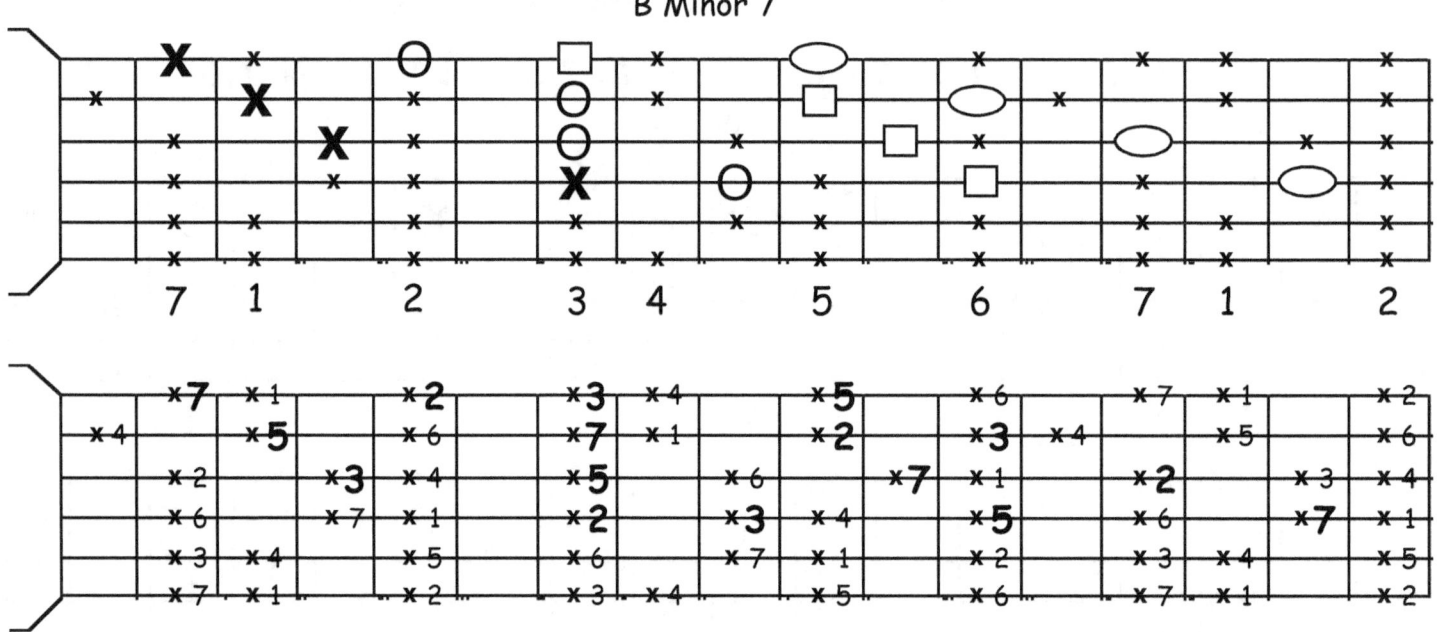

The only notes that you play are: 3, 5, 7, and 2 of the G major scale.

4321 STRING GROUPING
The "4" Chord: Major 7 Inversions In "G" Major
C Major 7

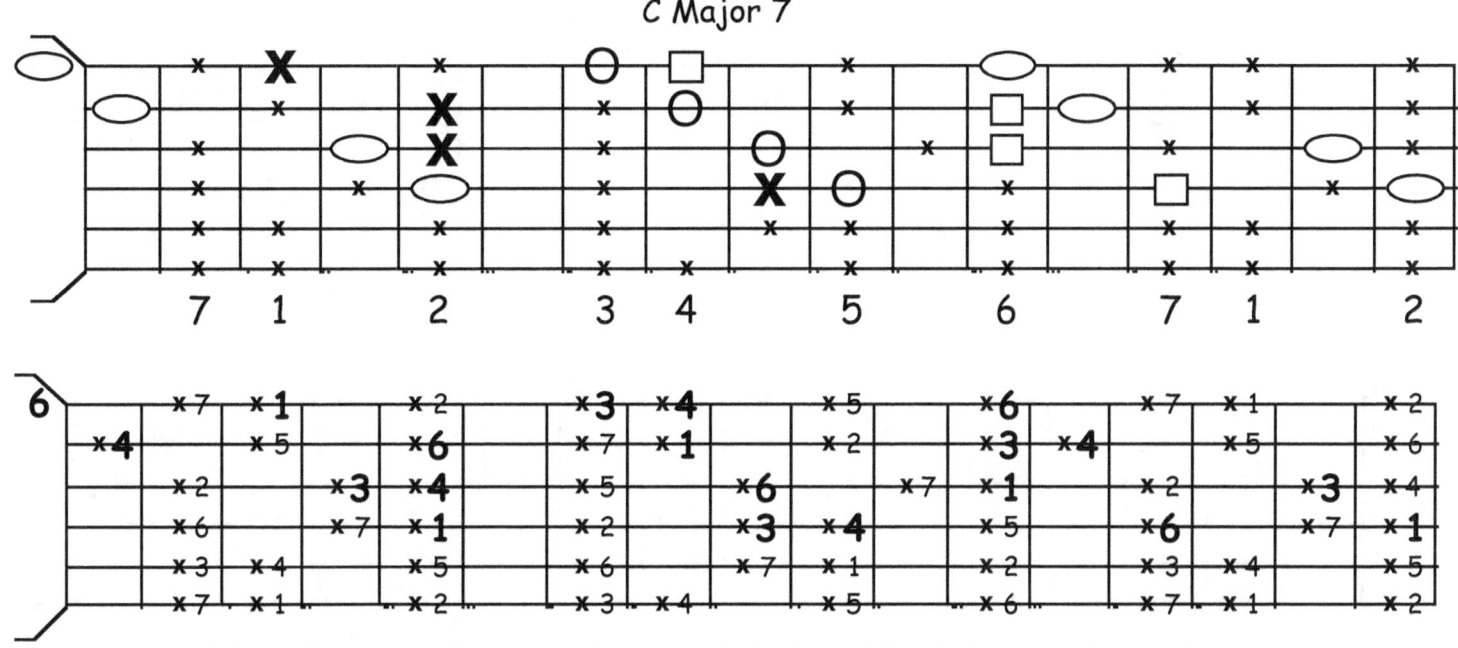

The only notes that you play are: 4, 6, 1, and 3 of the G major scale.

The "5" Chord: Dominant 7 Inversions In "G" Major
D Dominant 7

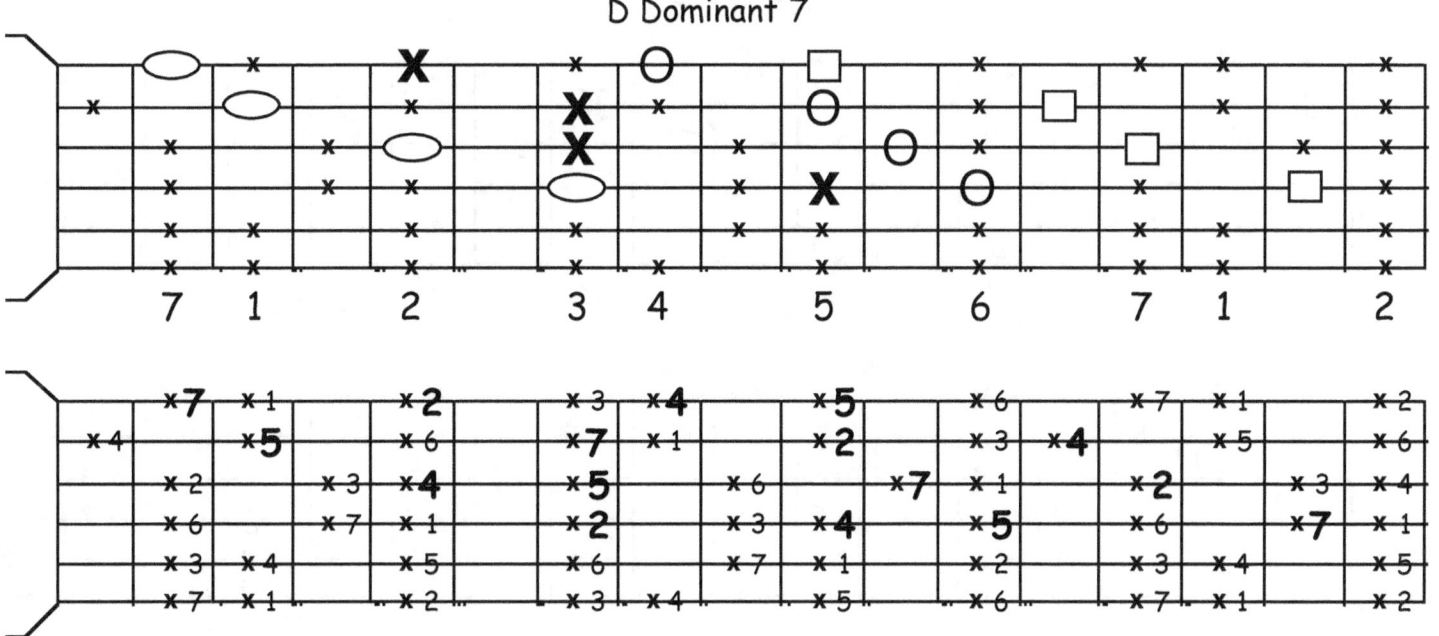

The only notes that you play are: 5, 7, 2, and 4 of the G major scale.

4321 STRING GROUPING
The "6" Chord: Minor 7 Inversions In "G" Major
E Minor 7

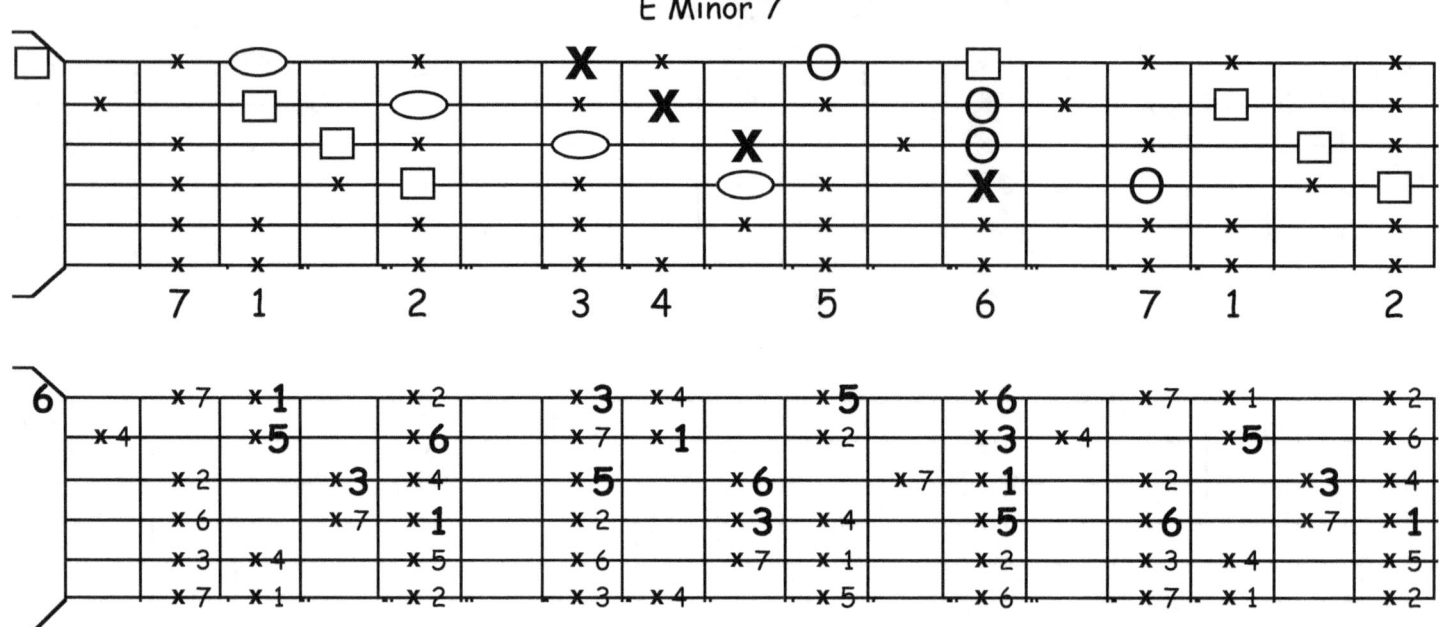

The only notes that you play are: 6, 1, 3, and 5 of the G major scale.

The "7" Chord: Minor 7b5 Inversions In "G" Major
F# Minor 7b5

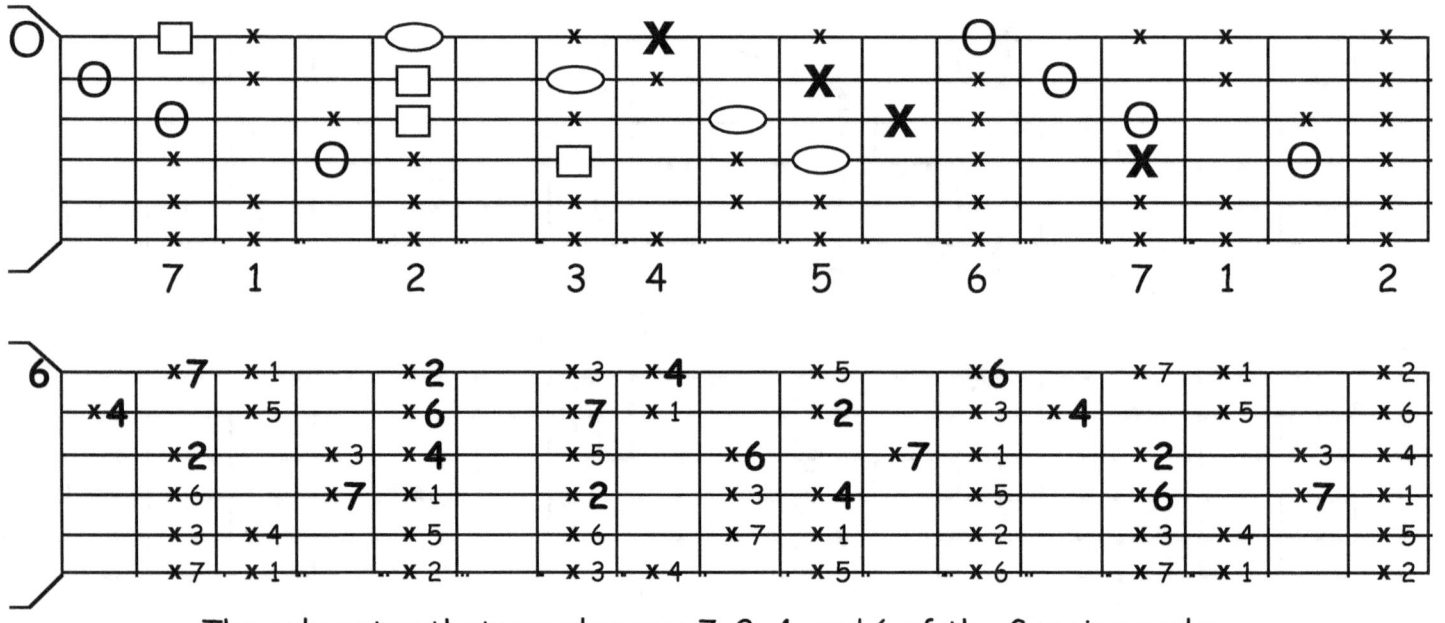

The only notes that you play are: 7, 2, 4, and 6 of the G major scale.

DROP 2:
6543 STRING GROUPING
The "1" Chord: Major 7 Inversions In "G" Major
G Major 7

The only notes that you play are: 1, 3, 5, and 7 of the G major scale.

The "2" Chord: Minor 7 Inversions In "G" Major
A Minor 7

The only notes that you play are: 2, 4, 6, and 1 of the G major scale.

6543 STRING GROUPING
The "3" Chord: Minor 7 Inversions In "G" Major
B Minor 7

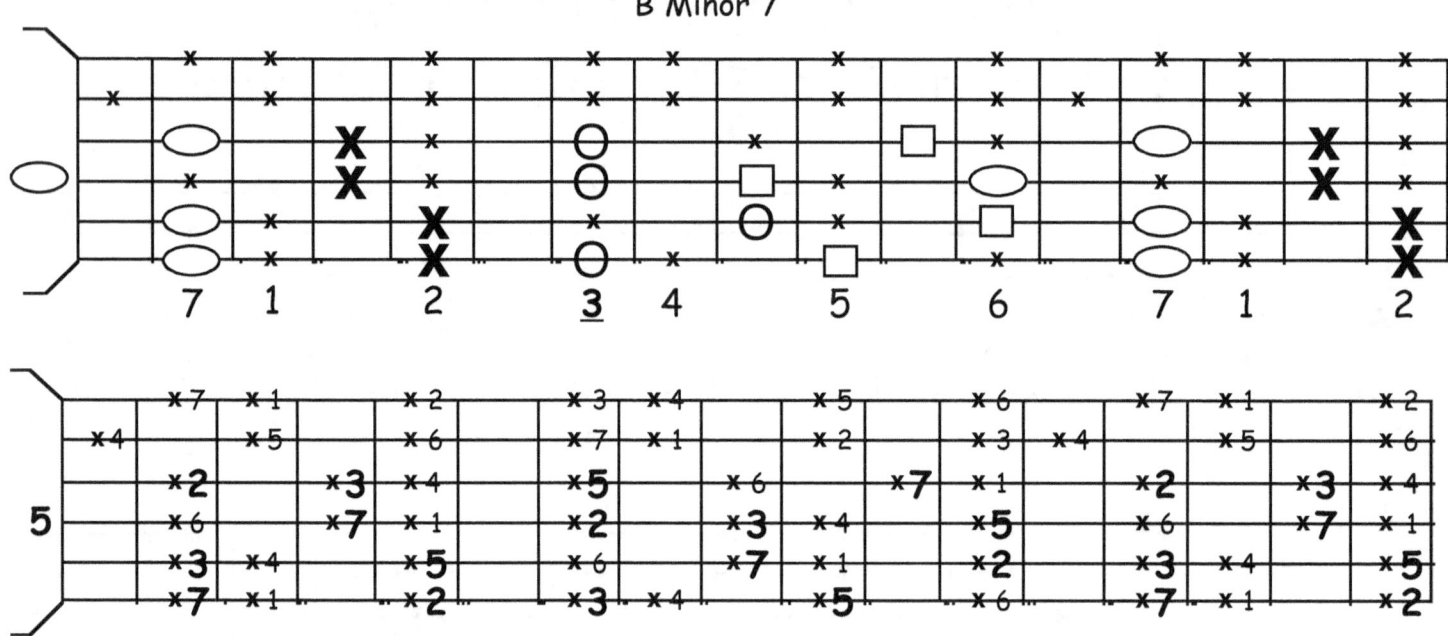

The only notes that you play are: 3, 5, 7, and 2 of the G major scale.

The "4" Chord: Major 7 Inversions In "G" Major
C Major 7

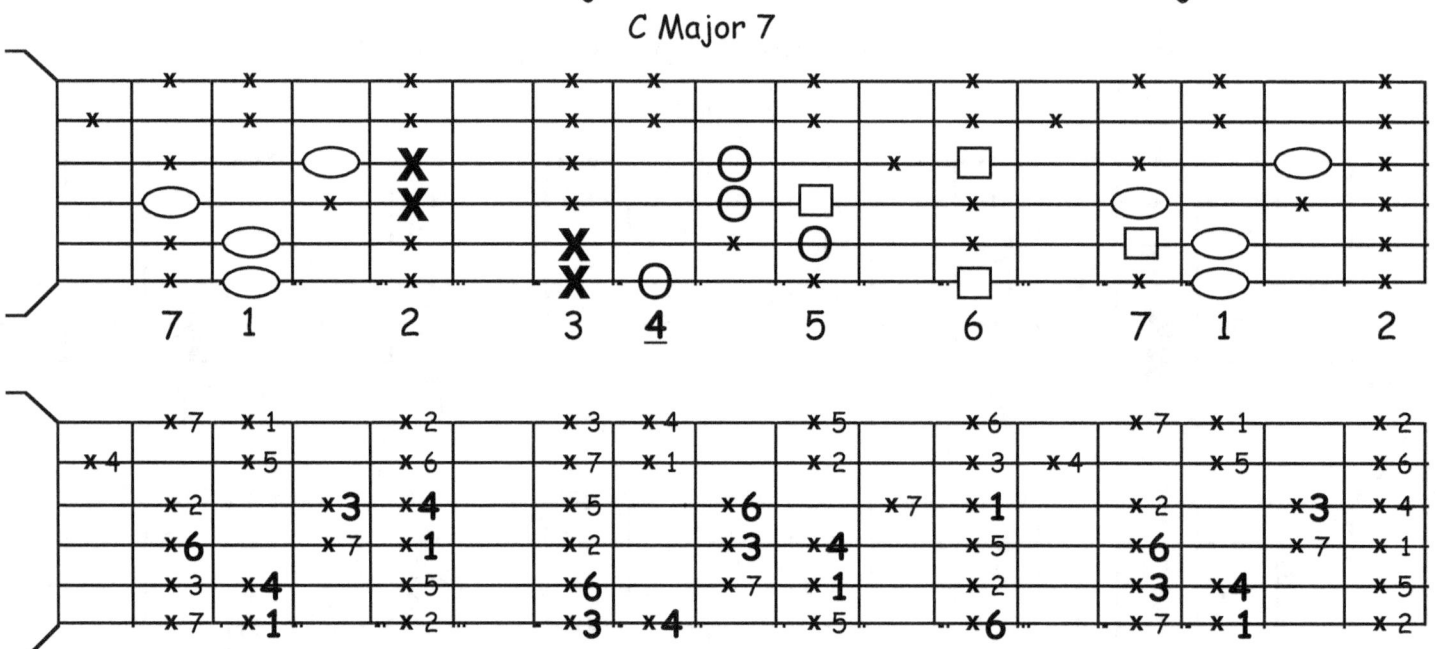

The only notes that you play are: 4, 6, 1, and 3 of the G major scale.

6543 STRING GROUPING

The "5" Chord: Dominant 7 Inversions In "G" Major
D Dominant 7

The only notes that you play are: 5, 7, 2, and 4 of the G major scale.

The "6" Chord: Minor 7 Inversions In "G" Major
E Minor 7

The only notes that you play are: 6, 1, 3, and 5 of the G major scale.

6543 STRING GROUPING
The "7" Chord: Minor 7b5 Inversions In "G" Major
F# Minor 7b5

The only notes that you play are: 7, 2, 4, and 6 of the G major scale.

DROP 2:
5432 STRING GROUPING
The "1" Chord: Major 7 Inversions In "G" Major
G Major 7

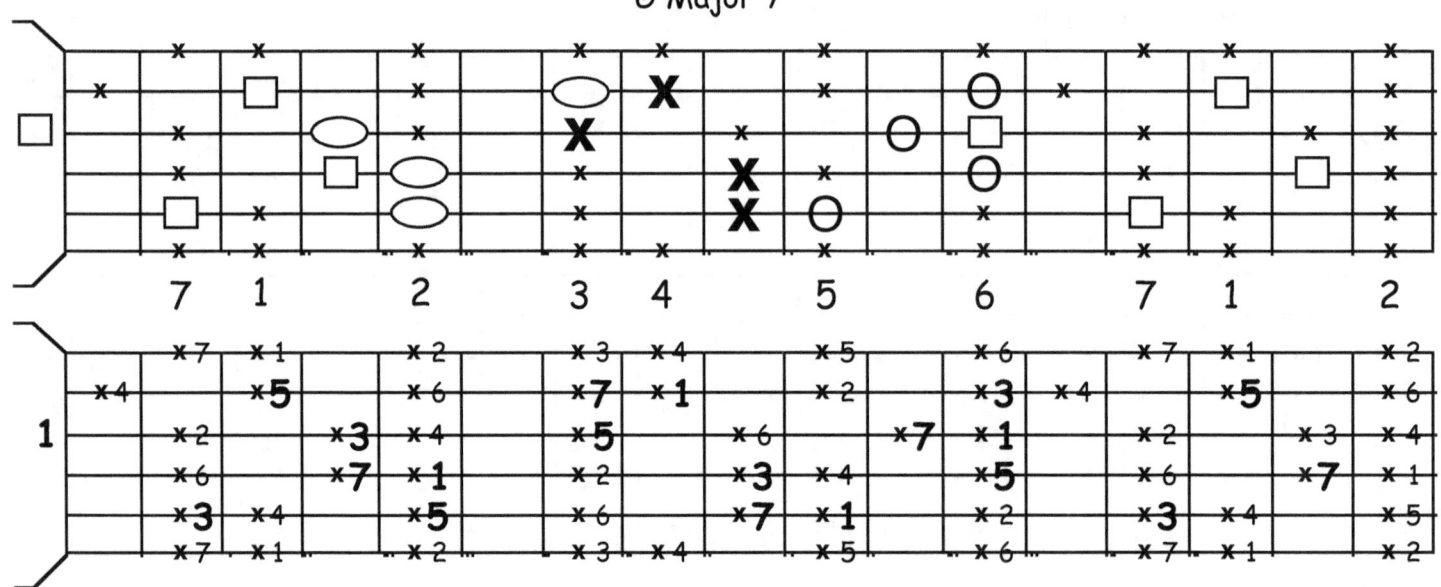

The only notes that you play are: 1, 3, 5, and 7 of the G major scale.

5432 STRING GROUPING

The "2" Chord: Minor 7 Inversions In "G" Major
A Minor 7

The only notes that you play are: 2, 4, 6, and 1 of the G major scale.

The "3" Chord: Minor 7 Inversions In "G" Major
B Minor 7

The only notes that you play are: 3, 5, 7, and 2 of the G major scale.

5432 STRING GROUPING
The "4" Chord: Major 7 Inversions In "G" Major
C Major 7

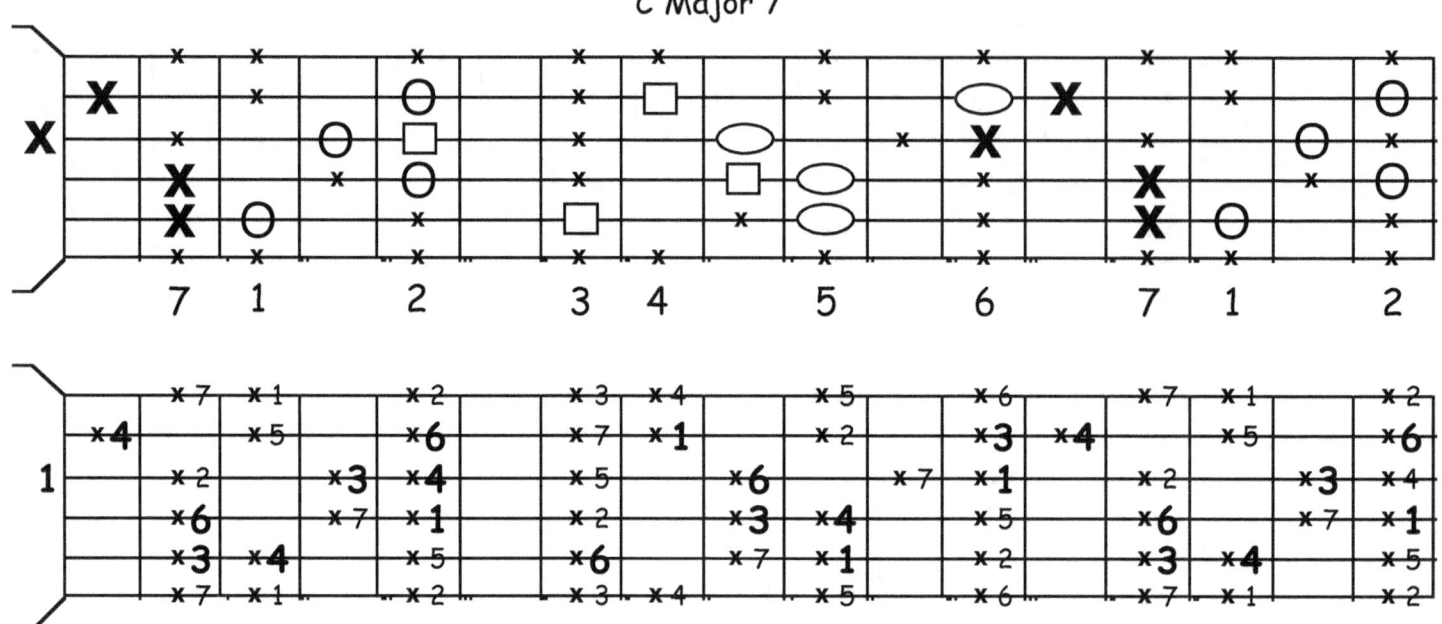

The only notes that you play are: 4, 6, 1, and 3 of the G major scale.

The "5" Chord: Dominant 7 Inversions In "G" Major
D Dominant 7

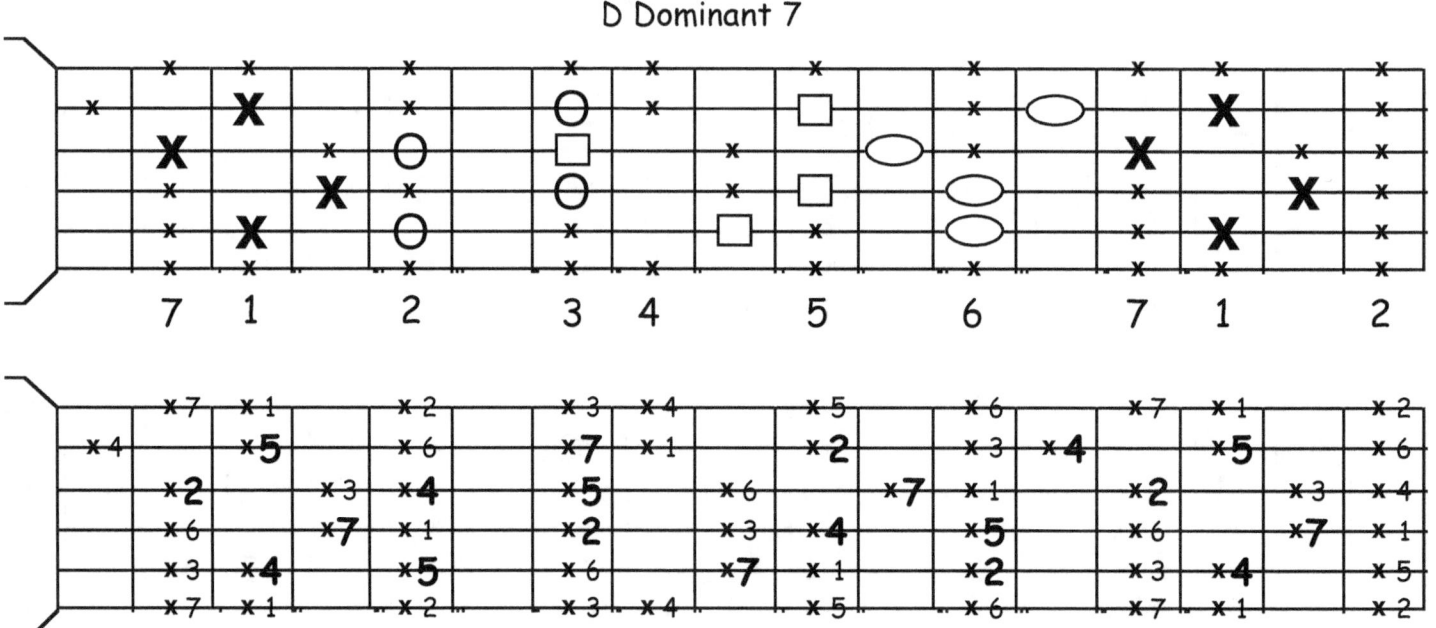

The only notes that you play are: 5, 7, 2, and 4 of the G major scale.

5432 STRING GROUPING

The "6" Chord: Minor 7 Inversions In "G" Major
E Minor 7

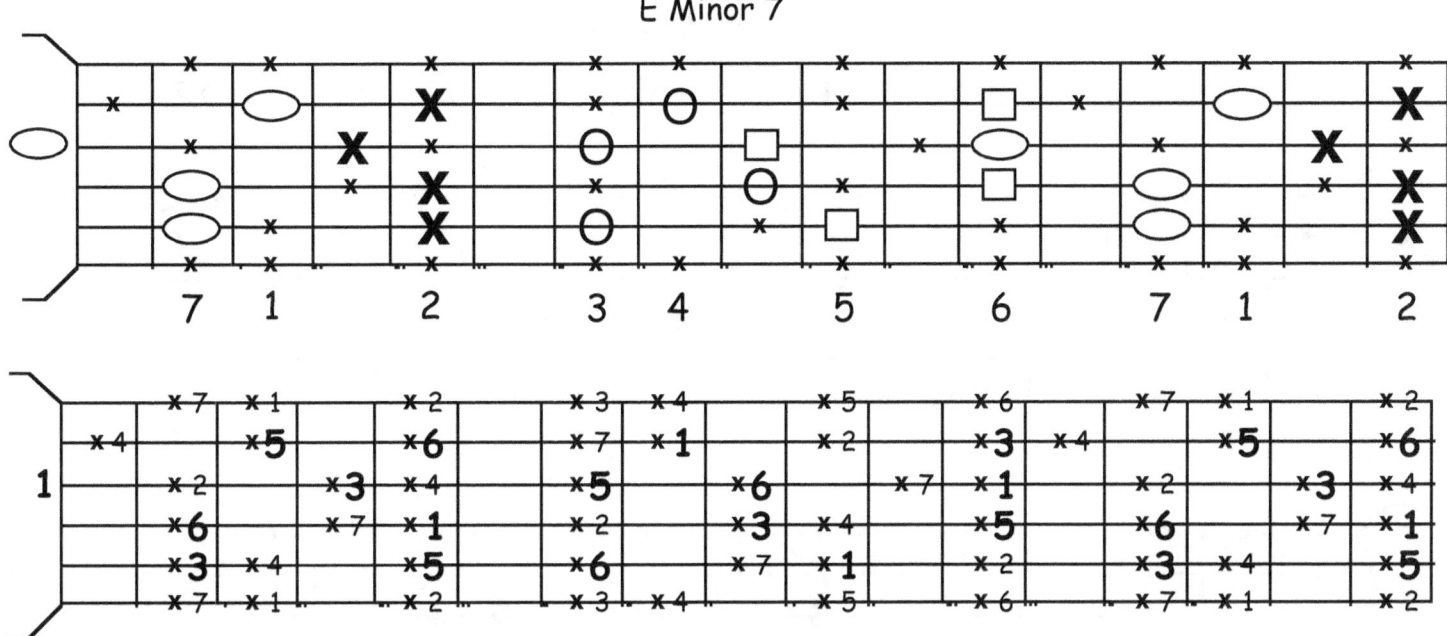

The only notes that you play are: 6, 1, 3, and 5 of the G major scale.

The "7" Chord: Minor 7b5 Inversions In "G" Major
F# Minor 7b5

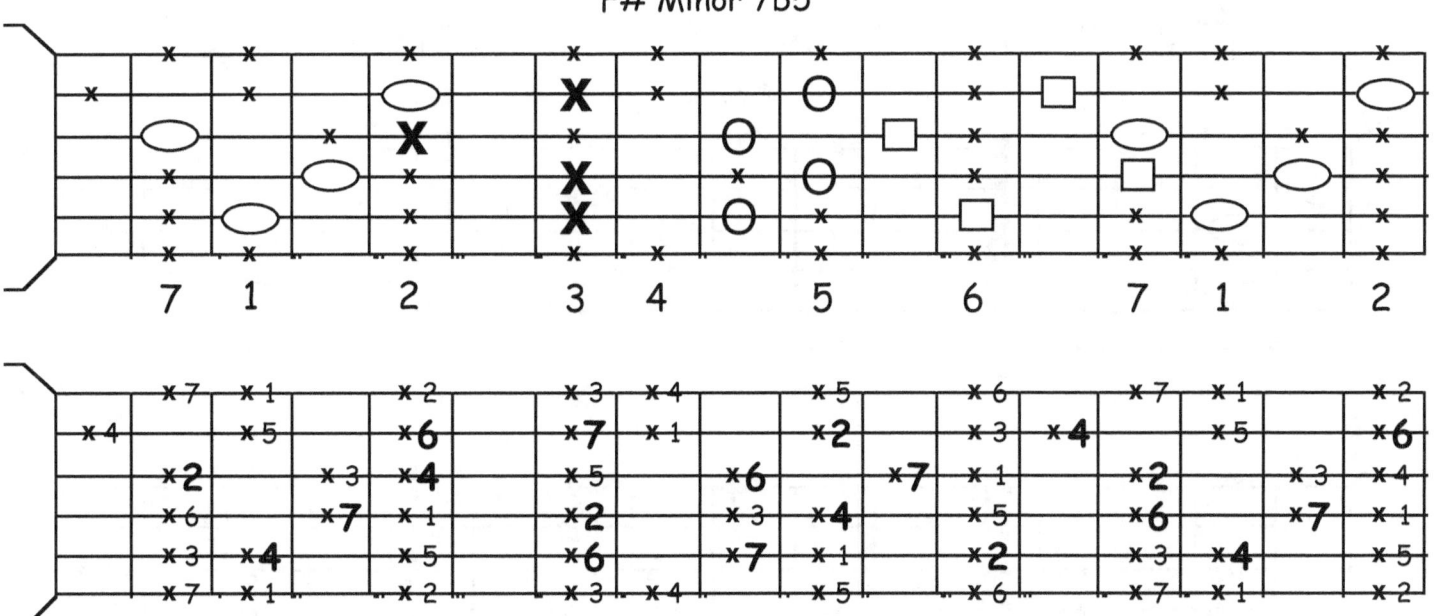

The only notes that you play are: 7, 2, 4, and 6 of the G major scale.

DROP 2:
4321 STRING GROUPING
The "1" Chord: Major 7 Inversions In "G" Major
G Major 7

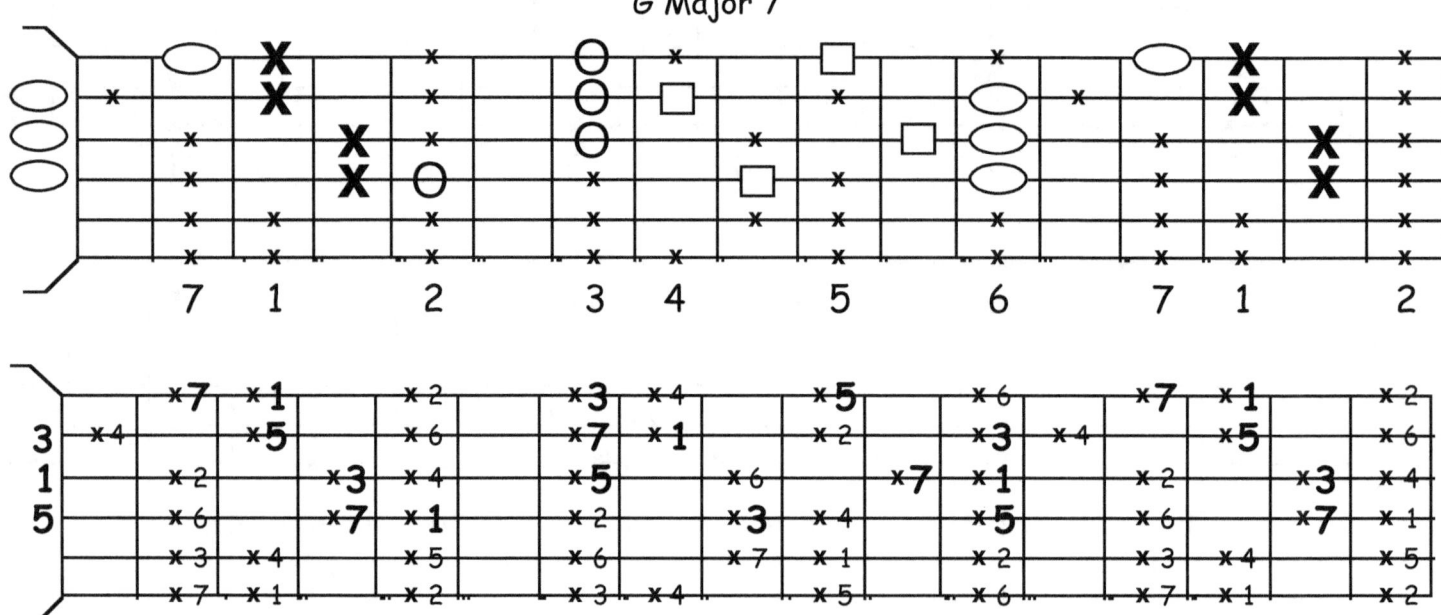

The only notes that you play are: 1, 3, 5, and 7 of the G major scale.

The "2" Chord: Minor 7 Inversions In "G" Major
A Minor 7

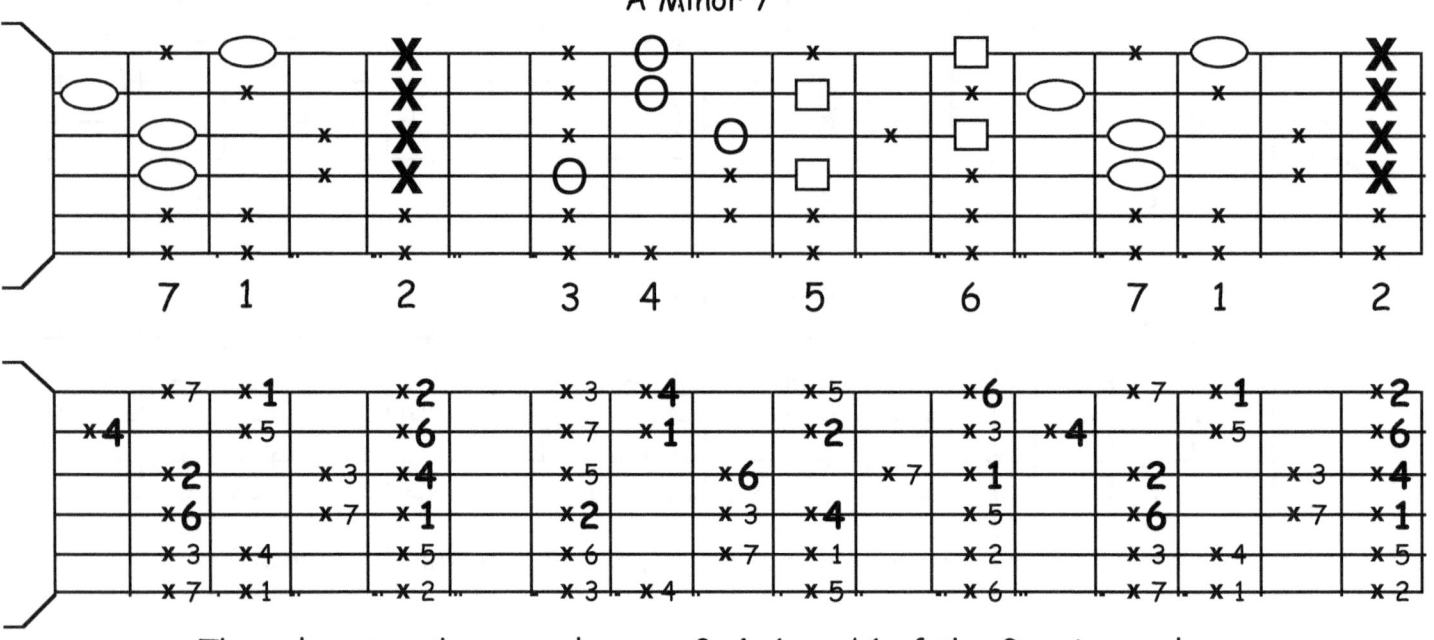

The only notes that you play are: 2, 4, 6, and 1 of the G major scale.

4321 STRING GROUPING
The "3" Chord: Minor 7 Inversions In "G" Major
B Minor 7

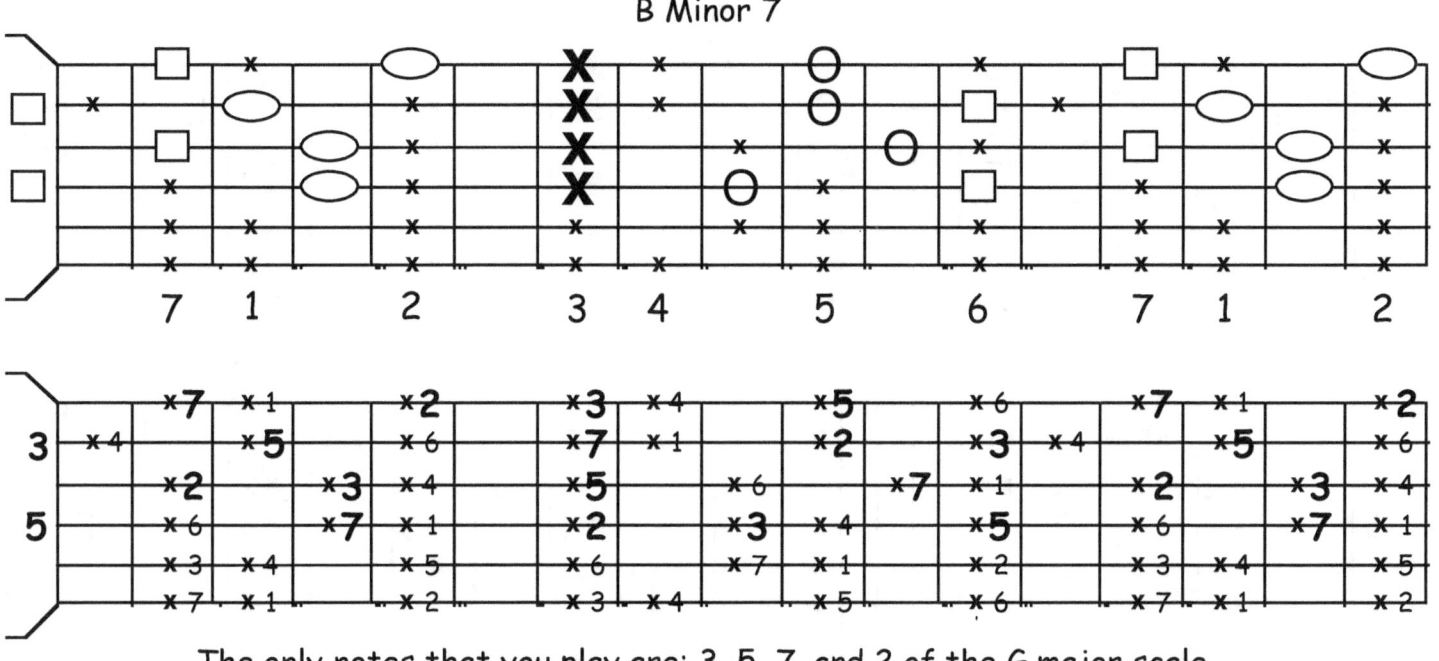

The only notes that you play are: 3, 5, 7, and 2 of the G major scale.

The "4" Chord: Major 7 Inversions In "G" Major
C Major 7

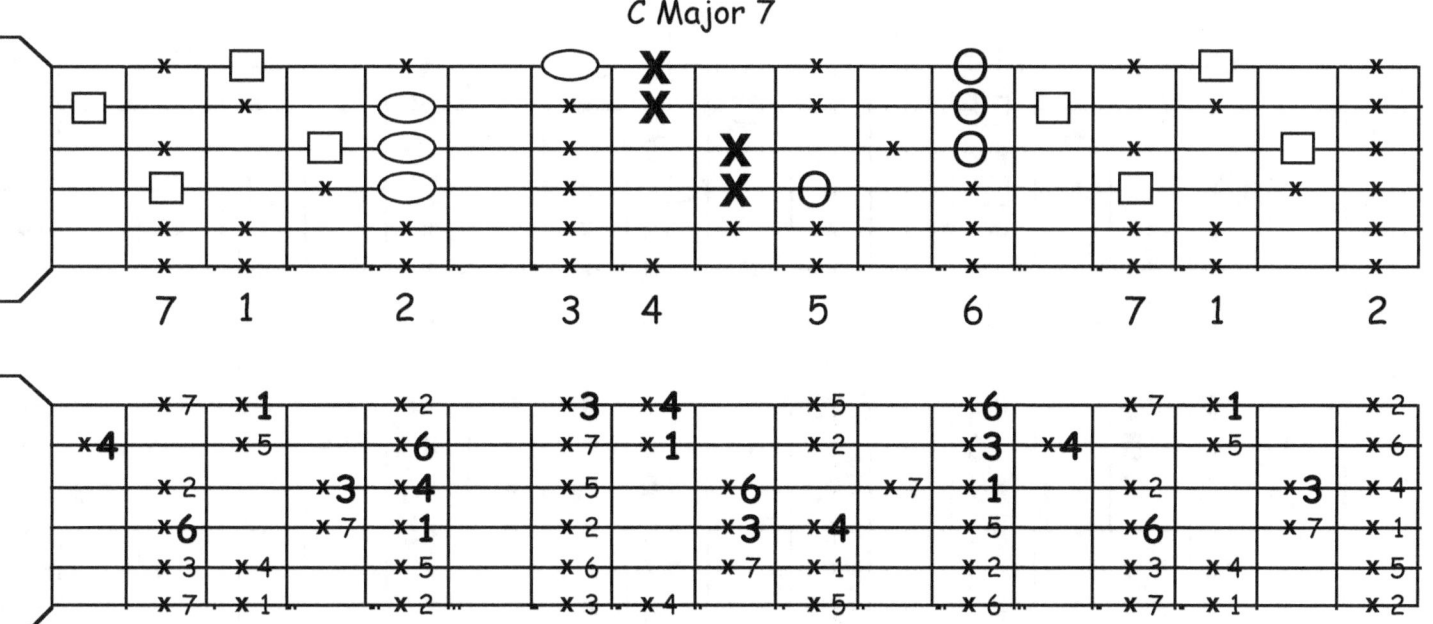

The only notes that you play are: 4, 6, 1, and 3 of the G major scale.

4321 STRING GROUPING

The "5" Chord: Dominant 7 Inversions In "G" Major

D Dominant 7

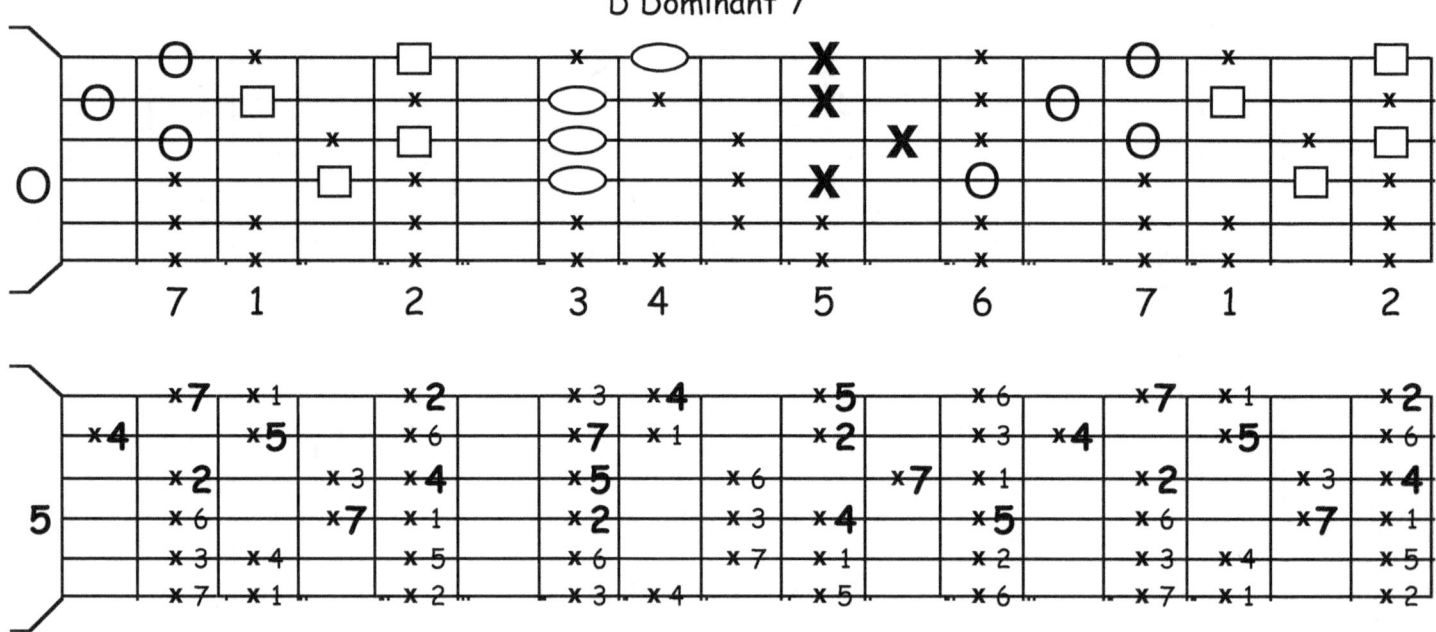

The only notes that you play are: 5, 7, 2, and 4 of the G major scale.

The "6" Chord: Minor 7 Inversions In "G" Major

E Minor 7

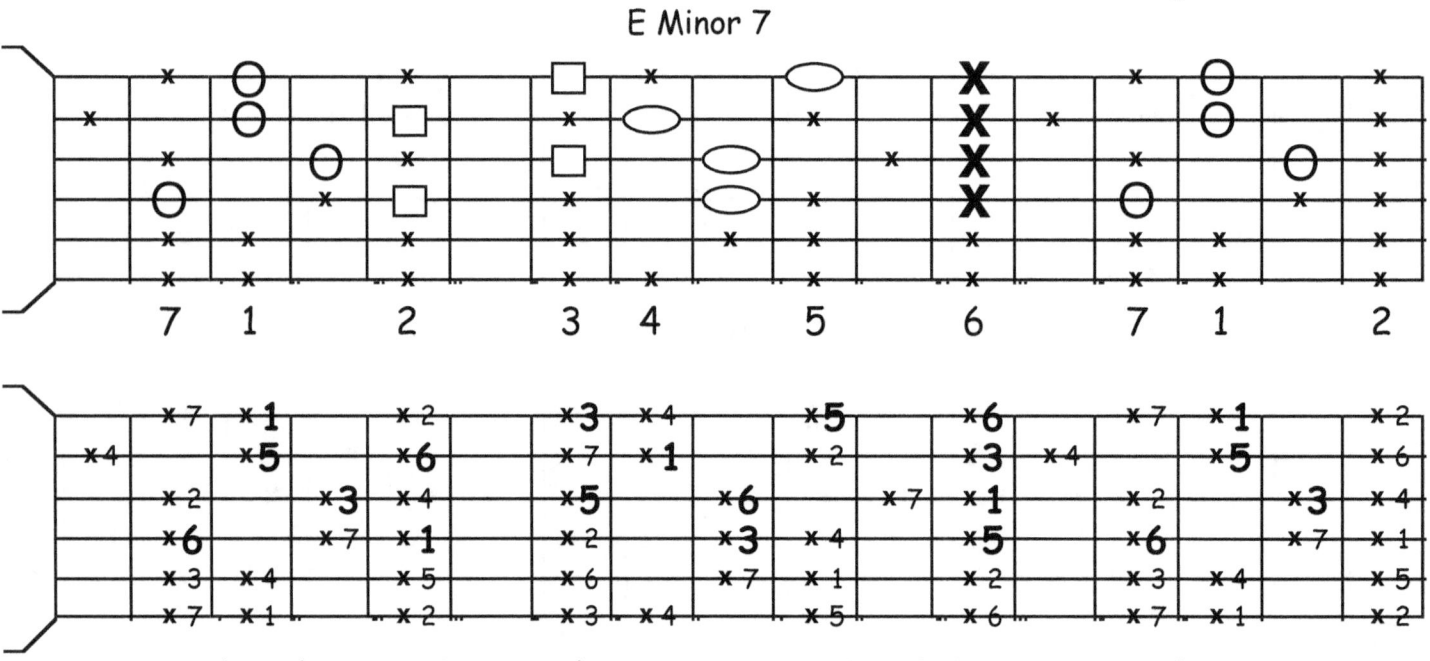

The only notes that you play are: 6, 1, 3, and 5 of the G major scale.

4321 STRING GROUPING
The "7" Chord: Minor 7b5 Inversions In "G" Major
F# Minor 7b5

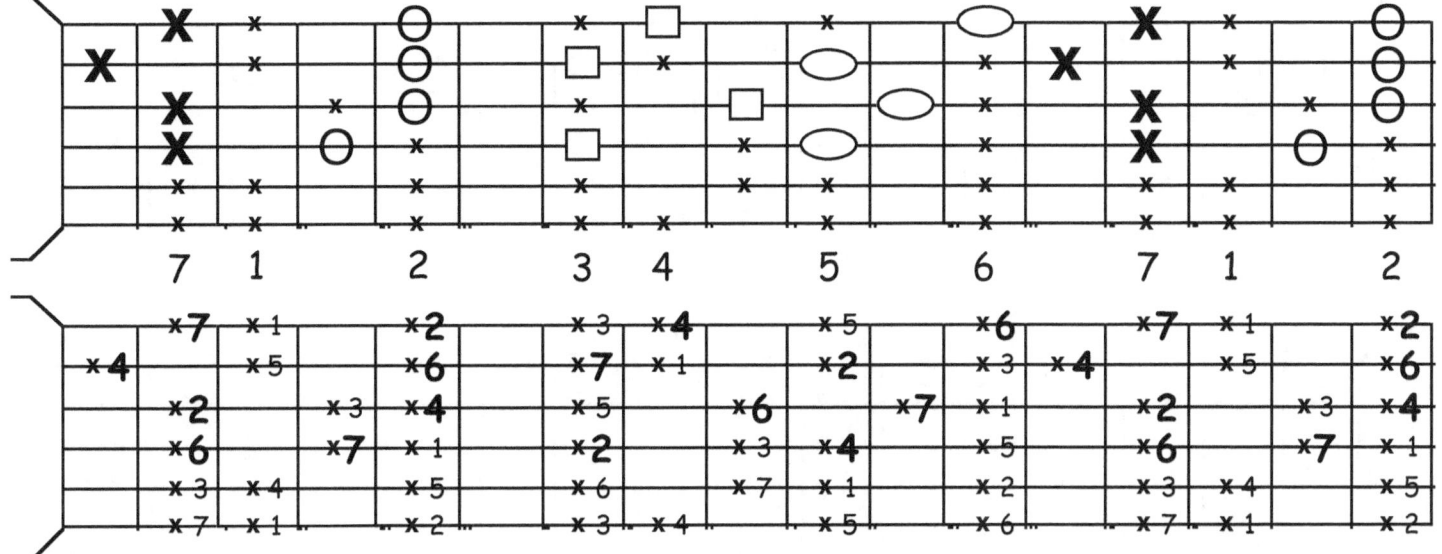

The only notes that you play are: 7, 2, 4, and 6 of the G major scale.

DROP 3:
6432 STRING GROUPING
The "1" Chord: Major 7 Inversions In "G" Major
G Major 7

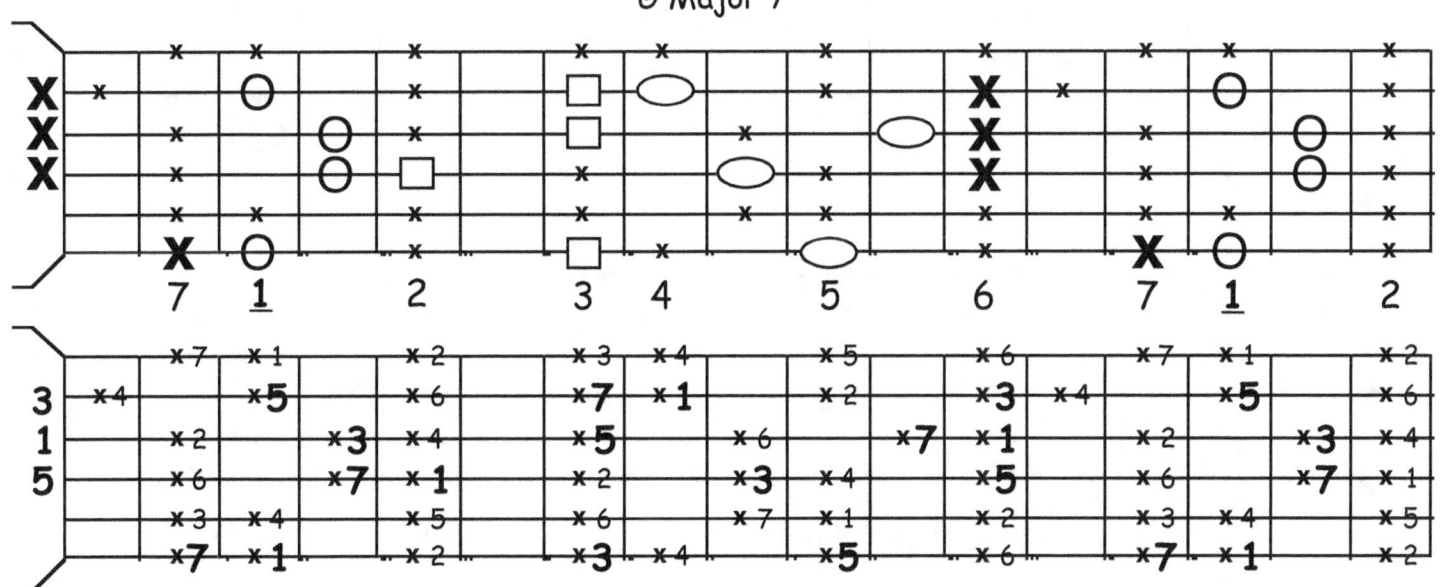

The only notes that you play are: 1, 3, 5, and 7 of the G major scale.

6432 STRING GROUPING

The "2" Chord: Minor 7 Inversions In "G" Major

A Minor 7

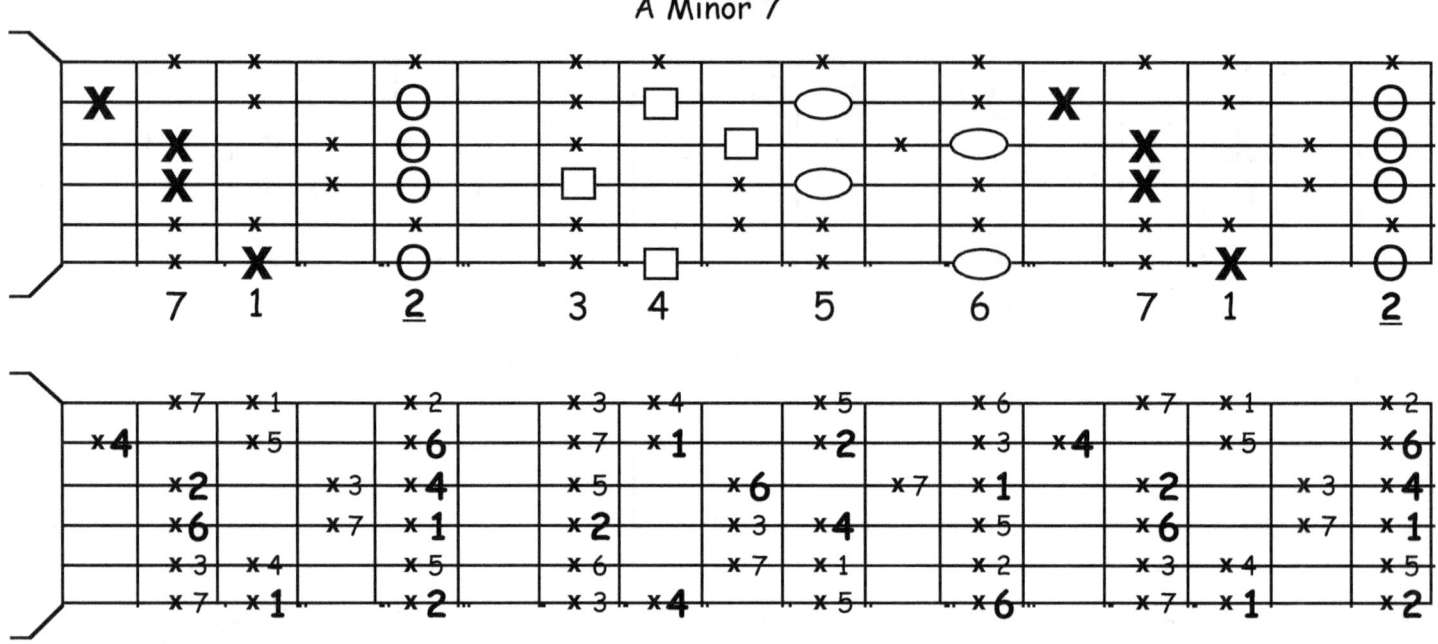

The only notes that you play are: 2, 4, 6, and 1 of the G major scale.

The "3" Chord: Minor 7 Inversions In "G" Major

B Minor 7

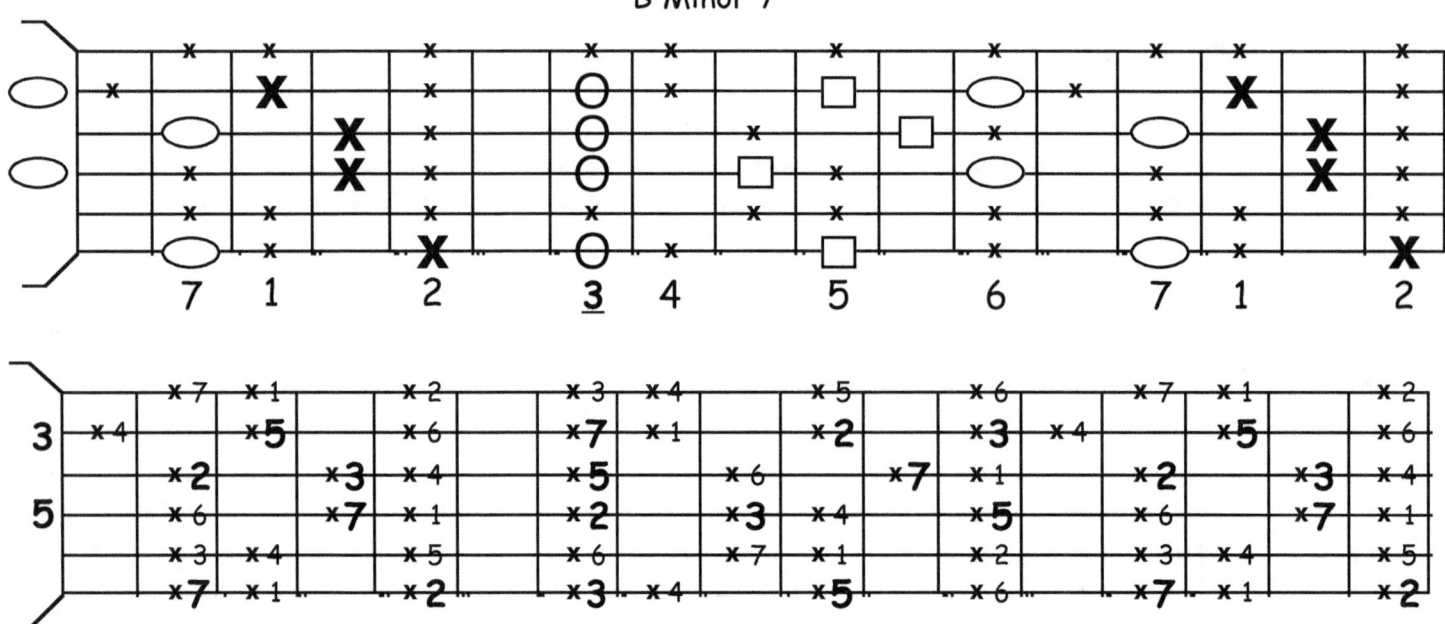

The only notes that you play are: 3, 5, 7, and 2 of the G major scale.

6432 STRING GROUPING
The "4" Chord: Major 7 Inversions In "G" Major
C Major 7

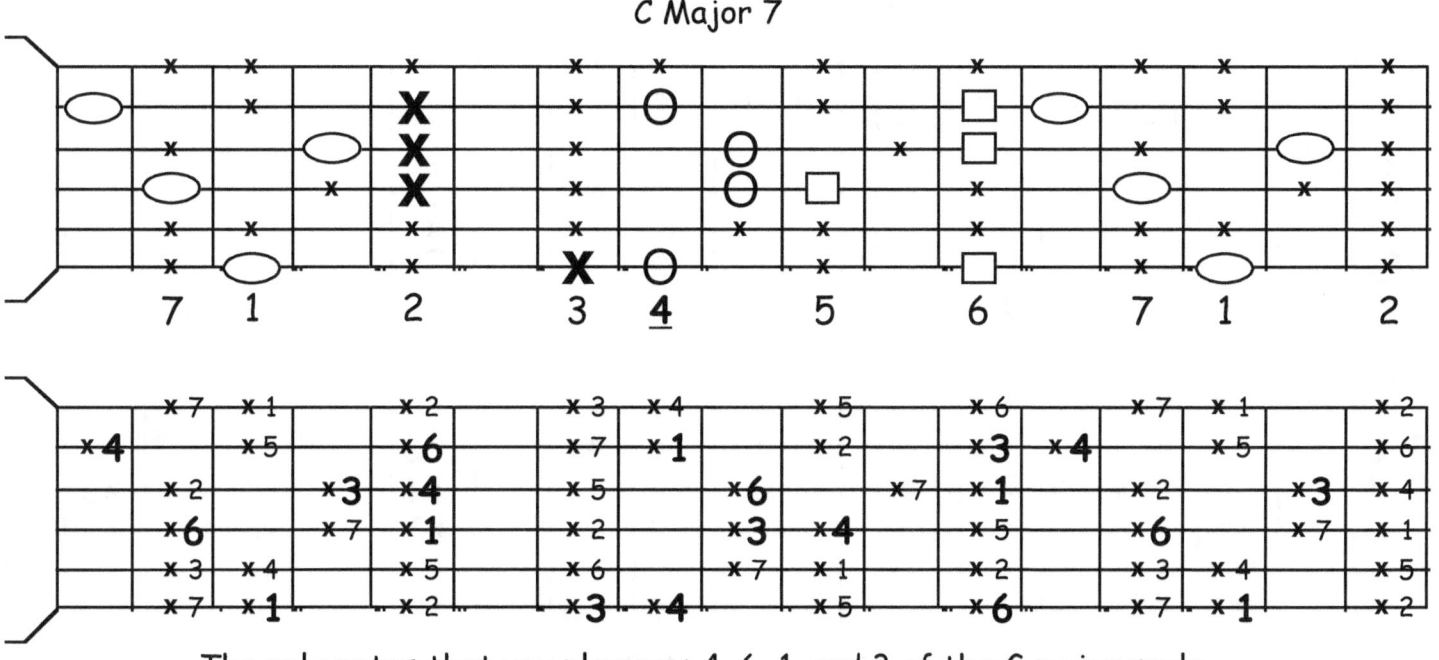

The only notes that you play are: 4, 6, 1, and 3 of the G major scale.

The "5" Chord: Dominant 7 Inversions In "G" Major
D Dominant 7

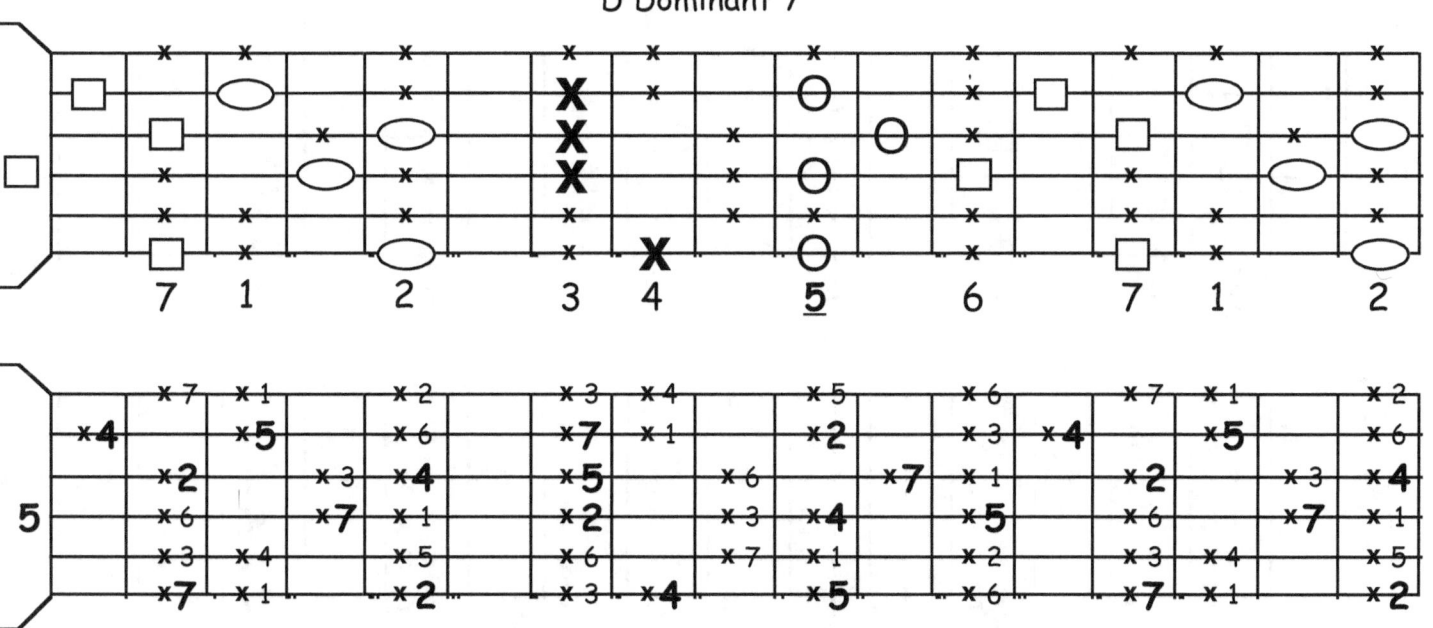

The only notes that you play are: 5, 7, 2, and 4 of the G major scale.

6432 STRING GROUPING

The "6" Chord: Minor 7 Inversions In "G" Major
E Minor 7

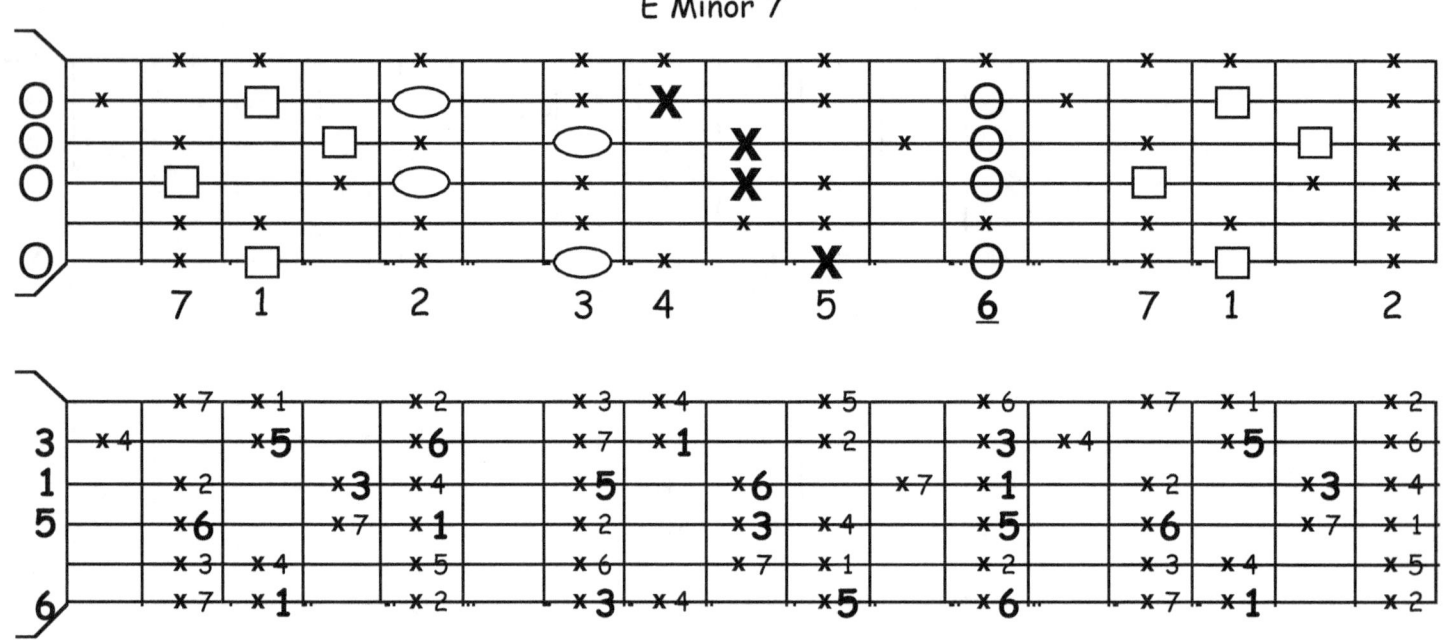

The only notes that you play are: 6, 1, 3, and 5 of the G major scale.

The "7" Chord: Minor 7b5 Inversions In "G" Major
F# Minor 7b5

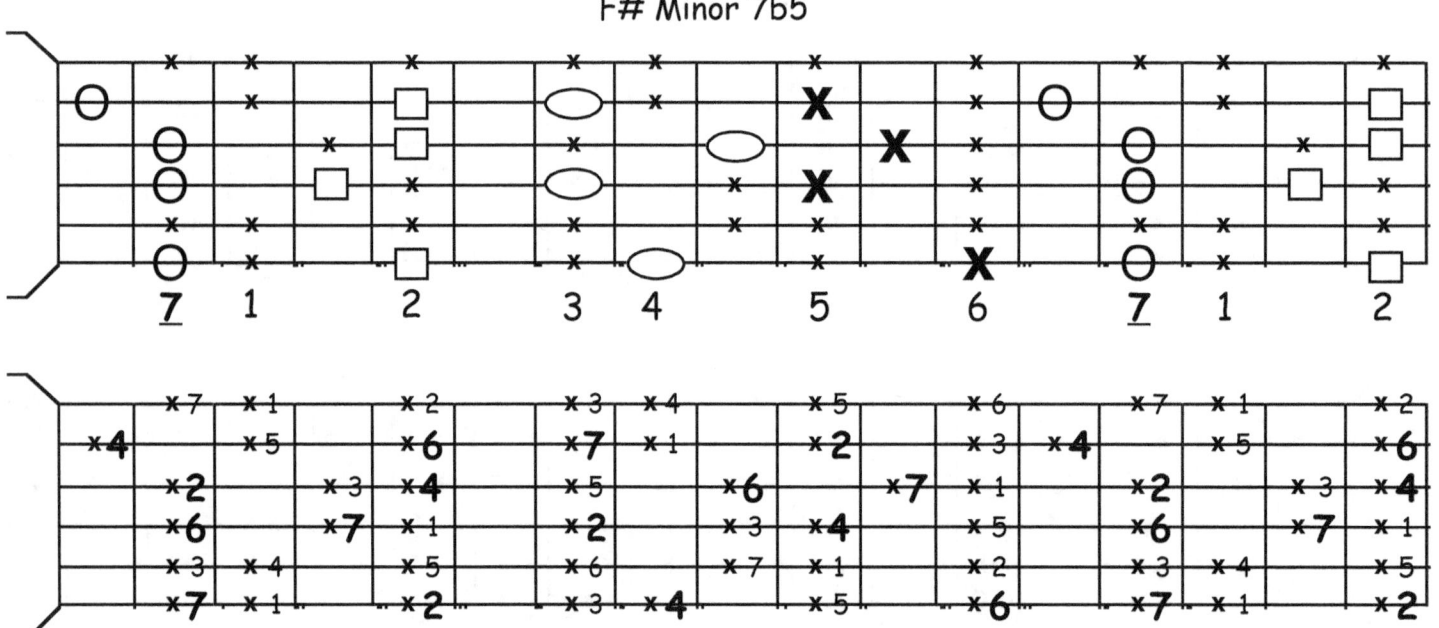

The only notes that you play are: 7, 2, 4, and 6 of the G major scale.

DROP 3:
5321 STRING GROUPING
The "1" Chord: Major 7 Inversions In "G" Major
G Major 7

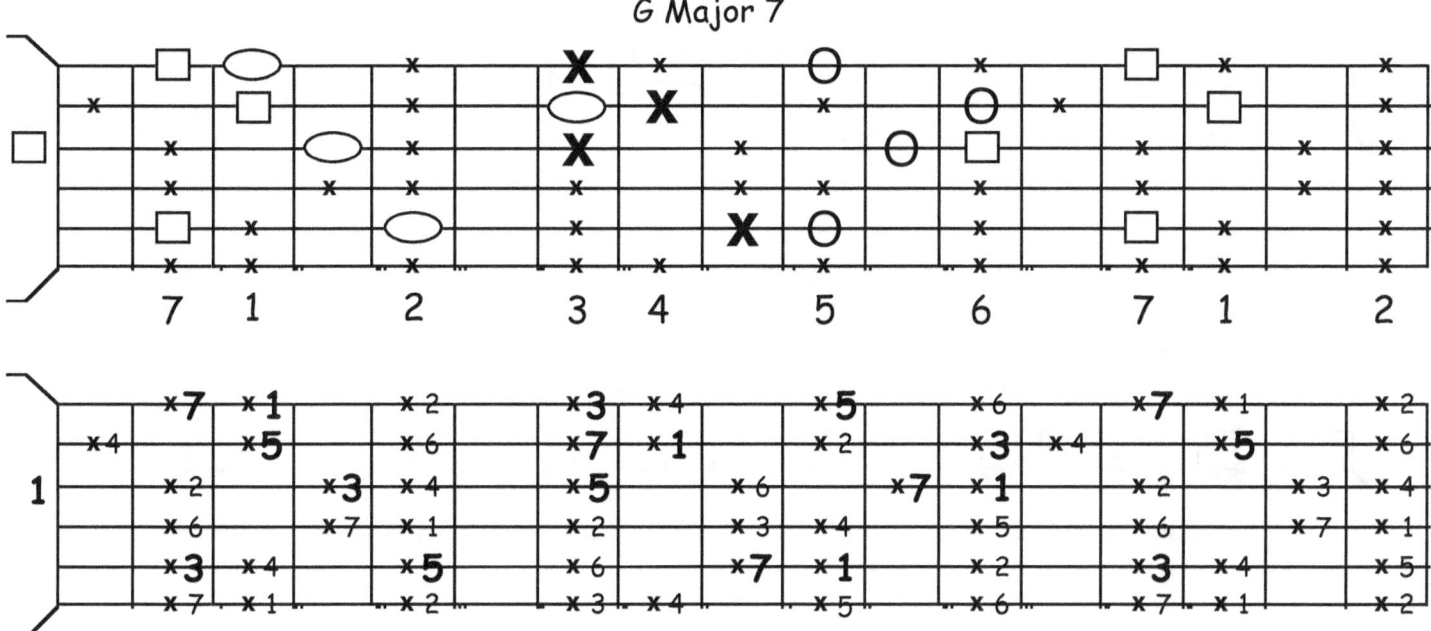

The only notes that you play are: 1, 3, 5, and 7 of the G major scale.

The "2" Chord: Minor 7 Inversions In "G" Major
A Minor 7

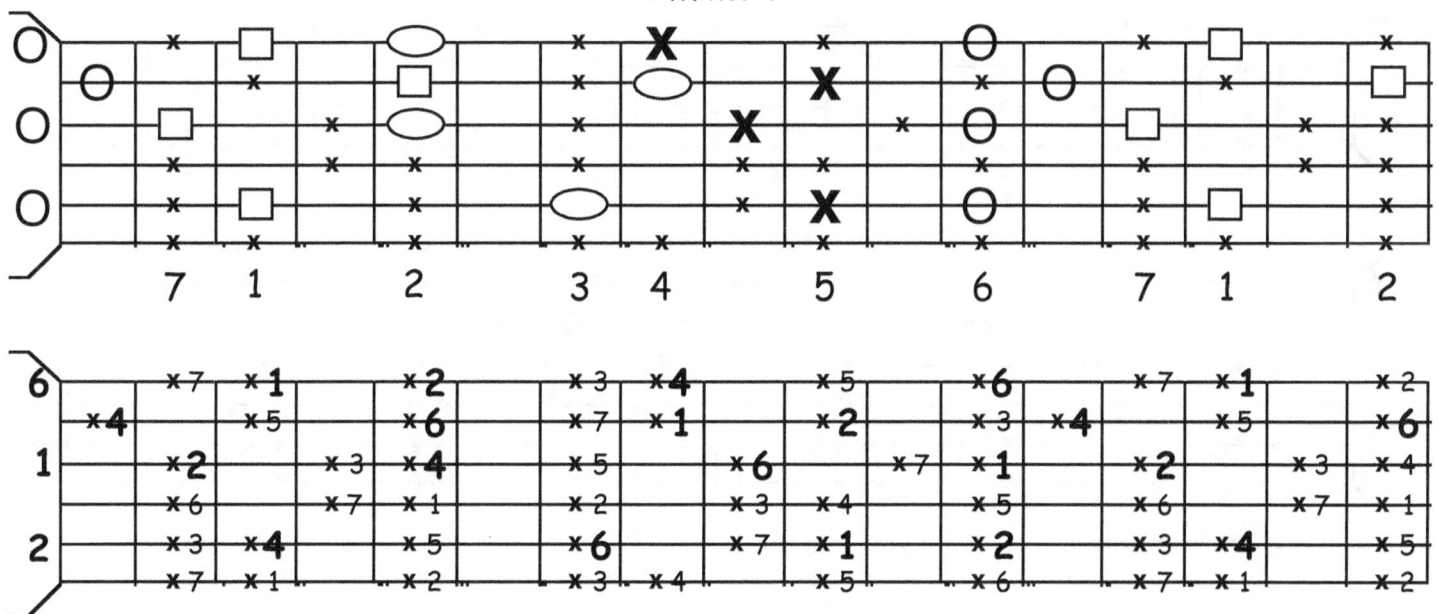

The only notes that you play are: 2, 4, 6, and 1 of the G major scale.

5321 STRING GROUPING
The "3" Chord: Minor 7 Inversions In "G" Major
B Minor 7

The only notes that you play are: 3, 5, 7, and 2 of the G major scale.

The "4" Chord: Major 7 Inversions In "G" Major
C Major 7

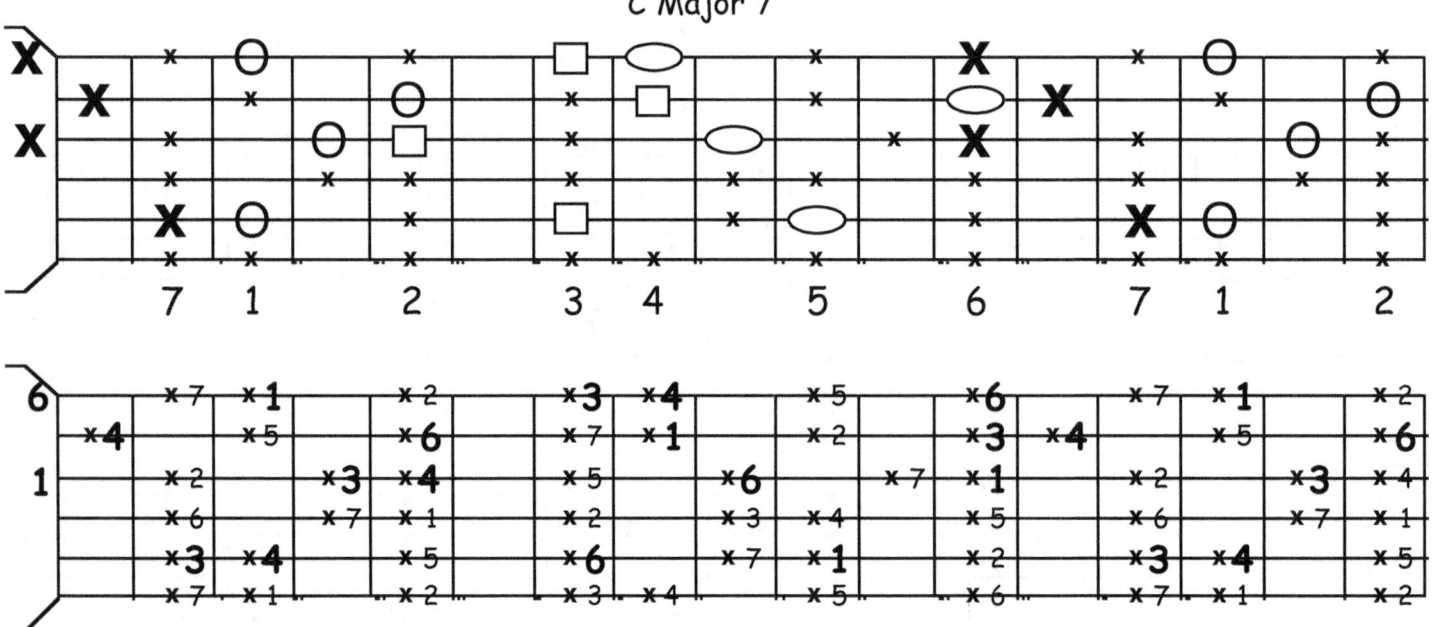

The only notes that you play are: 4, 6, 1, and 3 of the G major scale.

5321 STRING GROUPING

The "5" Chord: Dominant 7 Inversions In "G" Major

D Dominant 7

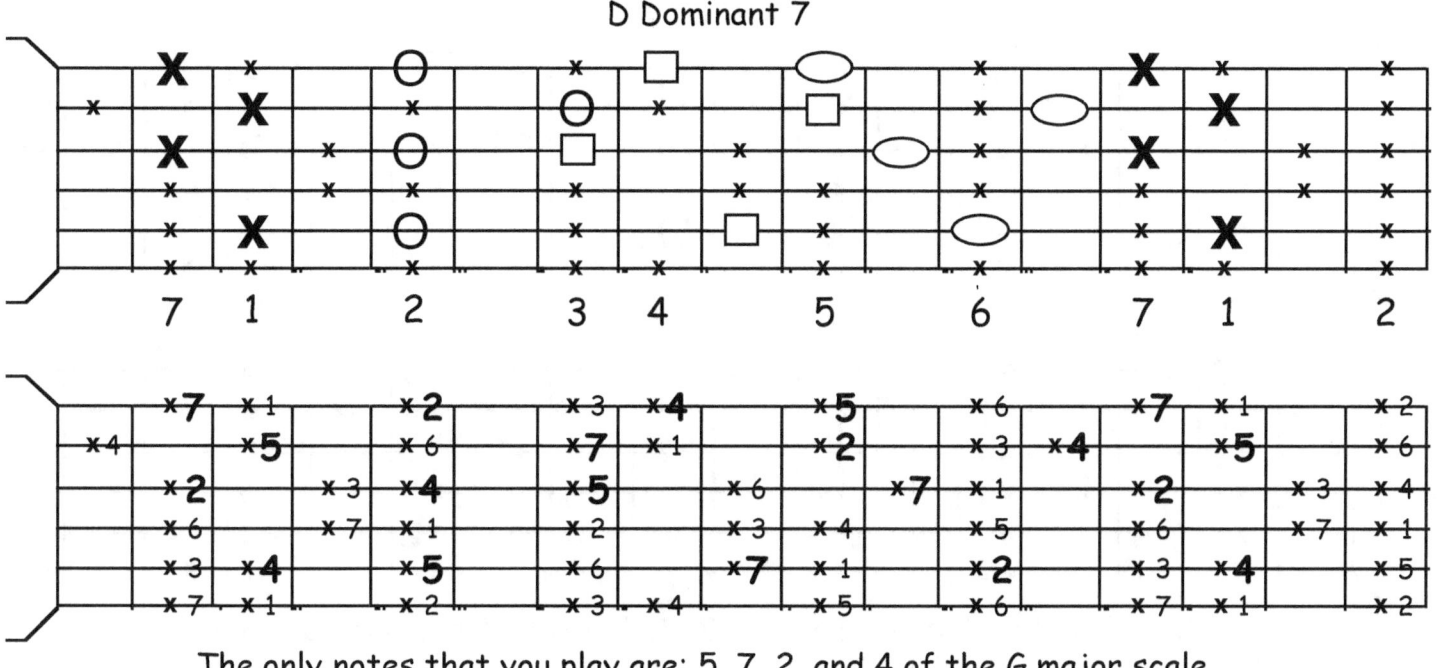

The only notes that you play are: 5, 7, 2, and 4 of the G major scale.

The "6" Chord: Minor 7 Inversions In "G" Major

E Minor 7

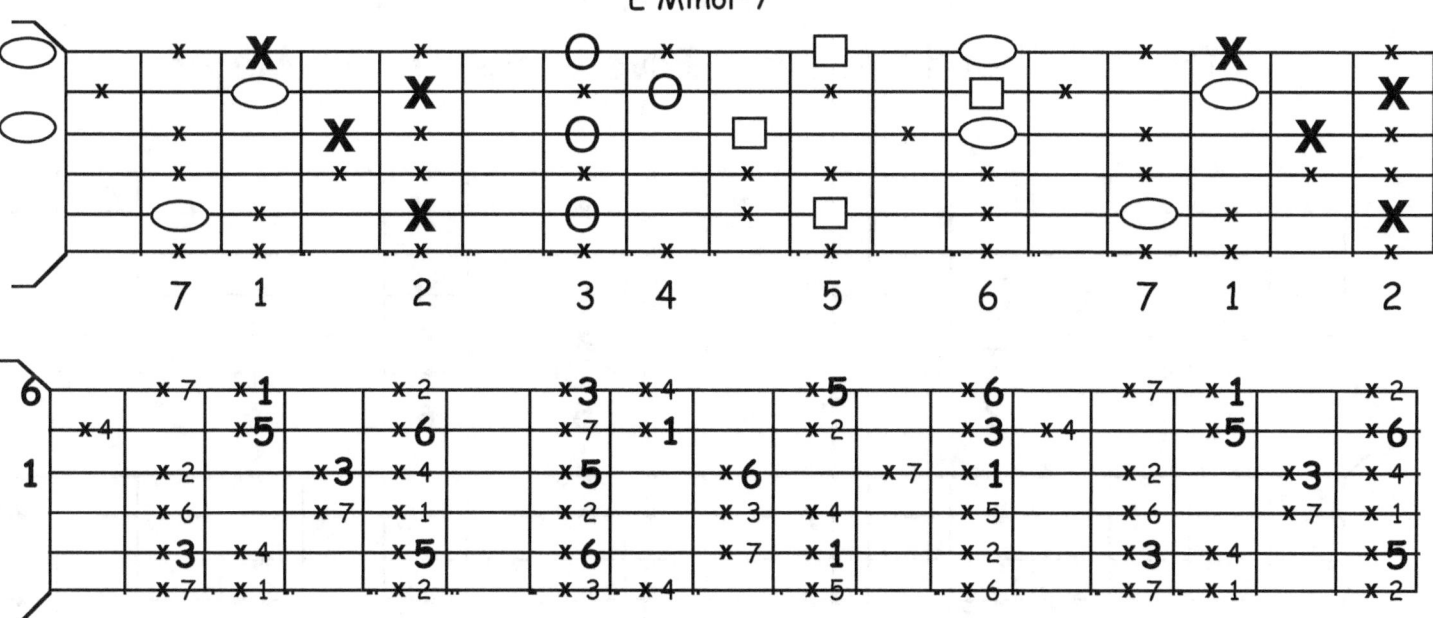

The only notes that you play are: 6, 1, 3, and 5 of the G major scale.

5321 STRING GROUPING
The "7" Chord: Minor 7b5 Inversions In "G" Major
F# Minor 7b5

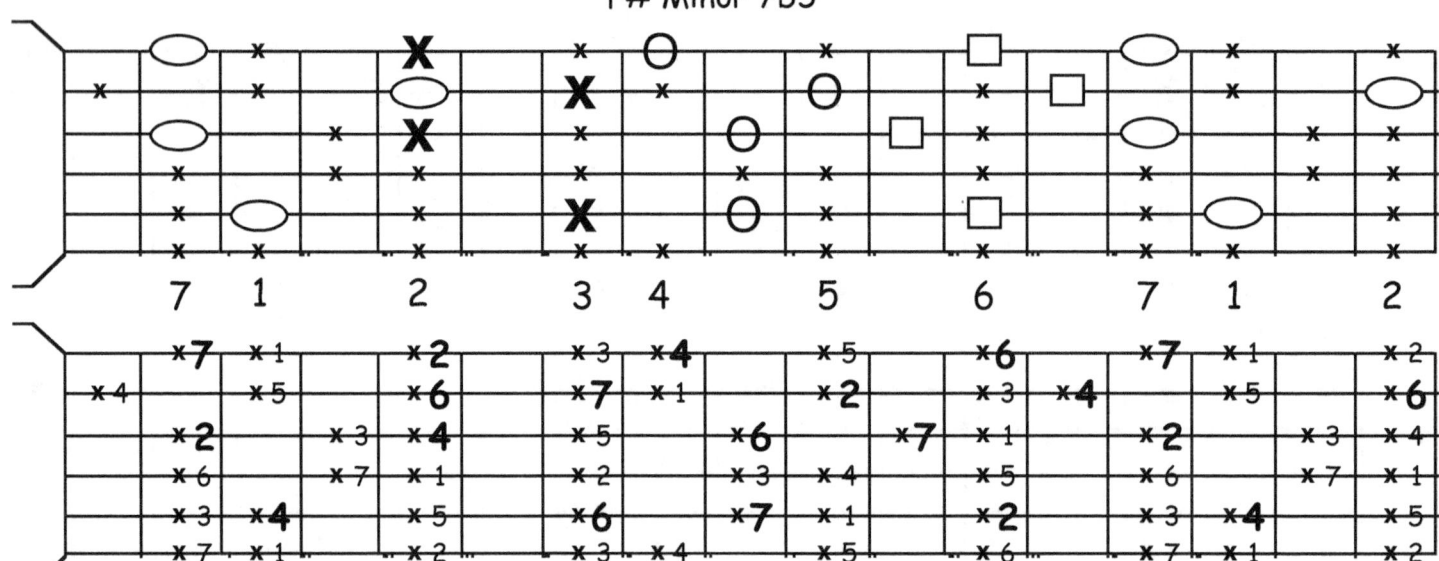

The only notes that you play are: 7, 2, 4, and 6 of the G major scale.

DROP 2 & 3:
6542 STRING GROUPING
The "1" Chord: Major 7 Inversions In "G" Major
G Major 7

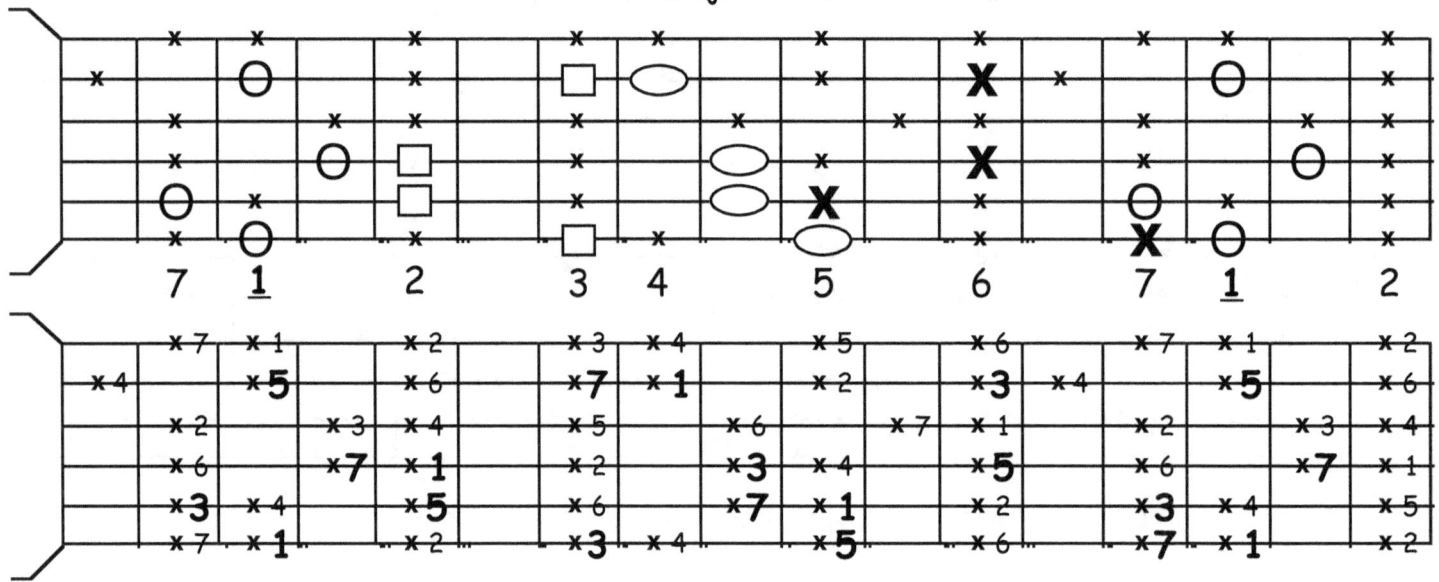

The only notes that you play are: 1, 3, 5, and 7 of the G major scale.

6542 STRING GROUPING

The "2" Chord: Minor 7 Inversions In "G" Major

A Minor 7

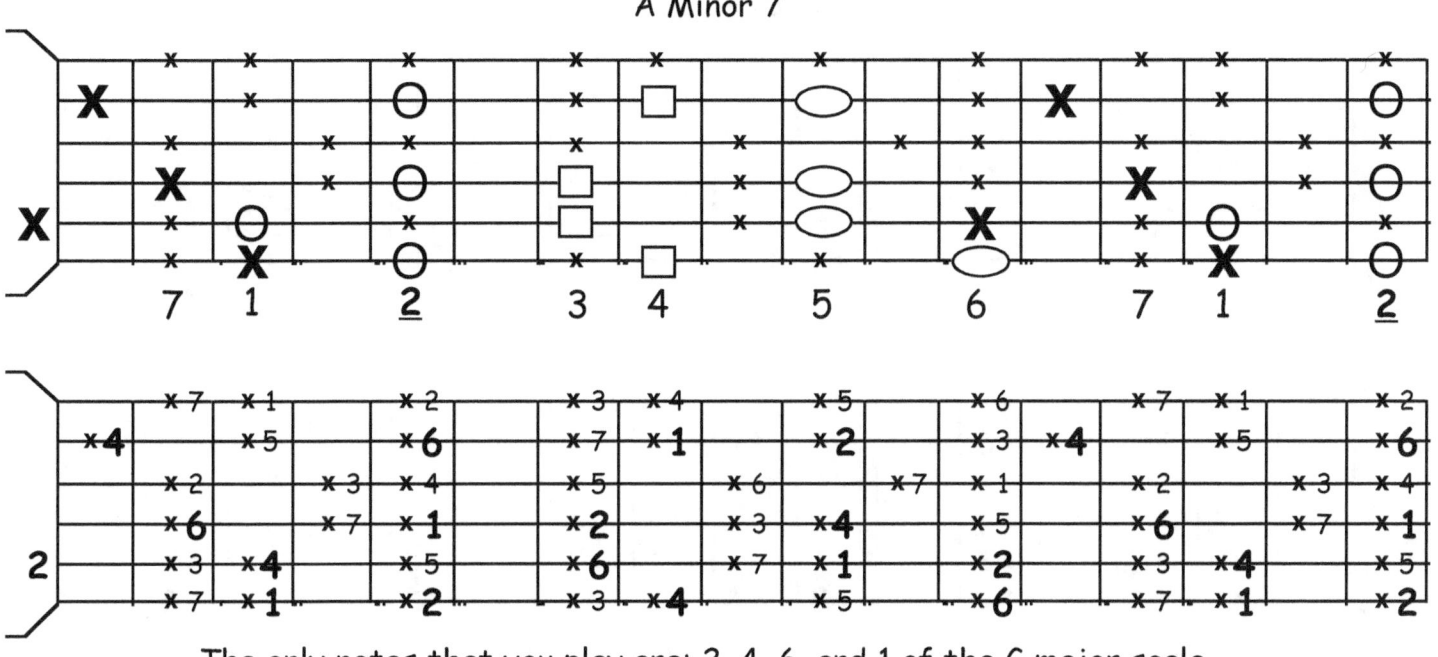

The only notes that you play are: 2, 4, 6, and 1 of the G major scale.

The "3" Chord: Minor 7 Inversions In "G" Major

B Minor 7

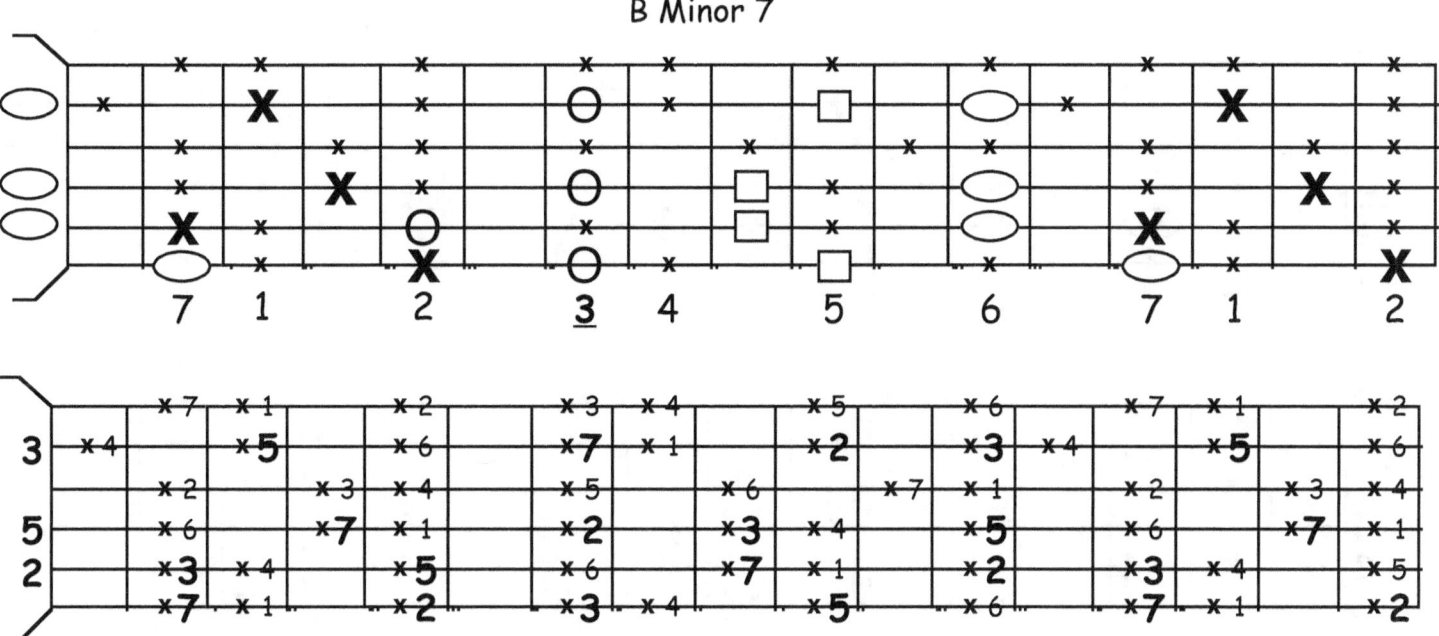

The only notes that you play are: 3, 5, 7, and 2 of the G major scale.

6542 STRING GROUPING

The "4" Chord: Major 7 Inversions In "G" Major
C Major 7

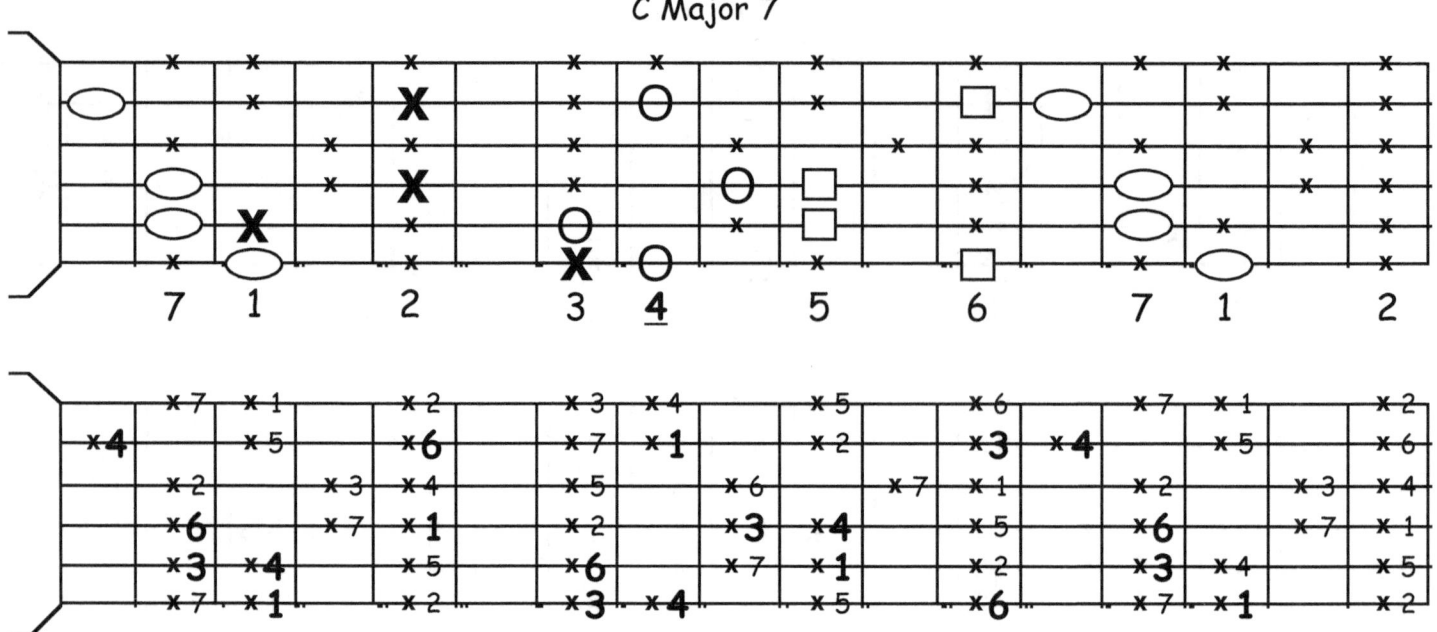

The only notes that you play are: 4, 6, 1, and 3 of the G major scale.

The "5" Chord: Dominant 7 Inversions In "G" Major
D Dominant 7

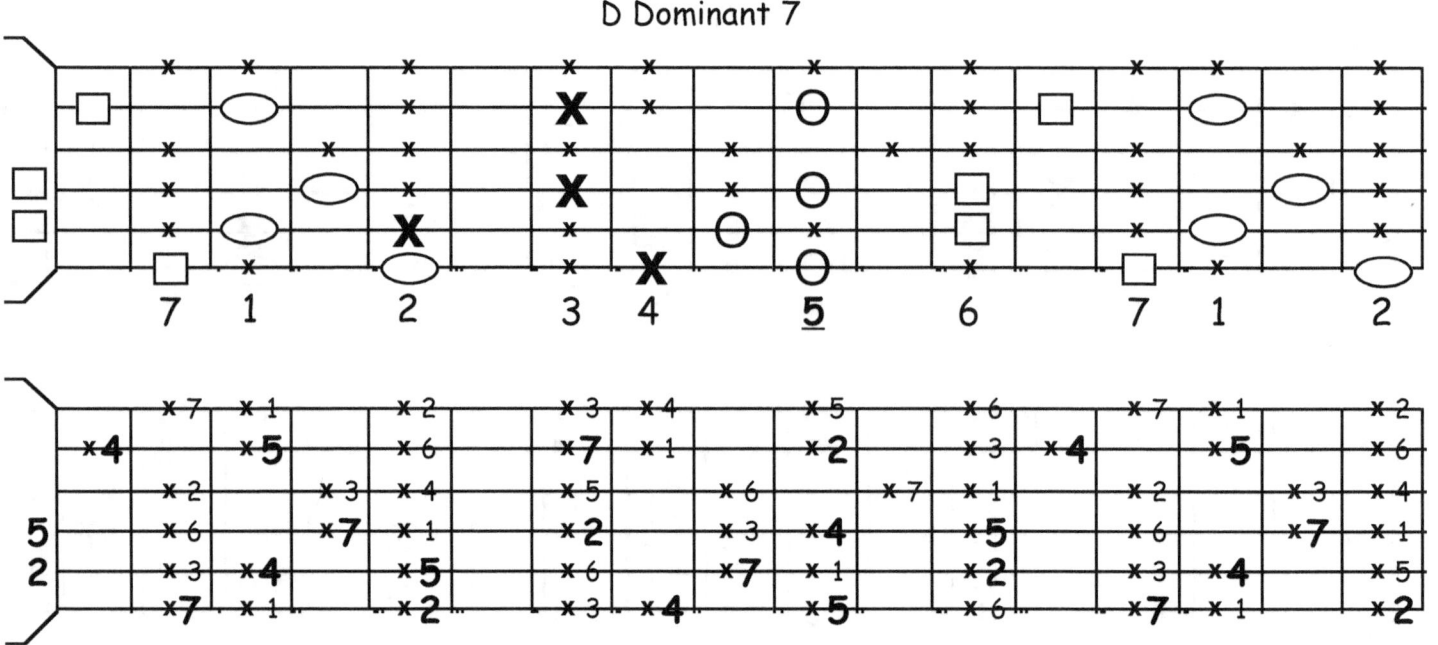

The only notes that you play are: 5, 7, 2, and 4 of the G major scale.

6542 STRING GROUPING

The "6" Chord: Minor 7 Inversions In "G" Major

E Minor 7

The only notes that you play are: 6, 1, 3, and 5 of the G major scale.

The "7" Chord: Minor 7b5 Inversions In "G" Major

F# Minor 7b5

The only notes that you play are: 7, 2, 4, and 6 of the G major scale.

DROP 2 & 3:
5431 STRING GROUPING
The "1" Chord: Major 7 Inversions In "G" Major
G Major 7

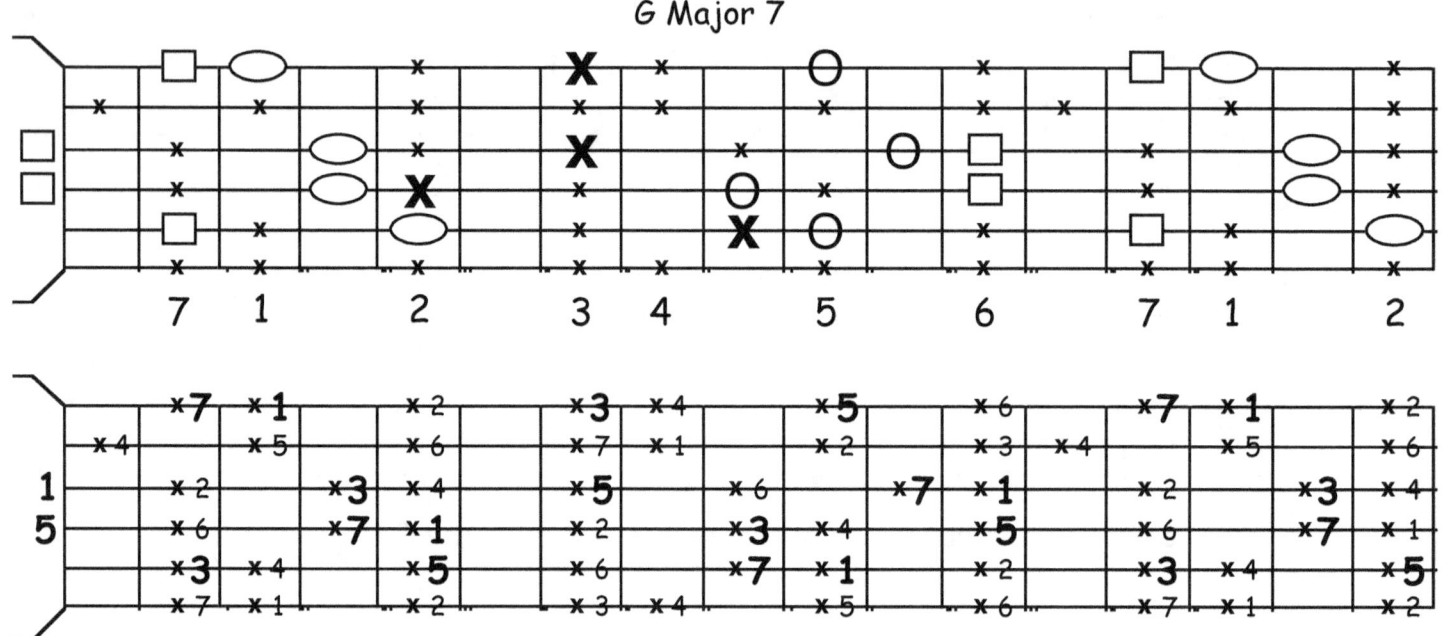

The only notes that you play are: 1, 3, 5, and 7 of the G major scale.

The "2" Chord: Minor 7 Inversions In "G" Major
A Minor 7

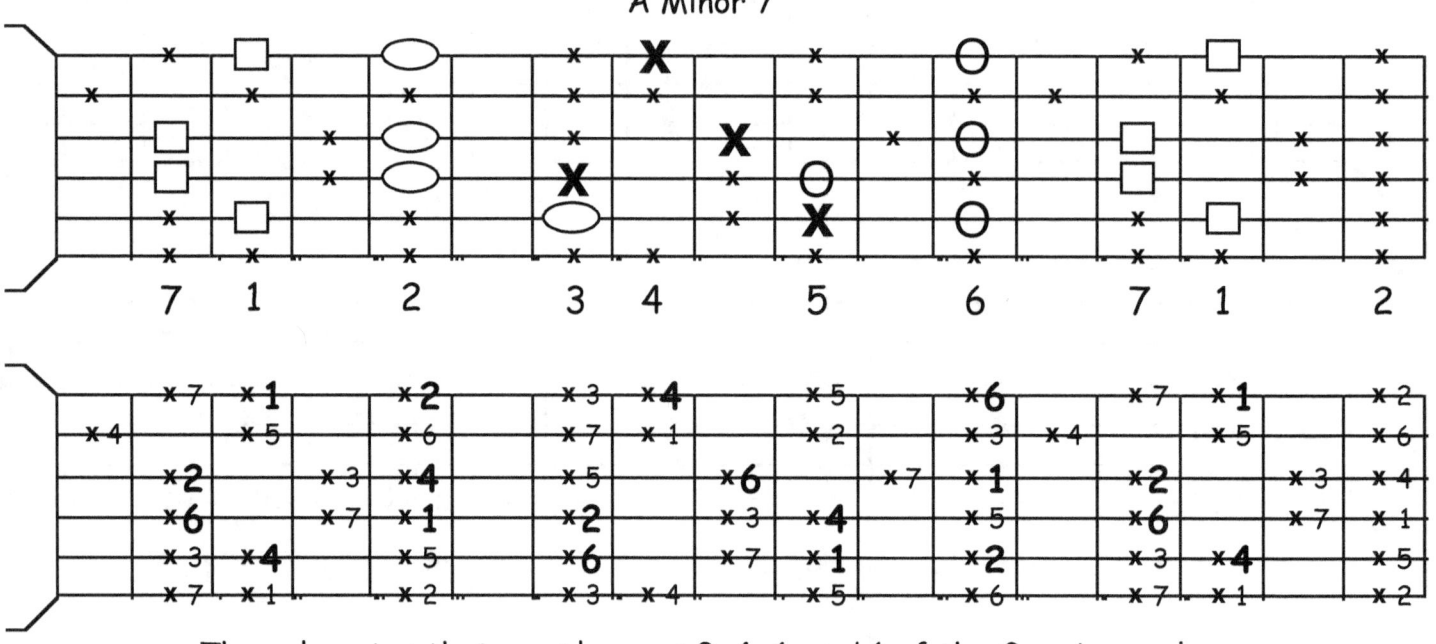

The only notes that you play are: 2, 4, 6, and 1 of the G major scale.

5431 STRING GROUPING
The "3" Chord: Minor 7 Inversions In "G" Major
B Minor 7

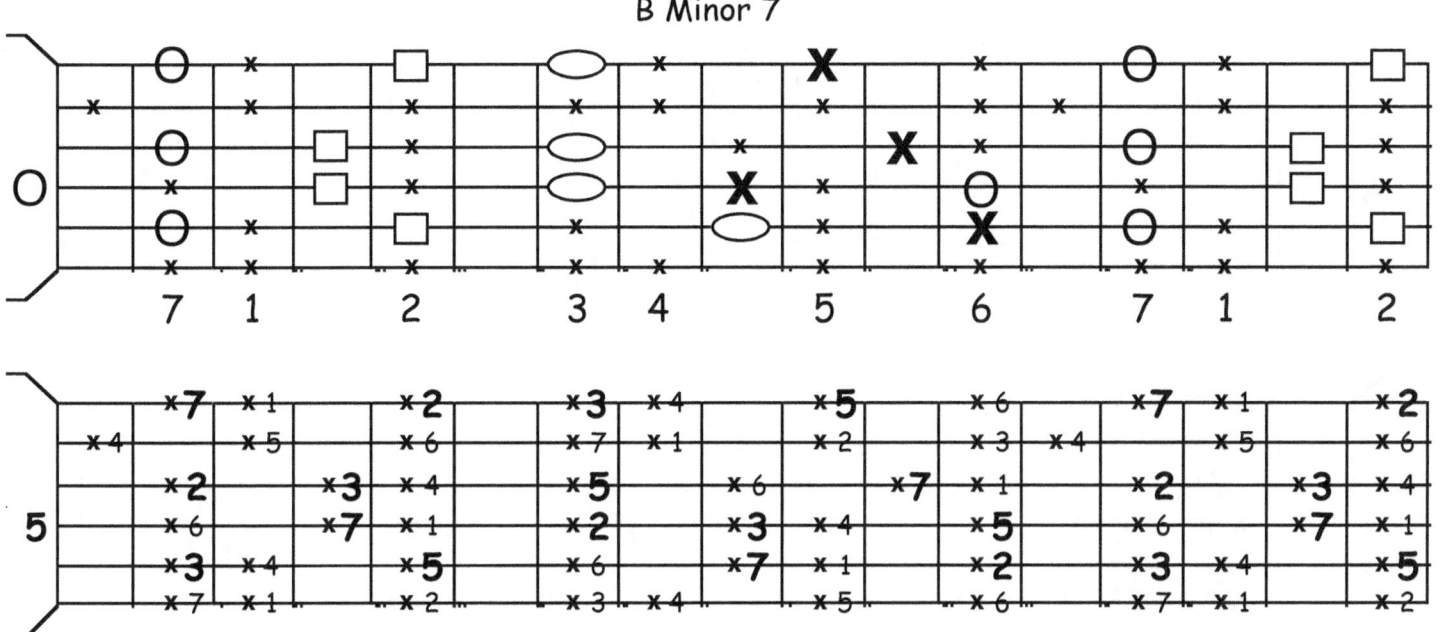

The only notes that you play are: 3, 5, 7, and 2 of the G major scale.

The "4" Chord: Major 7 Inversions In "G" Major
C Major 7

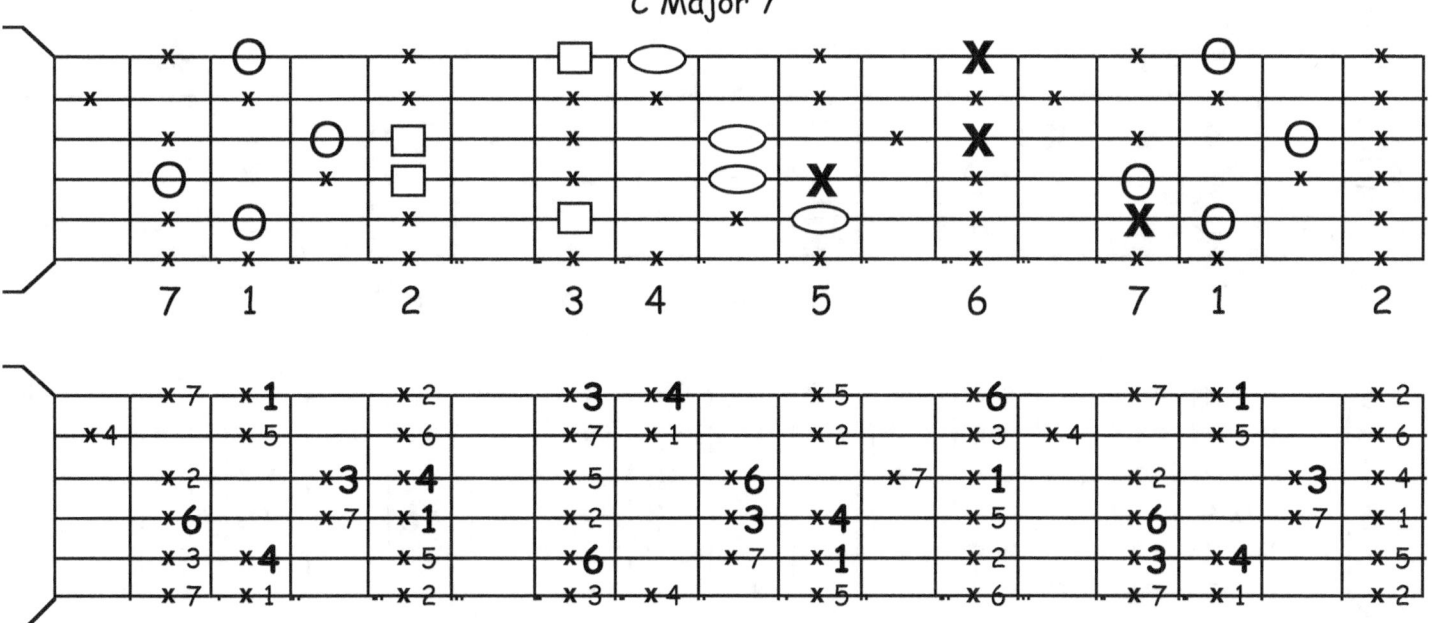

The only notes that you play are: 4, 6, 1, and 3 of the G major scale.

5431 STRING GROUPING
The "5" Chord: Dominant 7 Inversions In "G" Major
D Dominant 7

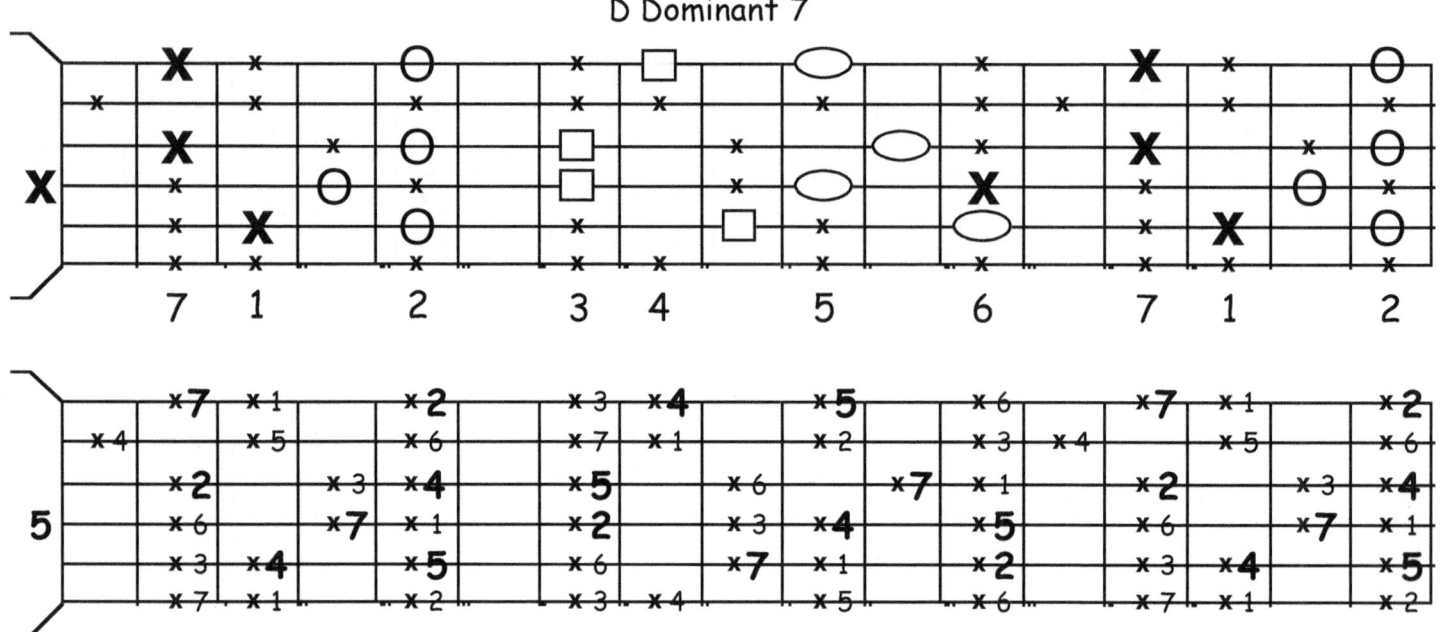

The only notes that you play are: 5, 7, 2, and 4 of the G major scale.

The "6" Chord: Minor 7 Inversions In "G" Major
E Minor 7

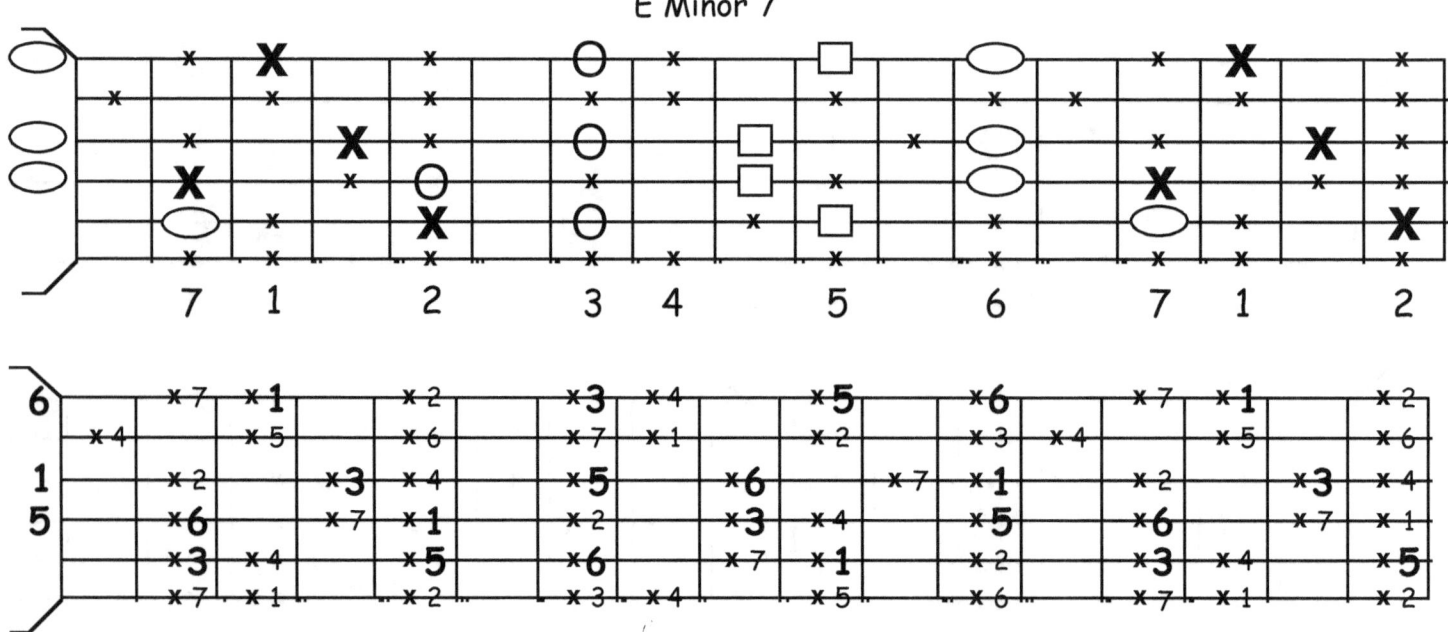

The only notes that you play are: 6, 1, 3, and 5 of the G major scale.

5431 STRING GROUPING
The "7" Chord: Minor 7b5 Inversions In "G" Major
F# Minor 7b5

The only notes that you play are: 7, 2, 4, and 6 of the G major scale.

DROP 4:
6321 STRING GROUPING
The "1" Chord: Major 7 Inversions In "G" Major
G Major 7

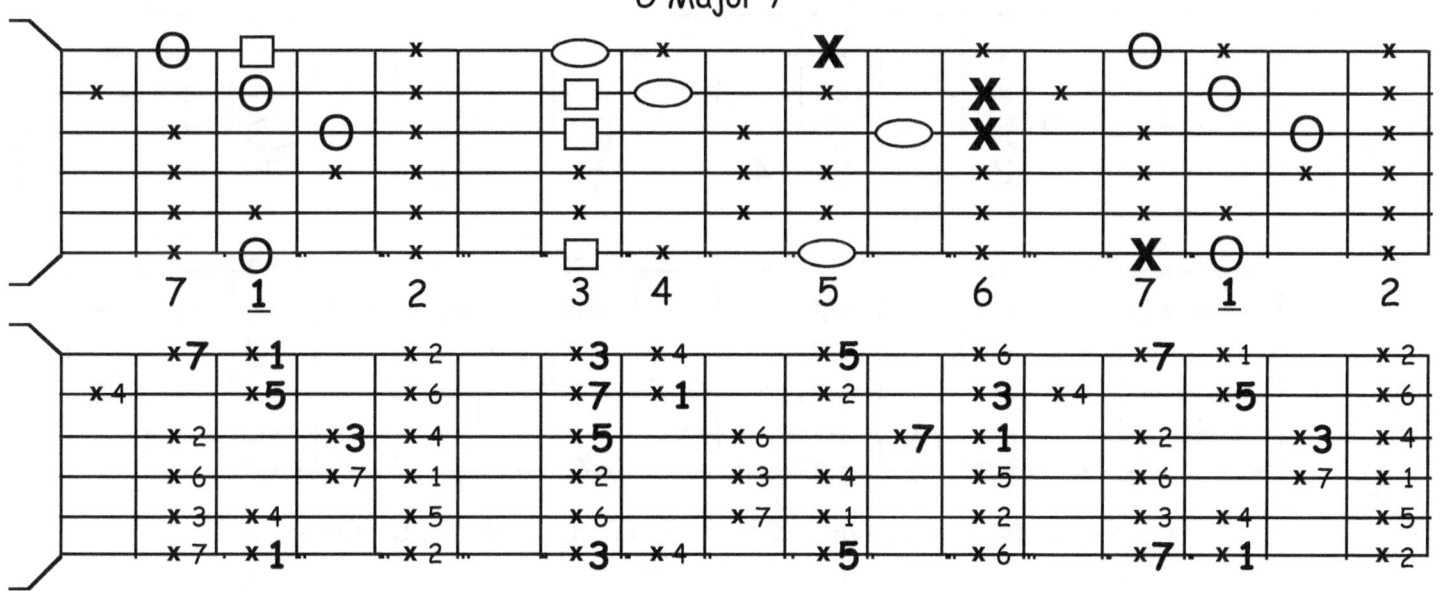

The only notes that you play are: 1, 3, 5, and 7 of the G major scale.

6321 STRING GROUPING
The "2" Chord: Minor 7 Inversions In "G" Major
A Minor 7

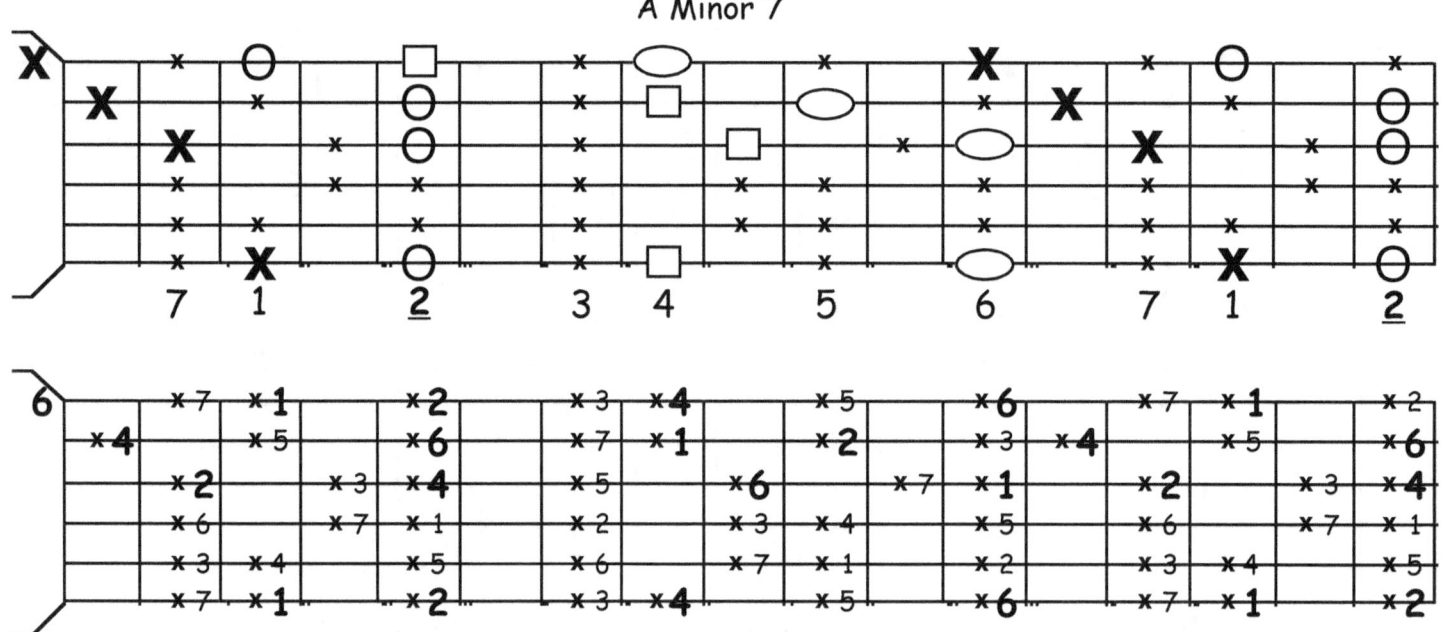

The only notes that you play are: 2, 4, 6, and 1 of the G major scale.

The "3" Chord: Minor 7 Inversions In "G" Major
B Minor 7

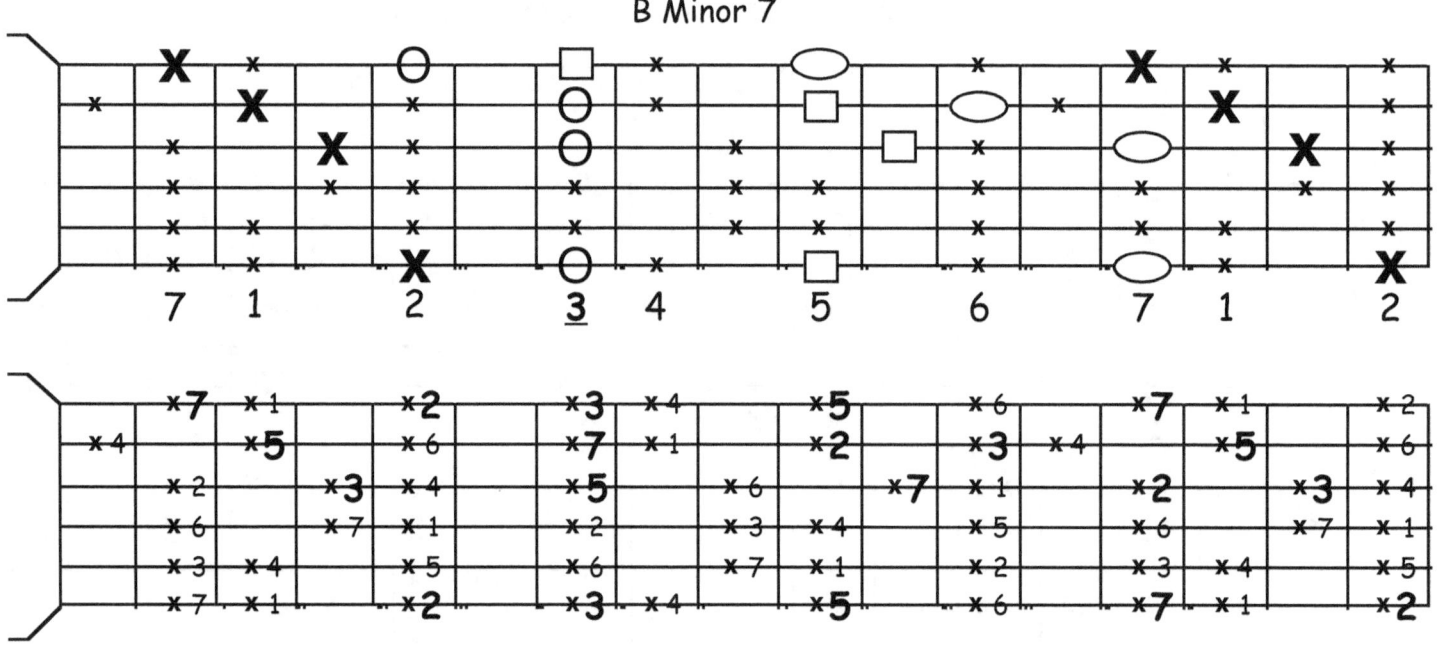

The only notes that you play are: 3, 5, 7, and 2 of the G major scale.

6321 STRING GROUPING
The "4" Chord: Major 7 Inversions In "G" Major
C Major 7

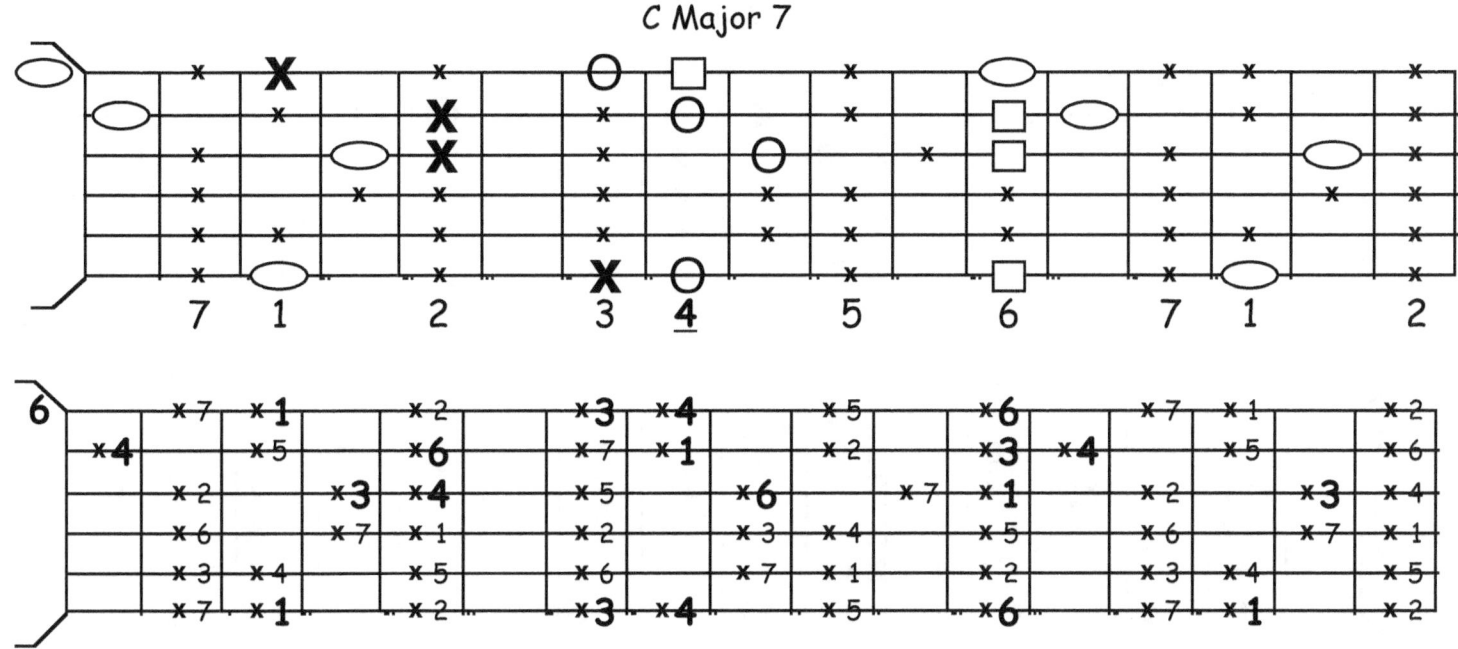

The only notes that you play are: 4, 6, 1, and 3 of the G major scale.

The "5" Chord: Dominant 7 Inversions In "G" Major
D Dominant 7

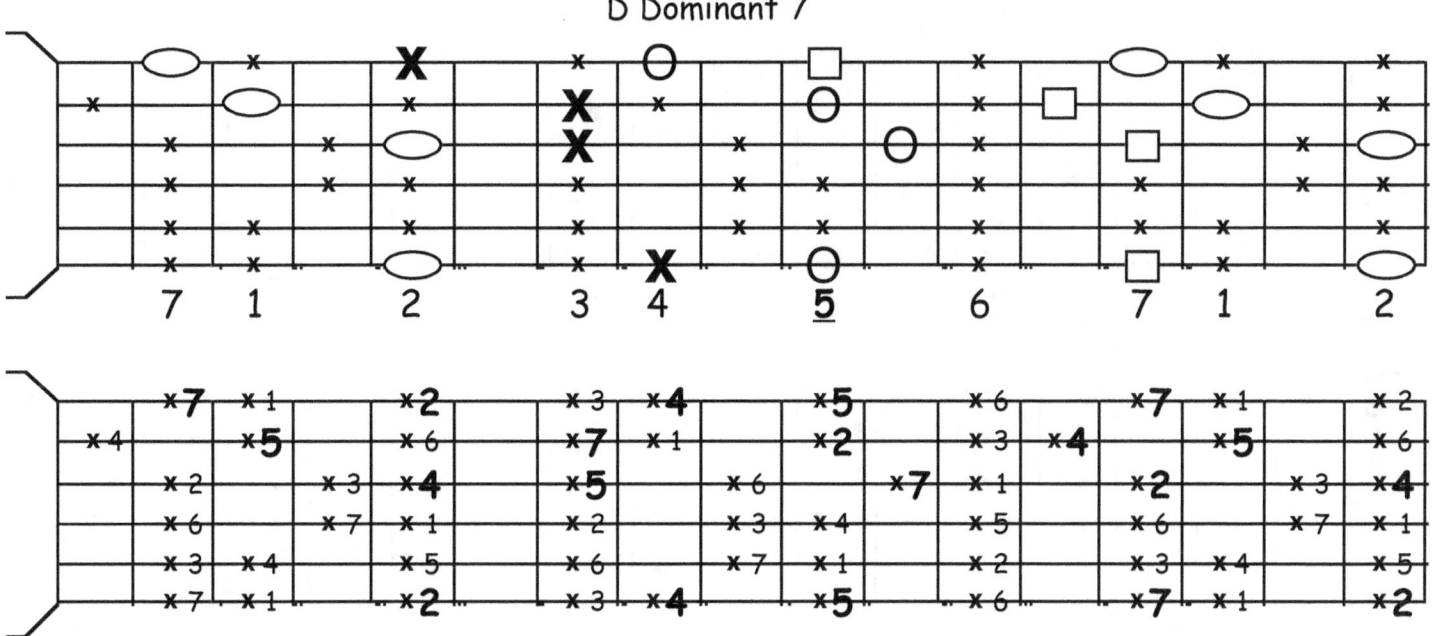

The only notes that you play are: 5, 7, 2, and 4 of the G major scale.

6321 STRING GROUPING
The "6" Chord: Minor 7 Inversions In "G" Major
E Minor 7

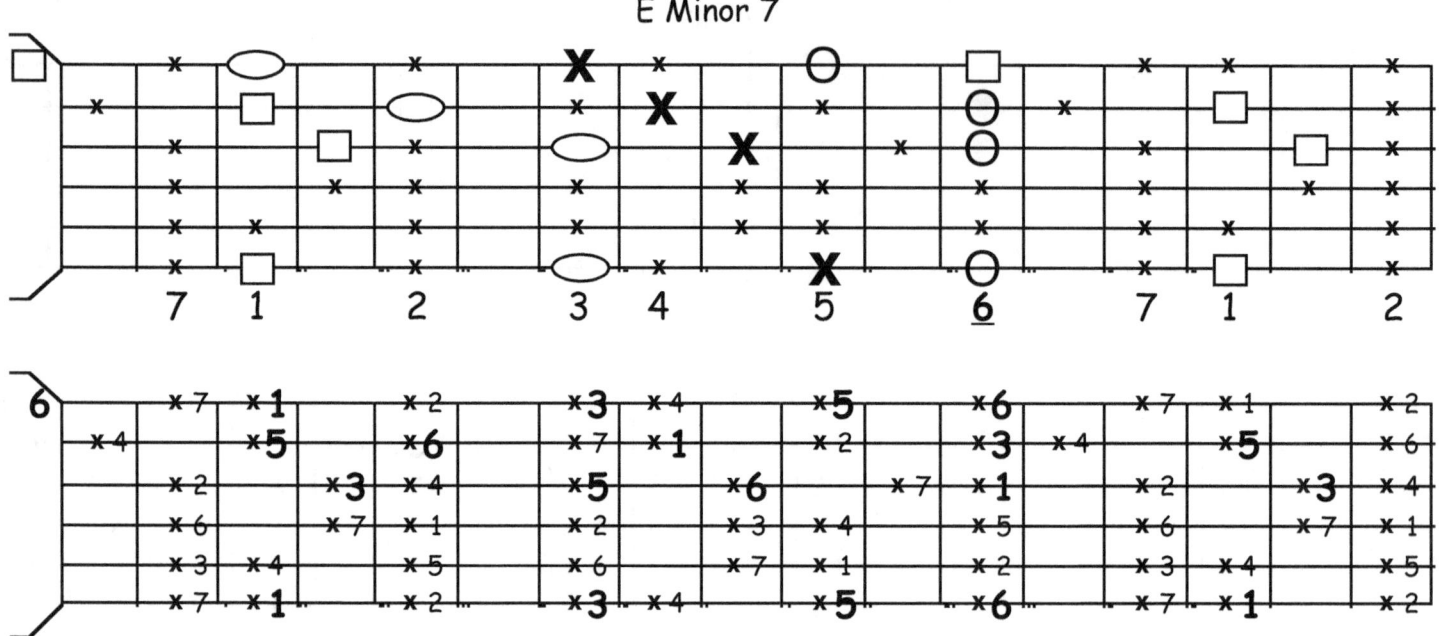

The only notes that you play are: 6, 1, 3, and 5 of the G major scale.

The "7" Chord: Minor 7b5 Inversions In "G" Major
F# Minor 7b5

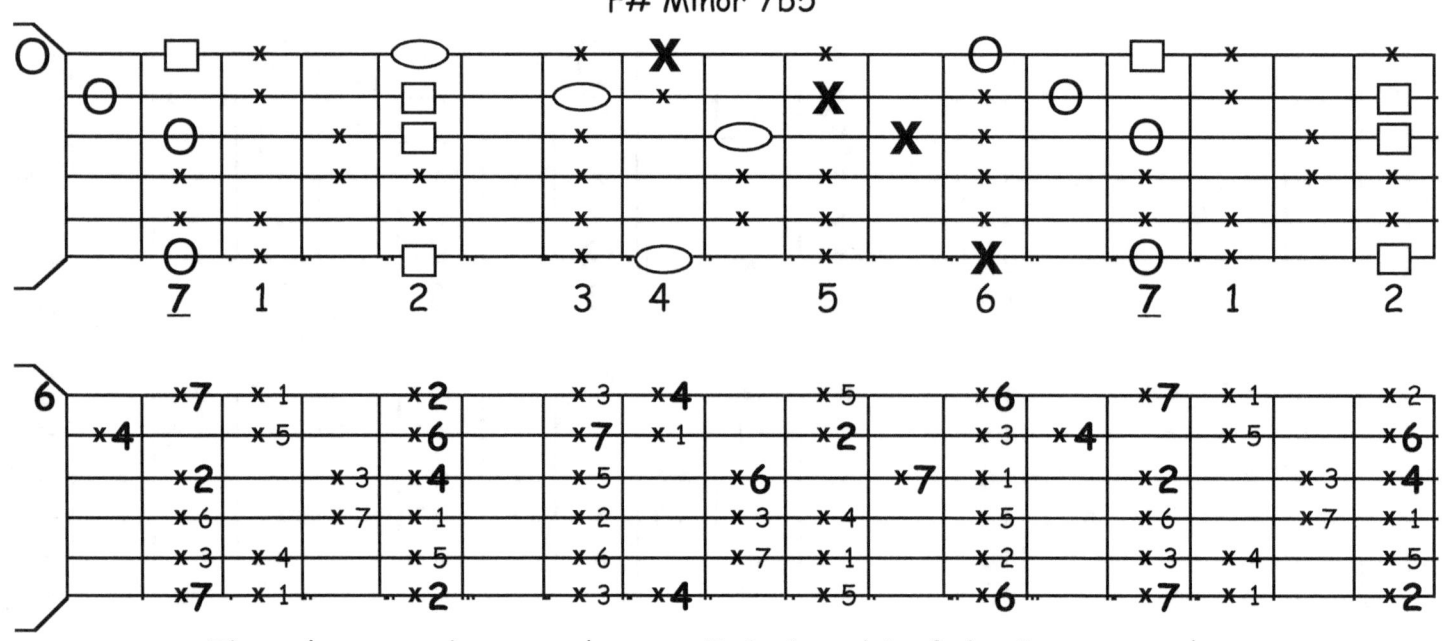

The only notes that you play are: 7, 2, 4, and 6 of the G major scale.

DROP 2 & 4:
6532 STRING GROUPING
The "1" Chord: Major 7 Inversions In "G" Major
G Major 7

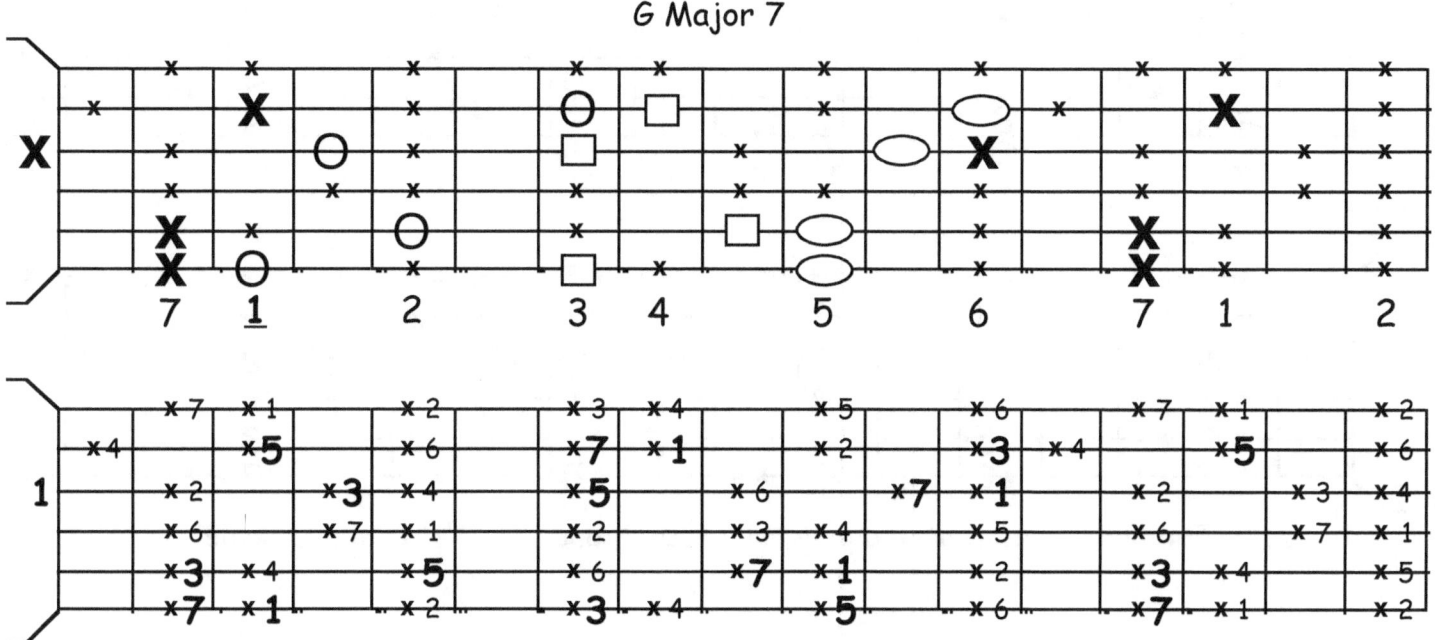

The only notes that you play are: 1, 3, 5, and 7 of the G major scale.

The "2" Chord: Minor 7 Inversions In "G" Major
A Minor 7

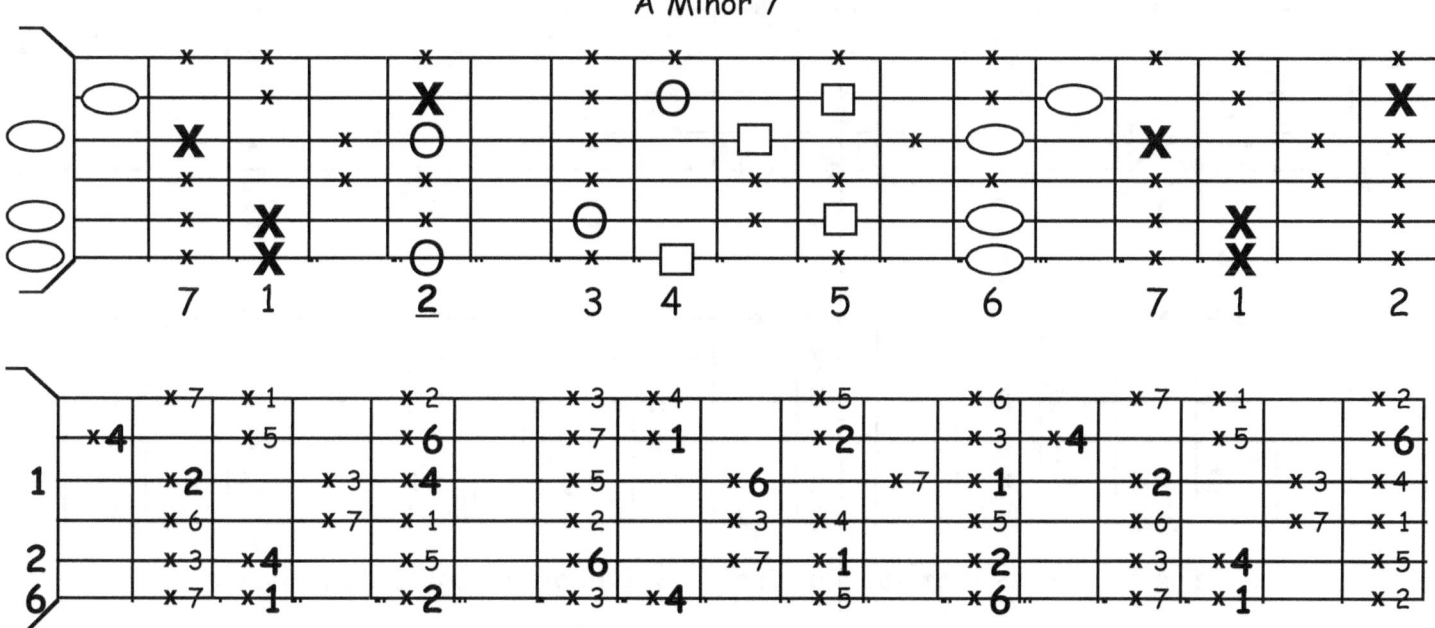

The only notes that you play are: 2, 4, 6, and 1 of the G major scale.

6532 STRING GROUPING
The "3" Chord: Minor 7 Inversions In "G" Major
B Minor 7

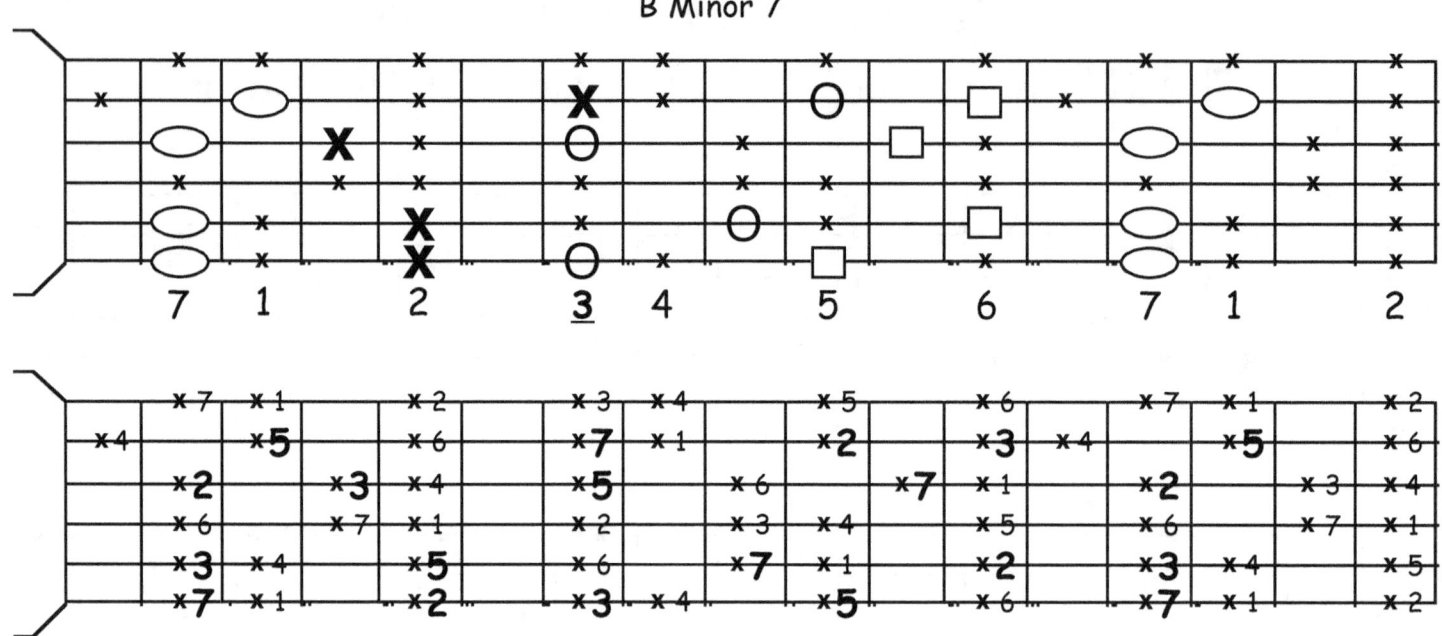

The only notes that you play are: 3, 5, 7, and 2 of the G major scale.

The "4" Chord: Major 7 Inversions In "G" Major
C Major 7

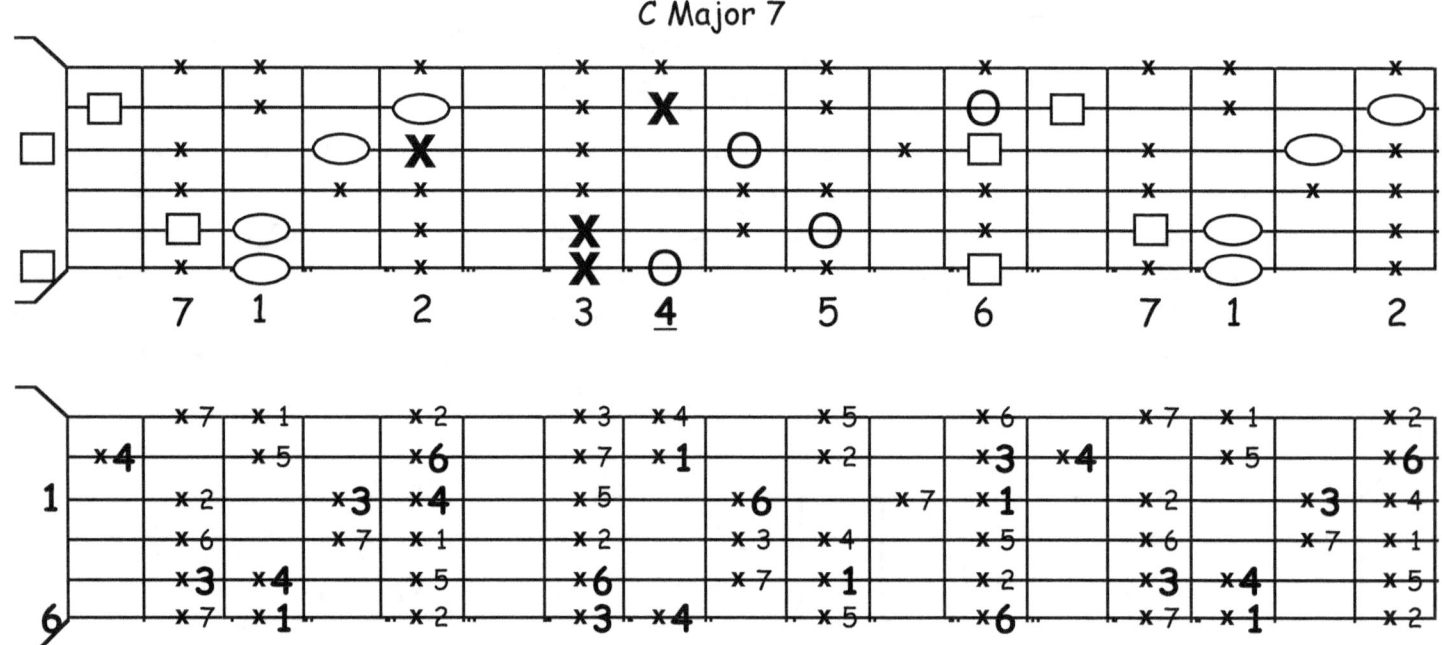

The only notes that you play are: 4, 6, 1, and 3 of the G major scale.

6532 STRING GROUPING

The "5" Chord: Dominant 7 Inversions In "G" Major
D Dominant 7

The only notes that you play are: 5, 7, 2, and 4 of the G major scale.

The "6" Chord: Minor 7 Inversions In "G" Major
E Minor 7

The only notes that you play are: 6, 1, 3, and 5 of the G major scale.

6532 STRING GROUPING
The "7" Chord: Minor 7b5 Inversions In "G" Major
F# Minor 7b5

The only notes that you play are: 7, 2, 4, and 6 of the G major scale.

DROP 2 & 4:
5421 STRING GROUPING
The "1" Chord: Major 7 Inversions In "G" Major
G Major 7

The only notes that you play are: 1, 3, 5, and 7 of the G major scale.

5421 STRING GROUPING
The "2" Chord: Minor 7 Inversions In "G" Major
A Minor 7

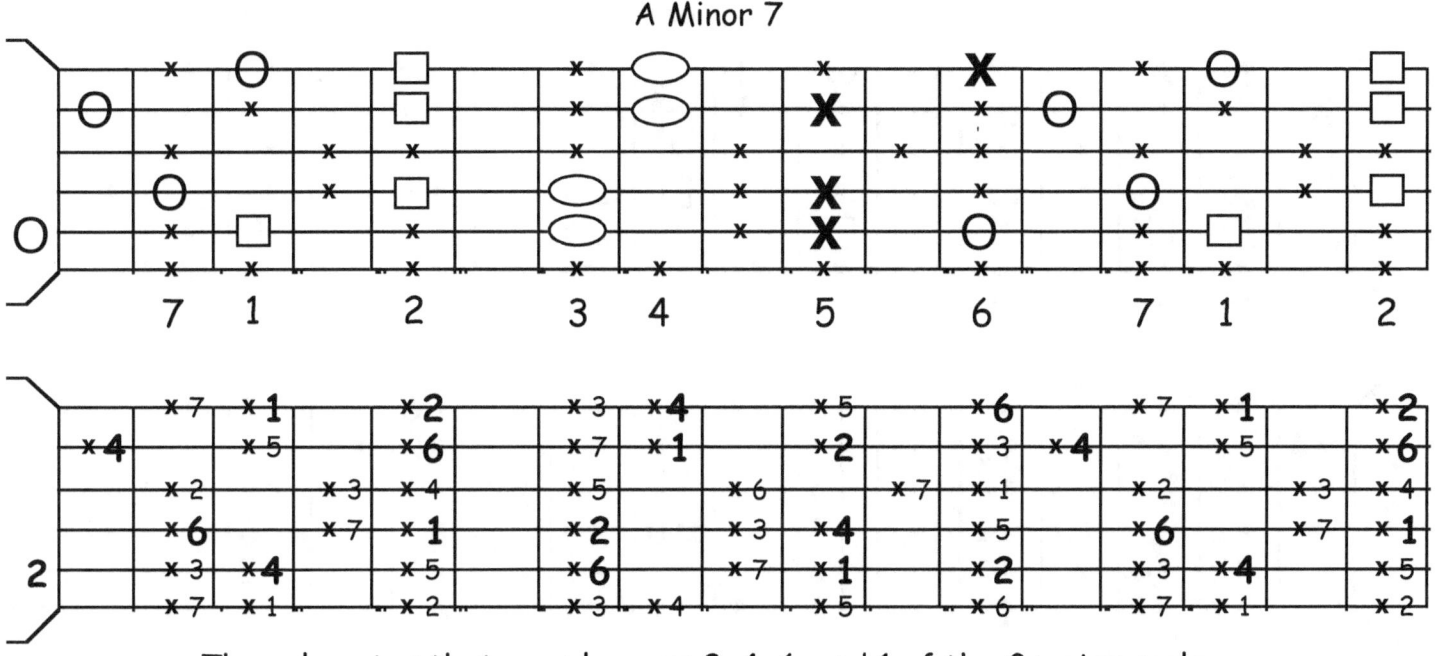

The only notes that you play are: 2, 4, 6, and 1 of the G major scale.

The "3" Chord: Minor 7 Inversions In "G" Major
B Minor 7

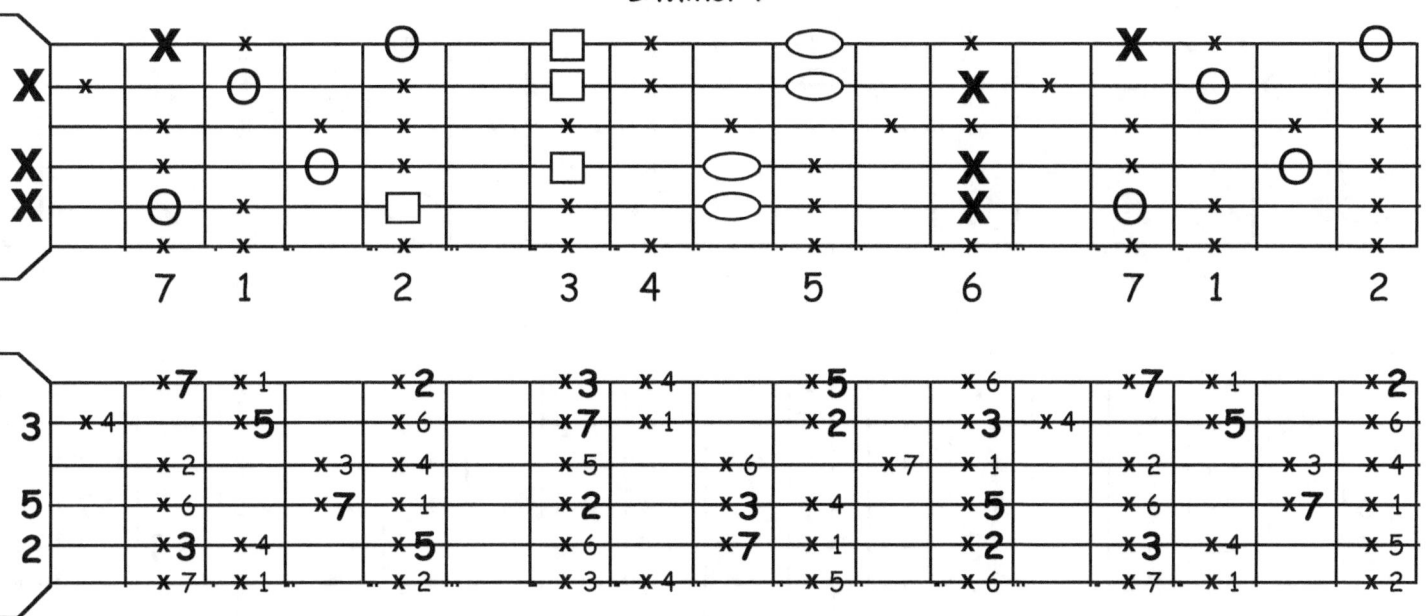

The only notes that you play are: 3, 5, 7, and 2 of the G major scale.

5421 STRING GROUPING
The "4" Chord: Major 7 Inversions In "G" Major
C Major 7

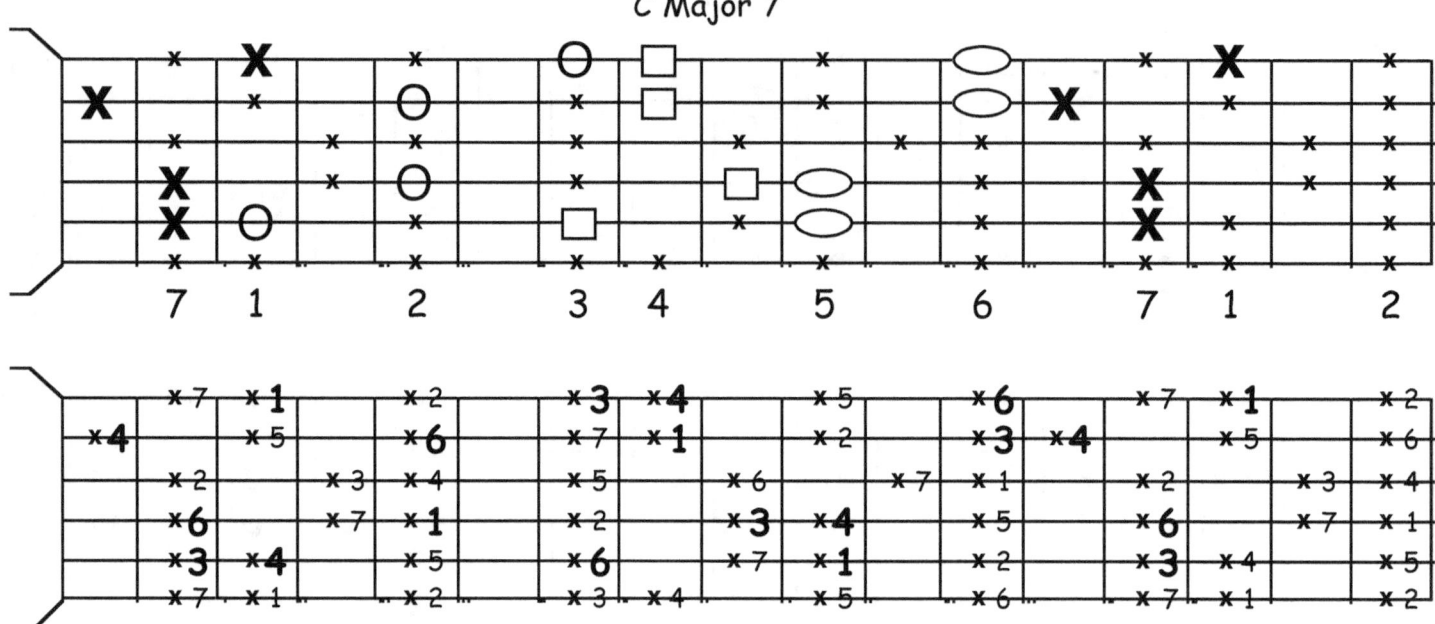

The only notes that you play are: 4, 6, 1, and 3 of the G major scale.

The "5" Chord: Dominant 7 Inversions In "G" Major
D Dominant 7

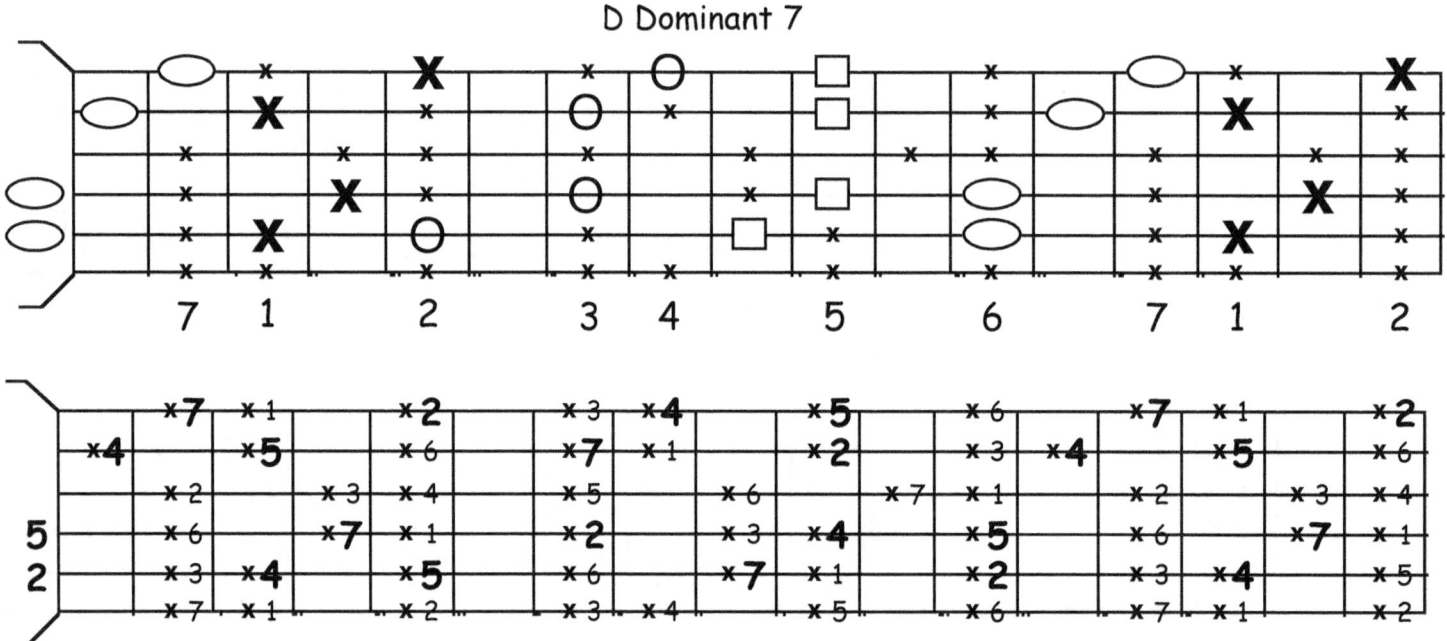

The only notes that you play are: 5, 7, 2, and 4 of the G major scale.

5421 STRING GROUPING
The "6" Chord: Minor 7 Inversions In "G" Major
E Minor 7

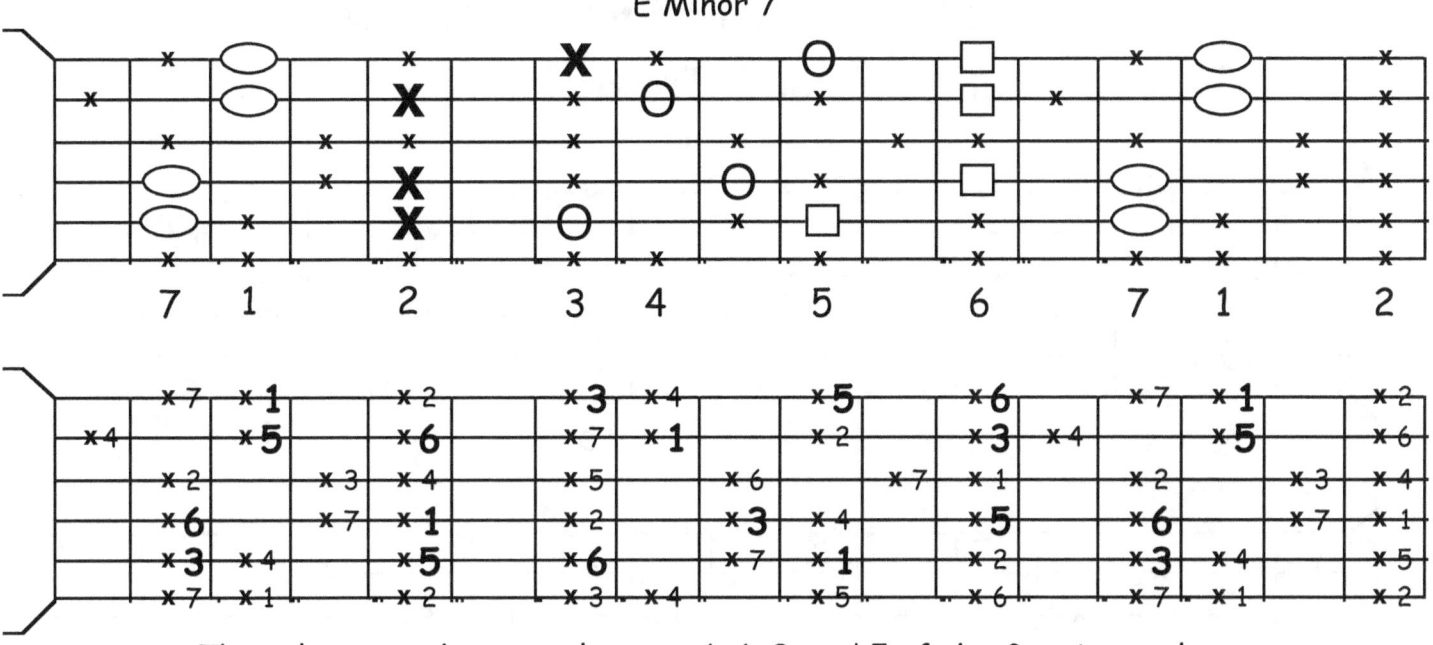

The only notes that you play are: 6, 1, 3, and 5 of the G major scale.

The "7" Chord: Minor 7b5 Inversions In "G" Major
F# Minor 7b5

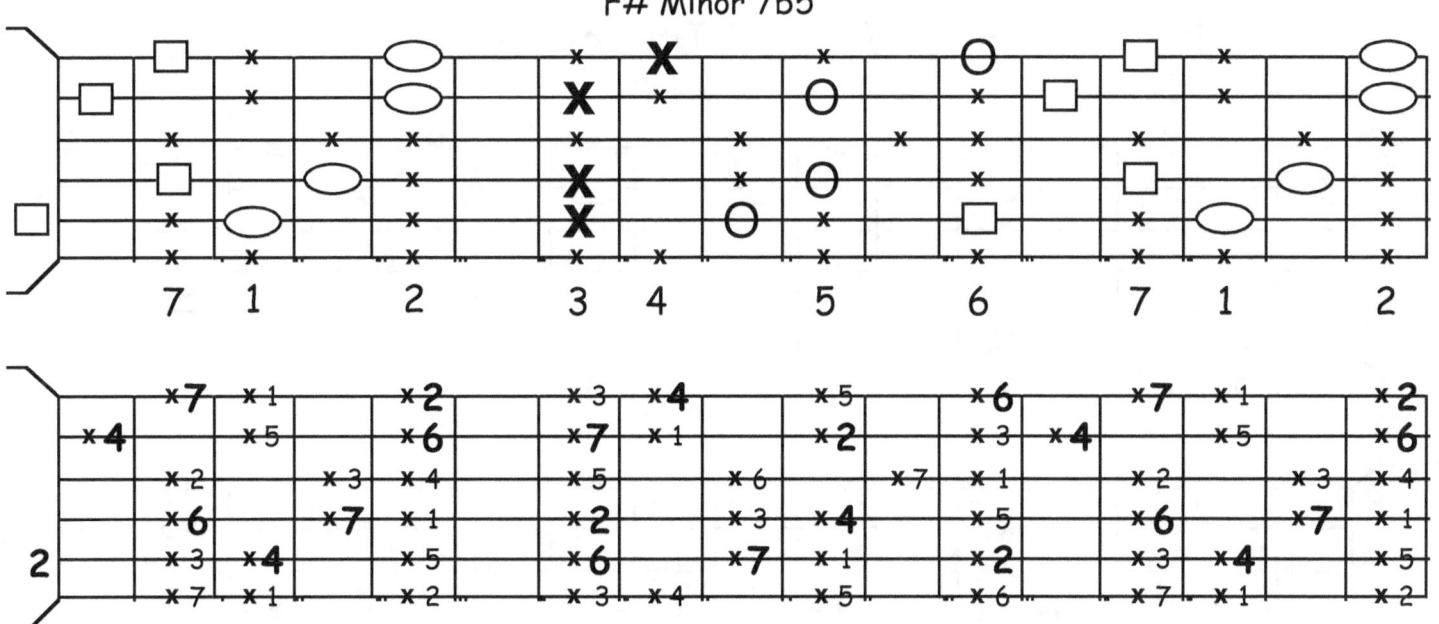

The only notes that you play are: 7, 2, 4, and 6 of the G major scale.

DROP 3 & 4:
6521 STRING GROUPING
The "1" Chord: Major 7 Inversions In "G" Major
G Major 7

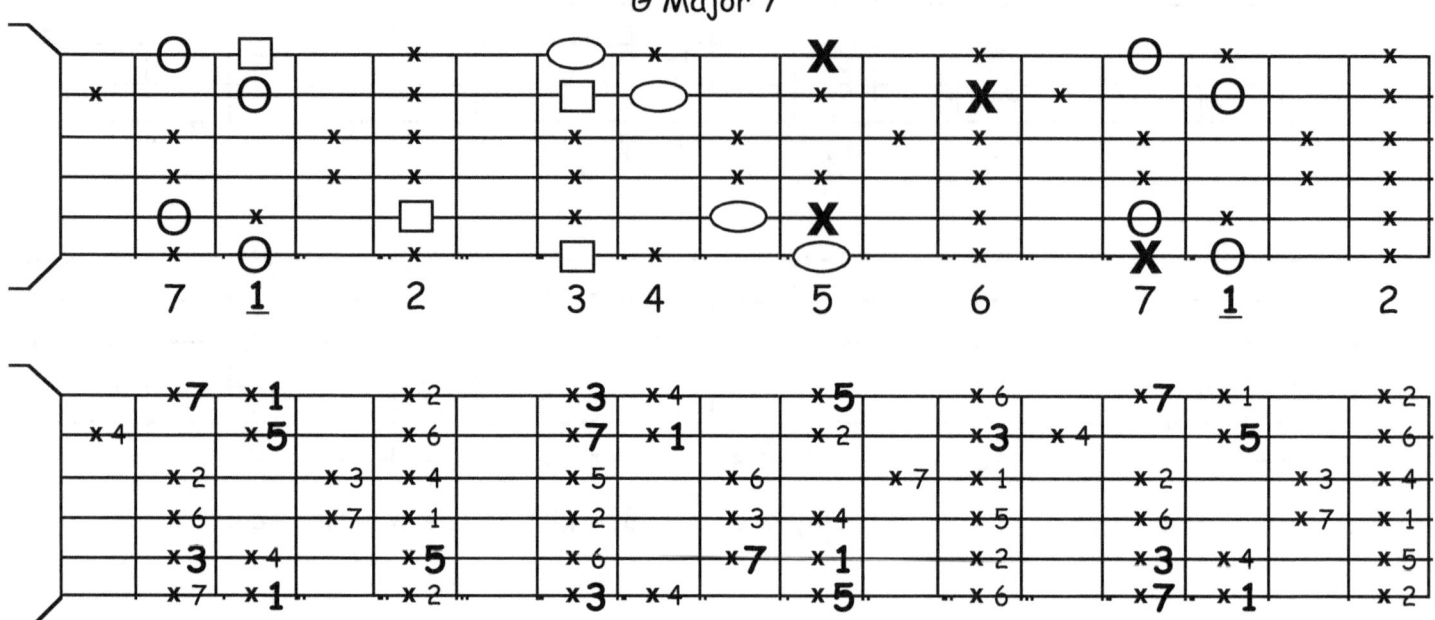

The only notes that you play are: 1, 3, 5, and 7 of the G major scale.

The "2" Chord: Minor 7 Inversions In "G" Major
A Minor 7

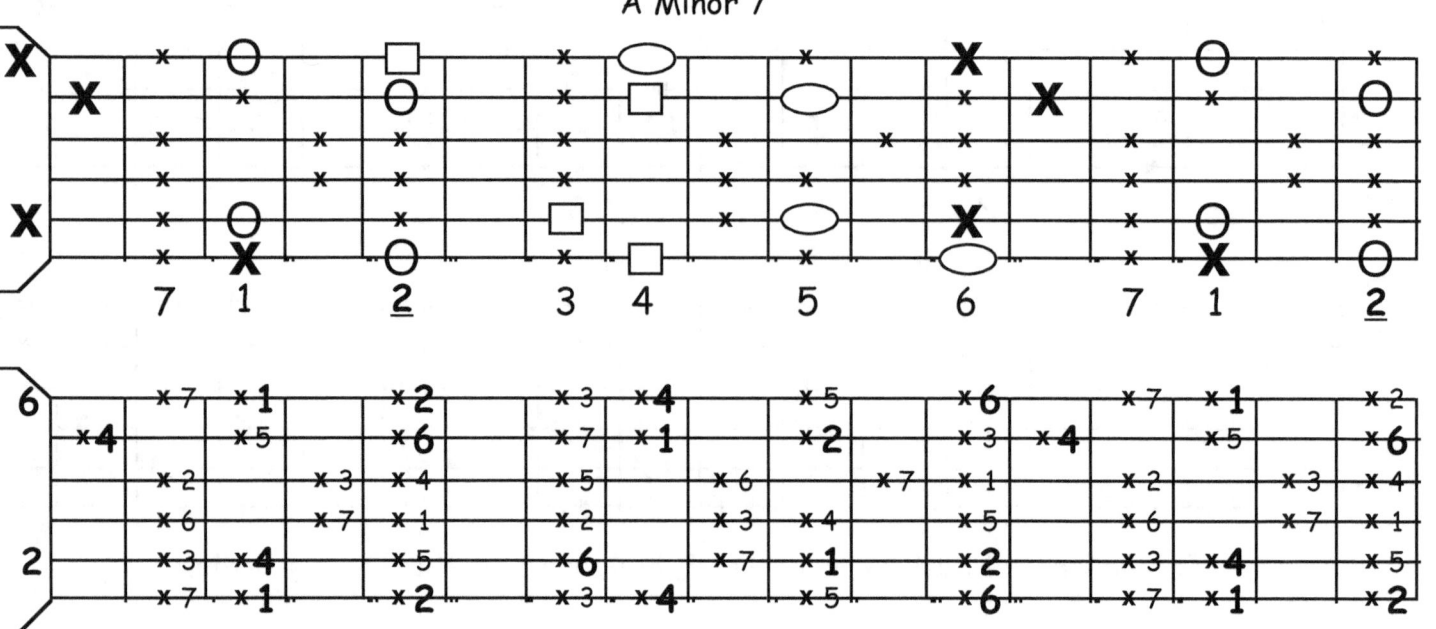

The only notes that you play are: 2, 4, 6, and 1 of the G major scale.

6521 STRING GROUPING
The "3" Chord: Minor 7 Inversions In "G" Major
B Minor 7

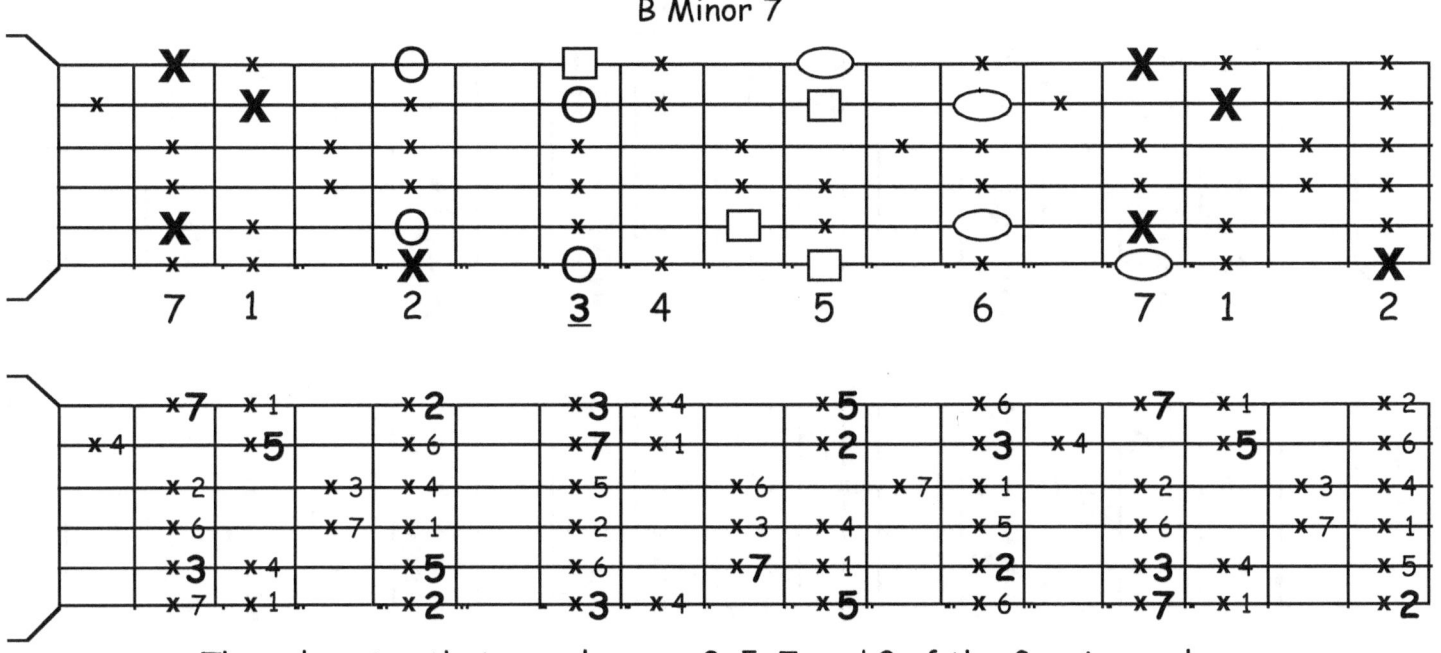

The only notes that you play are: 3, 5, 7, and 2 of the G major scale.

The "4" Chord: Major 7 Inversions In "G" Major
C Major 7

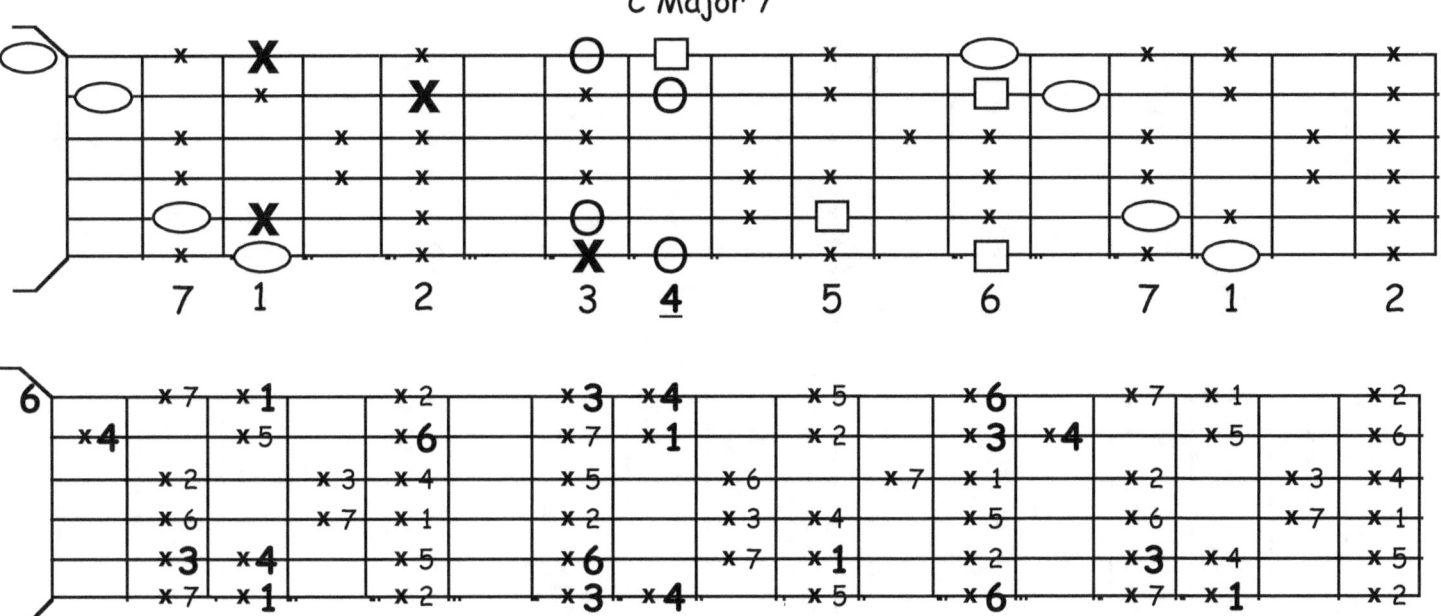

The only notes that you play are: 4, 6, 1, and 3 of the G major scale.

6521 STRING GROUPING

The "5" Chord: Dominant 7 Inversions In "G" Major

D Dominant 7

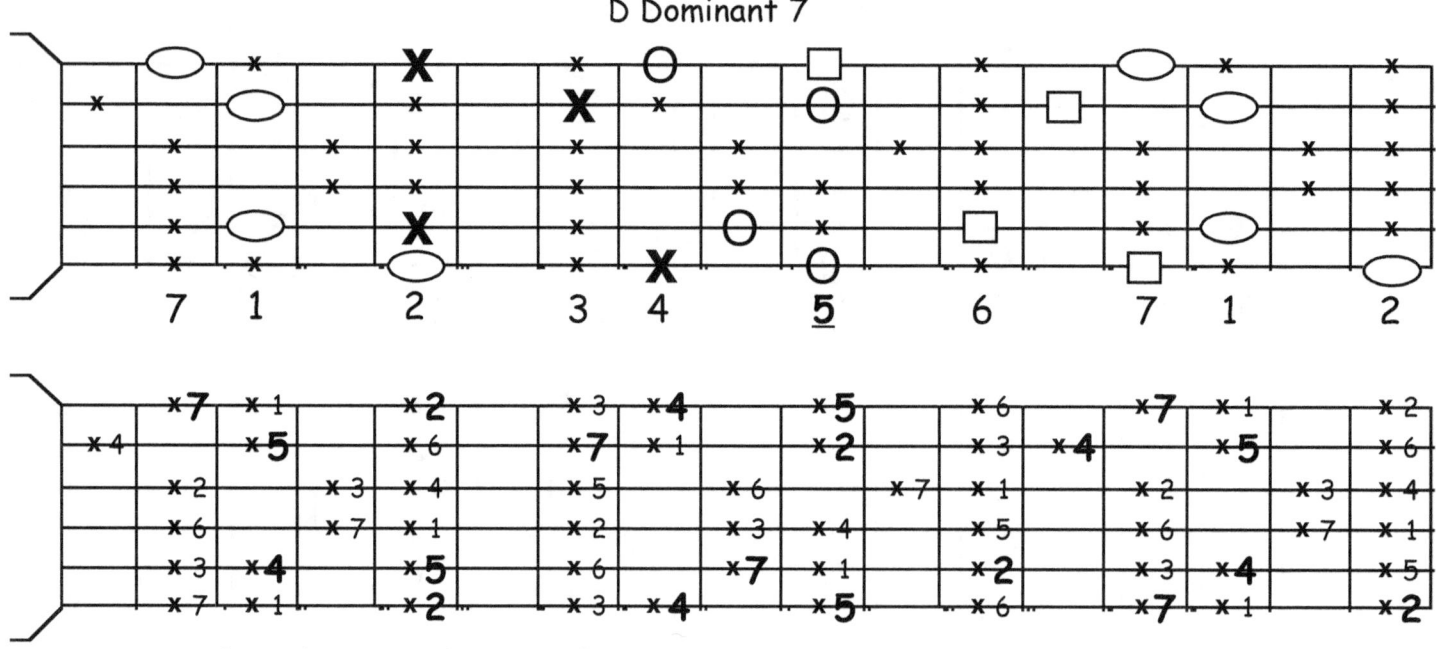

The only notes that you play are: 5, 7, 2, and 4 of the G major scale.

The "6" Chord: Minor 7 Inversions In "G" Major

E Minor 7

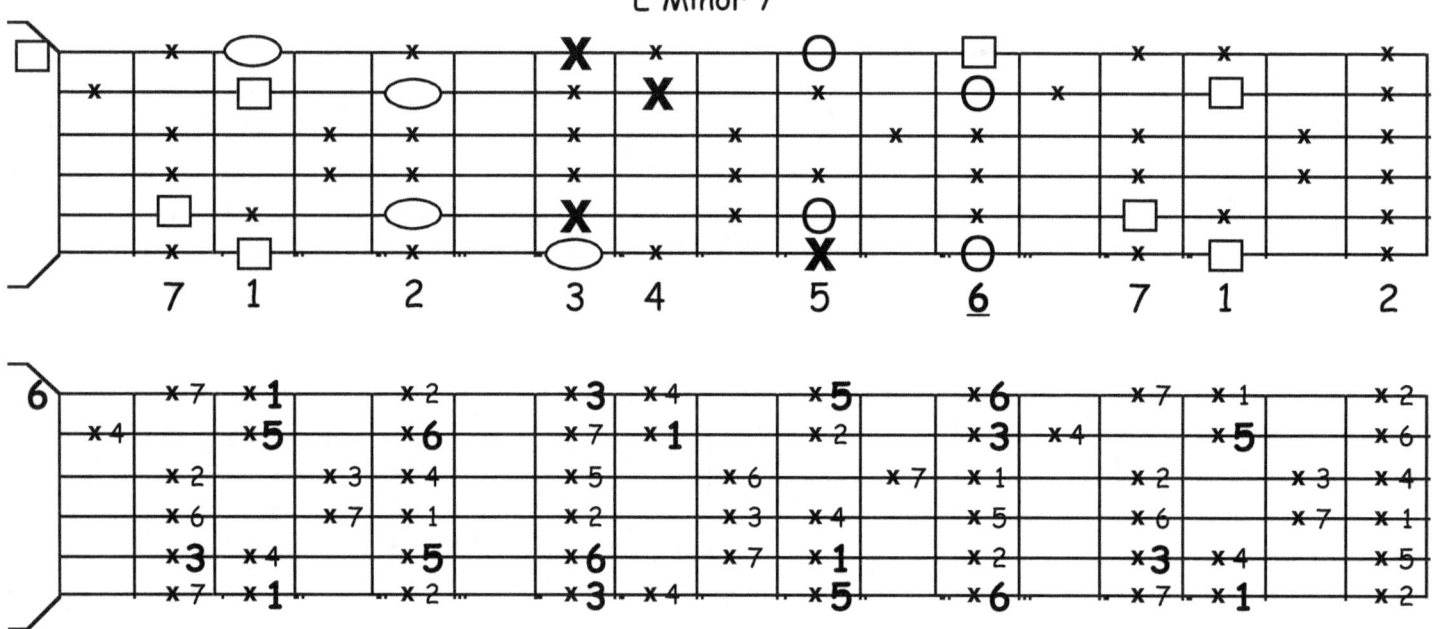

The only notes that you play are: 6, 1, 3, and 5 of the G major scale.

6521 STRING GROUPING
The "7" Chord: Minor 7b5 Inversions In "G" Major
F# Minor 7b5

The only notes that you play are: 7, 2, 4, and 6 of the G major scale.

DROP 2, 3, & 4:
6541 STRING GROUPING
The "1" Chord: Major 7 Inversions In "G" Major
G Major 7

The only notes that you play are: 1, 3, 5, and 7 of the G major scale.

6541 STRING GROUPING
The "2" Chord: Minor 7 Inversions In "G" Major
A Minor 7

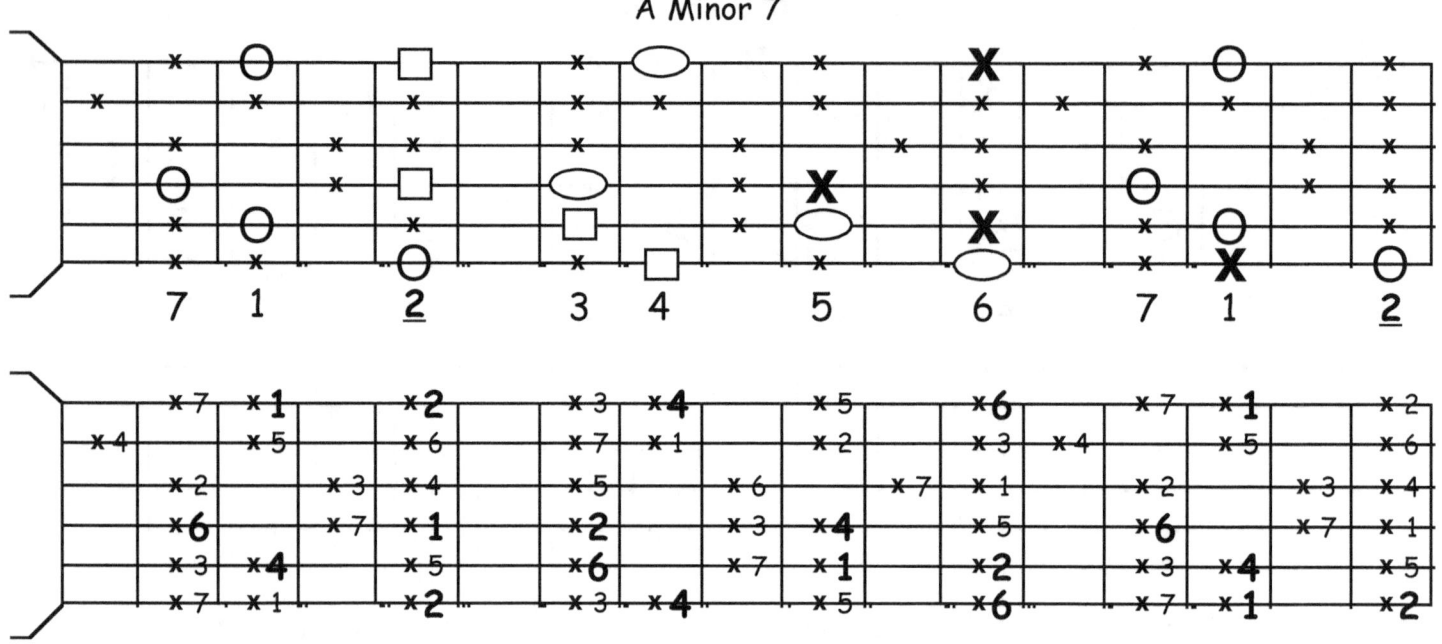

The only notes that you play are: 2, 4, 6, and 1 of the G major scale.

The "3" Chord: Minor 7 Inversions In "G" Major
B Minor 7

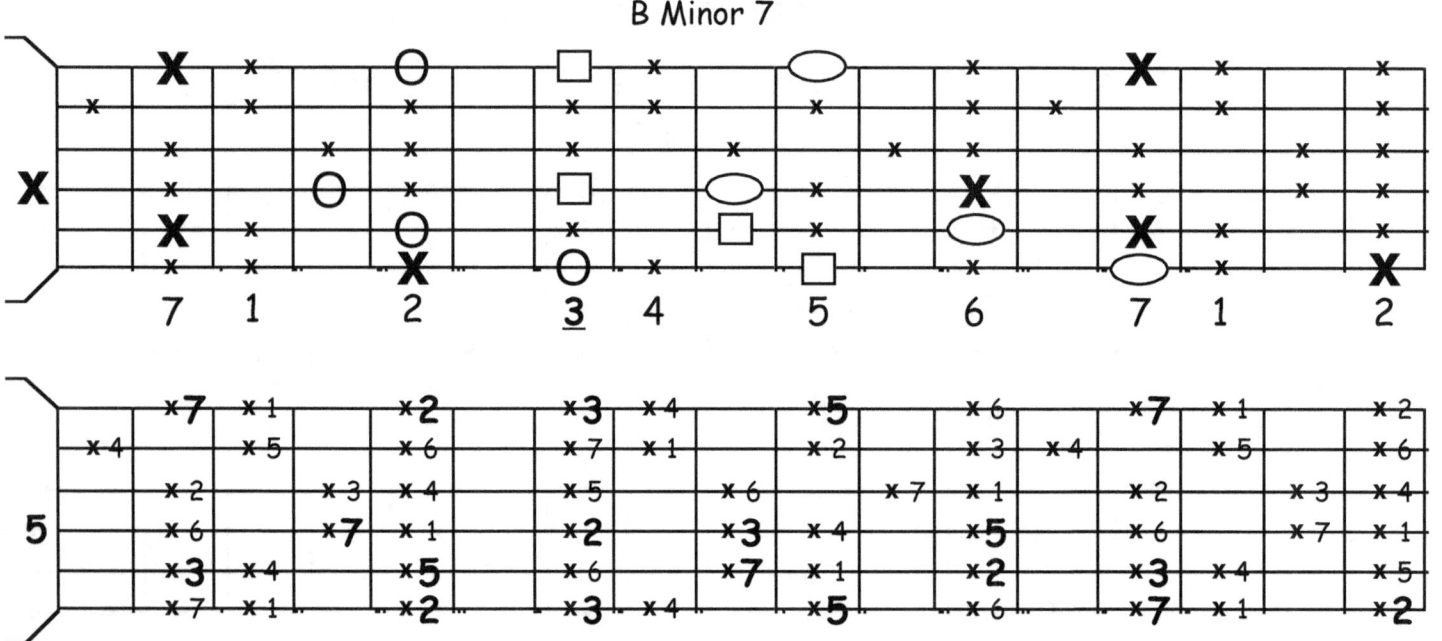

The only notes that you play are: 3, 5, 7, and 2 of the G major scale.

6541 STRING GROUPING
The "4" Chord: Major 7 Inversions In "G" Major
C Major 7

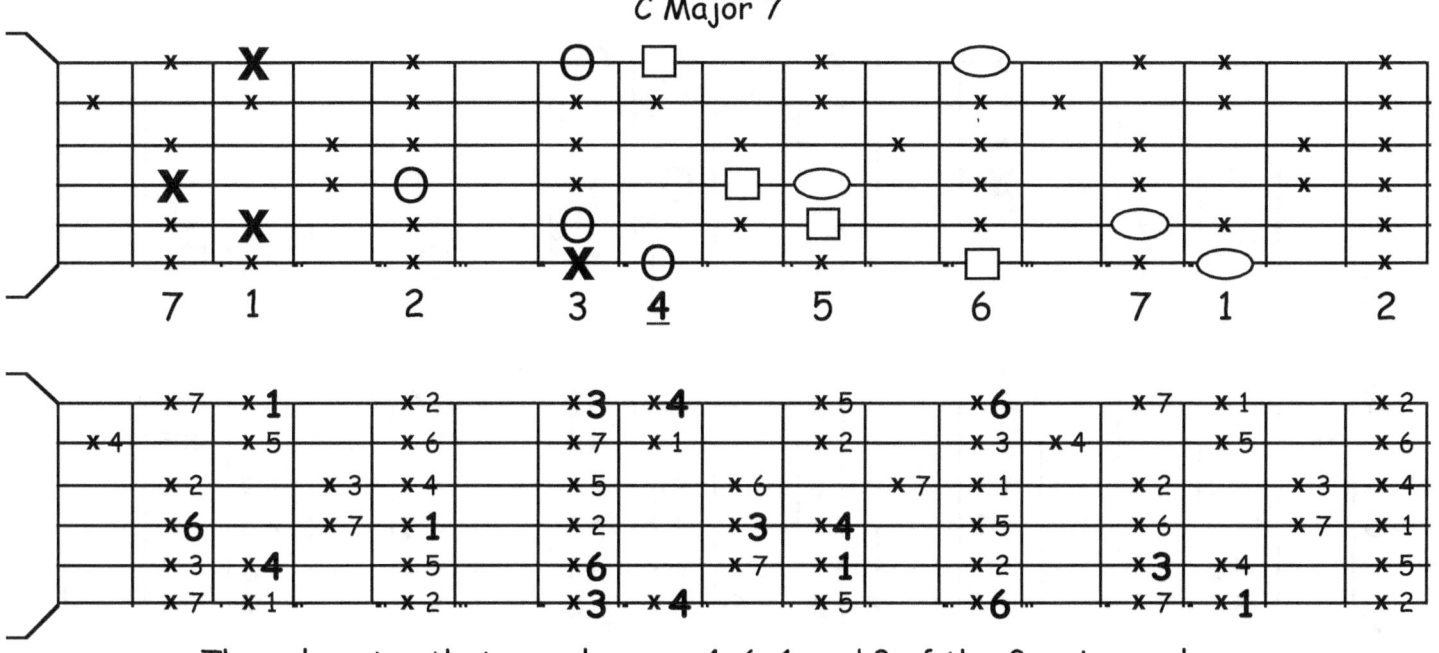

The only notes that you play are: 4, 6, 1, and 3 of the G major scale.

The "5" Chord: Dominant 7 Inversions In "G" Major
D Dominant 7

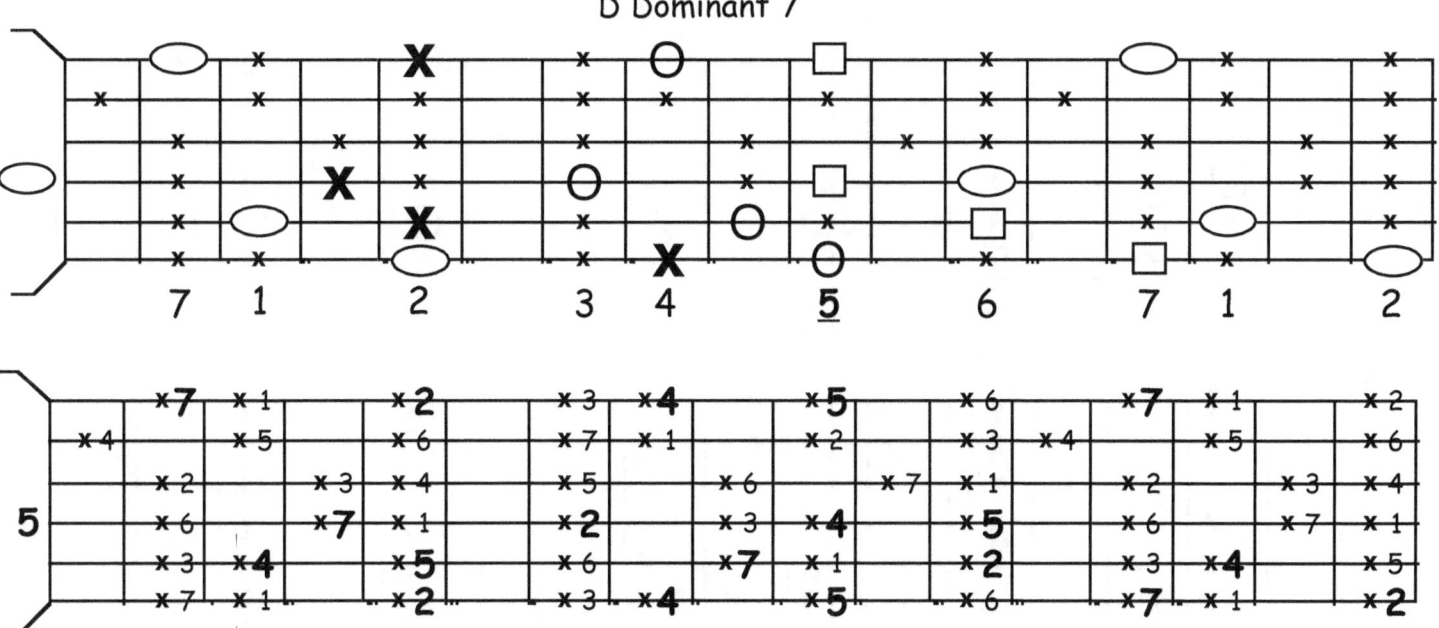

The only notes that you play are: 5, 7, 2, and 4 of the G major scale.

6541 STRING GROUPING

The "6" Chord: Minor 7 Inversions In "G" Major
E Minor 7

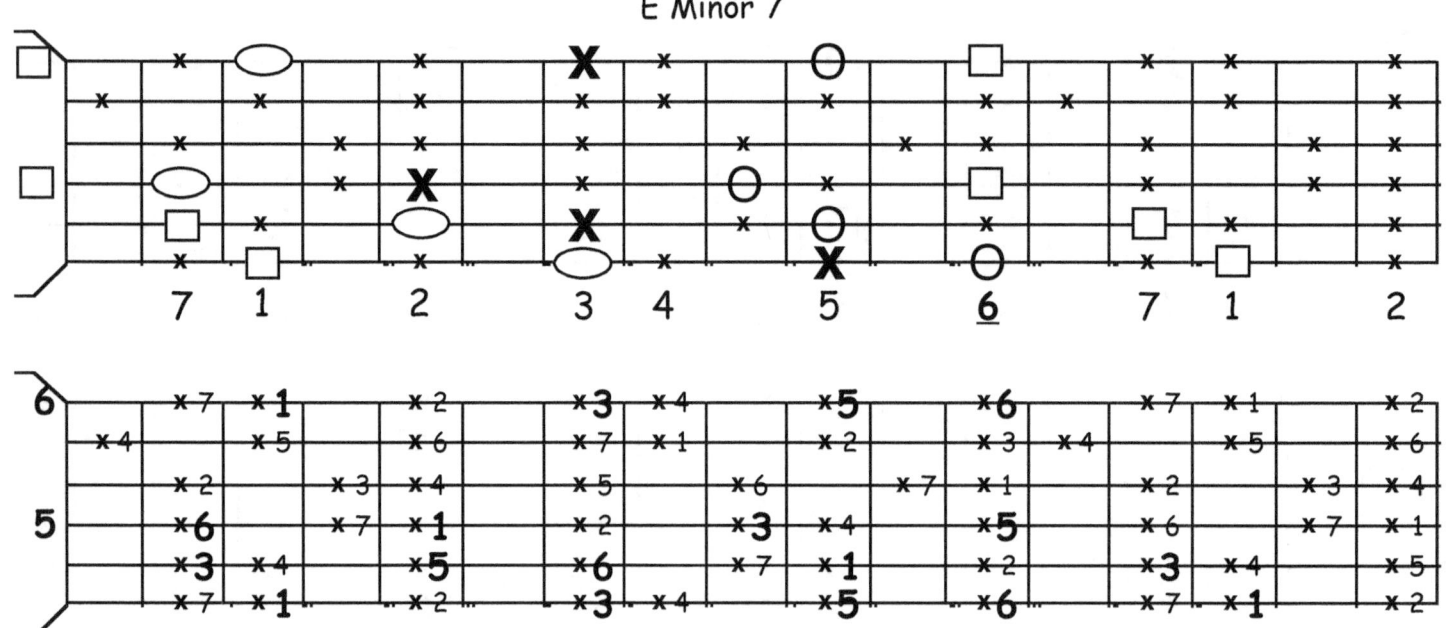

The only notes that you play are: 6, 1, 3, and 5 of the G major scale.

The "7" Chord: Minor 7b5 Inversions In "G" Major
F# Minor 7b5

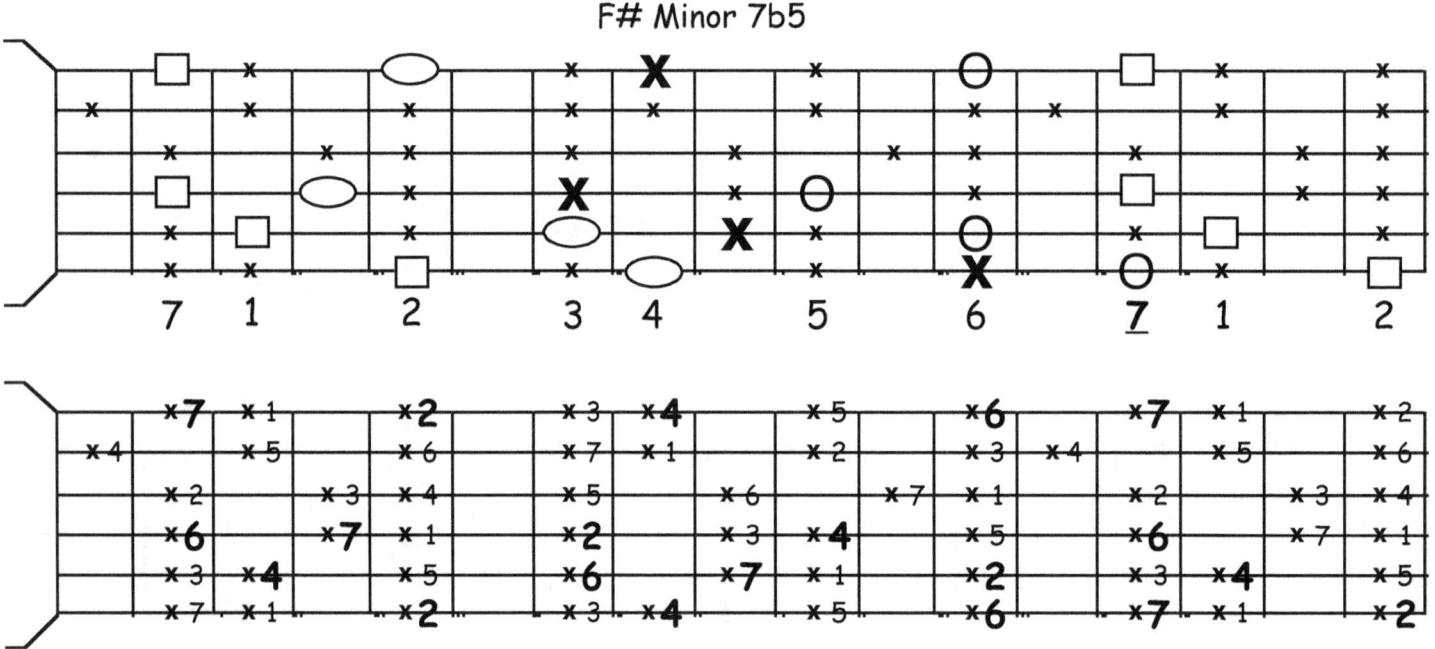

The only notes that you play are: 7, 2, 4, and 6 of the G major scale.

DOUBLE DROP 2 & DROP 4:
6521 STRING GROUPING
The "1" Chord: Major 7 Inversions In "G" Major
G Major 7

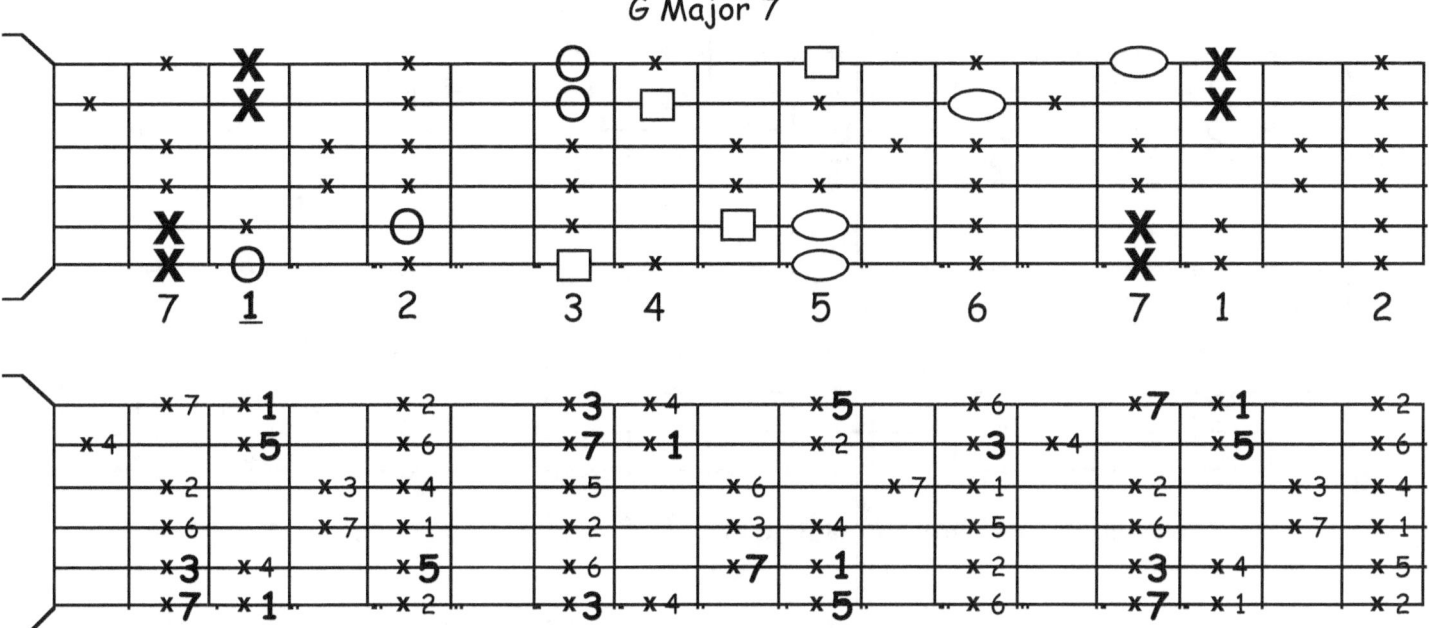

The only notes that you play are: 1, 3, 5, and 7 of the G major scale.

The "2" Chord: Minor 7 Inversions In "G" Major
A Minor 7

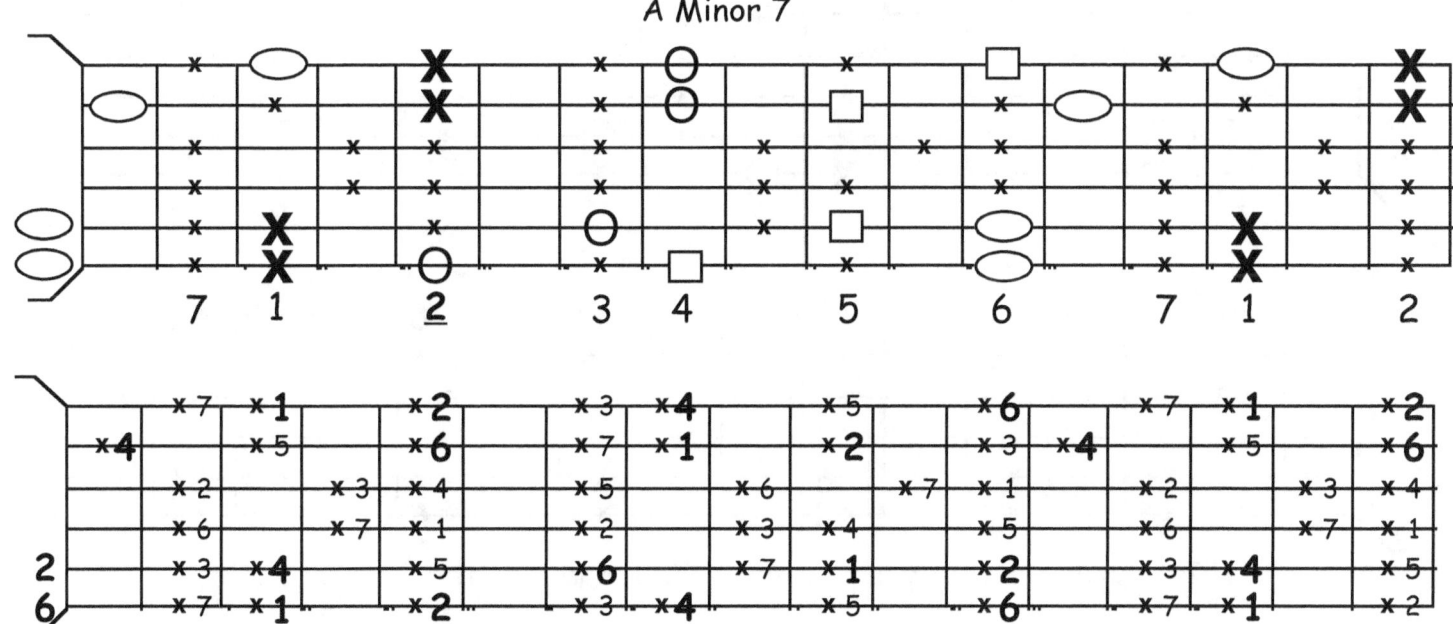

The only notes that you play are: 2, 4, 6, and 1 of the G major scale.

6521 STRING GROUPING

The "3" Chord: Minor 7 Inversions In "G" Major

B Minor 7

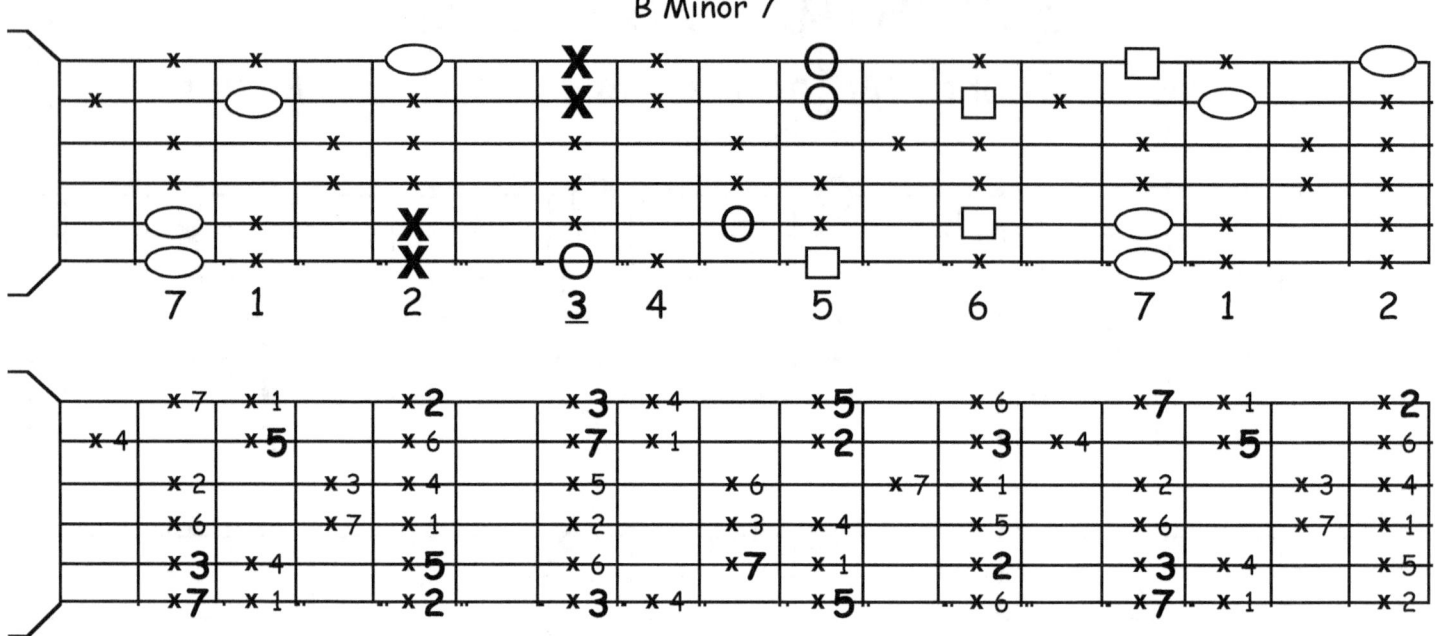

The only notes that you play are: 3, 5, 7, and 2 of the G major scale.

The "4" Chord: Major 7 Inversions In "G" Major

C Major 7

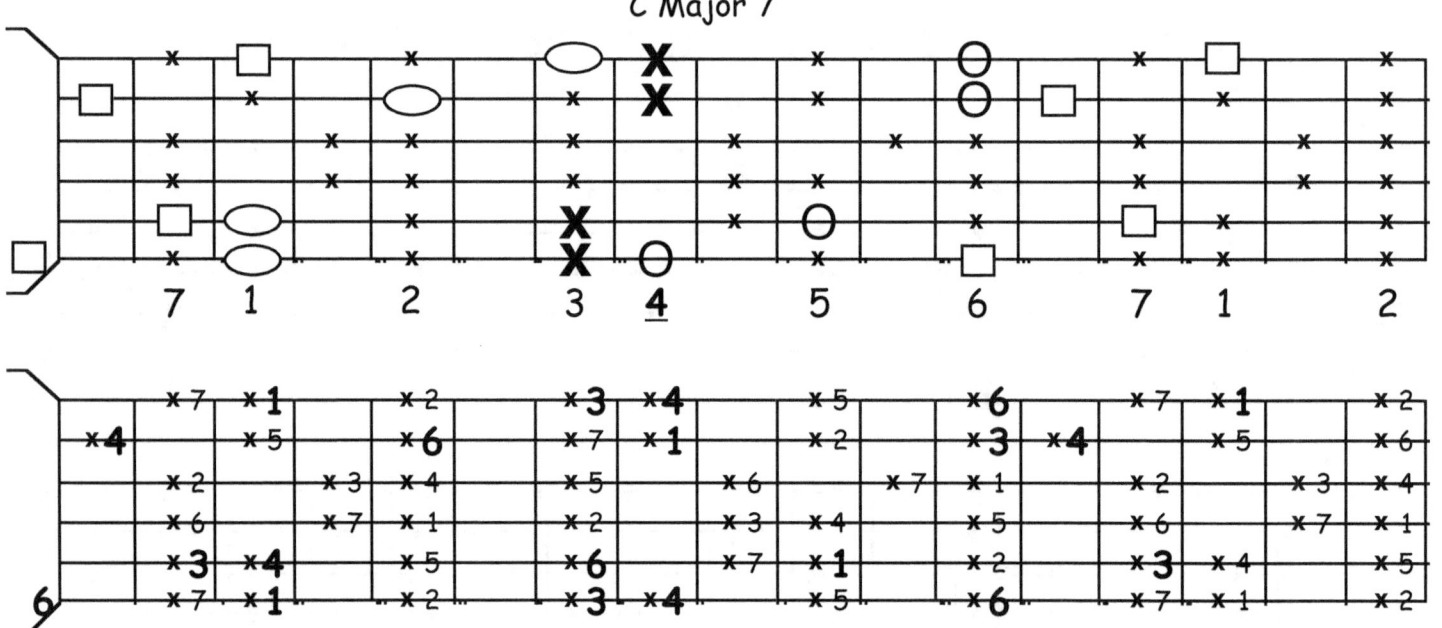

The only notes that you play are: 4, 6, 1, and 3 of the G major scale.

6521 STRING GROUPING

The "5" Chord: Dominant 7 Inversions In "G" Major

D Dominant 7

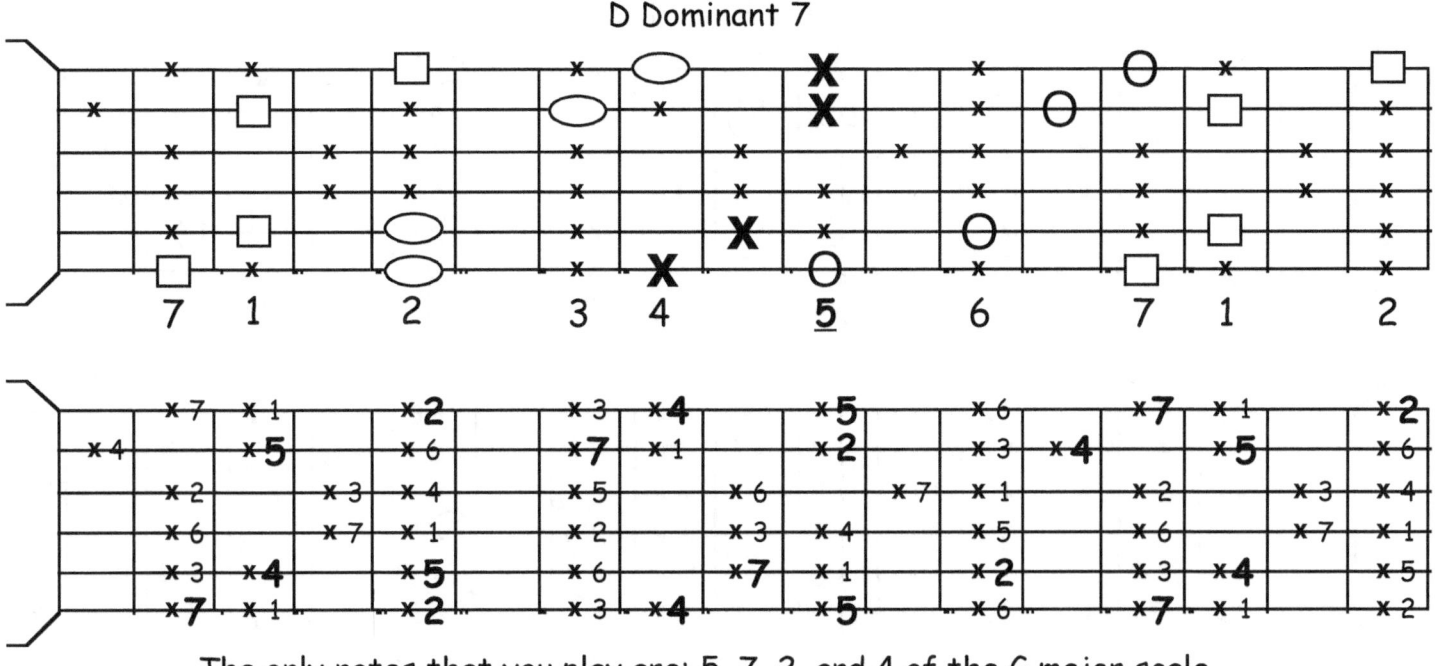

The only notes that you play are: 5, 7, 2, and 4 of the G major scale.

The "6" Chord: Minor 7 Inversions In "G" Major

E Minor 7

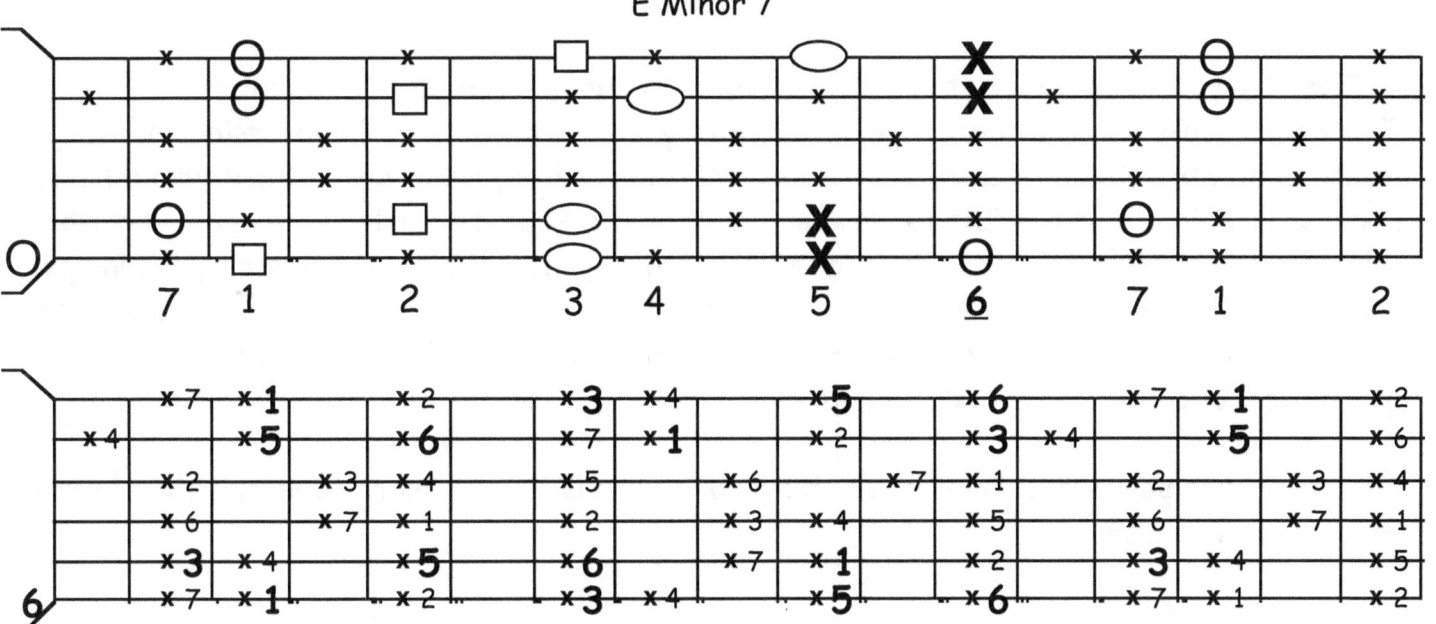

The only notes that you play are: 6, 1, 3, and 5 of the G major scale.

6521 STRING GROUPING
The "7" Chord: Minor 7b5 Inversions In "G" Major
F# Minor 7b5

The only notes that you play are: 7, 2, 4, and 6 of the G major scale.

NOTE: There are plenty of other diatonic seventh chord voicings on the guitar. This book focuses on the chord voicings that allow one to play all of the inversions on the neck. And even with this restriction, there are other voicings that are not presented here. For instance, it is also possible to play Double Drop 2 & Drop 3 chord voicings on the guitar. They are a bit of a stretch and in order to play them, you'll have to switch string groupings for a few of the inversions. Also remember that there are voicings that don't include all four chord tones and voicings that sound amazing by themselves but their inversions are impractical because of the finger stretches.

Of course, the point to learning all of this information is to have more tools and colors with which to make music!

CHORDAL EXTENSIONS

Chords are built from the notes of scales. Seventh chords are four-note chords that contain a root, a third, a fifth, and a seventh. These four notes are the "chord tones" of seventh chords. The first note is the root of the chord. Then, every other note of the scale is included until you have four notes. The chord tone after the root is called the 3rd. The chord tone after the 3rd is called the 5th. The chord tone after the 5th is called the 7th.

So, a G major 7 chord, in the key of G major, would look like this:

G Major Scale: G A B C D E F# G A B C D E F# G

The "G" is the root, the "B" is the 3rd, the "D" is the 5th, and the "F#" is the 7th.

The notes in between these chord tones can be added to the chord to add different colors to the basic chord. These "non-chord tones" are called extensions. For the most part, they add new colors to the basic chord without altering the function of the chord.

In the above example, the "non-chord tones" are:

"A" is called the 2nd or the 9th
"C" is called the 4th or the 11th
"E" is called the 6th or the 13th

Usually, the "A" is referred to as the 9th, BUT, sometimes you'll see "add 2" in a chord chart. These numbers are interchangeable.

Generally speaking, the "C" is called the 4th if the 3rd of the chord is not included in the chord voicing, i.e., "sus4". If the 3rd of the chord is included in the voicing, then the 4th is usually called the 11th.

The "E" is usually called the 6th if there is no 7th in the chord (so the chord just has a root, 3rd, 5th, and 6th). If there is a 7th in the chord, then the 6th is referred to as the 13th.

The challenge for guitar players is that we really only have four fingers available to play these chords on the neck of the guitar. So, sometimes we have to eliminate one of the "chord tones" in order to add one of these extensions to the chord. When playing an inversion that calls for the eliminated chord tone in the bass, the "extension" note will be the note in the bass.

9th (add 2) CHORDS

When playing a seventh chord, your fingers are on the root, the 3rd, the 5th, and the 7th of that chord. In order to include the 9th, one of the chord tones (hence one of your fingers) has to shift and play the note that is the 9th. The two notes that are closest to the 9th are the root and the 3rd. While it might seem counterintuitive, the root is the note that is more expendable. The 3rd of a chord gives the chord a lot of its color and strongly defines the chord's function. If a chord's function is clear, its root is not so important.

Now here's an interesting twist of events. If you shift your fingers, so that the finger that was playing the root is now playing the 9th, you will then actually be playing a different chord altogether. If we use the numbers of the major scale, you can see how this works. The major scale has seven different notes in it before the numbers start all over again in the next octave:

    Major Scale: 1 2 3 4 5 6 7 1 2 3 4 5 6 7

When you build chords, you build them with every other note of the scale. So a "1" chord is spelled 1, 3, 5, 7:

    "1" Chord: **1** 2 **3** 4 **5** 6 **7** 1 2 3 4 5 6 7

In order to turn this into a 9th chord, you can move the root of this chord (the 1) up to the 9th of this chord (the 2). And if you move the 1 up to the 2, you would then be playing a chord that is spelled: 2, 3, 5, 7. AND if you look at this set of numbers closely, you'll see that these are the exact same numbers that you need to create a "3" chord; 3, 5, 7, 2:

    "3" Chord: 1 2 **3** 4 **5** 6 **7** 1 **2** 3 4 5 6 7

What this means is that the "3" chord (minor 7 chord) can act as a "1" chord (major 9 chord). Another way of saying this is that the "3" chord can SUBSTITUTE for the "1" chord. AND if it does, it turns the "1" chord from a major 7 chord into a major 9 chord.

NOT ONLY can this happen for the "1" chord, but it can also happen to any of the other chords. So, if you want to turn any seventh chord into a 9th chord, and you understand how the seventh chord fits into a scale, you just play the diatonic seventh chord that is two chords up from the given chord:

                    Given "1" chord ... play "3" chord
                    Given "2" chord ... play "4" chord
                    Given "3" chord ... play "5" chord
                    Given "4" chord ... play "6" chord

Because guitar players are limited in the notes that we can play on the neck, this system works well. Are there other ways of playing 9th chords? YES. But this book is big enough!

6th CHORDS

In music theory, if you play a chord that has only a root, a 3rd, and a 5th, and you add the 6th to it, it is called a 6th chord. If you have a chord that has a root, a 3rd, a 5th, and a 7th, AND you add the 6th to it, it is called a 13th chord.

If you are asked to play a 6th chord and you only know your seventh chords, fear not! You actually know more than you think that you know. When playing a seventh chord, the two notes that are closest to the 6th are the 5th and the 7th. If you raise the 5th to the 6th, you'll end up with a 13th chord (because you'll still have the 7th in the chord). So, you should drop the 7th to the 6th instead. And if you do this, you'll actually be playing a different chord altogether. If we use the numbers of the major scale, you can see how this works. The major scale has seven different notes in it before the numbers start all over again in the next octave:

    Major Scale: 1 2 3 4 5 6 7 1 2 3 4 5 6 7

When you build chords, you build them with every other note of the scale. So a "1" chord is spelled 1, 3, 5, 7:

    "1" Chord: 1 2 **3** 4 **5** 6 **7** 1 2 3 4 5 6 7

In order to turn this into a 6th chord, you have to move the 7th down to the 6th. And if you move the 7 down to the 6, you would then be playing a chord that is spelled: 1, 3, 5, 6. AND if you look at this set of numbers closely, you'll see that these are the exact same numbers that you need to create a "6" chord; 6, 1, 3, 5:

    "6" Chord: 1 2 3 4 5 **6** 7 **1** 2 **3** 4 **5** 6 7

What this means is that the "6" chord (minor 7 chord) can act as a "1" chord (major 6 chord). Another way of saying this is that the "6" chord can SUBSTITUTE for the "1" chord. AND if it does, it turns the "1" chord from a major 7 chord into a major 6 chord.

NOT ONLY can this happen for the "1" chord, but it can also happen to any of the other chords. So, if you want to turn any seventh chord into a 6th chord, and you understand how the seventh chord fits into a scale, you just play the diatonic seventh chord that is two chords down from the given chord:

        Given "1" chord ... play "6" chord (counting down: 1...7...6)

        Given "2" chord ... play "7" chord (counting down: 2...1...7)

        Given "3" chord ... play "1" chord (counting down: 3...2...1)

        Given "4" chord ... play "2" chord (counting down: 4...3...2)

Are there other ways of playing 6th chords? YES. But, again, this book is big enough!

11th (sus4) CHORDS

If you're given a seventh chord and you want to add the note that appears between the 3rd and the 5th, this note is either called a 4th or an 11th. In general, if you raise the 3rd to play the 4th (eliminating the 3rd) it is called a sus4 chord. If the 5th is lowered to play the 4th (eliminating the 5th and keeping the 3rd in the chord voicing), it is called an 11th chord.

There are only four basic types of seventh chords: major 7, minor 7, dominant 7, and minor 7b5. Usually, major 7 and minor 7b5 chords don't get played as sus4 or 11th chords. The reason for this is that adding the 4th (or 11th) to these chords dramatically changes the color and function of these chords. Is it ever done? Yes … but not frequently.

I've only presented the diagrams for the "2" minor 11 chords (including the underlined root on the low E string) which are THE SAME as all of the "5" dominant 7(sus4) chords (no underlined root on the low E string). These are the two most commonly used 11th or sus4 chords AND, they share the same set of physical shapes. So, both the shapes and the fingerings are the same. The only difference is how the fingered notes function within each of these chords. I have only included 13 sets of these chords because the other voicings are physically impractical for the left hand. I have not taken the space to draw out the "3" minor 11 or the "6" minor 11 chords. The "3" minor 11 chords are exactly the same as the "2" minor 11 chords, only 2 frets up the neck of the guitar. And the "6" minor 11 chords are exactly the same as the "2" minor 11 chords, only down 5 frets on the neck of the guitar. AND, just in case you're curious, the "7" minor 7b5(11th) chords are exactly the same as the "2" minor 11th chords just down 3 frets on the neck of the guitar. HOWEVER, this version of these chords eliminates the "b5" sound, which changes the color/function of this chord.

13th CHORDS

The 13th is the note that comes between the 5th and the 7th of a chord. If we were to drop the 7th of the chord in order to include this note in our voicing, we would really be playing a 6th chord (which has a slightly different color than a 13th chord). If we raise the 5th of the chord up to the 6th, we would still have the 7th in the chord voicing, so this 6th pitch would now be called a 13th. This gives us a chord that includes: root, 3rd, 13th, and 7th. If the 13th is nine half steps above the root, it is simply called a 13th chord. If the 13th is eight half steps above the root, it is called a 7th chord with a flat 13th (b13). I have only presented 10 sets of these 13th chords because the other voicings are physically impractical for the left hand. **NOTE:** The diatonic "7" chord (min7b5) will lose its "b5" sound.

MINOR 11 & DOMINANT 7(sus4) CHORDS

For A Minor 11:
- O = Root Position Minor 11
- □ = First Inversion Minor 11
- ⬯ = Second Inversion Minor 11 (11th in bass)
- X = Third Inversion Minor 11

For D Dominant7(sus4):
- O = Second Inversion Dom.7(sus4)
- □ = Third Inversion Dom.7(sus4)
- ⬯ = Root Position Dom.7(sus4)
- X = First Inversion Dom.7(sus4) (4th in bass)

The "2" Chord: Minor 11 Inversions In "G" Major
The "5" Chord: Dominant 7(sus4) Inversions In "G" Major
The only notes that you play are the 2, 4, 5, 1 or the 5, 1, 2, 4 of the G major scale.

DROP 2
6543 STRING GROUPING
A Minor 11 & D Dominant 7(sus4)

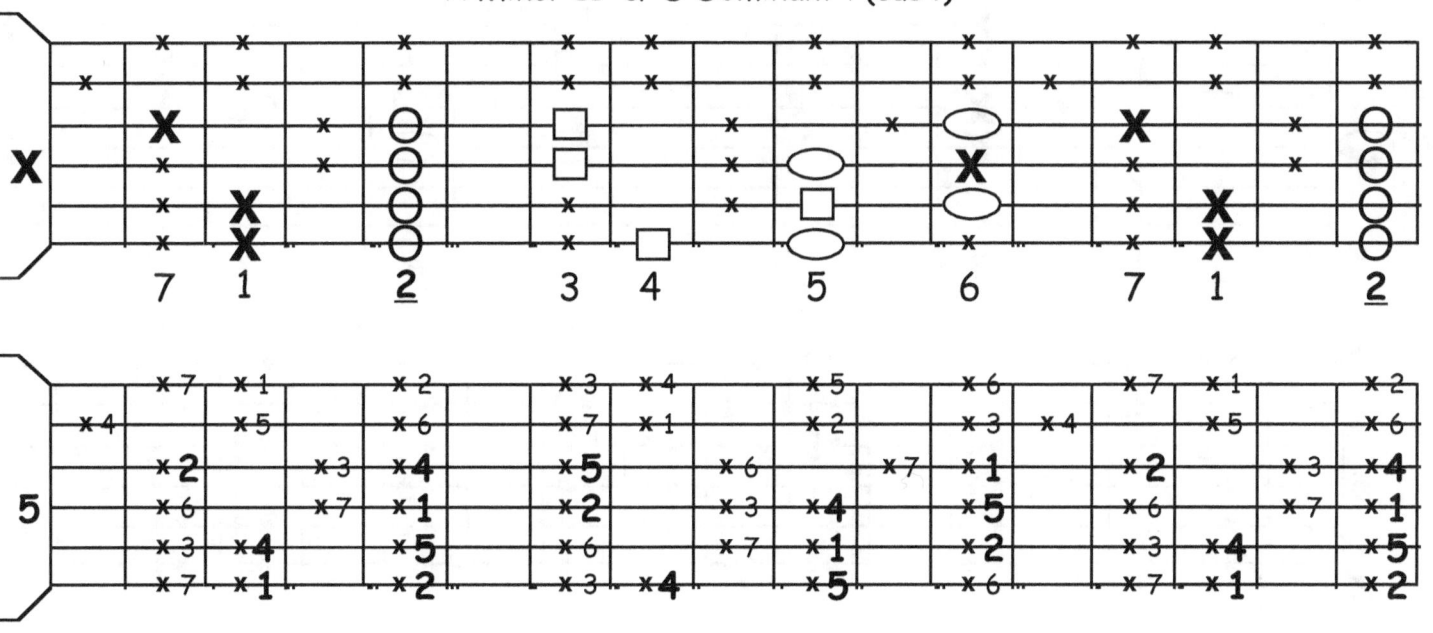

The "2" Chord: Minor 11 Inversions In "G" Major
The "5" Chord: Dominant 7(sus4) Inversions In "G" Major

The only notes that you play are the 2, 4, 5, 1 or the 5, 1, 2, 4 of the G major scale.

5432 STRING GROUPING
A Minor 11 & D Dominant 7(sus4)

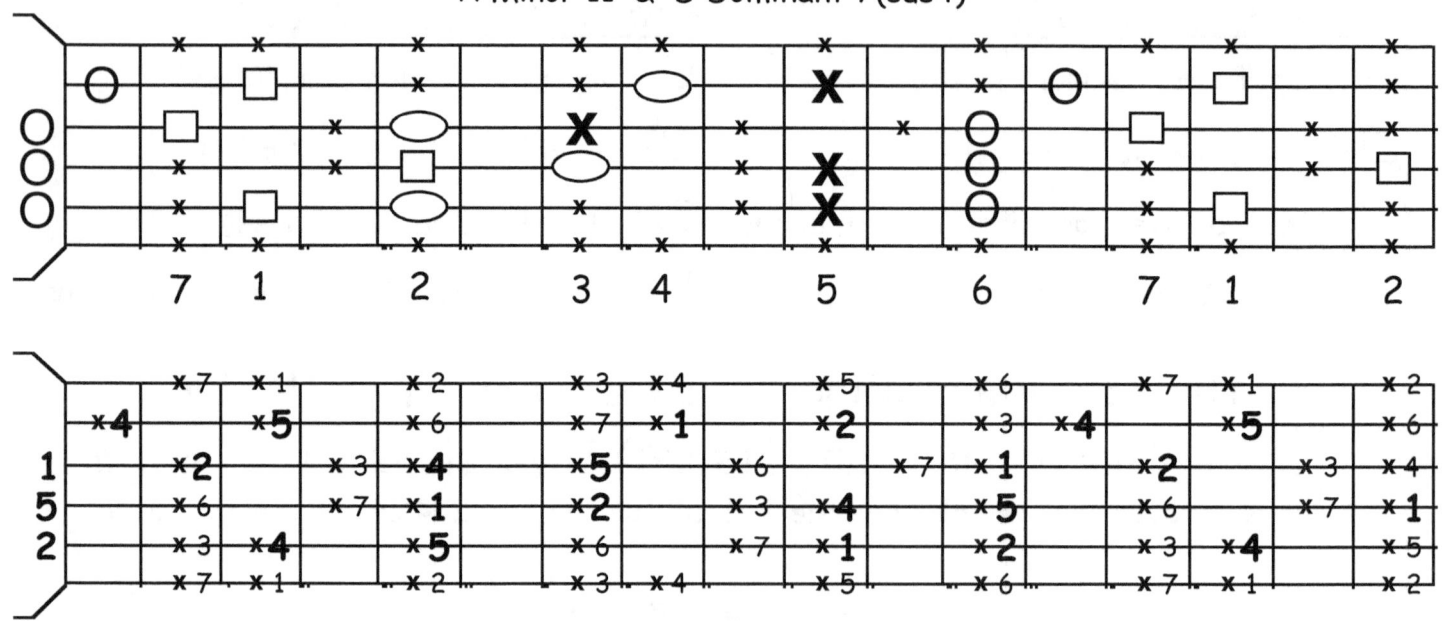

4321 STRING GROUPING
A Minor 11 & D Dominant 7(sus4)

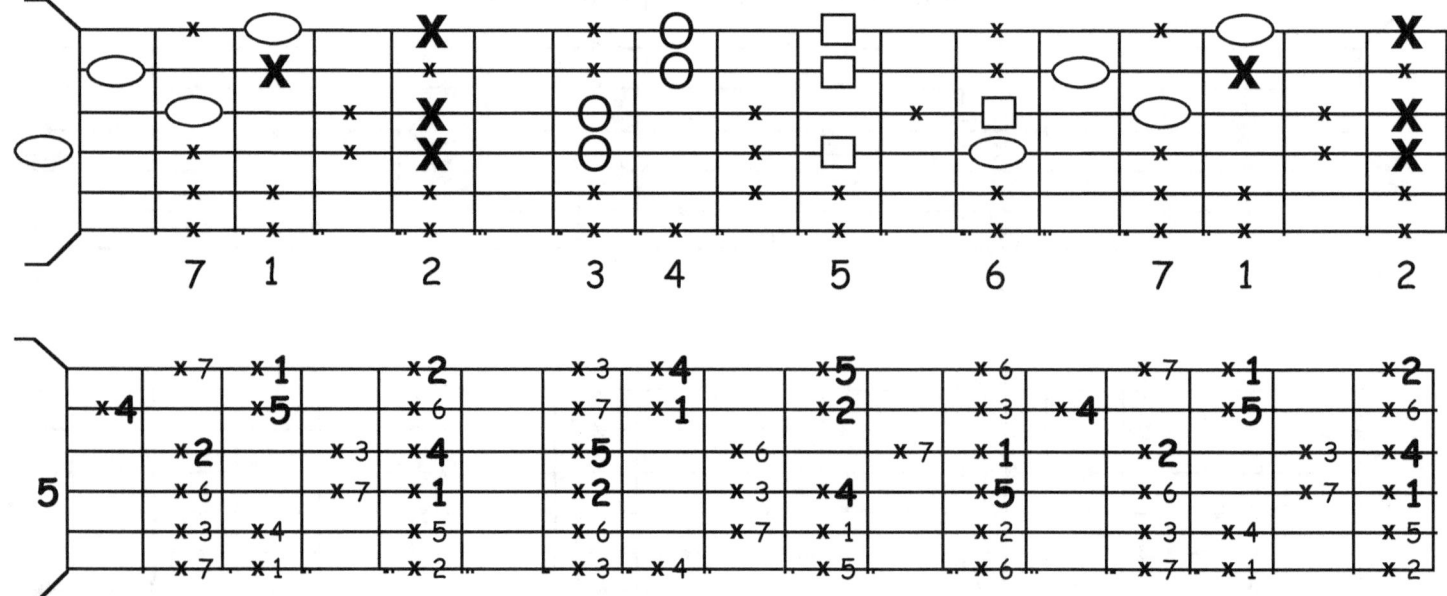

The "2" Chord: Minor 11 Inversions In "G" Major
The "5" Chord: Dominant 7(sus4) Inversions In "G" Major

The only notes that you play are the 2, 4, 5, 1 or the 5, 1, 2, 4 of the G major scale.

DROP 3

6432 STRING GROUPING
A Minor 11 & D Dominant 7(sus4)

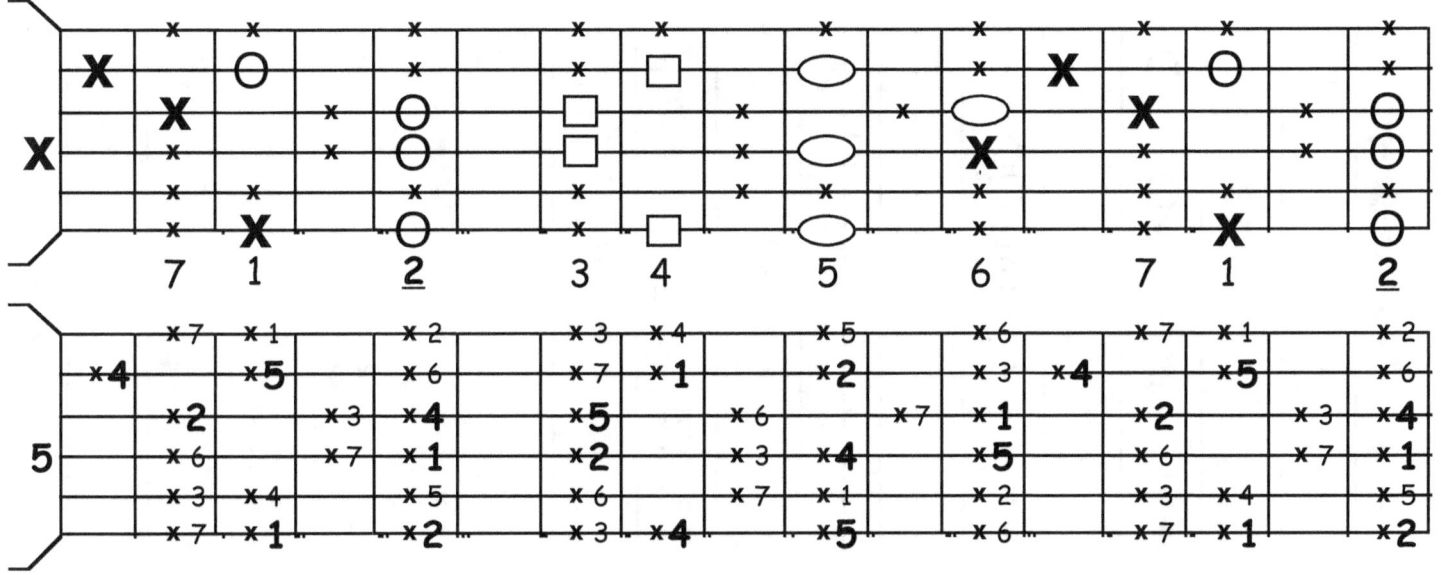

5321 STRING GROUPING
A Minor 11 & D Dominant 7(sus4)

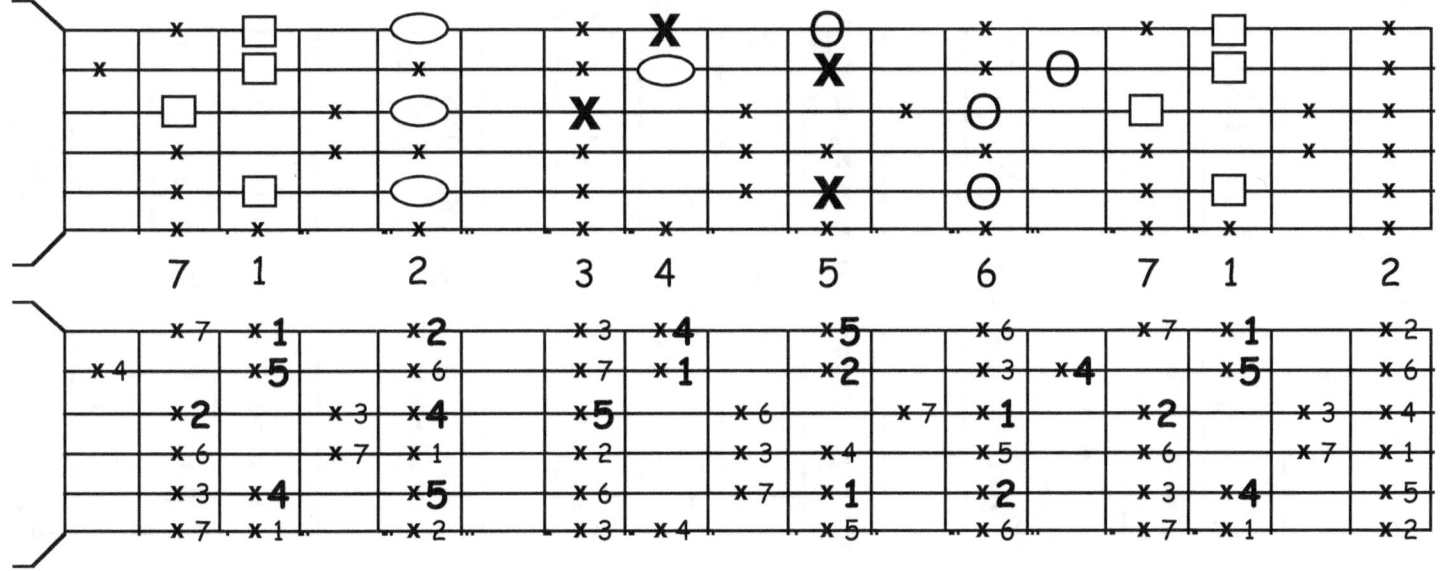

The "2" Chord: Minor 11 Inversions In "G" Major
The "5" Chord: Dominant 7(sus4) Inversions In "G" Major

The only notes that you play are the 2, 4, 5, 1 or the 5, 1, 2, 4 of the G major scale.

DROP 2 & 3

6542 STRING GROUPING
A Minor 11 & D Dominant 7(sus4)

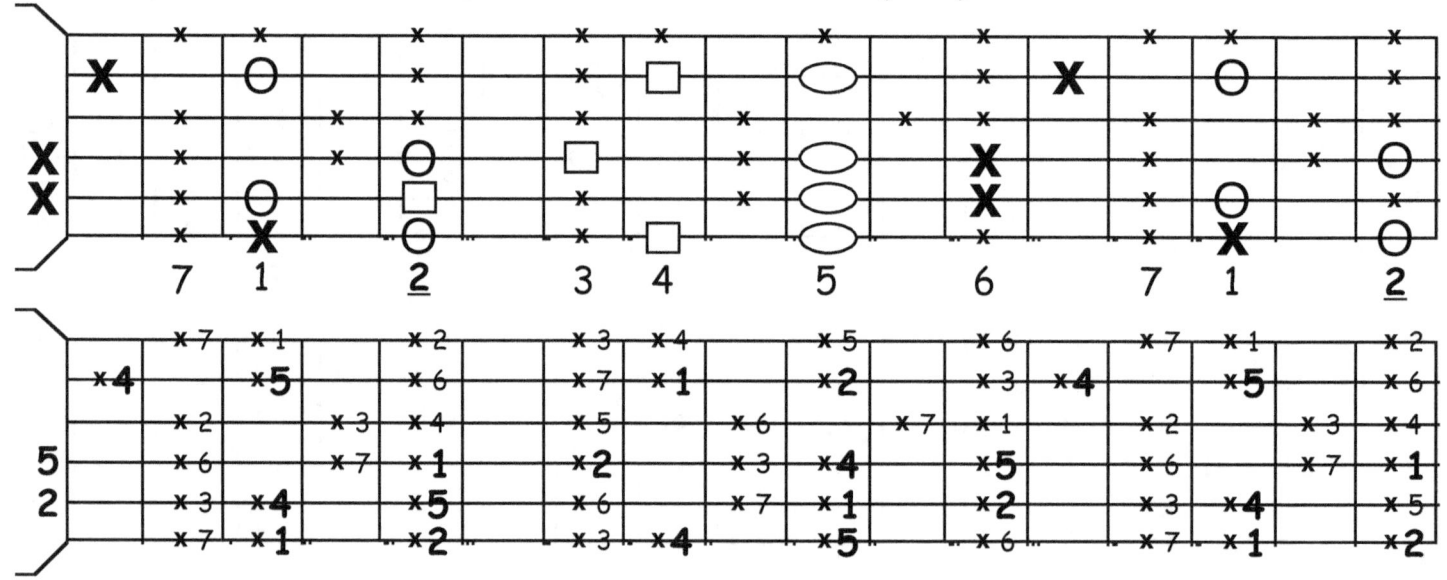

5431 STRING GROUPING
A Minor 11 & D Dominant 7(sus4)

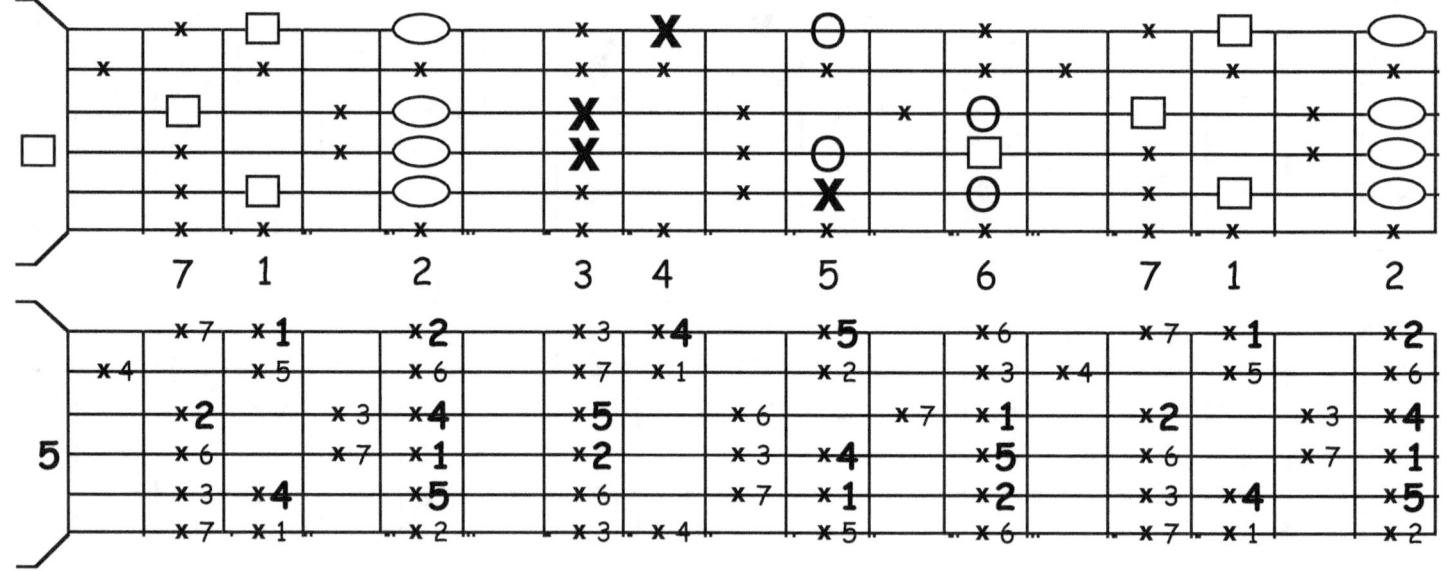

The "2" Chord: Minor 11 Inversions In "G" Major
The "5" Chord: Dominant 7(sus4) Inversions In "G" Major

The only notes that you play are the 2, 4, 5, 1 or the 5, 1, 2, 4 of the G major scale.

DROP 4
6321 STRING GROUPING
A Minor 11 & D Dominant 7(sus4)

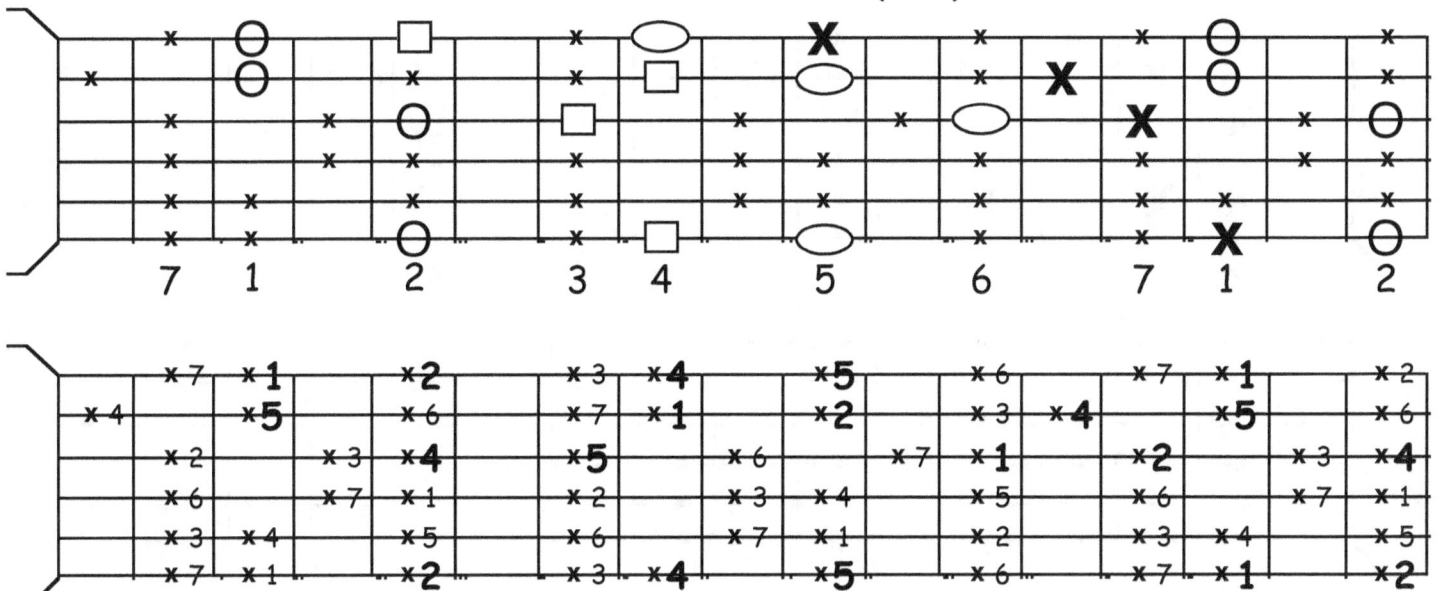

NOTE:
You'll notice that there aren't any closed voicings included in this "Chordal Extensions" section or in the next "Altered Seventh Chord" section. They were included in the earlier "Diatonic Seventh Chords" section of this book primarily because these are the voicings that are initially taught in traditional music theory classes. Many guitar players enroll in these classes thinking that they'll come away with a greater understanding of how music theory works on the neck of the guitar. Unfortunately, because of the fingering difficulties, these chords have a fairly limited use for guitarists (unless you use the tapping technique).

As I mentioned in the beginning "NOTES" section of this book, some of the drop 4, some of the drop 3 & 4, and most of the drop 2, 3, & 4 chord voicings can be awkward or even impossible to finger (unless you're using the tapping technique). HOWEVER, many of these voicings *are* playable. And whether you play all of the notes in these voicings or just some of them, use your ears to determine which ones you like and when to use them. OK, here are the rest of the Minor 11/Dominant 7(sus4) chord inversions.

The "2" Chord: Minor 11 Inversions In "G" Major
The "5" Chord: Dominant 7(sus4) Inversions In "G" Major

The only notes that you play are the 2, 4, 5, 1 or the 5, 1, 2, 4 of the G major scale.

DROP 2 & 4

6532 STRING GROUPING
A Minor 11 & D Dominant 7(sus4)

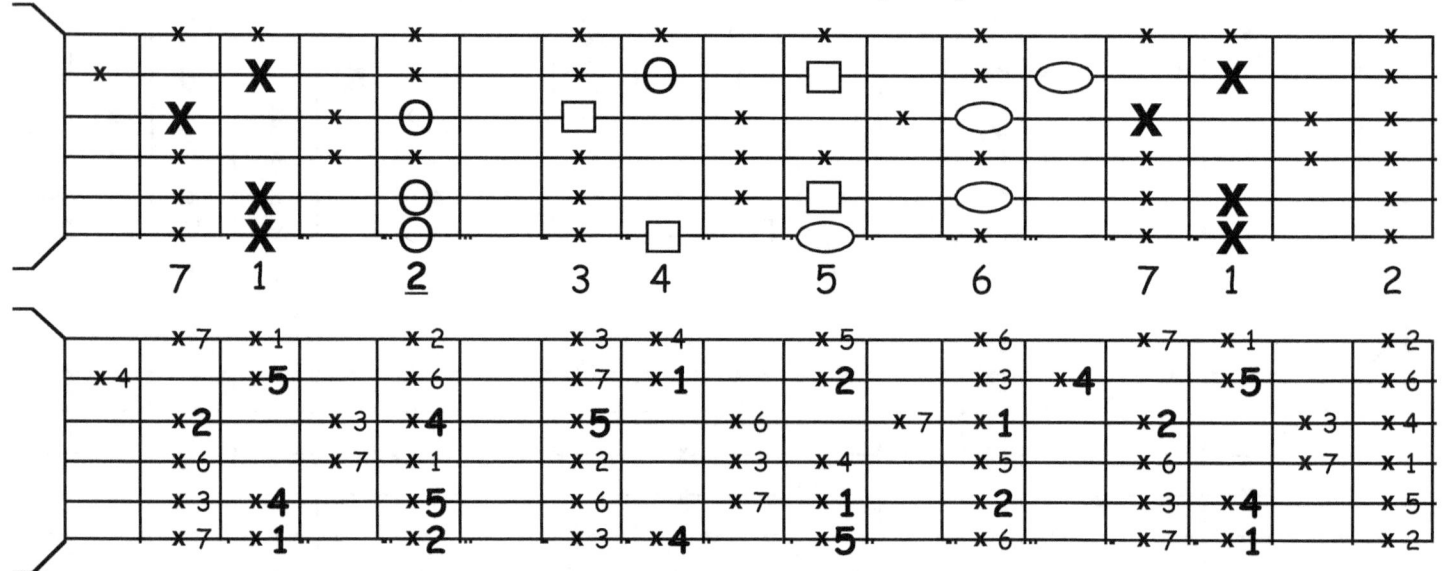

5421 STRING GROUPING
A Minor 11 & D Dominant 7(sus4)

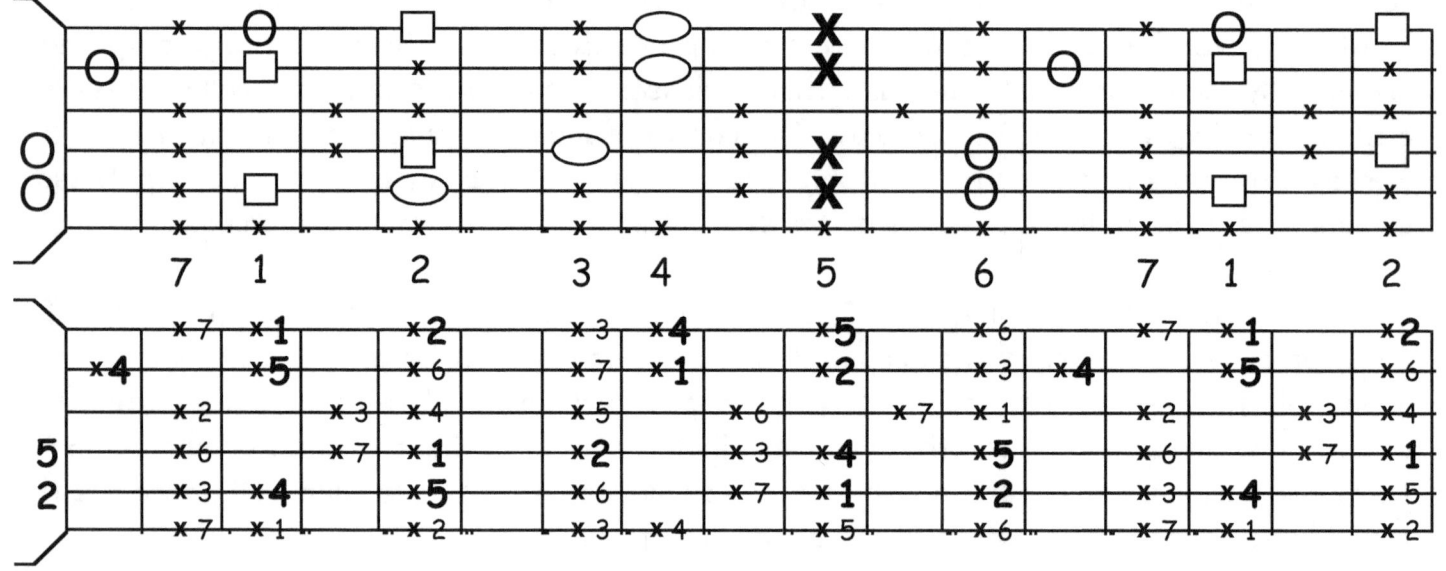

The "2" Chord: Minor 11 Inversions In "G" Major
The "5" Chord: Dominant 7(sus4) Inversions In "G" Major

The only notes that you play are the 2, 4, 5, 1 or the 5, 1, 2, 4 of the G major scale.

DROP 3 & 4
6521 STRING GROUPING
A Minor 11 & D Dominant 7(sus4)

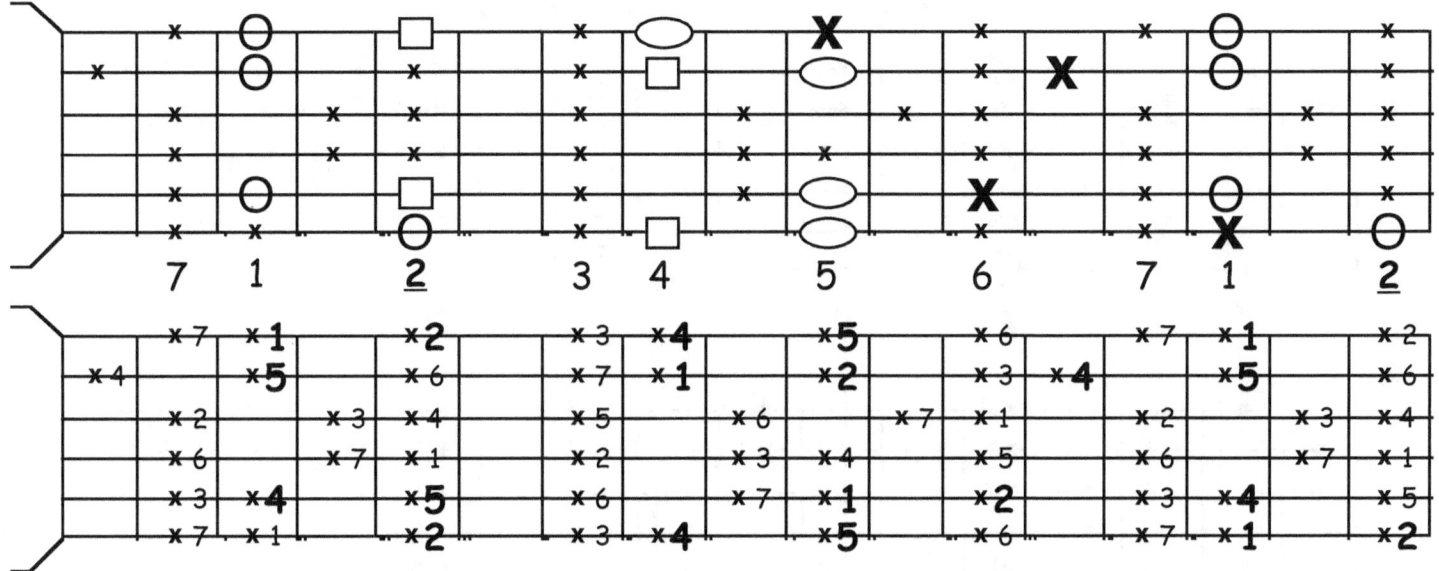

DROP 2, 3 & 4
6541 STRING GROUPING
A Minor 11 & D Dominant 7(sus4)

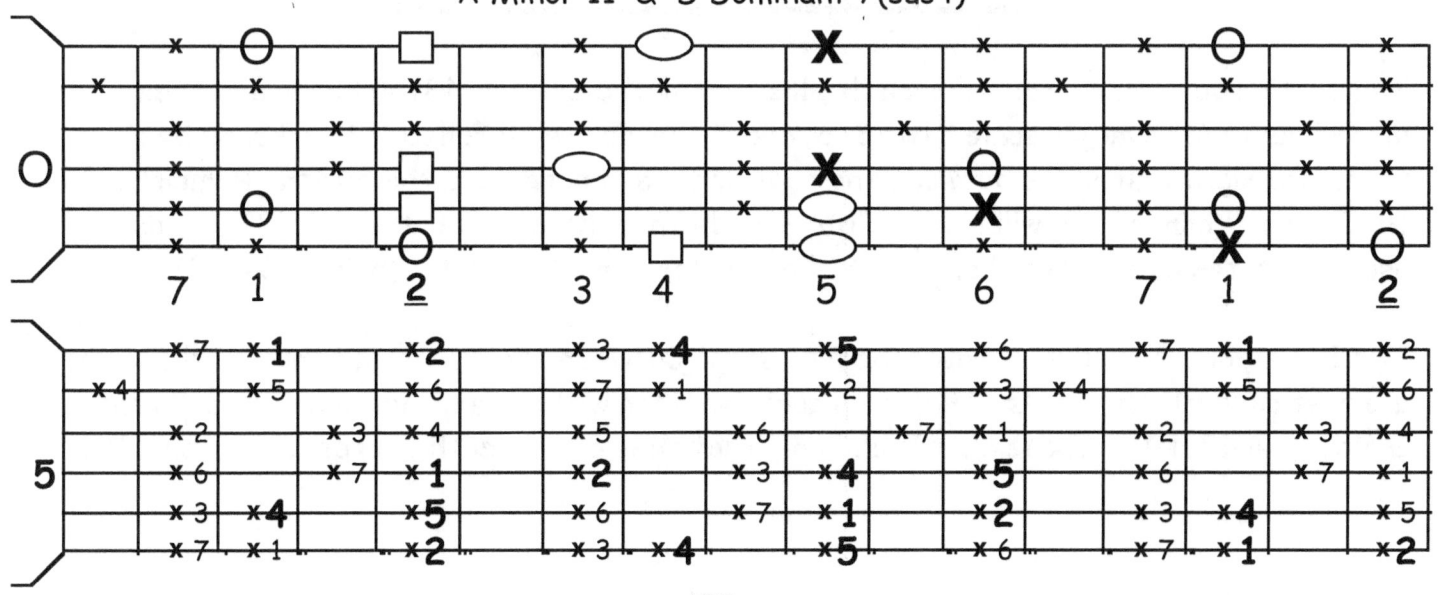

The "2" Chord: Minor 11 Inversions In "G" Major
The "5" Chord: Dominant 7(sus4) Inversions In "G" Major

The only notes that you play are the 2, 4, 5, 1 or the 5, 1, 2, 4 of the G major scale.

DOUBLE DROP 2 & DROP 4
6521 STRING GROUPING
A Minor 11 & D Dominant 7(sus4)

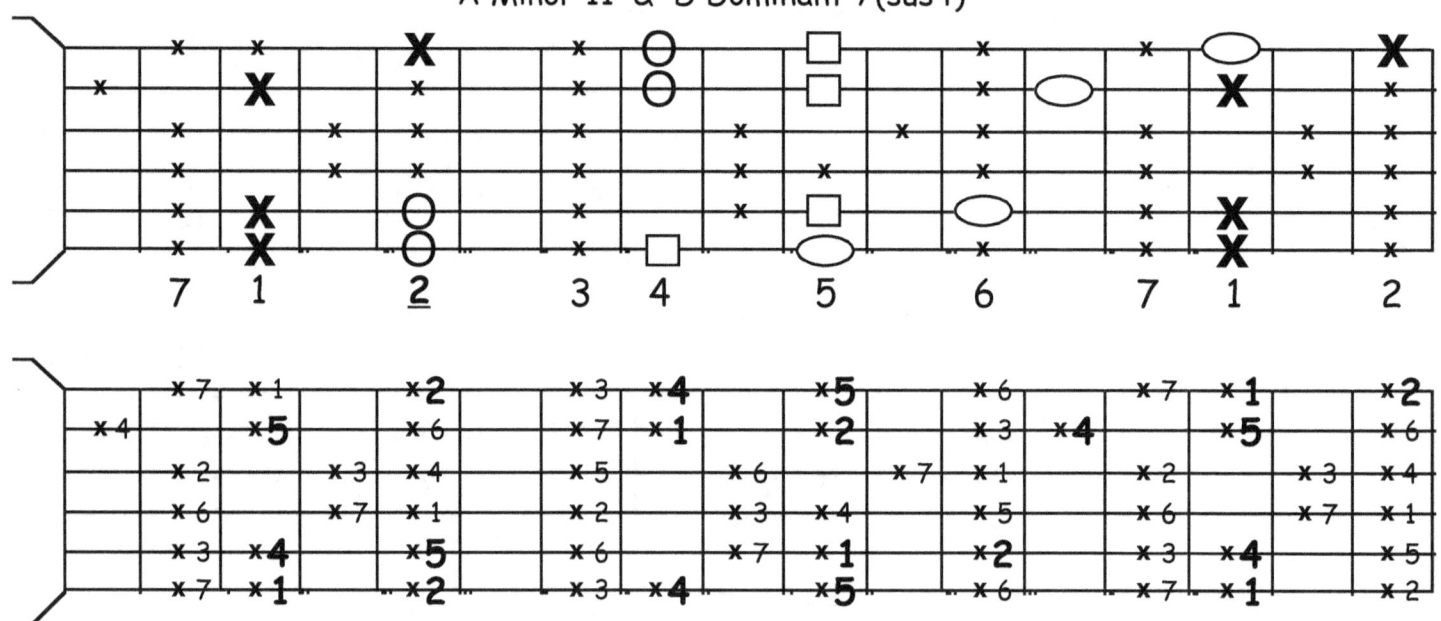

13th CHORDS

The section on 13th chords will include all seven of the diatonic 13th chords and their inversions for the major scale. The 3, 6, and 7 chords are all called "b13" chords because there are eight half steps between the root of these chords and their 13th. Remember that the 7 chord (minor 7b5) will lose its "b5" sound. In a chord chart, these "b13" chords are usually written as seventh chords with the "b13" in parenthesis: B-7(b13), E-7(b13).

The 1, 2, 4, and 5 chords all have nine half steps between their root and their 13th, so they are just called 13th chords. They are usually written without any mention of the seventh: G Maj13, A-13, D13. These chords all imply that they are seventh chords with the added 13th note.

13th CHORDS

○ = Root Position 13th Chord

□ = First Inversion 13th Chord

⬭ = Second Inversion 13th Chord (13th in the bass)

X = Third Inversion 13th Chord

DROP 2

6543 STRING GROUPING

The "1" Chord: Major 13 Inversions In "G" Major

G Major 13

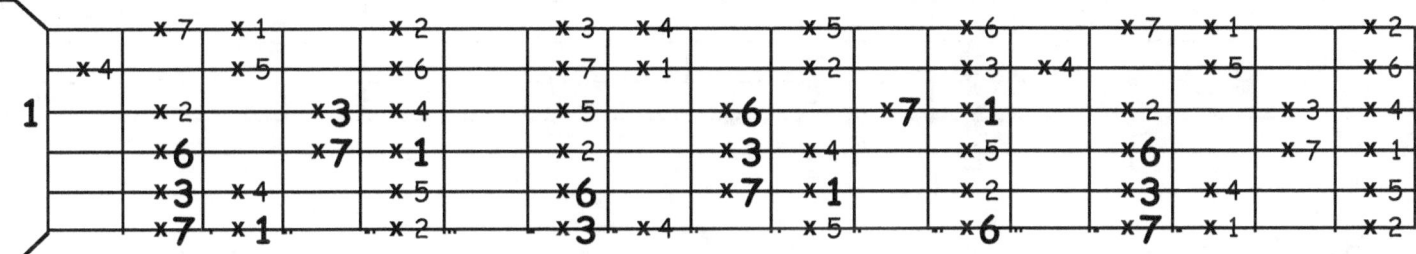

The only notes that you play are: 1, 3, 6, and 7 of the G major scale.

6543 STRING GROUPING

The "2" Chord: Minor 13 Inversions In "G" Major
A Minor 13

The only notes that you play are: 2, 4, 7, and 1 of the G major scale.

The "3" Chord: Minor 7 (b13) Inversions In "G" Major
B Minor 7 (b13)

The only notes that you play are: 3, 5, 1, and 2 of the G major scale.

6543 STRING GROUPING

The "4" Chord: Major 13 Inversions In "G" Major
C Major 13

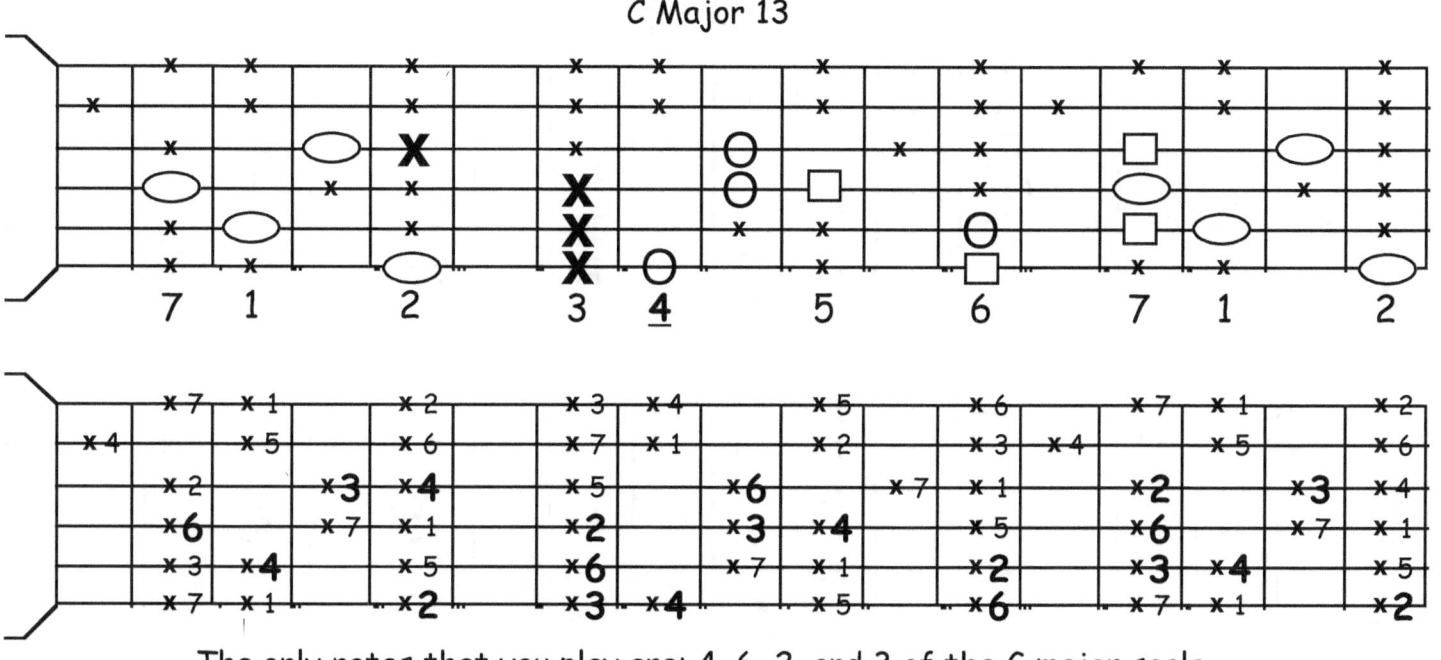

The only notes that you play are: 4, 6, 2, and 3 of the G major scale.

The "5" Chord: Dominant 13 Inversions In "G" Major
D Dominant 13

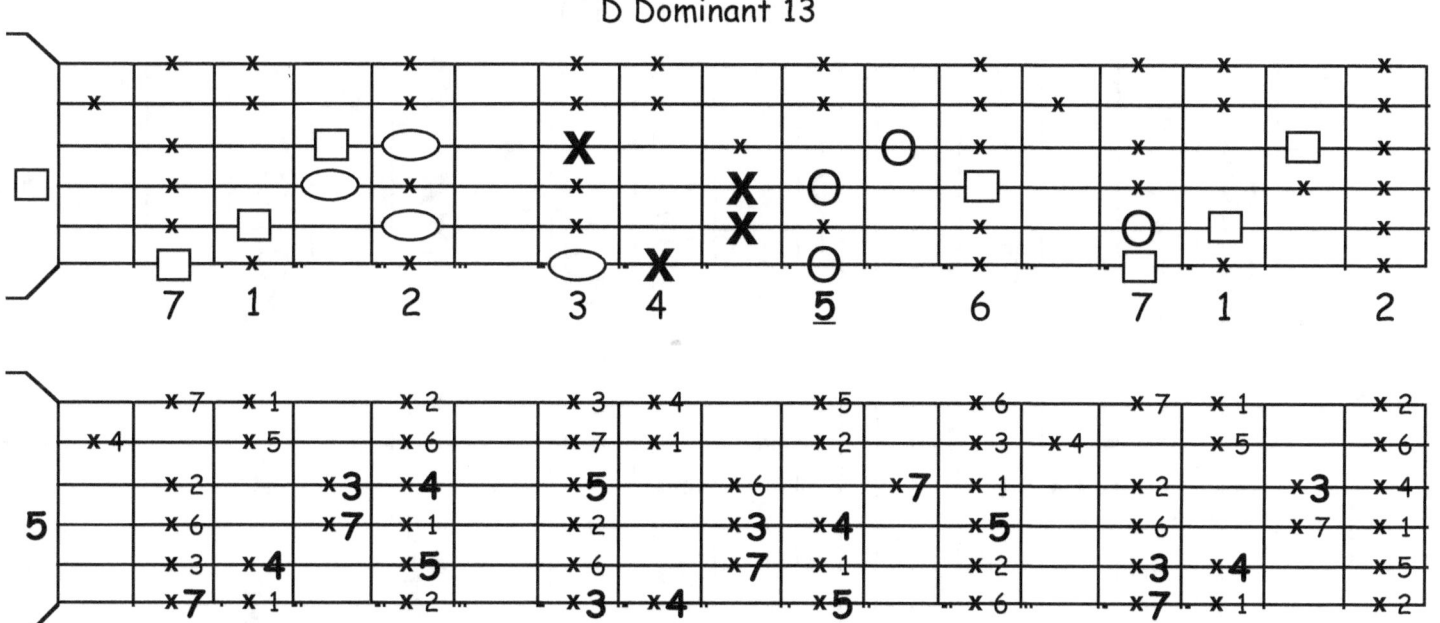

The only notes that you play are: 5, 7, 3, and 4 of the G major scale.

6543 STRING GROUPING

The "6" Chord: Minor 7 (b13) Inversions In "G" Major
E Minor 7 (b13)

The only notes that you play are: 6, 1, 4, and 5 of the G major scale.

The "7" Chord: Minor 7b5 (b13) Inversions In "G" Major
F# Minor 7b5 (b13)

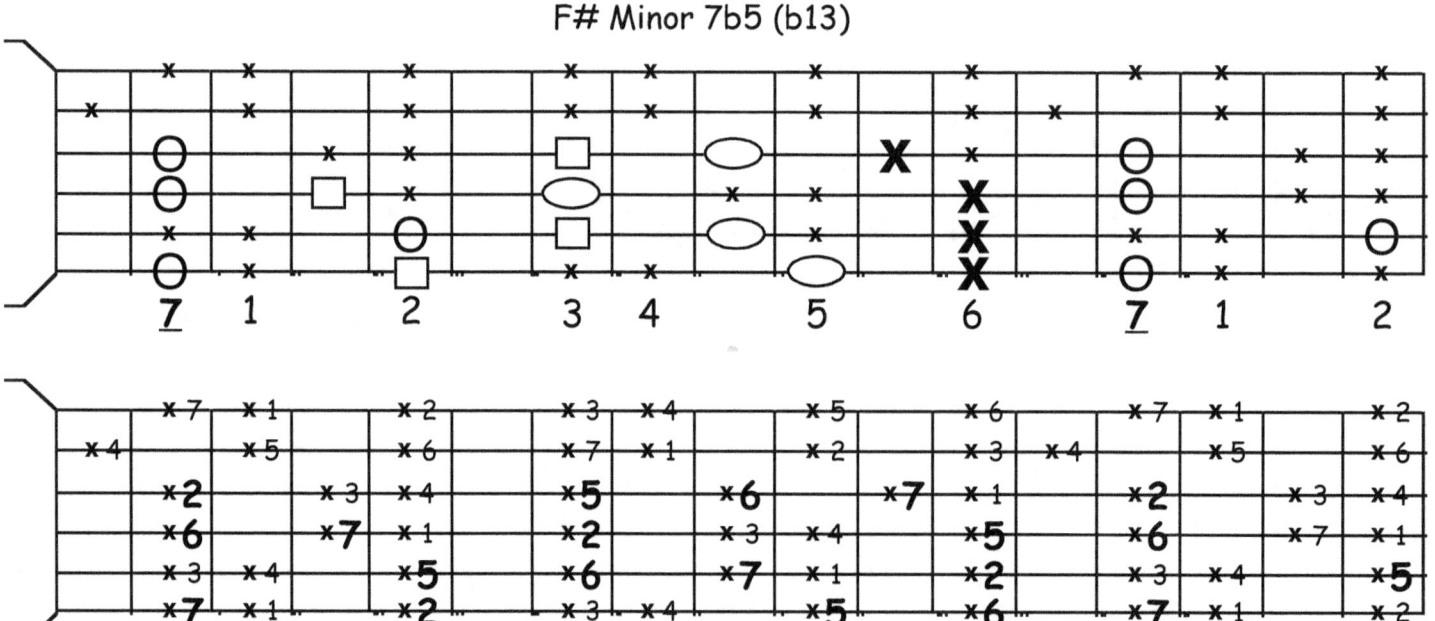

The only notes that you play are: 7, 2, 5, and 6 of the G major scale.

DROP 2
5432 STRING GROUPING
The "1" Chord: Major 13 Inversions In "G" Major
G Major 13

The only notes that you play are: 1, 3, 6, and 7 of the G major scale.

The "2" Chord: Minor 13 Inversions In "G" Major
A Minor 13

The only notes that you play are: 2, 4, 7, and 1 of the G major scale.

5432 STRING GROUPING

The "3" Chord: Minor 7 (b13) Inversions In "G" Major
B Minor 7 (b13)

The only notes that you play are: 3, 5, 1, and 2 of the G major scale.

The "4" Chord: Major 13 Inversions In "G" Major
C Major 13

The only notes that you play are: 4, 6, 2, and 3 of the G major scale.

5432 STRING GROUPING

The "5" Chord: Dominant 13 Inversions In "G" Major

D Dominant 13

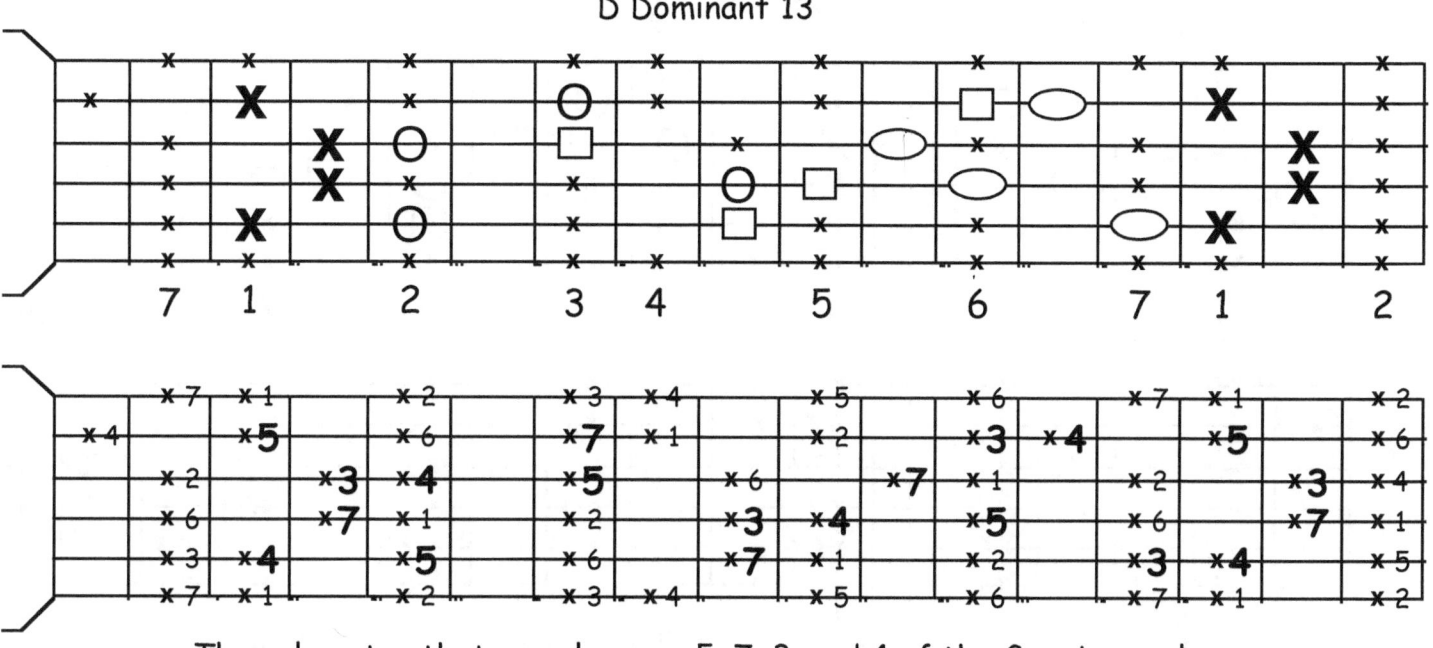

The only notes that you play are: 5, 7, 3, and 4 of the G major scale.

The "6" Chord: Minor 7 (b13) Inversions In "G" Major

E Minor 7 (b13)

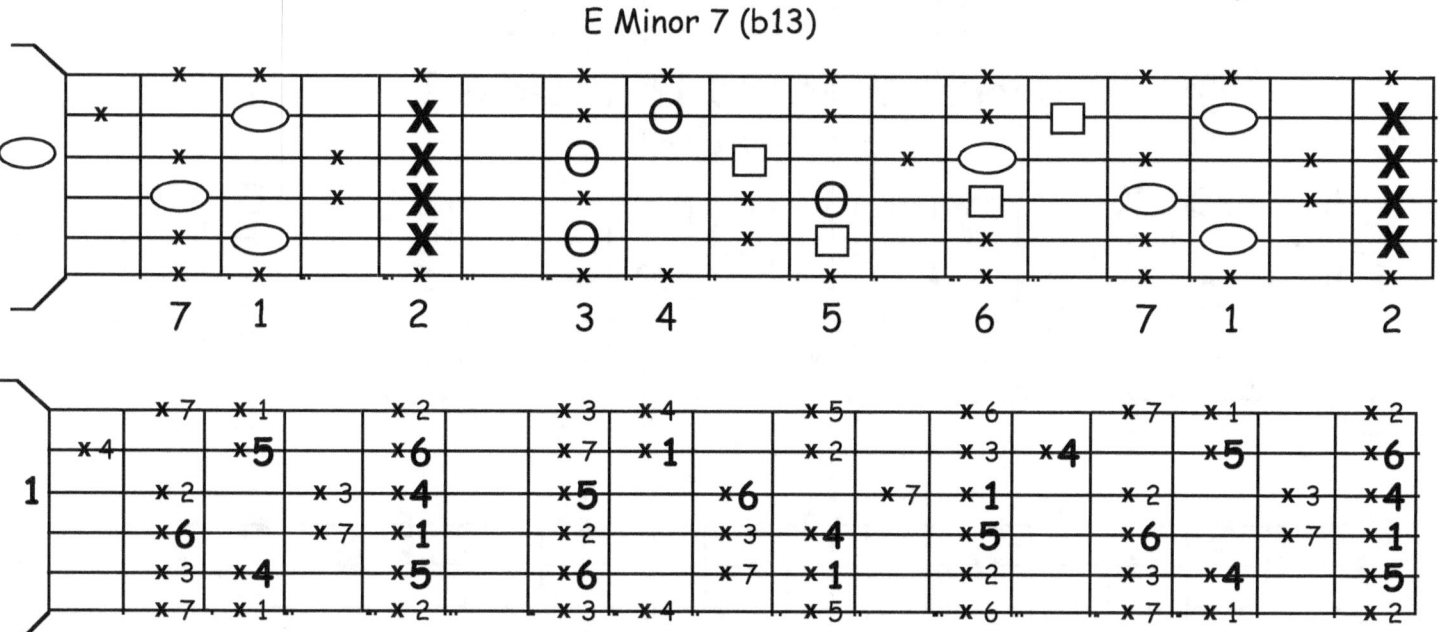

The only notes that you play are: 6, 1, 4, and 5 of the G major scale.

5432 STRING GROUPING
The "7" Chord: Minor 7b5 (b13) Inversions In "G" Major
F# Minor 7b5 (b13)

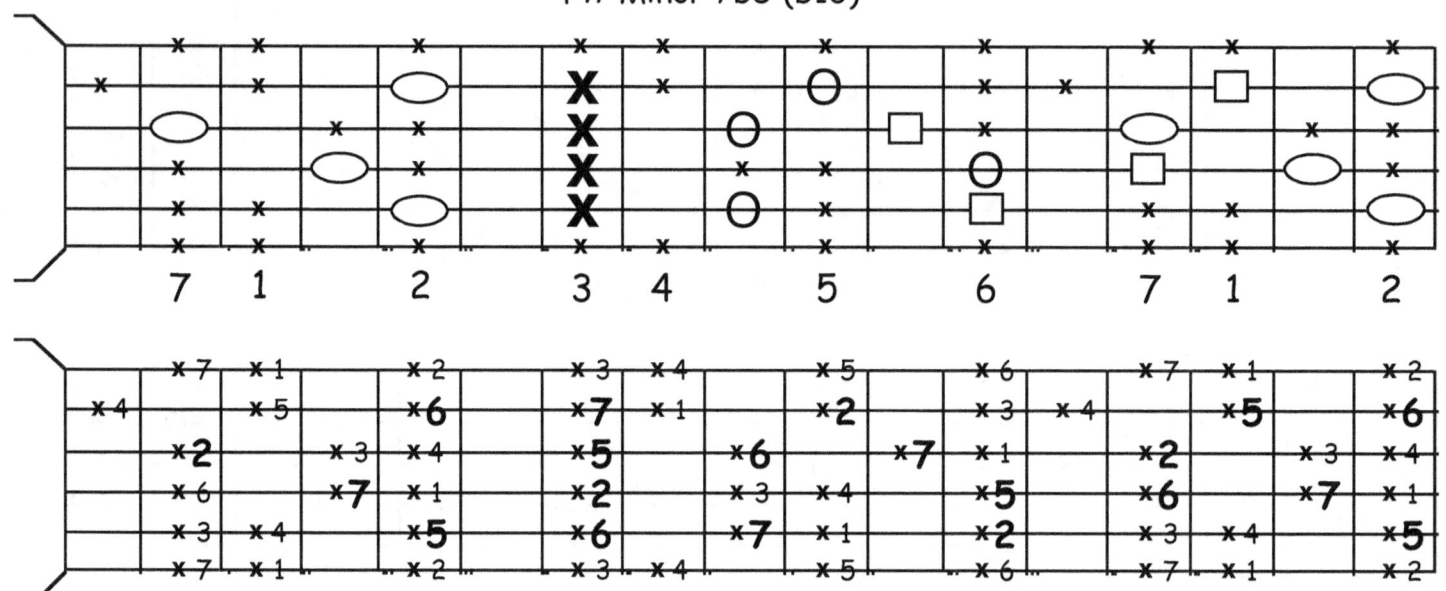

The only notes that you play are: 7, 2, 5, and 6 of the G major scale.

DROP 2

4321 STRING GROUPING
The "1" Chord: Major 13 Inversions In "G" Major
G Major 13

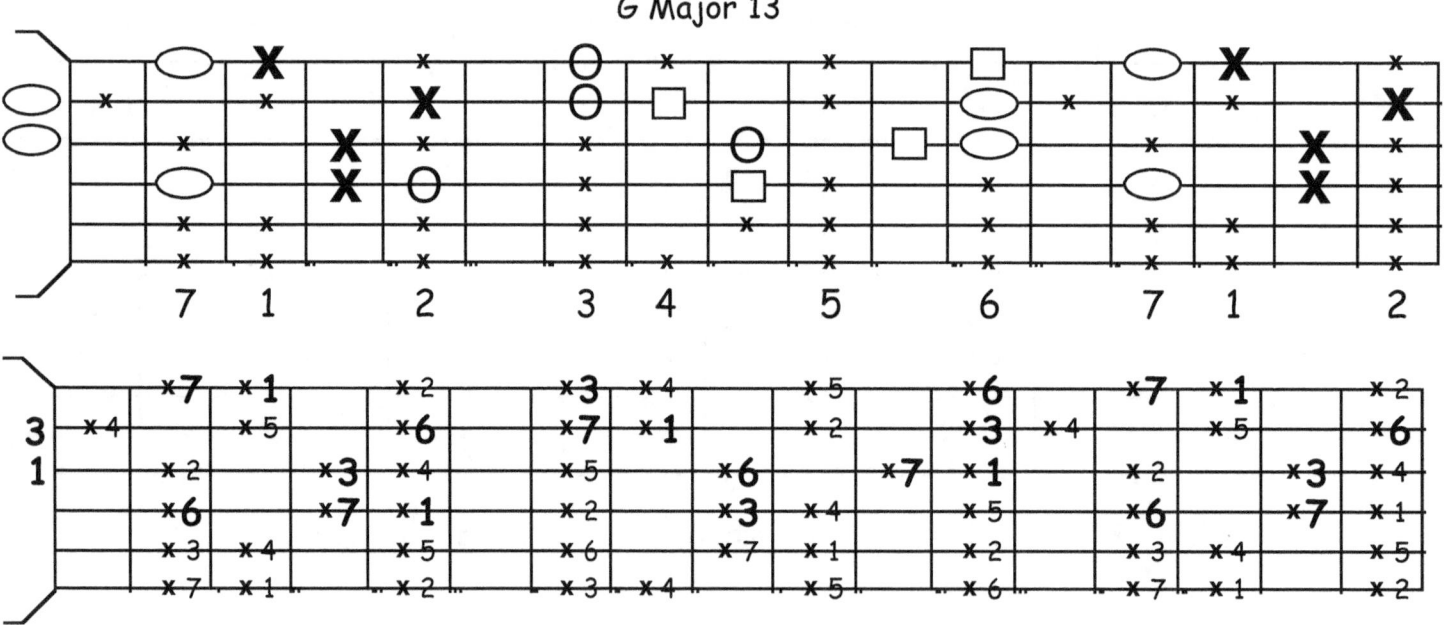

The only notes that you play are: 1, 3, 6, and 7 of the G major scale.

4321 STRING GROUPING

The "2" Chord: Minor 13 Inversions In "G" Major

A Minor 13

The only notes that you play are: 2, 4, 7, and 1 of the G major scale.

The "3" Chord: Minor 7 (b13) Inversions In "G" Major

B Minor 7 (b13)

The only notes that you play are: 3, 5, 1, and 2 of the G major scale.

4321 STRING GROUPING
The "4" Chord: Major 13 Inversions In "G" Major
C Major 13

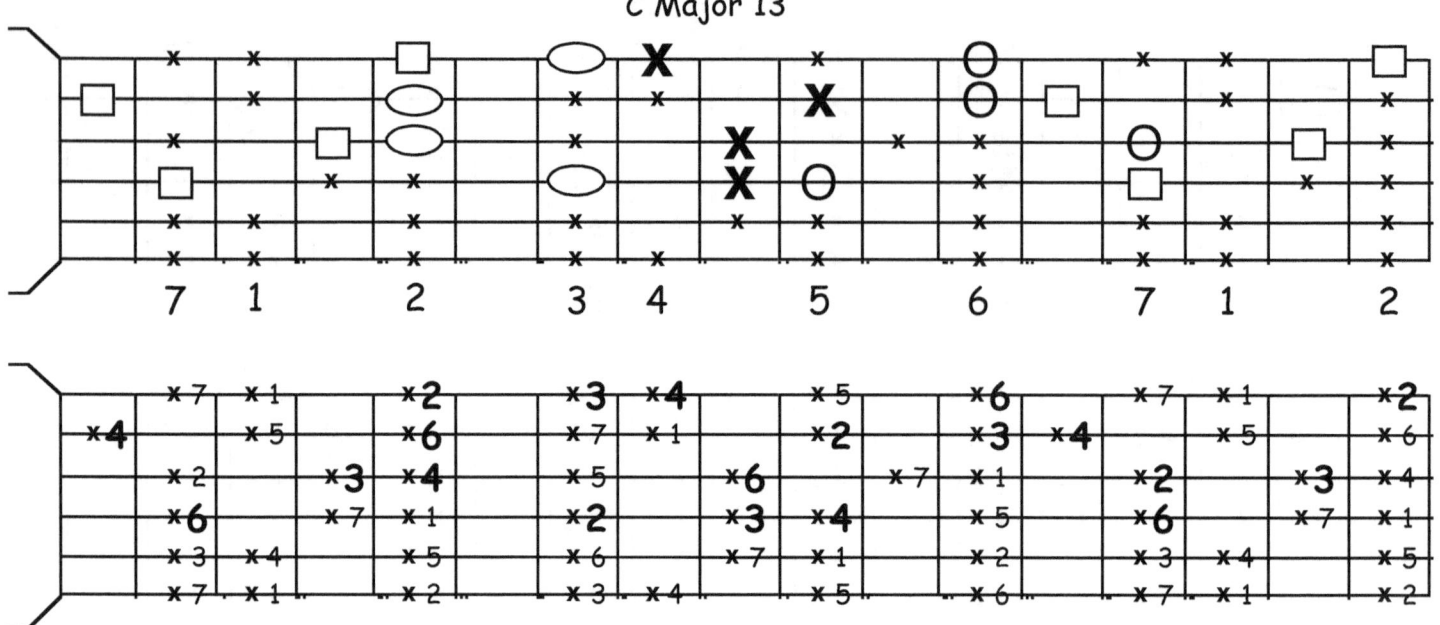

The only notes that you play are: 4, 6, 2, and 3 of the G major scale.

The "5" Chord: Dominant 13 Inversions In "G" Major
D Dominant 13

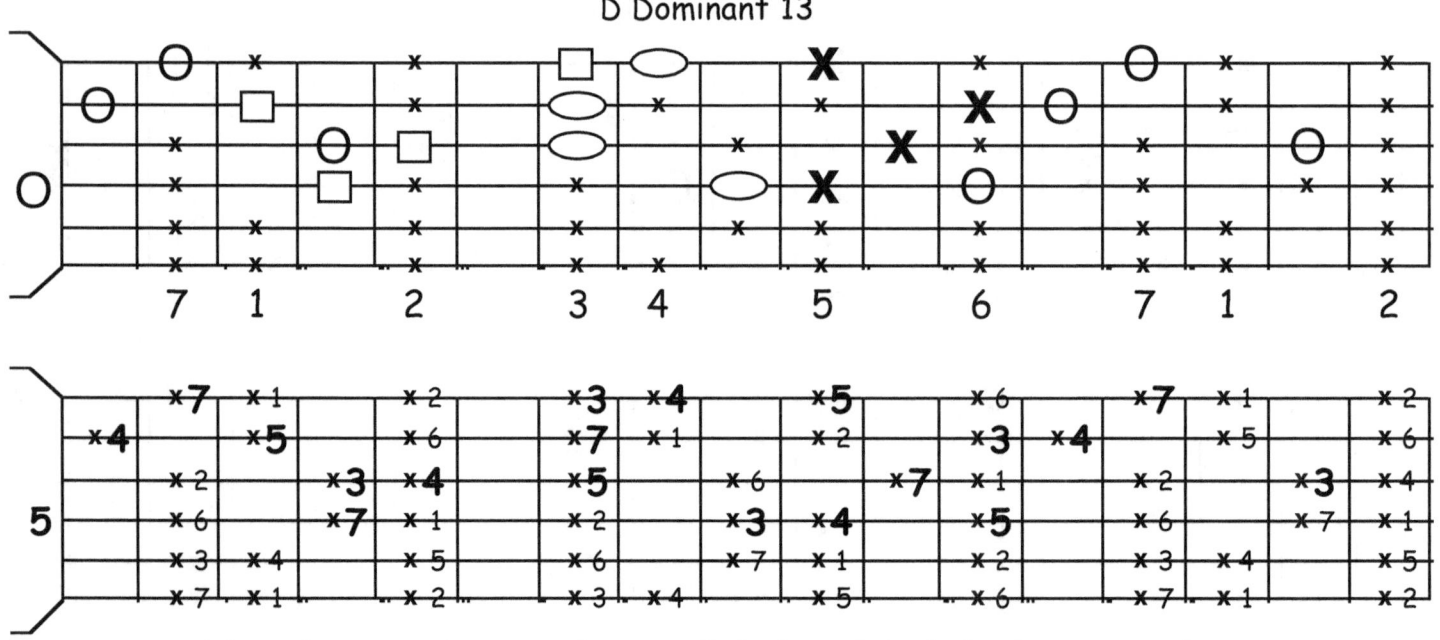

The only notes that you play are: 5, 7, 3, and 4 of the G major scale.

4321 STRING GROUPING

The "6" Chord: Minor 7 (b13) Inversions In "G" Major
E Minor 7 (b13)

The only notes that you play are: 6, 1, 4, and 5 of the G major scale.

The "7" Chord: Minor 7b5 (b13) Inversions In "G" Major
F# Minor 7b5 (b13)

The only notes that you play are: 7, 2, 5, and 6 of the G major scale.

DROP 3
6432 STRING GROUPING
The "1" Chord: Major 13 Inversions In "G" Major
G Major 13

The only notes that you play are: 1, 3, 6, and 7 of the G major scale.

The "2" Chord: Minor 13 Inversions In "G" Major
A Minor 13

The only notes that you play are: 2, 4, 7, and 1 of the G major scale.

6432 STRING GROUPING

The "3" Chord: Minor 7 (b13) Inversions In "G" Major

B Minor 7 (b13)

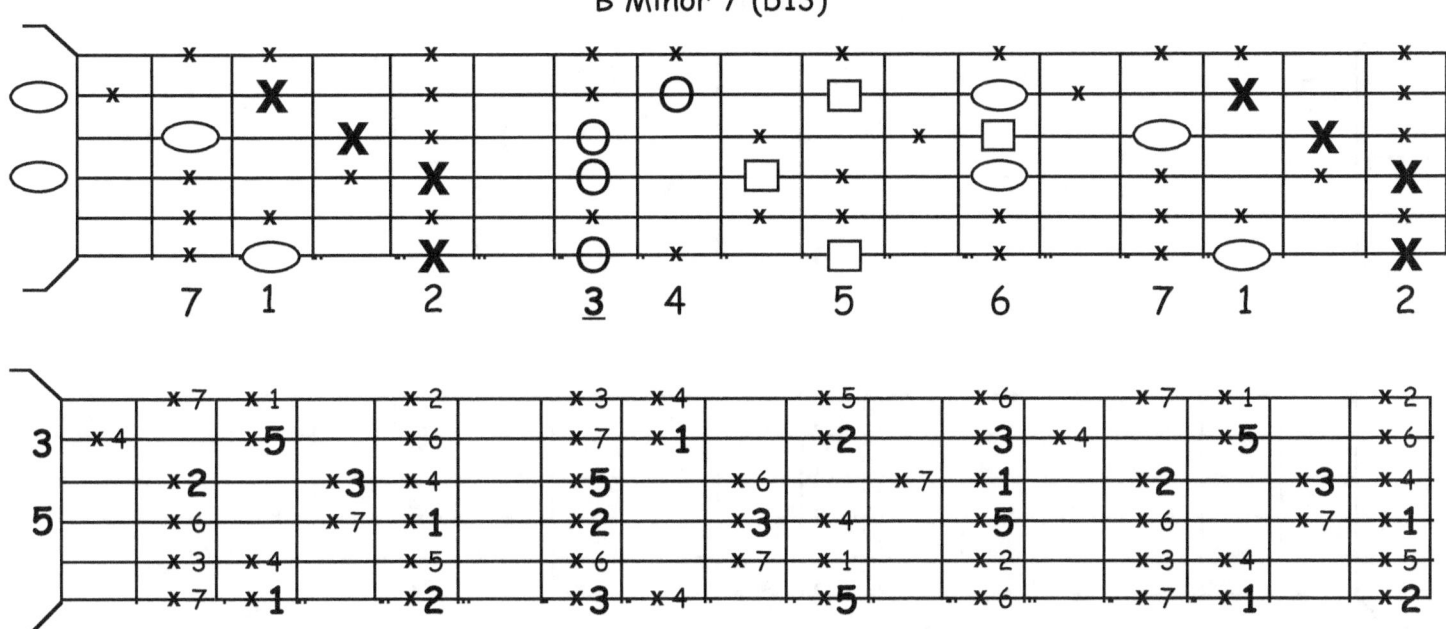

The only notes that you play are: 3, 5, 1, and 2 of the G major scale.

The "4" Chord: Major 13 Inversions In "G" Major

C Major 13

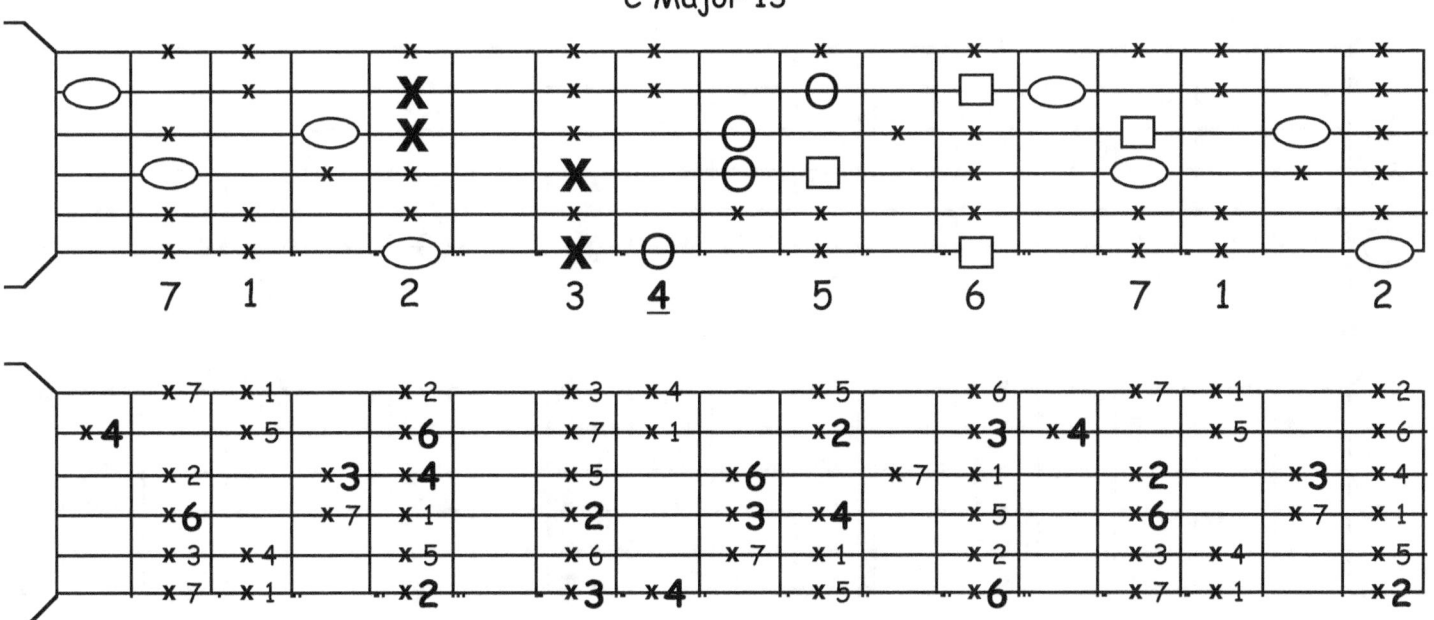

The only notes that you play are: 4, 6, 2, and 3 of the G major scale.

6432 STRING GROUPING

The "5" Chord: Dominant 13 Inversions In "G" Major
D Dominant 13

The only notes that you play are: 5, 7, 3, and 4 of the G major scale.

The "6" Chord: Minor 7 (b13) Inversions In "G" Major
E Minor 7 (b13)

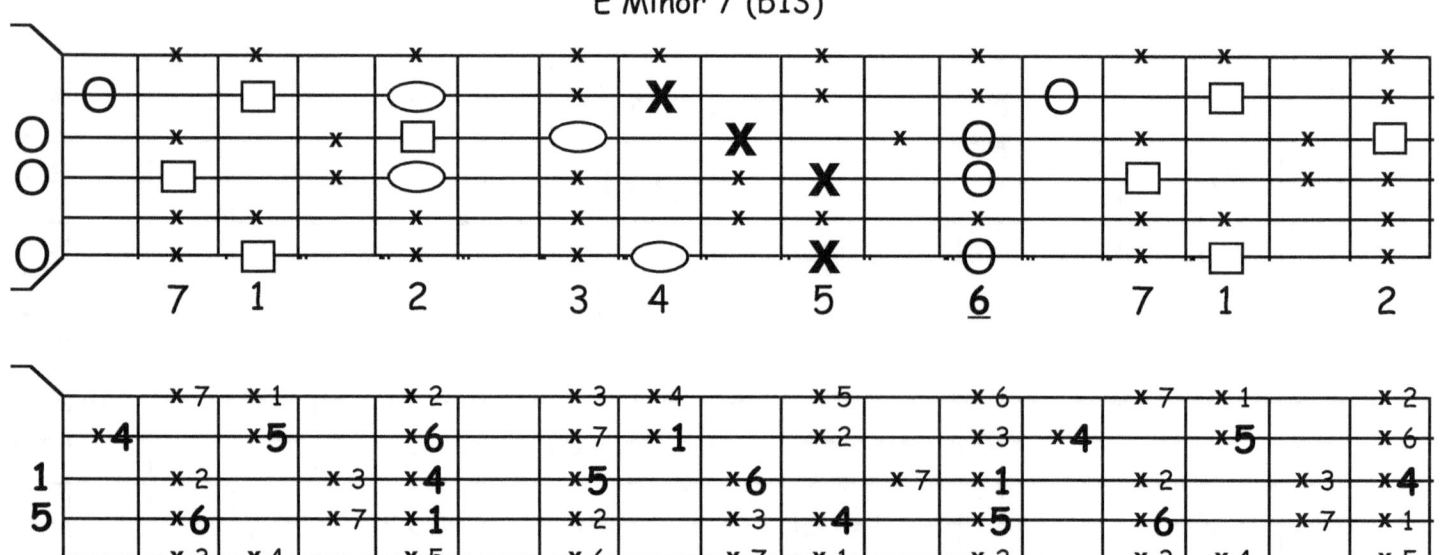

The only notes that you play are: 6, 1, 4, and 5 of the G major scale.

6432 STRING GROUPING
The "7" Chord: Minor 7b5 (b13) Inversions In "G" Major
F# Minor 7b5 (b13)

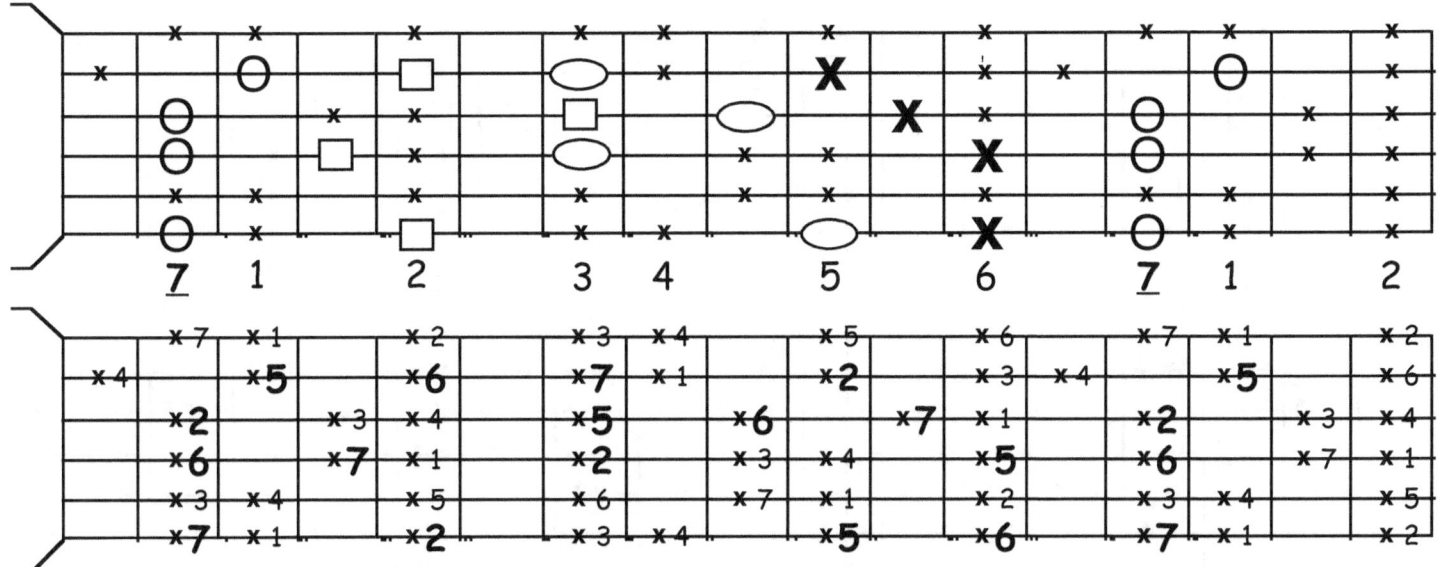

The only notes that you play are: 7, 2, 5, and 6 of the G major scale.

DROP 3

5321 STRING GROUPING
The "1" Chord: Major 13 Inversions In "G" Major
G Major 13

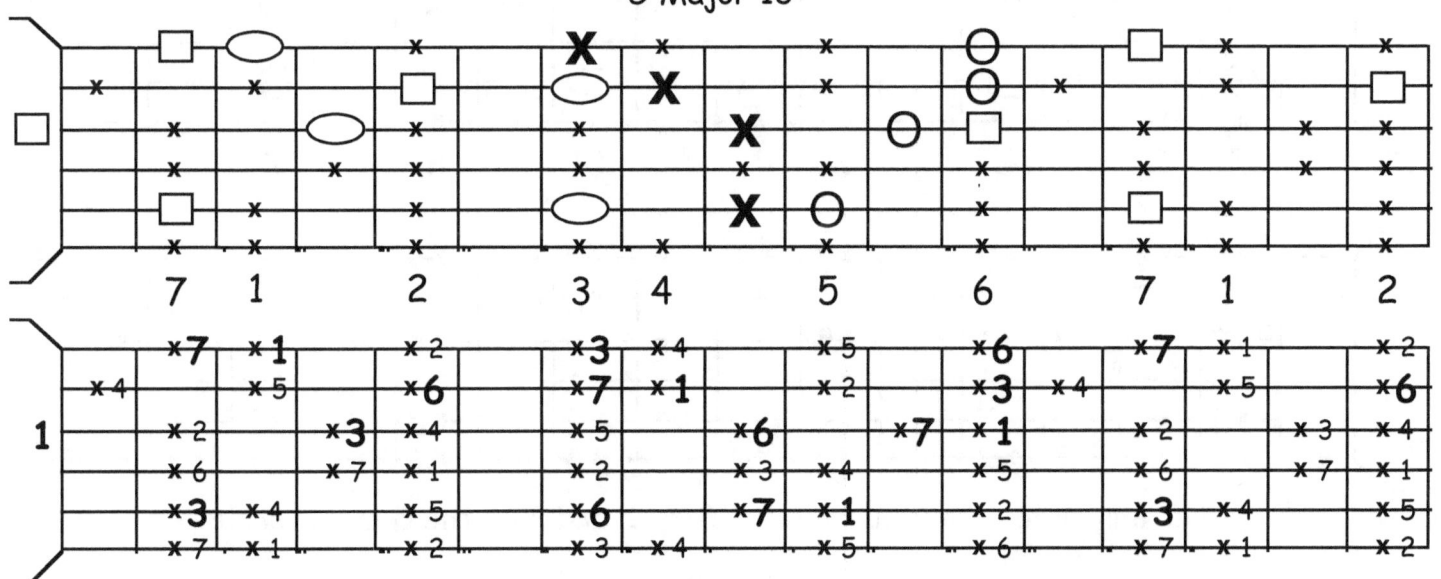

The only notes that you play are: 1, 3, 6, and 7 of the G major scale.

5321 STRING GROUPING
The "2" Chord: Minor 13 Inversions In "G" Major
A Minor 13

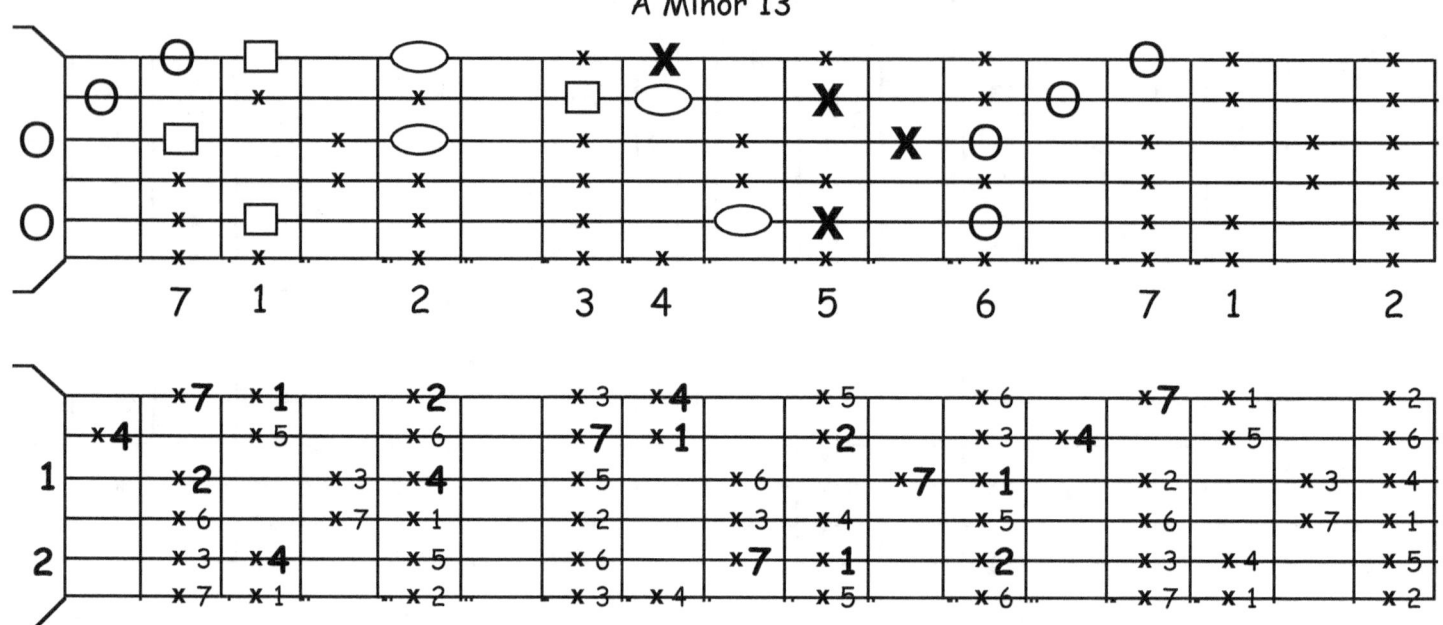

The only notes that you play are: 2, 4, 7, and 1 of the G major scale.

The "3" Chord: Minor 7 (b13) Inversions In "G" Major
B Minor 7 (b13)

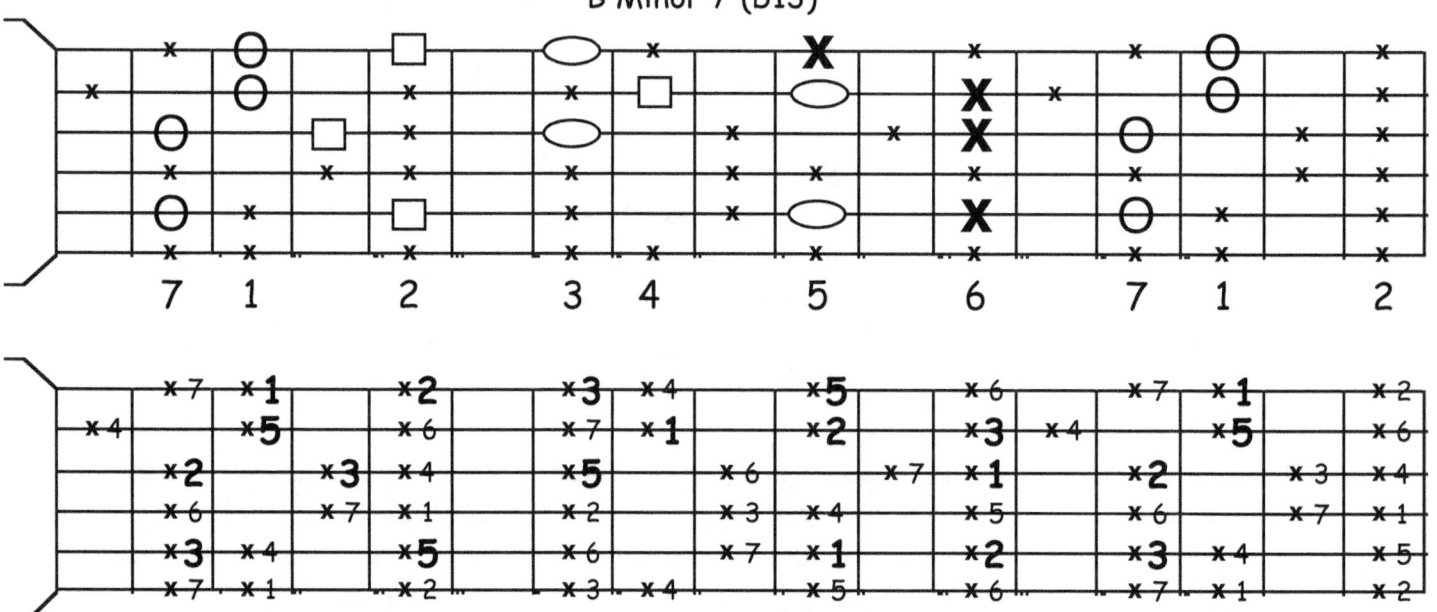

The only notes that you play are: 3, 5, 1, and 2 of the G major scale.

5321 STRING GROUPING

The "4" Chord: Major 13 Inversions In "G" Major

C Major 13

The only notes that you play are: 4, 6, 2, and 3 of the G major scale.

The "5" Chord: Dominant 13 Inversions In "G" Major

D Dominant 13

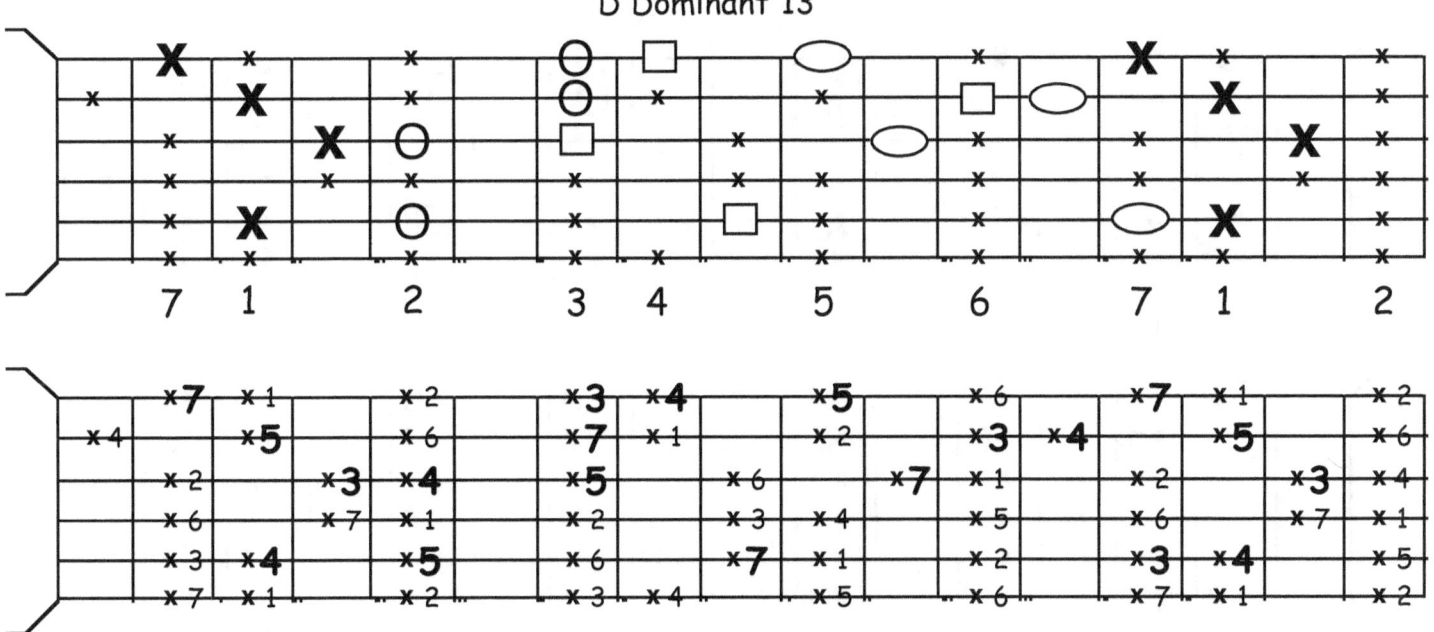

The only notes that you play are: 5, 7, 3, and 4 of the G major scale.

5321 STRING GROUPING

The "6" Chord: Minor 7 (b13) Inversions In "G" Major
E Minor 7 (b13)

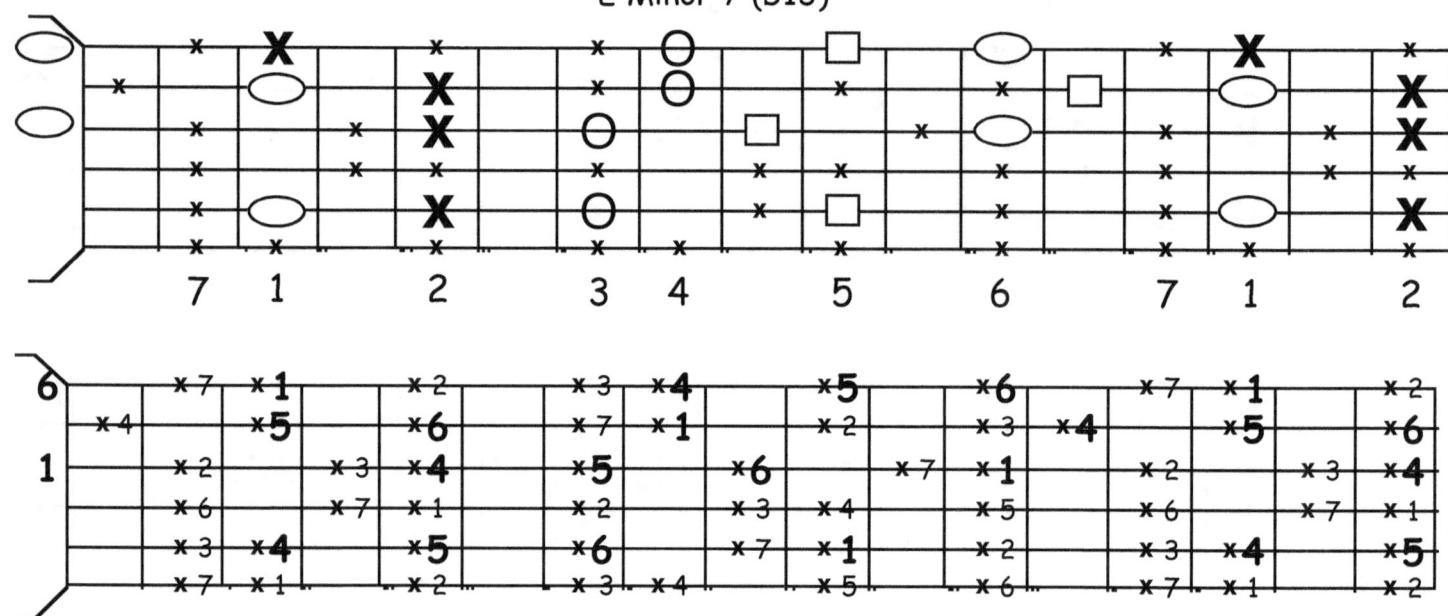

The only notes that you play are: 6, 1, 4, and 5 of the G major scale.

The "7" Chord: Minor 7b5 (b13) Inversions In "G" Major
F# Minor 7b5 (b13)

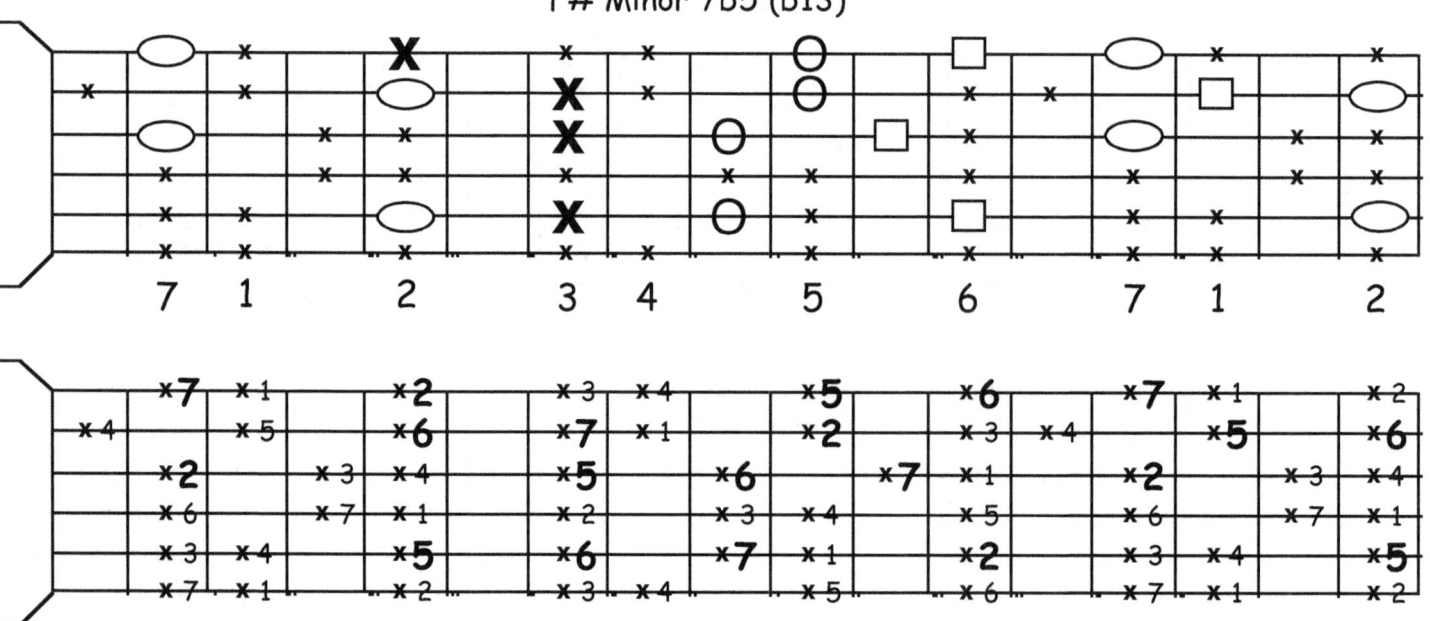

The only notes that you play are: 7, 2, 5, and 6 of the G major scale.

DROP 2 & 3
6542 STRING GROUPING
The "1" Chord: Major 13 Inversions In "G" Major
G Major 13

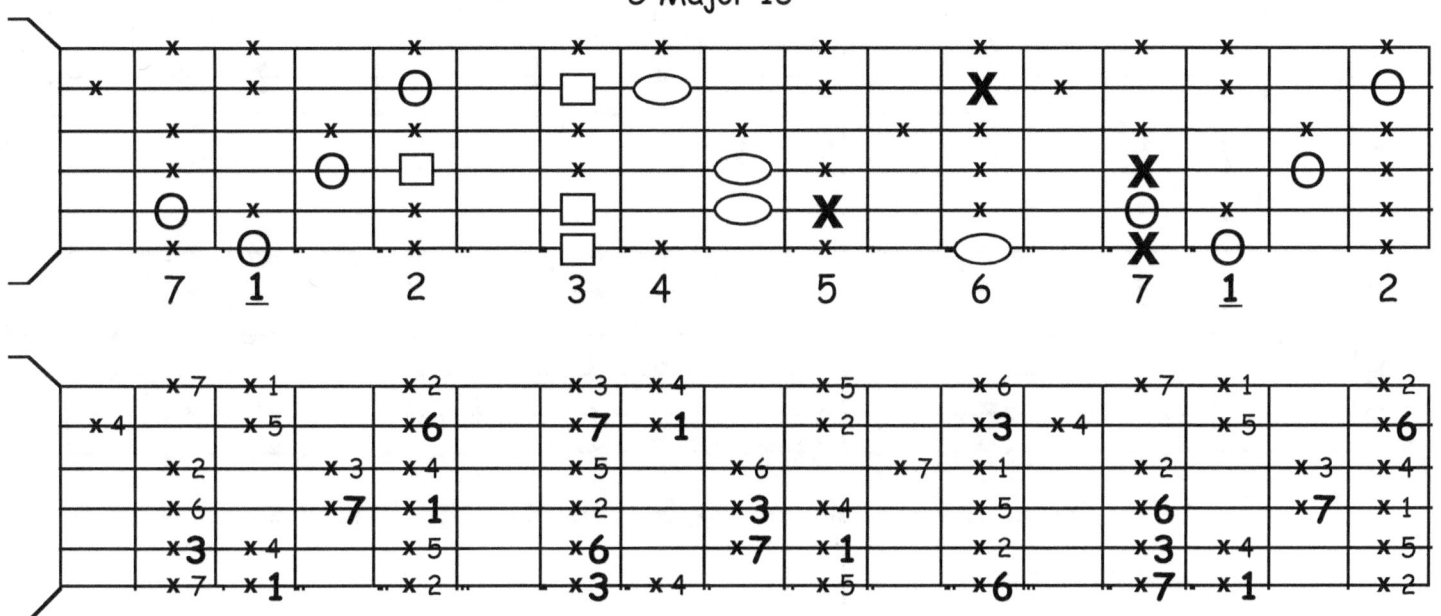

The only notes that you play are: 1, 3, 6, and 7 of the G major scale.

The "2" Chord: Minor 13 Inversions In "G" Major
A Minor 13

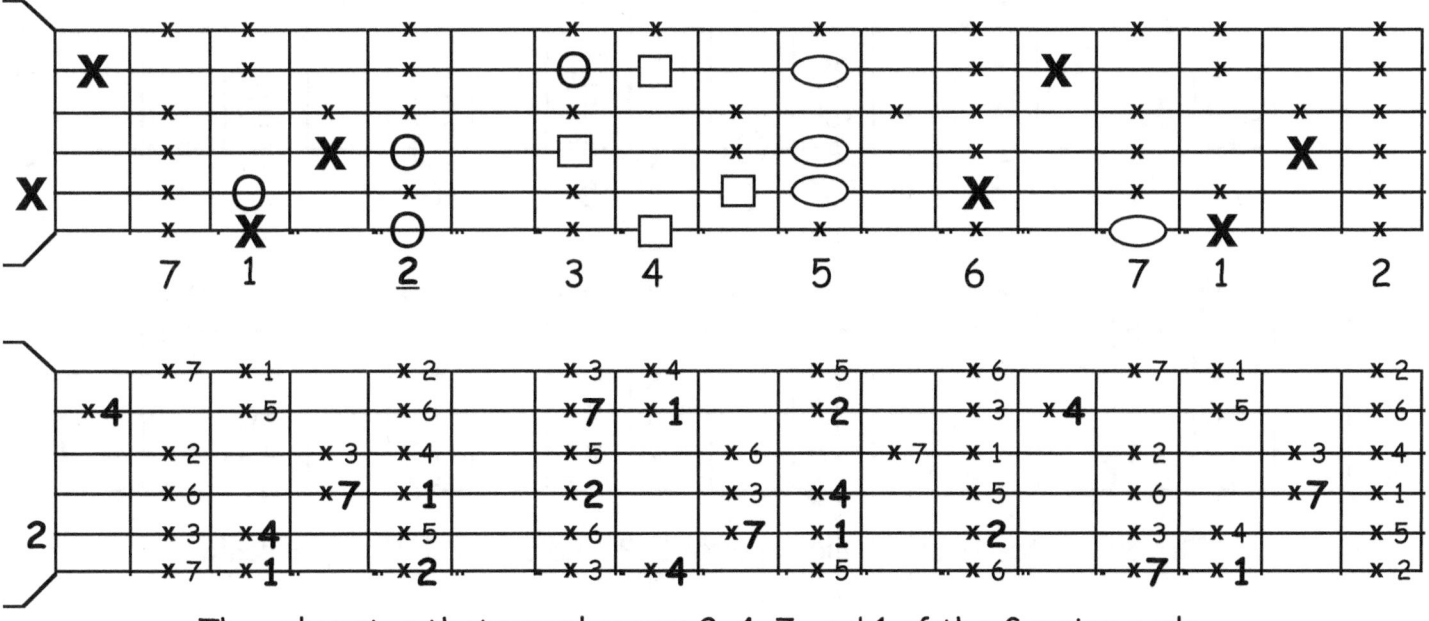

The only notes that you play are: 2, 4, 7, and 1 of the G major scale.

6542 STRING GROUPING

The "3" Chord: Minor 7 (b13) Inversions In "G" Major

B Minor 7 (b13)

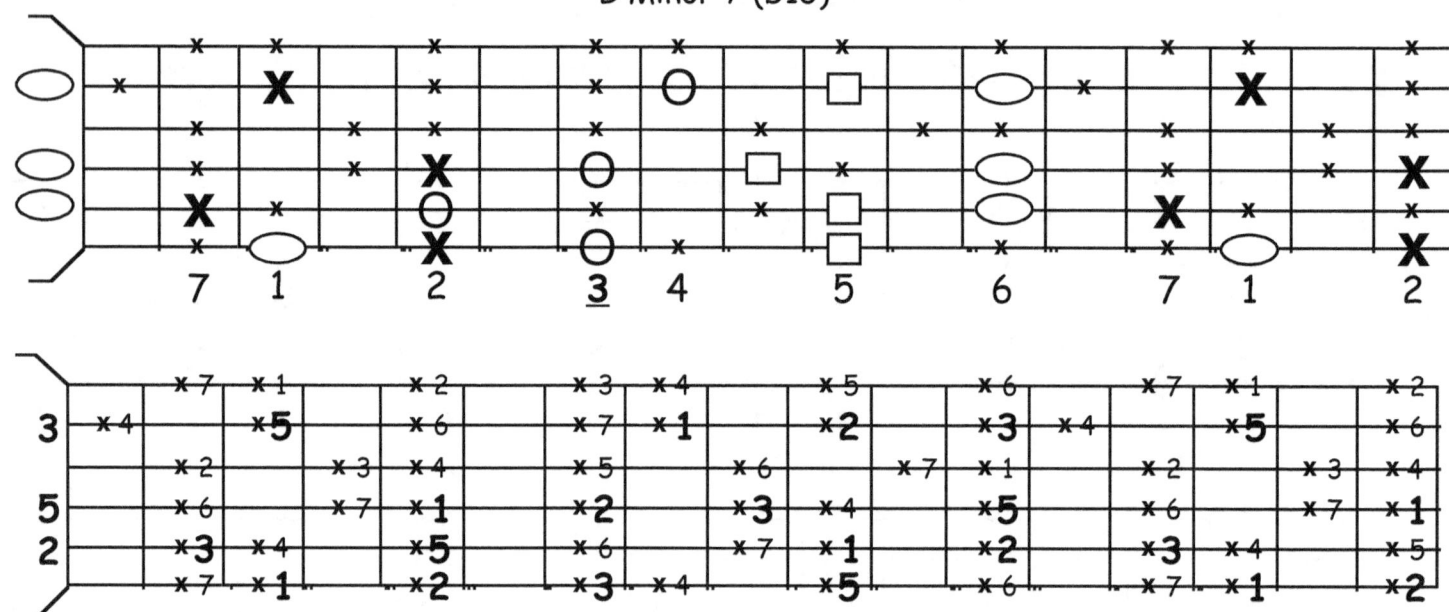

The only notes that you play are: 3, 5, 1, and 2 of the G major scale.

The "4" Chord: Major 13 Inversions In "G" Major

C Major 13

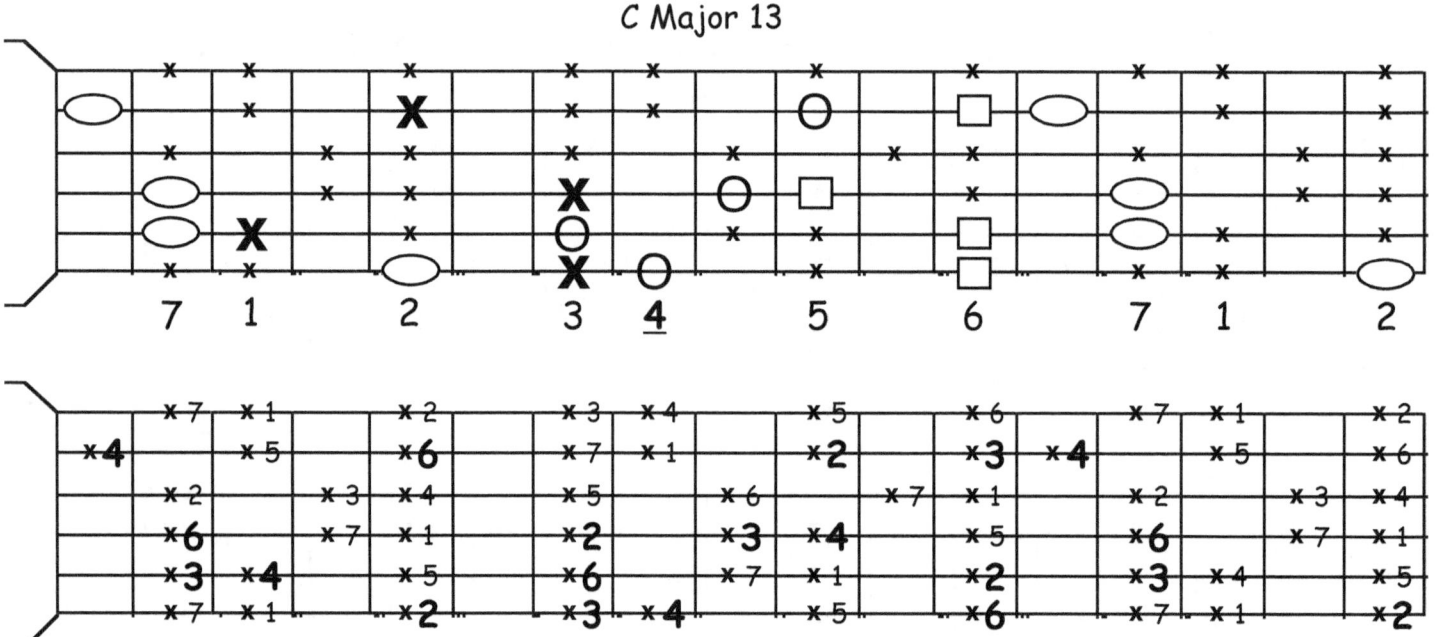

The only notes that you play are: 4, 6, 2, and 3 of the G major scale.

6542 STRING GROUPING

The "5" Chord: Dominant 13 Inversions In "G" Major

D Dominant 13

The only notes that you play are: 5, 7, 3, and 4 of the G major scale.

The "6" Chord: Minor 7 (b13) Inversions In "G" Major

E Minor 7 (b13)

The only notes that you play are: 6, 1, 4, and 5 of the G major scale.

6542 STRING GROUPING
The "7" Chord: Minor 7b5 (b13) Inversions In "G" Major
F# Minor 7b5 (b13)

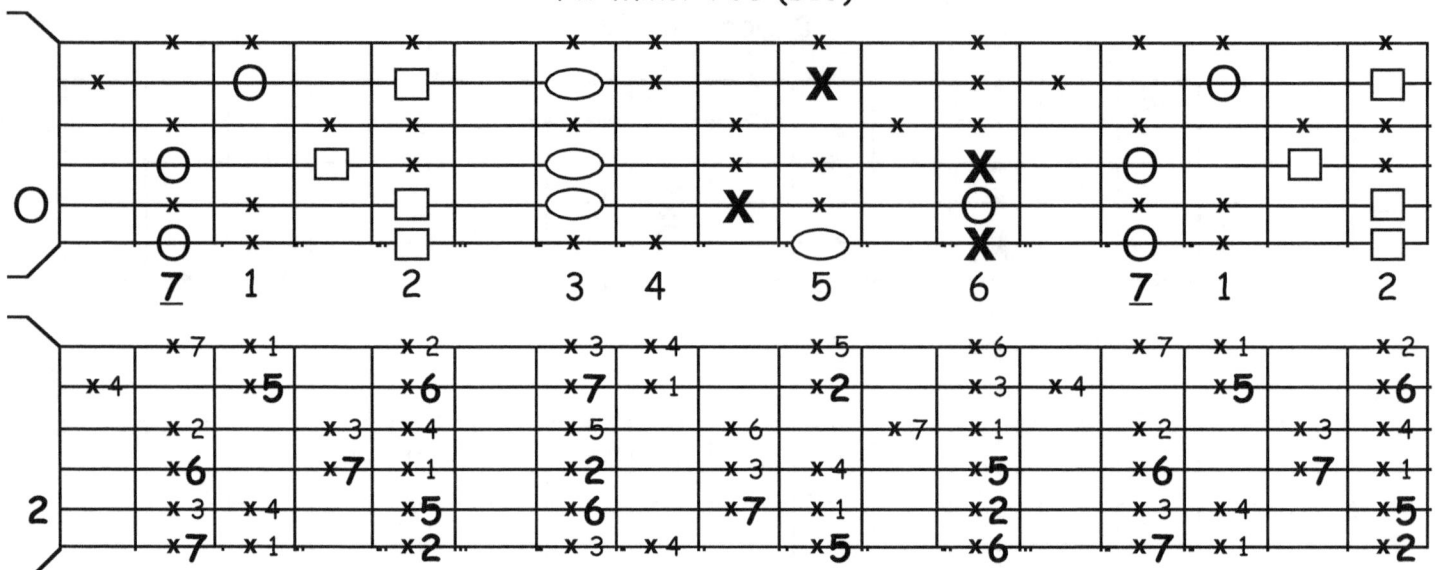

The only notes that you play are: 7, 2, 5, and 6 of the G major scale.

DROP 2 & 3

5431 STRING GROUPING
The "1" Chord: Major 13 Inversions In "G" Major
G Major 13

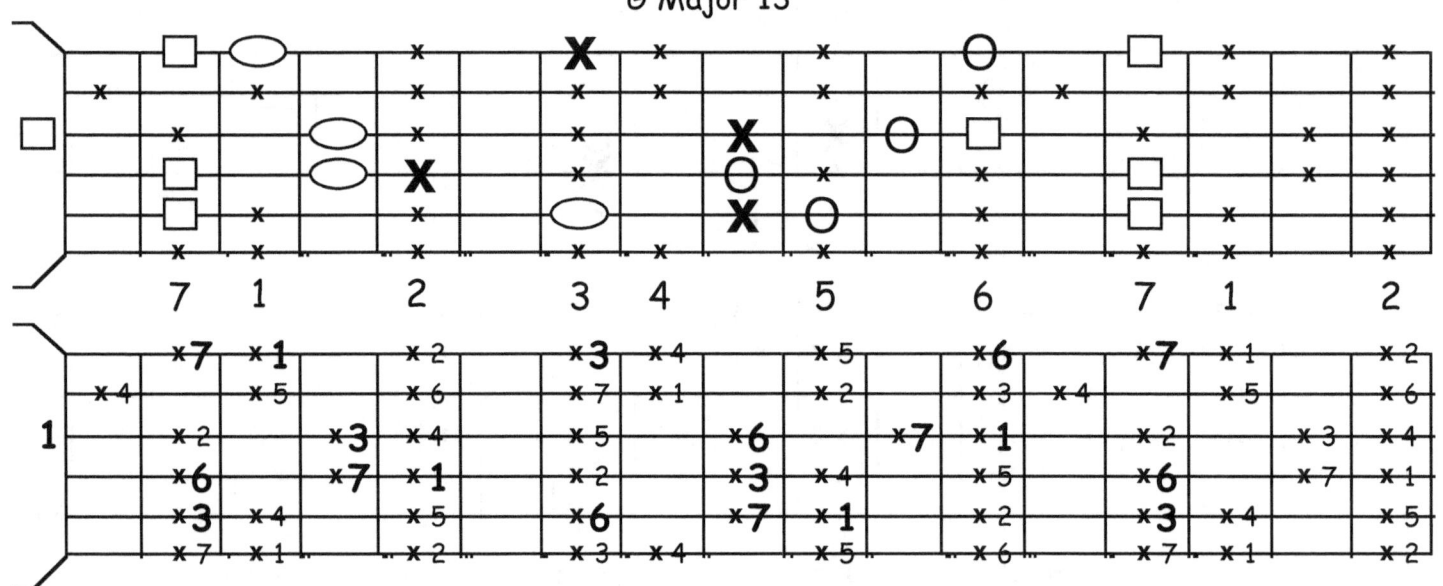

The only notes that you play are: 1, 3, 6, and 7 of the G major scale.

5431 STRING GROUPING

The "2" Chord: Minor 13 Inversions In "G" Major
A Minor 13

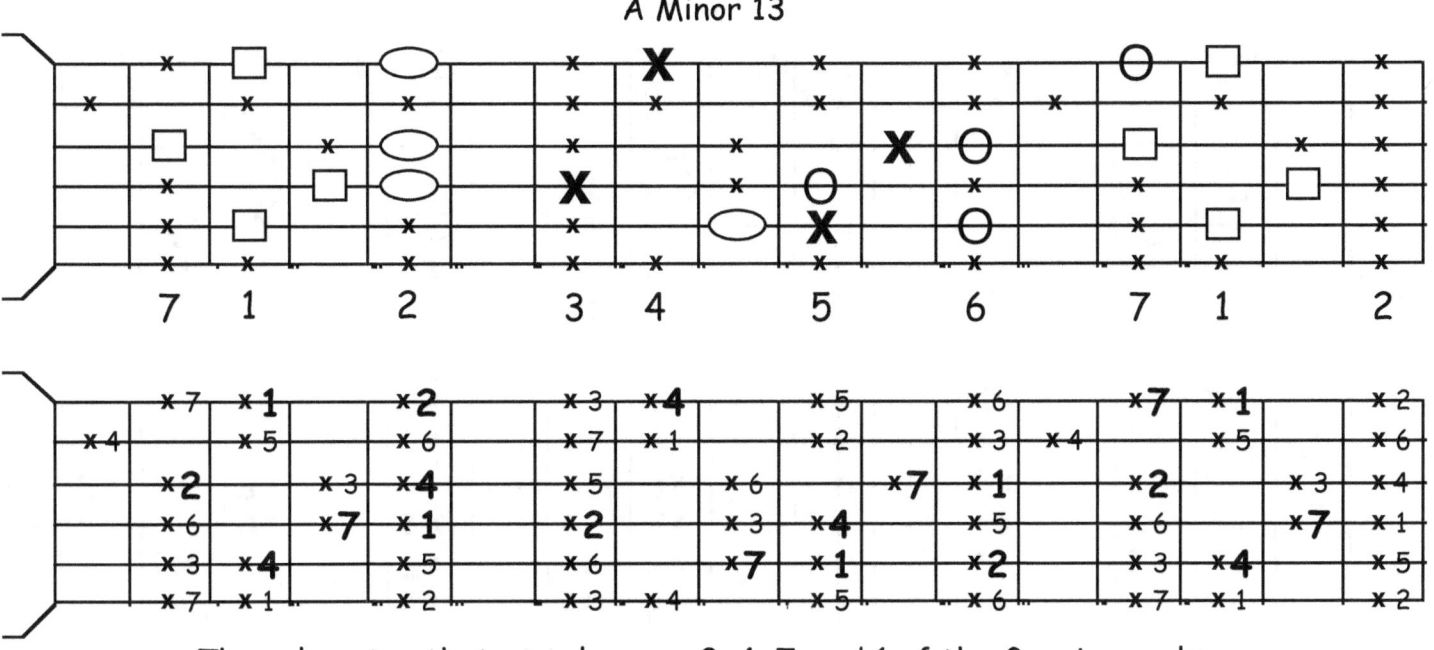

The only notes that you play are: 2, 4, 7, and 1 of the G major scale.

The "3" Chord: Minor 7 (b13) Inversions In "G" Major
B Minor 7 (b13)

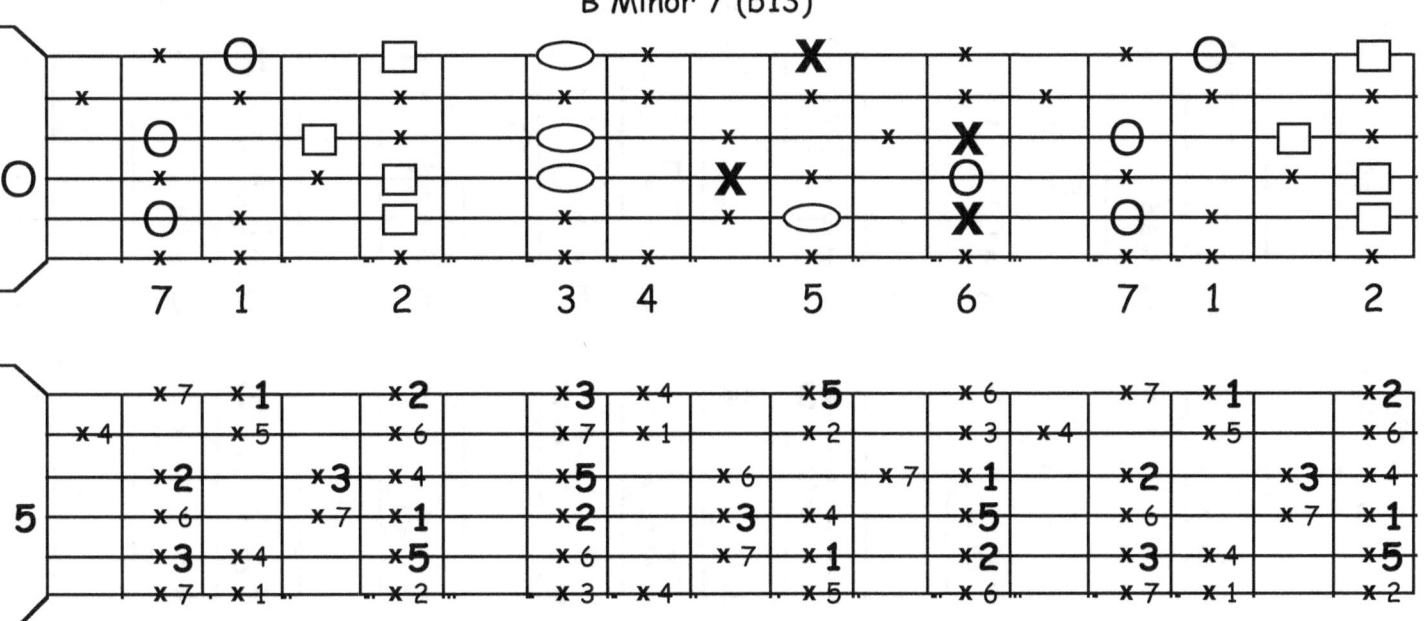

The only notes that you play are: 3, 5, 1, and 2 of the G major scale.

5431 STRING GROUPING

The "4" Chord: Major 13 Inversions In "G" Major

C Major 13

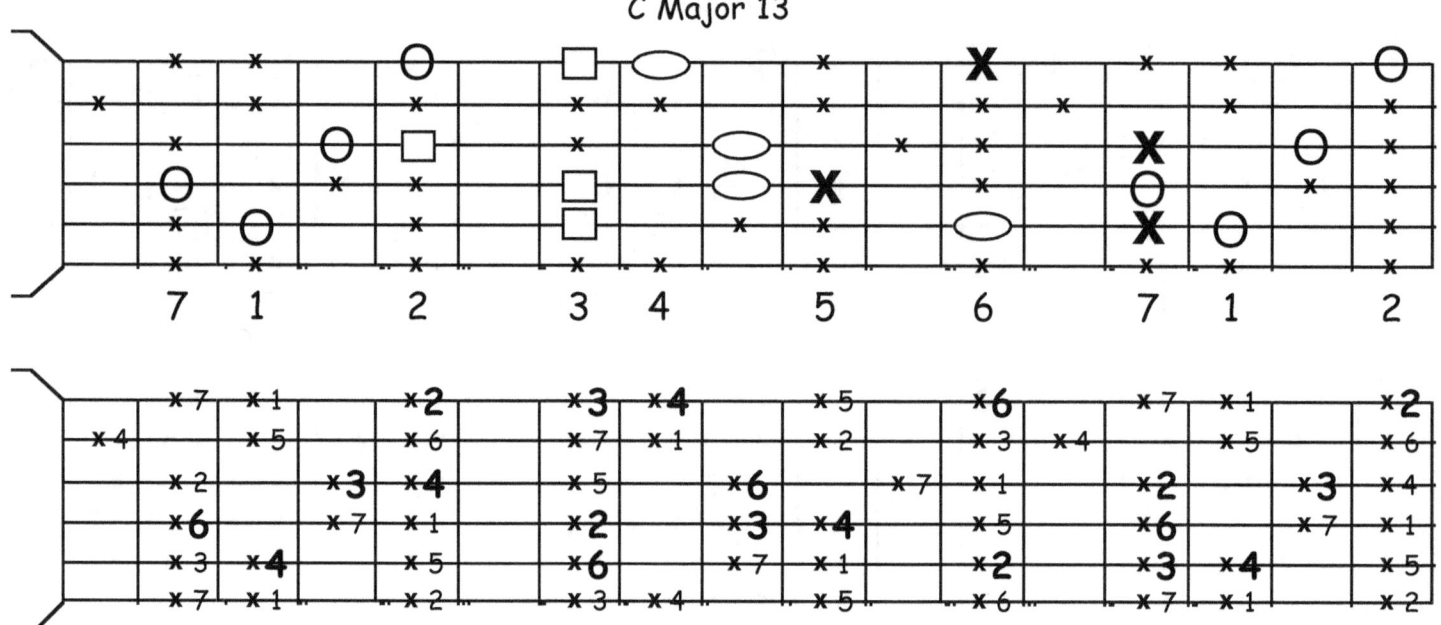

The only notes that you play are: 4, 6, 2, and 3 of the G major scale.

The "5" Chord: Dominant 13 Inversions In "G" Major

D Dominant 13

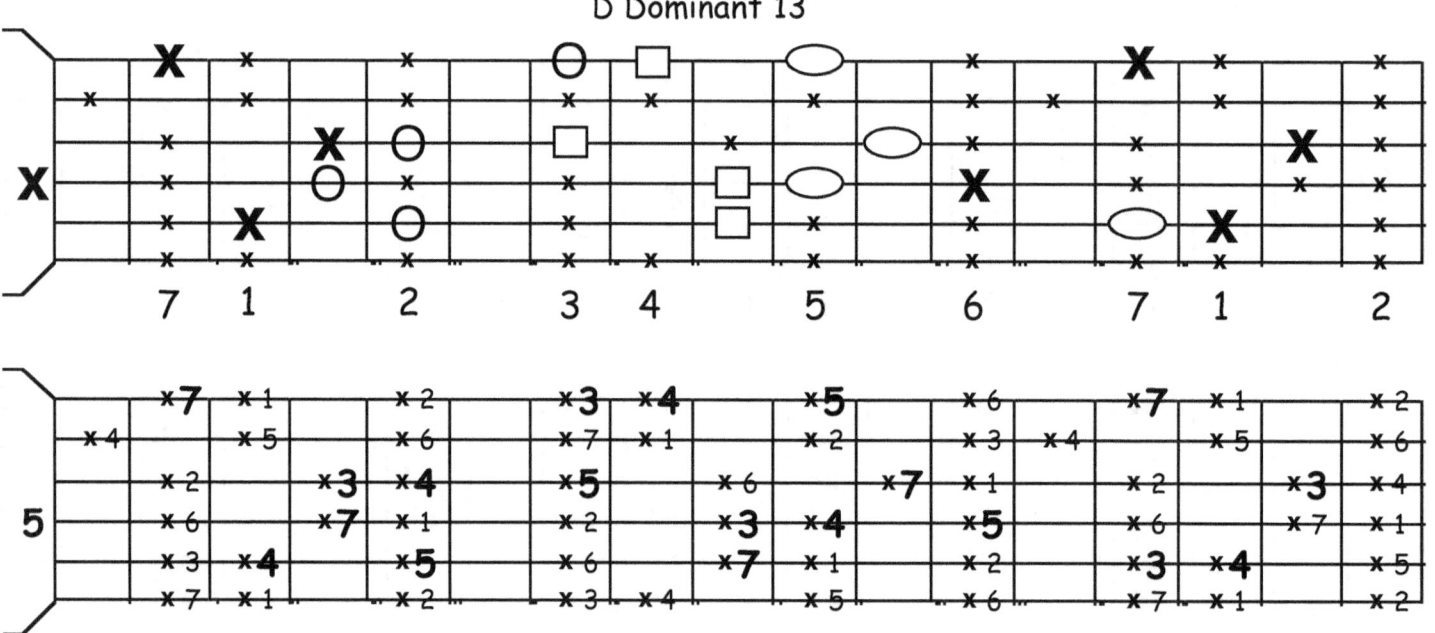

The only notes that you play are: 5, 7, 3, and 4 of the G major scale.

5431 STRING GROUPING

The "6" Chord: Minor 7 (b13) Inversions In "G" Major
E Minor 7 (b13)

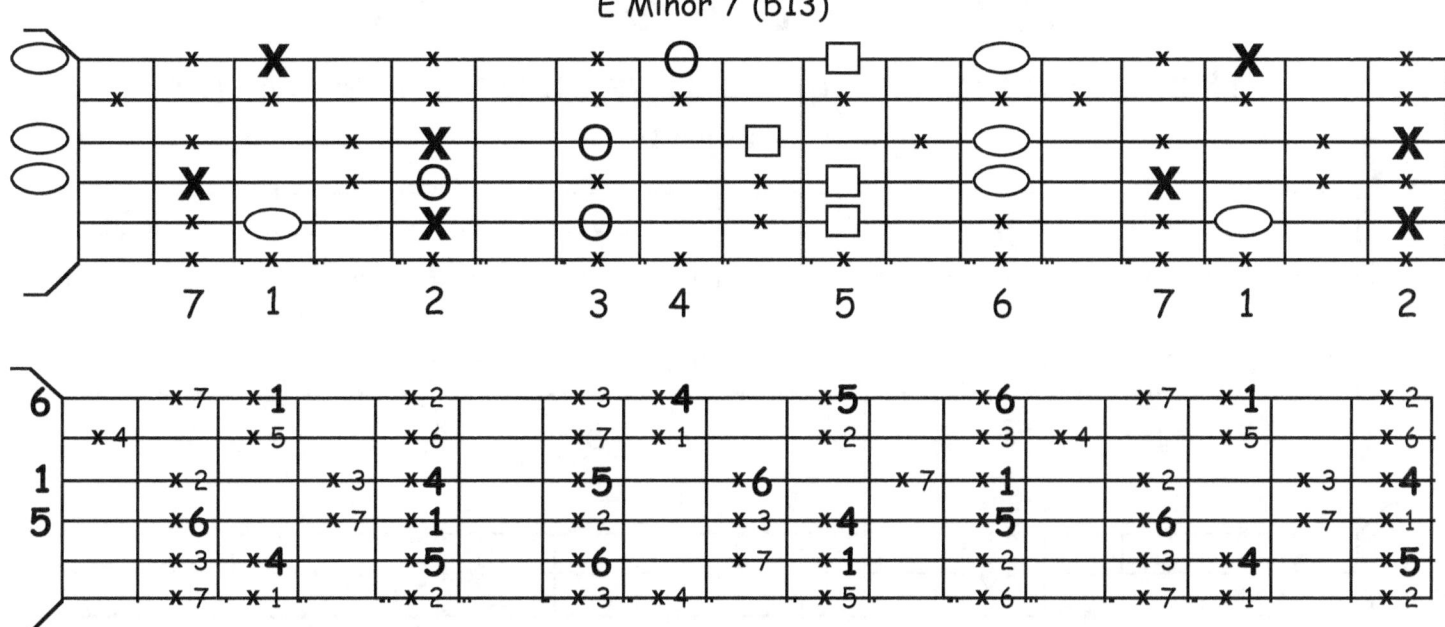

The only notes that you play are: 6, 1, 4, and 5 of the G major scale.

The "7" Chord: Minor 7b5 (b13) Inversions In "G" Major
F# Minor 7b5 (b13)

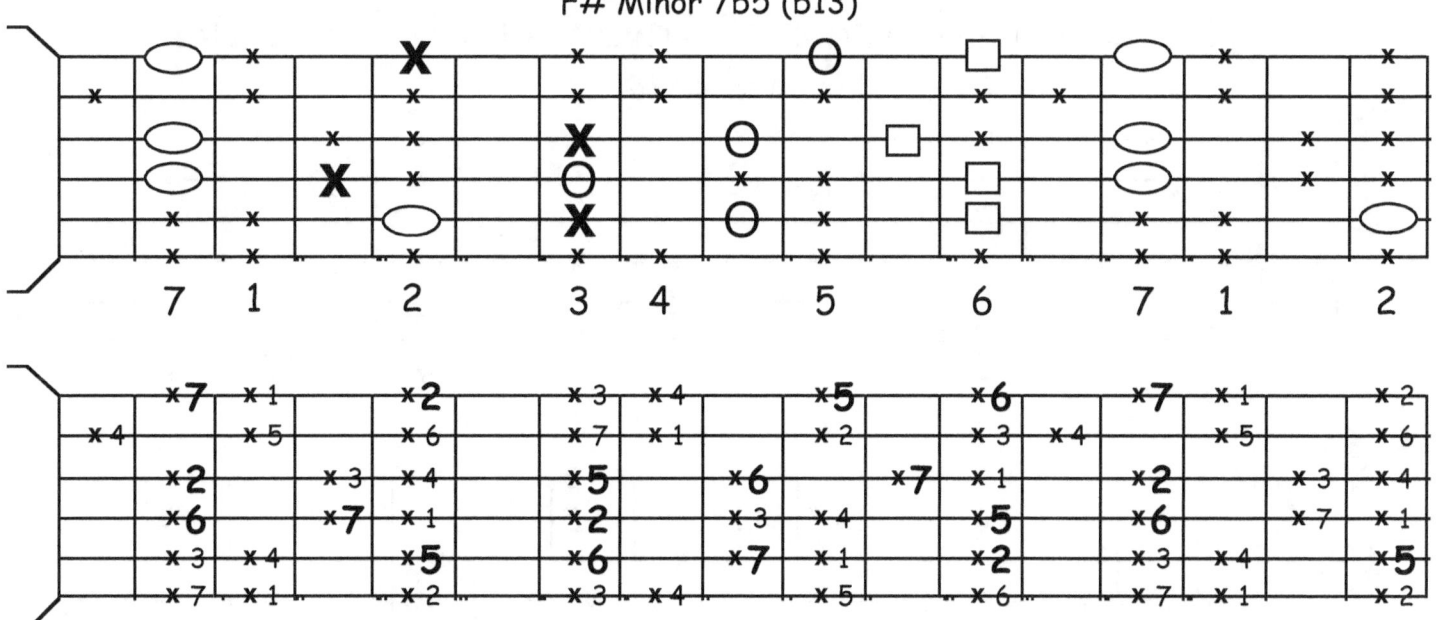

The only notes that you play are: 7, 2, 5, and 6 of the G major scale.

DROP 2 & 4
6532 STRING GROUPING
The "1" Chord: Major 13 Inversions In "G" Major
G Major 13

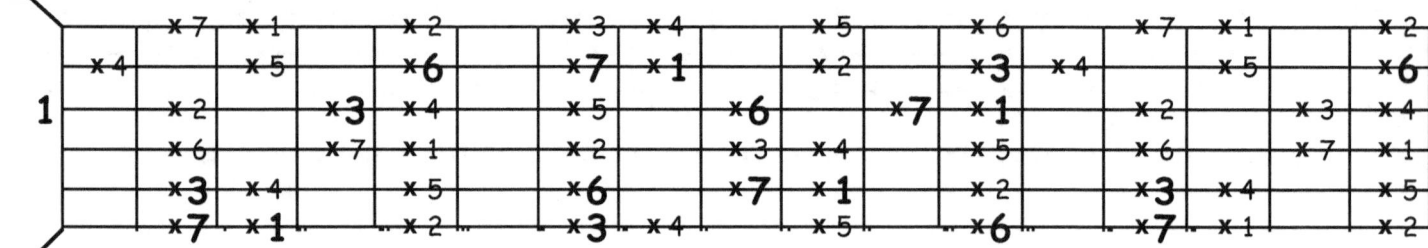

The only notes that you play are: 1, 3, 6, and 7 of the G major scale.

The "2" Chord: Minor 13 Inversions In "G" Major
A Minor 13

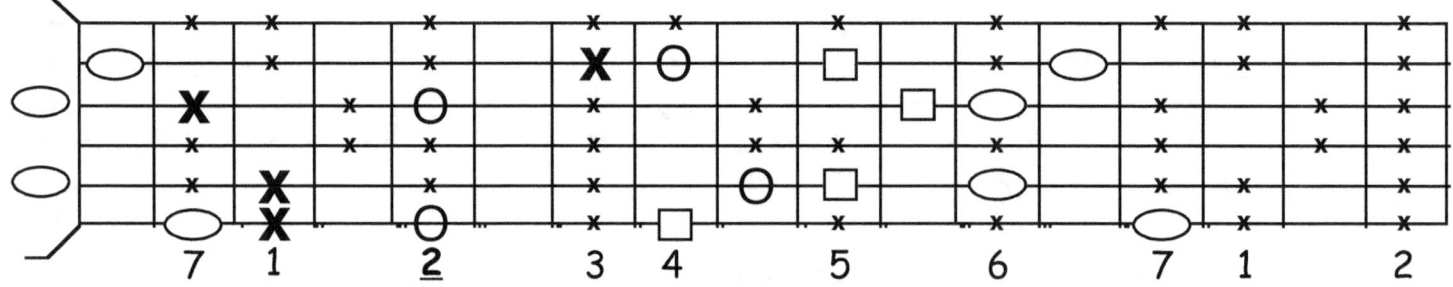

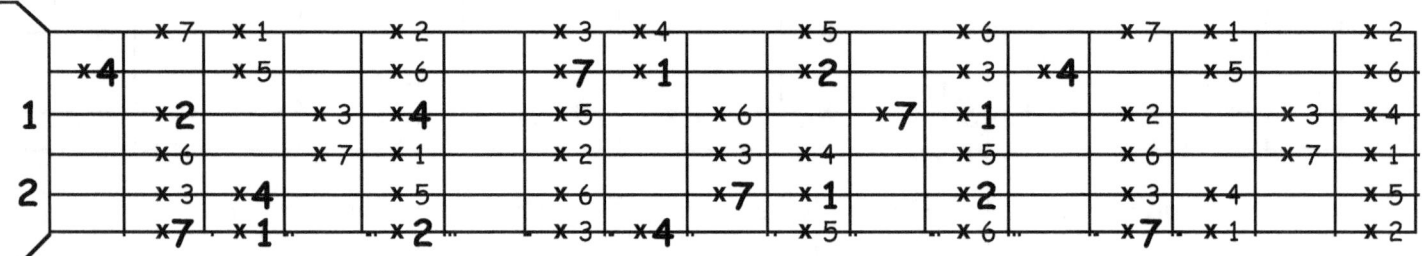

The only notes that you play are: 2, 4, 7, and 1 of the G major scale.

6532 STRING GROUPING

The "3" Chord: Minor 7 (b13) Inversions In "G" Major

B Minor 7 (b13)

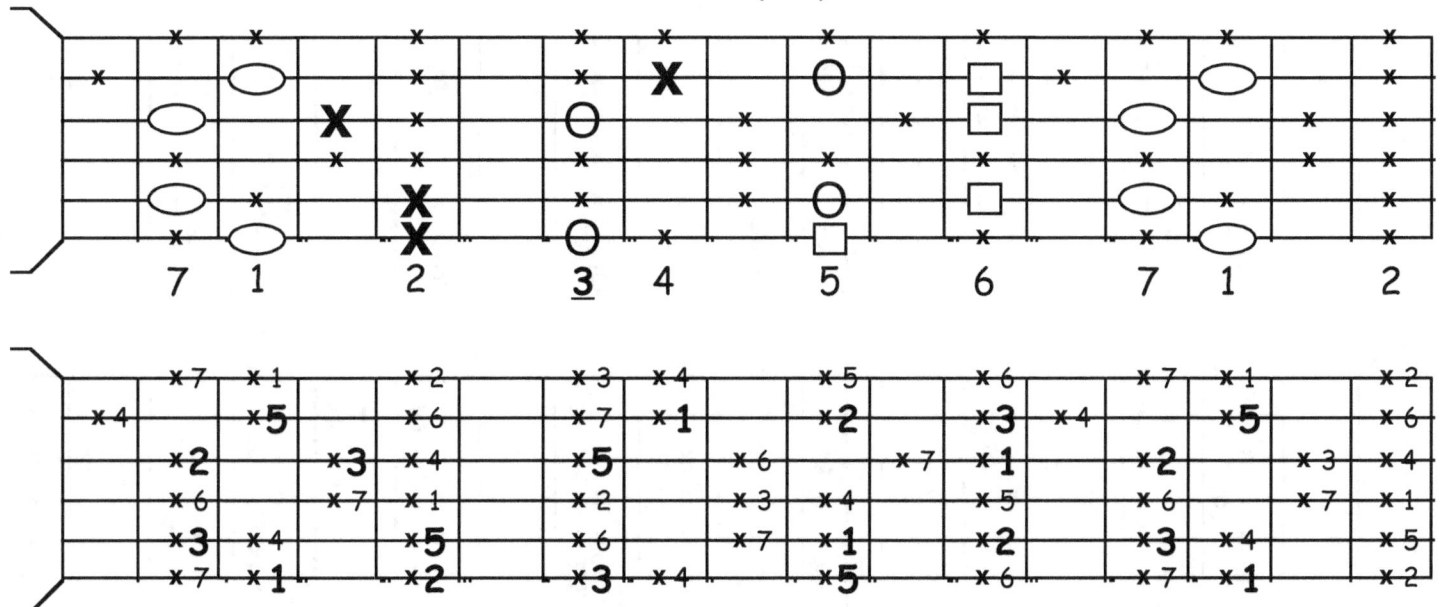

The only notes that you play are: 3, 5, 1, and 2 of the G major scale.

The "4" Chord: Major 13 Inversions In "G" Major

C Major 13

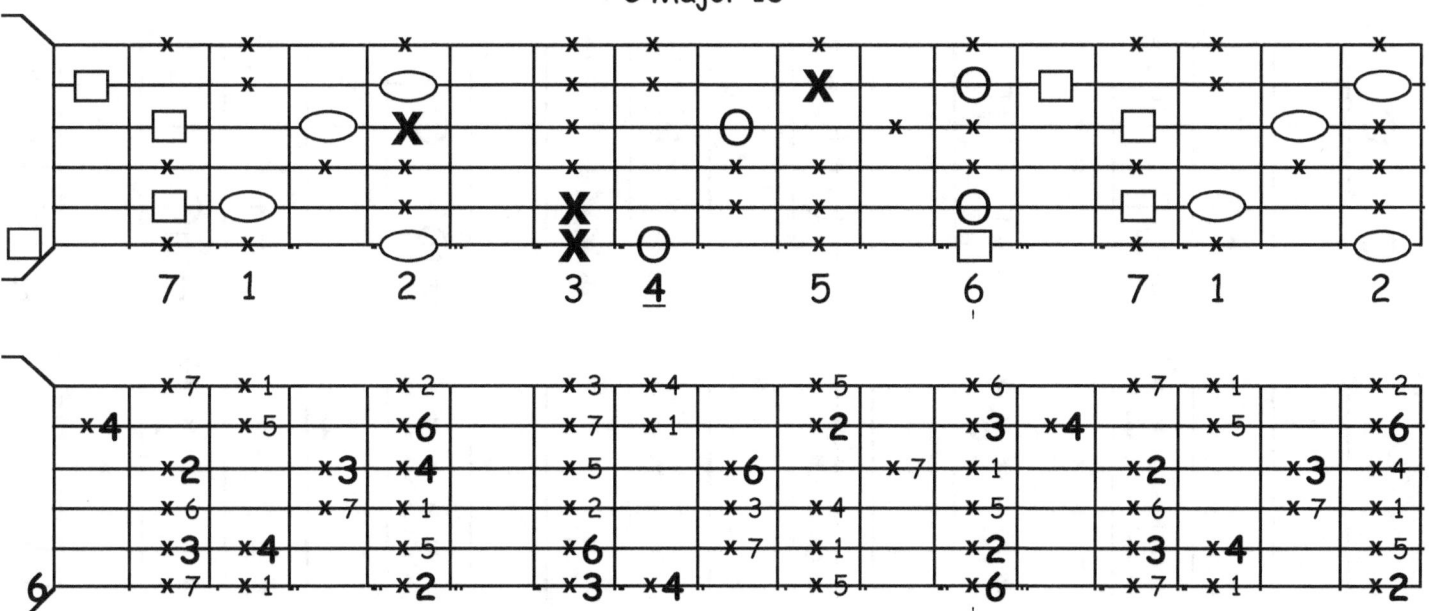

The only notes that you play are: 4, 6, 2, and 3 of the G major scale.

6532 STRING GROUPING
The "5" Chord: Dominant 13 Inversions In "G" Major
D Dominant 13

The only notes that you play are: 5, 7, 3, and 4 of the G major scale.

The "6" Chord: Minor 7 (b13) Inversions In "G" Major
E Minor 7 (b13)

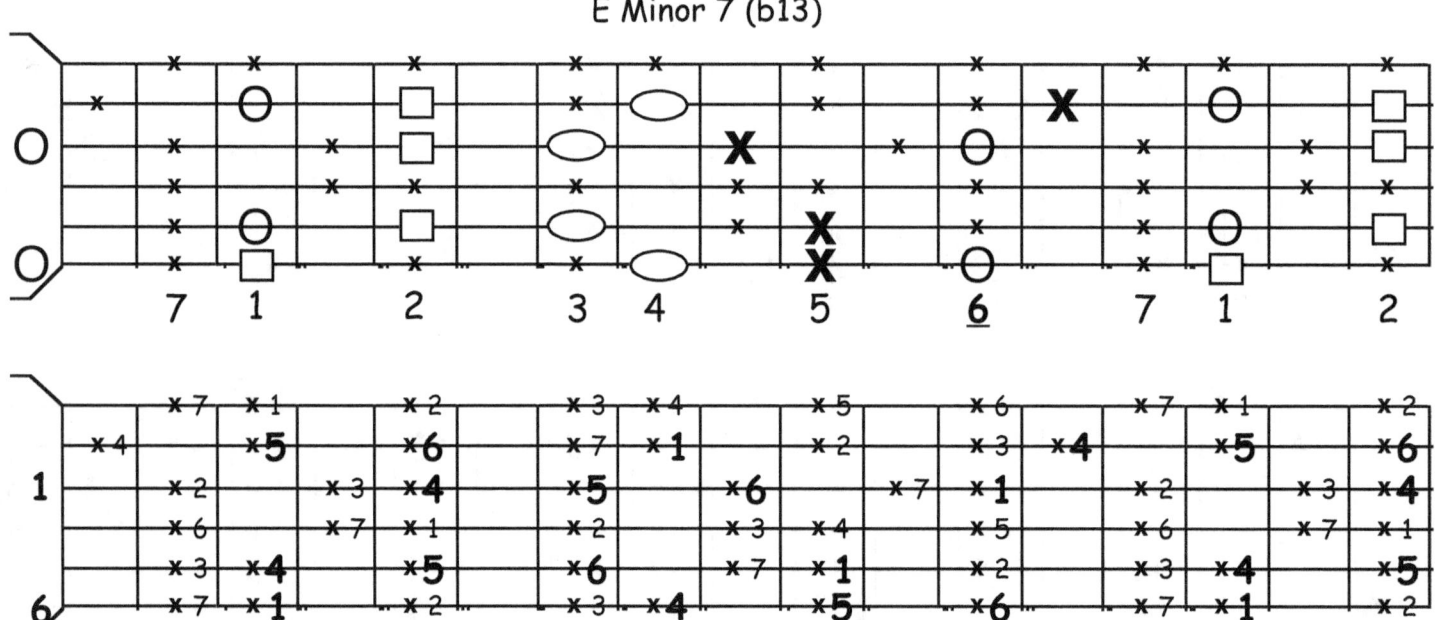

The only notes that you play are: 6, 1, 4, and 5 of the G major scale.

6532 STRING GROUPING

The "7" Chord: Minor 7b5 (b13) Inversions In "G" Major

F# Minor 7b5 (b13)

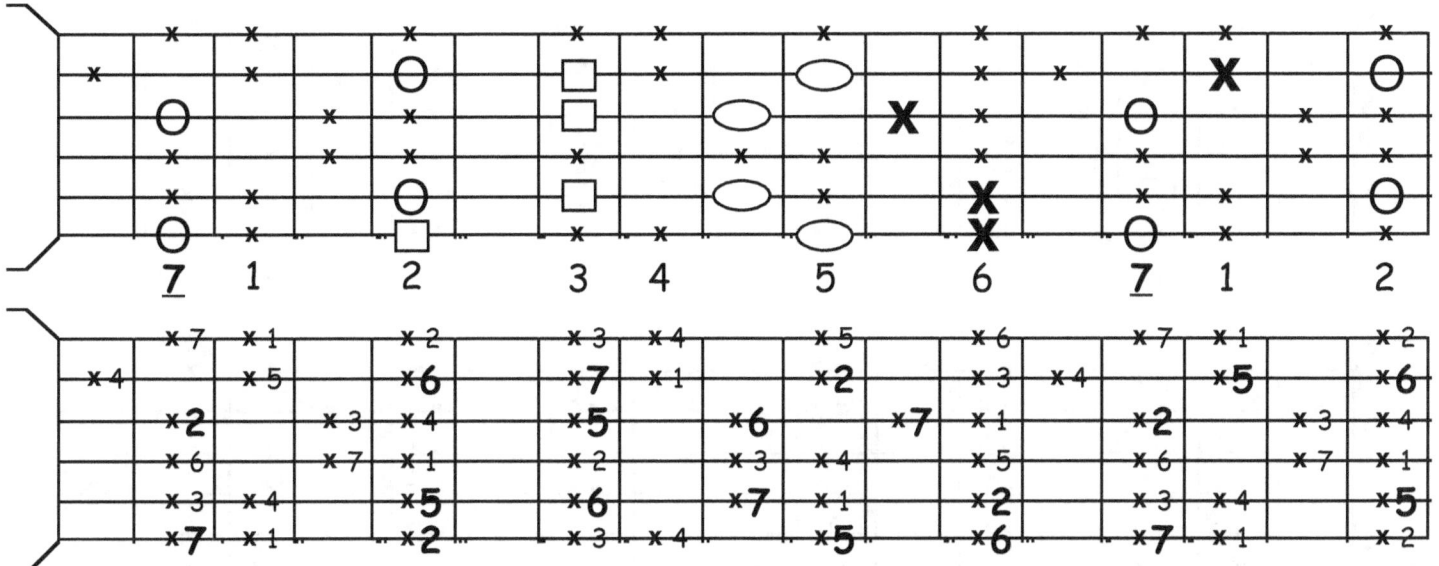

The only notes that you play are: 7, 2, 5, and 6 of the G major scale.

DROP 2 & 4

5421 STRING GROUPING

The "1" Chord: Major 13 Inversions In "G" Major

G Major 13

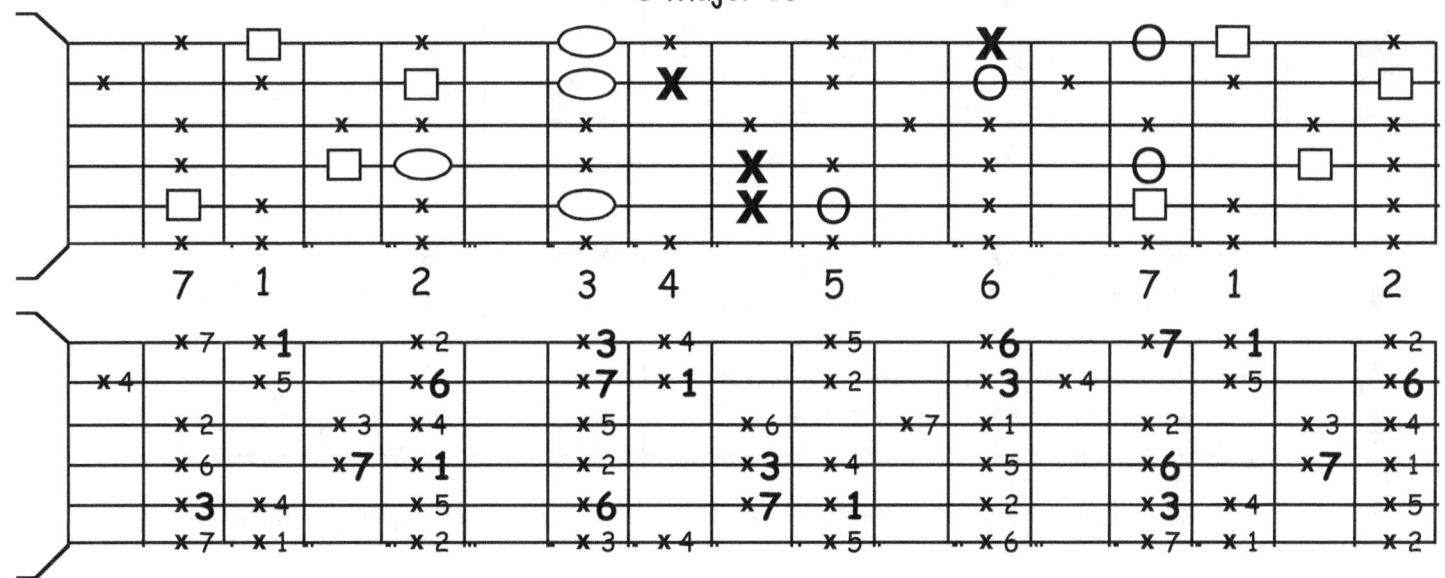

The only notes that you play are: 1, 3, 6, and 7 of the G major scale.

5421 STRING GROUPING
The "2" Chord: Minor 13 Inversions In "G" Major
A Minor 13

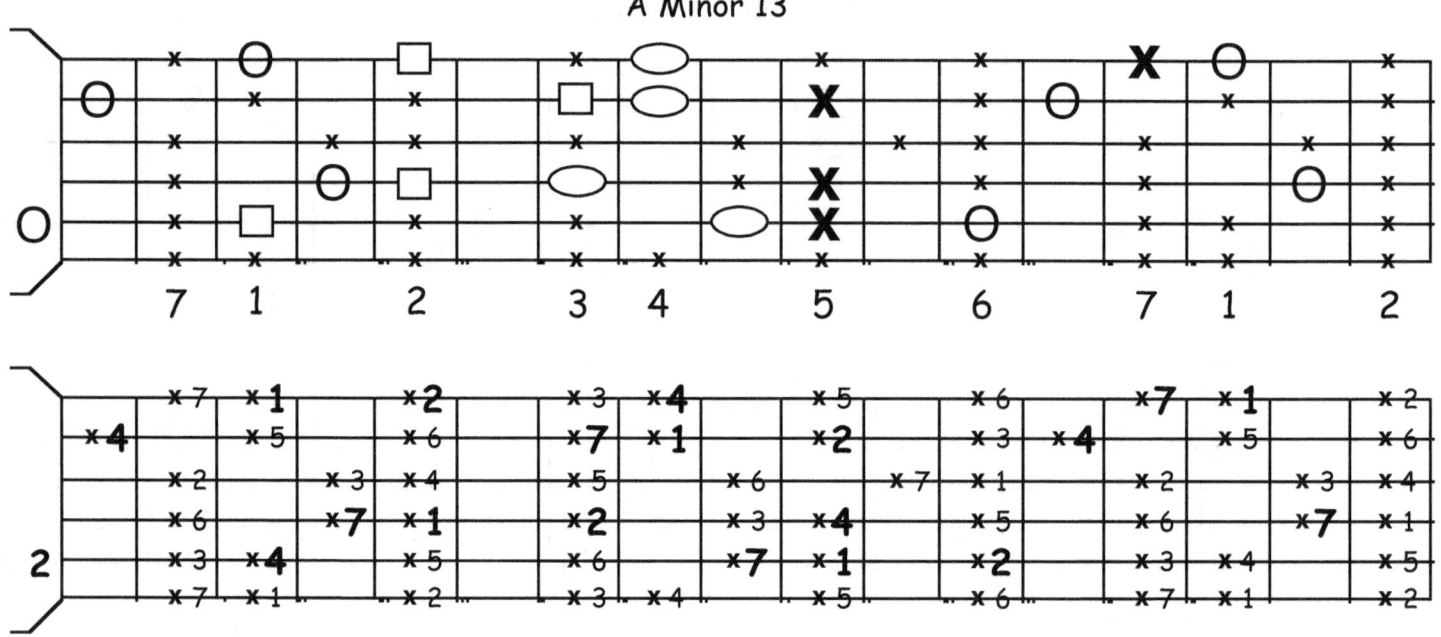

The only notes that you play are: 2, 4, 7, and 1 of the G major scale.

The "3" Chord: Minor 7 (b13) Inversions In "G" Major
B Minor 7 (b13)

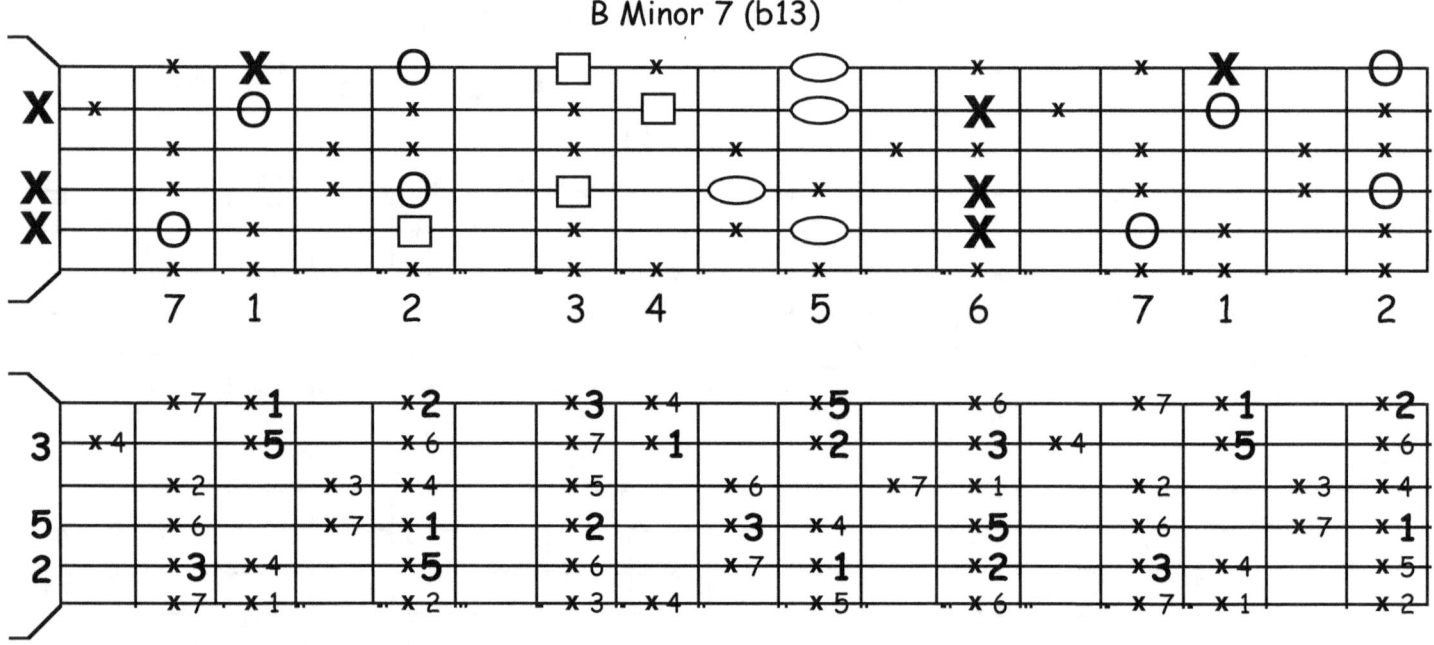

The only notes that you play are: 3, 5, 1, and 2 of the G major scale.

5421 STRING GROUPING

The "4" Chord: Major 13 Inversions In "G" Major

C Major 13

The only notes that you play are: 4, 6, 2, and 3 of the G major scale.

The "5" Chord: Dominant 13 Inversions In "G" Major

D Dominant 13

The only notes that you play are: 5, 7, 3, and 4 of the G major scale.

5421 STRING GROUPING

The "6" Chord: Minor 7 (b13) Inversions In "G" Major
E Minor 7 (b13)

The only notes that you play are: 6, 1, 4, and 5 of the G major scale.

The "7" Chord: Minor 7b5 (b13) Inversions In "G" Major
F# Minor 7b5 (b13)

The only notes that you play are: 7, 2, 5, and 6 of the G major scale.

DOUBLE DROP 2 & DROP 4
6521 STRING GROUPING
The "1" Chord: Major 13 Inversions In "G" Major
G Major 13

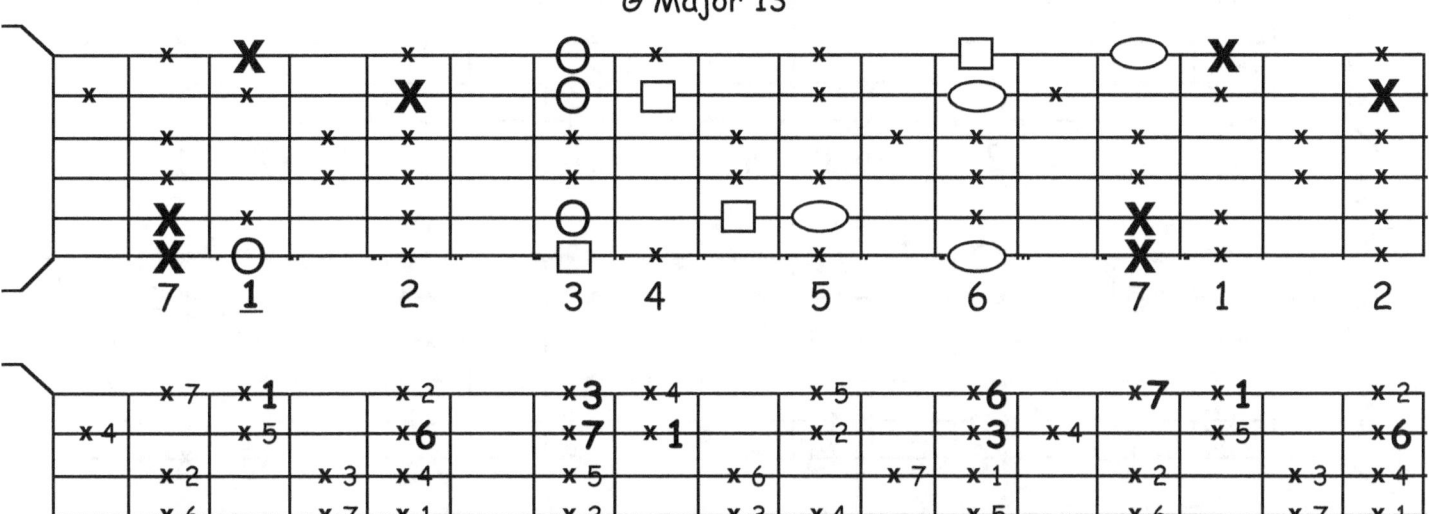

The only notes that you play are: 1, 3, 6, and 7 of the G major scale.

The "2" Chord: Minor 13 Inversions In "G" Major
A Minor 13

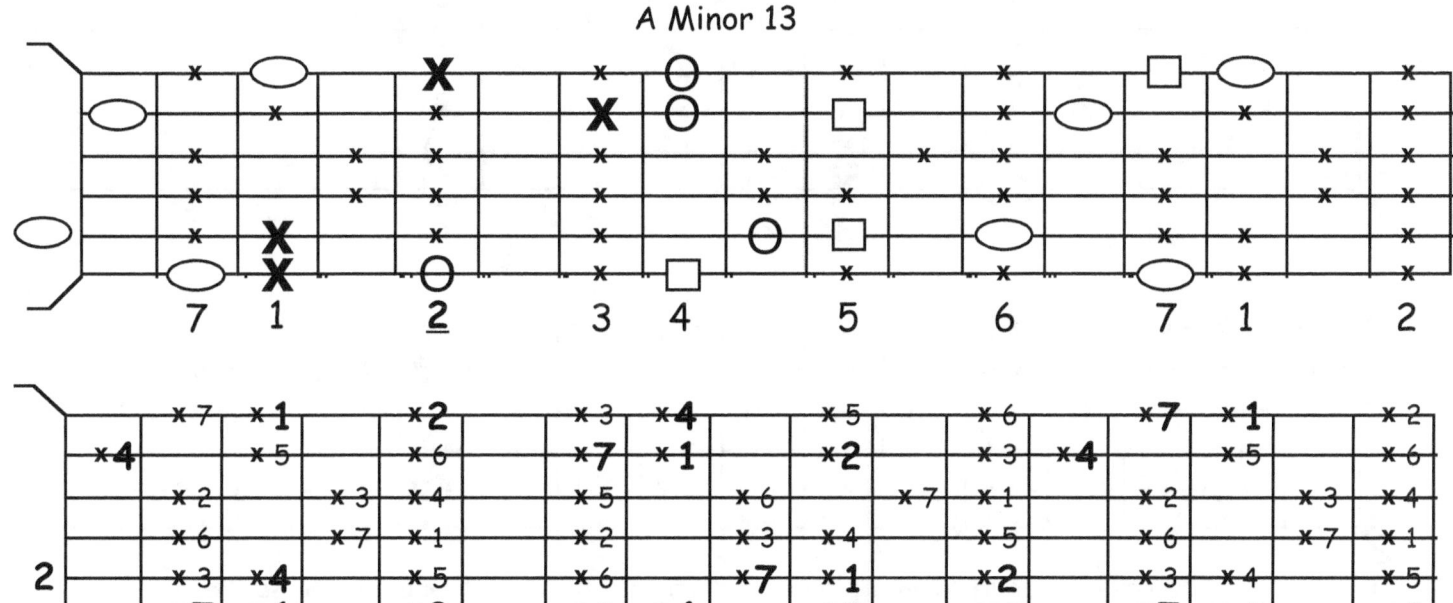

The only notes that you play are: 2, 4, 7, and 1 of the G major scale.

6521 STRING GROUPING

The "3" Chord: Minor 7 (b13) Inversions In "G" Major

B Minor 7 (b13)

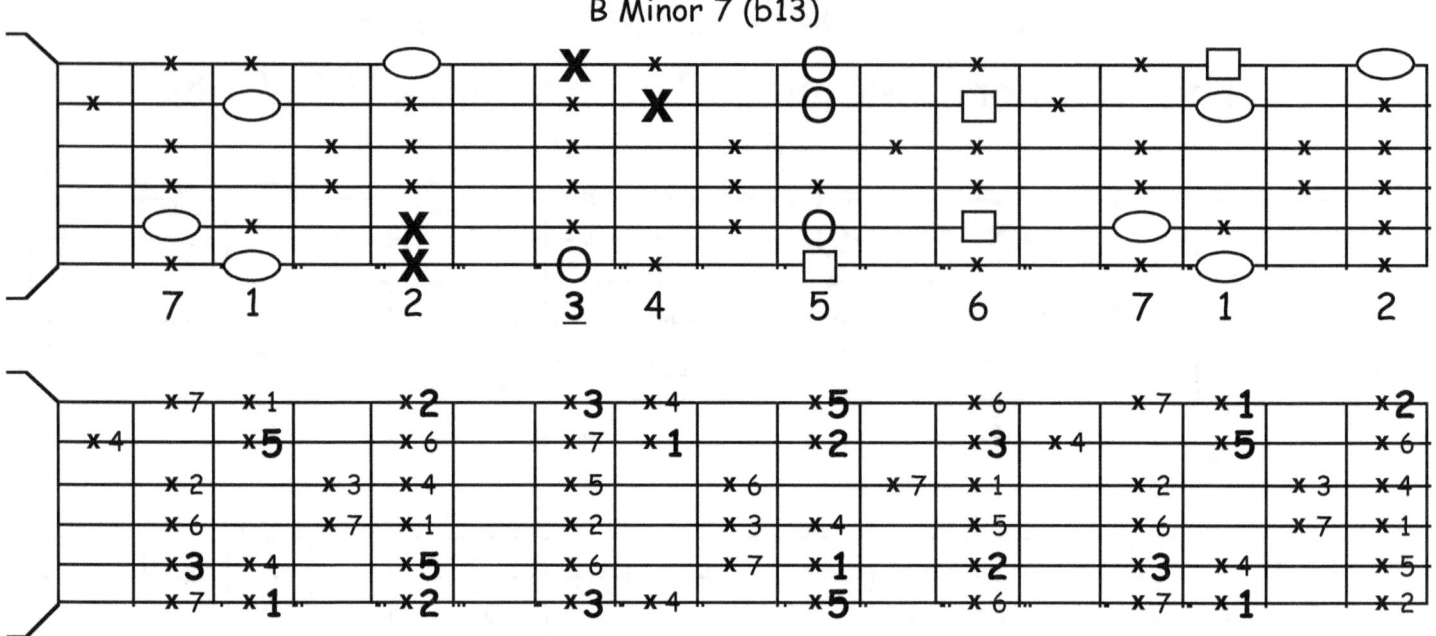

The only notes that you play are: 3, 5, 1, and 2 of the G major scale.

The "4" Chord: Major 13 Inversions In "G" Major

C Major 13

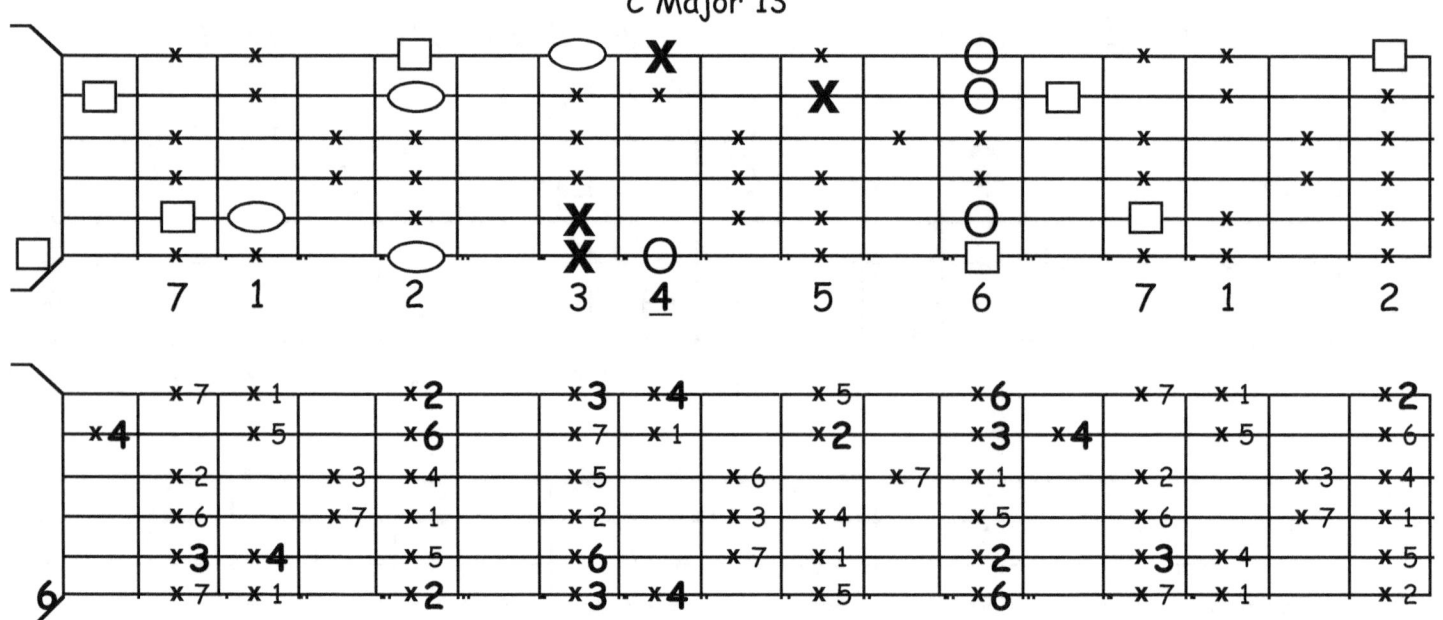

The only notes that you play are: 4, 6, 2, and 3 of the G major scale.

6521 STRING GROUPING

The "5" Chord: Dominant 13 Inversions In "G" Major

D Dominant 13

The only notes that you play are: 5, 7, 3, and 4 of the G major scale.

The "6" Chord: Minor 7 (b13) Inversions In "G" Major

E Minor 7 (b13)

The only notes that you play are: 6, 1, 4, and 5 of the G major scale.

6521 STRING GROUPING
The "7" Chord: Minor 7b5 (b13) Inversions In "G" Major
F# Minor 7b5 (b13)

The only notes that you play are: 7, 2, 5, and 6 of the G major scale.

ALTERED SEVENTH CHORDS

There are many ways to "alter" seventh chords. Categorizing all of these different ways would require an entire book (or two). The most common ways to alter seventh chords can be reduced to 7 basic altered chord types. These basic altered chords are:

> Major 7#11
> Major 7#5
> Minor Major 7
> Dominant 7#11
> Dominant 7#5
> Dominant 7#9
> Dominant 7b9

These are the only altered seventh chord voicings and inversions that are included in this book. There are also chords that combine multiple alterations. However, remember that we guitarists usually only have four fingers with which to play these chords (unless we're using the tapping method). Sometimes when a chord chart calls for multiple alterations, its because the arranger doesn't know how to write for guitar, so they have given us a chord symbol that represents what they would like, but not what is possible for the guitar. Sometimes, however, these multiple alterations are included to inform us of what harmonies appear in the other written parts, so we can pick and choose how to alter the chord appropriately without clashing with the other musical parts.

Earlier in this book, all 7 diatonic seventh chords of the major scale were presented with their inversions (1 chord, 2 chord, 3 chord, etc ...). The parent scales that contain the altered seventh chords also contain some un-altered diatonic seventh chords. While presenting ALL of the chords (both altered and un-altered diatonic seventh chords) that come from these scales would provide you with a clear context of where the altered chords come from and how all of the chords relate to these scales, it would also triple the size of this book. So, the altered seventh chords and their inversions are presented individually with only one of their potential parent scales underneath them.

ALSO, at this point in the book, I trust that you have gotten used to the shapes that I am using to distinguish between the root position, first inversion, second inversion, and third inversion chords. Keep in mind that with the altered chords, one of the chord tones will be raised or lowered in order to create the desired "altered" note. When playing an inversion that calls for the affected chord tone in the bass, the "altered" note will be the note in the bass.

Now what you need to know is:
1) What do these chords look like on a chord chart?
2) What do these chords look like on the neck of the guitar?

NOTE:
ALL of the "#11" chords are interchangeable with their corresponding "b5" chords. And all of the dominant 7#5 chords are interchangeable with dominant 7b13 chords. There are music theorists who will argue until the end of time that these are all completely different chord types, BUT, because of the fingering limitations on the guitar, these chords are interchangeable.

While there is no one standard notation for writing out chord symbols on chord charts, there are some symbols that are used more frequently then others. Here are some of the common ways that you will see these altered chords depicted in chord charts. I'll use the letter "C" as a constant to show you some of these symbols:

C Major 7#11 = C Maj7#11, C M7#11, C△7#11, C Ma7#11
C Maj7b5, C M7b5, C△7b5, C Ma7b5

C Major 7#5 = C Maj7#5, C M7#5, C△7#5, C Ma7#5, C Maj7+5

C Minor Major 7 = C-maj7, C min/maj7, C mi△7, C min-maj7, C-Maj7

C Dominant 7#11 = C7#11, C7b5

C Dominant 7#5 = C7#5, C+7, C7b13

C Dominant 7#9 = C7#9, C7+9

C Dominant 7b9 = C7b9

Here now are the altered seventh chords ...

MAJOR 7#11

The major 7#11 (major 7b5) chords need to include the note that exists between the 4th and the 5th of the basic major 7 chord voicing. The closest chord tone to the #11 is the 5th of the chord. The easiest way to create the #11 (or b5) sound is to lower the 5th of the chord a half step (one fret). In the major scale, both the "1" chord and the "4" chord are major 7 chords. When you play the "4" chord (spelled: 4, 6, 1, 3), the 5th of the chord is the 1 of the scale. You can lower it a half step (to the 7), without changing the scale. This gives you a chord that has a root, a 3rd, a #11th (or b5), and a 7th (4 = root, 6 = 3rd, 7 = #11th, 3 = 7th). When playing the second inversion, the #11th will be the note in the bass.

O = Root Position Major 7#11 Chord
□ = First Inversion Major 7#11 Chord
⬭ = Second Inversion Major 7#11 Chord (#11 in the bass)
X = Third Inversion Major 7#11 Chord

DROP 2

The "4" Chord: Major 7#11 Inversions In "G" Major
6543 STRING GROUPING
C Major 7#11

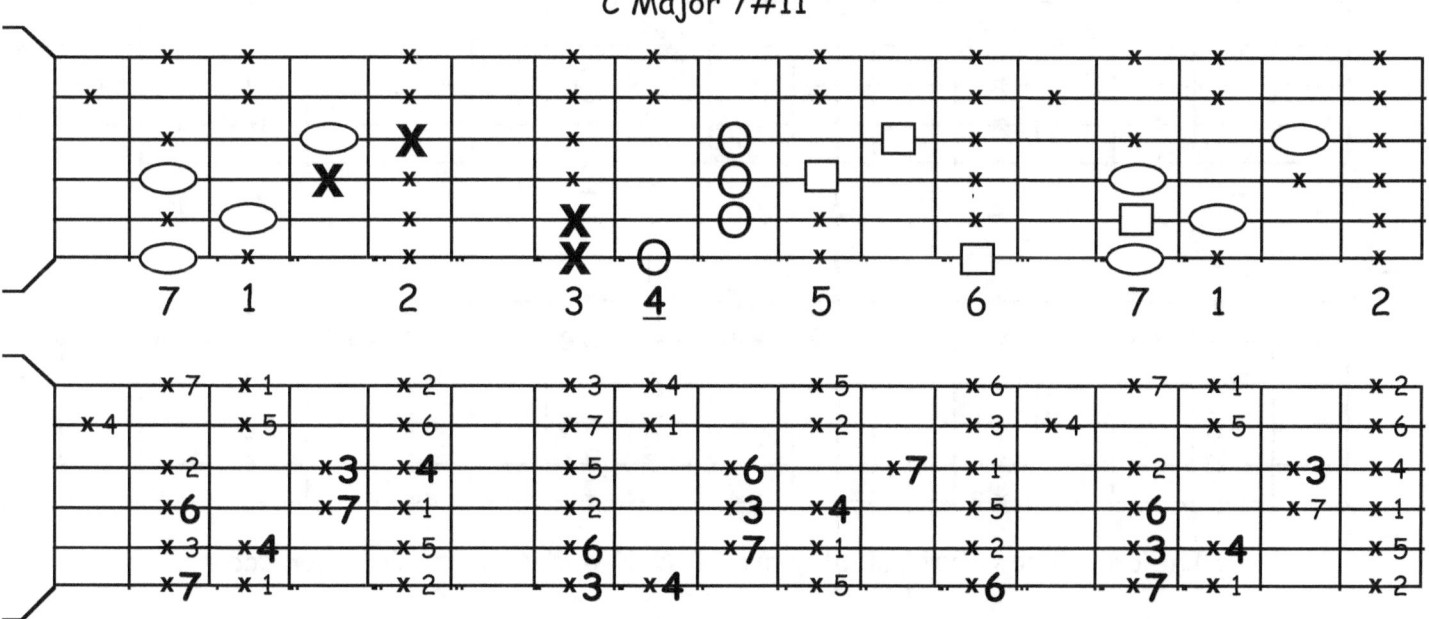

The only notes that you play are: 4, 6, 7, and 3 of the G major scale.

The "4" Chord: Major 7#11 Inversions In "G" Major
5432 STRING GROUPING
C Major 7#11

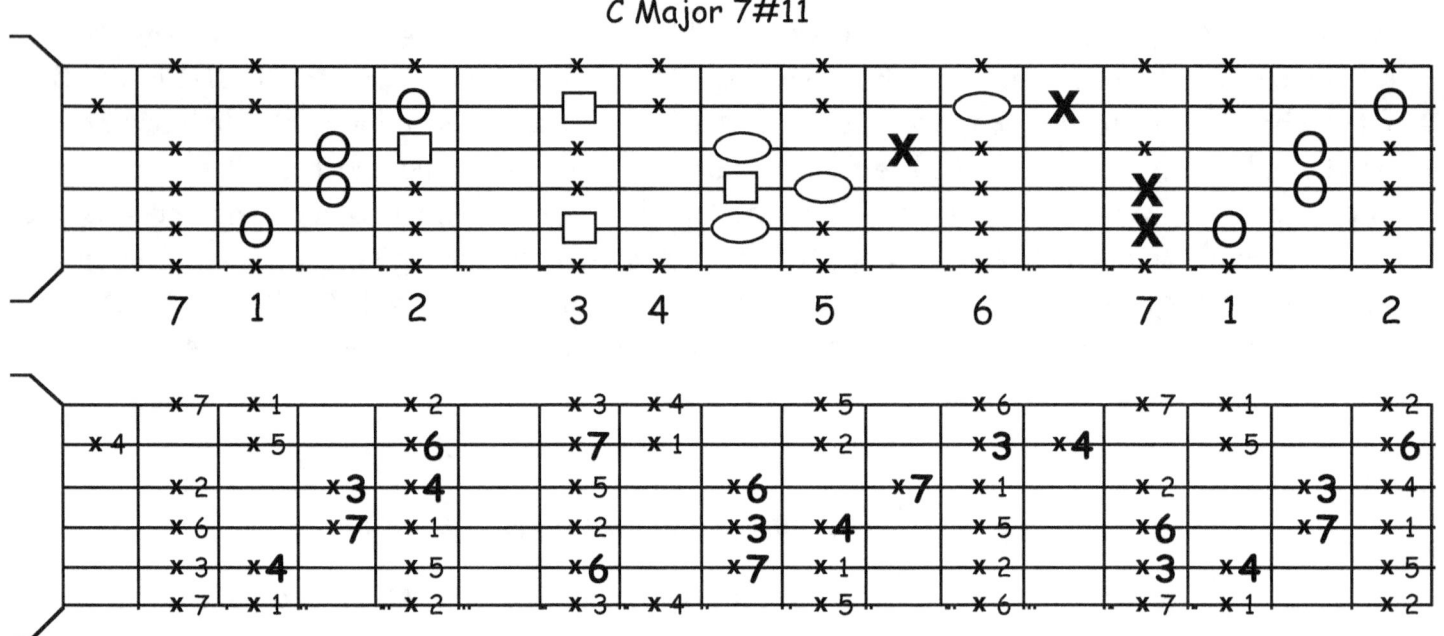

The only notes that you play are: 4, 6, 7, and 3 of the G major scale.

4321 STRING GROUPING
C Major 7#11

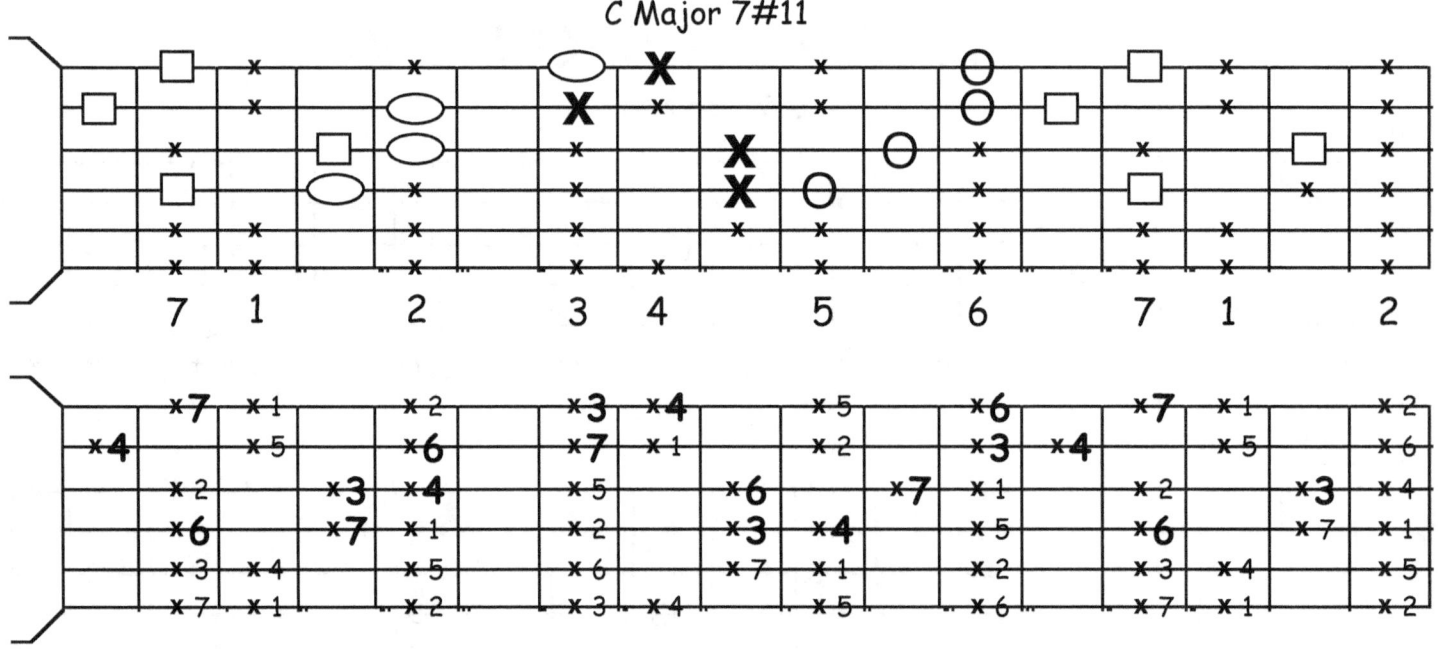

The only notes that you play are: 4, 6, 7, and 3 of the G major scale.

The "4" Chord: Major 7#11 Inversions In "G" Major

DROP 3

6432 STRING GROUPING
C Major 7#11

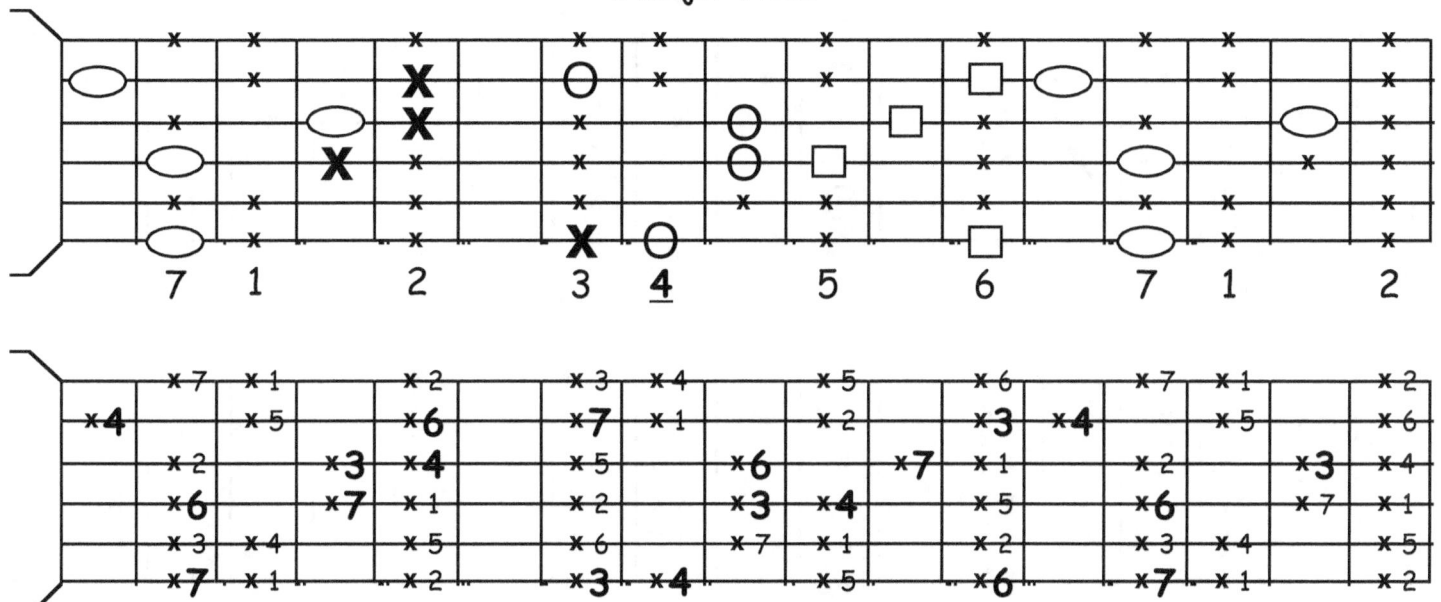

The only notes that you play are: 4, 6, 7, and 3 of the G major scale.

5321 STRING GROUPING
C Major 7#11

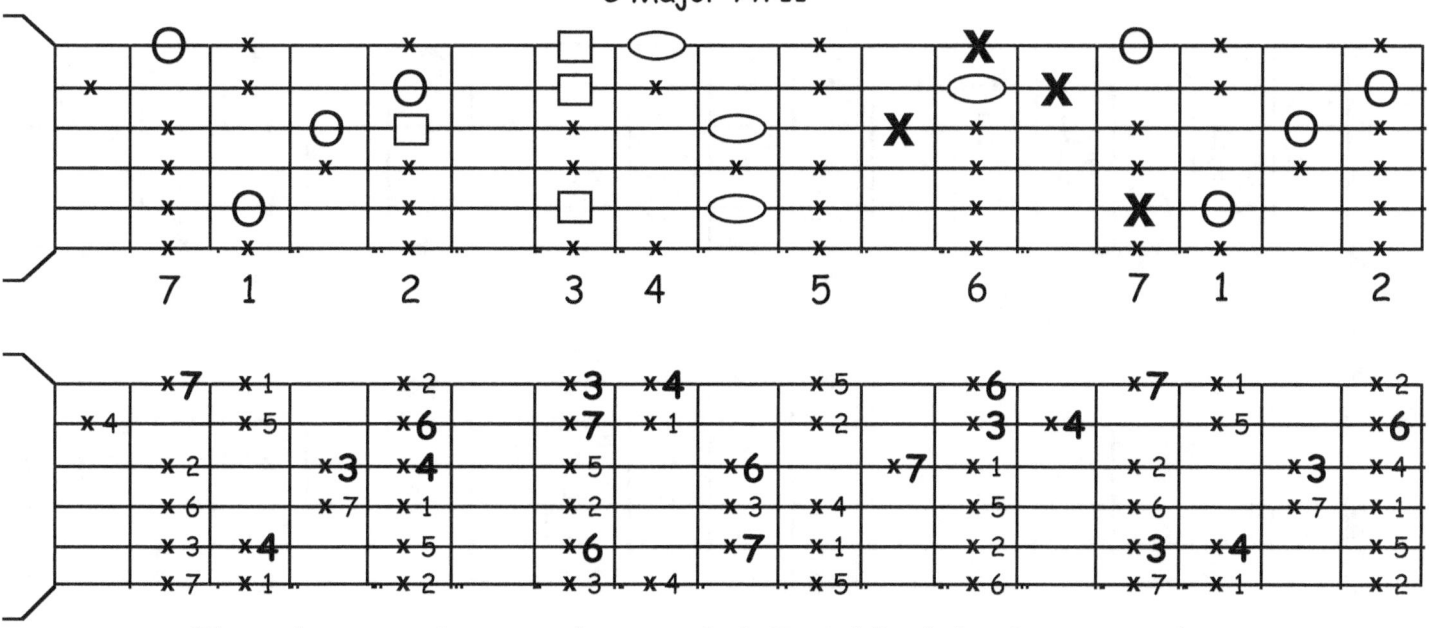

The only notes that you play are: 4, 6, 7, and 3 of the G major scale.

The "4" Chord: Major 7#11 Inversions In "G" Major
DROP 2 & 3
6542 STRING GROUPING
C Major 7#11

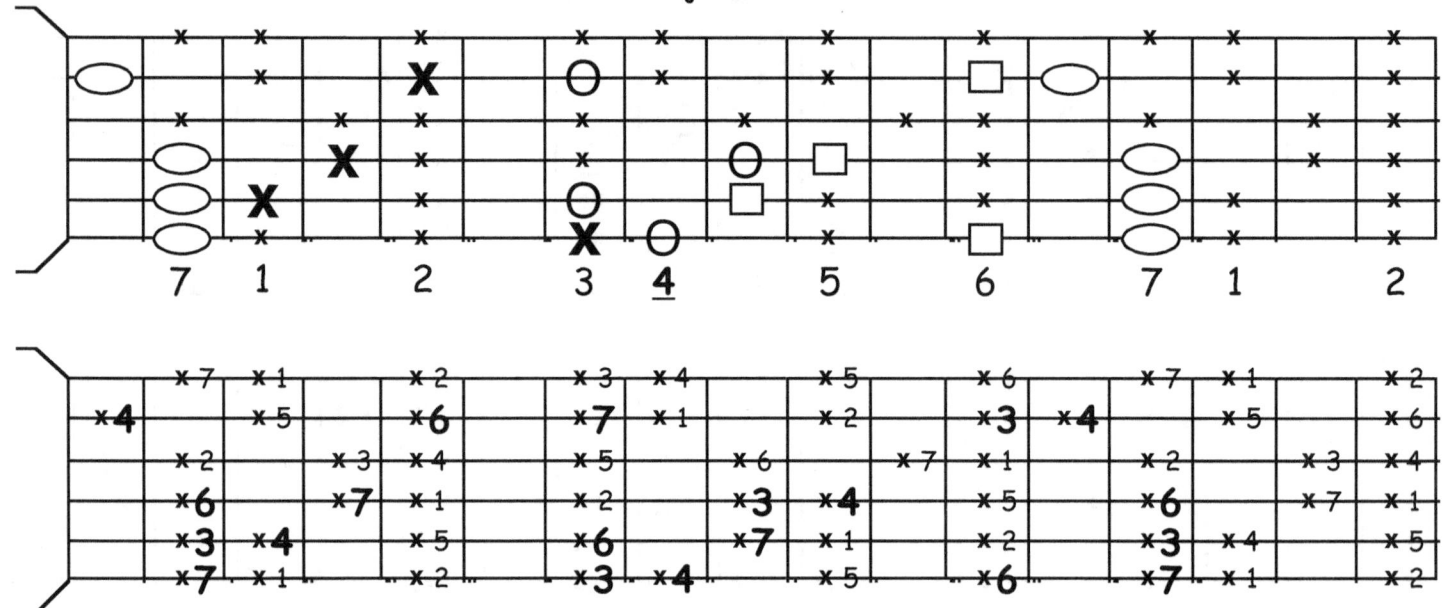

The only notes that you play are: 4, 6, 7, and 3 of the G major scale.

5431 STRING GROUPING
C Major 7#11

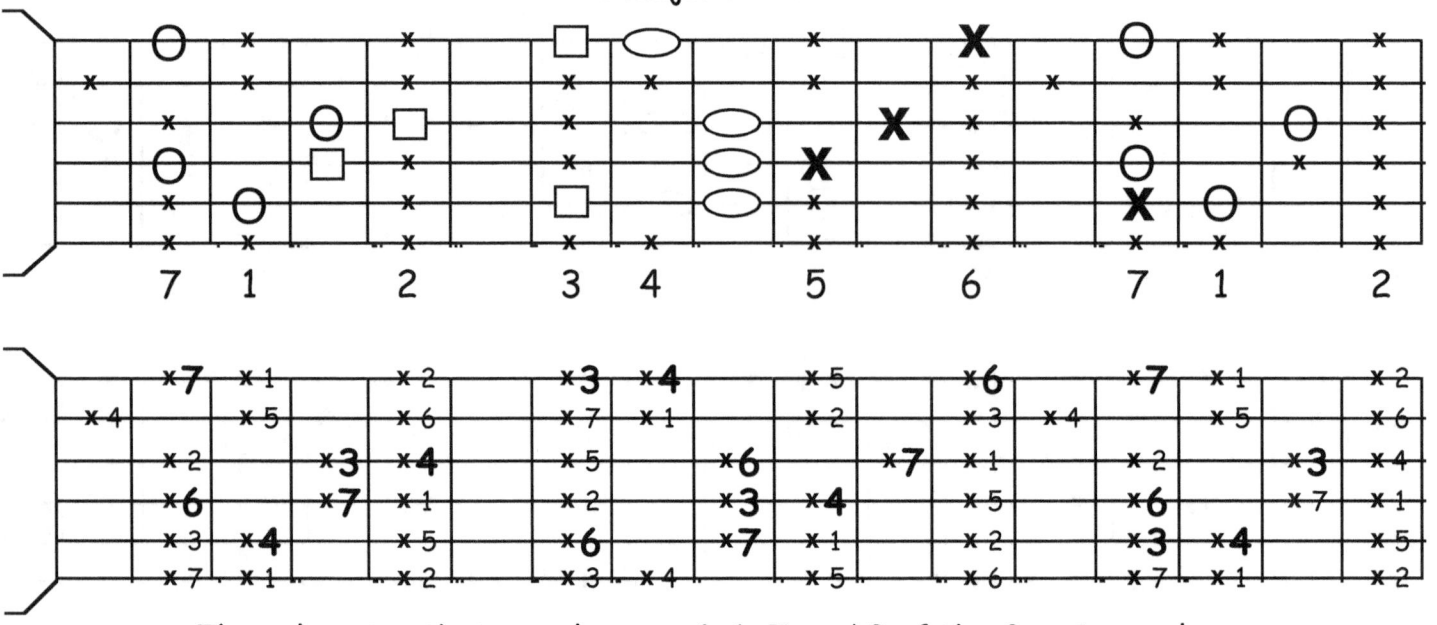

The only notes that you play are: 4, 6, 7, and 3 of the G major scale.

The "4" Chord: Major 7#11 Inversions In "G" Major
DROP 2 & 4

6532 STRING GROUPING
C Major 7#11

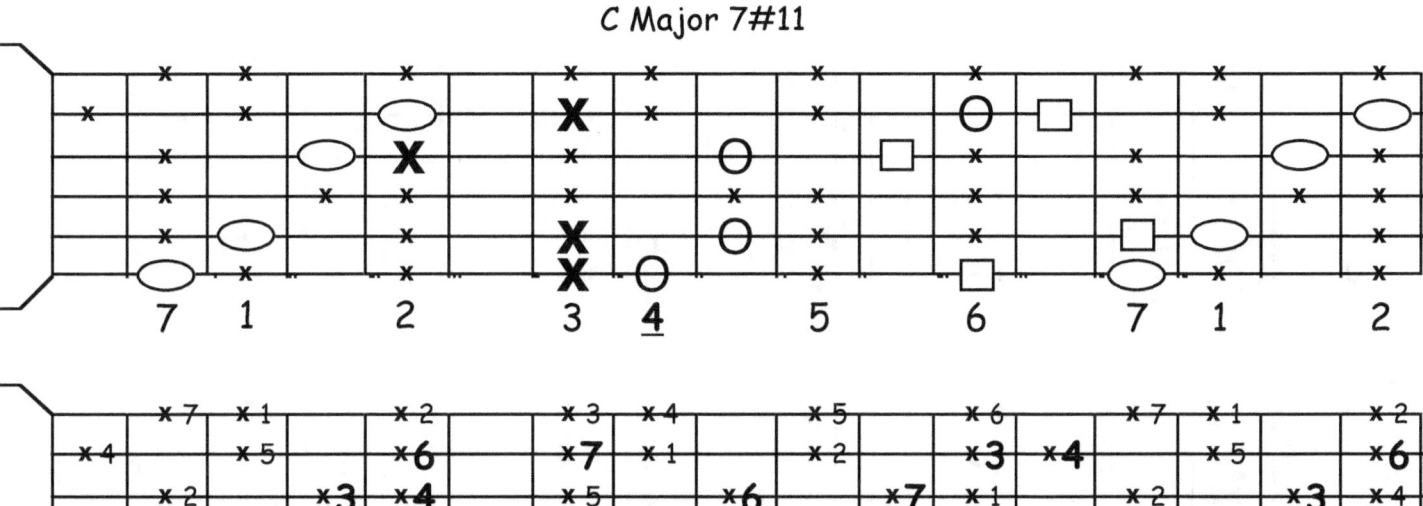

The only notes that you play are: 4, 6, 7, and 3 of the G major scale.

5421 STRING GROUPING
C Major 7#11

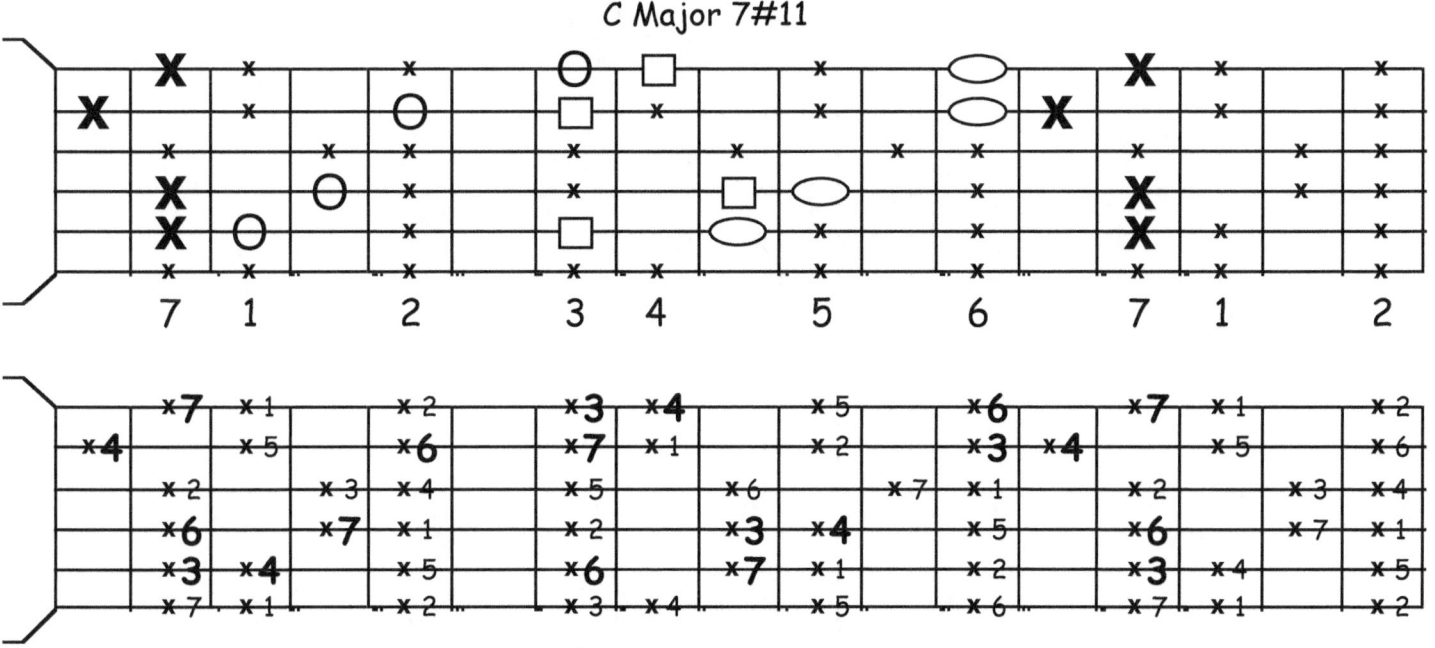

The only notes that you play are: 4, 6, 7, and 3 of the G major scale.

The "4" Chord: Major 7#11 Inversions In "G" Major
DOUBLE DROP 2 & DROP 4
6521 STRING GROUPING

C Major 7#11

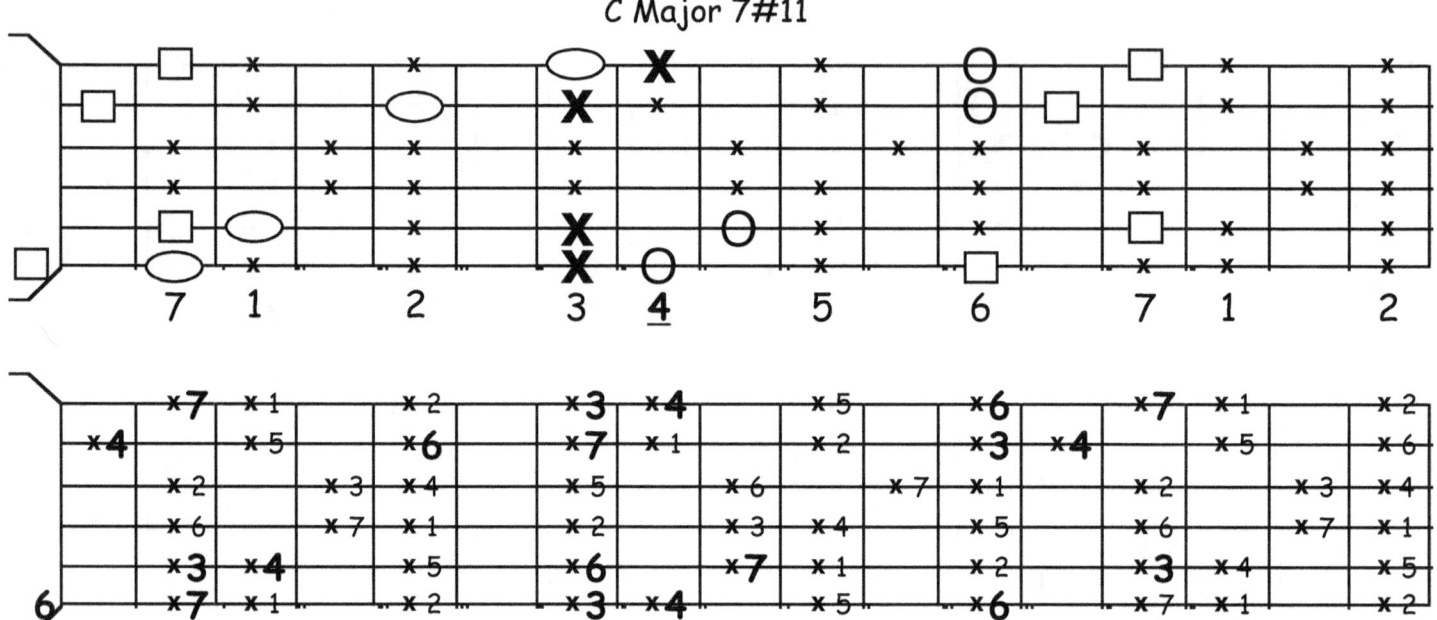

The only notes that you play are: 4, 6, 7, and 3 of the G major scale.

MAJOR 7#5

As the name states, a "major 7#5" chord is a major 7 chord with a raised 5th.
The major 7#5 chord occurs naturally in the harmonic minor and melodic minor scales.
I have presented them within the harmonic minor scale. In the MAJOR METHOD, the
E harmonic minor scale = the G major scale with a #5. So, the "1" chord in E harmonic minor
IS a G major 7#5 chord spelled: 1, 3, #5, 7 (1 = root, 3 = 3rd, #5 = #5th, 7 = 7th).
When playing the second inversion, the #5 will be the note in the bass.

O = Root Position Major 7#5 Chord

□ = First Inversion Major 7#5 Chord

◯ = Second Inversion Major 7#5 Chord (#5 in the bass)

X = Third Inversion Major 7#5 Chord

DROP 2

The "1" Chord: Major 7#5 Inversions In "E" Harmonic Minor
6543 STRING GROUPING

G Major 7#5 Chord

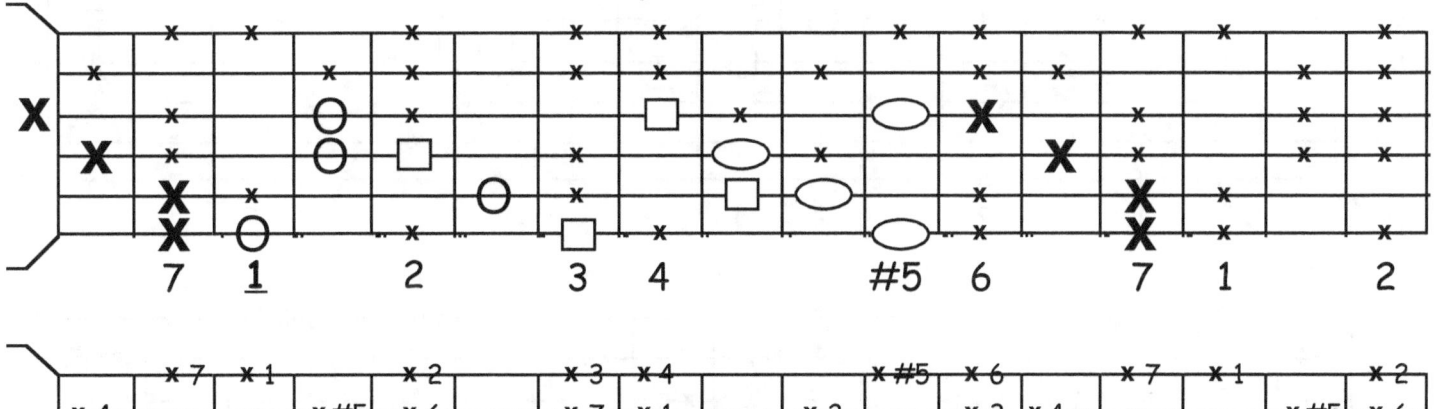

The only notes that you play are: 1, 3, #5, and 7 of the E harmonic minor scale.

199

The "1" Chord: Major 7#5 Inversions In "E" Harmonic Minor
5432 STRING GROUPING
G Major 7#5 Chord

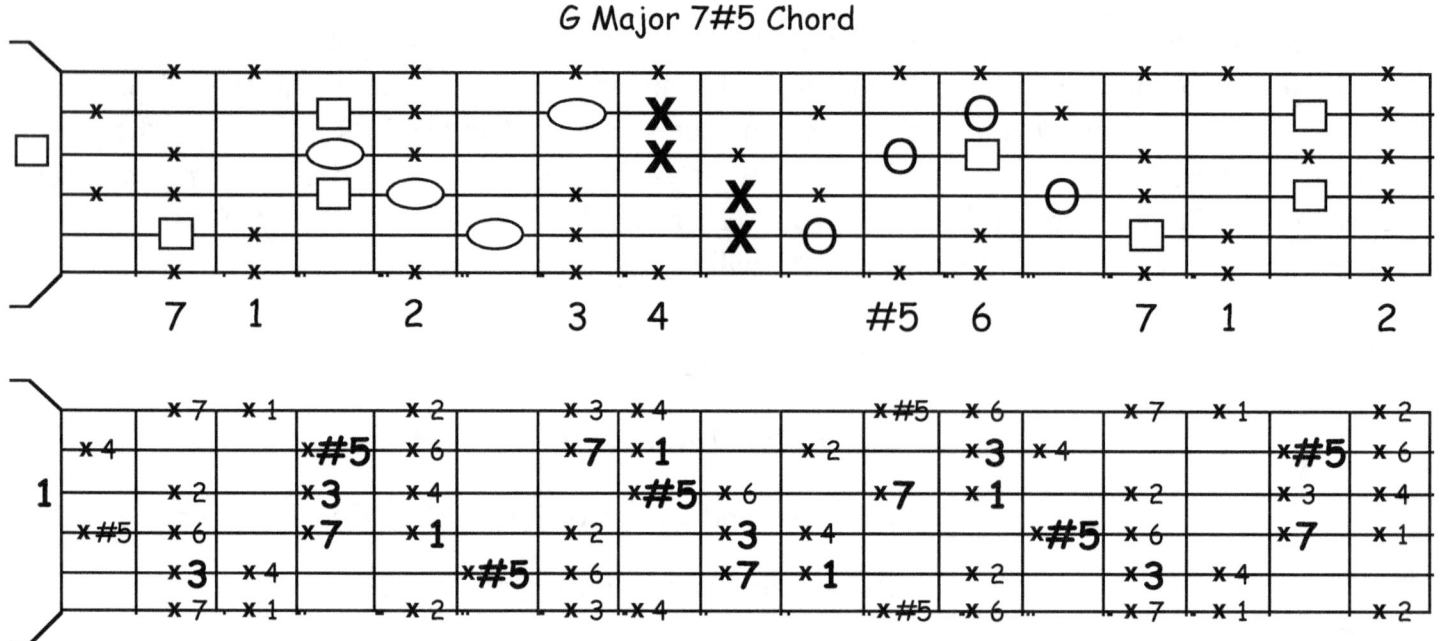

The only notes that you play are: 1, 3, #5, and 7 of the E harmonic minor scale.

4321 STRING GROUPING
G Major 7#5 Chord

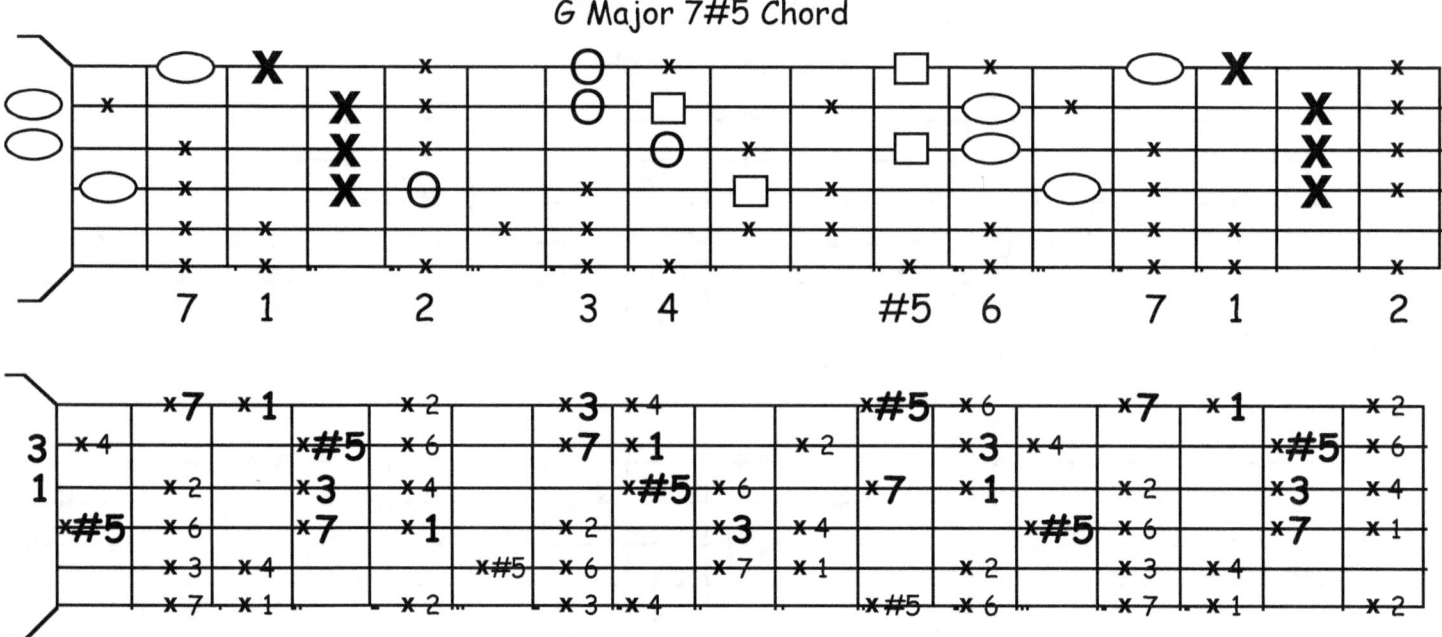

The only notes that you play are: 1, 3, #5, and 7 of the E harmonic minor scale.

The "1" Chord: Major 7#5 Inversions In "E" Harmonic Minor
DROP 3

6432 STRING GROUPING
G Major 7#5 Chord

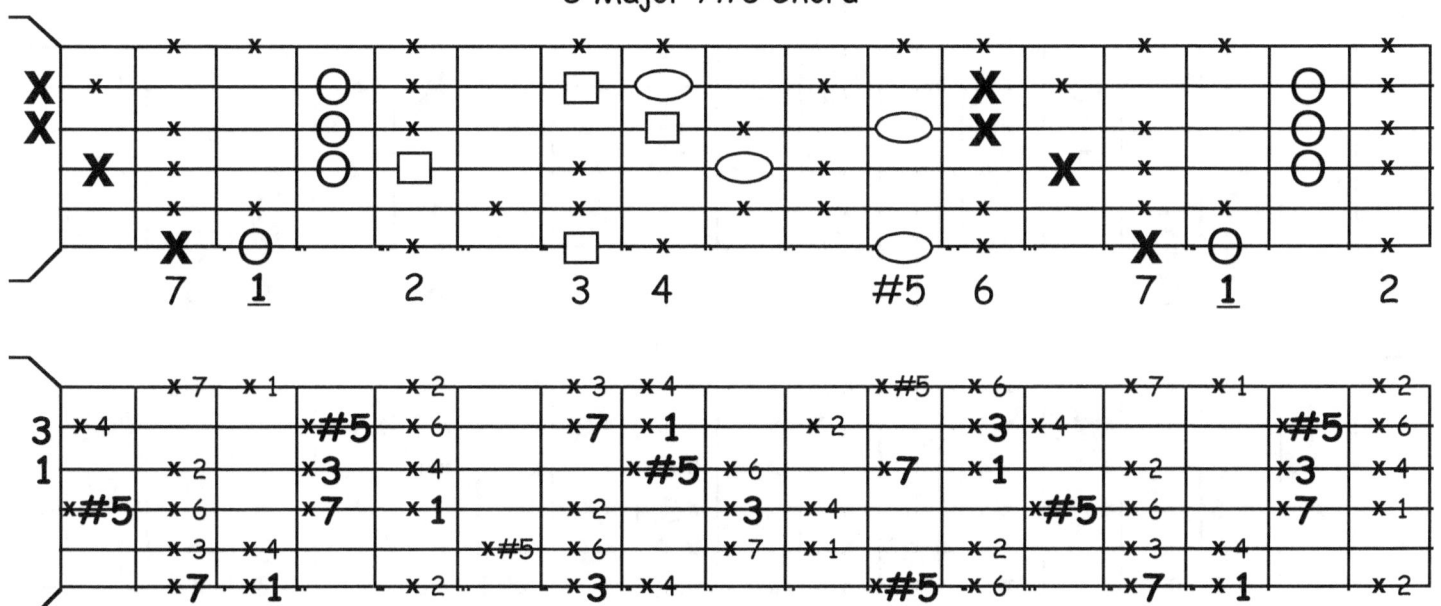

The only notes that you play are: 1, 3, #5, and 7 of the E harmonic minor scale.

5321 STRING GROUPING
G Major 7#5 Chord

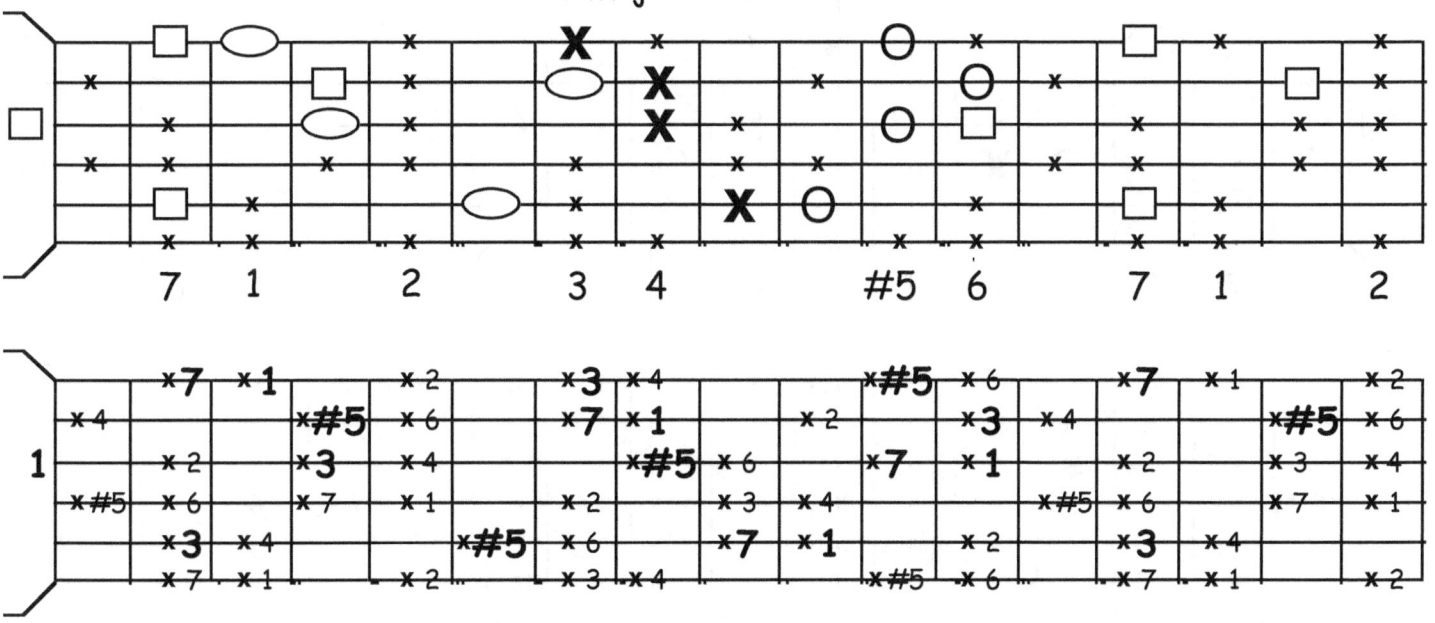

The only notes that you play are: 1, 3, #5, and 7 of the E harmonic minor scale.

The "1" Chord: Major 7#5 Inversions In "E" Harmonic Minor
DROP 2 & 3
6542 STRING GROUPING
G Major 7#5 Chord

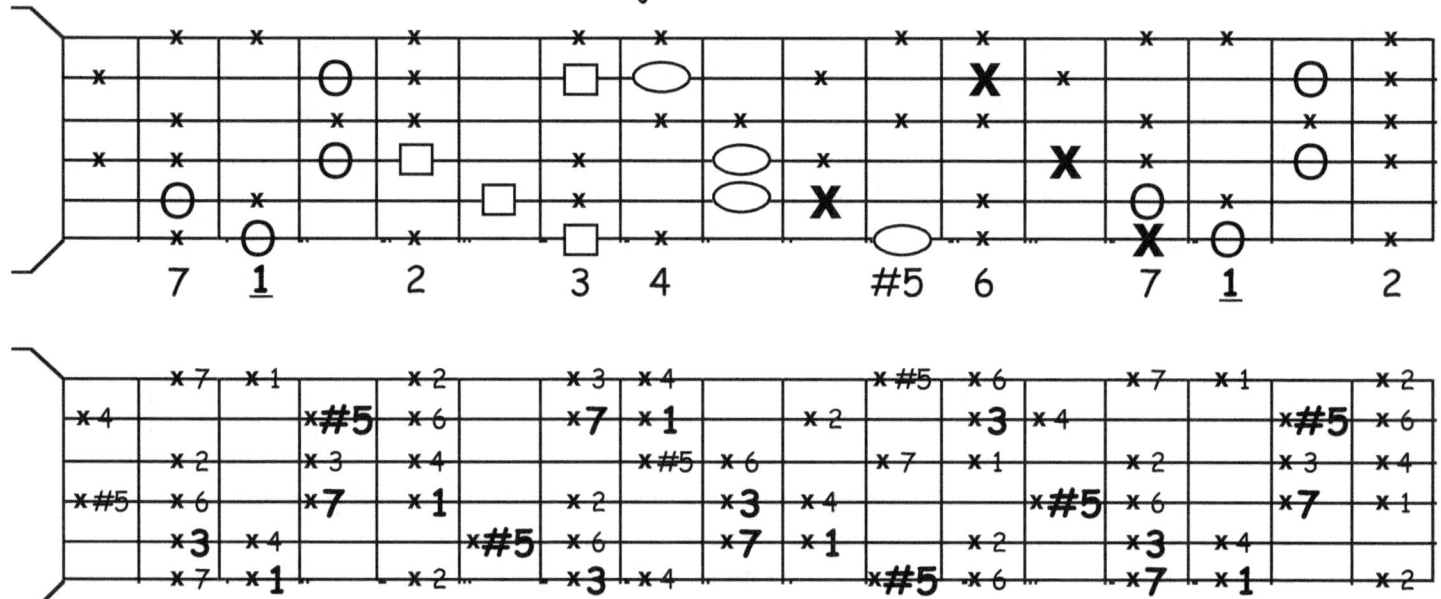

The only notes that you play are: 1, 3, #5, and 7 of the E harmonic minor scale.

5431 STRING GROUPING
G Major 7#5 Chord

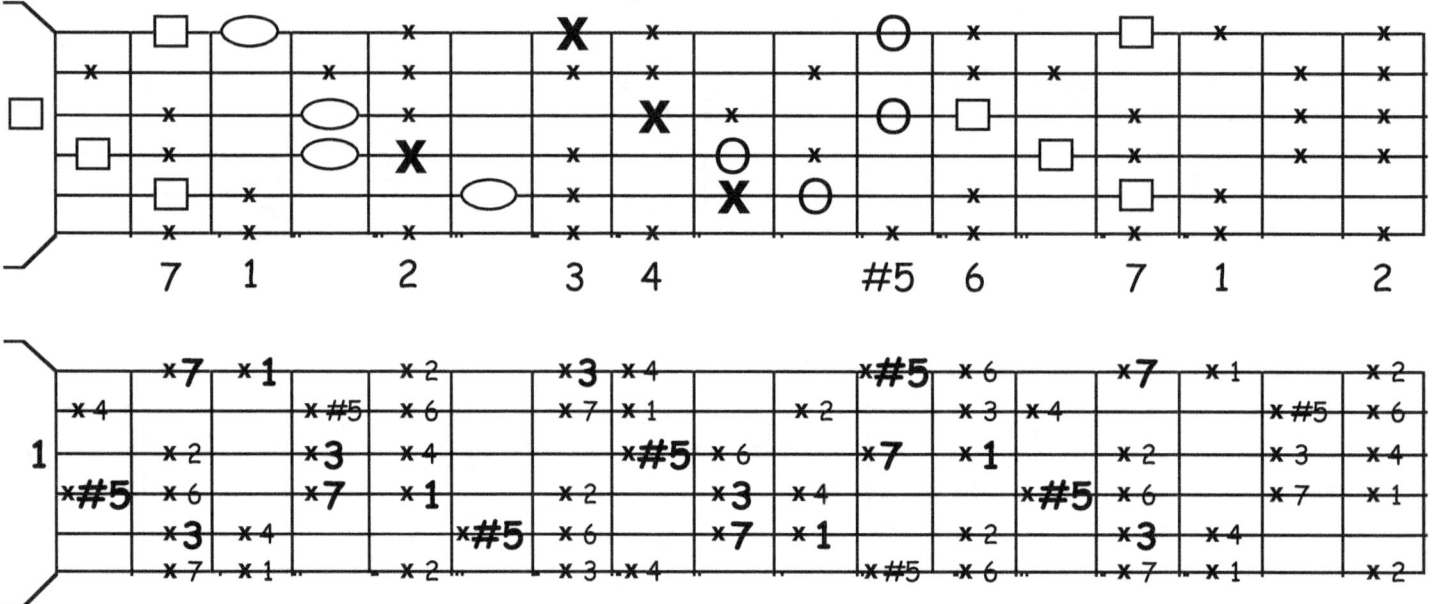

The only notes that you play are: 1, 3, #5, and 7 of the E harmonic minor scale.

The "1" Chord: Major 7#5 Inversions In "E" Harmonic Minor
DROP 2 & 4

6532 STRING GROUPING
G Major 7#5 Chord

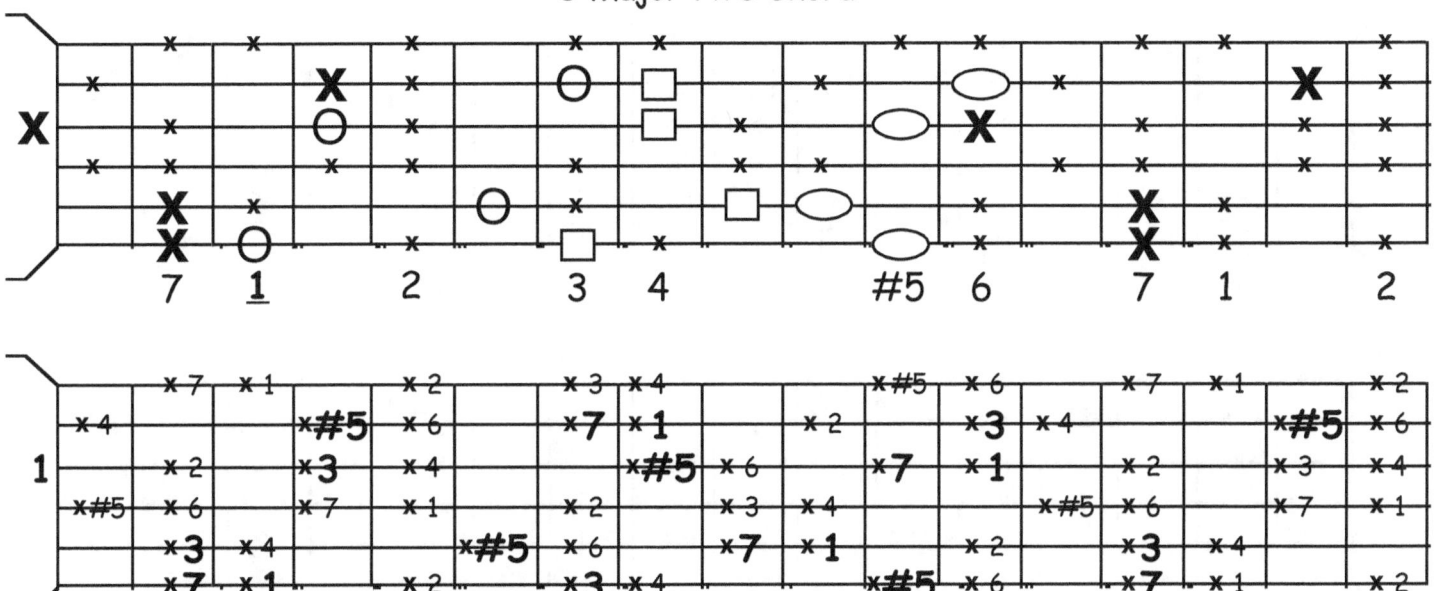

The only notes that you play are: 1, 3, #5, and 7 of the E harmonic minor scale.

5421 STRING GROUPING
G Major 7#5 Chord

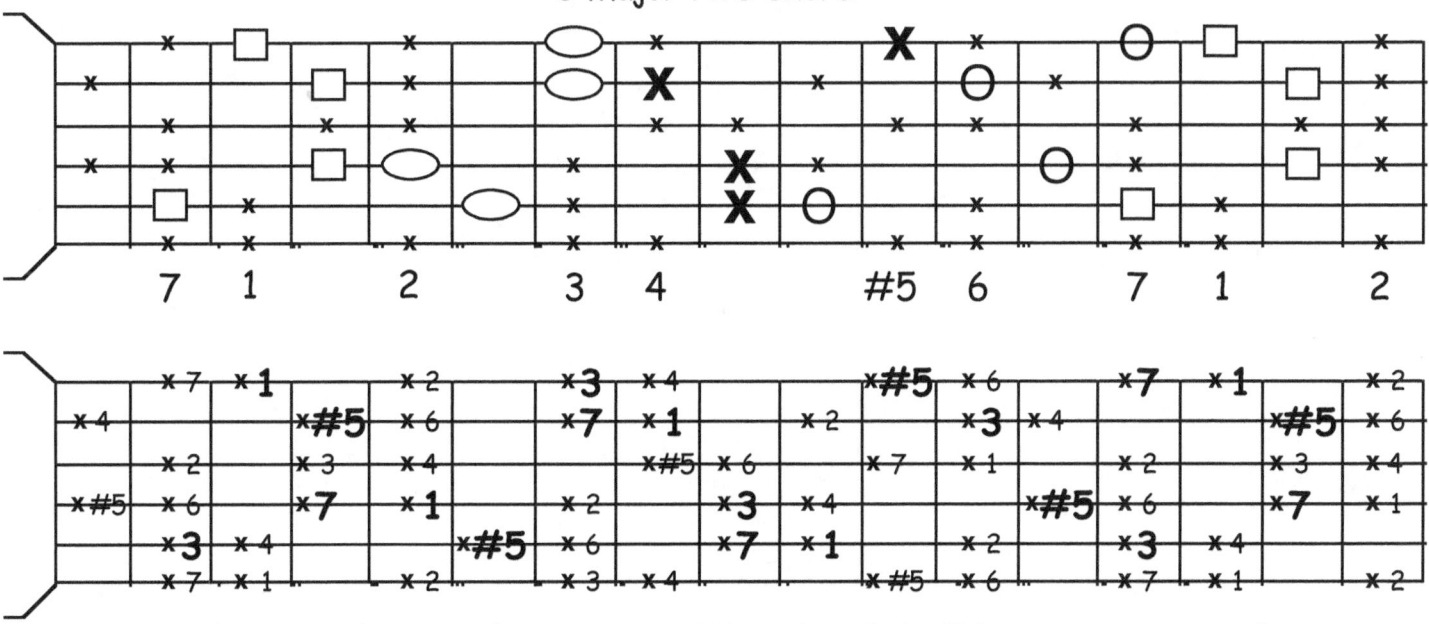

The only notes that you play are: 1, 3, #5, and 7 of the E harmonic minor scale.

The "1" Chord: Major 7#5 Inversions In "E" Harmonic Minor
DOUBLE DROP 2 & DROP 4
6521 STRING GROUPING
G Major 7#5 Chord

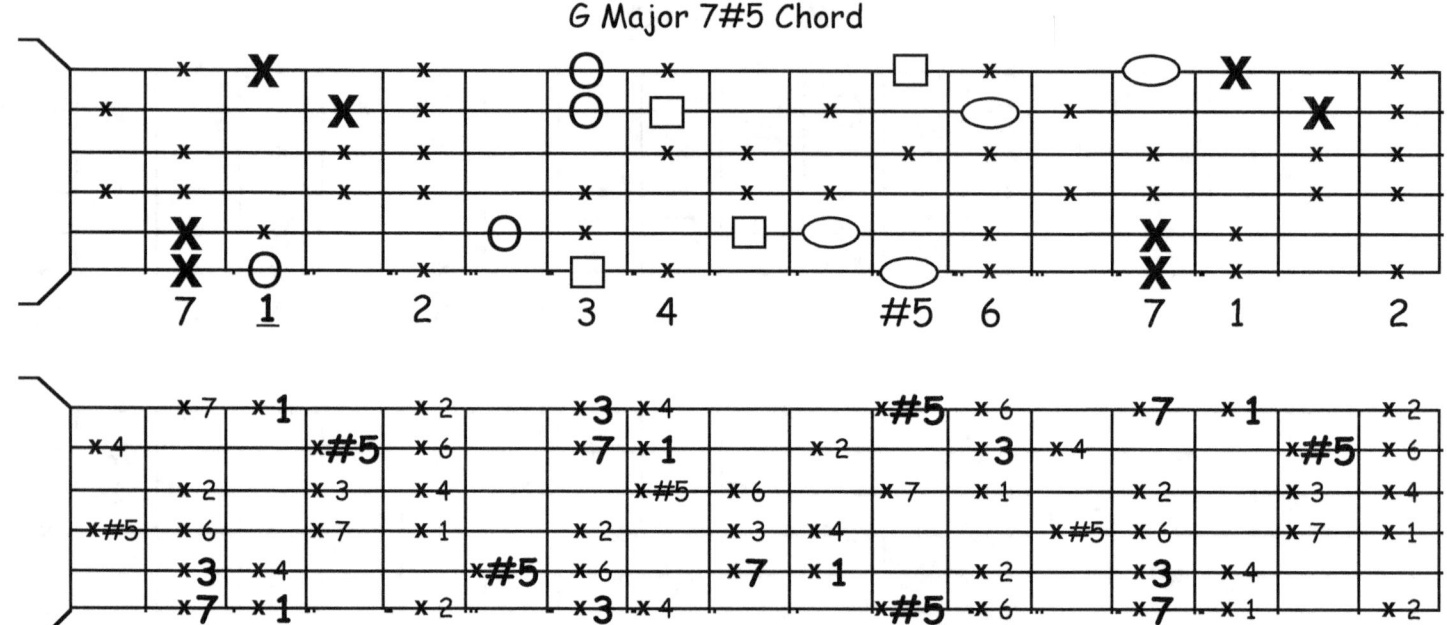

The only notes that you play are: 1, 3, #5, and 7 of the E harmonic minor scale.

MINOR MAJOR 7

You can either think of a "minor major 7" chord as a minor 7 chord with a raised 7th or as a major 7 chord with a flatted 3rd. The minor major 7 chord occurs naturally in the harmonic minor and melodic minor scales. I have presented them within the melodic minor scale.
In the MAJOR METHOD, the G melodic minor scale = the G major scale with a b3.
So, the "1" chord in G melodic minor IS a G minor major 7 chord spelled: 1, b3, 5, 7
(1 = root, b3 = 3rd, 5 = 5th, 7 = 7th).
When playing the first inversion, the b3 will be the note in the bass.

O = Root Position Minor Major 7 Chord

□ = First Inversion Minor Major 7 Chord (b3 in the bass)

⬭ = Second Inversion Minor Major 7 Chord

X = Third Inversion Minor Major 7 Chord

DROP 2

The "1" Chord: Minor Major 7 Inversions In "G" Melodic Minor
6543 STRING GROUPING

G Minor Major 7 Chord

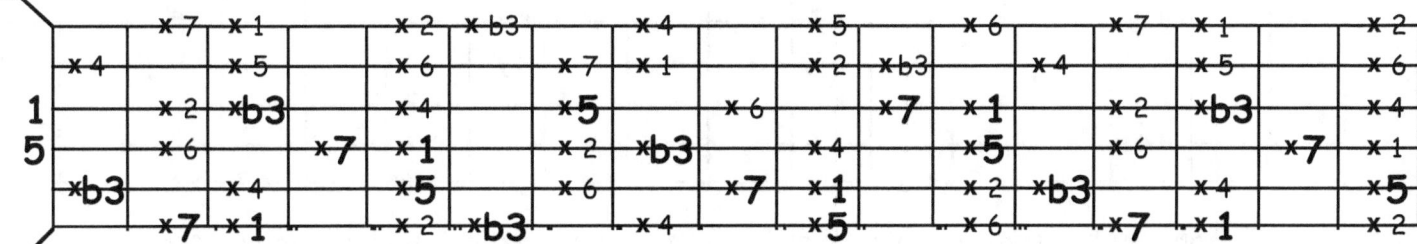

The only notes that you play are: 1, b3, 5, and 7 of the G melodic minor scale.

205

The "1" Chord: Minor Major 7 Inversions In "G" Melodic Minor
5432 STRING GROUPING
G Minor Major 7 Chord

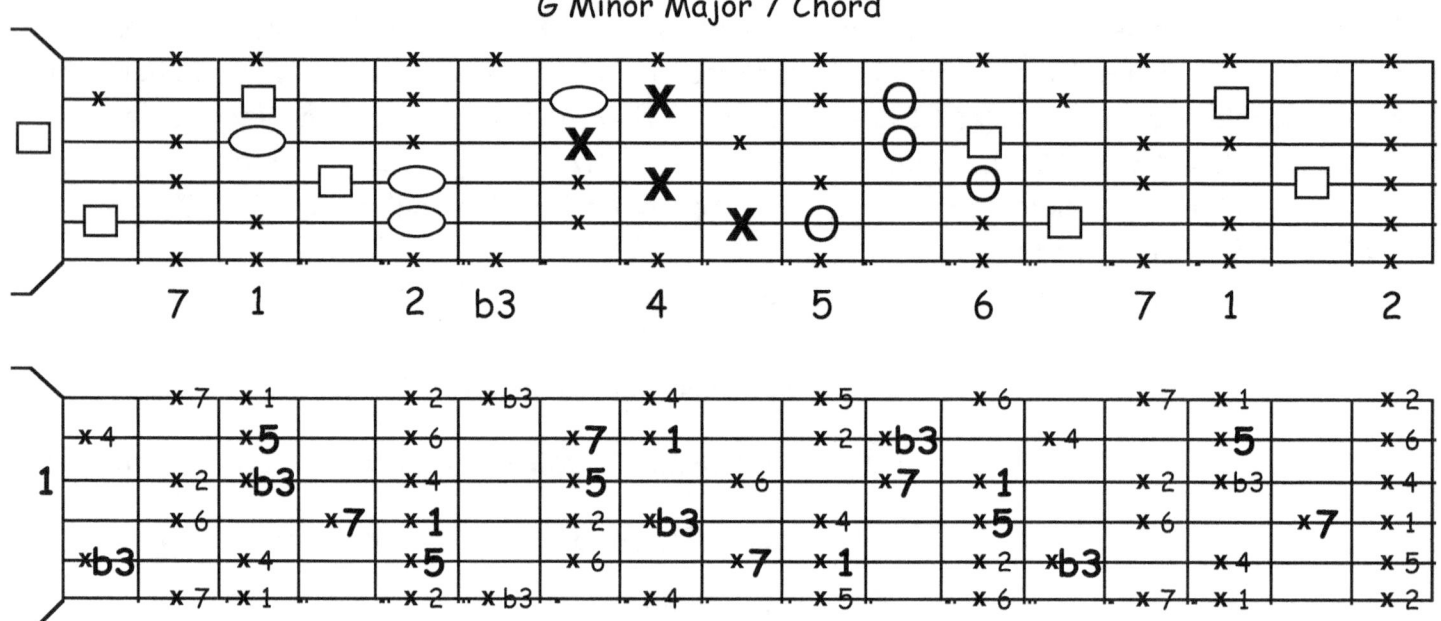

The only notes that you play are: 1, b3, 5, and 7 of the G melodic minor scale.

4321 STRING GROUPING
G Minor Major 7 Chord

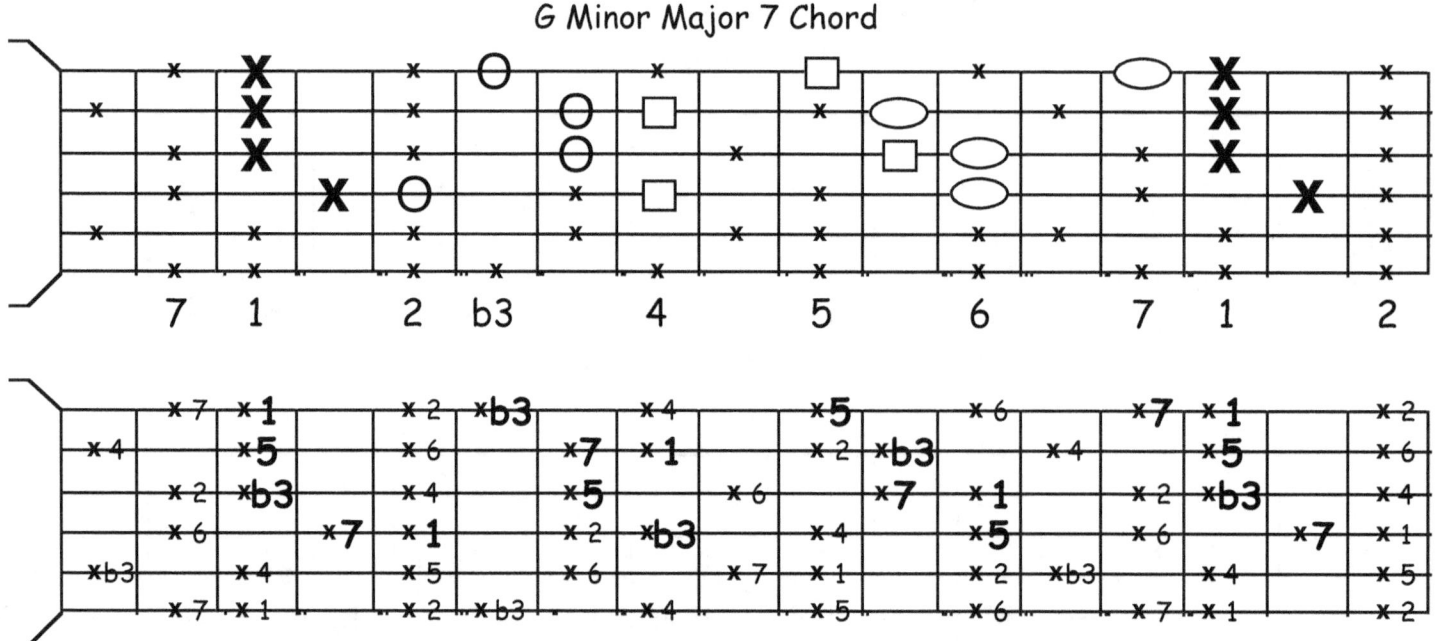

The only notes that you play are: 1, b3, 5, and 7 of the G melodic minor scale.

The "1" Chord: Minor Major 7 Inversions In "G" Melodic Minor
DROP 3

6432 STRING GROUPING
G Minor Major 7 Chord

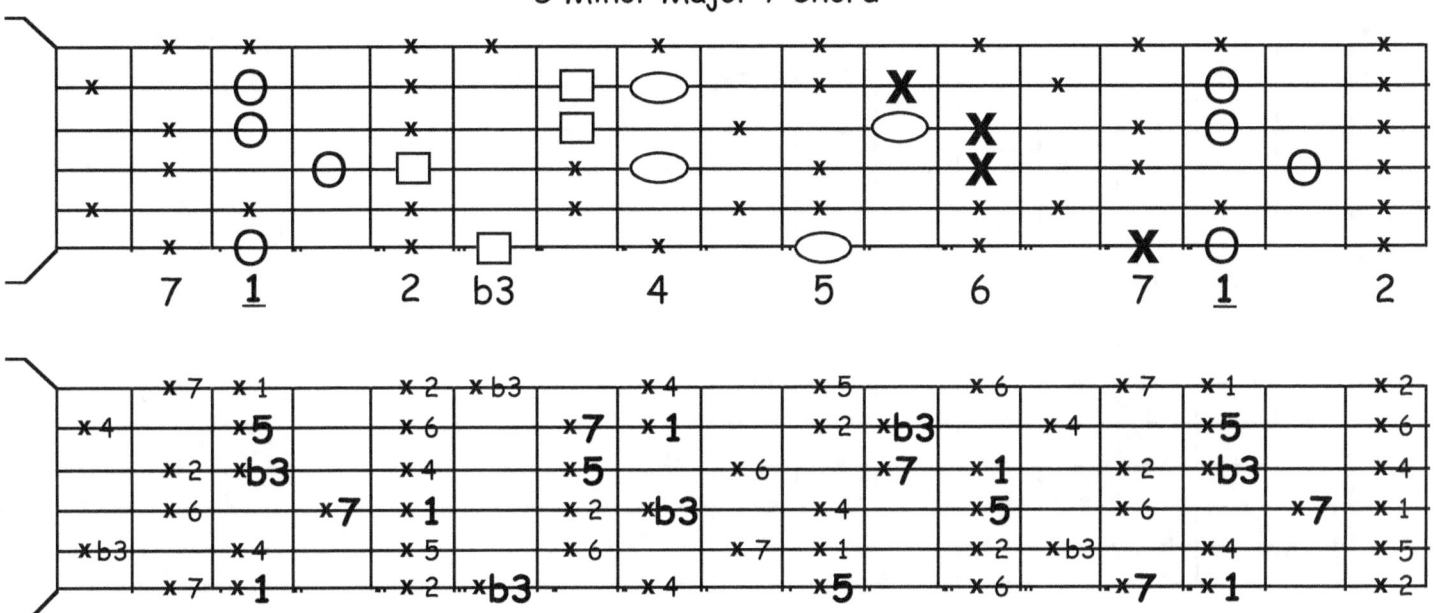

The only notes that you play are: 1, b3, 5, and 7 of the G melodic minor scale.

5321 STRING GROUPING
G Minor Major 7 Chord

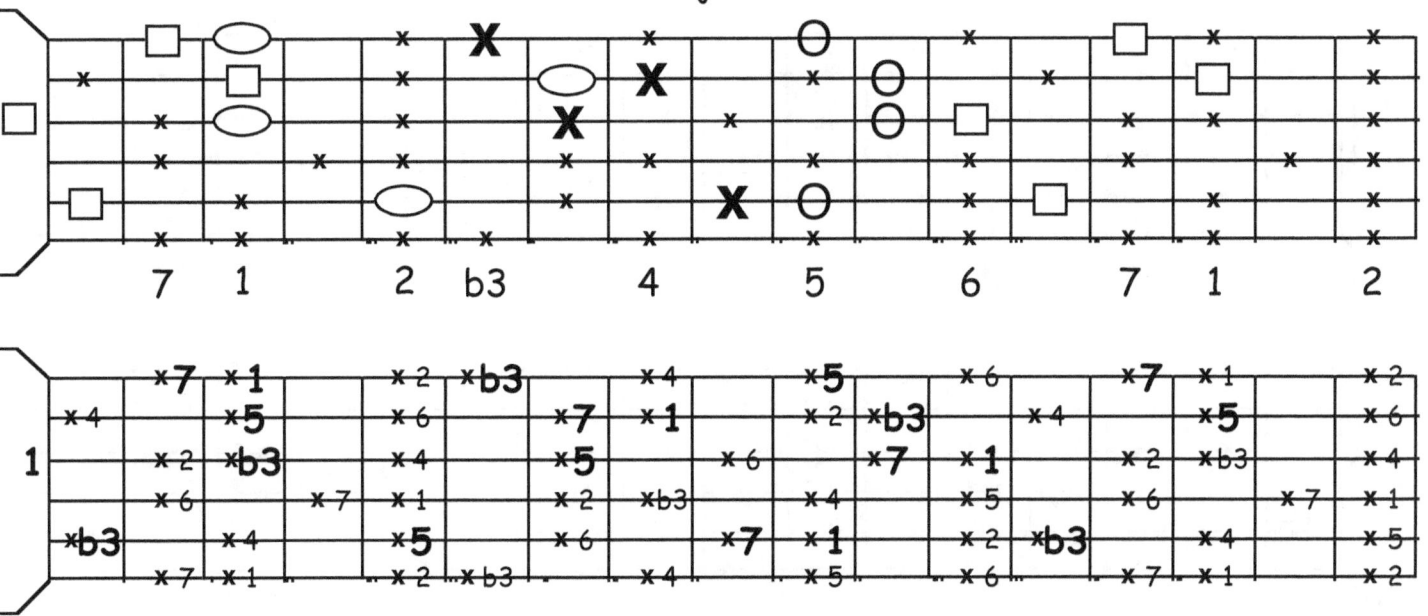

The only notes that you play are: 1, b3, 5, and 7 of the G melodic minor scale.

The "1" Chord: Minor Major 7 Inversions In "G" Melodic Minor
DROP 2 & 3
6542 STRING GROUPING
G Minor Major 7 Chord

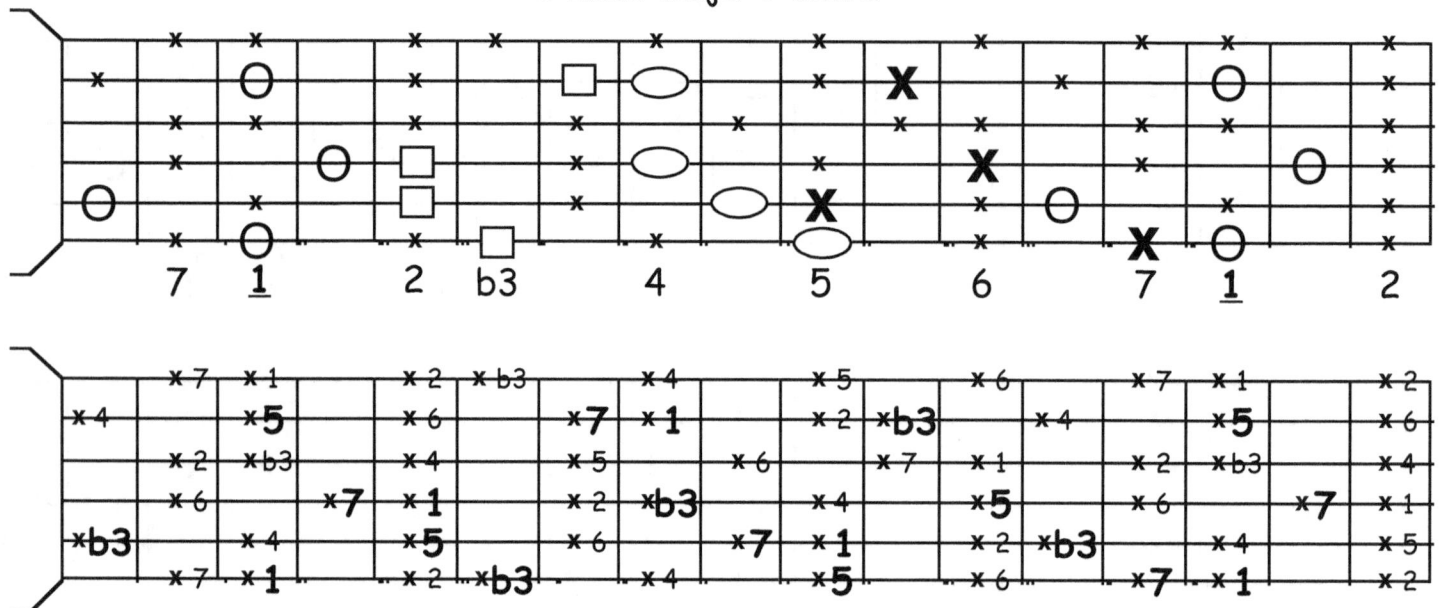

The only notes that you play are: 1, b3, 5, and 7 of the G melodic minor scale.

5431 STRING GROUPING
G Minor Major 7 Chord

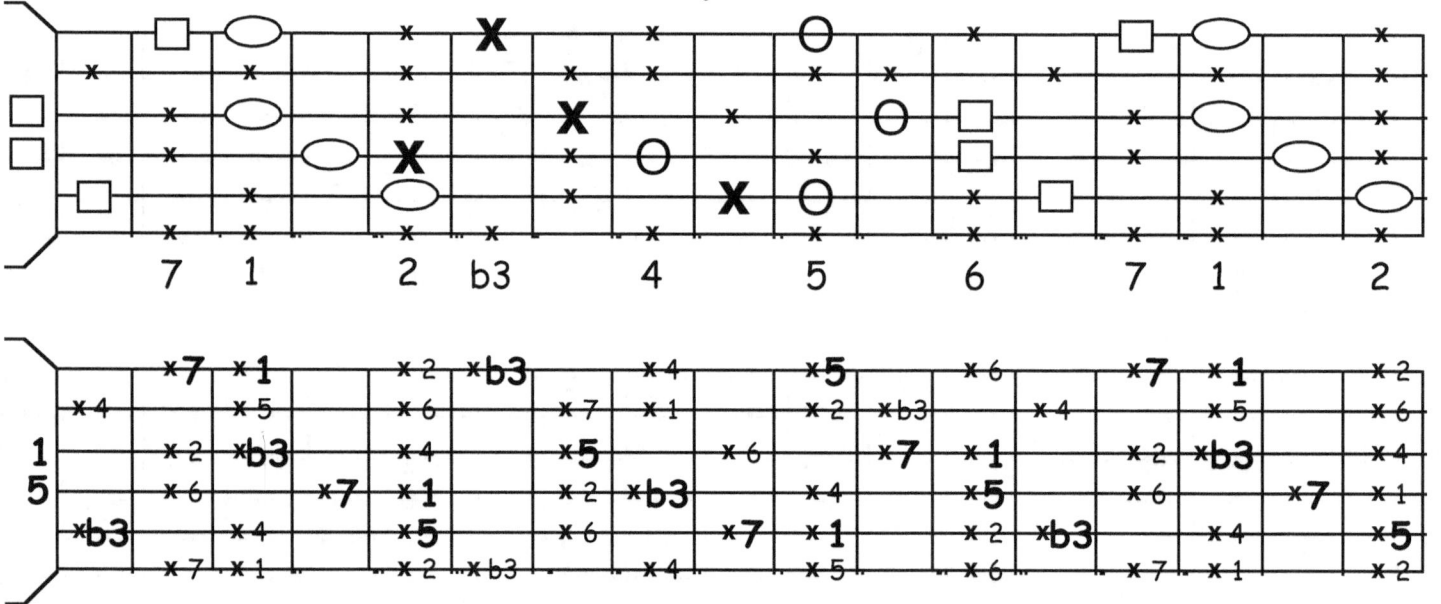

The only notes that you play are: 1, b3, 5, and 7 of the G melodic minor scale.

The "1" Chord: Minor Major 7 Inversions In "G" Melodic Minor
DROP 2 & 4

6532 STRING GROUPING
G Minor Major 7 Chord

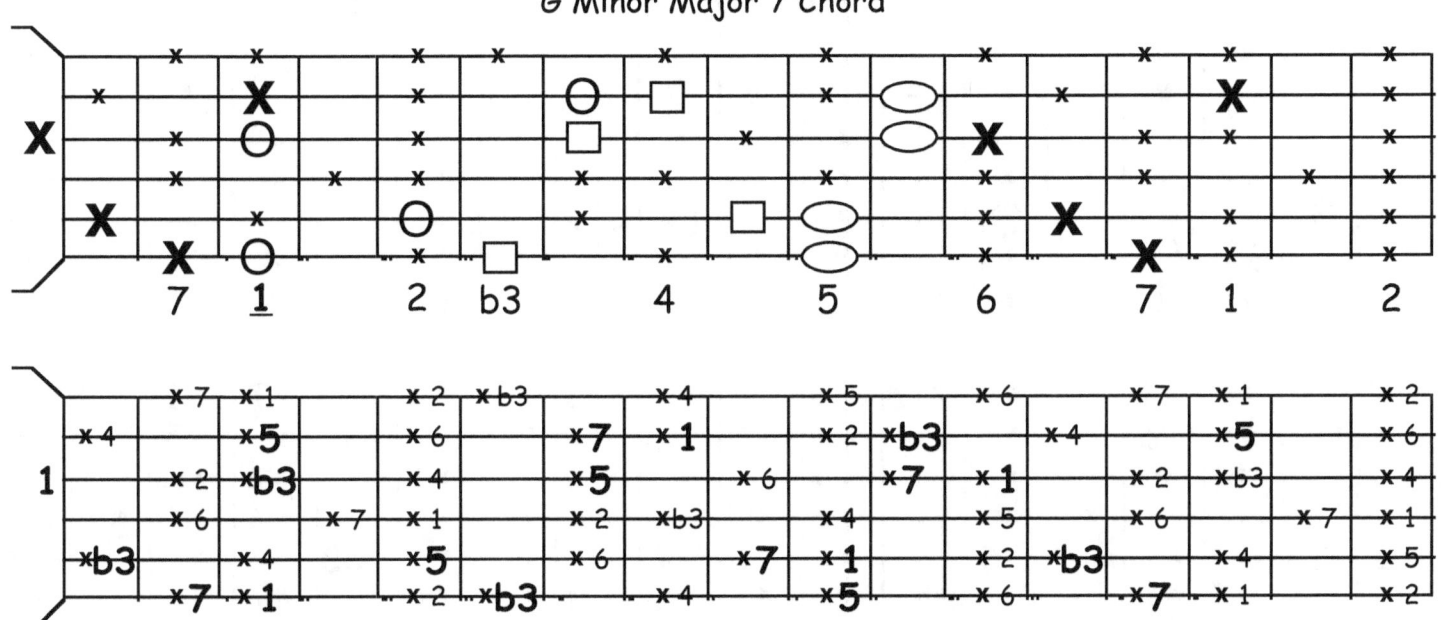

The only notes that you play are: 1, b3, 5, and 7 of the G melodic minor scale.

5421 STRING GROUPING
G Minor Major 7 Chord

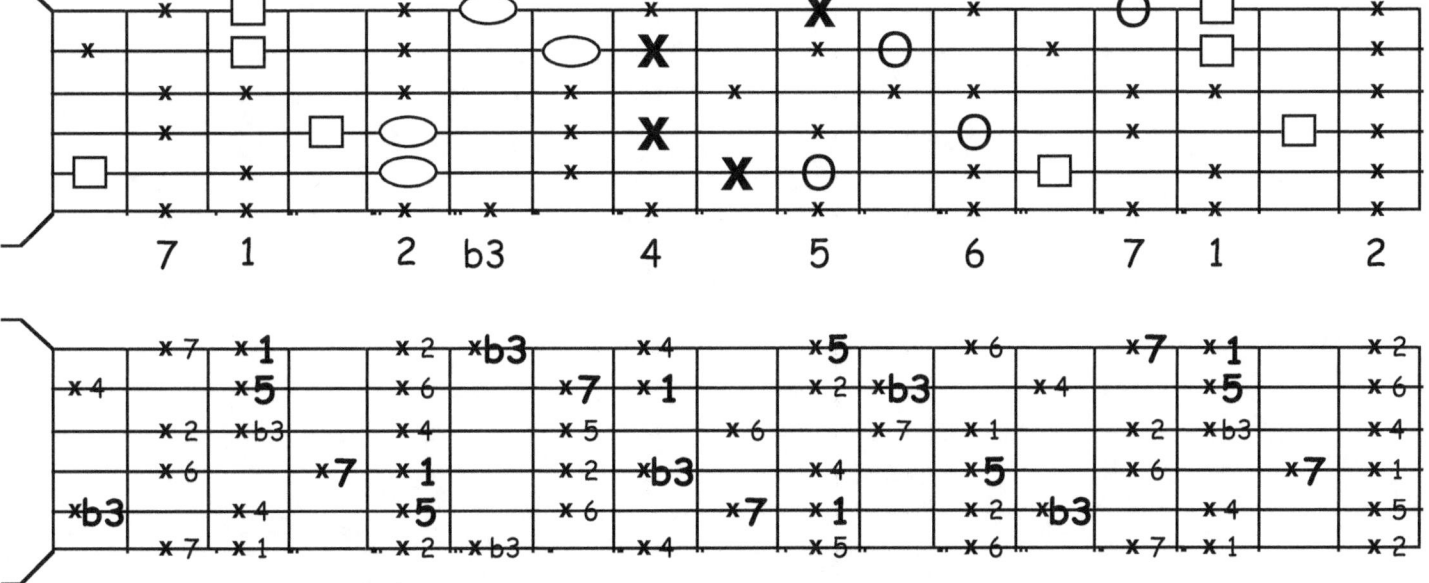

The only notes that you play are: 1, b3, 5, and 7 of the G melodic minor scale.

The "1" Chord: Minor Major 7 Inversions In "G" Melodic Minor
DOUBLE DROP 2 & DROP 4
6521 STRING GROUPING

G Minor Major 7 Chord

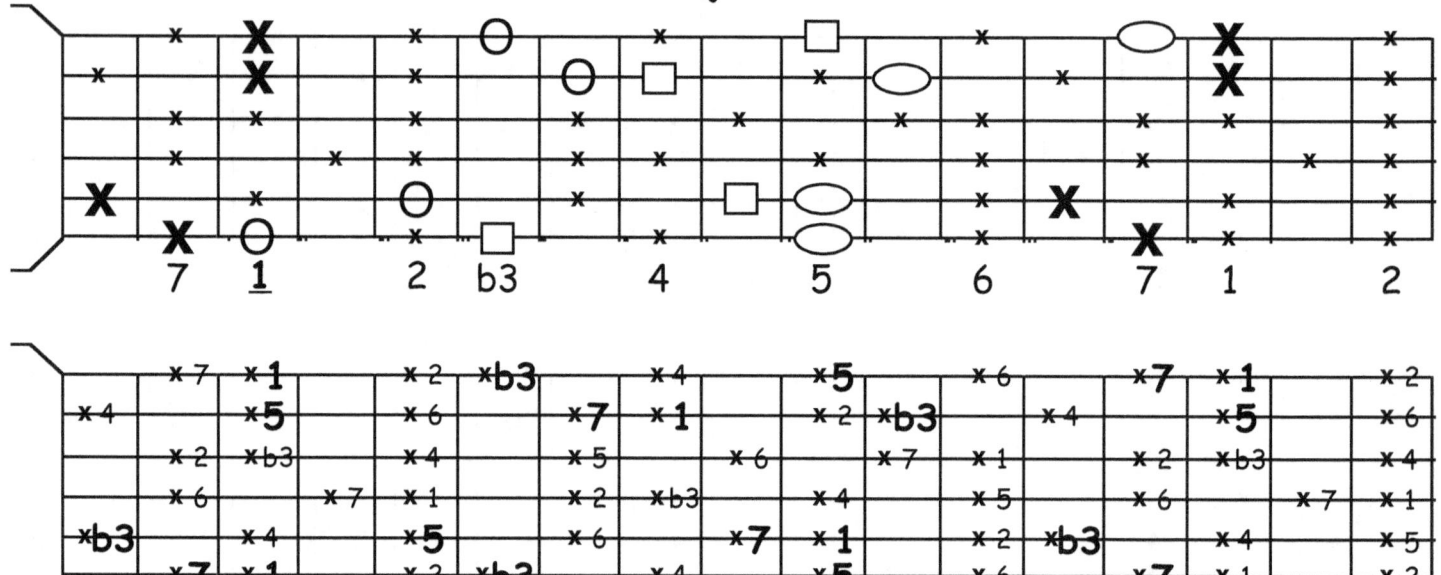

The only notes that you play are: 1, b3, 5, and 7 of the G melodic minor scale.

DOMINANT 7#11

The dominant 7#11 (dominant 7b5) chord can occur in the whole tone and melodic minor scales. I have presented them within the melodic minor scale.

In the melodic minor scale, both the "4" chord and the "5" chord are dominant 7 chords. When you play the "4" chord dominant 7 (spelled: 4, 6, 1, b3), the 5th of the chord is a 1, which can be lowered a half step to the 7 without changing the scale. This gives you a chord that has a root, a 3rd, a #11th (or b5th), and a 7th: (4 = root, 6 = 3rd, 7 = #11th, b3 = 7th). When playing the second inversion, the #11 will be the note in the bass.

- O = Root Position Dominant 7#11 Chord
- □ = First Inversion Dominant 7#11 Chord
- ⬯ = Second Inversion Dominant 7#11 Chord (#11 in the bass)
- X = Third Inversion Dominant 7#11 Chord

DROP 2

The "4" Chord: Dominant 7#11 Inversions In "G" Melodic Minor

6543 STRING GROUPING

C Dominant 7#11

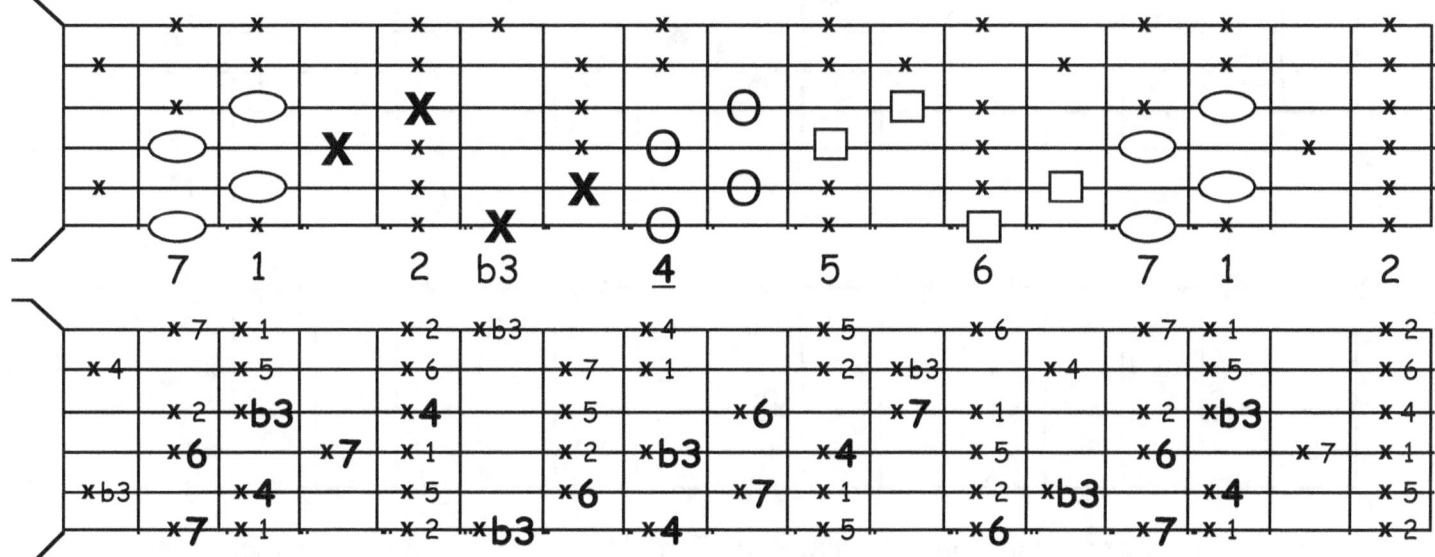

The only notes that you play are: 4, 6, 7, and b3 of the G melodic minor scale.

The "4" Chord: Dominant 7#11 Inversions In "G" Melodic Minor

5432 STRING GROUPING
C Dominant 7#11

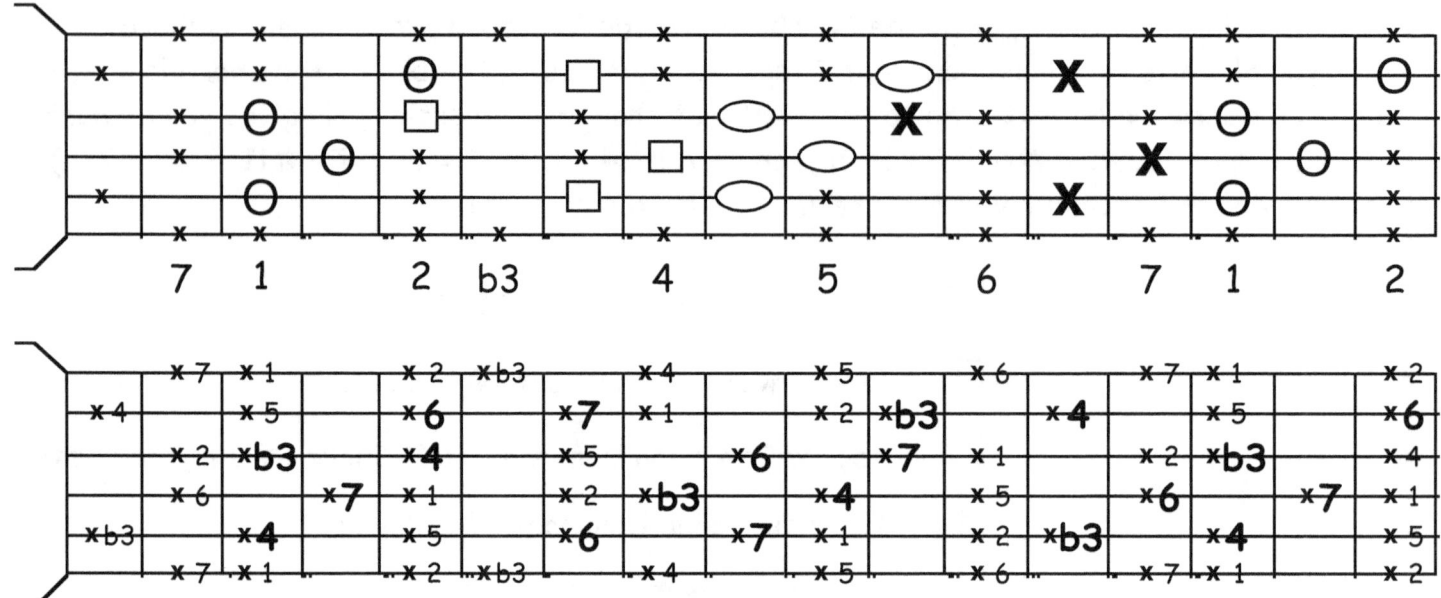

The only notes that you play are: 4, 6, 7, and b3 of the G melodic minor scale.

4321 STRING GROUPING
C Dominant 7#11

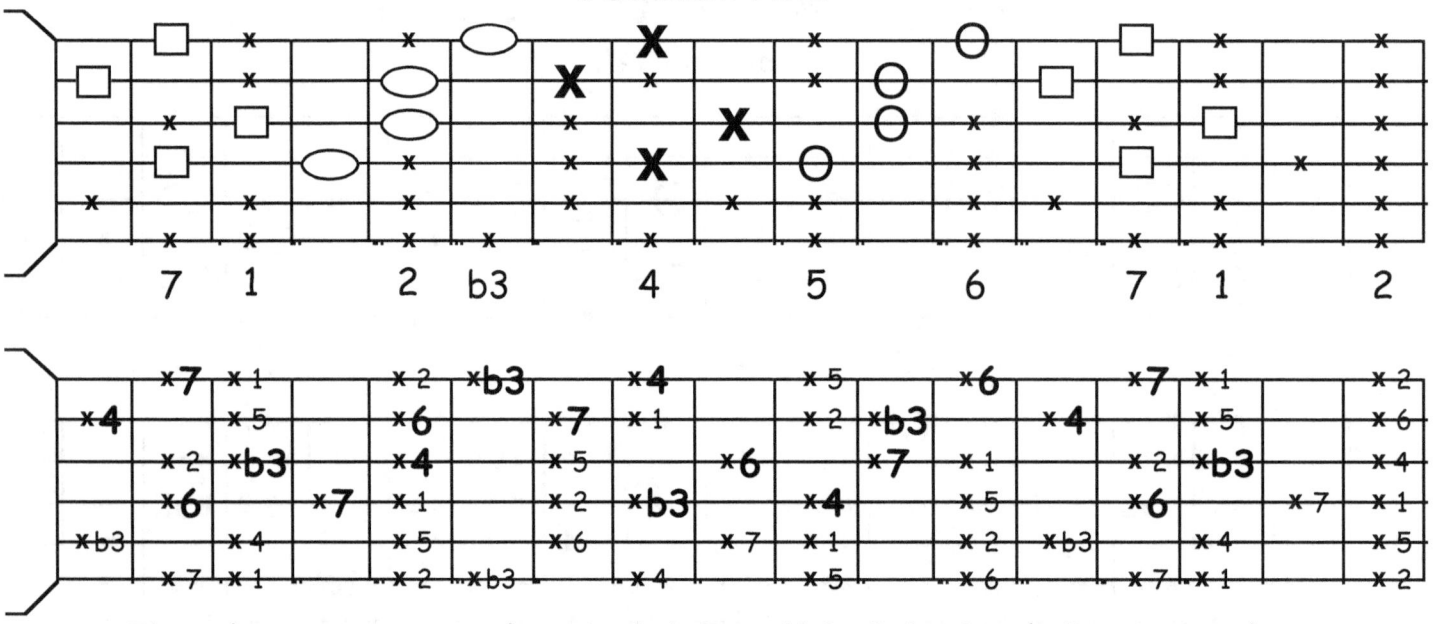

The only notes that you play are: 4, 6, 7, and b3 of the G melodic minor scale.

The "4" Chord: Dominant 7#11 Inversions In "G" Melodic Minor
DROP 3

6432 STRING GROUPING
C Dominant 7#11

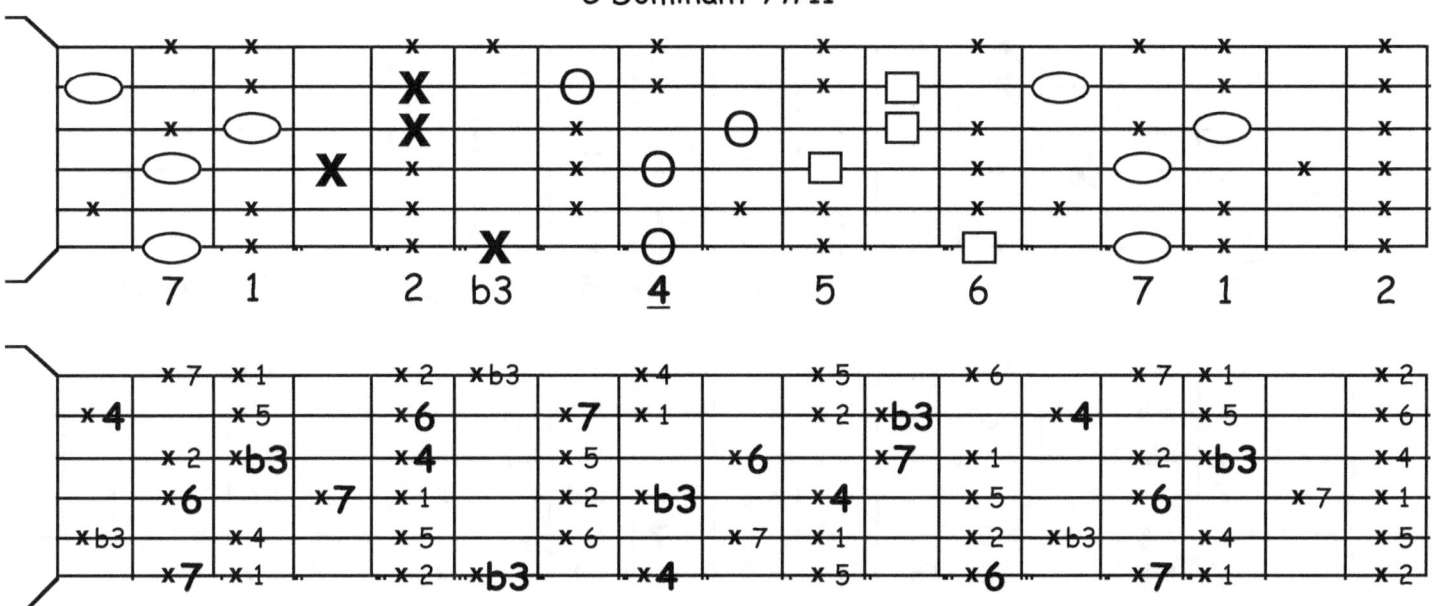

The only notes that you play are: 4, 6, 7, and b3 of the G melodic minor scale.

5321 STRING GROUPING
C Dominant 7#11

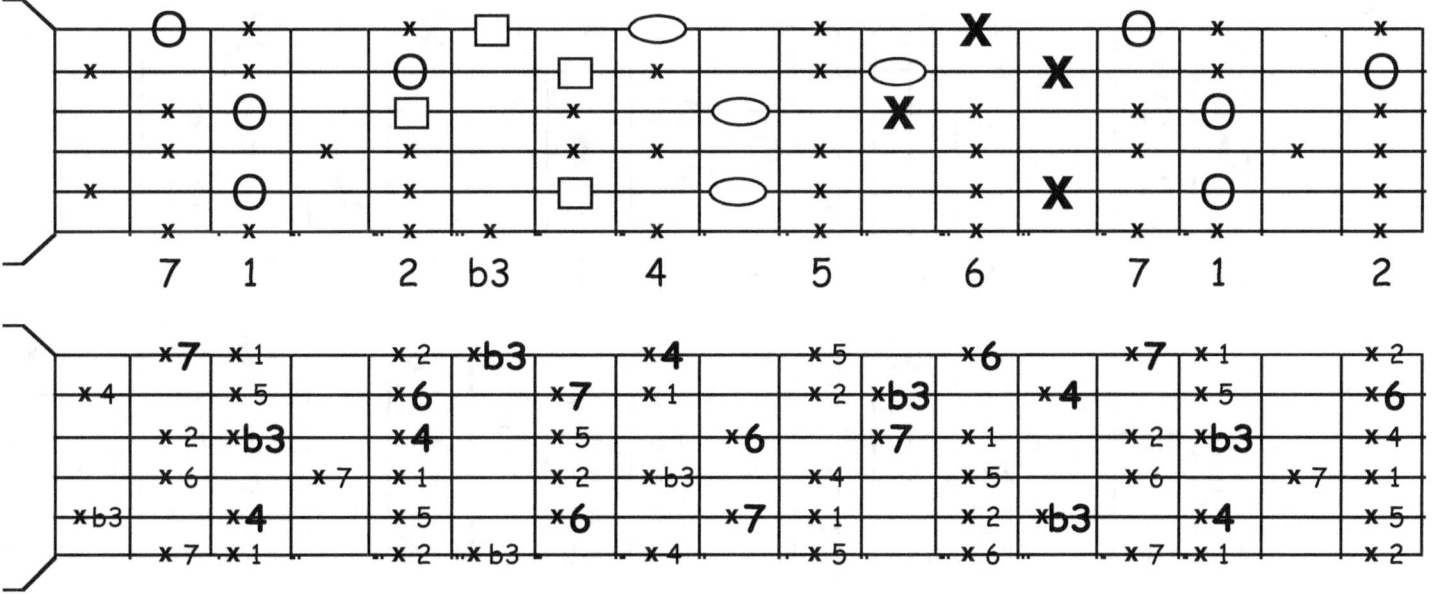

The only notes that you play are: 4, 6, 7, and b3 of the G melodic minor scale.

The "4" Chord: Dominant 7#11 Inversions In "G" Melodic Minor

DROP 2 & 3

6542 STRING GROUPING
C Dominant 7#11

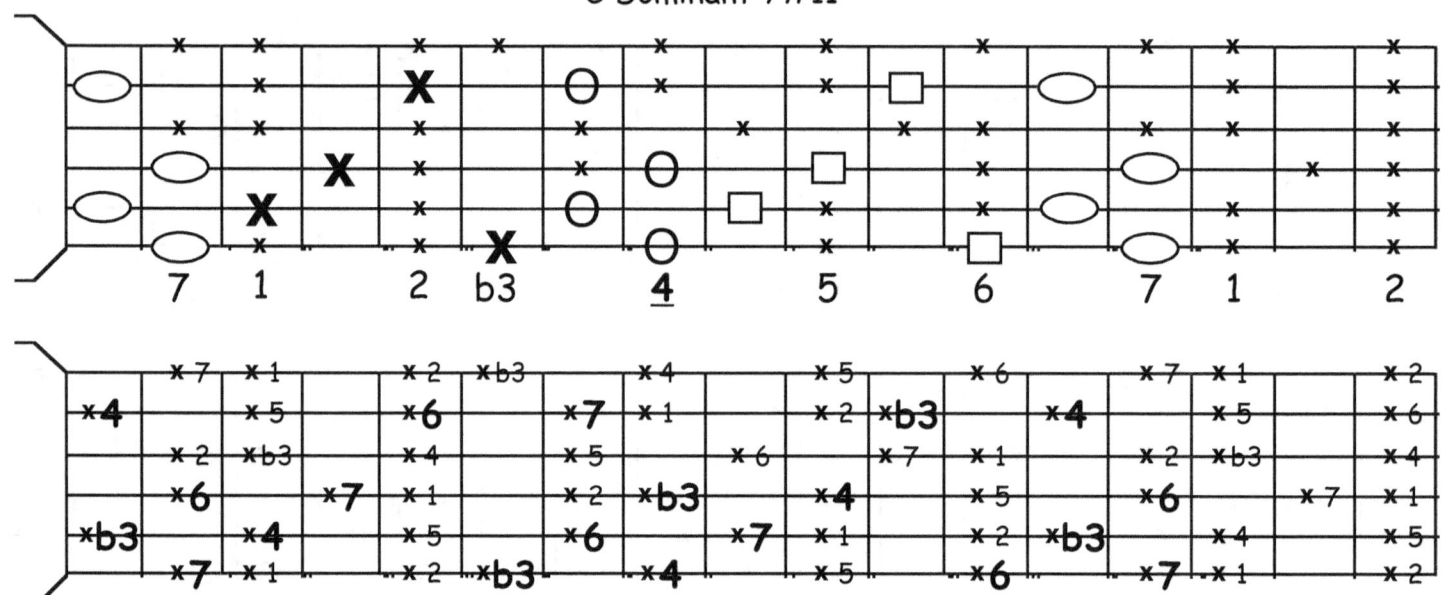

The only notes that you play are: 4, 6, 7, and b3 of the G melodic minor scale.

5431 STRING GROUPING
C Dominant 7#11

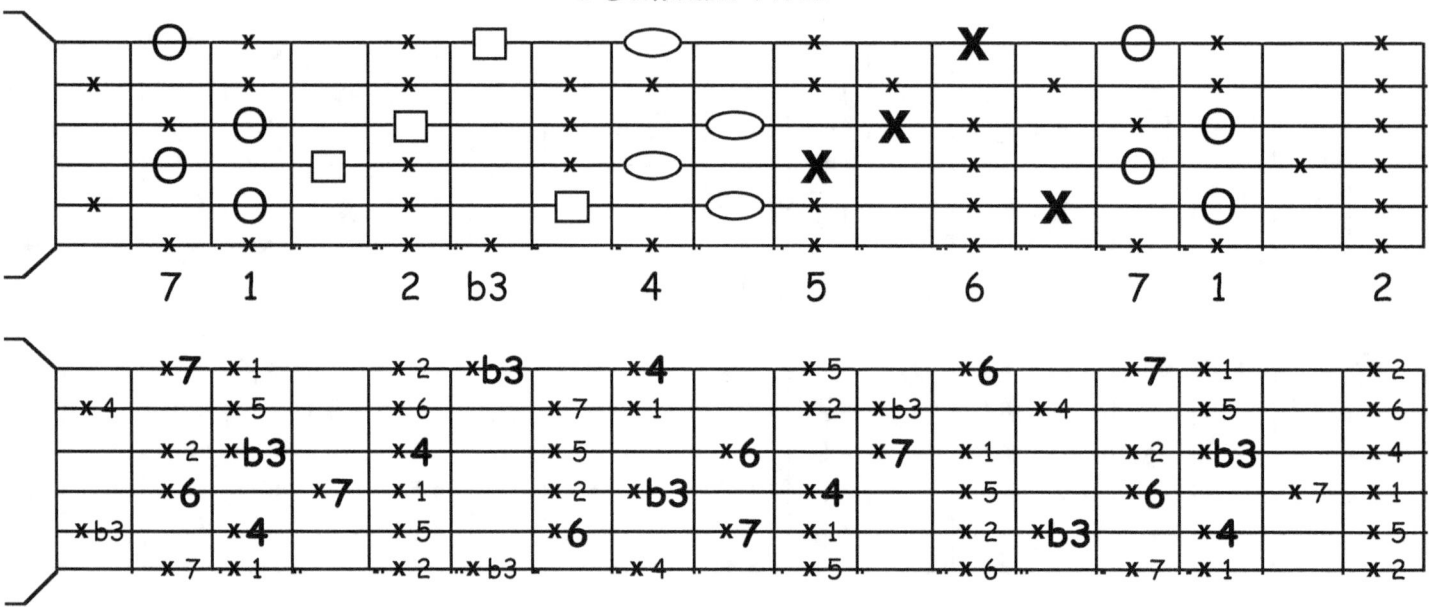

The only notes that you play are: 4, 6, 7, and b3 of the G melodic minor scale.

214

The "4" Chord: Dominant 7#11 Inversions In "G" Melodic Minor

DROP 2 & 4

6532 STRING GROUPING
C Dominant 7#11

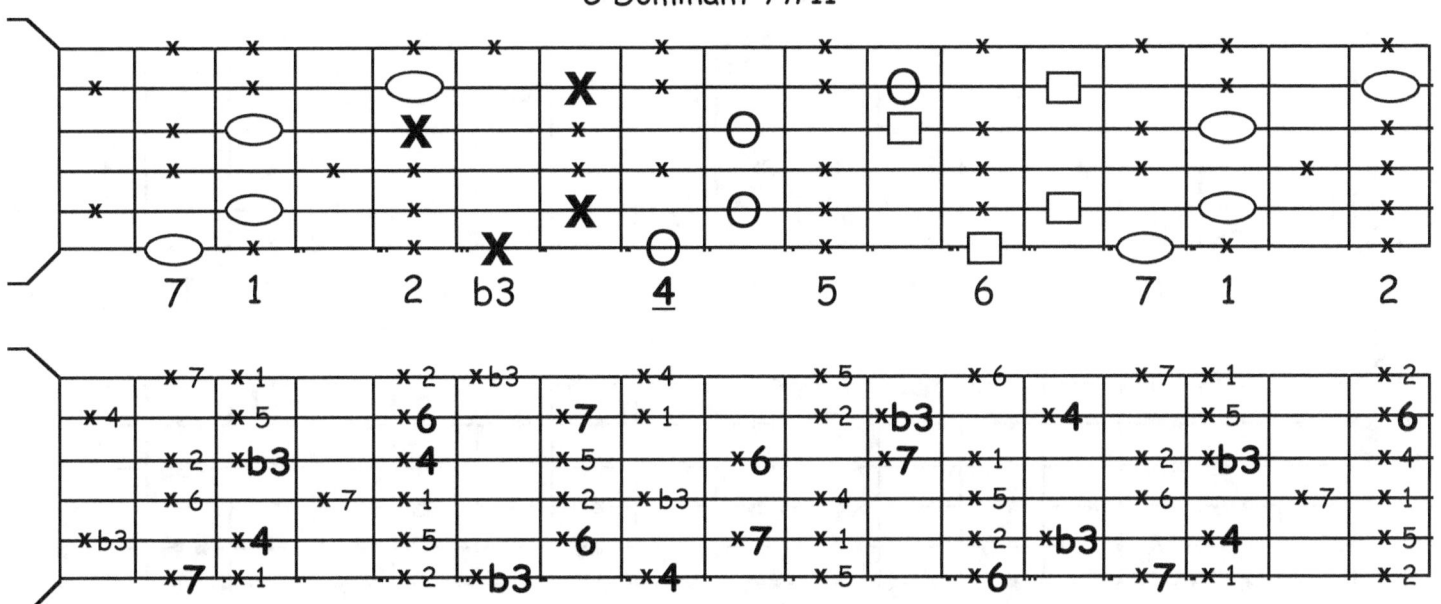

The only notes that you play are: 4, 6, 7, and b3 of the G melodic minor scale.

5421 STRING GROUPING
C Dominant 7#11

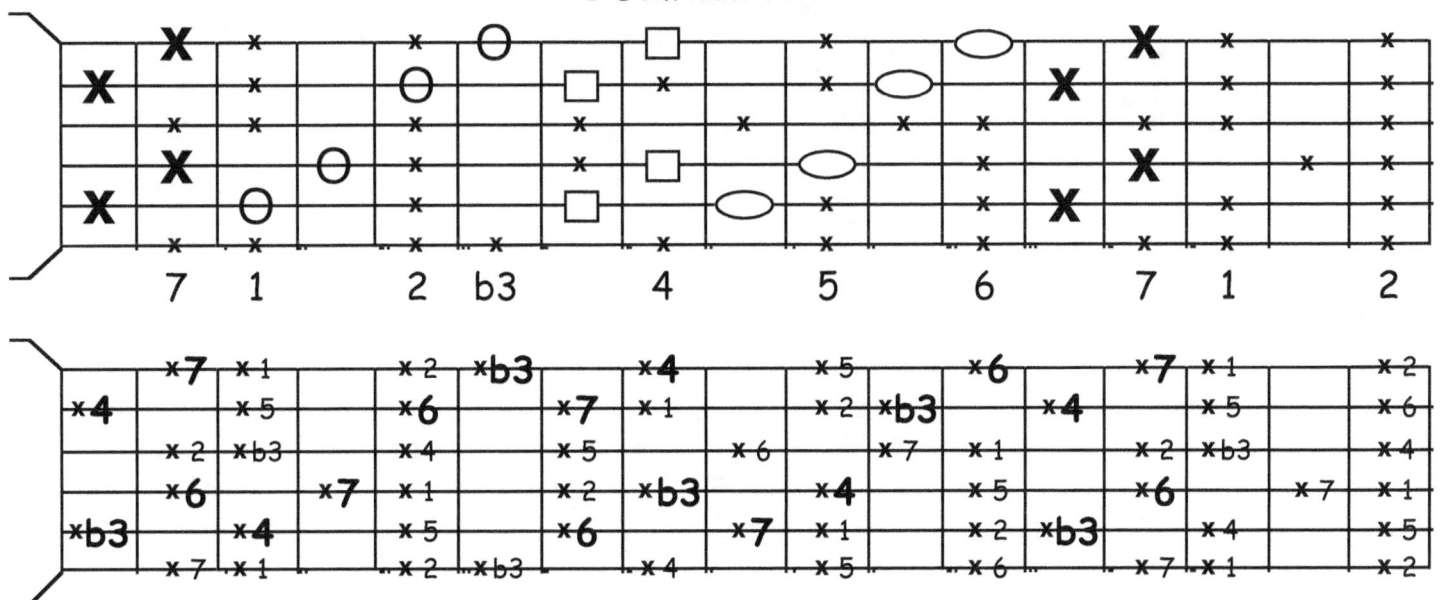

The only notes that you play are: 4, 6, 7, and b3 of the G melodic minor scale.

The "4" Chord: Dominant 7#11 Inversions In "G" Melodic Minor
DOUBLE DROP 2 & DROP 4
6521 STRING GROUPING
C Dominant 7#11

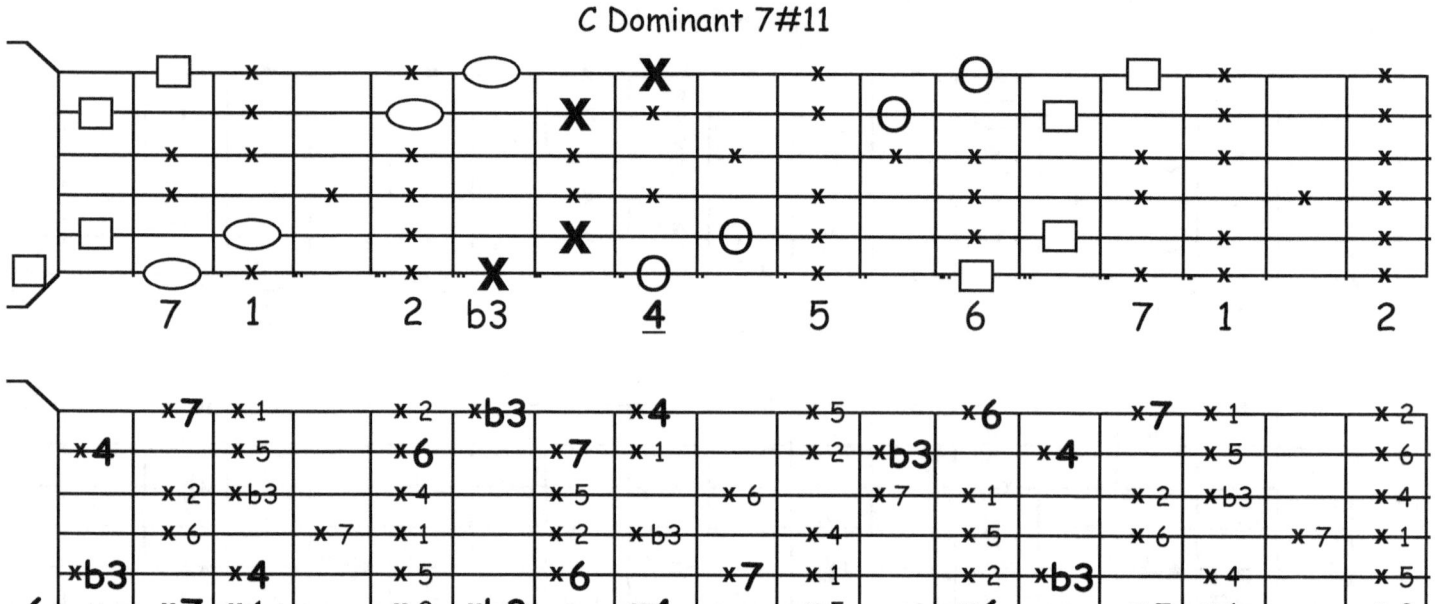

The only notes that you play are: 4, 6, 7, and b3 of the G melodic minor scale.

DOMINANT 7#5

The dominant 7#5 chords (augmented 7 chord) can occur naturally in the whole tone, melodic minor, and harmonic minor scales. I have presented them within the harmonic minor scale. In the MAJOR METHOD, the E harmonic minor scale = the G major scale with a #5. So the "3" chord in E harmonic minor is a B dominant 7 chord spelled: 3, #5, 7, 2. The 5th of the chord is a 7, which can be raised a half step to the 1 without changing the scale. This dominant 7#5 chord is spelled: 3, #5, 1, 2 (3 = root, #5 = 3rd, 1 = #5th, 2 = 7th). When playing the second inversion, the #5th will be the note in the bass.

○ = Root Position Dominant 7#5 Chord

□ = First Inversion Dominant 7#5 Chord

⬭ = Second Inversion Dominant 7#5 Chord (#5 in the bass)

X = Third Inversion Dominant 7#5 Chord

DROP 2

The "3" Chord: Dominant 7#5 Inversions
In "E" Harmonic Minor
6543 STRING GROUPING
B Dominant 7#5

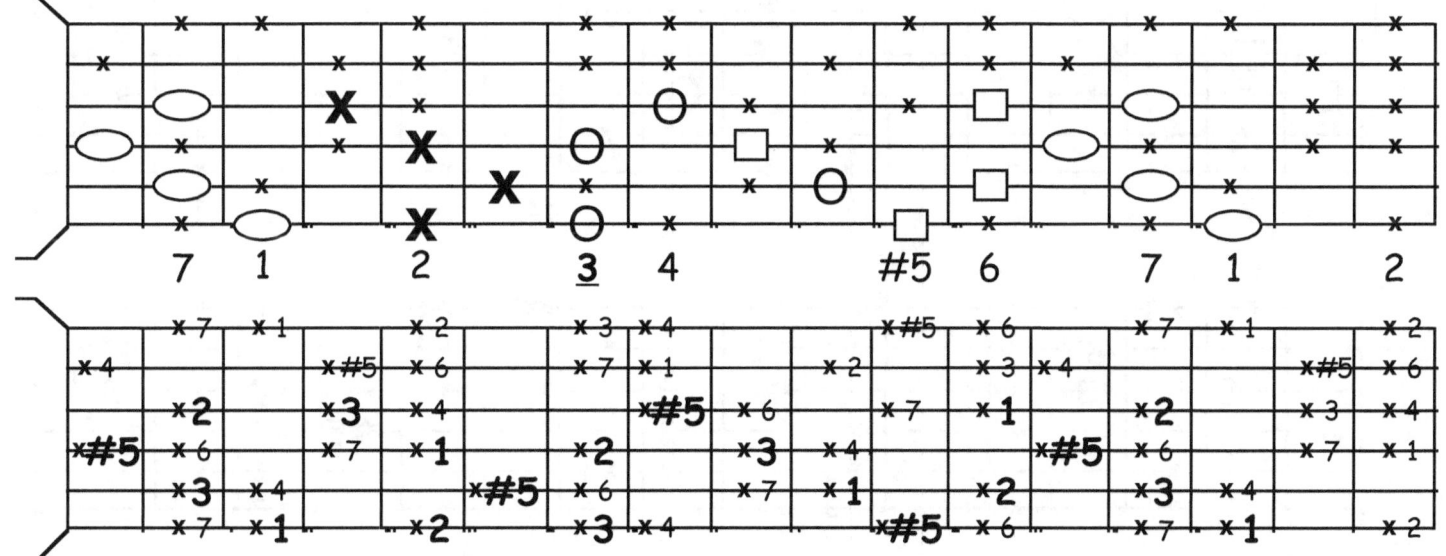

The only notes that you play are: 3, #5, 1, and 2 of the E harmonic minor scale.

The "3" Chord: Dominant 7#5 Inversions In "E" Harmonic Minor
5432 STRING GROUPING
B Dominant 7#5

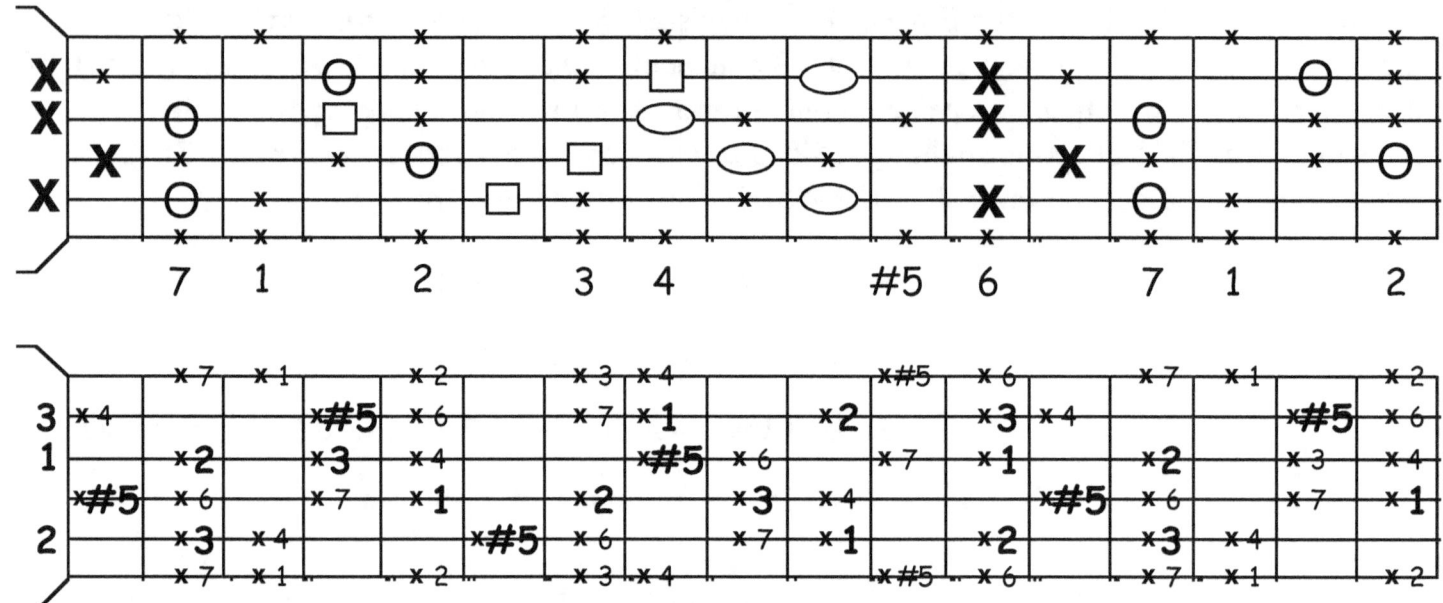

The only notes that you play are: 3, #5, 1, and 2 of the E harmonic minor scale.

4321 STRING GROUPING
B Dominant 7#5

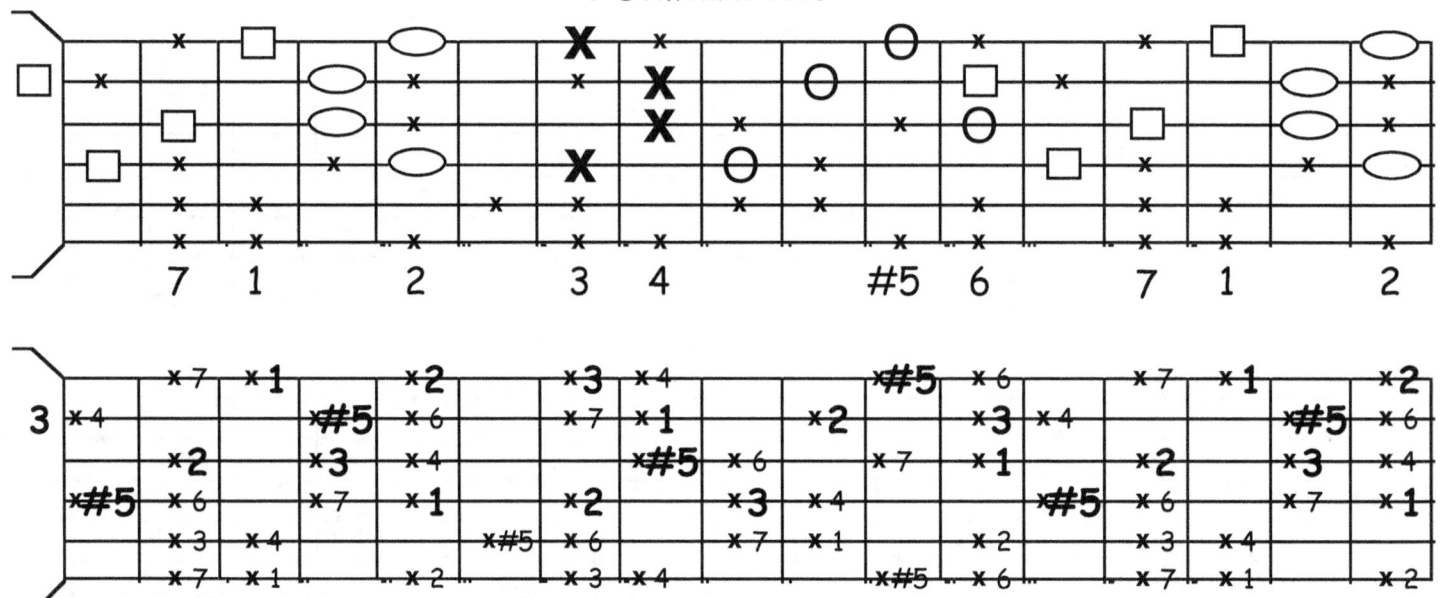

The only notes that you play are: 3, #5, 1, and 2 of the E harmonic minor scale.

The "3" Chord: Dominant 7#5 Inversions In "E" Harmonic Minor
DROP 3
6432 STRING GROUPING
B Dominant 7#5

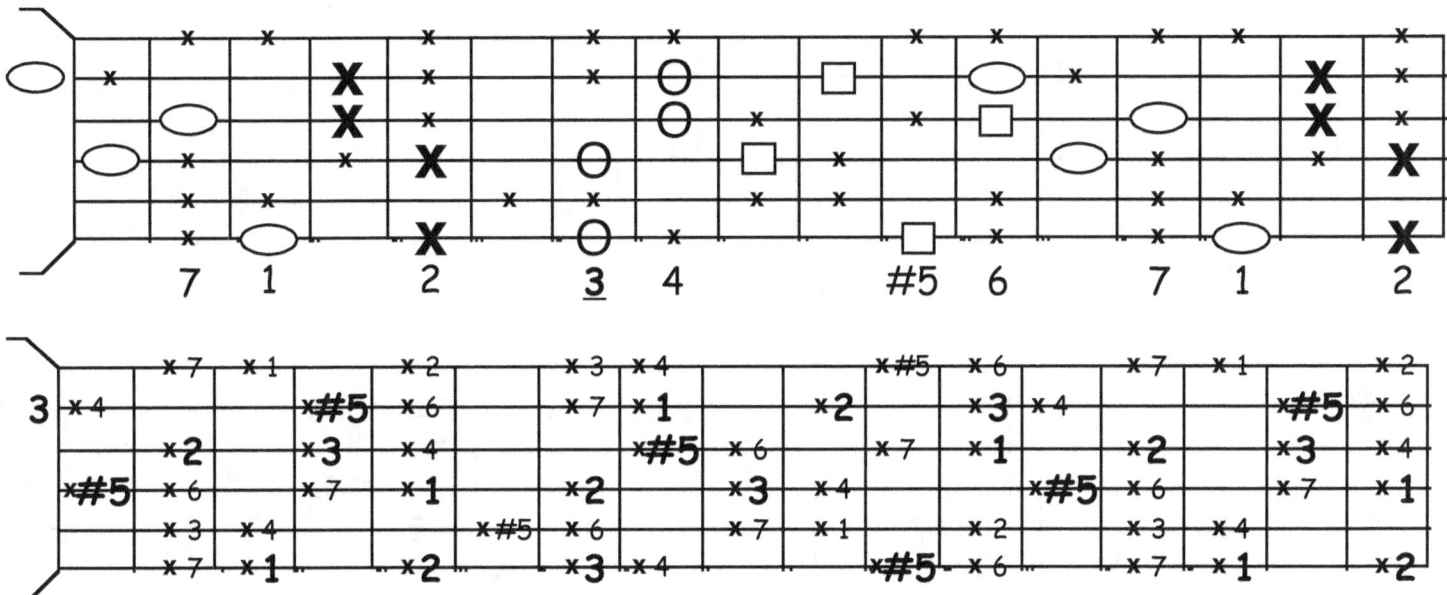

The only notes that you play are: 3, #5, 1, and 2 of the E harmonic minor scale.

5321 STRING GROUPING
B Dominant 7#5

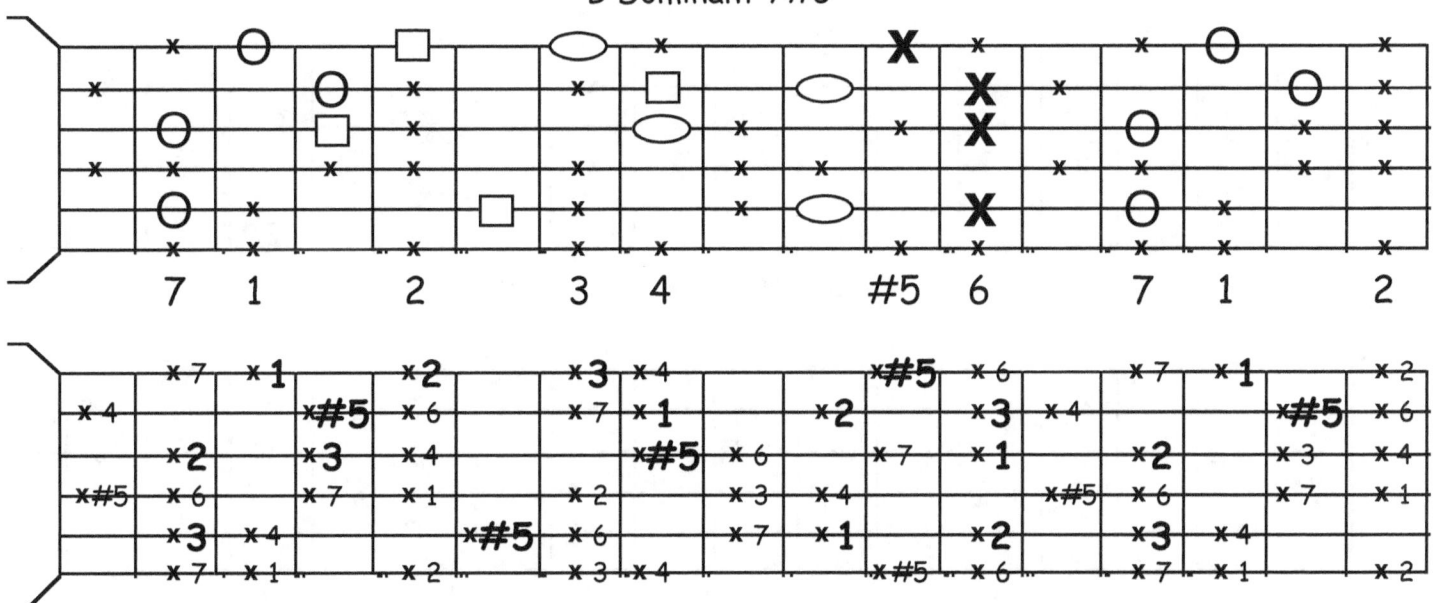

The only notes that you play are: 3, #5, 1, and 2 of the E harmonic minor scale.

The "3" Chord: Dominant 7#5 Inversions In "E" Harmonic Minor
DROP 2 & 3
6542 STRING GROUPING
B Dominant 7#5

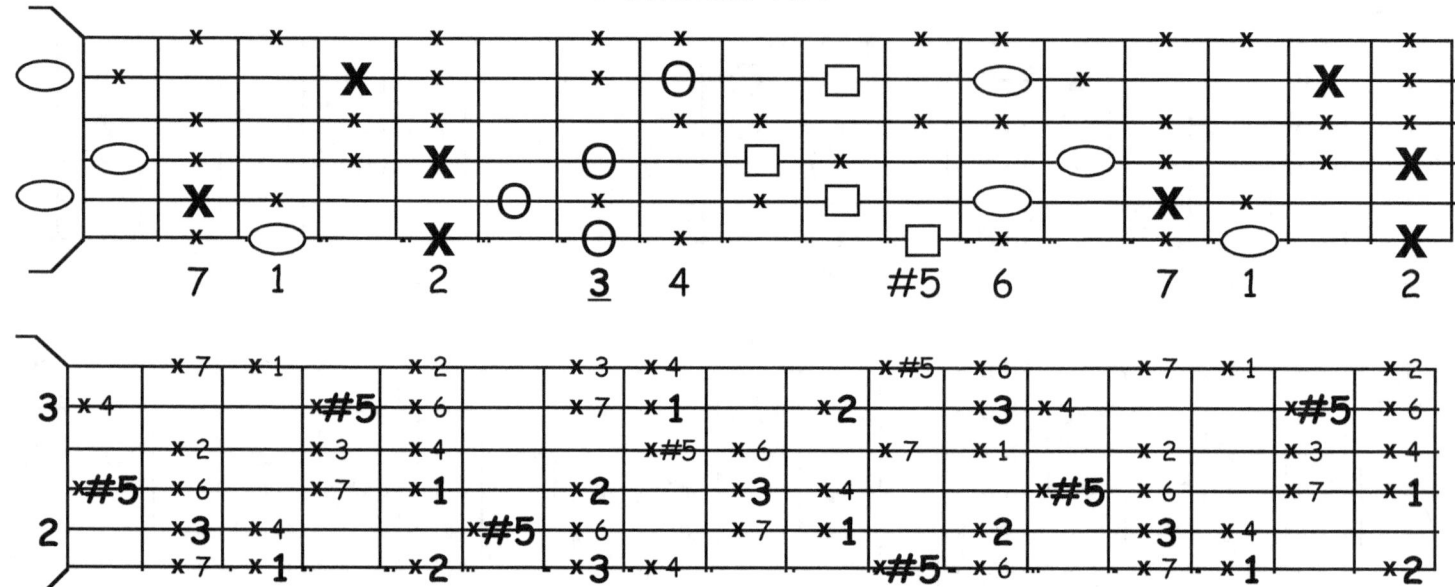

The only notes that you play are: 3, #5, 1, and 2 of the E harmonic minor scale.

5431 STRING GROUPING
B Dominant 7#5

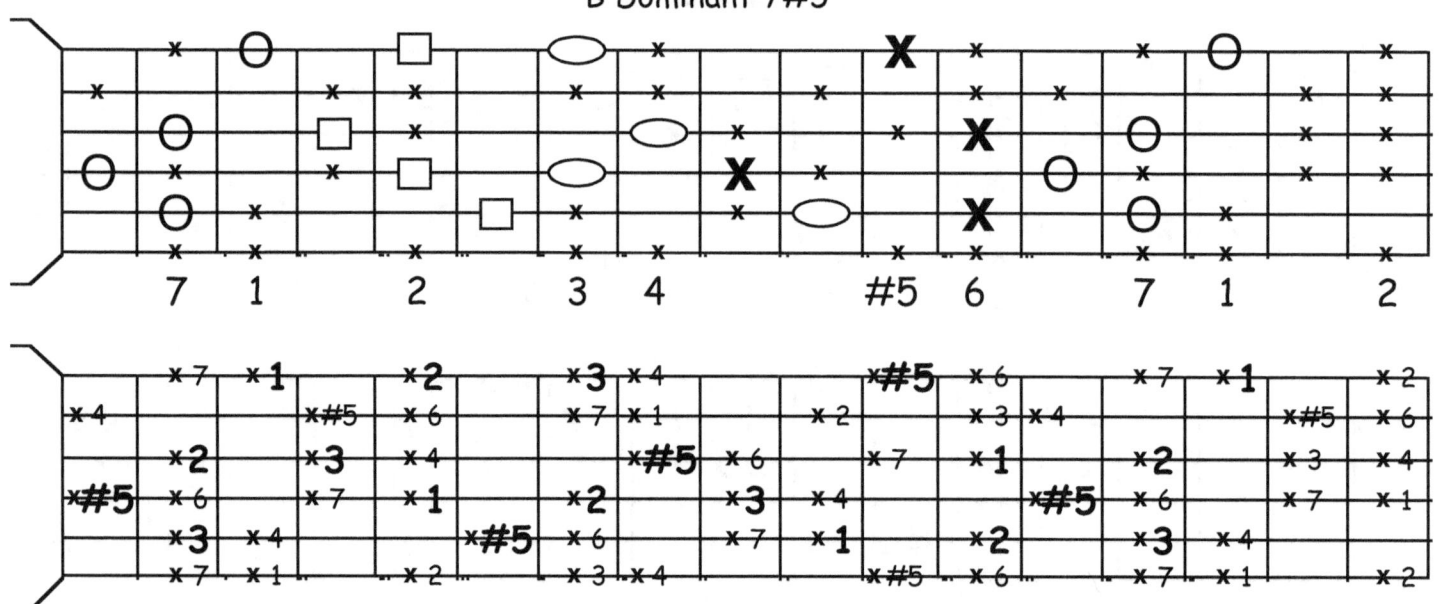

The only notes that you play are: 3, #5, 1, and 2 of the E harmonic minor scale.

The "3" Chord: Dominant 7#5 Inversions In "E" Harmonic Minor
DROP 2 & 4

6532 STRING GROUPING
B Dominant 7#5

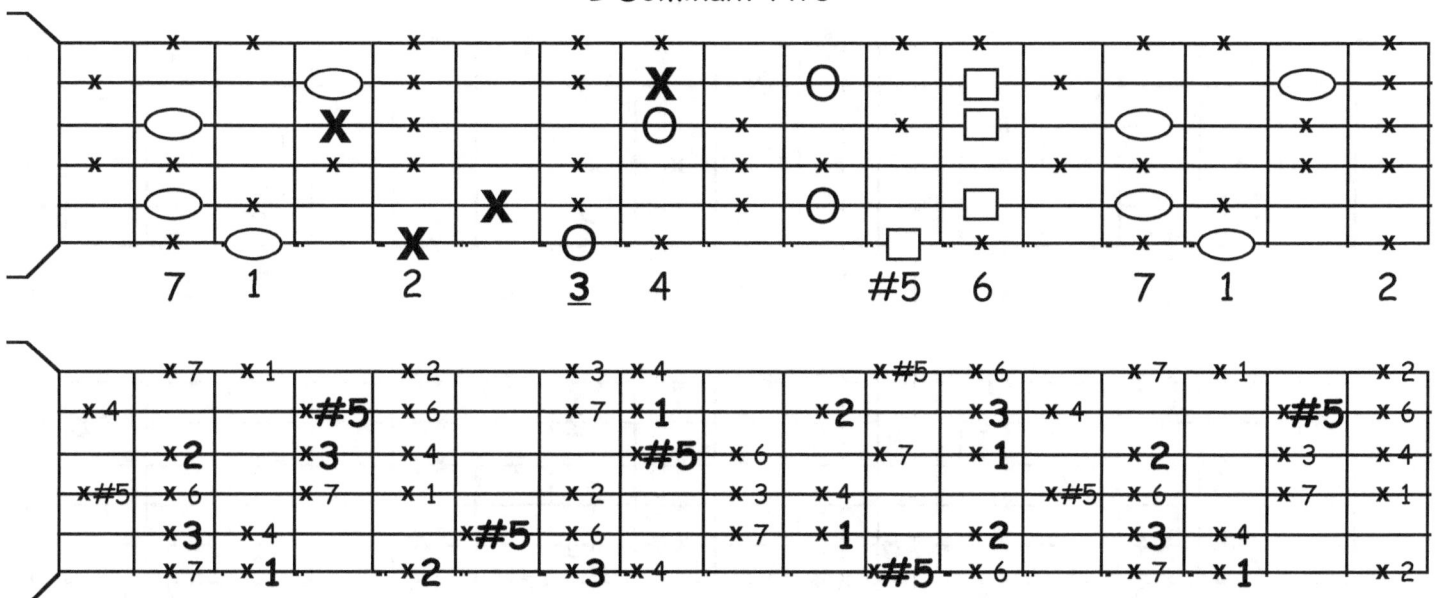

The only notes that you play are: 3, #5, 1, and 2 of the E harmonic minor scale.

5421 STRING GROUPING
B Dominant 7#5

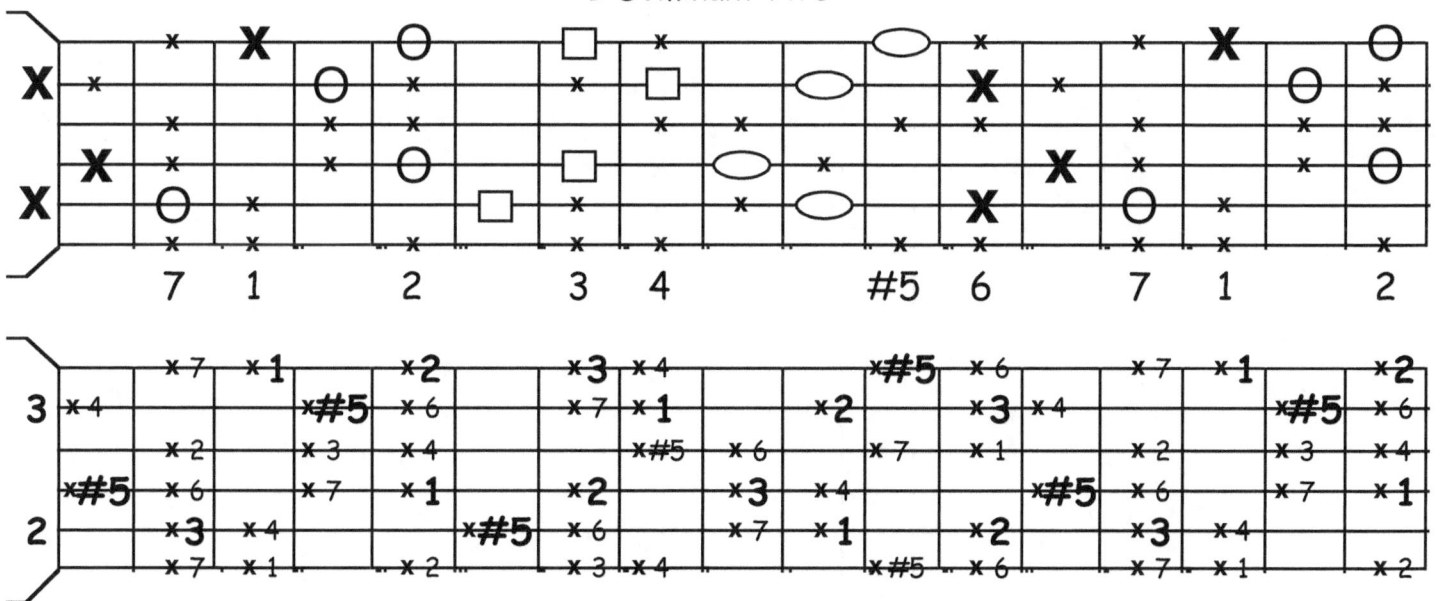

The only notes that you play are: 3, #5, 1, and 2 of the E harmonic minor scale.

The "3" Chord: Dominant 7#5 Inversions In "E" Harmonic Minor
DOUBLE DROP 2 & DROP 4
6521 STRING GROUPING
B Dominant 7#5

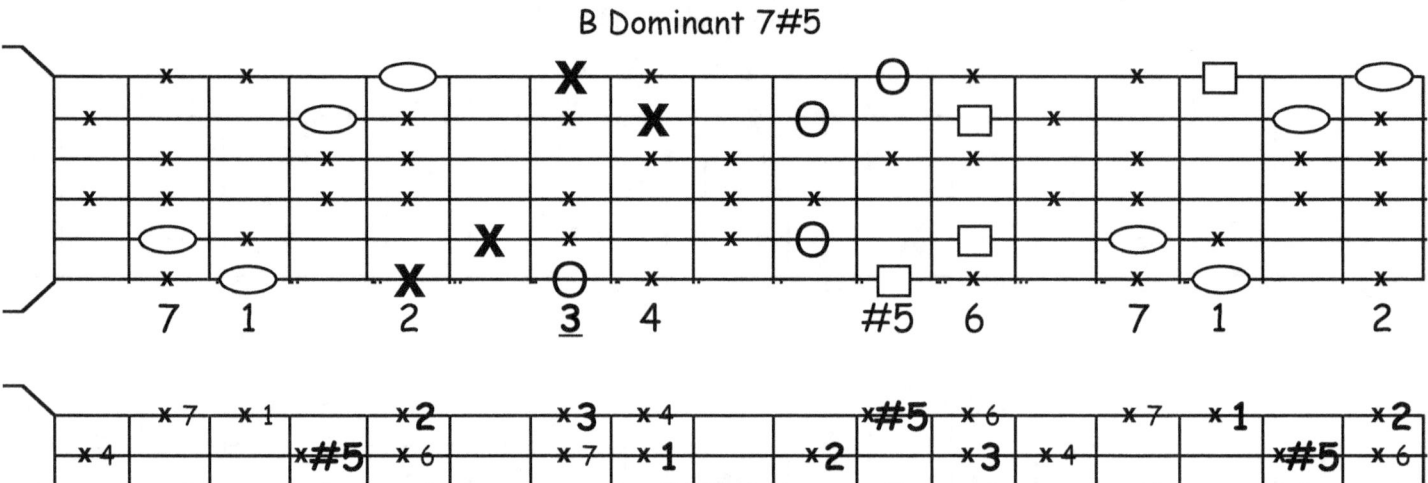

The only notes that you play are: 3, #5, 1, and 2 of the E harmonic minor scale.

DOMINANT 7#9

There are a number of different ways to voice a dominant 7#9 chord on the guitar. The note that functions as the #9 is between the 9th and the 3rd of the chord. The closest chord tone to the #9 is the 3rd of the chord. HOWEVER, the 3rd of the chord is vital to the chord's color and function. So, in order to play the #9 of this chord, we are going to raise the root of the chord a minor 3rd (up 3 frets).

This means that all of the chords that would otherwise be in root position, will now have the #9 in the bass (because the root has been raised in order to play the #9).

This way of playing a dominant 7#9 chord may seem a little strange, but this way you have both the 3rd and the #9 in the chord voicing. Also, this way of voicing the dominant 7#9 chords produces some really weird and pretty odd sounding chords (something that I love).

One of the scales that can accommodate these chords is the diminished scale. So, all of these chords are presented within the G diminished scale. There are 4 dominant 7#9 chords that can fit into the G diminished scale: F#7#9, A7#9, C7#9. Eb7#9. All of these chords are a minor 3rd apart. The F#7#9 is the chord that is presented here.

Remember that the diminished scale is one of the two scales in the MAJOR METHOD that is NOT related back to the major scale. Since we are NOT using the major scale pitch numbers, I have labeled the notes of the dominant 7#9 chords with their functions: #9, 3, 5, 7.

#9 = the #9 of the chord
3 = the 3rd of the chord
5 = the 5th of the chord
7 = the 7th of the chord

And don't forget that when you are playing the root position in these chords, the #9 will be the note in the bass. Here now are those dominant 7#9 chords.

DOMINANT 7#9

○ = Root Position Dominant 7#9 Chord (#9 in the bass)
□ = First Inversion Dominant 7#9 Chord
⬭ = Second Inversion Dominant 7#9 Chord
X = Third Inversion Dominant 7#9 Chord

DROP 2

The Dominant 7#9 Chord Inversions In "G" Diminished
6543 STRING GROUPING
F# Dominant 7#9

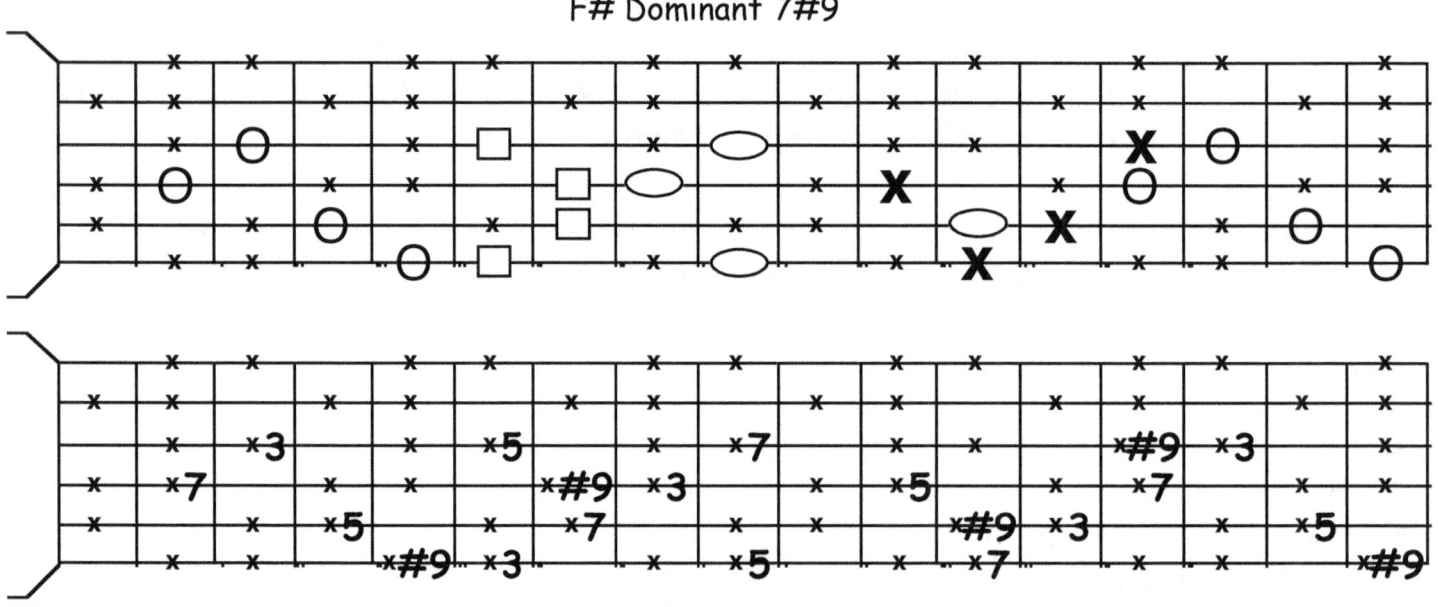

The numbers represent the chord tones and alteration: #9 = #9th, 3 = 3rd, 5 = 5th, 7 = 7th.

REMEMBER: The numbers in all of these lower diagrams are NOT scale numbers. The dominant 7#9 chord inversions are drawn on top of the diminished scale. The diminished scale does not relate back to the major scale. The numbers that are shown are the chord tones and alteration:

#9 = the sharp ninth of the chord
3 = the third of the chord
5 = the fifth of the chord
7 = the seventh of the chord

The Dominant 7#9 Chord Inversions In "G" Diminished

5432 STRING GROUPING
F# Dominant 7#9

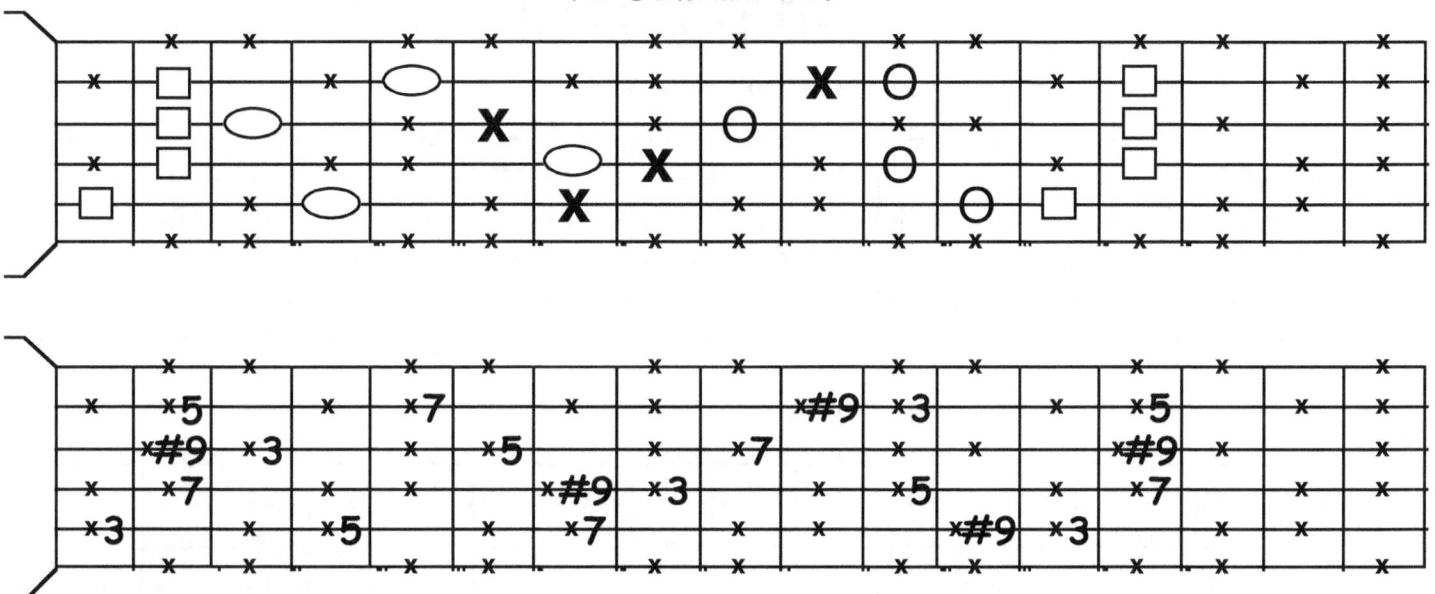

The numbers represent the chord tones and alteration: #9 = #9th, 3 = 3rd, 5 = 5th, 7 = 7th.

4321 STRING GROUPING
F# Dominant 7#9

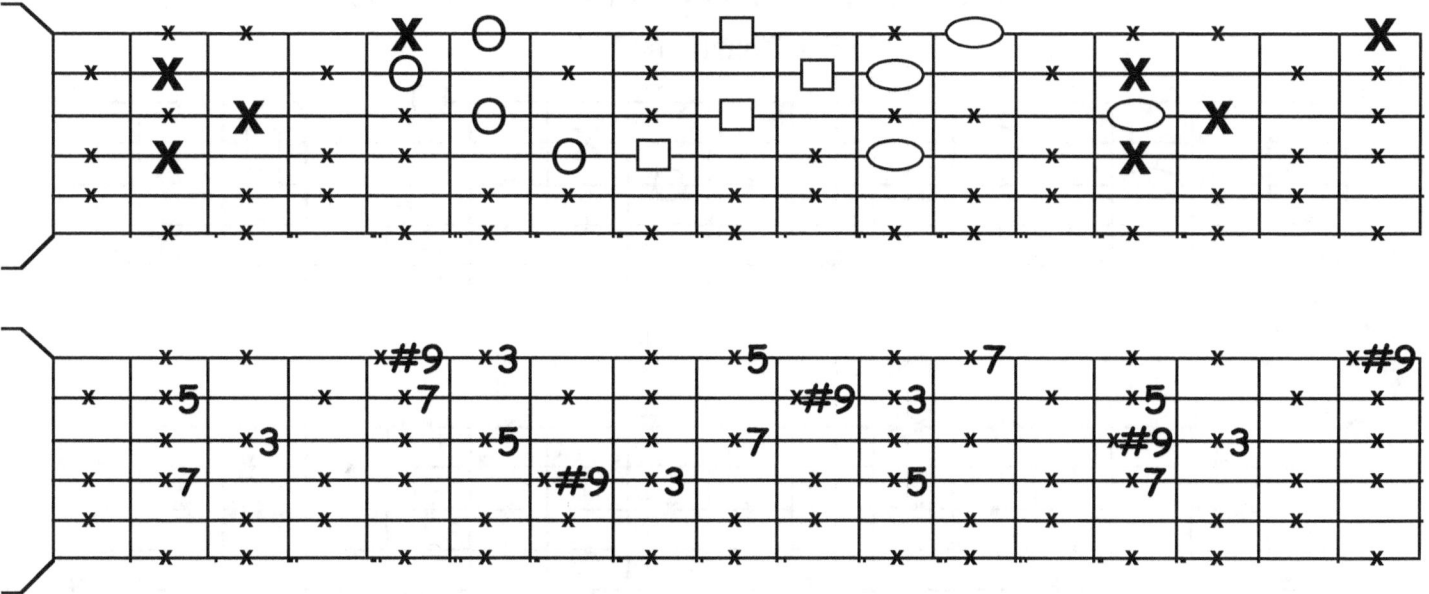

The numbers represent the chord tones and alteration: #9 = #9th, 3 = 3rd, 5 = 5th, 7 = 7th.

The Dominant 7#9 Chord Inversions In "G" Diminished
DROP 3

6432 STRING GROUPING
F# Dominant 7#9

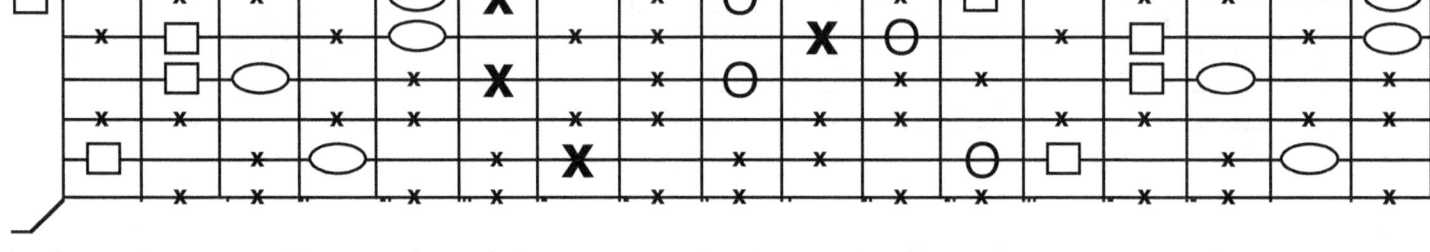

The numbers represent the chord tones and alteration: #9 = #9th, 3 = 3rd, 5 = 5th, 7 = 7th.

5321 STRING GROUPING
F# Dominant 7#9

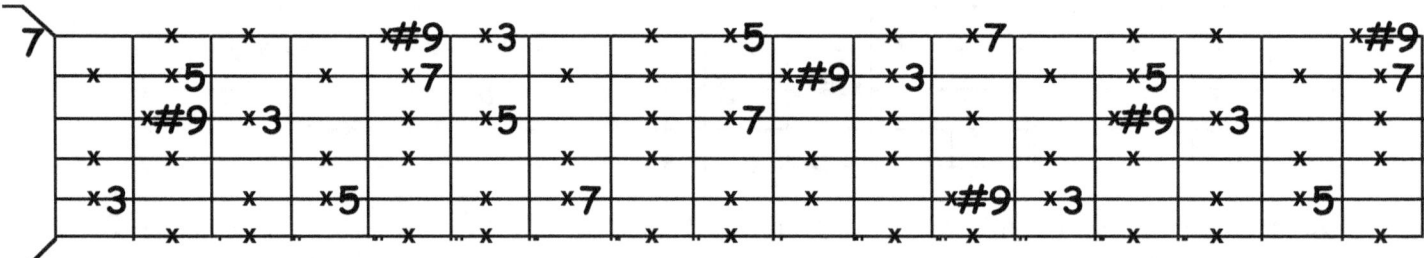

The numbers represent the chord tones and alteration: #9 = #9th, 3 = 3rd, 5 = 5th, 7 = 7th.

The Dominant 7#9 Chord Inversions In "G" Diminished
DROP 2 & 3

6542 STRING GROUPING
F# Dominant 7#9

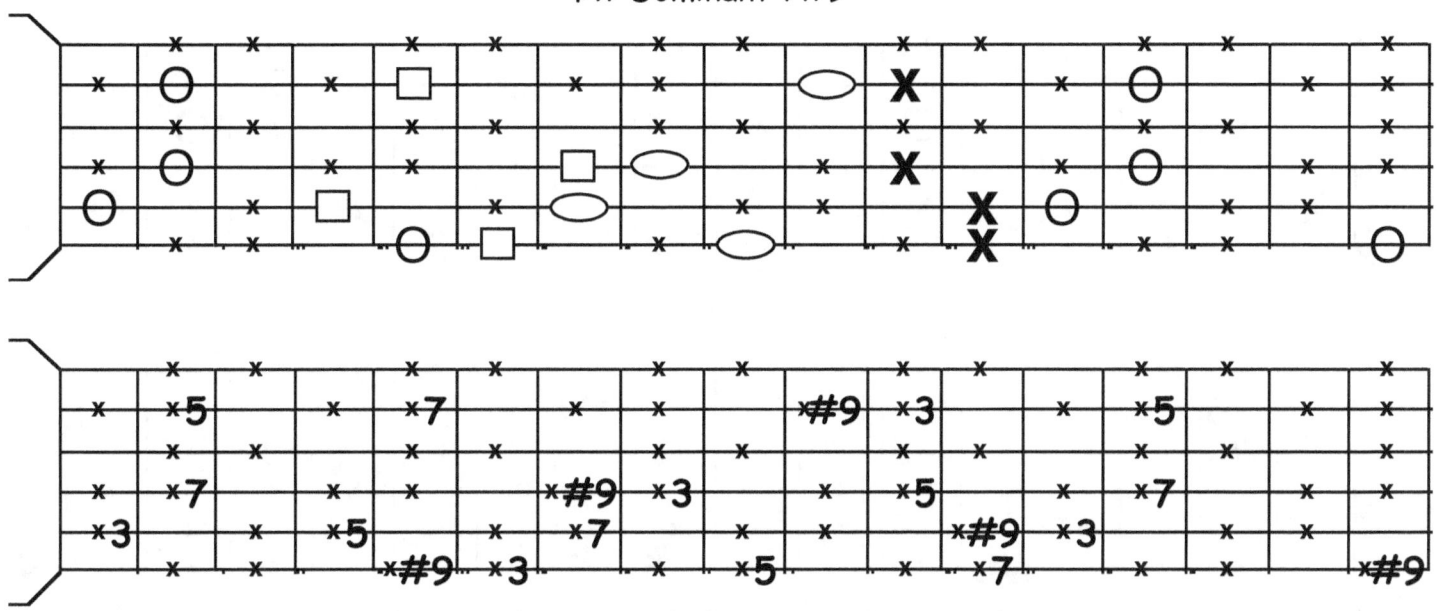

The numbers represent the chord tones and alteration: #9 = #9th, 3 = 3rd, 5 = 5th, 7 = 7th.

5431 STRING GROUPING
F# Dominant 7#9

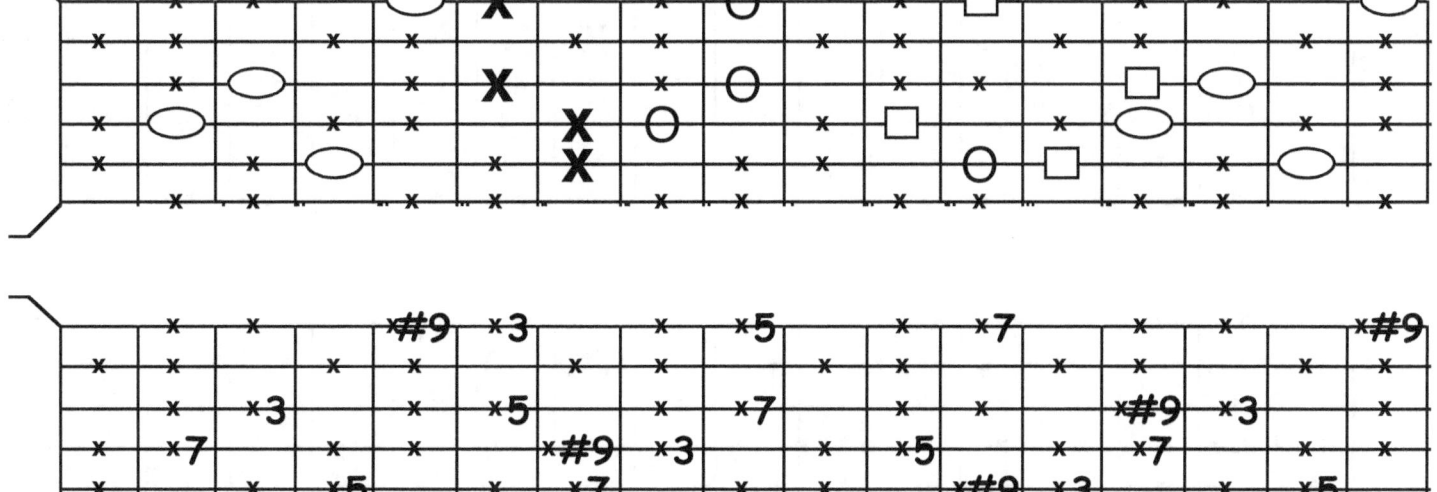

The numbers represent the chord tones and alteration: #9 = #9th, 3 = 3rd, 5 = 5th, 7 = 7th.

The Dominant 7#9 Chord Inversions In "G" Diminished
DROP 2 & 4

6532 STRING GROUPING
F# Dominant 7#9

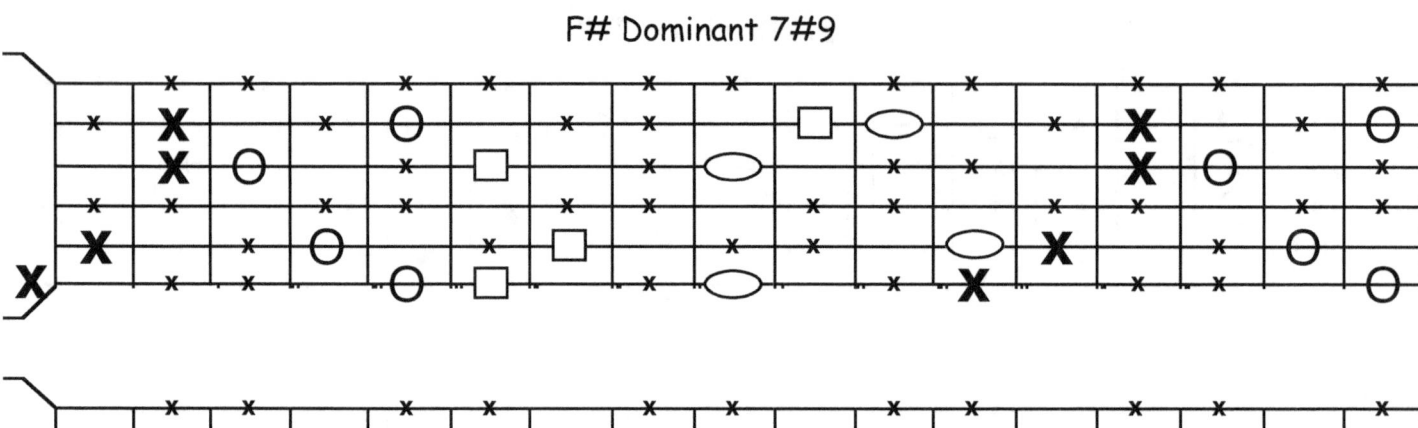

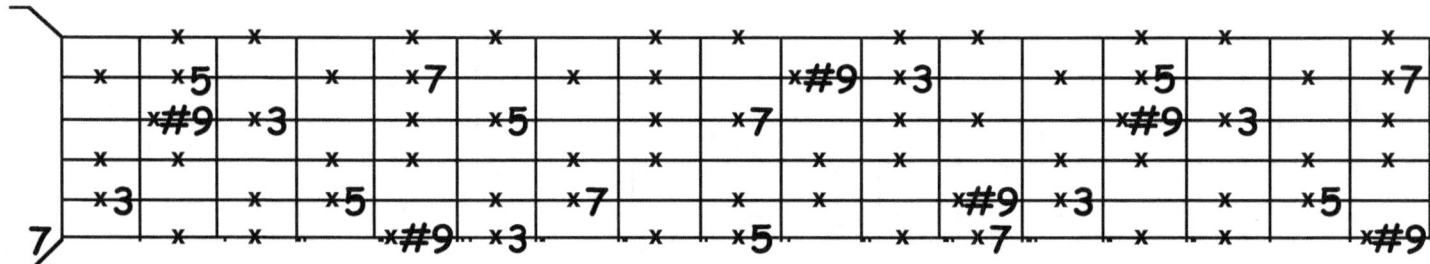

The numbers represent the chord tones and alteration: #9 = #9th, 3 = 3rd, 5 = 5th, 7 = 7th.

5421 STRING GROUPING
F# Dominant 7#9

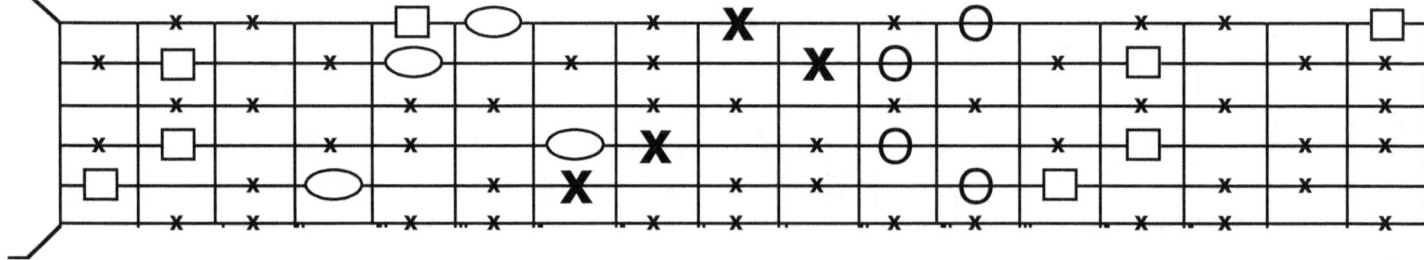

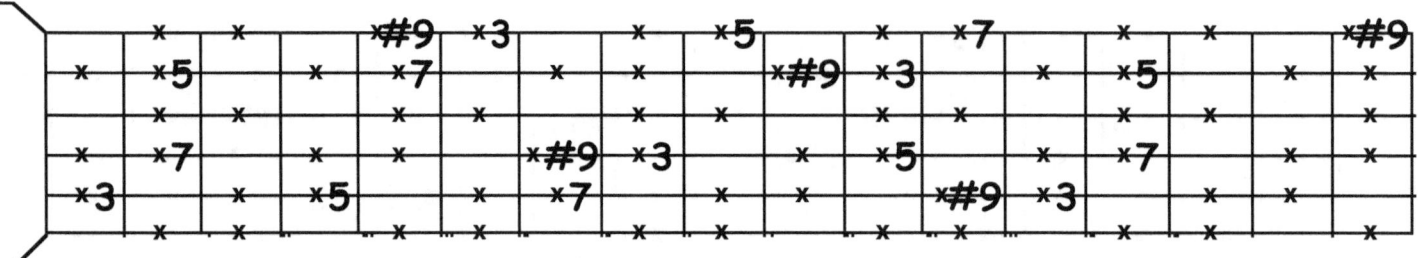

The numbers represent the chord tones and alteration: #9 = #9th, 3 = 3rd, 5 = 5th, 7 = 7th.

The Dominant 7#9 Chord Inversions In "G" Diminished
DOUBLE DROP 2 & DROP 4
6521 STRING GROUPING
F# Dominant 7#9

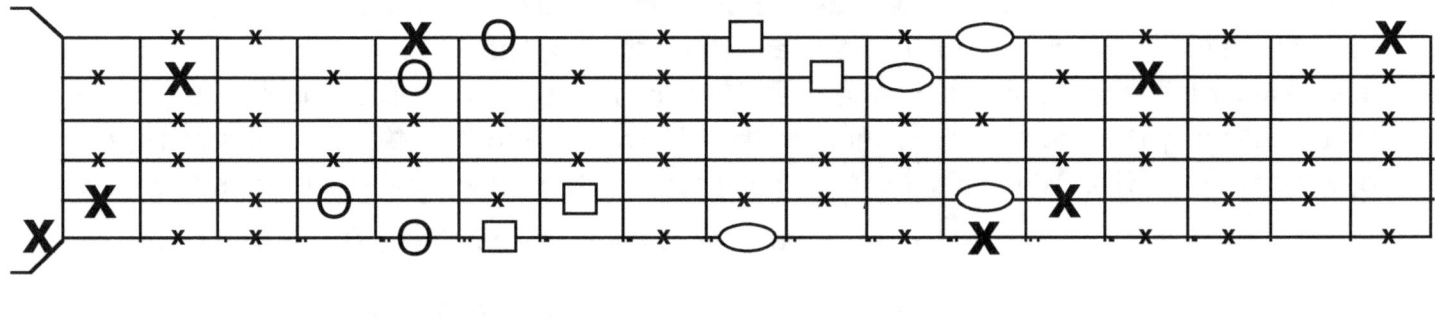

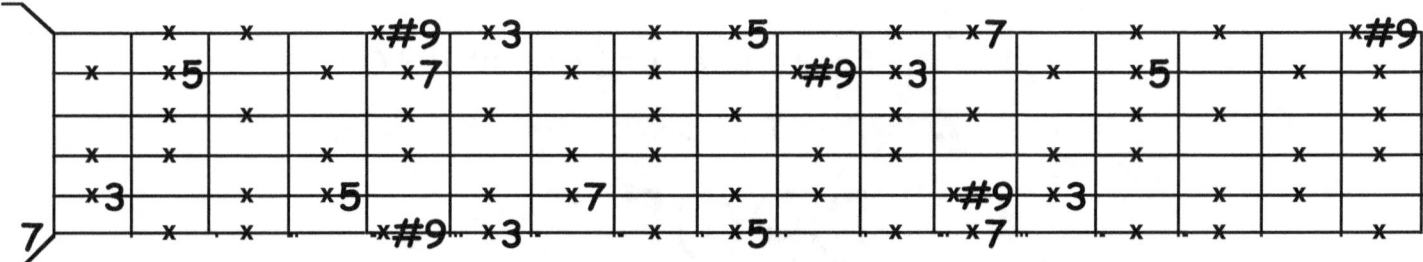

The numbers represent the chord tones and alteration: #9 = #9th, 3 = 3rd, 5 = 5th, 7 = 7th.

DOMINANT 7b9

You can raise the root of a regular dominant 7 chord a half step (1 fret) to get the b9 sound. The dominant 7b9 chord can occur in the diminished and the harmonic minor scales. In fact, these ARE the diminished 7 chords on the guitar. It's more useful to see these within the harmonic minor scale, so that's how they are presented here. In the MAJOR METHOD, the E harmonic minor scale = the G major scale with a #5. So, the "3" chord in E harmonic minor is a B dominant 7 chord spelled: 3, #5, 7, 2. You can raise the root (3) a half step (to the 4), without changing the scale. This dominant 7b9 chord is spelled: 4, #5, 7, 2 (4 = b9th, #5 = 3rd, 7 = 5th, 2 = 7th). When playing the root position, the b9 will be the note in the bass.

O = Root Position Dominant 7b9 Chord (b9 in the bass)

□ = First Inversion Dominant 7b9 Chord

⬯ = Second Inversion Dominant 7b9 Chord

X = Third Inversion Dominant 7b9 Chord

DROP 2

The "3" Chord: Dominant 7b9 Inversions
In "E" Harmonic Minor

6543 STRING GROUPING

B Dominant 7b9 Chord

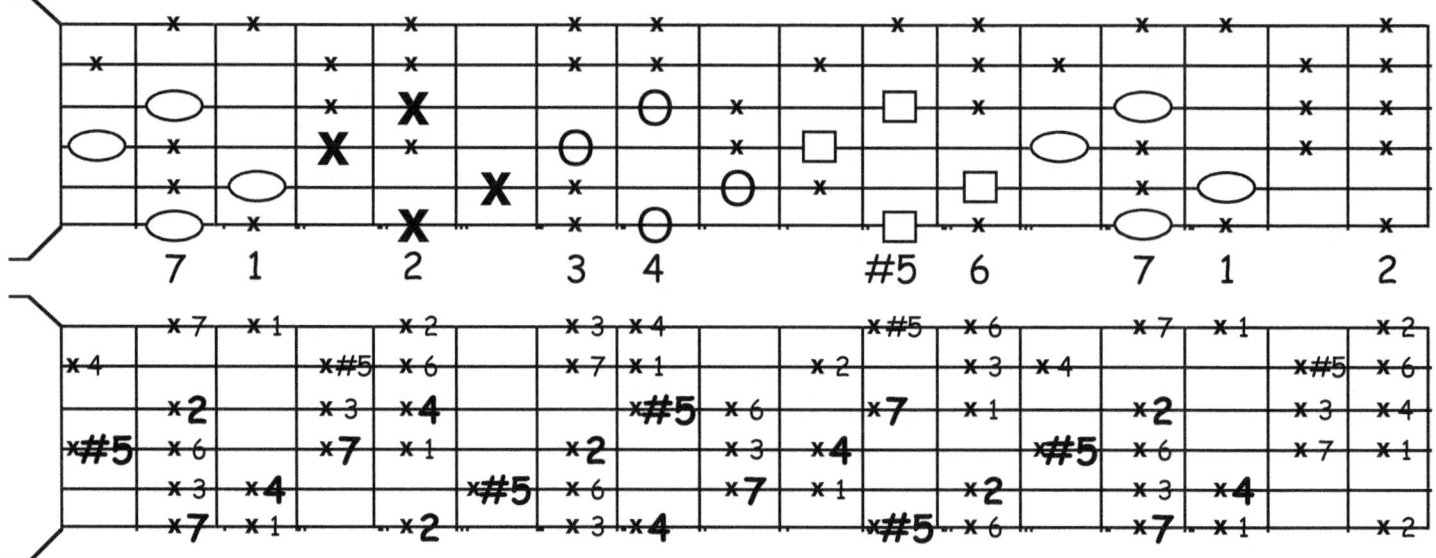

The only notes that you play are: 4, #5, 7, and 2 of the E harmonic minor scale.

The "3" Chord: Dominant 7b9 Inversions
In "E" Harmonic Minor
5432 STRING GROUPING
B Dominant 7b9 Chord

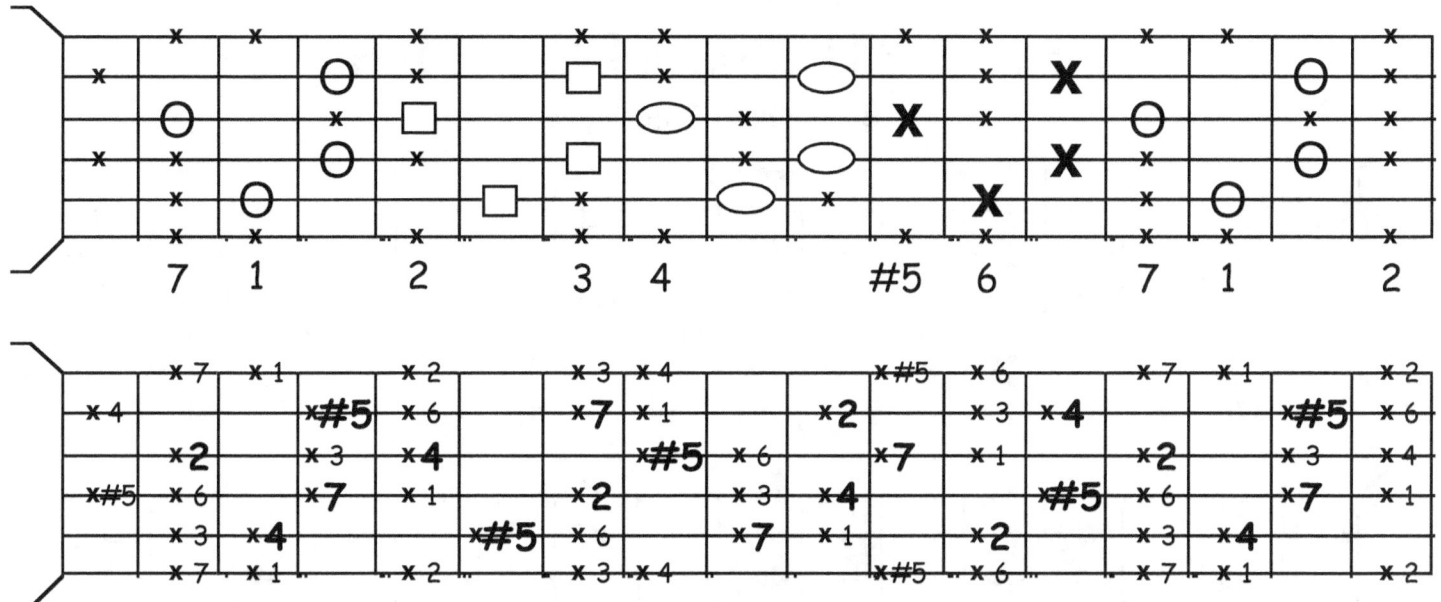

The only notes that you play are: 4, #5, 7, and 2 of the E harmonic minor scale.

4321 STRING GROUPING
B Dominant 7b9 Chord

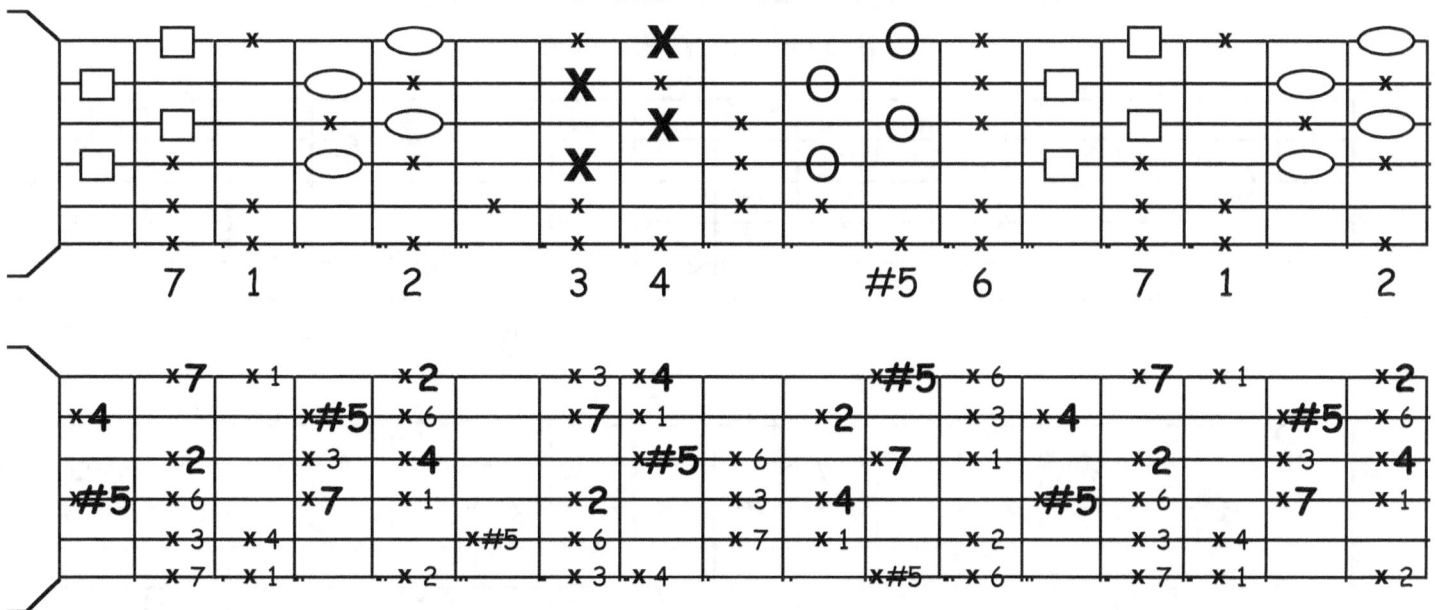

The only notes that you play are: 4, #5, 7, and 2 of the E harmonic minor scale.

The "3" Chord: Dominant 7b9 Inversions In "E" Harmonic Minor
DROP 3
6432 STRING GROUPING
B Dominant 7b9 Chord

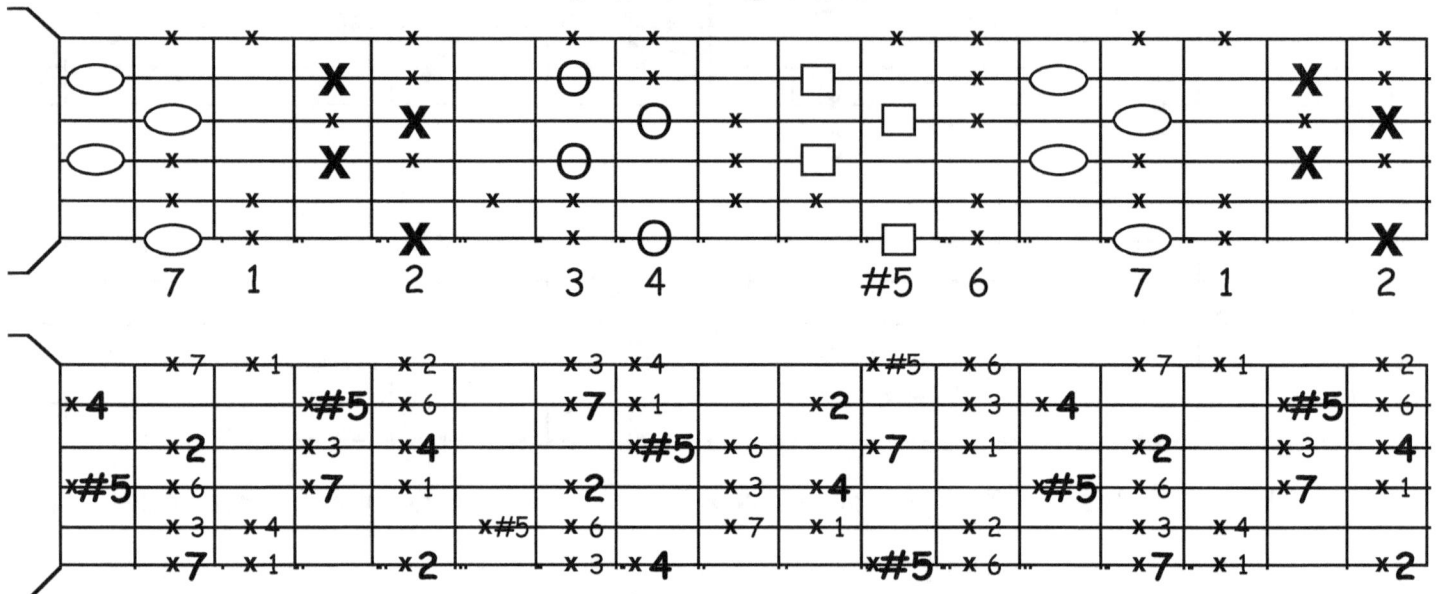

The only notes that you play are: 4, #5, 7, and 2 of the E harmonic minor scale.

5321 STRING GROUPING
B Dominant 7b9 Chord

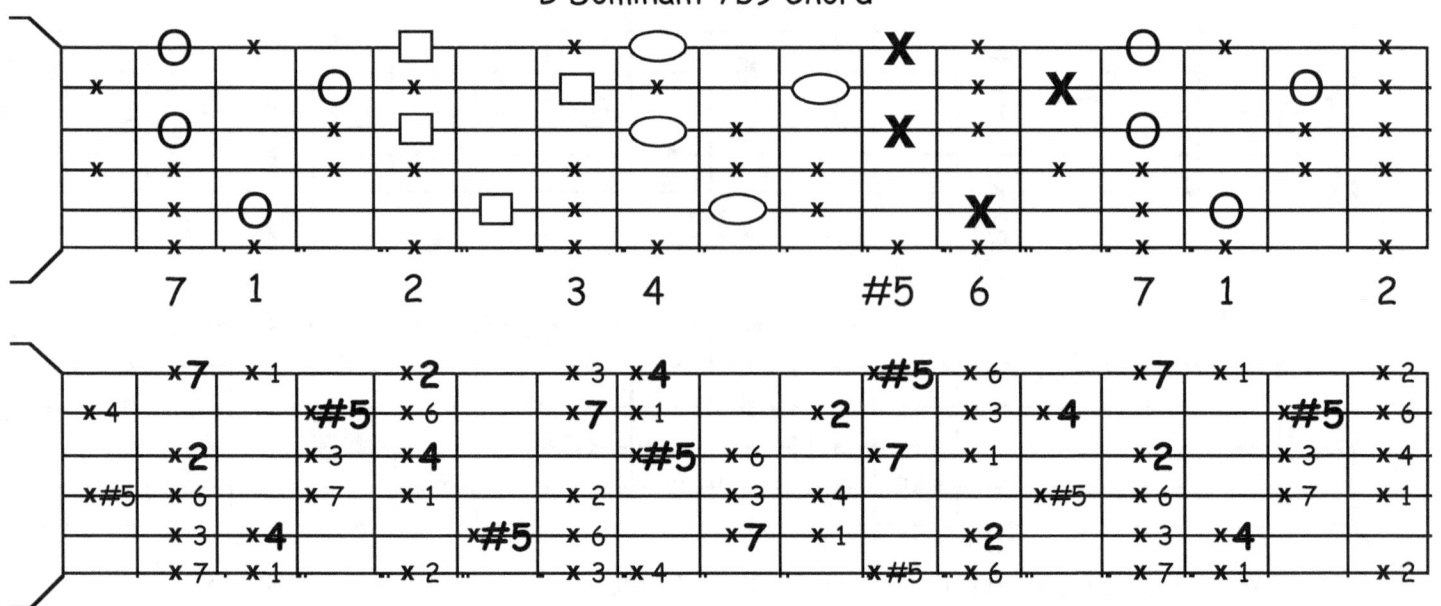

The only notes that you play are: 4, #5, 7, and 2 of the E harmonic minor scale.

The "3" Chord: Dominant 7b9 Inversions In "E" Harmonic Minor
DROP 2 & 3

6542 STRING GROUPING
B Dominant 7b9 Chord

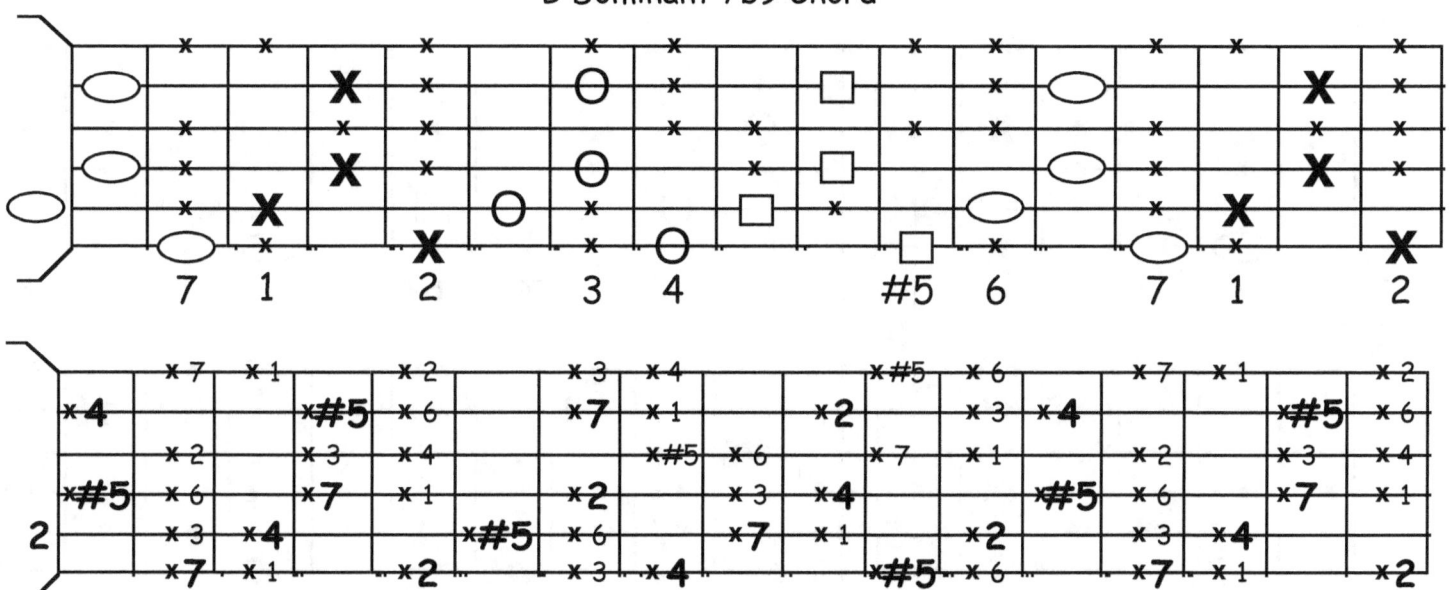

The only notes that you play are: 4, #5, 7, and 2 of the E harmonic minor scale.

5431 STRING GROUPING
B Dominant 7b9 Chord

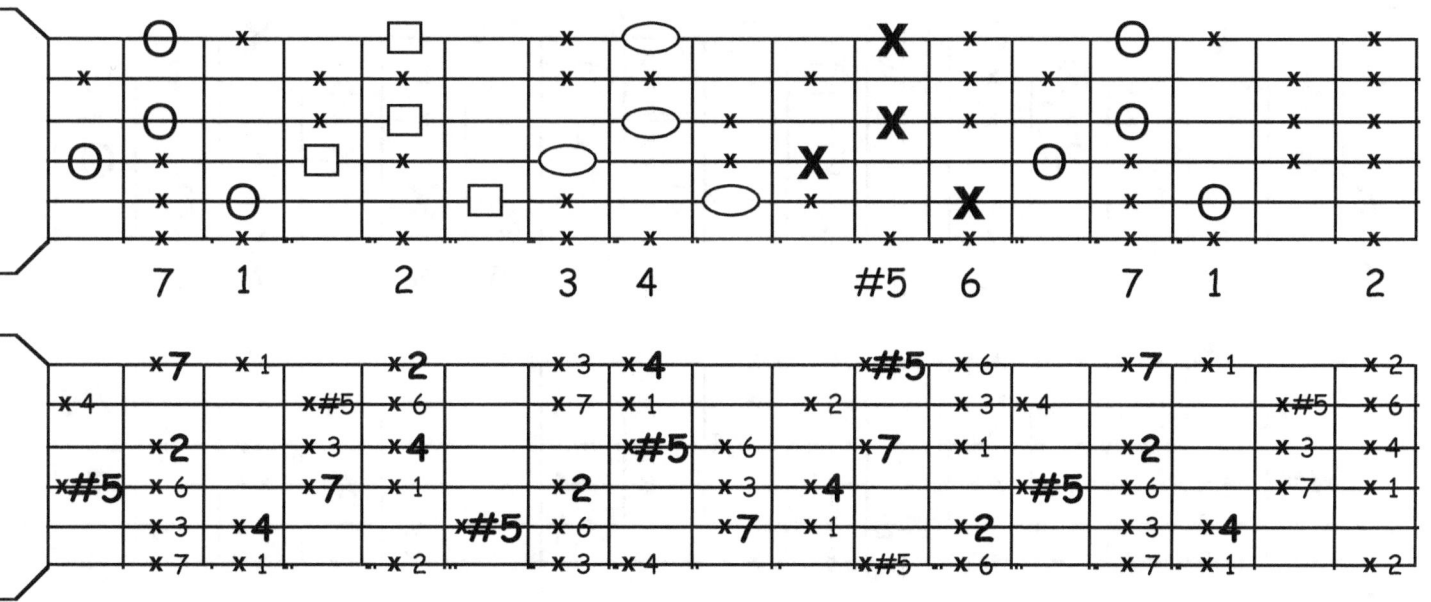

The only notes that you play are: 4, #5, 7, and 2 of the E harmonic minor scale.

The "3" Chord: Dominant 7b9 Inversions In "E" Harmonic Minor

DROP 2 & 4

6532 STRING GROUPING
B Dominant 7b9 Chord

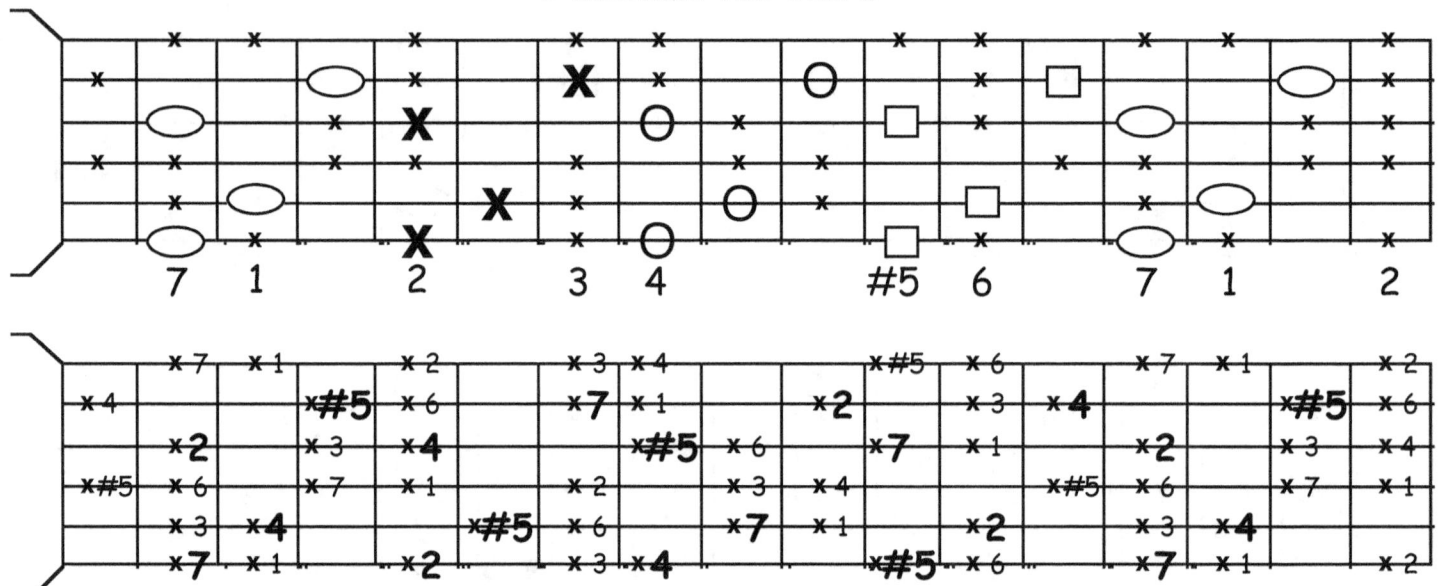

The only notes that you play are: 4, #5, 7, and 2 of the E harmonic minor scale.

5421 STRING GROUPING
B Dominant 7b9 Chord

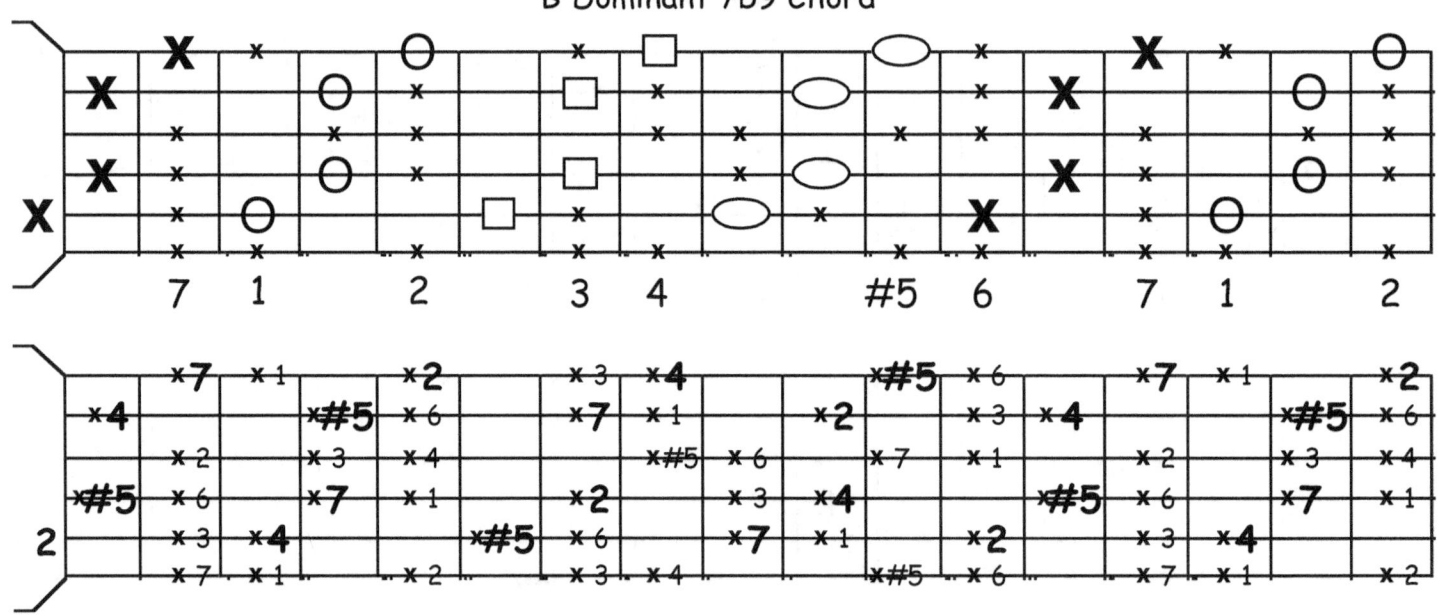

The only notes that you play are: 4, #5, 7, and 2 of the E harmonic minor scale.

The "3" Chord: Dominant 7b9 Inversions In "E" Harmonic Minor
DOUBLE DROP 2 & DROP 4
6521 STRING GROUPING
B Dominant 7b9 Chord

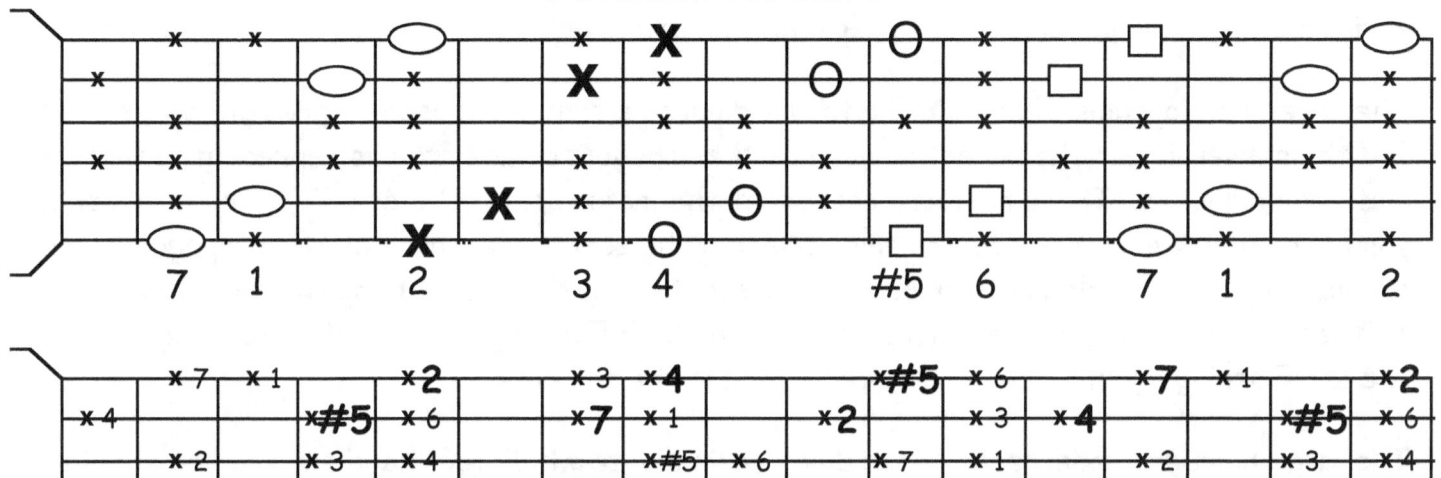

The only notes that you play are: 4, #5, 7, and 2 of the E harmonic minor scale.

DIATONIC SEVENTH CHORD ARPEGGIOS

Arpeggios are the missing link between chords and scales. You play an arpeggio one note at a time (like a scale), but you only play the chord tones of a given chord within a scale, not the entire scale. Some people refer to arpeggios as broken chords.

The arpeggio diagrams will be similar to the diagrams that were used to present the chords and their inversions. The parent scale that the arpeggio comes from is represented with "X"s and small numbers. These numbers represent the major scale pitches (1-7). The notes that you need to play are presented as circles within the scale. To practice these arpeggios, you should play these circle notes one at a time, starting on the low E string (where I have written "Start Here"), play them up through the high E string notes, and return back down to the low E string again. You don't have to repeat the top note.

The large numbers underneath these diagrams indicate which left hand fingers you should use. Remember, the thumb does not count as a finger. Your pointer (index) finger is 1, your middle finger is 2, your ring finger is 3, and your little finger is 4. There will be patterns where you will have to stretch your first finger or your fourth finger in order to play a note. If this happens, try to make sure that you still play the remaining notes with the recommended fingers. The fingerings that are given actually reduce the amount of stretching that is required to play these arpeggios within these patterns. If you have to shift your left hand back and forth a little to use these fingerings, it's OK. As you're practicing, monitor your left hand. If you feel ANY pain or fatigue, take a break and give your hand a rest. Playing the guitar is physical and you need to take care of your hands.

After you memorize these arpeggios, you'll need to tie them together and be able to shift from one pattern to another. This will take some time. To help speed this process along, I have grouped all of the "1" chord arpeggios together, then all of the "2" chord arpeggios, then all of the "3" chord arpeggios, until you have all seven sets of diatonic arpeggios. Try soloing using only the "1" chord arpeggios. Then try soloing using only the "2" chord arpeggios, and so on. Eventually you'll want to try soloing throughout an entire tune using only the arpeggios of that tune's chords. This may seem fairly limiting compared to soloing with entire scales, but it provides for a very different sound and approach to soloing. It also comes in handy when the chords of a tune go by so fast that there isn't enough time to use an entire scale. Besides, we guitar players are frequently criticized as being too "scalar" (always using scales) in our improvisations and not intervallic enough. Using arpeggios is one way to break out of this tendency.

For the diatonic seventh chord arpeggios, I have used the G major scale as the constant. So, all of the diatonic arpeggios presented here come from the seven chords of the G major scale. After learning these, you will have to transpose all of this information into the other keys. **NOTE:** There are seven different chords in a major scale, each with its own tonality:

>1 Chord = Major 7
>2 Chord = Minor 7
>3 Chord = Minor 7
>4 Chord = Major 7
>5 Chord = Dominant 7
>6 Chord = Minor 7
>7 Chord = Minor 7b5 (Half Diminished)

The seven arpeggios that come from any major scale outline each one of these seven chords. If you want to play a "1" chord arpeggio, you play all of the notes that make up a "1" chord. Remember that chords are built in thirds, which means that they are built from every other note following the root of the chord. This means that a "1" chord is spelled: 1, 3, 5, 7. The "1" chord arpeggio will have the sound or tonality of the "1" chord (a major 7 tonality). Here are the seven arpeggio tonalities and spellings:

>1 Chord = Major 7 Arpeggio: 1, 3, 5, 7
>2 Chord = Minor 7 Arpeggio: 2, 4, 6, 1
>3 Chord = Minor 7 Arpeggio: 3, 5, 7, 2
>4 Chord = Major 7 Arpeggio: 4, 6, 1, 3
>5 Chord = Dominant 7 Arpeggio: 5, 7, 2, 4
>6 Chord = Minor 7 Arpeggio: 6, 1, 3, 5
>7 Chord = Minor 7b5 (Half Diminished) Arpeggio: 7, 2, 4, 6

As you look through this list, you'll notice that some of the chords/arpeggios have the same tonality. Here is a summary of the different chord/arpeggio tonalities:

>1 & 4 Chords = Major 7
>2, 3, & 6 Chords = Minor 7
>5 Chord = Dominant 7
>7 Chord = Minor 7b5 (or Half Diminished)

This means that the "1" chord arpeggios and the "4" chord arpeggios will be built from the exact same physical shapes (the major 7 shapes). The "1" and "4" chord arpeggio shapes will just happen at different places on the neck of the guitar. This is also true for the "2", "3", and "6" chord arpeggios (all minor 7 shapes). This will all be much clearer once you start playing the actual arpeggios. Here they are ...

"1" Chord Arpeggio In "G" Major
G Major 7 Arpeggio: 1, 3, 5, 7

Pattern 7

This is labeled as "Pattern 7" because your 1st finger starts on the 7th scale degree.

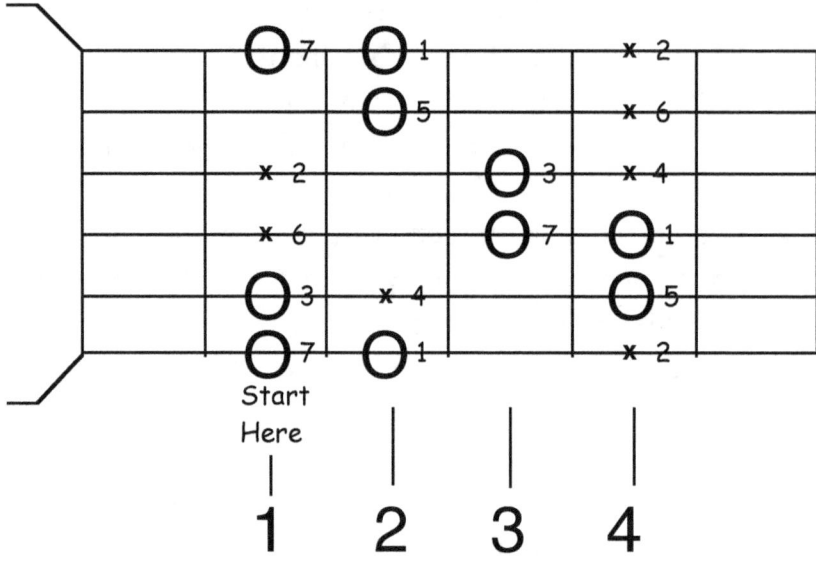

Pattern 1

This is labeled as "Pattern 1" because your 1st finger starts on the 1st scale degree.

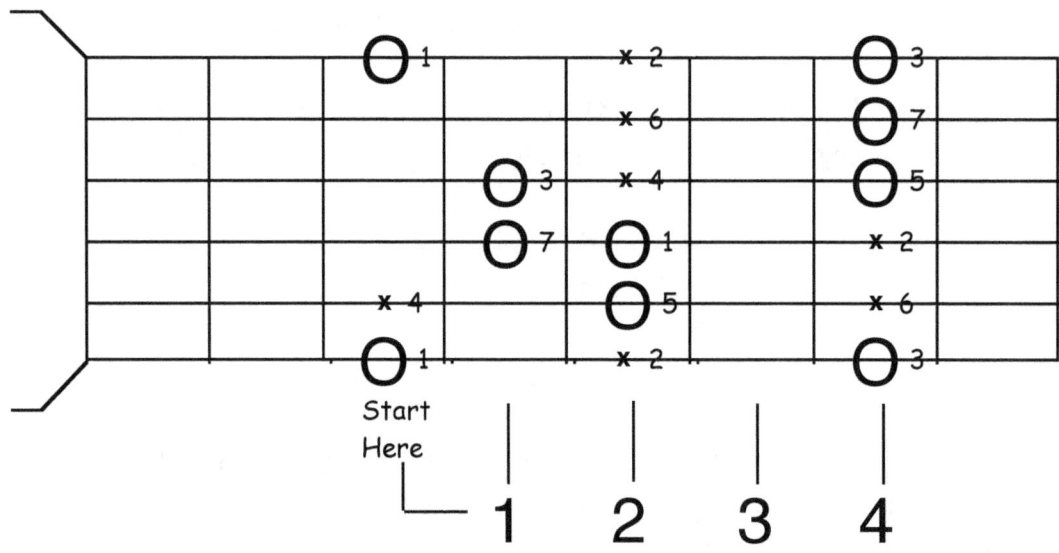

The first finger must "stretch" to play the notes on the third fret.

"1" Chord Arpeggio In "G" Major
G Major 7 Arpeggio: 1, 3, 5, 7

Pattern 2

This is labeled as "Pattern 2" because your 1st finger would start on the 2nd scale degree if the 2nd scale degree was in this arpeggio.

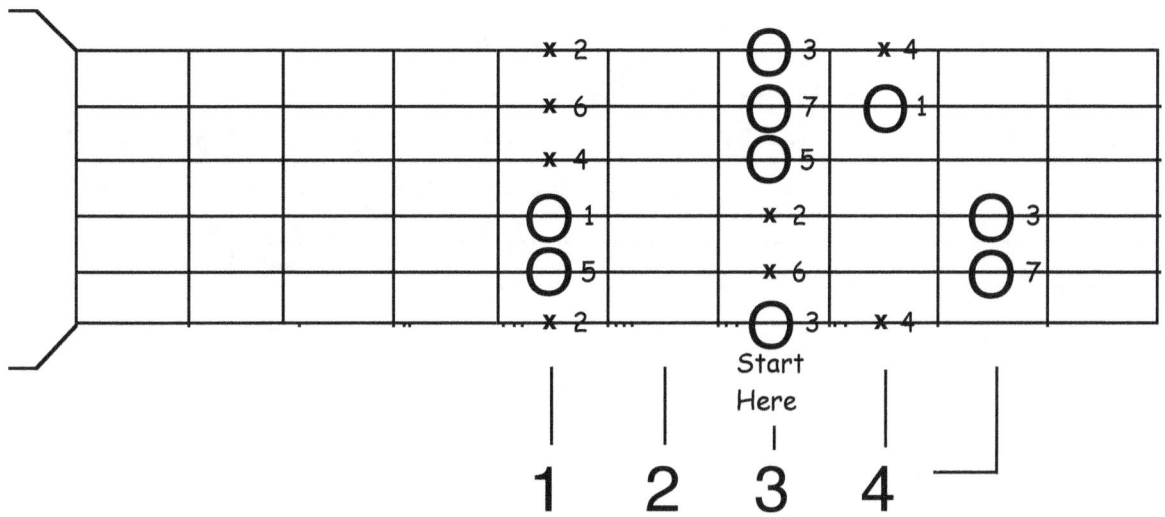

The 4th finger must "stretch" to play the notes on the 9th fret.

Pattern 3

This is labeled as "Pattern 3" because your 1st finger starts on the 3rd scale degree.

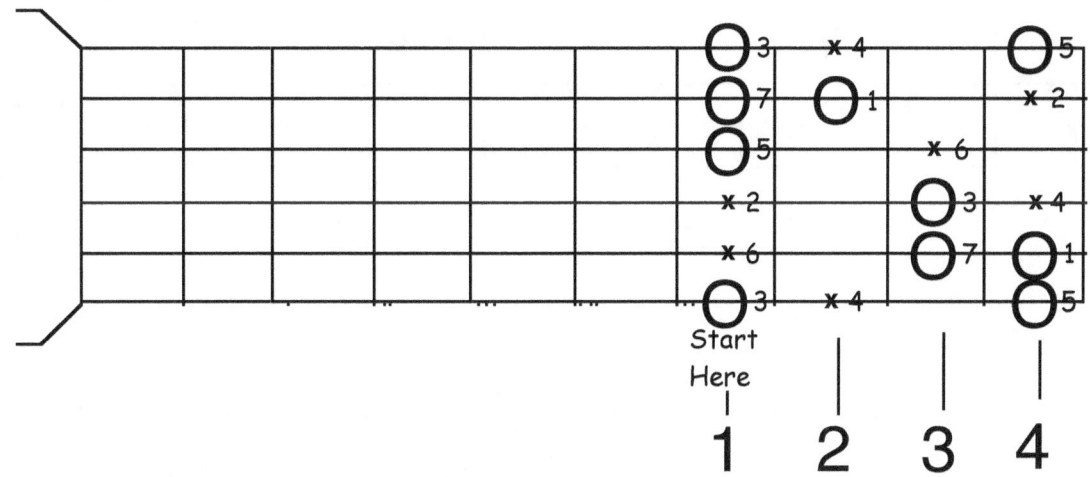

239

"1" Chord Arpeggio In "G" Major
G Major 7 Arpeggio: 1, 3, 5, 7

Pattern 4

This is labeled as "Pattern 4" because your 1st finger would start on the 4th scale degree if the 4th scale degree was in this arpeggio.

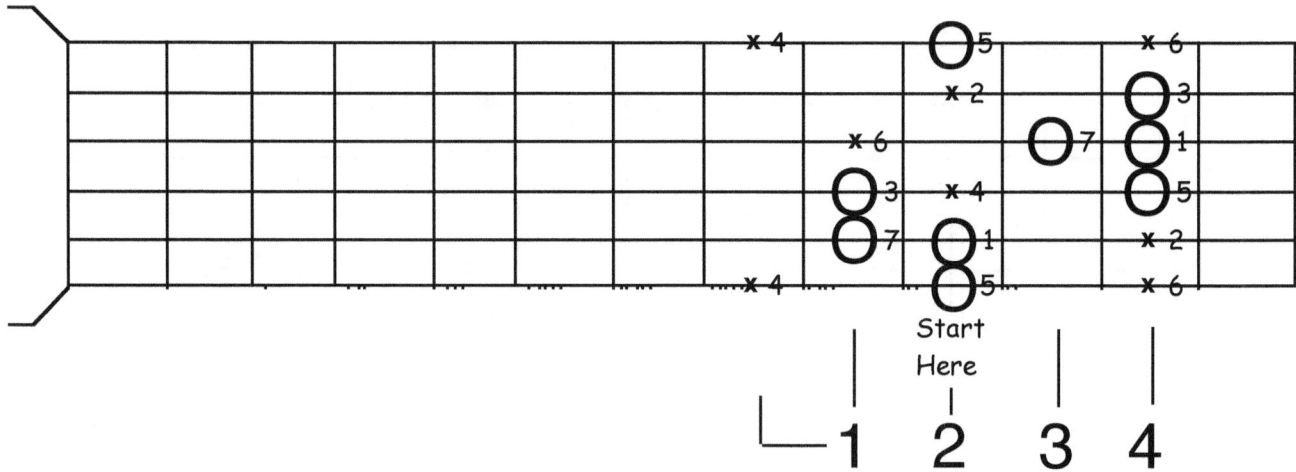

Pattern 5

This is labeled as "Pattern 5" because your 1st finger starts on the 5th scale degree.

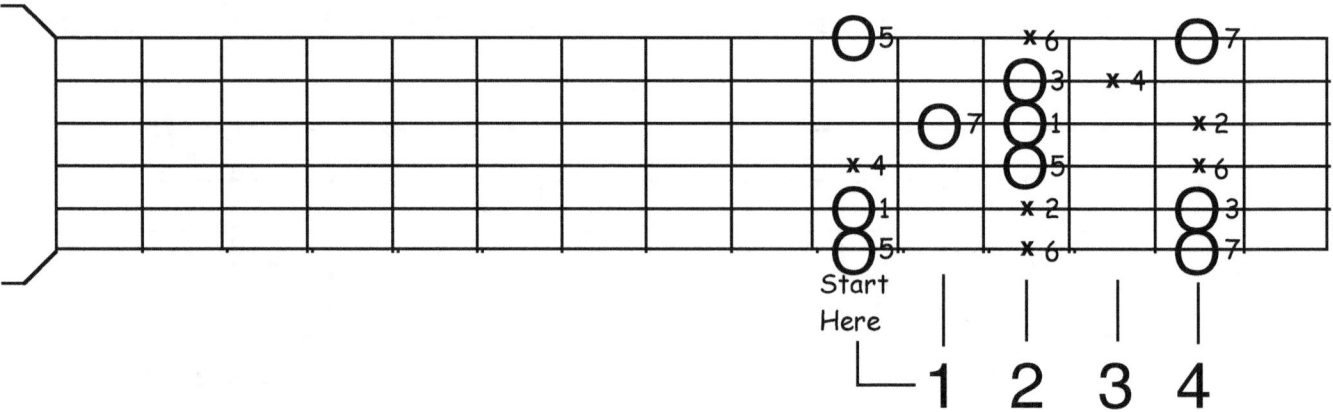

Once again, the first finger must stretch in order to play the notes on the eighth fret in pattern 4 and the tenth fret in pattern 5. When doing this, make sure that your middle finger is still being used to play the notes on the tenth and twelfth frets respectively. At this point, you get the idea of how these diagrams work, so I won't include these little finger-stretching reminders on future patterns.

"1" Chord Arpeggio In "G" Major

G Major 7 Arpeggio: 1, 3, 5, 7

Pattern 6

This is labeled as "Pattern 6" because your 1st finger would start on the 6th scale degree if the 6th scale degree was in this arpeggio.

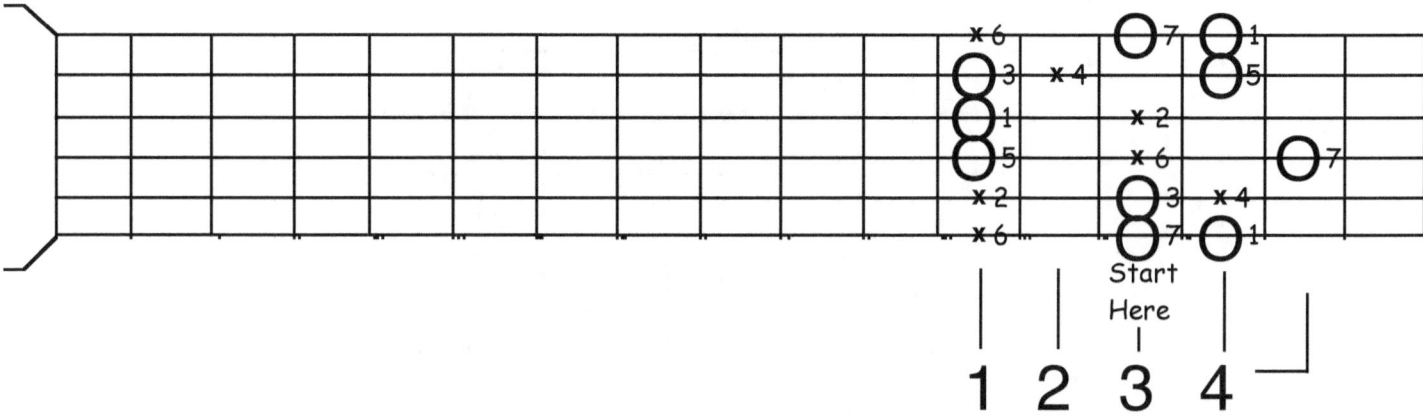

Pattern 6 is way up there on the neck. If you just can't reach these notes on the guitar that you have right now, run this pattern on a lower spot on the neck. But if there is any way humanly possible, run it in place on the neck. Since the frets are so close together up there, playing this is almost like playing a different instrument, and you're going to have to be comfortable with this part of the neck sooner or later.

Below is a diagram of the "1" chord arpeggios on the entire neck.

G Major 7 Arpeggio
(1 CHORD ON THE ENTIRE NECK)

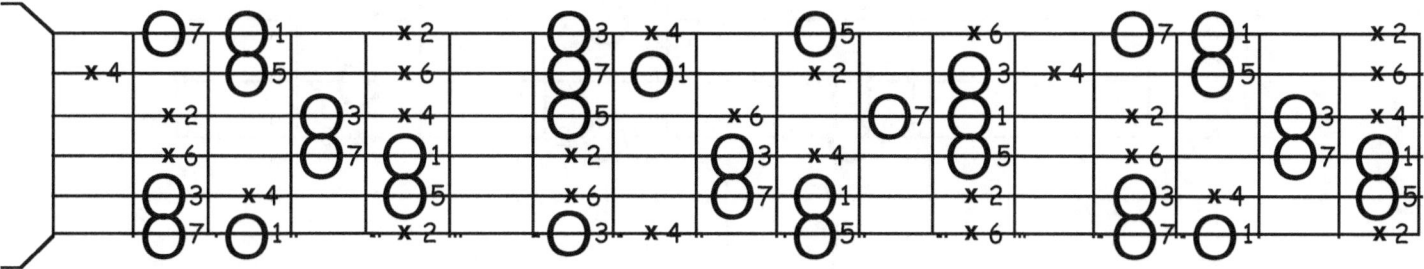

"2" Chord Arpeggio In "G" Major
A Minor 7 Arpeggio: 2, 4, 6, 1

Pattern 7

This is labeled as "Pattern 7" because your 1st finger would start on the 7th scale degree if the 7th scale degree was in this arpeggio.

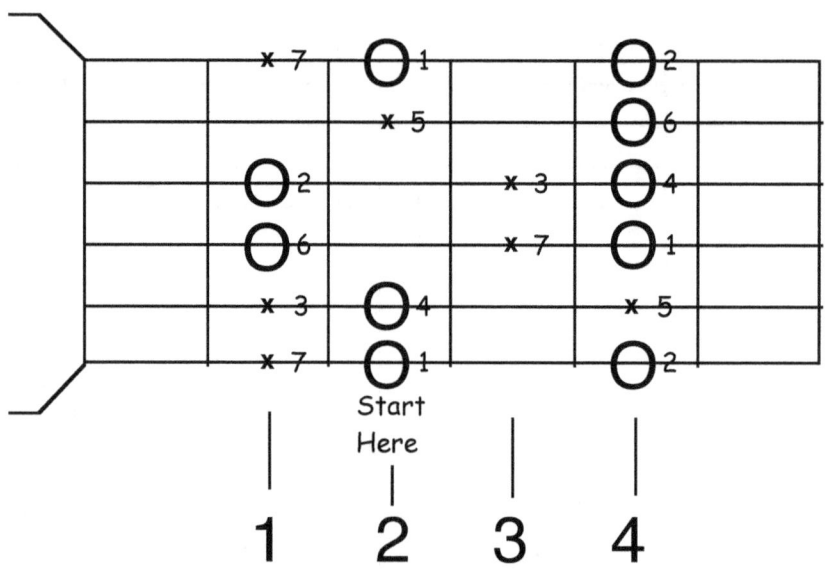

Pattern 1

This is labeled as "Pattern 1" because your 1st finger starts on the 1st scale degree.

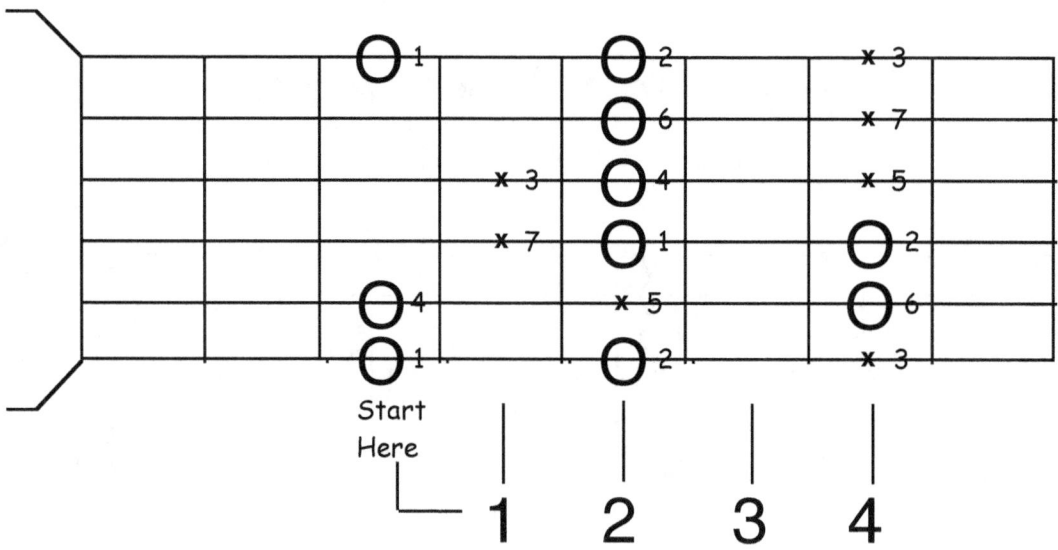

"2" Chord Arpeggio In "G" Major
A Minor 7 Arpeggio: 2, 4, 6, 1

Pattern 2
This is labeled as "Pattern 2" because your 1st finger starts on the 2nd scale degree.

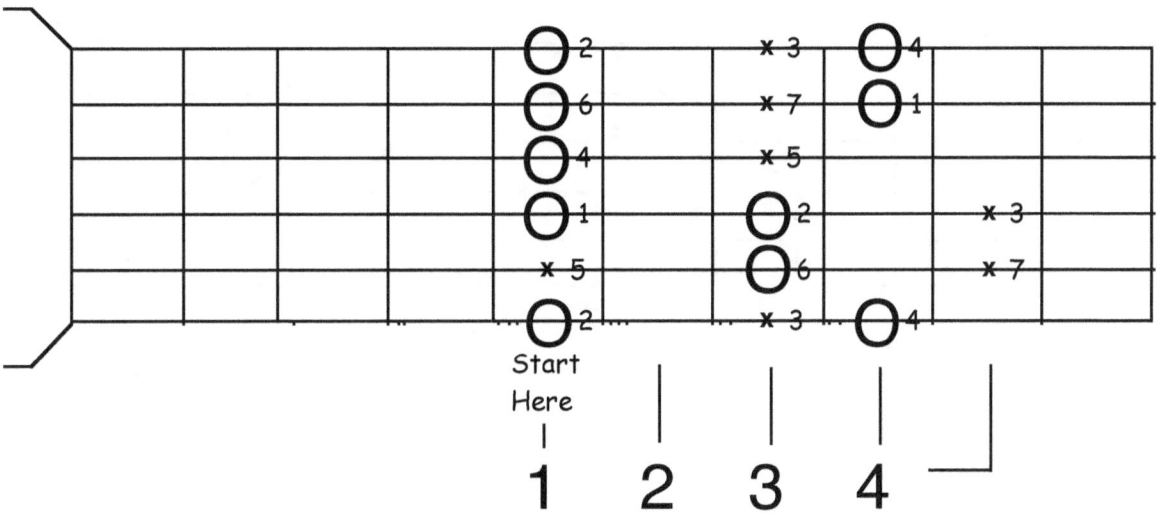

Pattern 3
This is labeled as "Pattern 3" because your 1st finger would start on the 3rd scale degree if the 3rd scale degree was in this arpeggio.

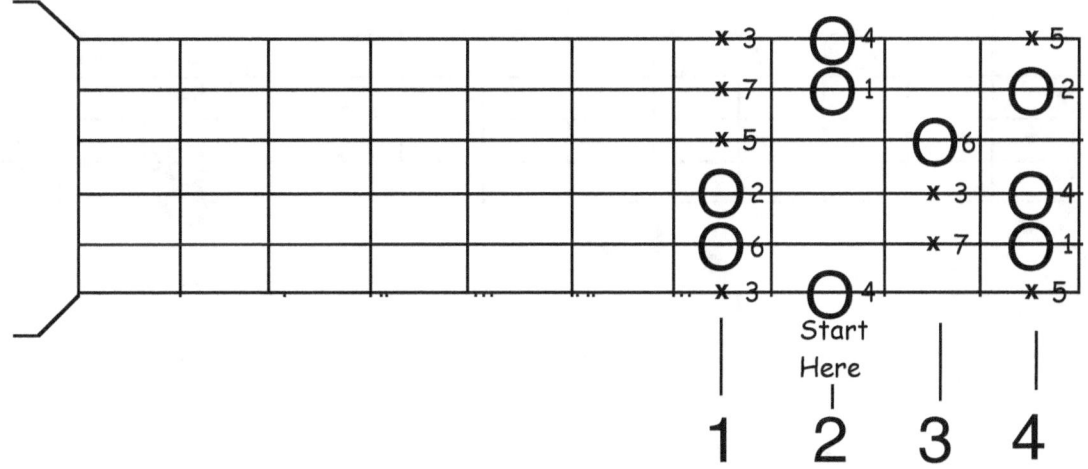

"2" Chord Arpeggio In "G" Major
A Minor 7 Arpeggio: 2, 4, 6, 1

Pattern 4

This is labeled as "Pattern 4" because your 1st finger starts on the 4th scale degree.

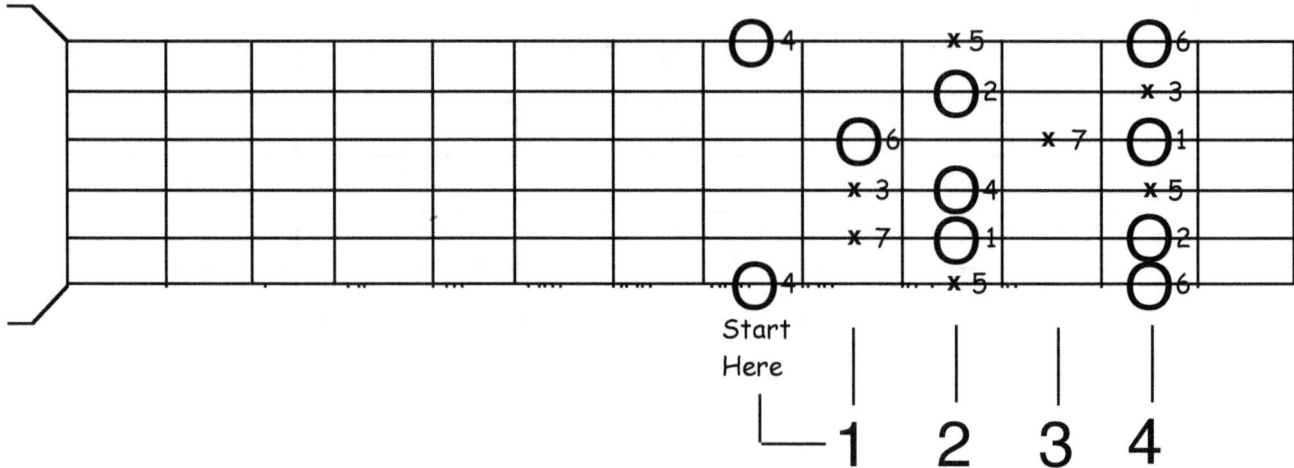

Pattern 5

This is labeled as "Pattern 5" because your 1st finger would start on the 5th scale degree if the 5th scale degree was in this arpeggio.

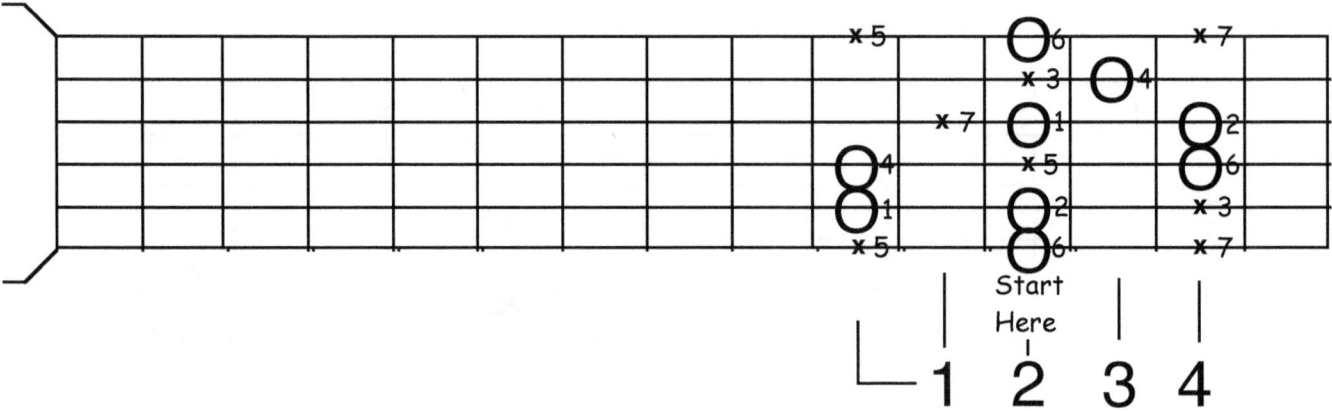

"2" Chord Arpeggio In "G" Major
A Minor 7 Arpeggio: 2, 4, 6, 1

Pattern 6

This is labeled as "Pattern 6" because your 1st finger starts on the 6th scale degree.

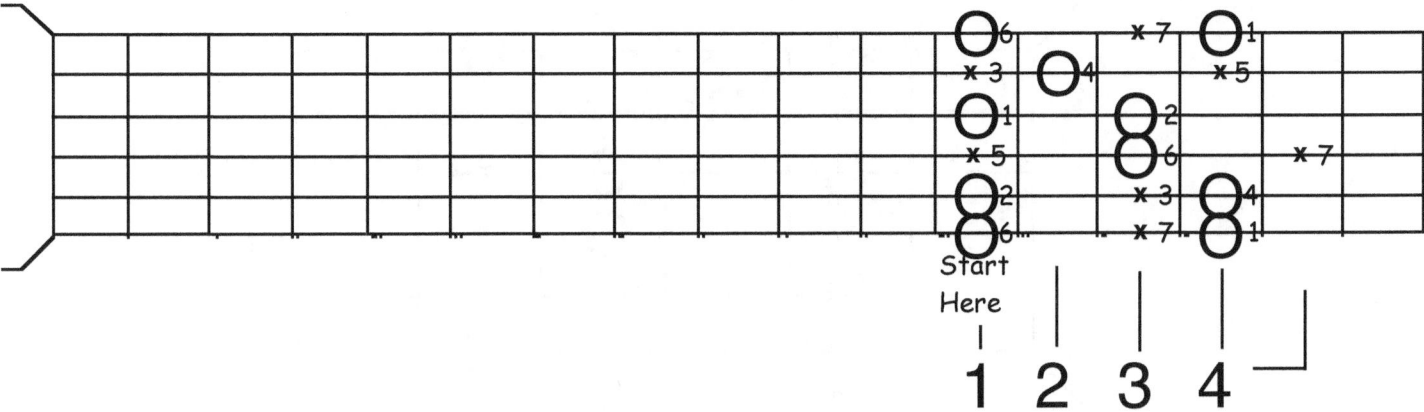

Again, if you just can't reach these notes on the guitar that you have right now, run this pattern on a lower spot on the neck. But if there is any way humanly possible, run it way up there on the neck.

Below is a diagram of the "2" chord arpeggios on the entire neck.

A Minor 7 Arpeggio
(2 CHORD ON THE ENTIRE NECK)

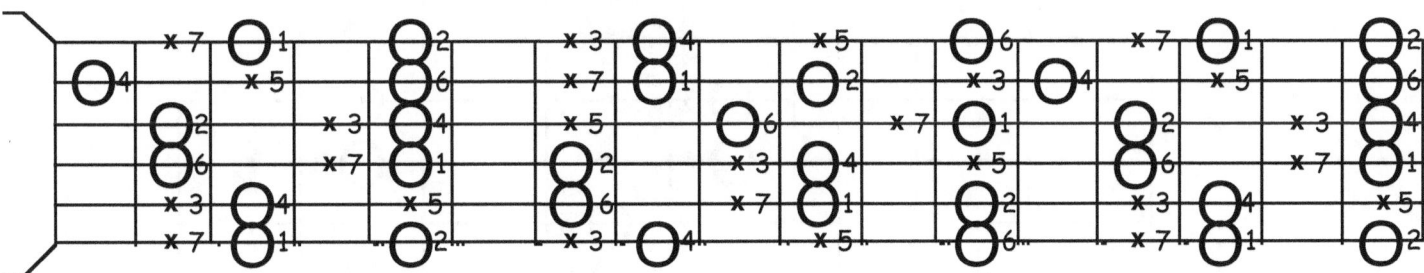

"3" Chord Arpeggio In "G" Major
B Minor 7 Arpeggio: 3, 5, 7, 2

Pattern 7
This is labeled as "Pattern 7" because your 1st finger starts on the 7th scale degree.

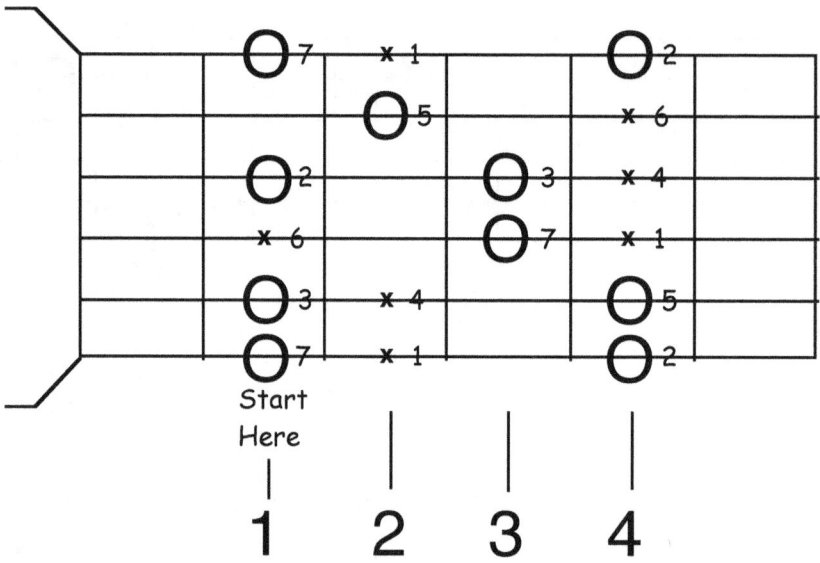

Pattern 1
This is labeled as "Pattern 1" because your 1st finger would start on the 1st scale degree if the 1st scale degree was in this arpeggio.

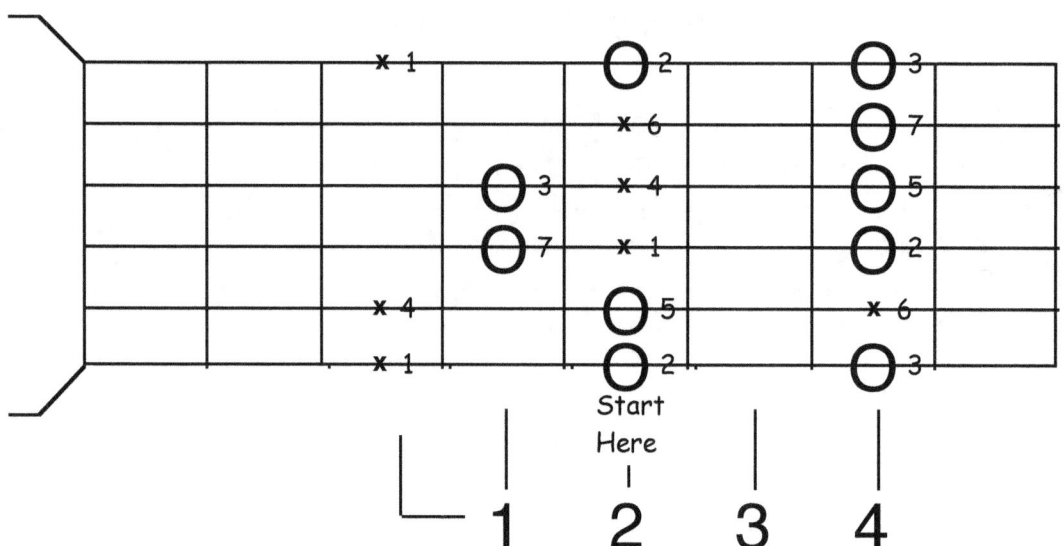

"3" Chord Arpeggio In "G" Major

B Minor 7 Arpeggio: 3, 5, 7, 2

Pattern 2

This is labeled as "Pattern 2" because your 1st finger starts on the 2nd scale degree.

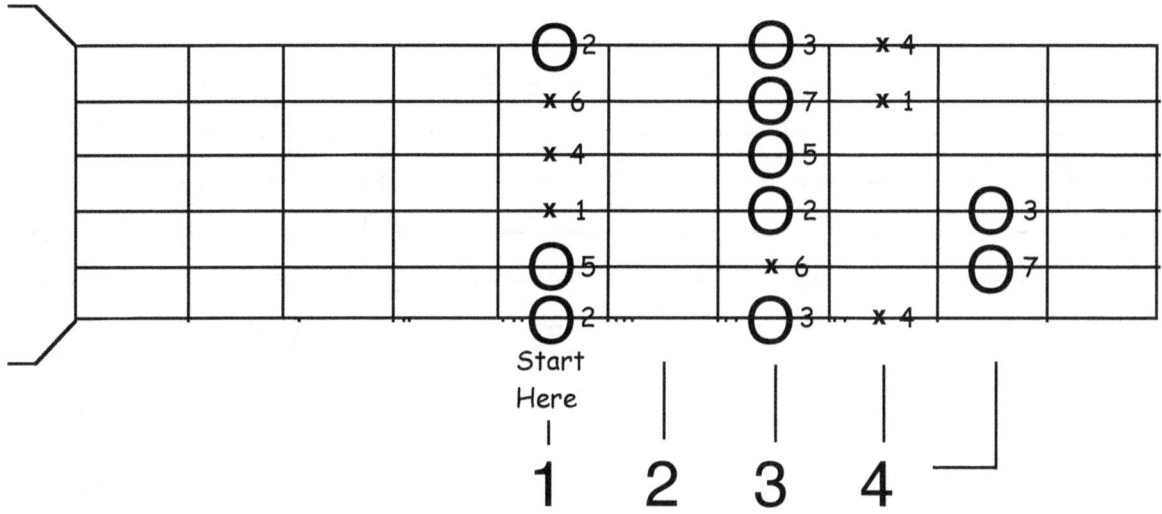

Pattern 3

This is labeled as "Pattern 3" because your 1st finger starts on the 3rd scale degree.

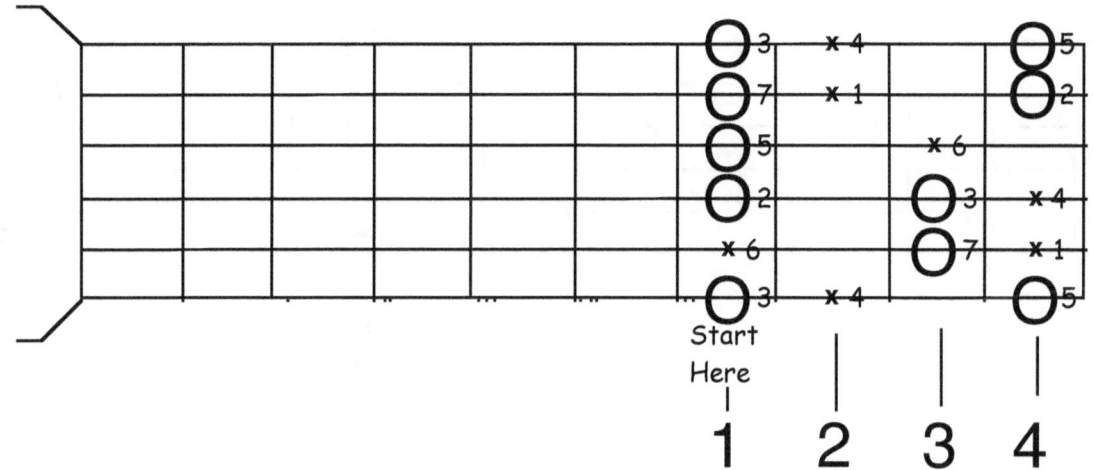

"3" Chord Arpeggio In "G" Major

B Minor 7 Arpeggio: 3, 5, 7, 2

Pattern 4

This is labeled as "Pattern 4" because your 1st finger would start on the 4th scale degree if the 4th scale degree was in this arpeggio.

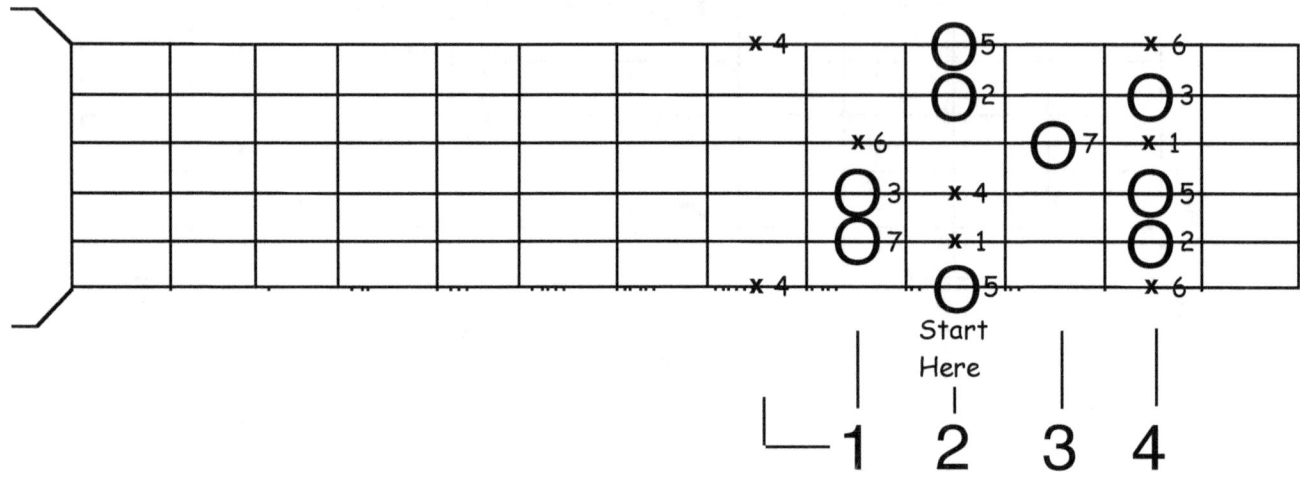

Pattern 5

This is labeled as "Pattern 5" because your 1st finger starts on the 5th scale degree.

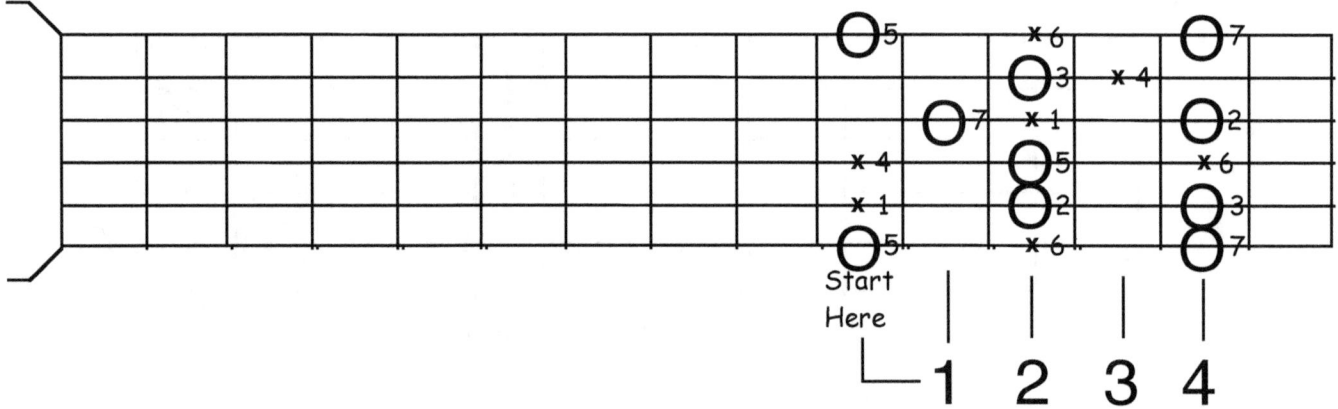

"3" Chord Arpeggio In "G" Major
B Minor 7 Arpeggio: 3, 5, 7, 2

Pattern 6

This is labeled as "Pattern 6" because your 1st finger would start on the 6th scale degree if the 6th scale degree was in this arpeggio.

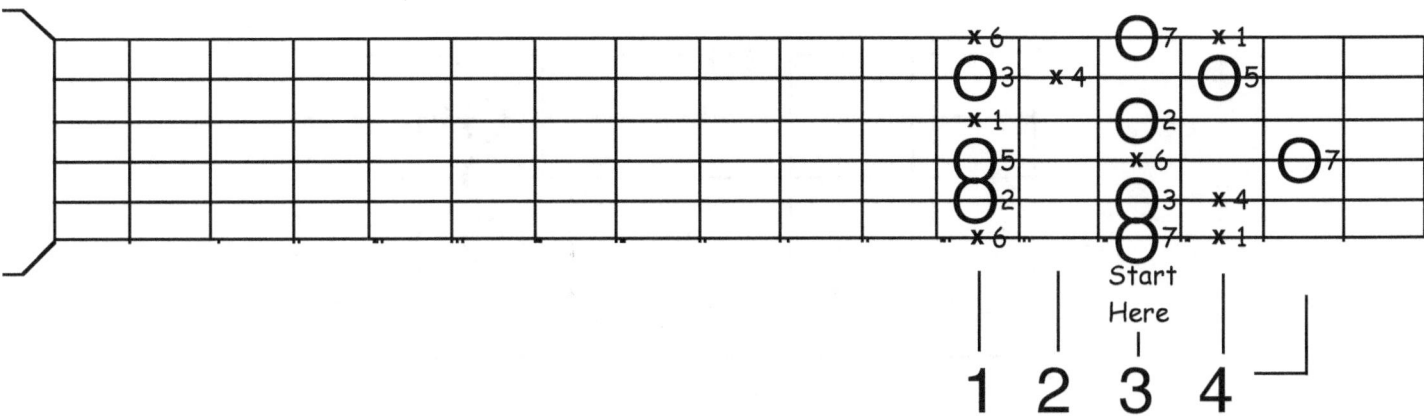

And again, if you just can't reach these notes on the guitar that you have right now, run this pattern on a lower spot on the neck. But if there is any way humanly possible, run it way up there on the neck.

Below is a diagram of the "3" chord arpeggios on the entire neck.

B Minor 7 Arpeggio
(3 CHORD ON THE ENTIRE NECK)

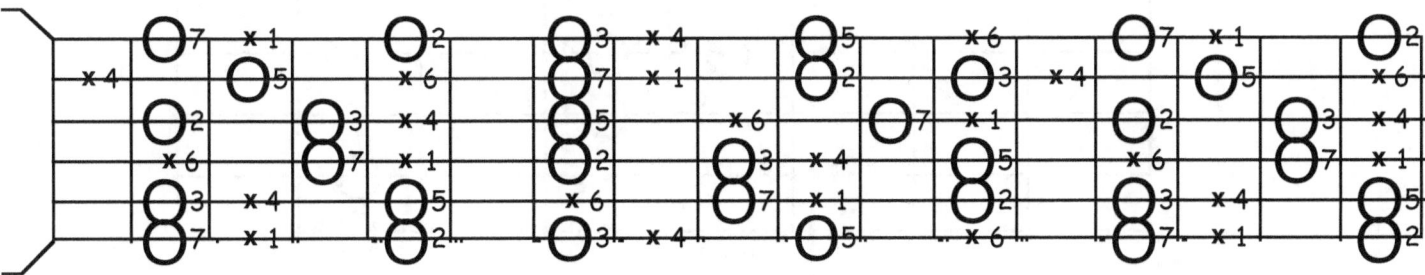

"4" Chord Arpeggio In "G" Major
C Major 7 Arpeggio: 4, 6, 1, 3

Pattern 7

This is labeled as "Pattern 7" because your 1st finger would start on the 7th scale degree if the 7th scale degree was in this arpeggio.

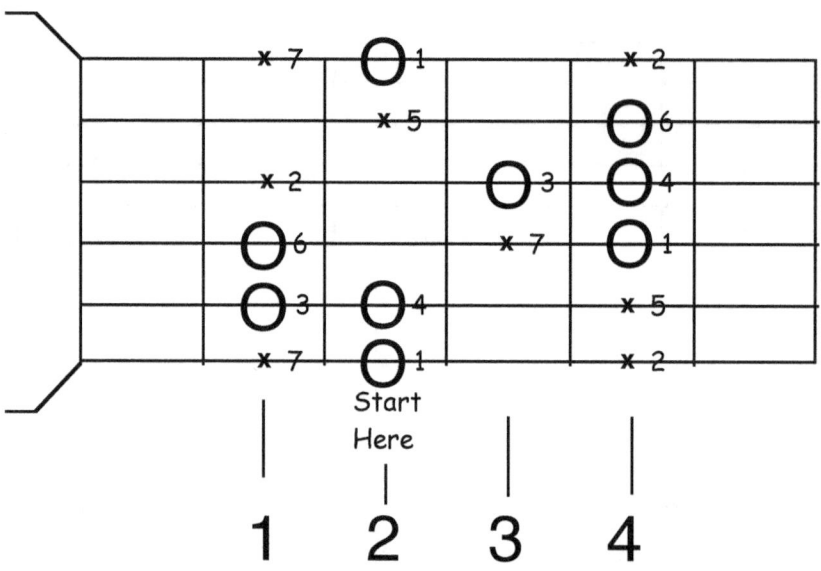

Pattern 1

This is labeled as "Pattern 1" because your 1st finger starts on the 1st scale degree.

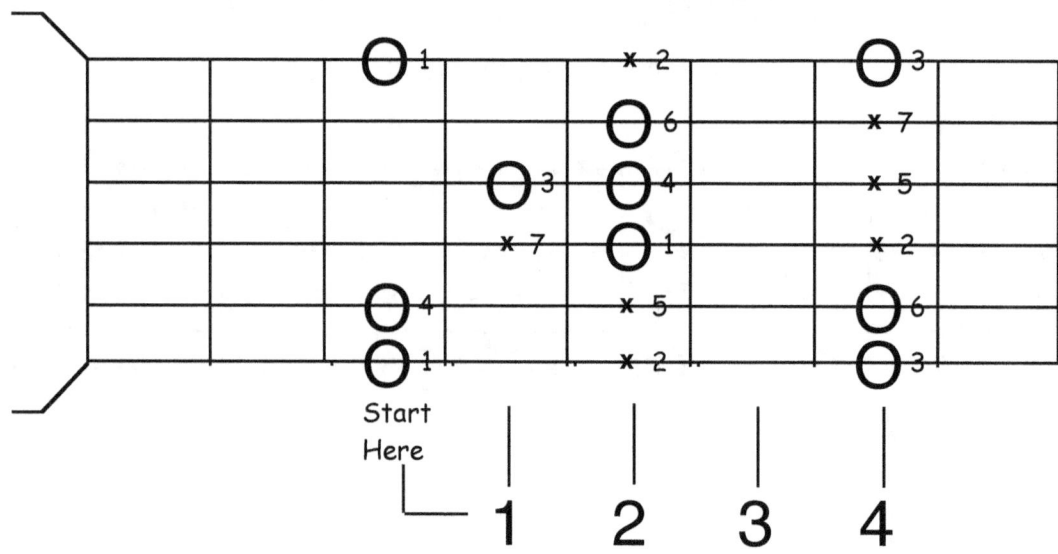

"4" Chord Arpeggio In "G" Major
C Major 7 Arpeggio: 4, 6, 1, 3

Pattern 2

This is labeled as "Pattern 2" because your 1st finger would start on the 2nd scale degree if the 2nd scale degree was in this arpeggio.

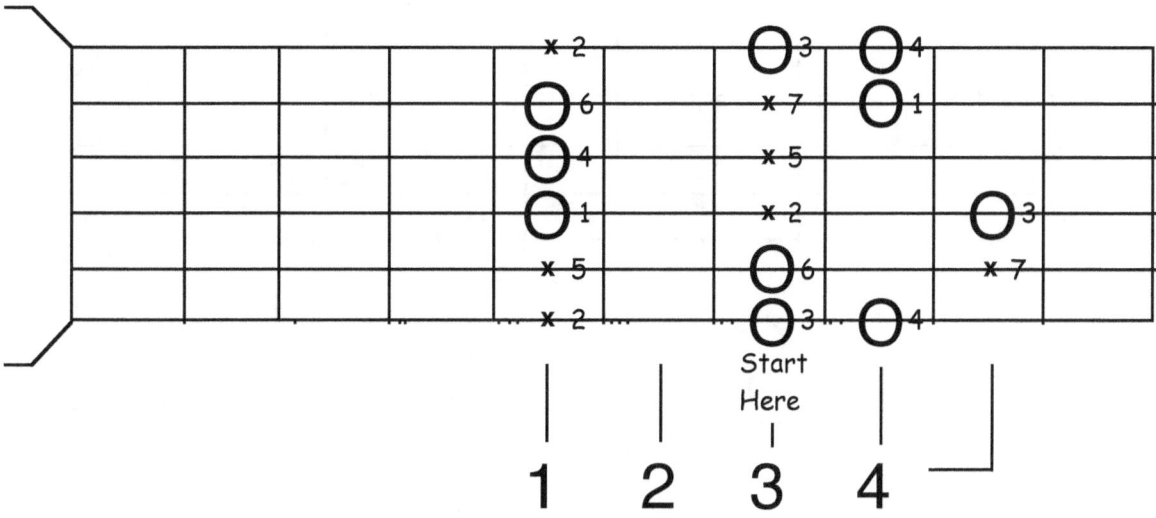

Pattern 3

This is labeled as "Pattern 3" because your 1st finger starts on the 3rd scale degree.

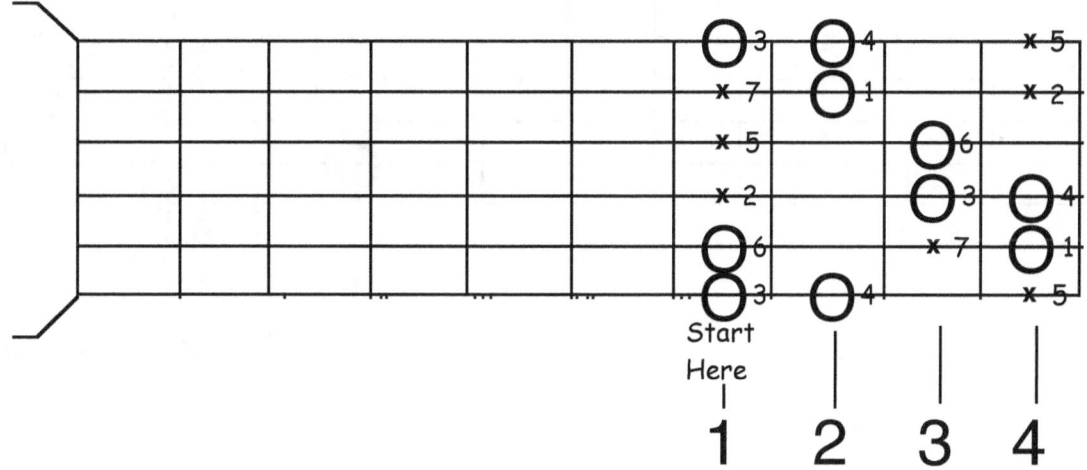

"4" Chord Arpeggio In "G" Major
C Major 7 Arpeggio: 4, 6, 1, 3

Pattern 4

This is labeled as "Pattern 4" because your 1st finger starts on the 4th scale degree.

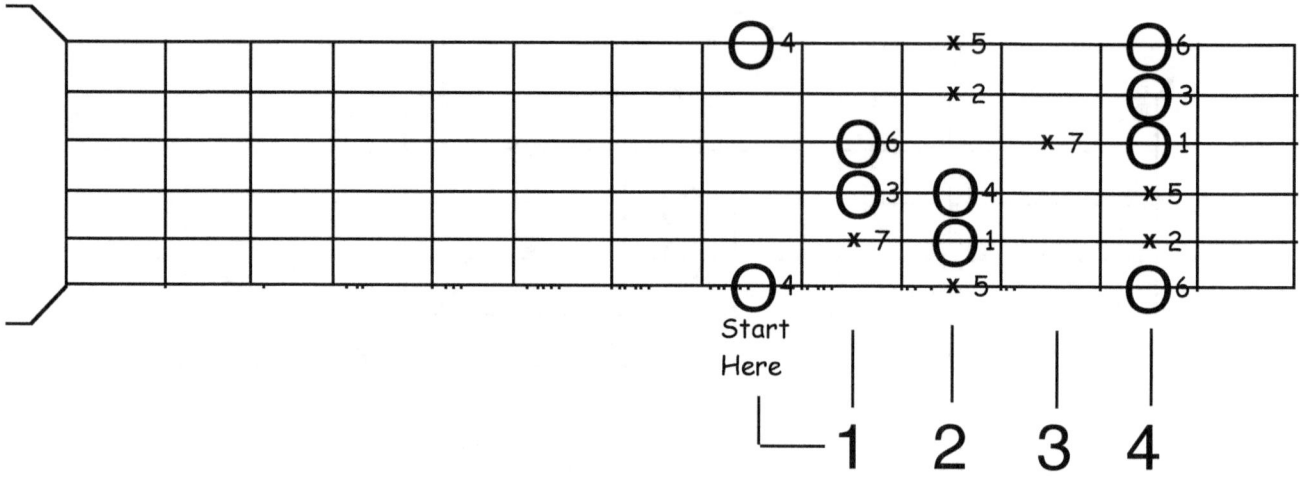

Pattern 5

This is labeled as "Pattern 5" because your 1st finger would start on the 5th scale degree if the 5th scale degree was in this arpeggio.

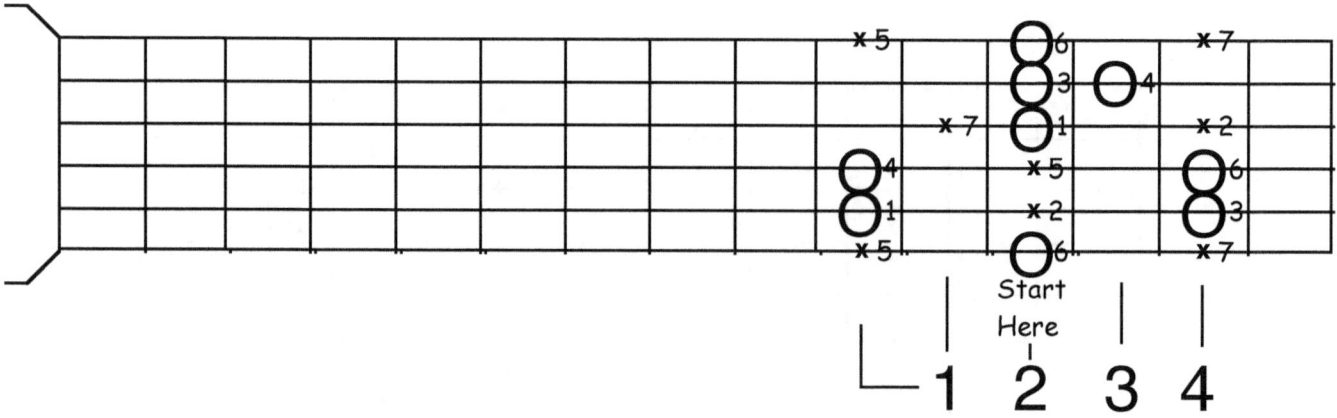

"4" Chord Arpeggio In "G" Major
C Major 7 Arpeggio: 4, 6, 1, 3

Pattern 6

This is labeled as "Pattern 6" because your 1st finger starts on the 6th scale degree.

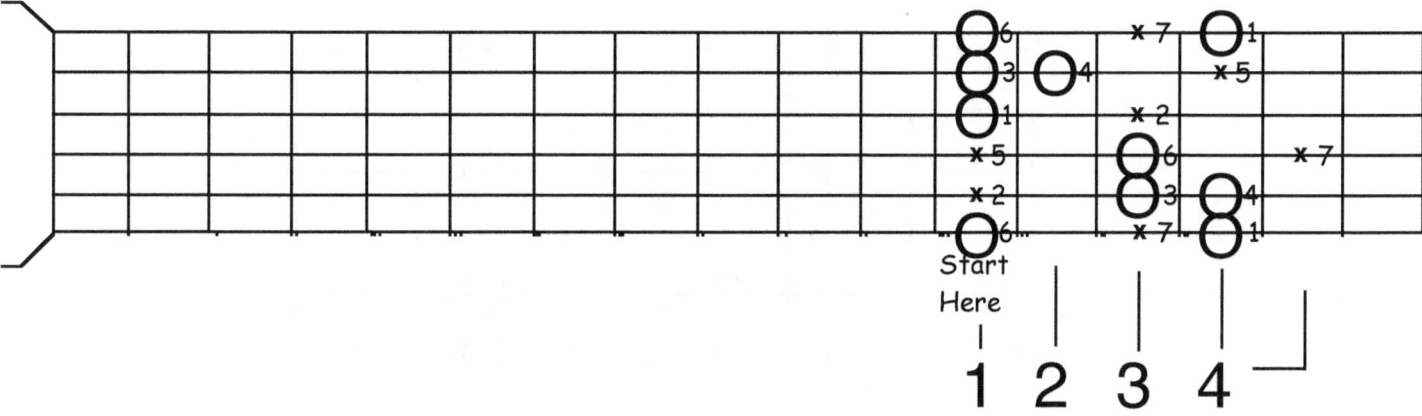

And, yet again, if you just can't reach these notes on the guitar that you have right now, run this pattern on a lower spot on the neck. But if there is any way humanly possible, run it way up there on the neck.

Below is a diagram of the "4" chord arpeggios on the entire neck.

C Major 7 Arpeggio
(4 CHORD ON THE ENTIRE NECK)

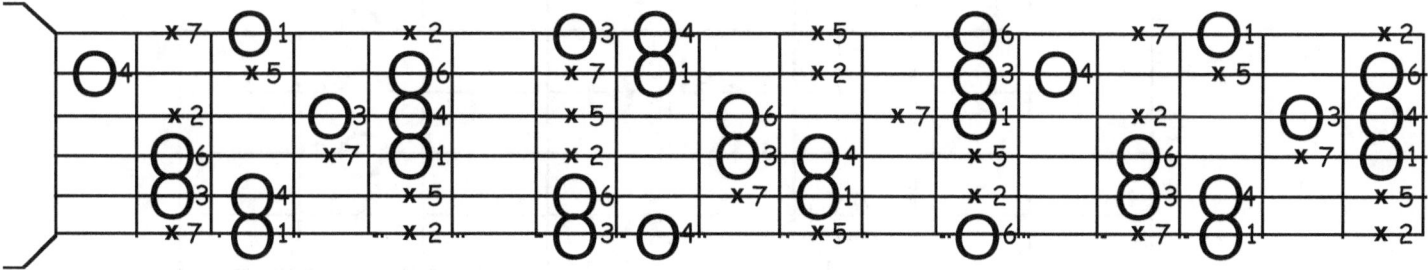

"5" Chord Arpeggio In "G" Major

D Dominant 7 Arpeggio: 5, 7, 2, 4

Pattern 7

This is labeled as "Pattern 7" because your 1st finger starts on the 7th scale degree.

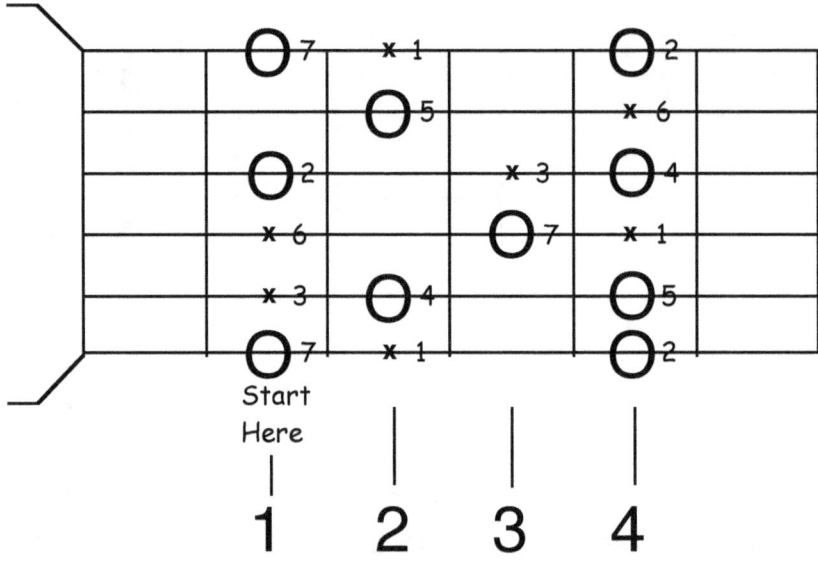

Pattern 1

This is labeled as "Pattern 1" because your 1st finger would start on the 1st scale degree if the 1st scale degree was in this arpeggio.

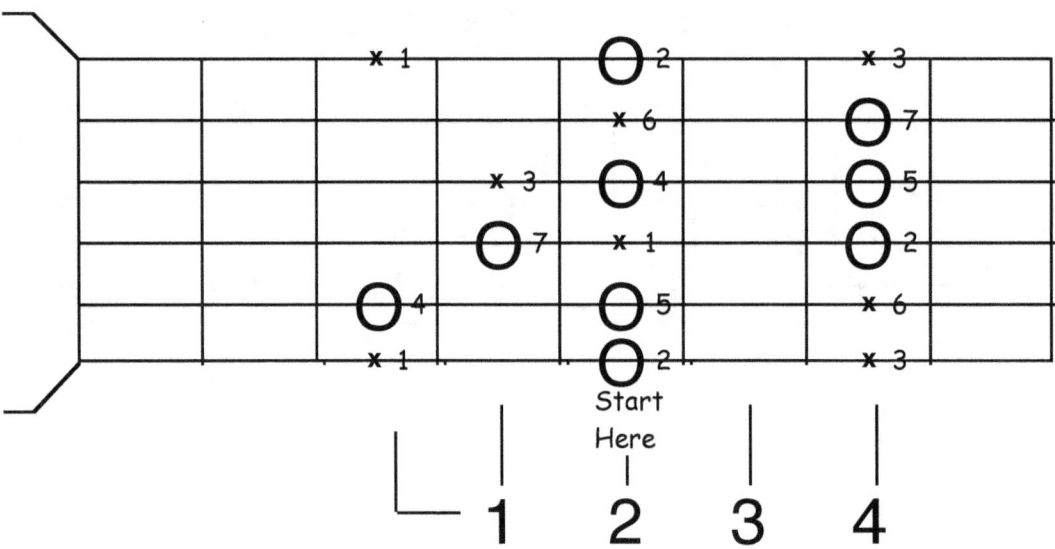

254

"5" Chord Arpeggio In "G" Major

D Dominant 7 Arpeggio: 5, 7, 2, 4

Pattern 2

This is labeled as "Pattern 2" because your 1st finger starts on the 2nd scale degree.

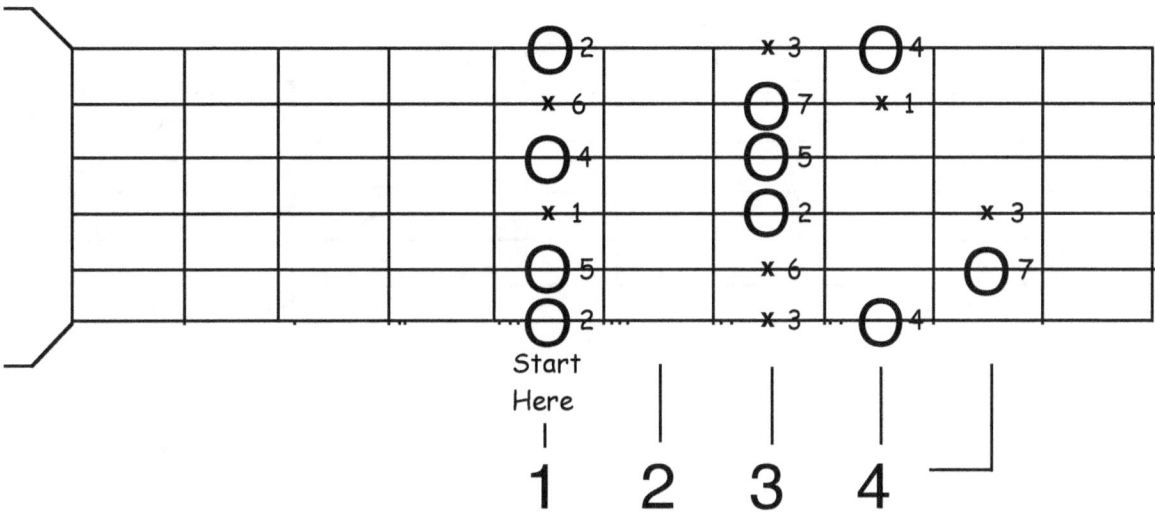

Pattern 3

This is labeled as "Pattern 3" because your 1st finger would start on the 3rd scale degree if the 3rd scale degree was in this arpeggio.

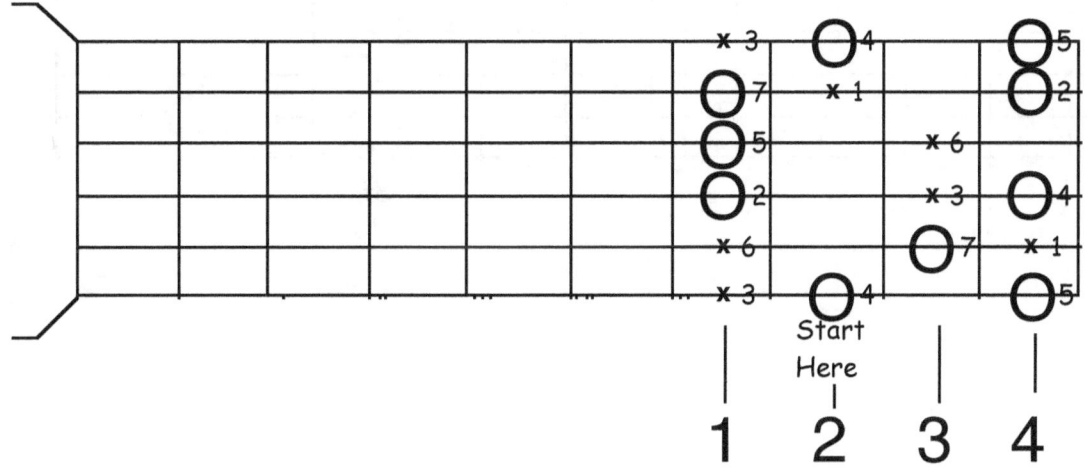

"5" Chord Arpeggio In "G" Major
D Dominant 7 Arpeggio: 5, 7, 2, 4

Pattern 4

This is labeled as "Pattern 4" because your 1st finger starts on the 4th scale degree.

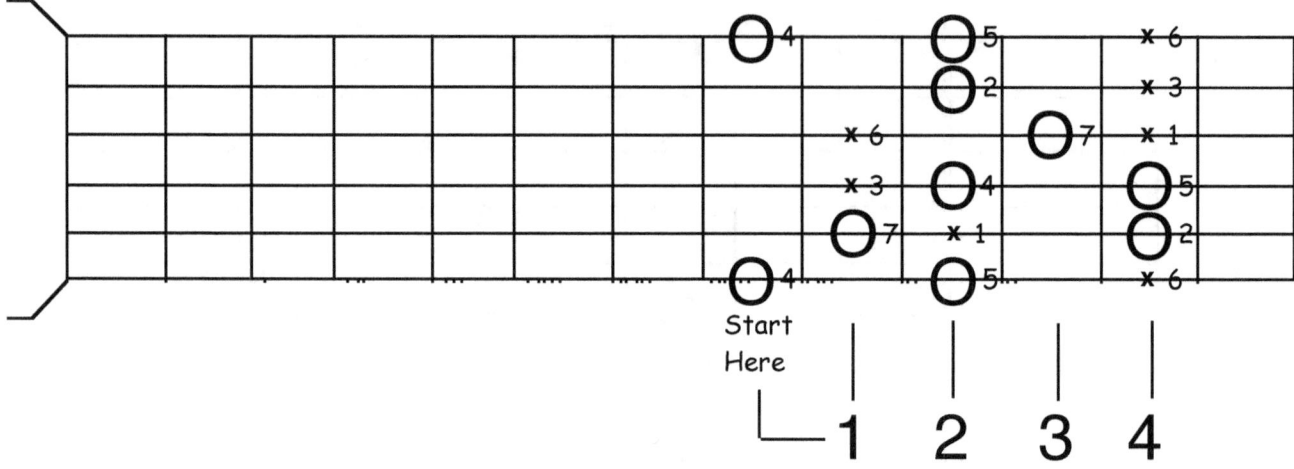

Pattern 5

This is labeled as "Pattern 5" because your 1st finger starts on the 5th scale degree.

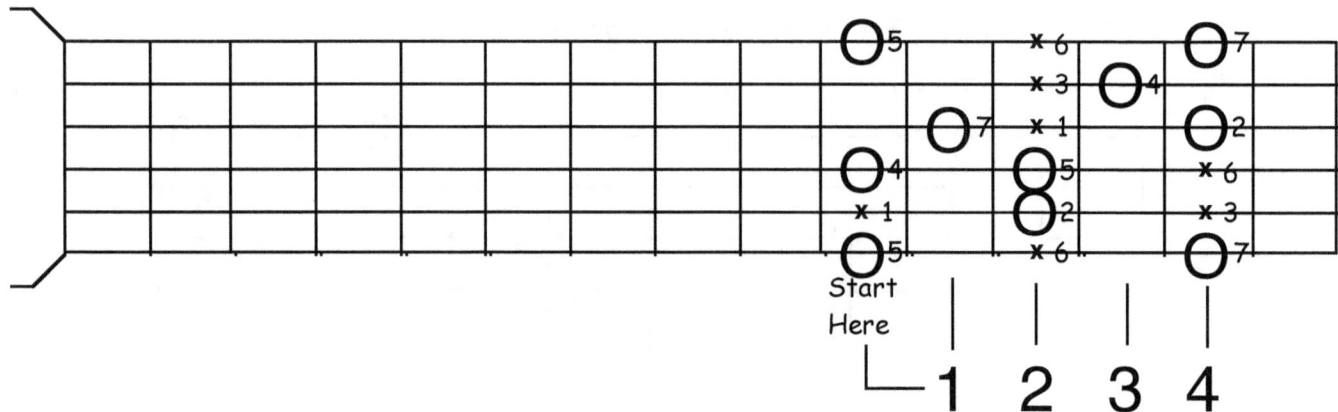

"5" Chord Arpeggio In "G" Major
D Dominant 7 Arpeggio: 5, 7, 2, 4

Pattern 6

This is labeled as "Pattern 6" because your 1st finger would start on the 6th scale degree if the 6th scale degree was in this arpeggio.

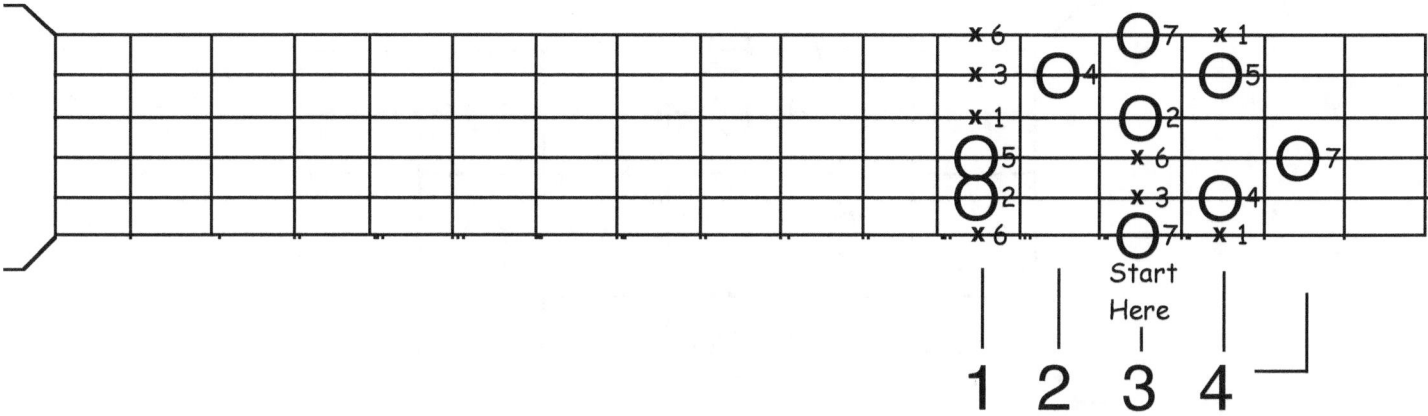

You guessed it, if you just can't reach these notes on the guitar that you have, run this pattern on a lower spot on the neck. But if there is any way humanly possible, run it way up there on the neck.

Below is a diagram of the "5" chord arpeggios on the entire neck.

D Dominant 7 Arpeggio
(5 CHORD ON THE ENTIRE NECK)

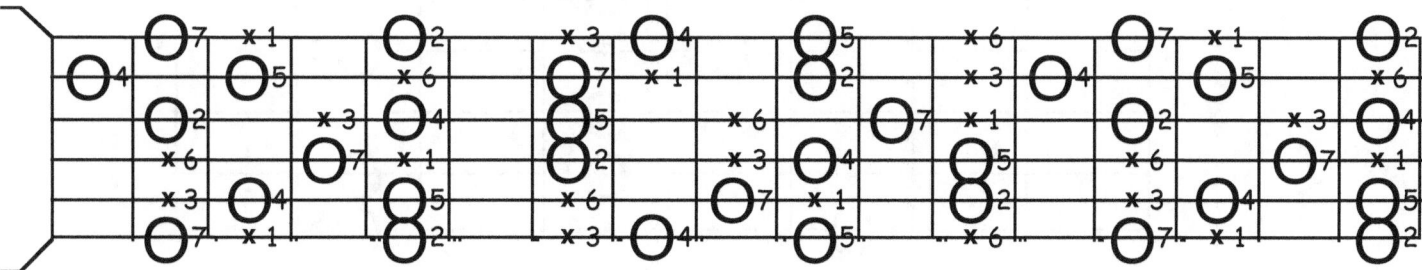

"6" Chord Arpeggio In "G" Major

E Minor 7 Arpeggio: 6, 1, 3, 5

Pattern 7

This is labeled as "Pattern 7" because your 1st finger would start on the 7th scale degree if the 7th scale degree was in this arpeggio.

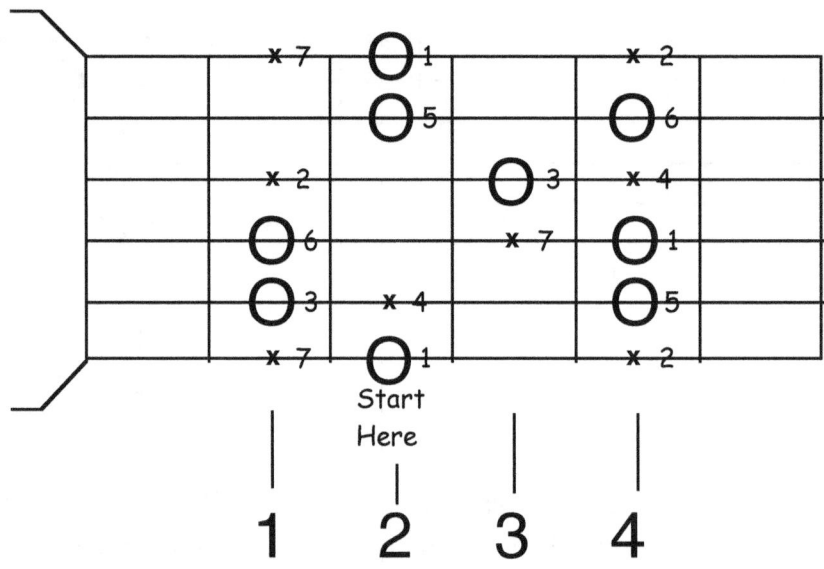

Pattern 1

This is labeled as "Pattern 1" because your 1st finger starts on the 1st scale degree.

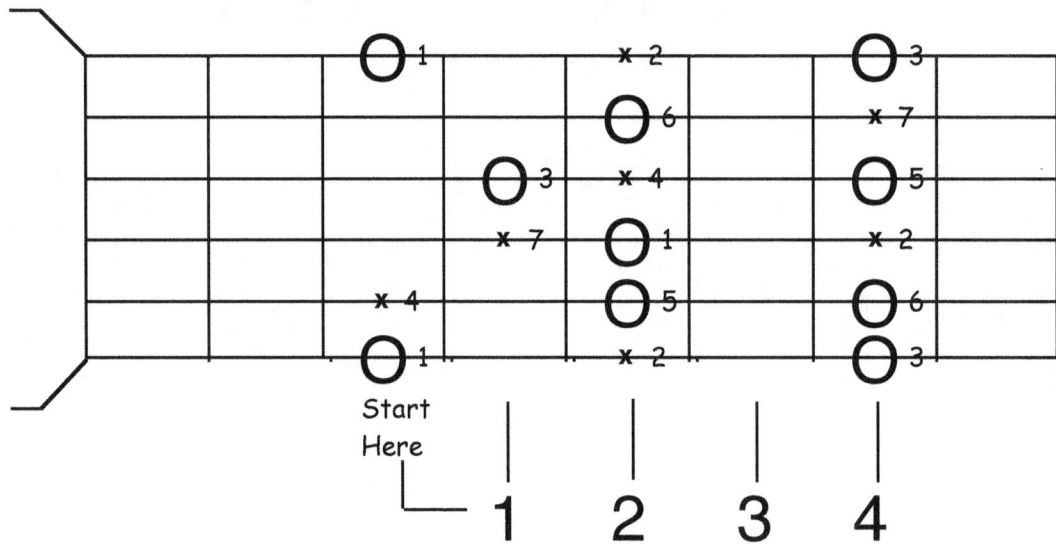

"6" Chord Arpeggio In "G" Major
E Minor 7 Arpeggio: 6, 1, 3, 5

Pattern 2

This is labeled as "Pattern 2" because your 1st finger would start on the 2nd scale degree if the 2nd scale degree was in this arpeggio.

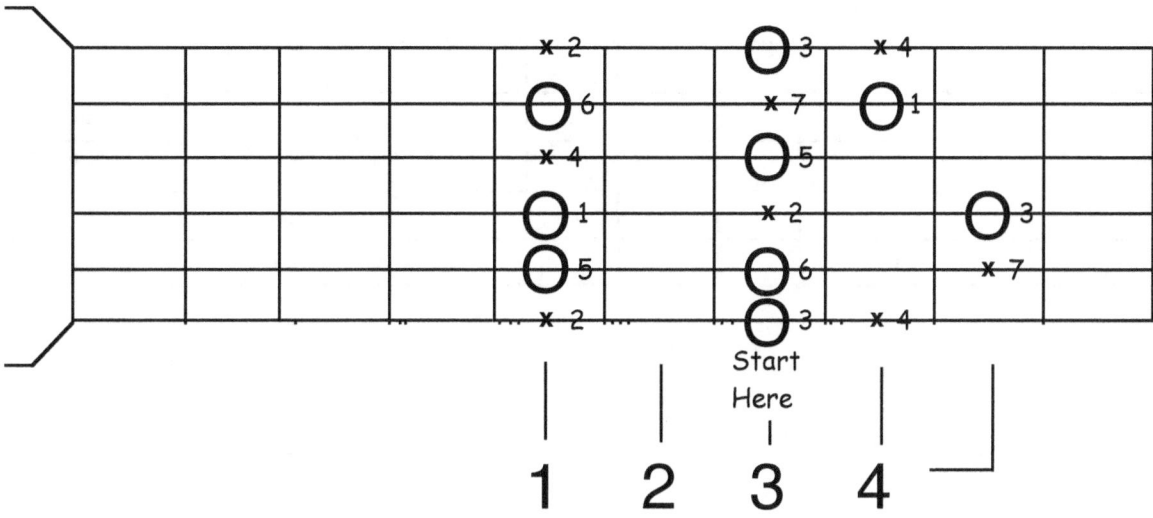

Pattern 3

This is labeled as "Pattern 3" because your 1st finger starts on the 3rd scale degree.

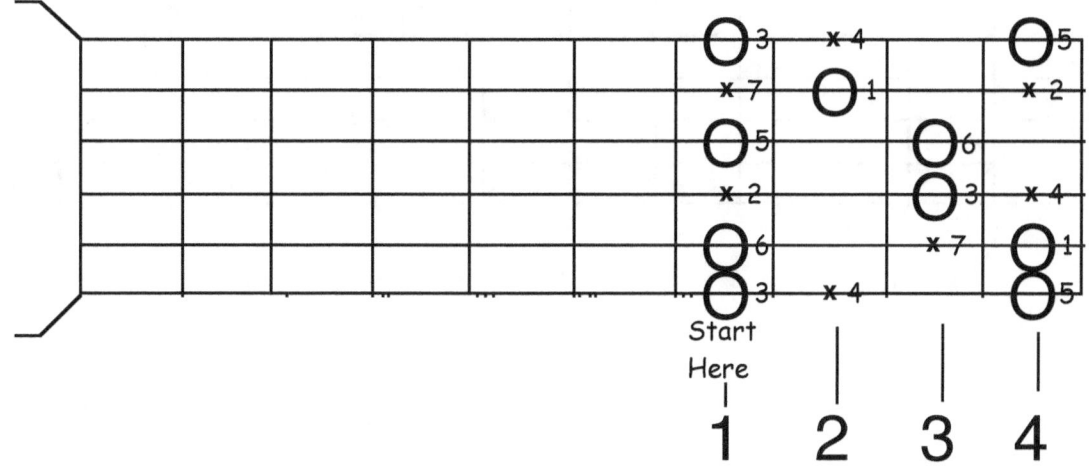

"6" Chord Arpeggio In "G" Major
E Minor 7 Arpeggio: 6, 1, 3, 5

Pattern 4

This is labeled as "Pattern 4" because your 1st finger would start on the 4th scale degree if the 4th scale degree was in this arpeggio.

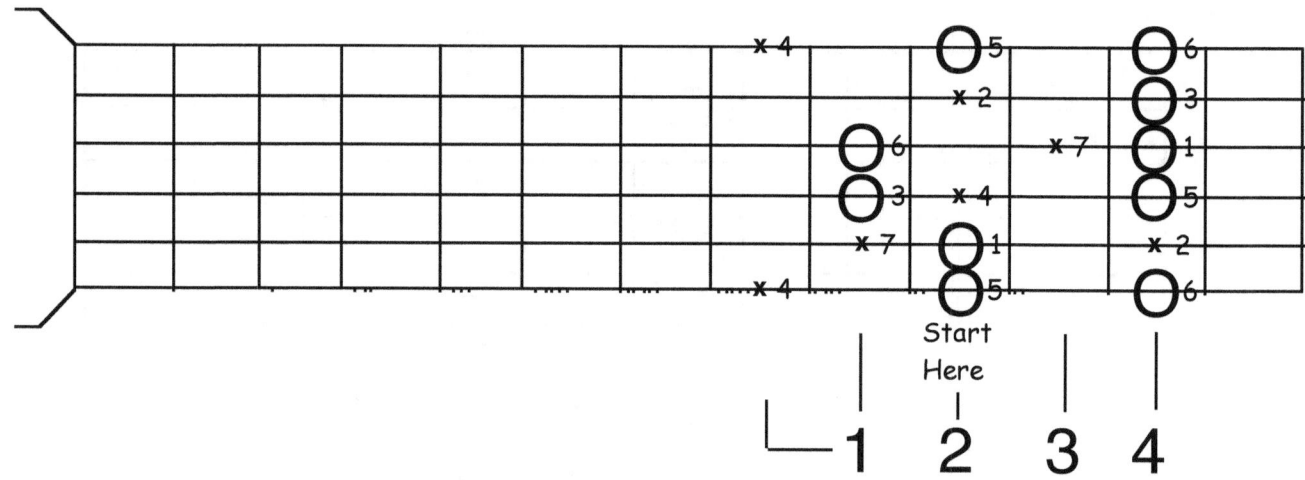

Pattern 5

This is labeled as "Pattern 5" because your 1st finger starts on the 5th scale degree.

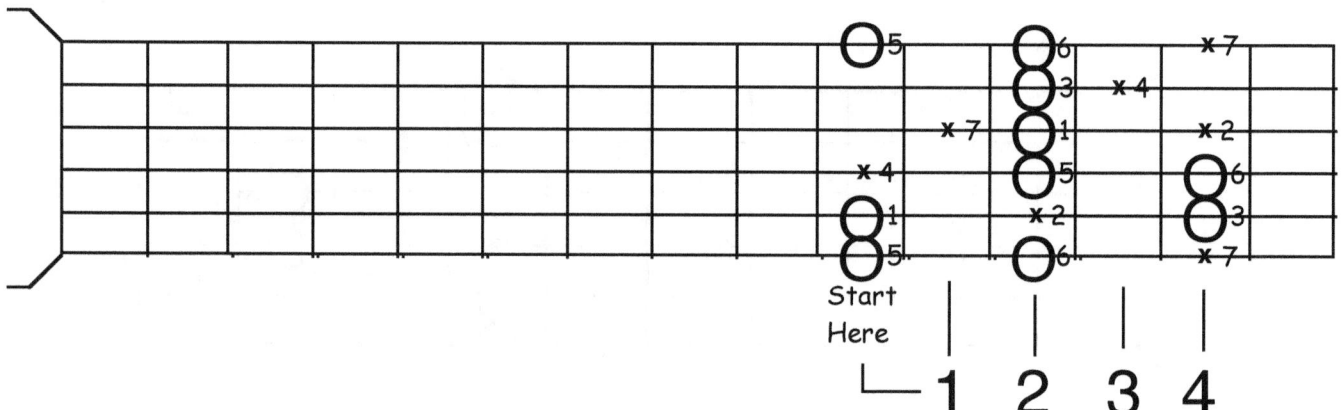

"6" Chord Arpeggio In "G" Major
E Minor 7 Arpeggio: 6, 1, 3, 5

Pattern 6

This is labeled as "Pattern 6" because your 1st finger starts on the 6th scale degree.

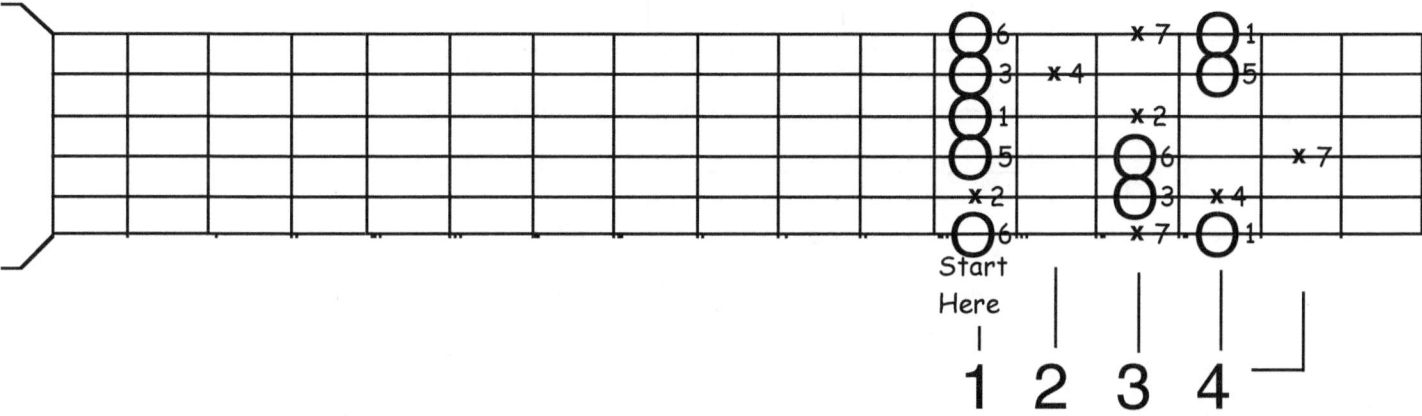

If you just can't reach these notes on your guitar, you know what to do ... (run this pattern on a lower spot on the neck). But if there is any way humanly possible, run it way up there on the neck.

Below is a diagram of the "6" chord arpeggios on the entire neck.

E Minor 7 Arpeggio
(6 CHORD ON THE ENTIRE NECK)

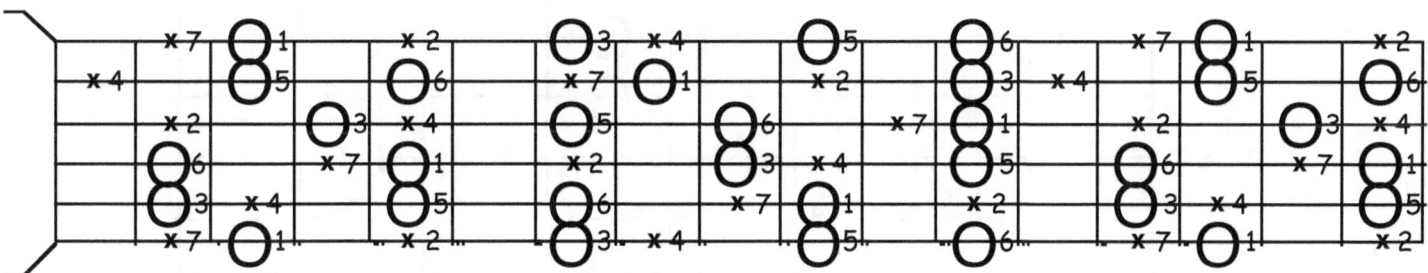

"7" Chord Arpeggio In "G" Major

F# Minor 7b5 Arpeggio: 7, 2, 4, 6

Pattern 7

This is labeled as "Pattern 7" because your 1st finger starts on the 7th scale degree.

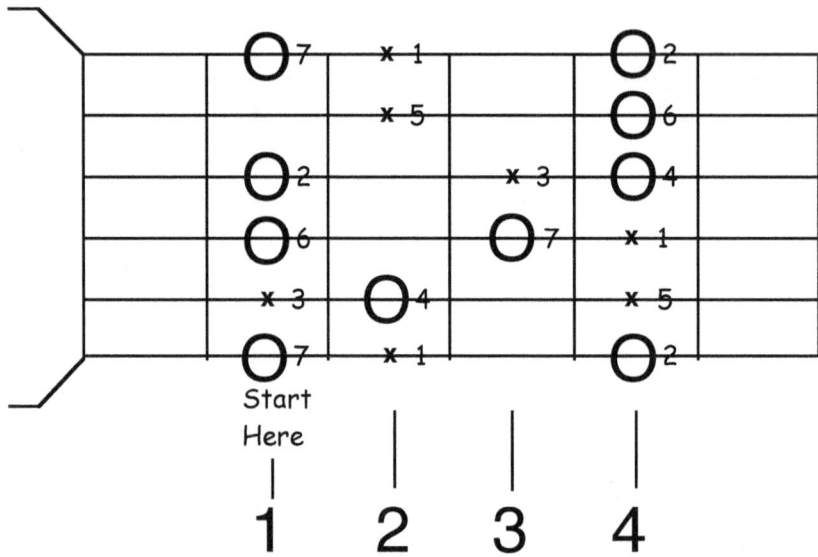

Pattern 1

This is labeled as "Pattern 1" because your 1st finger would start on the 1st scale degree if the 1st scale degree was in this arpeggio.

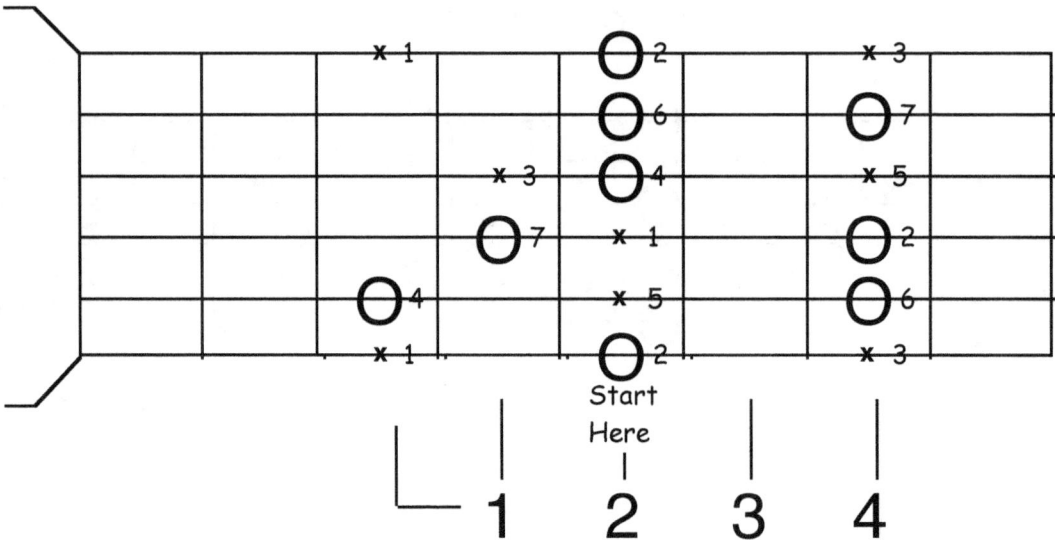

"7" Chord Arpeggio In "G" Major
F# Minor 7b5 Arpeggio: 7, 2, 4, 6

Pattern 2
This is labeled as "Pattern 2" because your 1st finger starts on the 2nd scale degree.

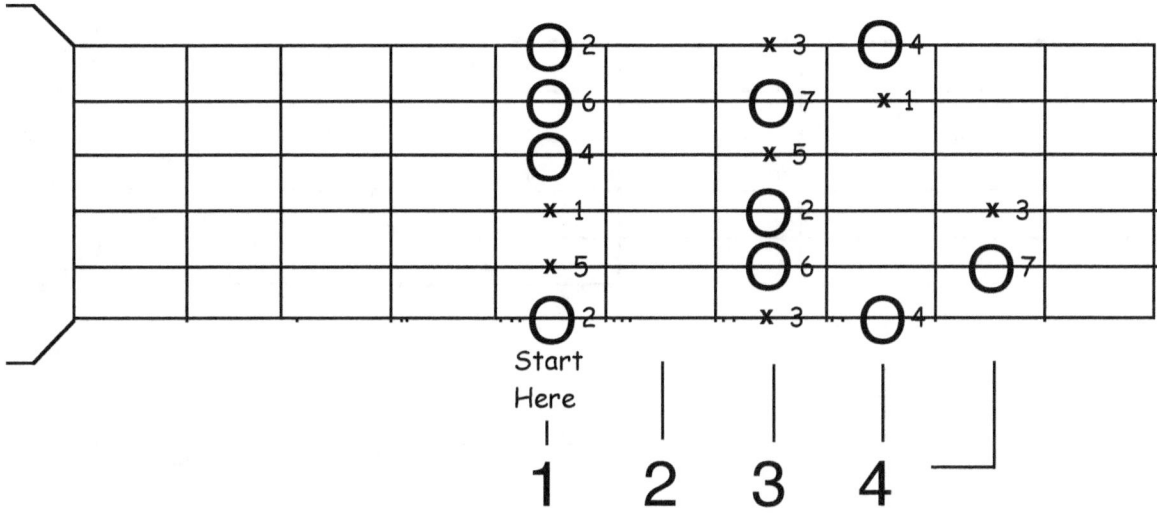

Pattern 3
This is labeled as "Pattern 3" because your 1st finger would start on the 3rd scale degree if the 3rd scale degree was in this arpeggio.

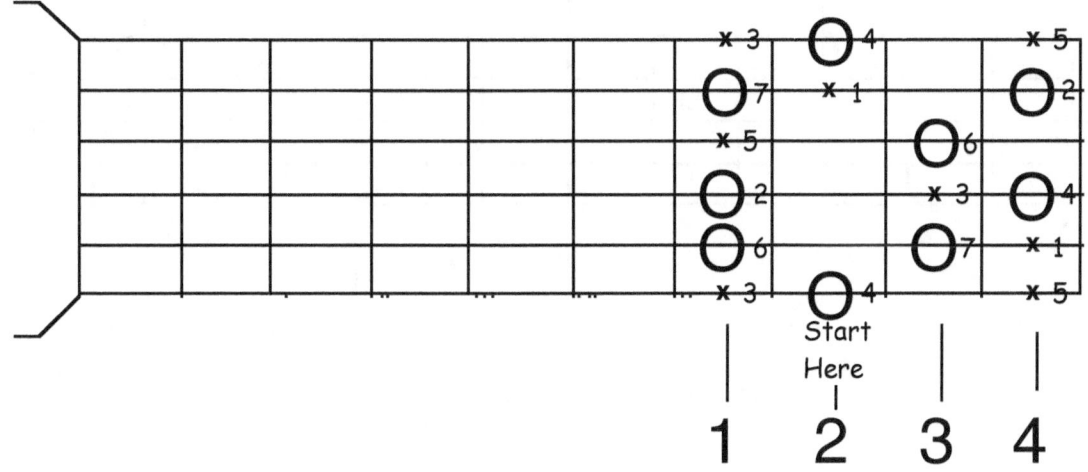

"7" Chord Arpeggio In "G" Major
F# Minor 7b5 Arpeggio: 7, 2, 4, 6

Pattern 4
This is labeled as "Pattern 4" because your 1st finger starts on the 4th scale degree.

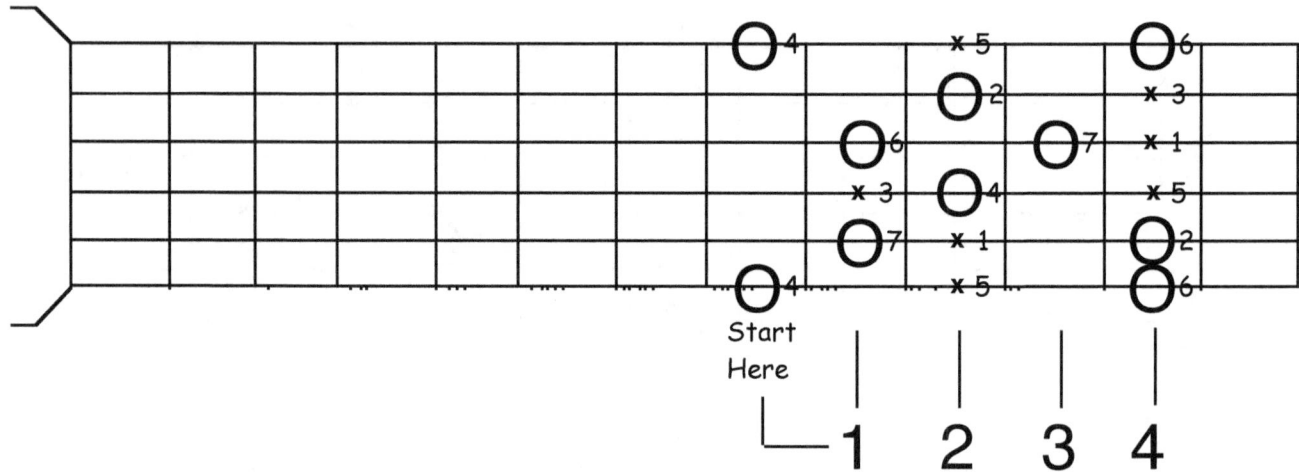

Pattern 5
This is labeled as "Pattern 5" because your 1st finger would start on the 5th scale degree if the 5th scale degree was in this arpeggio.

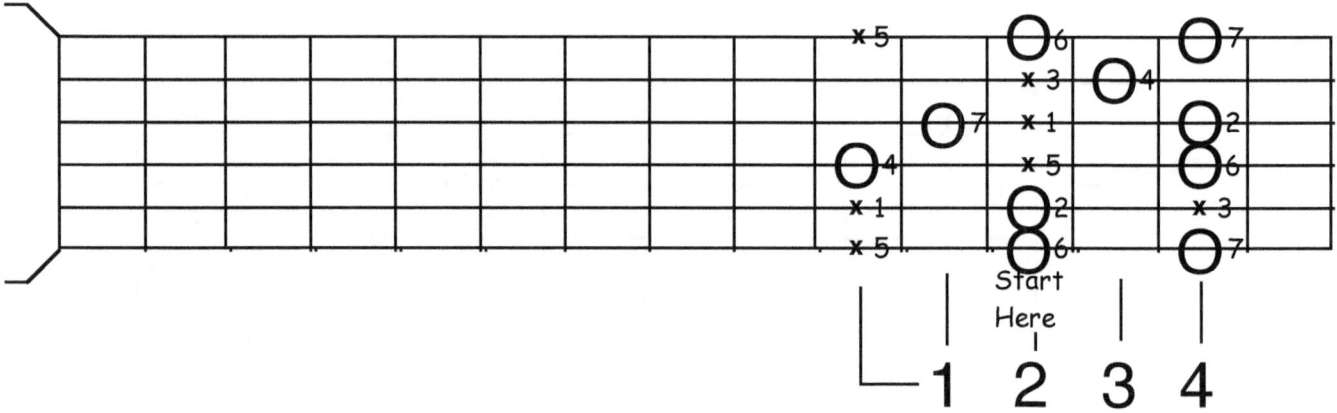

"7" Chord Arpeggio In "G" Major

F# Minor 7b5 Arpeggio: 7, 2, 4, 6

Pattern 6

This is labeled as "Pattern 6" because your 1st finger starts on the 6th scale degree.

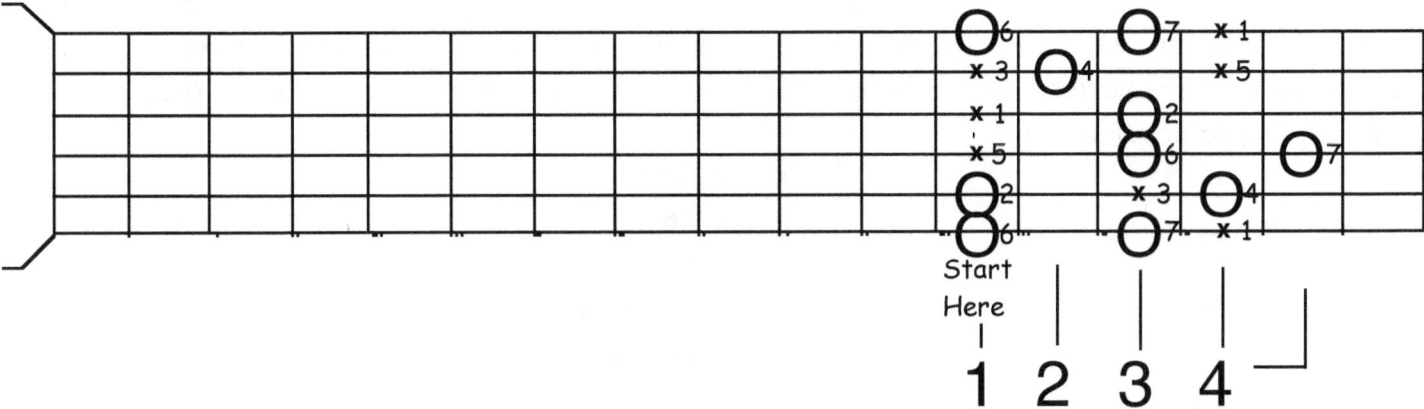

If you just can't reach these notes on your guitar ... run this pattern on a lower spot on the neck. But try to run it way up there on the neck if you can.

Below is a diagram of the "7" chord arpeggios on the entire neck.

F# Minor 7b5 Arpeggio
(7 CHORD ON THE ENTIRE NECK)

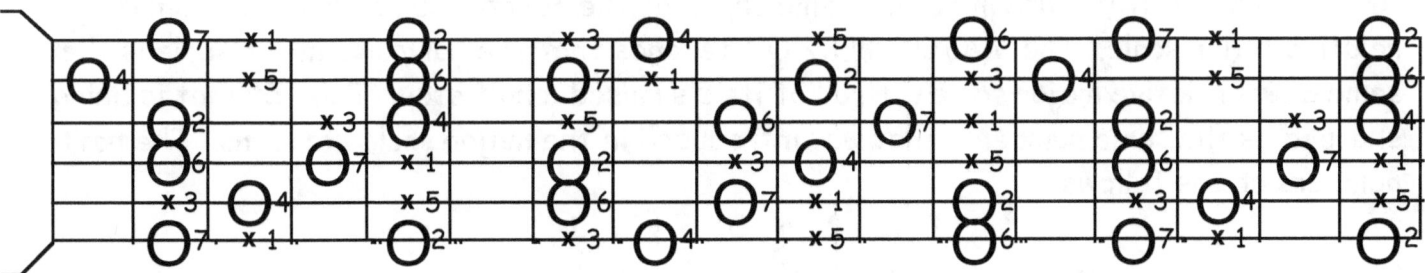

ALTERED SEVENTH CHORD ARPEGGIOS

As mentioned in the "Altered Seventh Chords" section of this book, there are many ways to "alter" seventh chords. The most common ways to alter seventh chords can be reduced to seven basic alterations. These seven basic alterations for seventh chords are going to be examined in this section about altered arpeggios. The seven basic altered arpeggios that we're going to cover are:

>Major 7#11
>Major 7#5
>Minor Major 7
>Dominant 7#11
>Dominant 7#5
>Dominant 7#9
>Dominant 7b9

Most of these arpeggios are drawn on diagrams that are labeled with "pattern numbers". All of the pattern numbers come from the MAJOR METHOD numbering system. If your first finger starts on the first scale degree of the major scale, you are in pattern 1. If your first finger starts on the second scale degree of the major scale, you are in pattern 2. So, the pattern number is determined by which scale degree your first finger starts on in that scale pattern (even if your first finger isn't used when playing a particular arpeggio within that pattern).

AND remember, if you are in harmonic minor, all of the pattern numbers come from its relative major scale. The MAJOR METHOD teaches that the harmonic minor scale is the same as its relative major scale with all of its 5's raised a half step. This "5" that is being sharped, is the same number 5 that was introduced in the major scale patterns. The pattern numbers are as follows:

```
                  1  2  3  4  5  6  7   1
        G major:  G  A  B  C  D  E  F#  G

                         6   7  1  2  3  4  5  6
        E natural minor: E   F# G  A  B  C  D  E

                         6   7  1  2  3  4  #5  6
        E harmonic minor: E  F# G  A  B  C  D#  E
```

The MAJOR METHOD teaches the melodic minor scale as a major scale with a b3. This "3" that is being flatted, is the same 3 that was introduced in the major scale patterns. Remember that the pattern number is determined by which scale degree your first finger starts on in that scale pattern (even if your first finger isn't used when playing a particular arpeggio within that pattern). The pattern numbers are as follows:

	1	2	3	4	5	6	7	1
E major:	E	F#	G#	A	B	C#	D#	E

	1	2	b3	4	5	6	7	1
E melodic minor:	E	F#	G	A	B	C#	D#	E

The only two scales that are not related back to the major scale in the MAJOR METHOD are the whole tone and the diminished scales. Neither of these scales will be used when introducing the altered arpeggios.

The dominant 7b9 arpeggios are the same as the diminished 7 arpeggios. These arpeggios were introduced in the MAJOR METHOD Volume 1 within the diminished scale. To provide a different parent scale for these arpeggios, the dominant 7b9 arpeggios are presented here within the harmonic minor scale.

The dominant 7#9 arpeggios appear naturally within the diminished scale. However, in order to more clearly show how the #9 note relates to the regular dominant 7 arpeggios, I have taken the liberty to present them within the regular major scale patterns. The #9 will appear as an extra note added to the regular dominant 7 arpeggios, so the root of the chord will not be eliminated in order to create the #9. This extra #9 note is drawn as a circle with a star in its middle. The underlying major scale with this extra note is not a common scale. It is only used here to clearly show the shapes of the dominant 7#9 arpeggios.

For those guitarists who learned basic music theory in a more traditional fashion, you can ignore the numbers presented in these altered seventh arpeggio diagrams and concentrate on the shapes and patterns. All of the patterns of the underlying harmonic minor, melodic minor, and major scales are EXACTLY the same as the traditionally learned patterns.

When dividing the neck up into individual patterns, some of these arpeggio shapes become a bit awkward. Because of this, I have not included any left hand fingering numbers underneath these diagrams. There are many ways to finger these arpeggios AND once you start tying them together on the neck, you'll come up with even more ways to finger them. Some of these other ways may be a lot easier on your left hand.

Here are the "Altered Seventh Chord Arpeggios"...

MAJOR 7#11 ARPEGGIO

The major 7#11 (major 7b5) arpeggio needs to include the note that exists between the 4th and the 5th of the basic major 7 arpeggio. The closest chord tone to the #11 is the 5th of the chord. The easiest way to create the #11 (or b5) sound is to lower the 5th of the chord a half step (one fret). In the major scale, both the "1" chord arpeggio and the "4" chord arpeggio are major 7 arpeggios. When you play the "4" chord arpeggio (spelled: 4, 6, 1, 3), the 5th of the arpeggio is the 1 of the scale. You can lower it a half step (to the 7), without changing the scale. This gives you an arpeggio that has a root, a 3rd, a #11th (or b5th), and a 7th: (4 = root, 6 = 3rd, 7 = #11th, 3 = 7th).

Major 7#11 Arpeggio In "G" Major
C Major 7#11 Arpeggio: 4, 6, 7, 3

Pattern 7

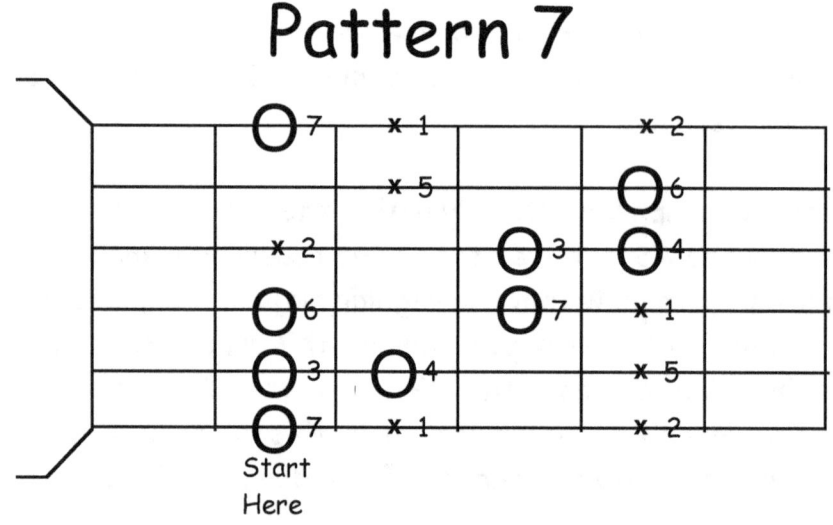

Pattern 1

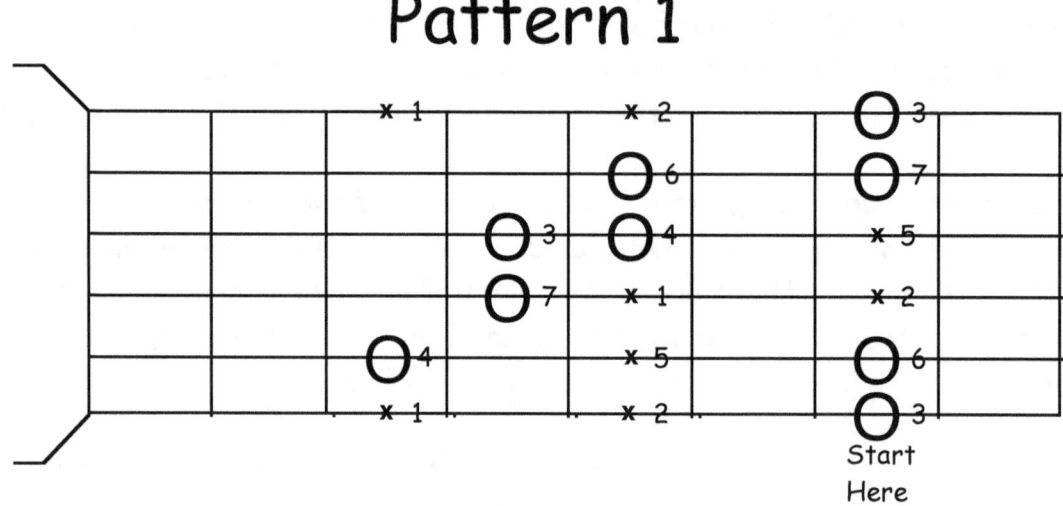

268

Major 7#11 Arpeggio In "G" Major
C Major 7#11 Arpeggio: 4, 6, 7, 3

Pattern 2

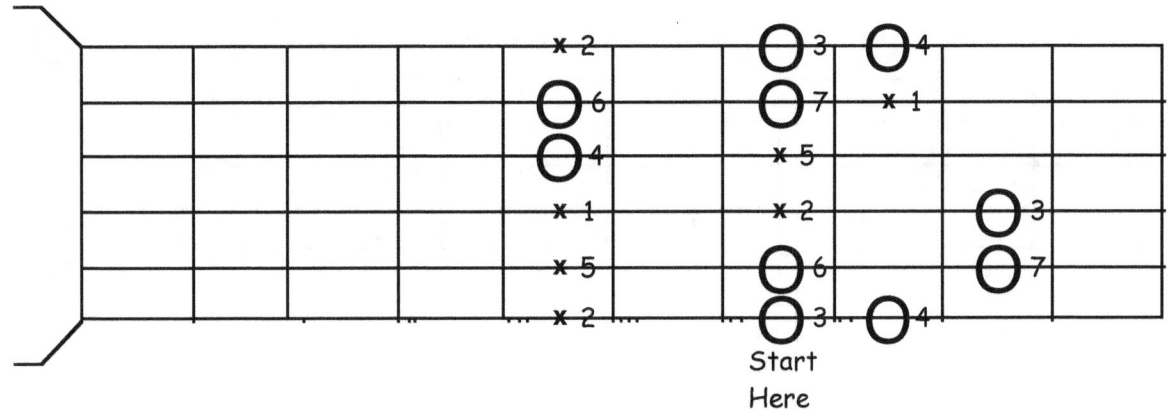

Pattern 3

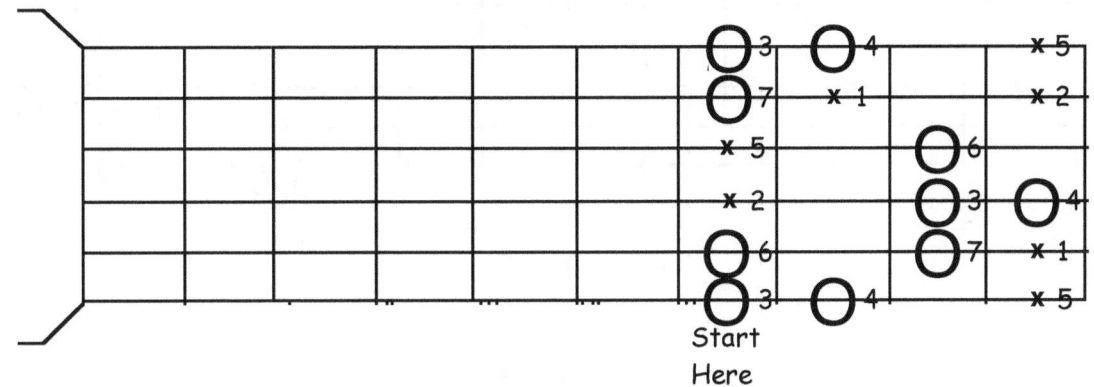

Pattern 4

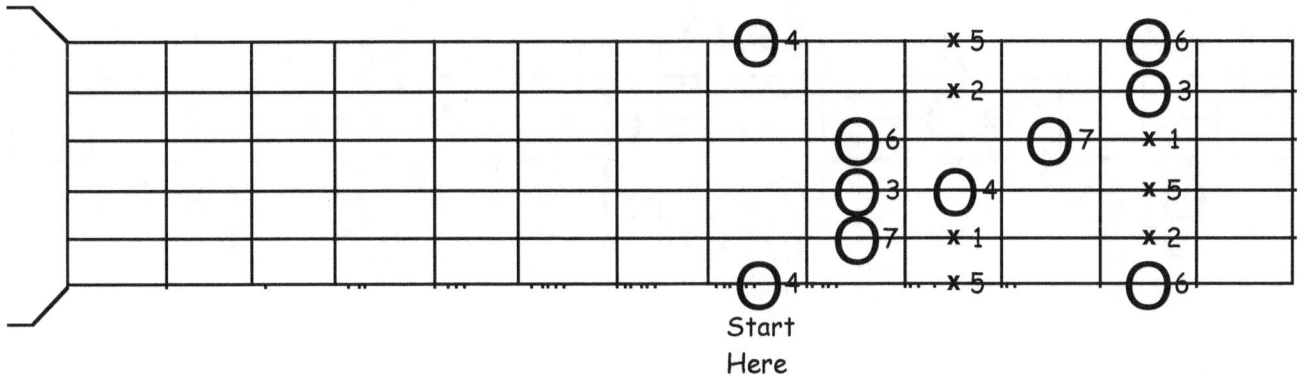

Major 7#11 Arpeggio In "G" Major

C Major 7#11 Arpeggio: 4, 6, 7, 3

Pattern 5

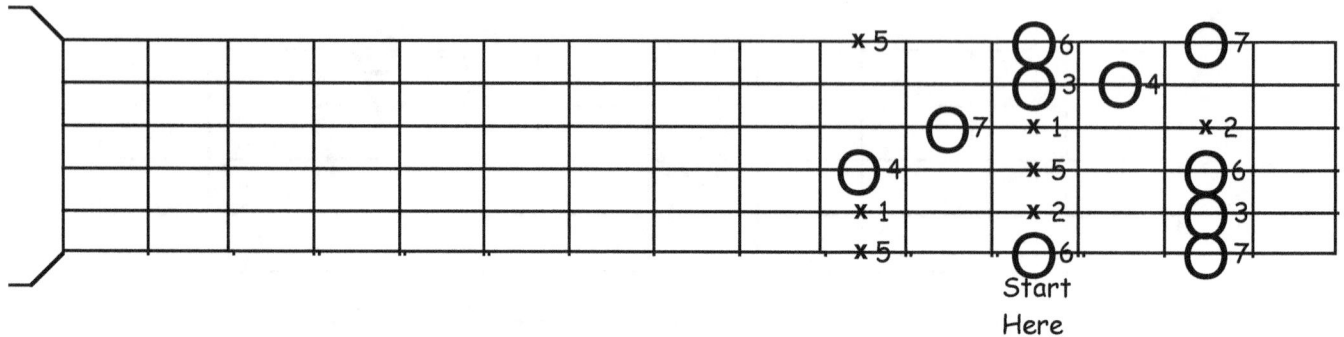

Pattern 6

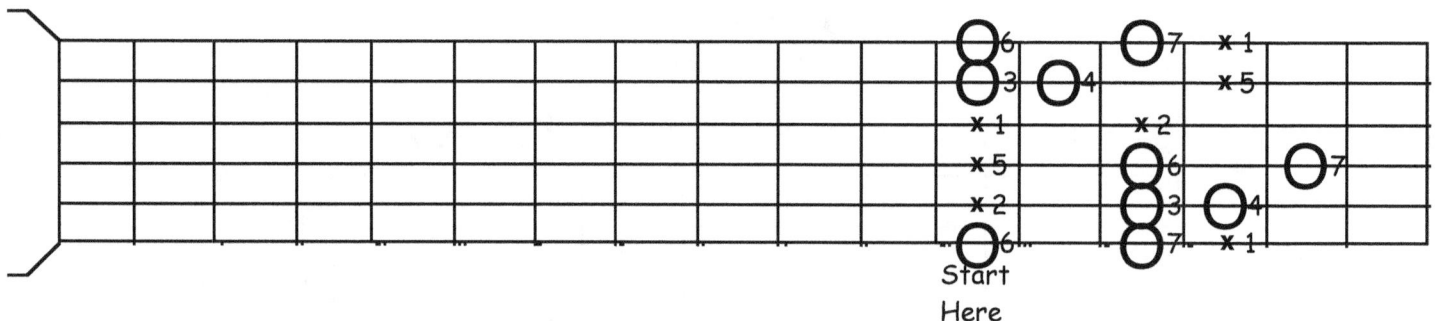

C Major 7#11 Arpeggio
(ENTIRE NECK)

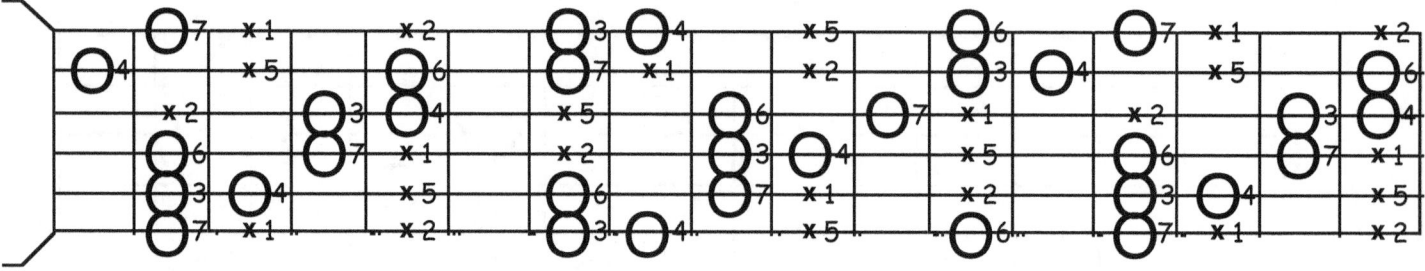

MAJOR 7#5 ARPEGGIO

As the name states, the "major 7#5" arpeggio is a major 7 arpeggio with a raised 5th.
The major 7#5 arpeggio occurs naturally in the melodic minor and harmonic minor scales.
I have presented them within the harmonic minor scale.
In the MAJOR METHOD, the E harmonic minor scale = the G major scale with a #5.
So, the "1" chord arpeggio in E harmonic minor IS a G major 7#5 arpeggio, spelled:
1, 3, #5, 7 (1 = root, 3 = 3rd, #5 = #5th, 7 = 7th).

Major 7#5 Arpeggio In "E" Harmonic Minor

G Major 7#5: Arpeggio: 1, 3, #5, 7

Pattern 7

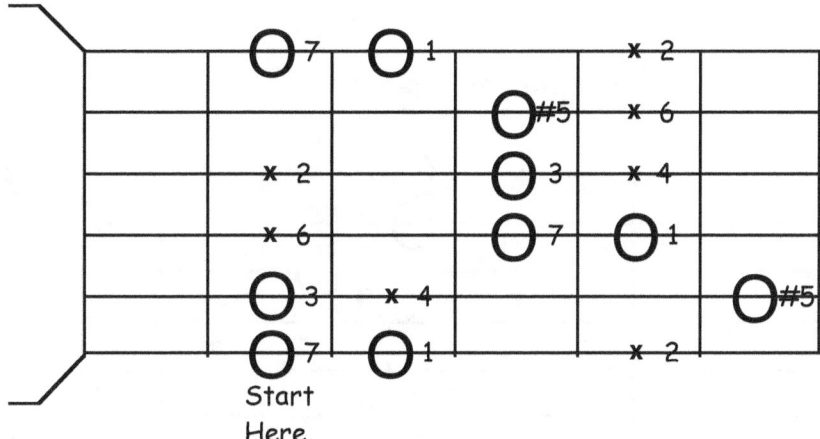

Start Here

Pattern 1

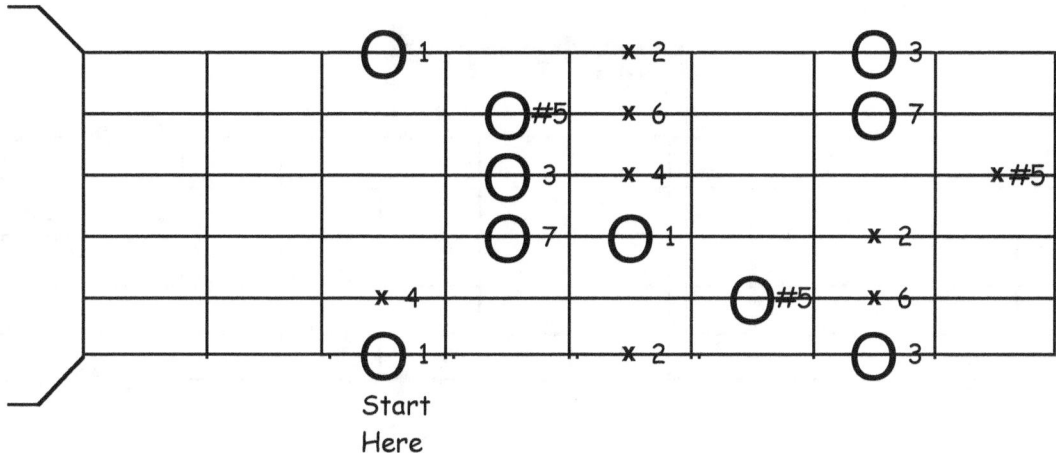

Start Here

271

Major 7#5 Arpeggio
In "E" Harmonic Minor

G Major 7#5 Arpeggio: 1, 3, #5, 7

Pattern 2

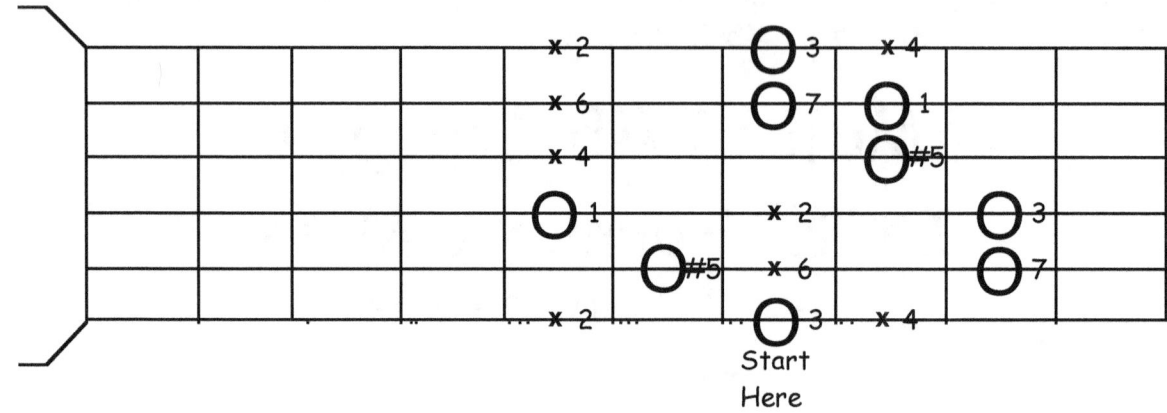

Pattern 3

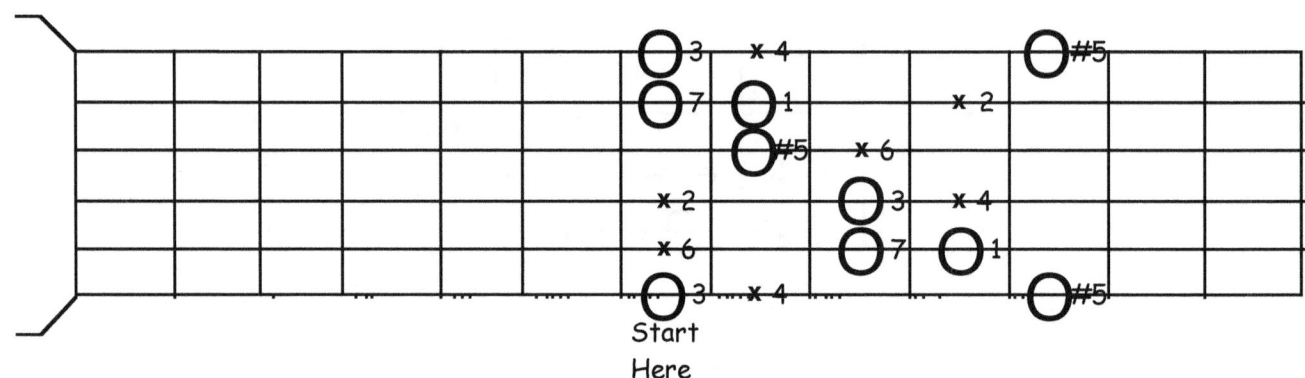

Pattern 4

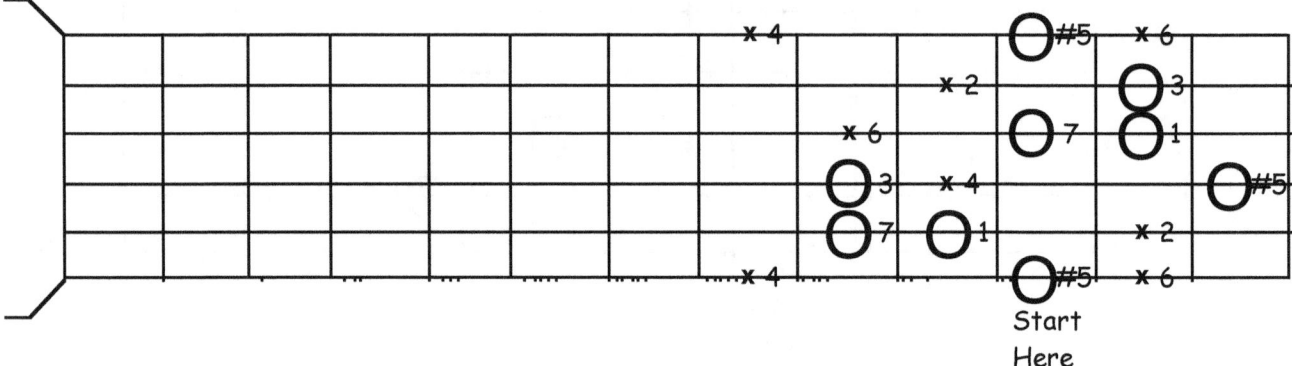

Major 7#5 Arpeggio
In "E" Harmonic Minor

G Major 7#5 Arpeggio: 1, 3, #5, 7

Pattern #5

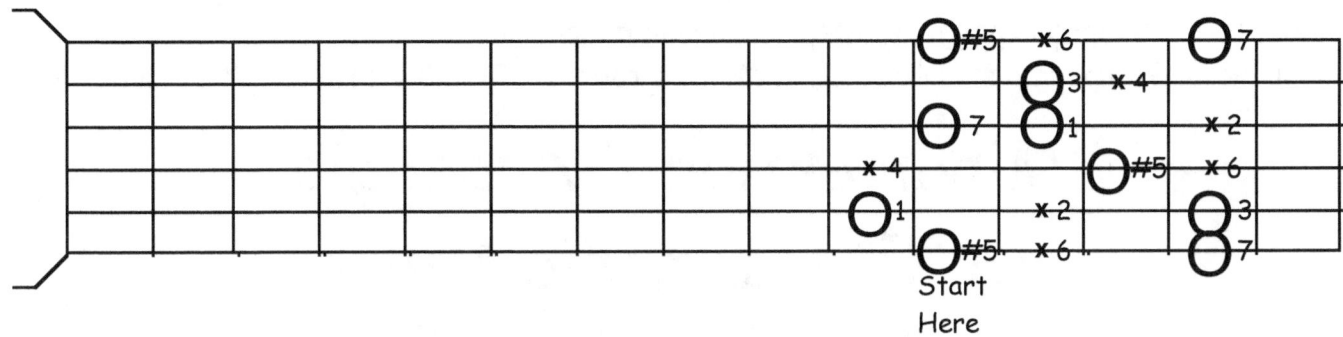

Pattern 6

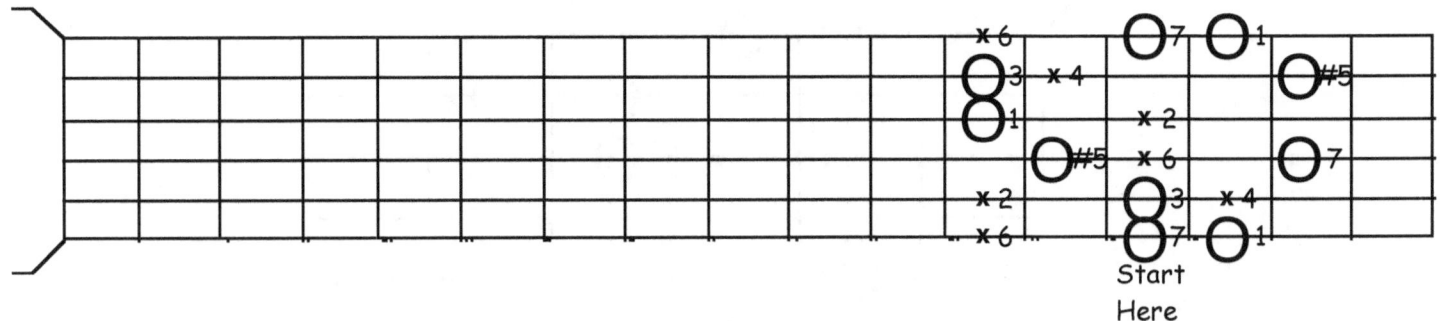

G Major 7#5 Arpeggio
(ENTIRE NECK)

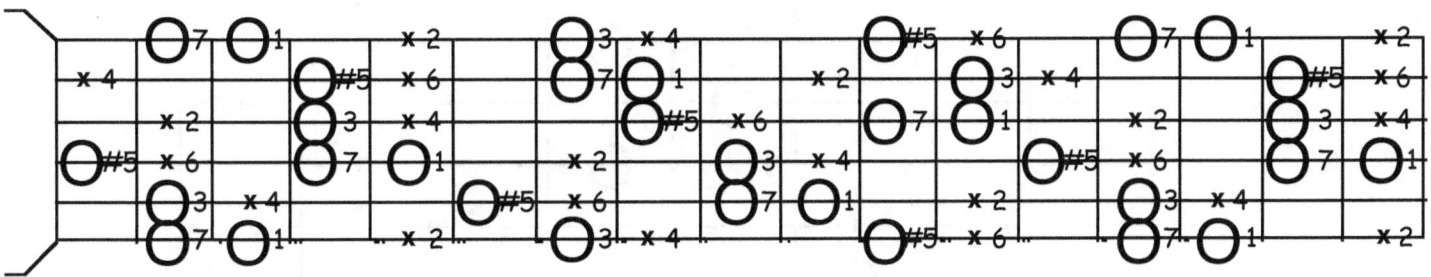

MINOR MAJOR 7 ARPEGGIO

You can either think of the "minor major 7" arpeggio as a minor 7 arpeggio with a raised 7th or as a major 7 arpeggio with a flatted 3rd. The minor major 7 arpeggio occurs naturally in the melodic minor and harmonic minor scales. The minor major 7 *chord* was presented within the melodic minor scale. The minor major 7 *arpeggio* is presented here within the harmonic minor scale. In the MAJOR METHOD the E harmonic minor scale = the G major scale with a #5. So, the "6" chord arpeggio in the E harmonic minor scale IS an E minor major 7 arpeggio spelled: 6, 1, 3, #5 (6 = root, 1 = 3rd, 3 = 5th, and #5 = major 7th).

Minor Major 7 Arpeggio
In "E" Harmonic Minor

E Minor Major 7 Arpeggio: 6, 1, 3, #5

Pattern 7

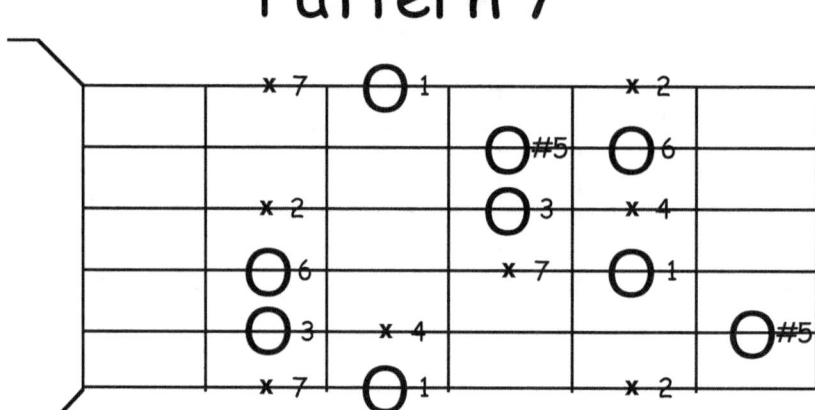

Pattern 1

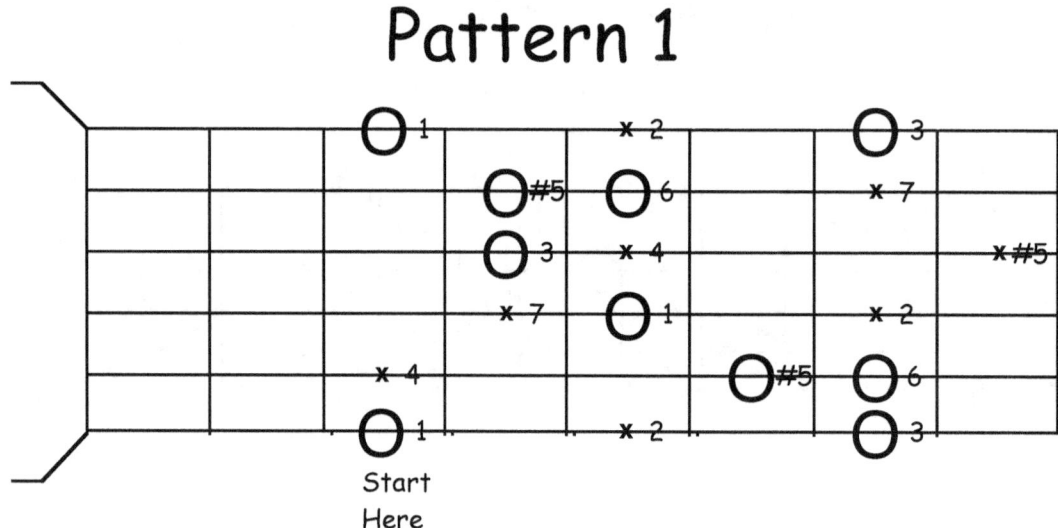

Minor Major 7 Arpeggio
In "E" Harmonic Minor

E Minor Major 7 Arpeggio: 6, 1, 3, #5

Pattern 2

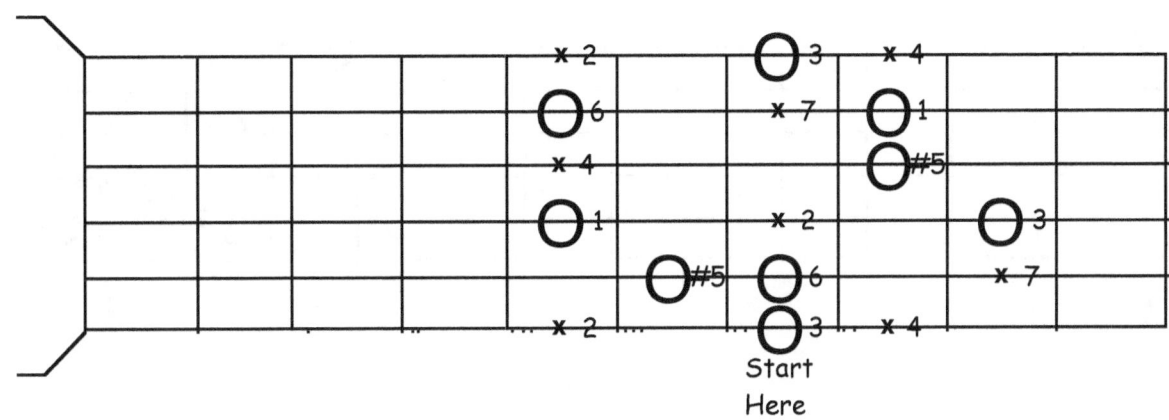

Pattern 3

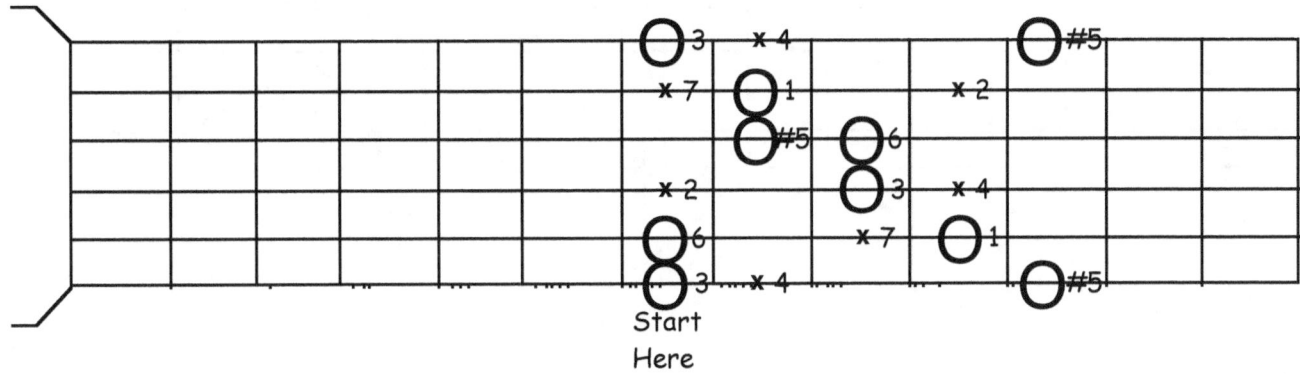

Pattern 4

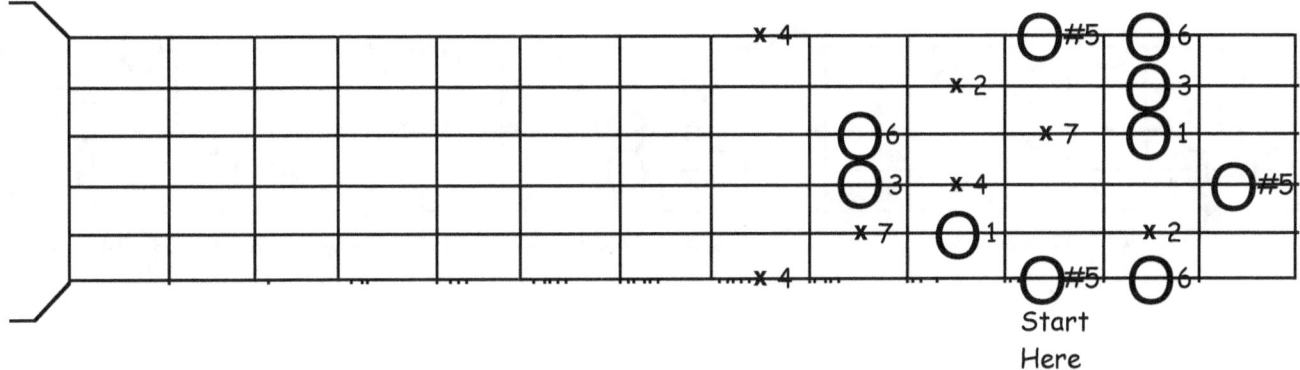

Minor Major 7 Arpeggio
In "E" Harmonic Minor

E Minor Major 7 Arpeggio: 6, 1, 3, #5

Pattern 5

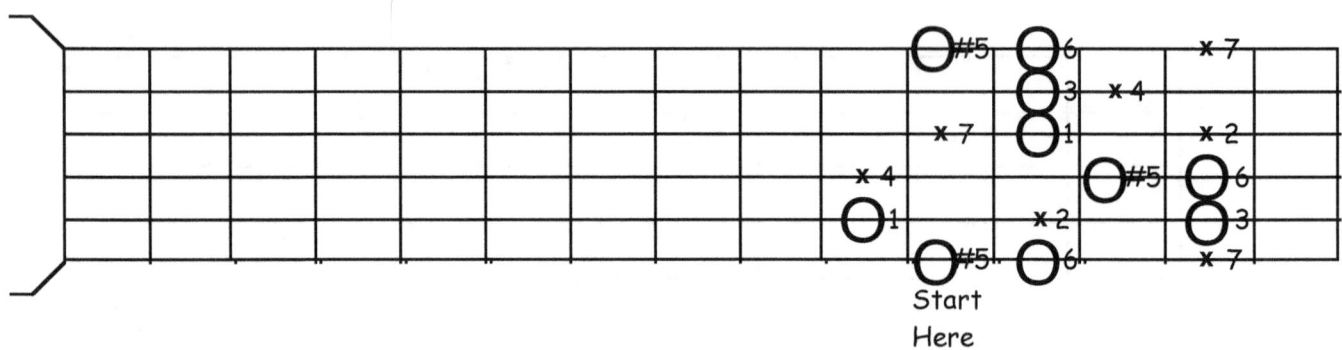

Pattern 6

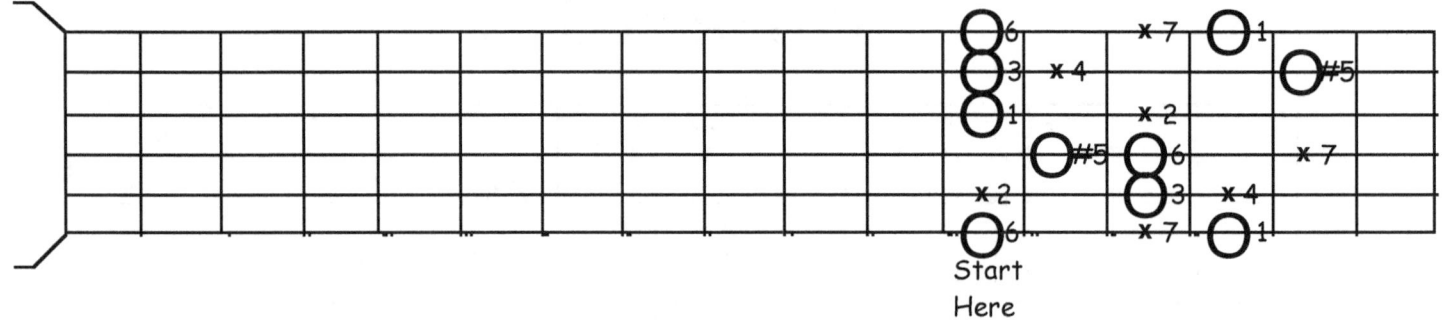

E Minor Major 7 Arpeggio
(ENTIRE NECK)

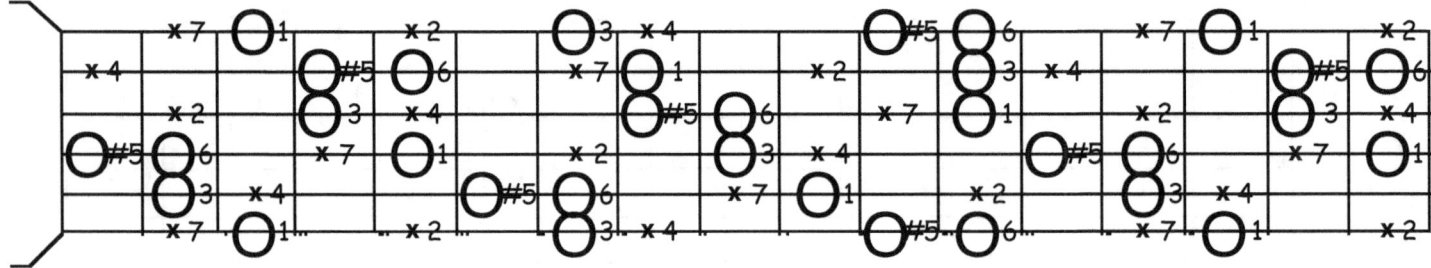

DOMINANT 7#11 ARPEGGIO

The dominant 7#11 (dominant 7b5) arpeggio can occur in the whole tone and melodic minor scales. I have presented them within the melodic minor scale. In the melodic minor scale, both the "4" chord and the "5" chord are dominant 7 chords. When you play the "4" chord arpeggio (spelled: 4, 6, 1, b3), the 5th of the arpeggio is a 1, which can be lowered a half step to the 7 without changing the scale. This gives you an arpeggio that has a root, a 3rd, a #11th (or b5th), and a 7th: (4 = Root, 6 = 3rd, 7 = #11th, b3 = 7th).

Dominant 7#11 Arpeggio In "G" Melodic Minor
C Dominant 7#11 Arpeggio: 4, 6, 7, b3

Pattern 7

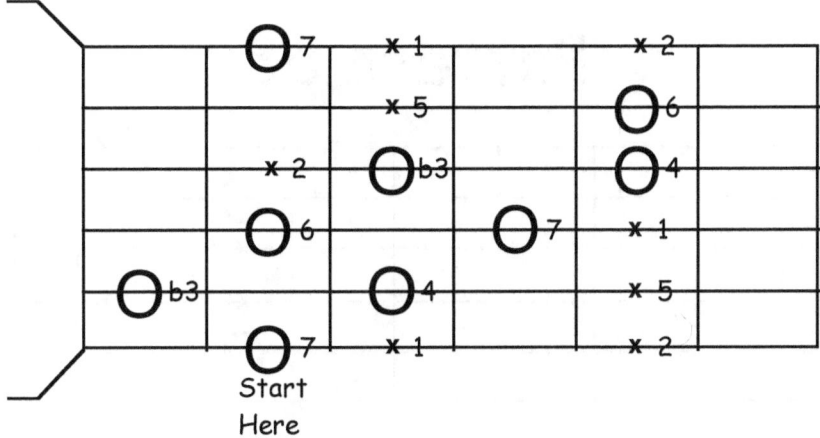

Pattern 1

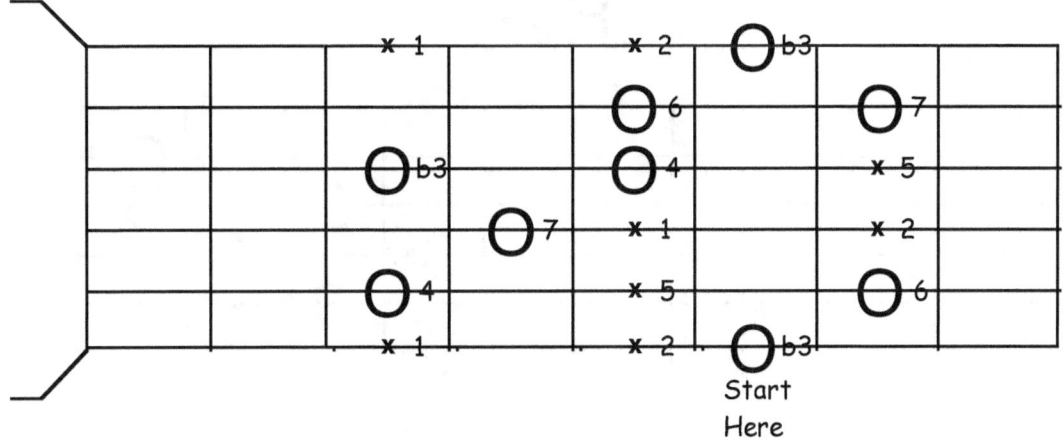

277

Dominant 7#11 Arpeggio
In "G" Melodic Minor

C Dominant 7#11 Arpeggio: 4, 6, 7, b3

Pattern 2

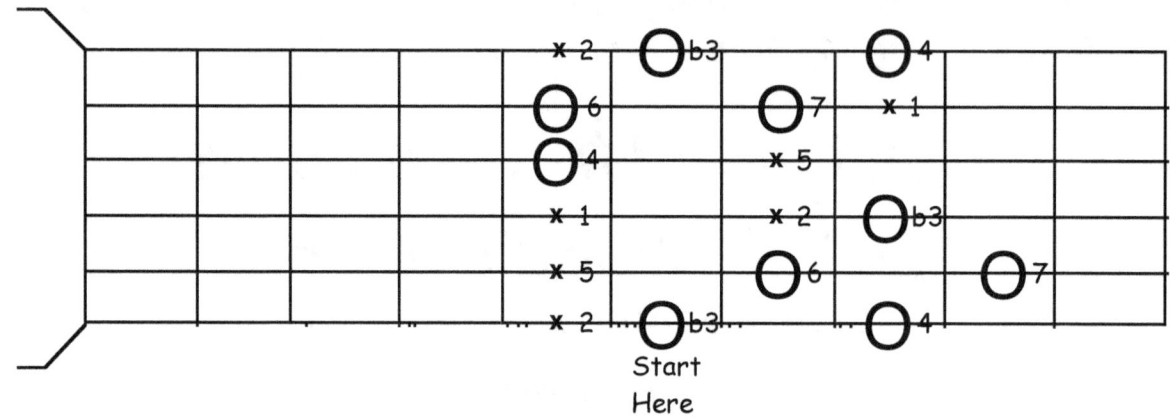

Pattern b3

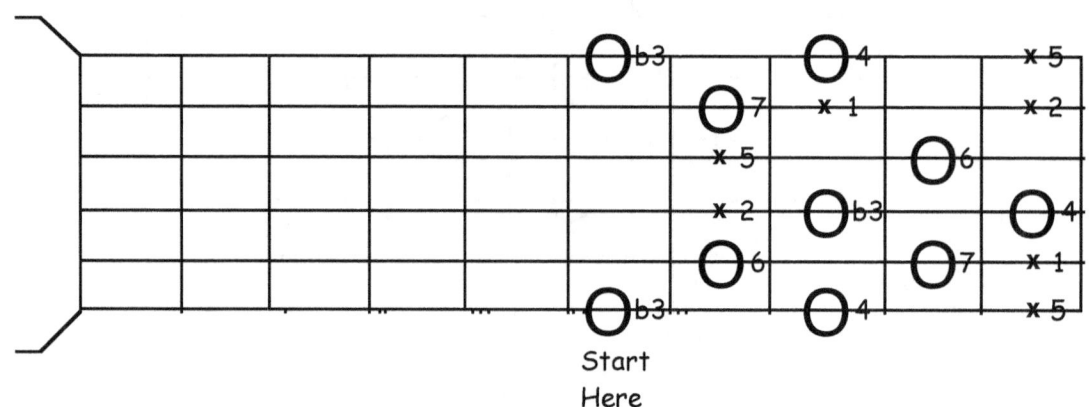

Pattern 4

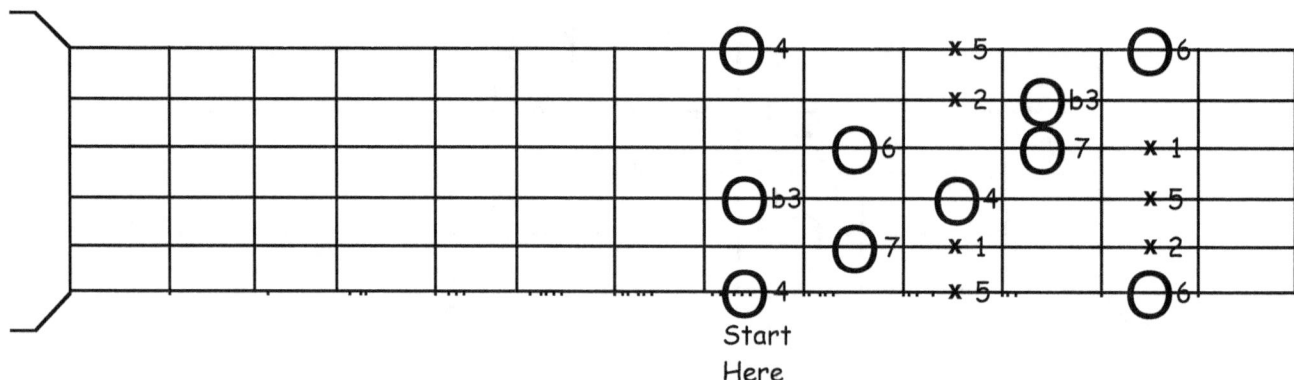

Dominant 7#11 Arpeggio
In "G" Melodic Minor

C Dominant 7#11 Arpeggio: 4, 6, 7, b3

Pattern 5

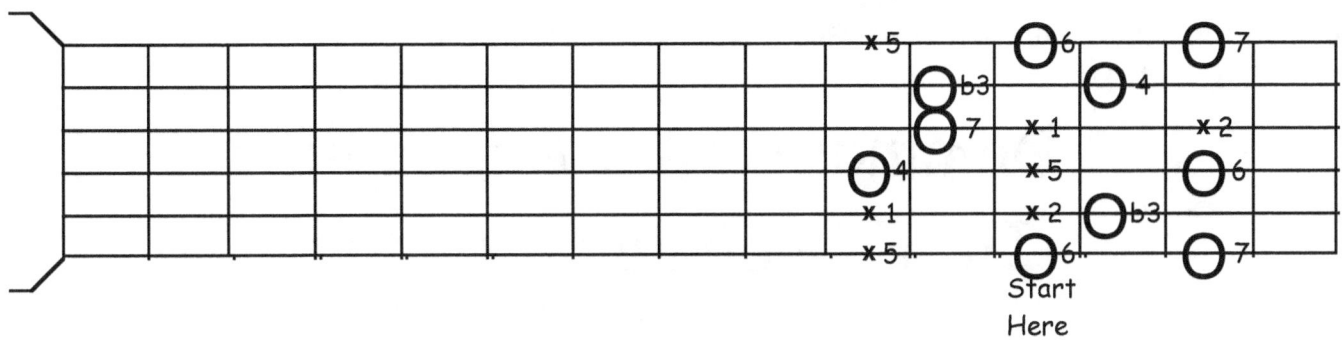

Pattern 6

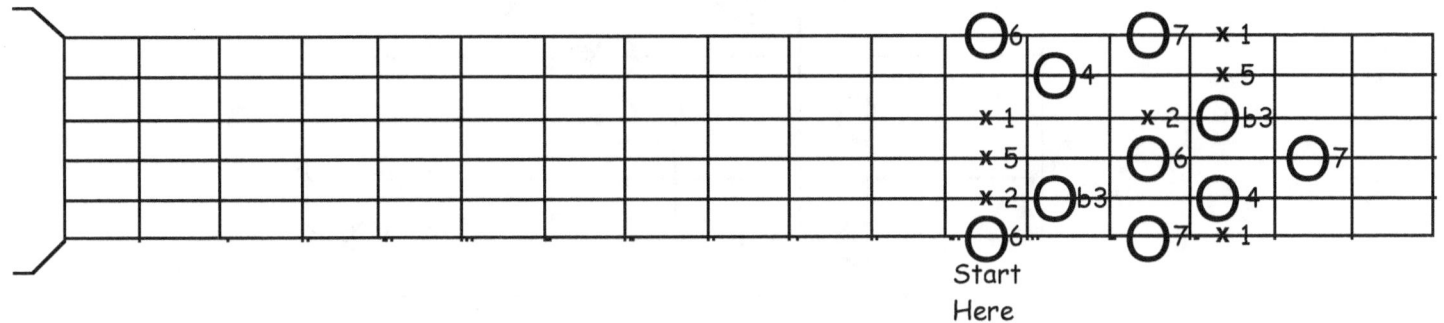

C Dominant 7#11 Arpeggio
(ENTIRE NECK)

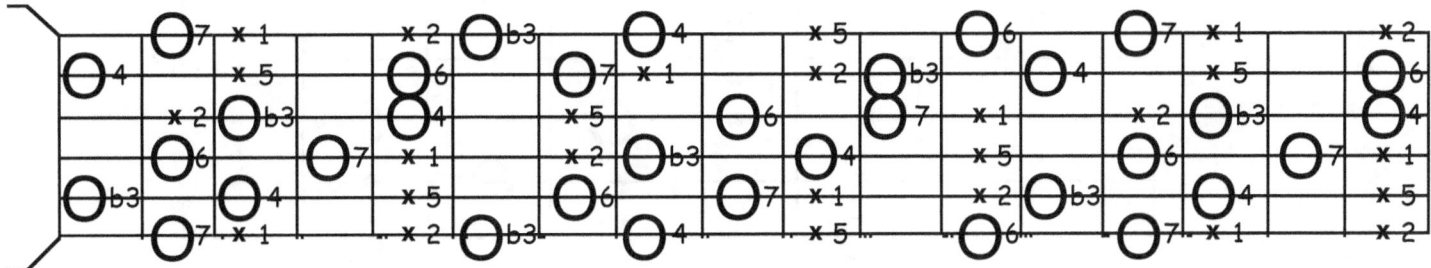

DOMINANT 7#5 ARPEGGIO

The dominant 7#5 arpeggio (augmented 7 arpeggio) can occur naturally in the whole tone, melodic minor and harmonic minor scales. I have presented them within the harmonic minor scale. In the MAJOR METHOD, the E harmonic minor scale = the G major scale with a #5. So, the "3" chord arpeggio in E harmonic minor is a B dominant 7 arpeggio, spelled: 3, #5, 7, 2. The 5th of the arpeggio is a 7, which can be raised a half step to the 1 without changing the scale. This dominant 7#5 arpeggio is spelled: 3, #5, 1, 2 (3 = root, #5 = 3rd, 1 = #5th, 2 = 7th).

Dominant 7#5 Arpeggio
In "E" Harmonic Minor

B Dominant 7#5 Arpeggio: 3, #5, 1, 2

Pattern 7

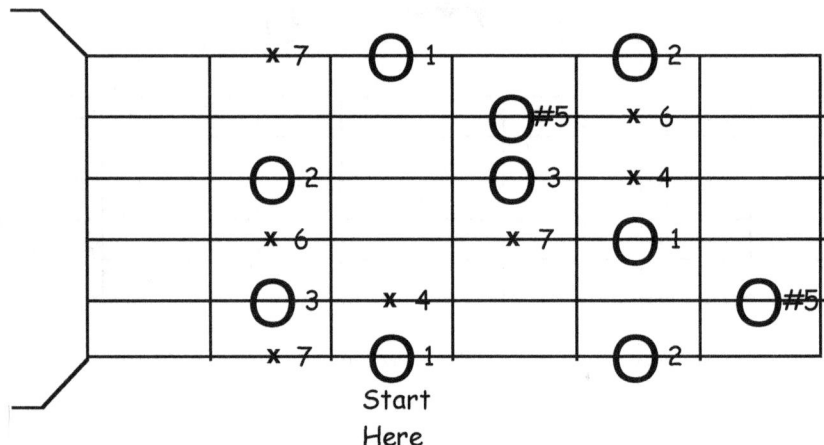

Pattern 1

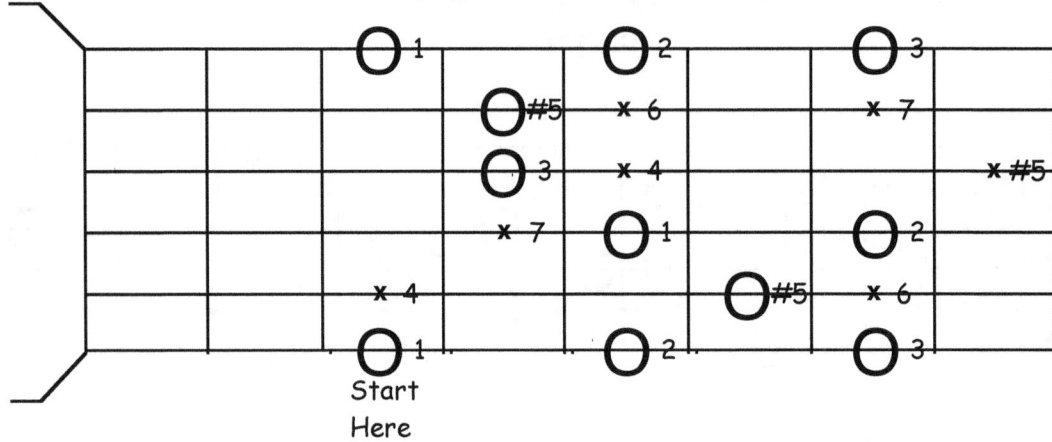

Dominant 7#5 Arpeggio
In "E" Harmonic Minor

B Dominant 7#5 Arpeggio: 3, #5, 1, 2

Pattern 2

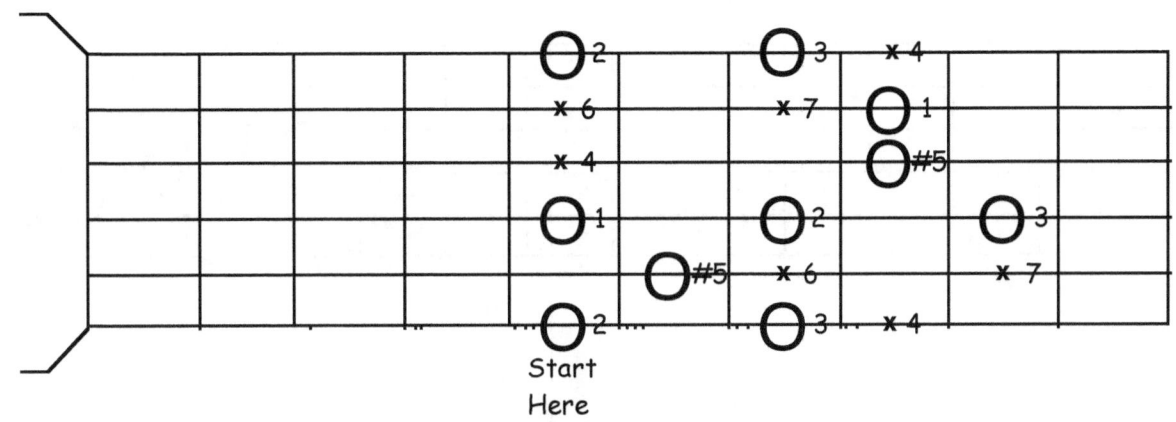

Pattern 3

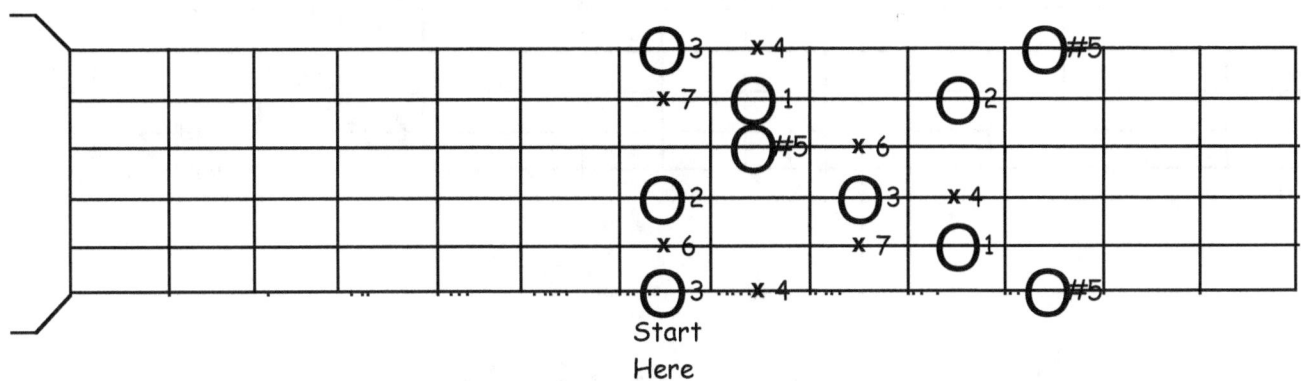

Pattern 4

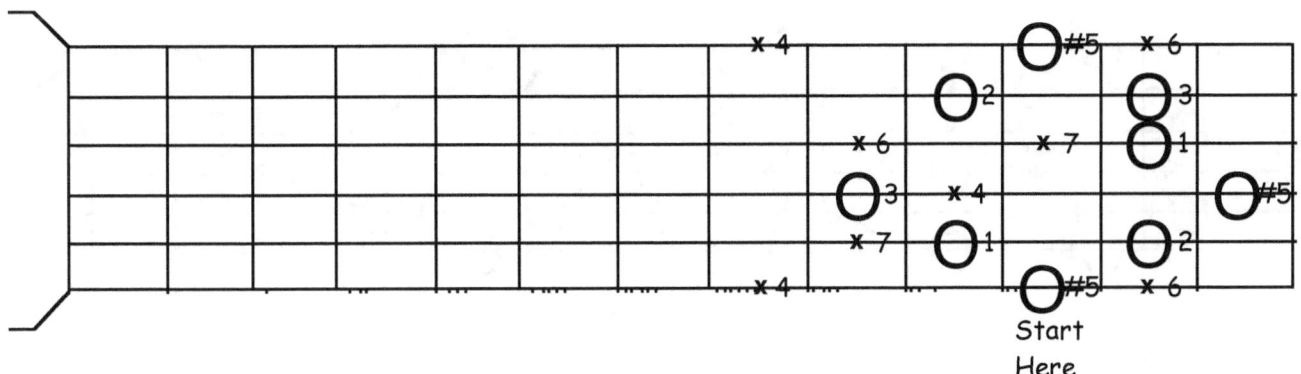

Dominant 7#5 Arpeggio
In "E" Harmonic Minor

B Dominant 7#5 Arpeggio: 3, #5, 1, 2

Pattern #5

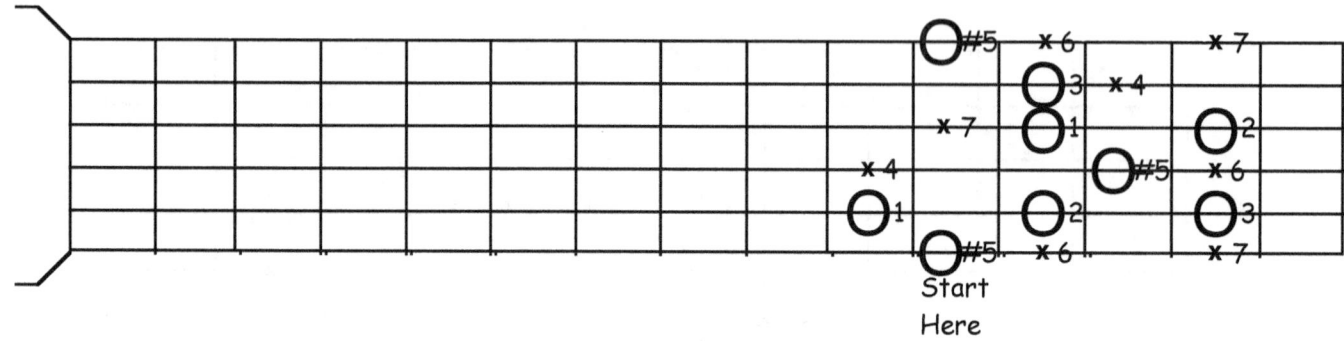

Pattern 6

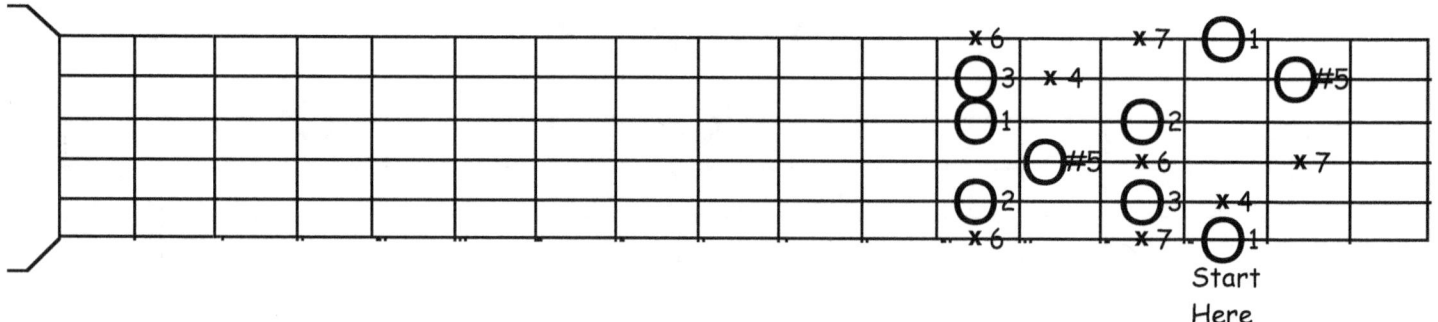

B Dominant 7#5 Arpeggio
(ENTIRE NECK)

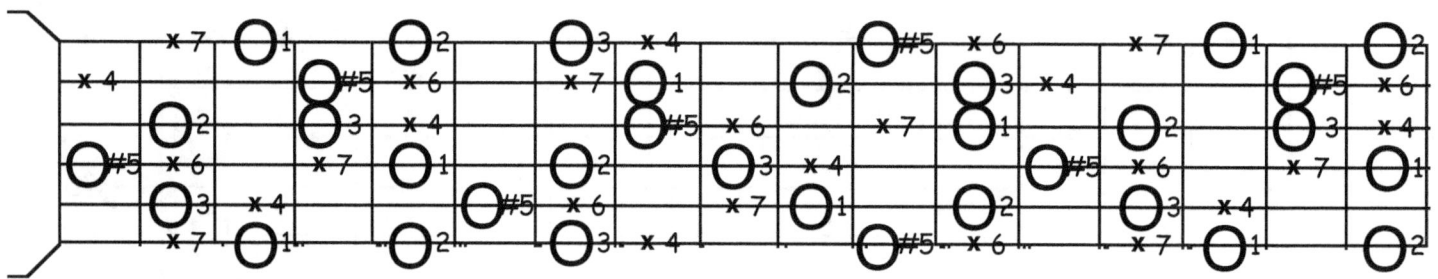

DOMINANT 7#9 ARPEGGIO

The dominant 7#9 arpeggio can occur naturally within the diminished scale. However, in order to clearly show how all of the #9 notes relate to the regular dominant 7 arpeggios, I have presented them within the regular major scale patterns. The #9 appears as an extra note added to these regular dominant 7 arpeggios. This extra (#9) note is drawn as a circle with a star in its middle. The underlying major scale with this extra note is not a common scale. It is only used here to clearly show the shapes of the dominant 7#9 arpeggios. This dominant 7#9 arpeggio is spelled: 5, *, 7, 2, 4 (5 = root, * = #9th, 7 = 3rd, 2 = 5th, 4 = 7th).

Dominant 7#9 Arpeggio In "G" Major

D Dominant 7#9 Arpeggio: 5, (#9), 7, 2, 4

Pattern 7

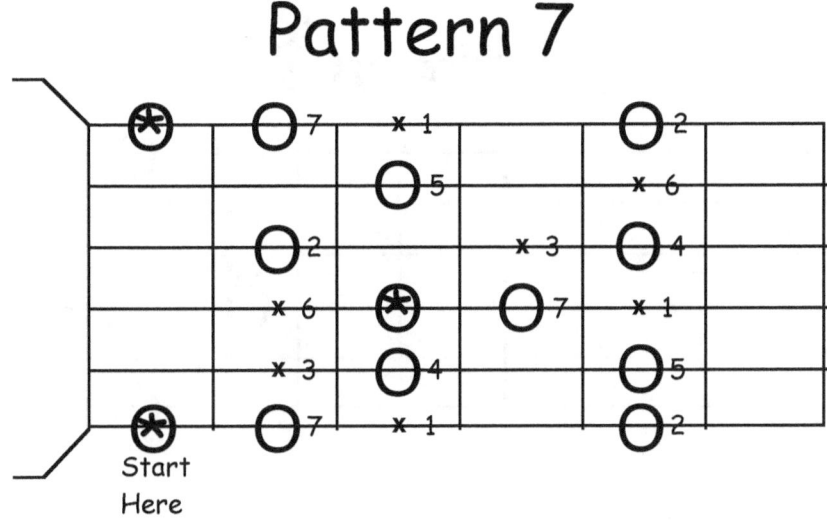

Pattern 1

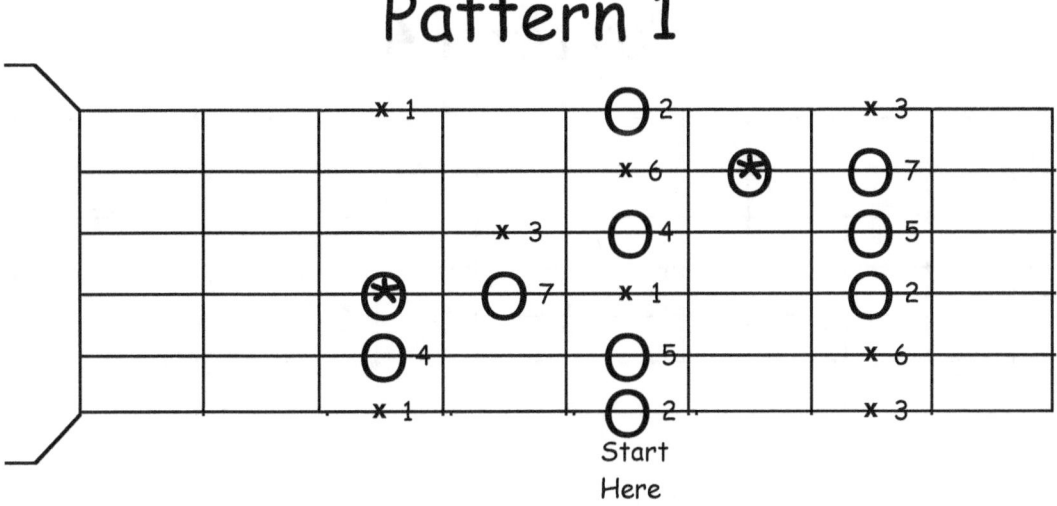

Dominant 7#9 Arpeggio In "G" Major

D Dominant 7#9 Arpeggio: 5, (#9), 7, 2, 4

Pattern 2

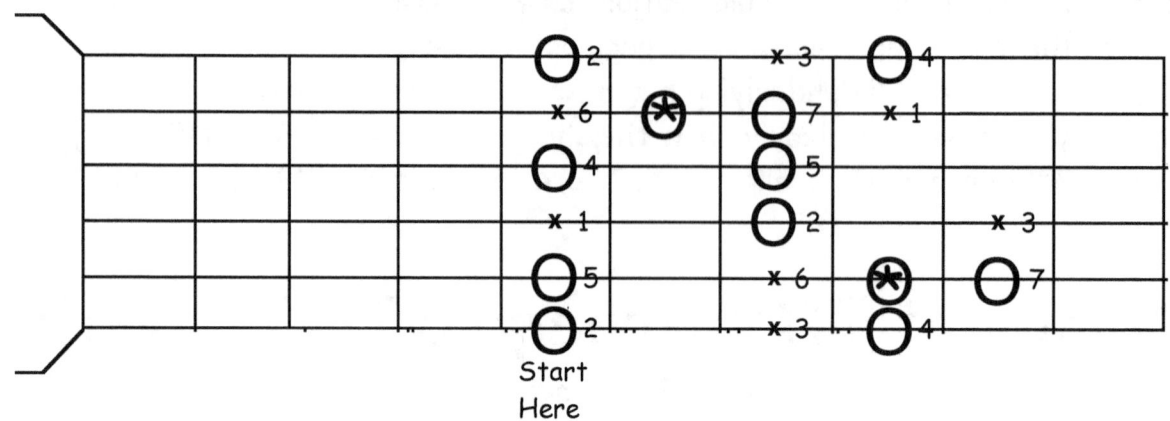

Pattern 3

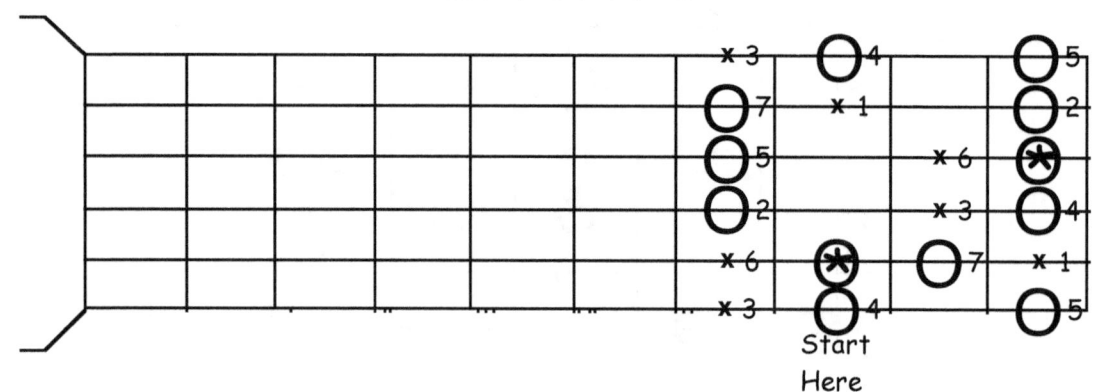

Pattern 4

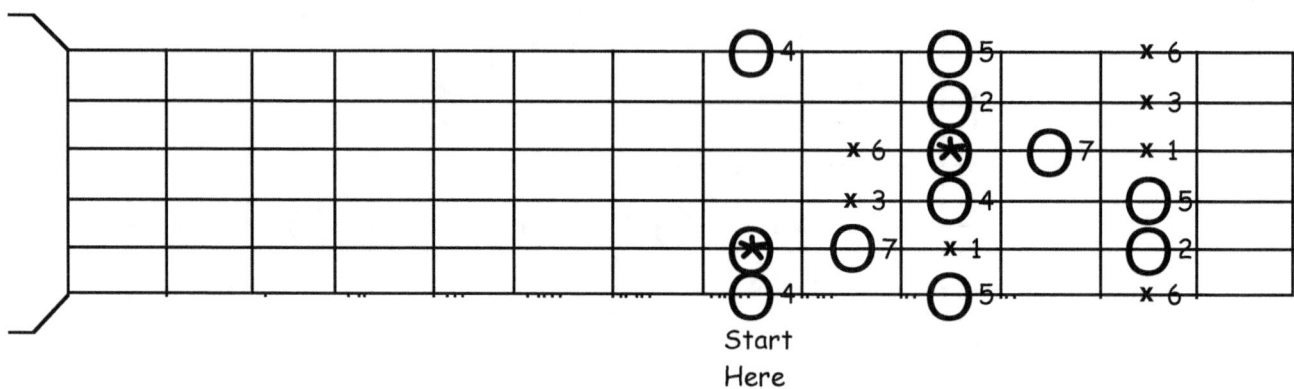

Dominant 7#9 Arpeggio In "G" Major

D Dominant 7#9 Arpeggio: 5, (#9), 7, 2, 4

Pattern 5

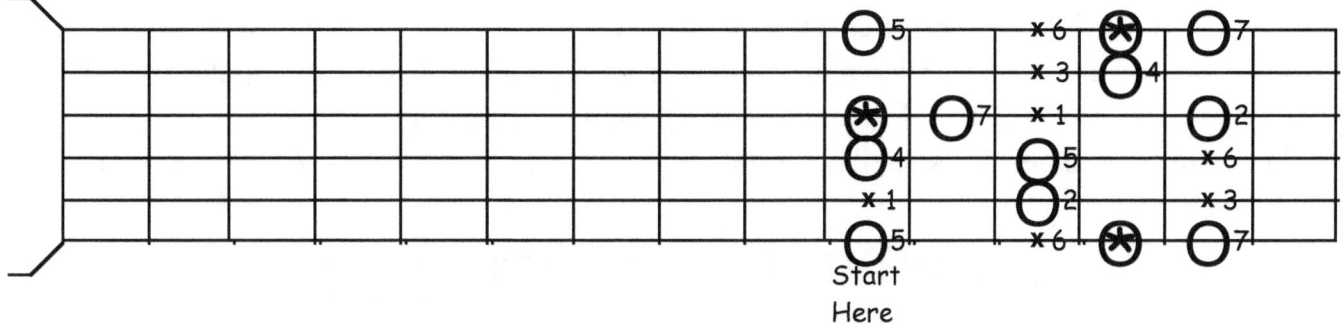

Pattern 6

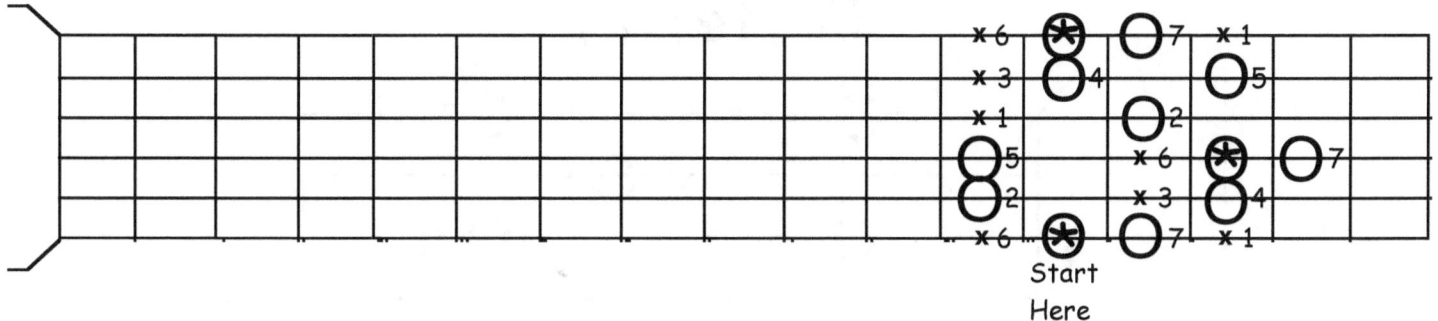

D Dominant 7#9 Arpeggio
(ENTIRE NECK)

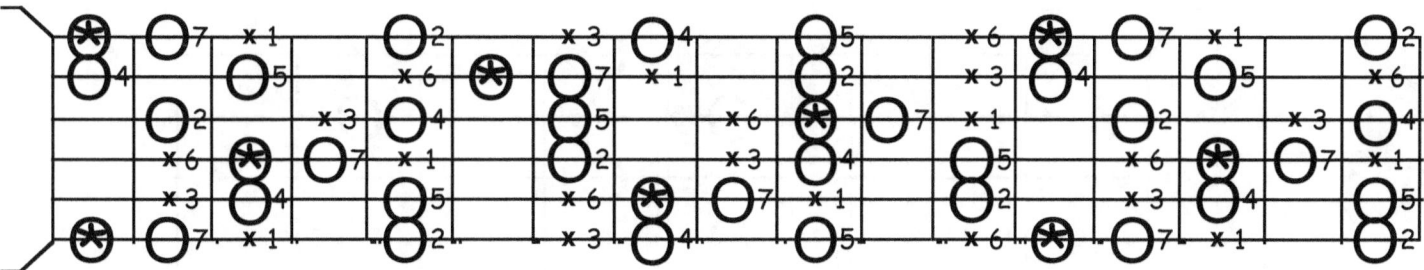

DOMINANT 7b9 ARPEGGIO

The dominant 7b9 arpeggio (diminished arpeggio) can occur in the diminished and harmonic minor scales. I have presented them within the harmonic minor scale.
The dominant 7b9 arpeggios are just regular dominant 7 arpeggios with a raised root.
In the MAJOR METHOD, the E harmonic minor scale = the G major scale with a #5.
So, the "3" chord arpeggio in E harmonic minor is a B dominant 7 arpeggio spelled: 3, #5, 7, 2.
You can raise the root (3) a half step (to the 4), without changing the scale.
This dominant 7b9 arpeggio is spelled: 4, #5, 7, 2 (4 = b9th, #5 = 3rd, 7 = 5th, 2 = 7th).

Dominant 7b9 Arpeggio
In "E" Harmonic Minor

B Dominant 7b9 Arpeggio: 4, #5, 7, 2

Pattern 7

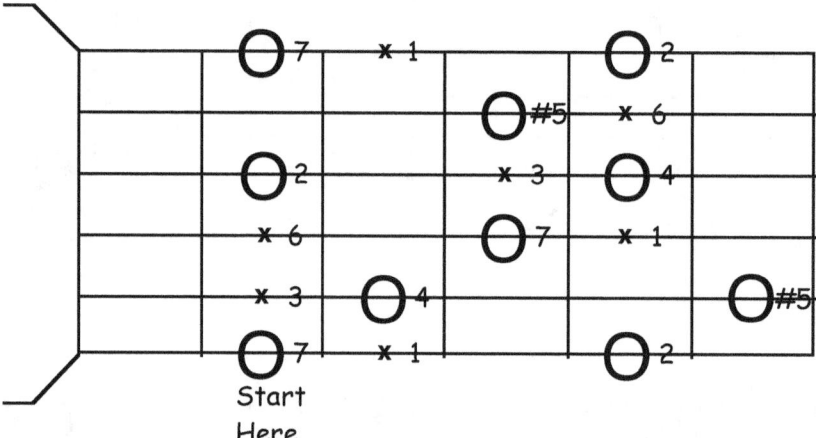

Pattern 1

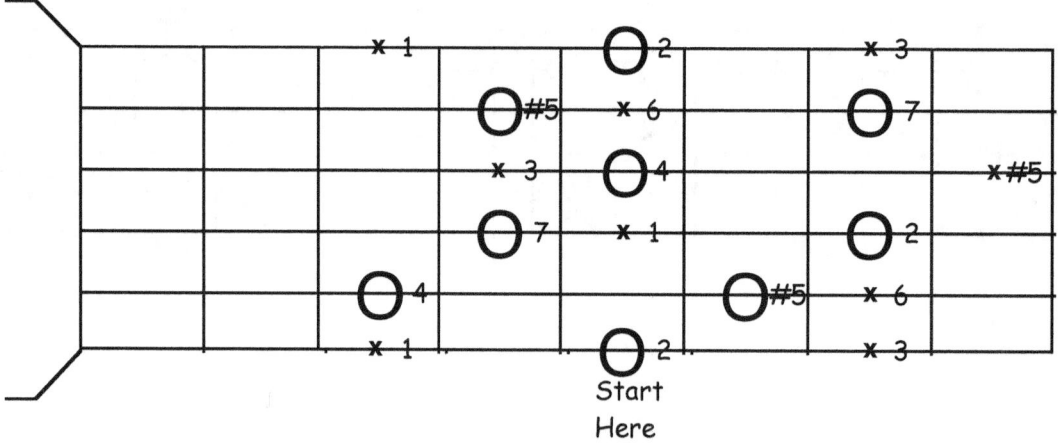

Dominant 7b9 Arpeggio In "E" Harmonic Minor

B Dominant 7b9 Arpeggio: 4, #5, 7, 2

Pattern 2

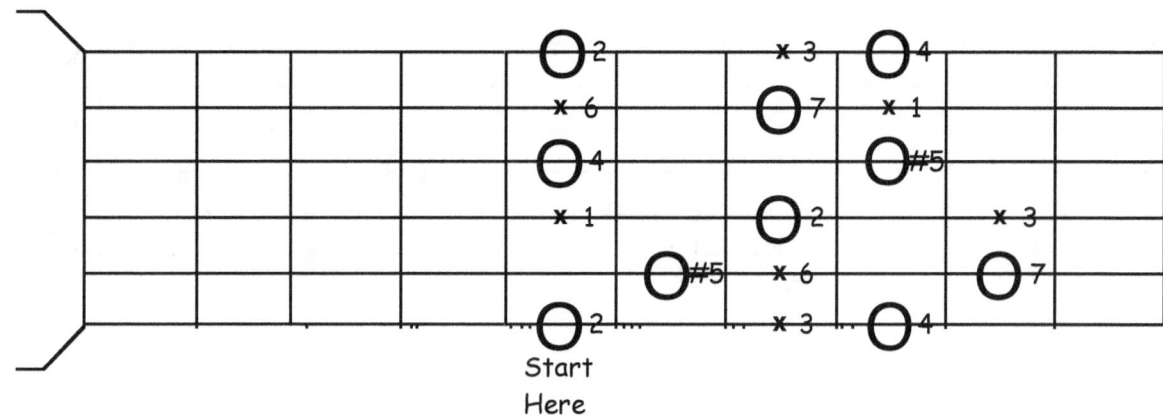

Pattern 3

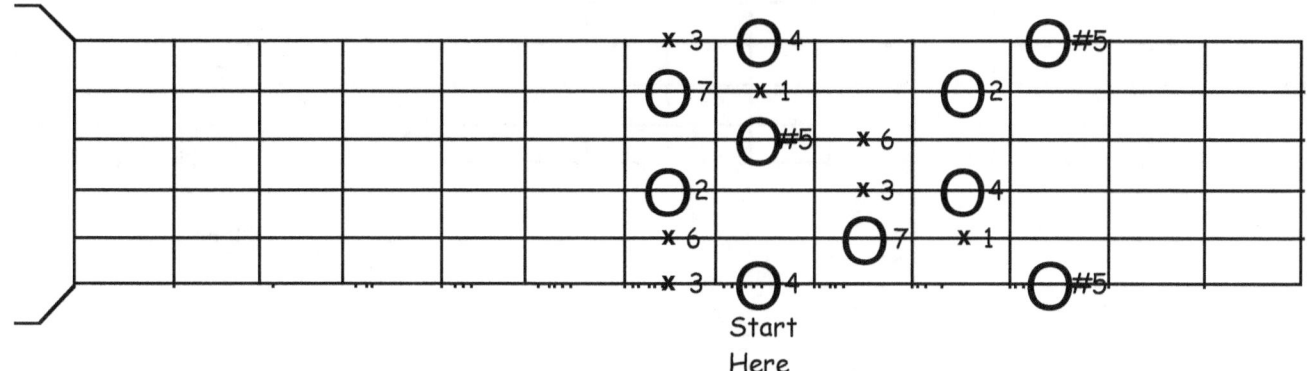

Pattern 4

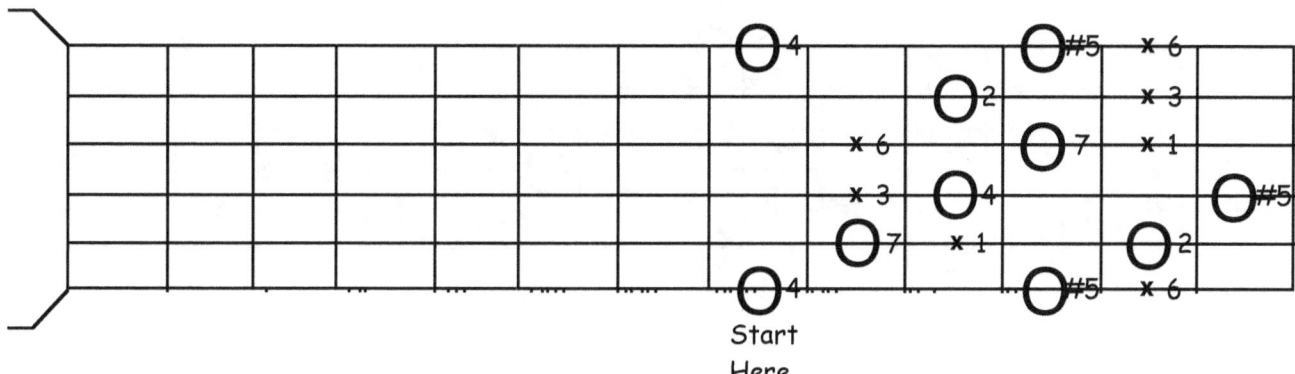

Dominant 7b9 Arpeggio In "E" Harmonic Minor

B Dominant 7b9 Arpeggio: 4, #5, 7, 2

Pattern 5

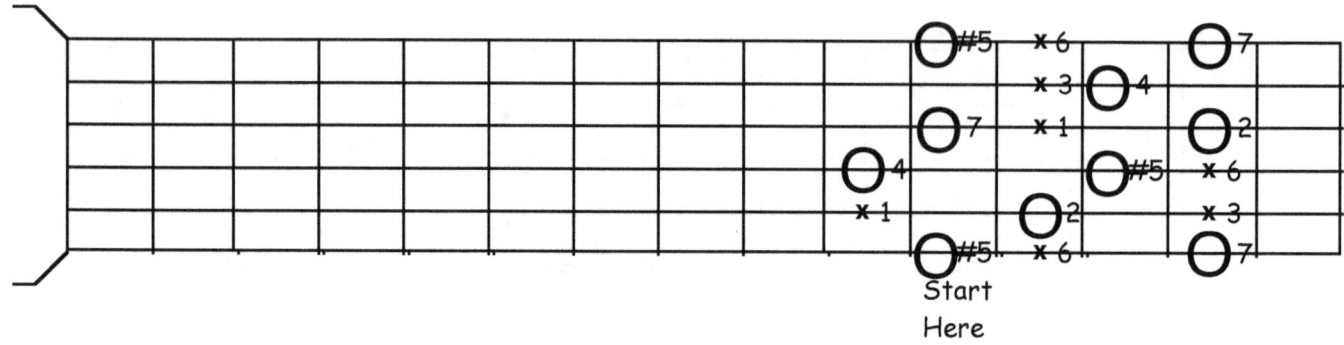

Pattern 6

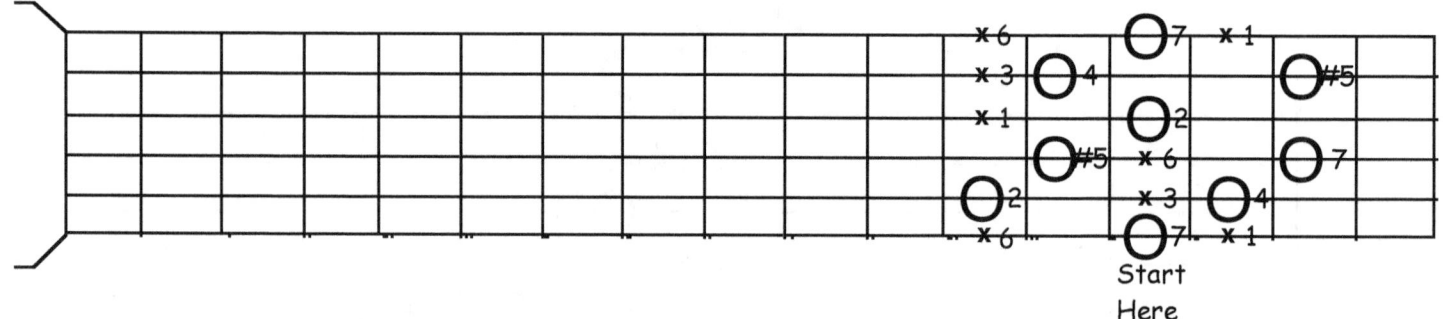

B Dominant 7b9 Arpeggio
(ENTIRE NECK)

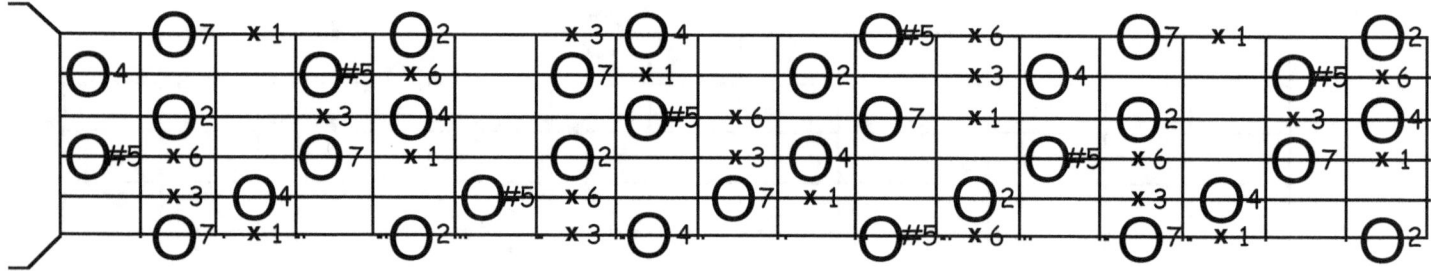

WHAT TO DO...

You now know (or are getting to know):

I <u>TRIADS</u>:
   1) Diatonic Triads
   2) Altered Triads

II <u>SEVENTH CHORDS</u>:
   1) Diatonic Seventh Chords
   2) Chordal Extensions for Diatonic Seventh Chords
   3) Altered Seventh Chords

III <u>ARPEGGIOS</u>
   1) Diatonic Seventh Chord Arpeggios
   2) Altered Seventh Chord Arpeggios

Now, what you'll want to do is start applying all of this information to your playing. At the end of this volume, I have written out a handful of chord charts for you. These charts can be used to work on everything that you've learned from this book.

TRIADS: Even if you are looking at a chord chart filled with seventh chords, remember that every seventh chord has a basic triad at its core. All major 7 and dominant 7 chords are built on major triads: C major7 is built on a C major triad. G dominant7 is built on a G major triad.

All minor 7 chords are built on minor triads: A minor 7 is built on an A minor triad.

All minor 7b5 chords are built on diminished triads: B minor 7b5 is built on a B diminished triad.

All major 7#5 and dominant 7#5 chords are built on major #5 triads (augmented):
C major 7#5 is built on a C major #5 triad (augmented) AND C dominant 7#5 is also built on a C major #5 triad (augmented).

All major 7#11 and dominant 7#11 chords are built on major #11 triads: C major 7#11 is built on a C major #11 triad AND C dominant 7#11 is also built on a C major #11 triad.

It is possible to play other triads over these chords when considering the upper extensions and/or the alterations, but these are concepts that we'll get into in the MAJOR METHOD Volume 3.

For now, see how many basic types of triad voicings you remember for each of the chords in a chart. Don't worry about playing the chart with a beat. After you are able to play all of the chord voicings that you can remember for each chord, try playing though the whole chart using only one string grouping or only one voicing type at a time (drop 2 or drop 3, etc ...).

SEVENTH CHORDS:
First, see how many types of seventh chord voicings you remember for each of the chords in a chart. Don't worry about playing the chart with a beat. After you are able to play all of the chord voicings that you can remember for each chord, try playing though the whole chart using only one string grouping or only one voicing type at a time (drop 2 or drop 3, etc ...). Does this paragraph sound familiar?

As you're doing this, see if you can shift as few notes as possible when switching between chords. Also, try moving your left hand as little as possible when chord switching. These are excellent ways of testing your knowledge AND playing through a chord chart with smooth voice leading (something that tends to be a challenge for guitarists).

ARPEGGIOS:
Try playing through each of these chord charts using only arpeggios. First try playing the arpeggio for each given chord all over the neck of the guitar. Spend some time on each chord and make sure that you don't have any blind spots on the neck (where you've forgotten the shapes of the arpeggio for that chord). Once you feel fairly comfortable with this, try soloing through the chart using only arpeggios. When a chord changes to another chord, try to play the next chord tone in the arpeggio for the new chord that is the closest to where your hand is located. See if you can smoothly change into the new arpeggio without shifting your hand. Avoid starting each arpeggio on the low E string.

Here now are some chord charts to work on:

JAZZ BLUES CHORD CHART

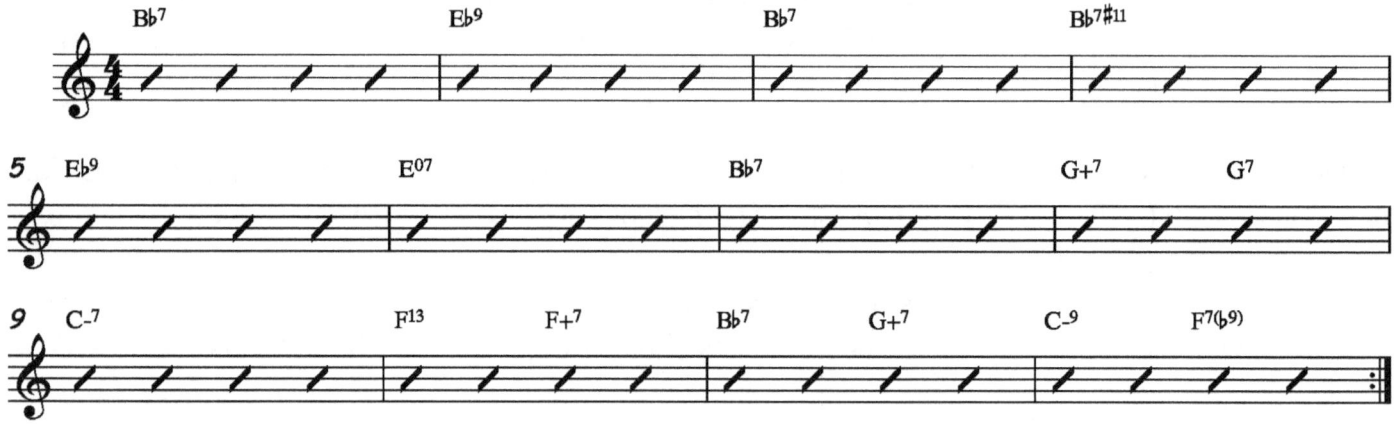

ALL THE CHORDS YOU KNOW

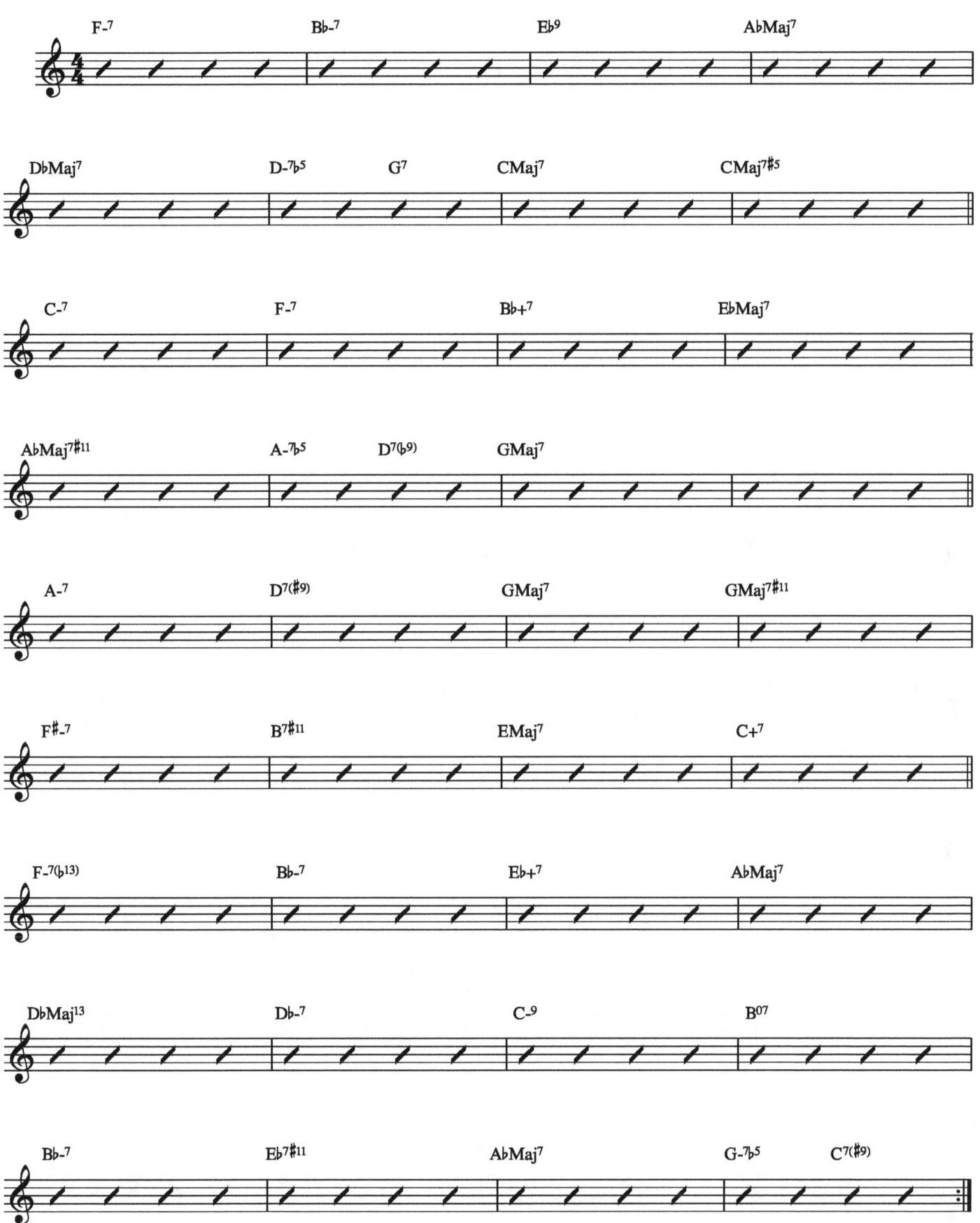

DAYS OF SEVENTH CHORDS

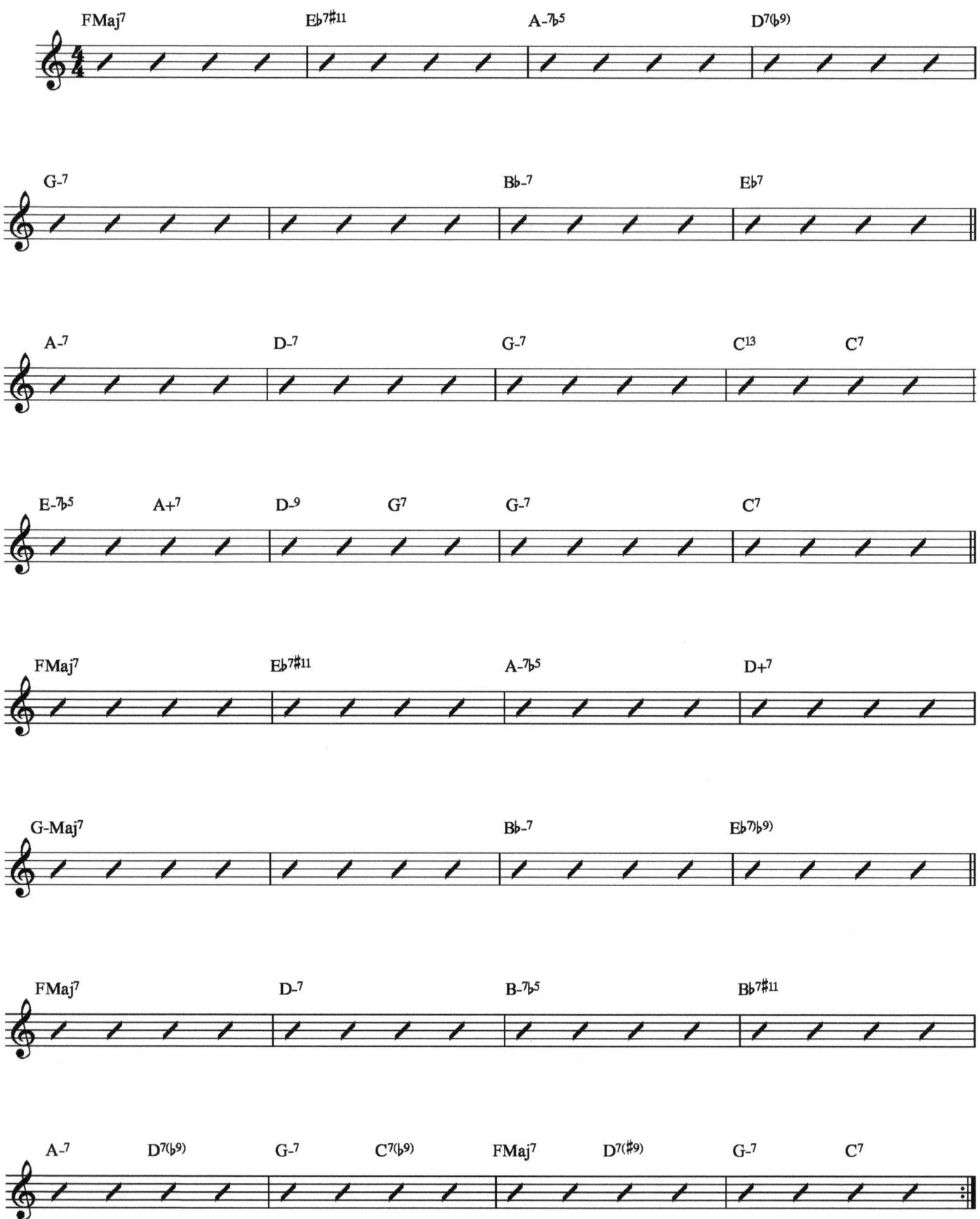

ALL OF THESE

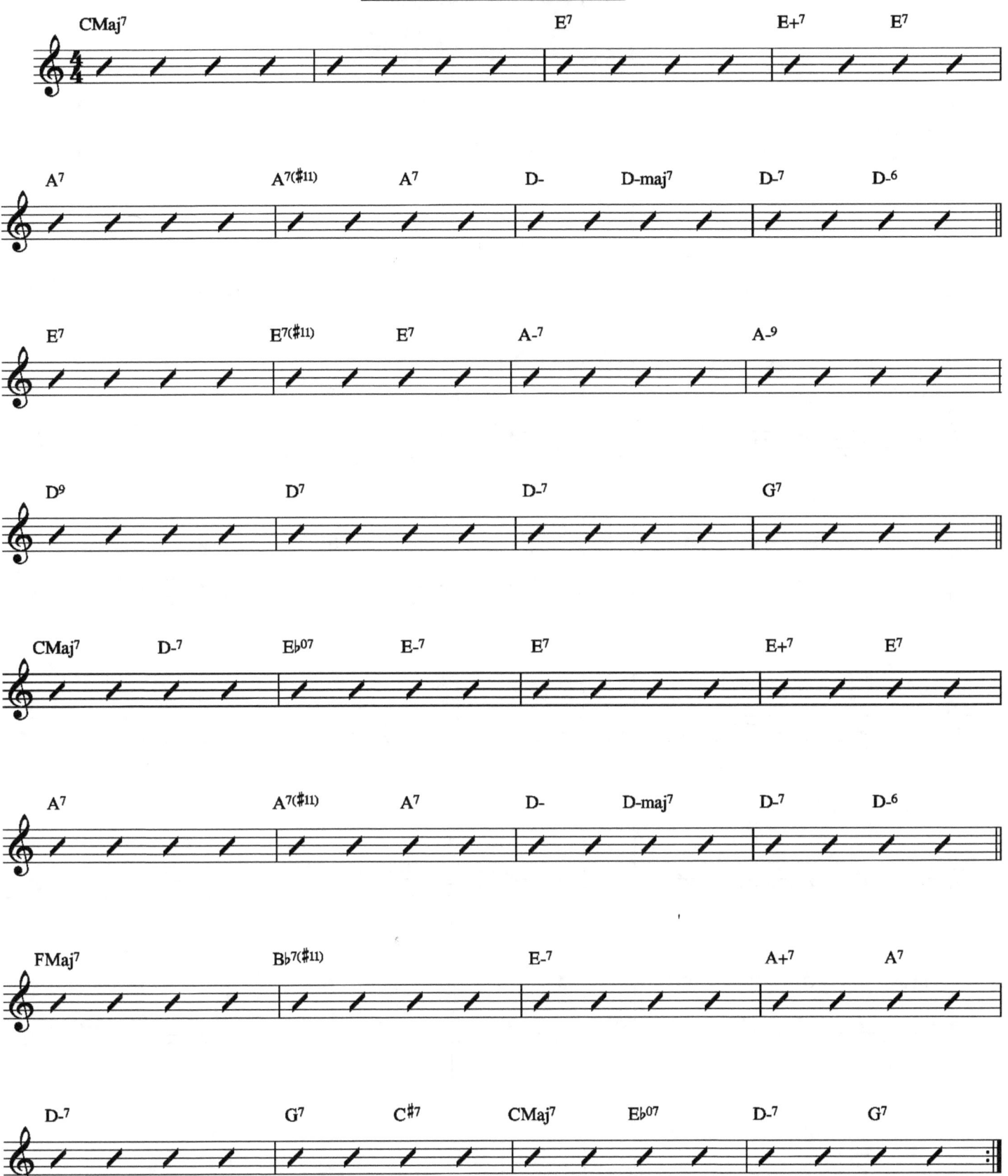

Here is a chart with no added extensions or alterations. Try adding some.

RHYTHM CHANGES

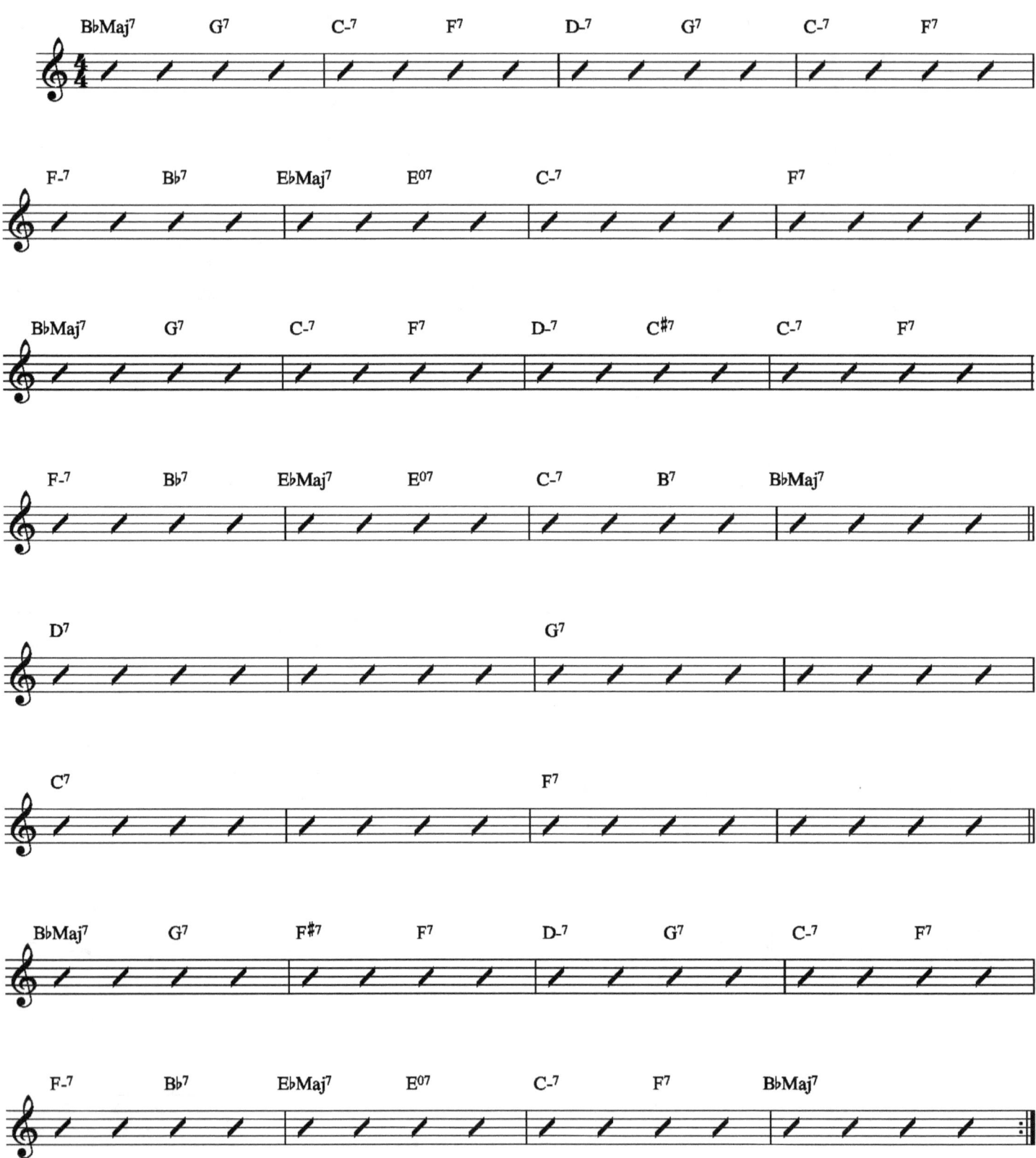

ABOUT THE AUTHOR

Rolf Sturm is a NJ area guitarist who has performed and/or toured with the Tony Trischka Band, Anthony Braxton, the Argentinean tango group New York-Buenos Aires Connection, drummer Billy Martin, country singer Eddy Arnold, The Washington Street Players, Strike Anywhere Performance Ensemble, Tomas Ulrich's Cargo Cult, the Grateful Dead big band Illuminati, the Walter Thompson Orchestra, and klezmer clarinetist Giora Feidman. He has led his own NYC area bands Feed The Meter and Just Cause. He co-leads the jazz trio Tricycle, is a member of the 4 Five VI ensemble and he was the featured guitarist in *Night Music for John Lennon* under the baton of its composer, Lukas Foss.

Rolf has toured North America and Europe, performing at numerous jazz and jam band festivals, the World Expo 2000 in Hannover, Germany, at Lincoln Center and Town Hall in NYC, and at the Kennedy Center in Washington, D.C. He has performed on soundtracks for both film and television and has released numerous CDs on the Water Street Music label: www.waterstreetmusic.org. Rolf has also recorded dozens of CDs as a sideman, appearing on recordings that have featured Tony Trischka, Glen Velez, Maggie Roche, Dave Douglas, Loudon Wainwright, Cameron Brown, Jorma Kaukonen, David Johansen, Ike Willis, Buddy Cage, and members of the Grateful Dead.

Rolf graduated from Ithaca College, with a BFA in Jazz Guitar, where he studied with Steve Brown. Since then he has studied with John Abercrombie, Jim Hall, Joe Pass, Bill Frisell, and Harry Leahey.

Rolf performs and teaches in the NYC area. He also teaches jazz guitar at the Hoff-Barthelson Music School in Scarsdale, NY.

To learn more about Rolf Sturm and his music visit:
www.rolfsturm.org
www.waterstreetmusic.org